ASCENT

CENTER FOR TECHNICAL KNOWLEDGE

Creo Parametric 6.0
Advanced Part Design

Learning Guide
1ˢᵗ Edition

ASCENT - Center for Technical Knowledge®
Creo Parametric 6.0
Advanced Part Design
1st Edition

Prepared and produced by:

ASCENT Center for Technical Knowledge
630 Peter Jefferson Parkway, Suite 175
Charlottesville, VA 22911

866-527-2368
www.ASCENTed.com

Lead Contributor: Scott Hendren

ASCENT - Center for Technical Knowledge (a division of Rand Worldwide Inc.) is a leading developer of professional learning materials and knowledge products for engineering software applications. ASCENT specializes in designing targeted content that facilitates application-based learning with hands-on software experience. For over 25 years, ASCENT has helped users become more productive through tailored custom learning solutions.

We welcome any comments you may have regarding this guide, or any of our products. To contact us please email: feedback@ASCENTed.com.

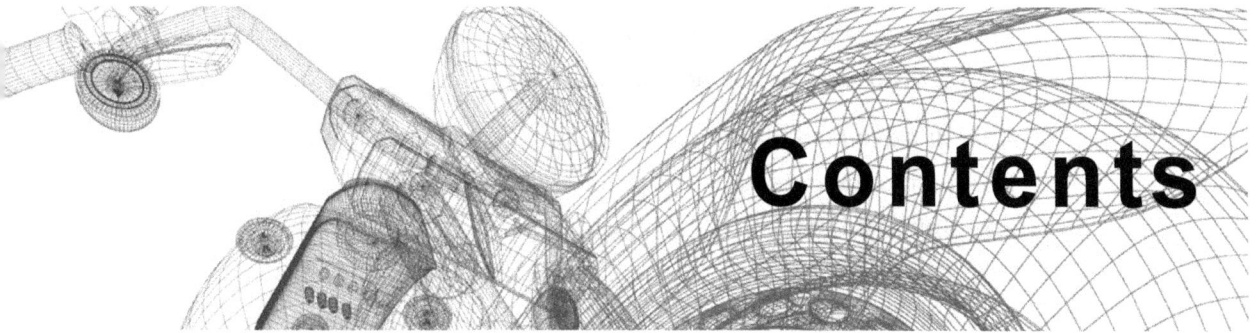

Contents

Preface

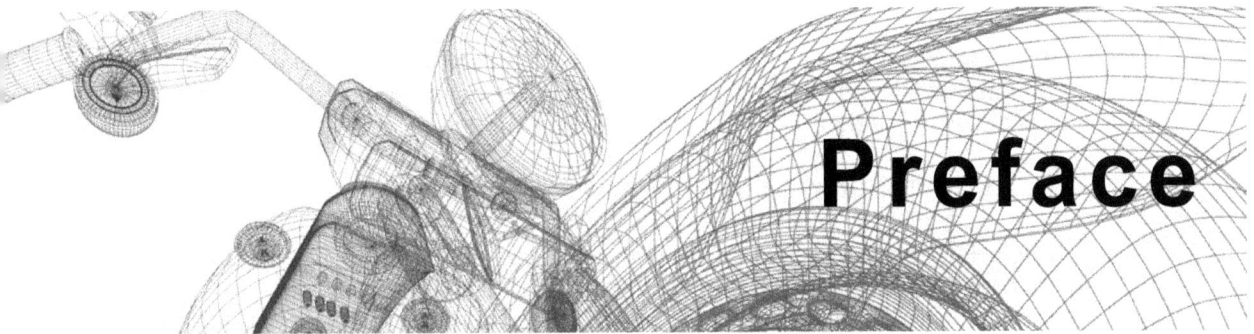

As an experienced user in the basics of Creo Parametric 6.0, the *Creo Parametric 6:0: Advanced Part Design* learning guide enables you to become more productive by extending your modeling abilities with advanced functionality and techniques. This extensive hands-on learning guide contains numerous labs and practices to give you practical experience that will improve your job performance.

Topics Covered

- Advanced datum features
- Advanced bends
- Sweeps with variable sections and helical sweeps
- Rotational and swept blends
- Designing with rounds
- Advanced round functionality
- Drafts
- Basic surface design
- Part family tables
- User-defined features (UDFs)
- Date sharing
- View Manager
- Automation (Appendix)

Prerequisites

- Access to the Creo Parametric 6.0 software. The practices and files included with this guide might not be compatible with prior versions. Practice files included with this guide are compatible with the commercial version of the software, but not the student edition.

- Completing the *Creo Parametric 6.0: Introduction to Solid Modeling* learning guide, or the equivalent Creo Parametric experience.

Note on Software Setup

This guide assumes a standard installation of the software using the default preferences during installation. Lectures and practices use the standard software templates and default options for the Content Libraries.

Lead Contributor: Scott Hendren

Scott Hendren has been a trainer and curriculum developer in the PLM industry for over 20 years, with experience on multiple CAD systems, including Pro/ENGINEER, Creo Parametric, and CATIA. Trained in Instructional Design, Scott uses his skills to develop instructor-led and web-based training products.

Scott has held training and development positions with several high profile PLM companies, and has been with the ASCENT team since 2013.

Scott holds a Bachelor of Mechanical Engineering Degree as well as a Bachelor of Science in Mathematics from Dalhousie University, Nova Scotia, Canada.

Scott Hendren has been the Lead Contributor for *Creo Parametric: Advanced Part Design* since 2013.

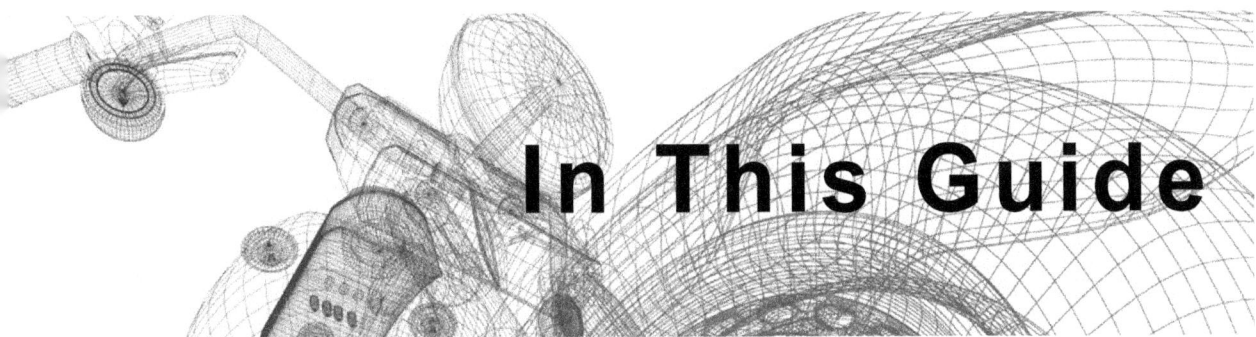

In This Guide

The following highlights the key features of this guide.

Feature	Description
Practice Files	The Practice Files page includes a link to the practice files and instructions on how to download and install them. The practice files are required to complete the practices in this guide.
Chapters	A chapter consists of the following - Learning Objectives, Instructional Content, Practices, Chapter Review Questions, and Command Summary. • **Learning Objectives** define the skills you can acquire by learning the content provided in the chapter. • **Instructional Content**, which begins right after Learning Objectives, refers to the descriptive and procedural information related to various topics. Each main topic introduces a product feature, discusses various aspects of that feature, and provides step-by-step procedures on how to use that feature. Where relevant, examples, figures, helpful hints, and notes are provided. • **Practice** for a topic follows the instructional content. Practices enable you to use the software to perform a hands-on review of a topic. It is required that you download the practice files (using the link found on the Practice Files page) prior to starting the first practice. • **Chapter Review Questions**, located close to the end of a chapter, enable you to test your knowledge of the key concepts discussed in the chapter.
Appendices	Appendices provide additional information to the main course content. It could be in the form of instructional content, practices, tables, projects, or skills assessment.

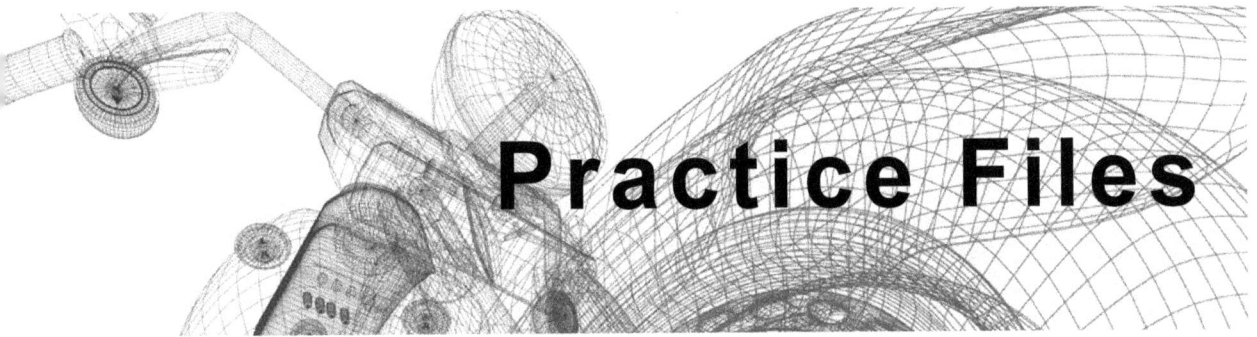

Practice Files

To download the practice files for this guide, use the following steps:

1. Type the URL *exactly as shown below* into the address bar of your Internet browser, to access the Course File Download page.

   Note: If you are using the ebook, you do not have to type the URL. Instead, you can access the page simply by clicking the URL below.

   ## https://www.ascented.com/getfile/id/didyma

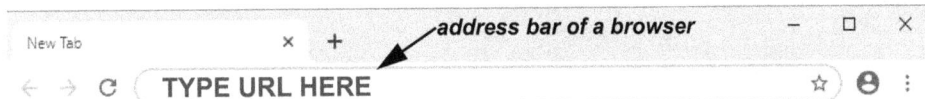

2. On the Course File Download page, click the **DOWNLOAD NOW** button, as shown below, to download the .ZIP file that contains the practice files.

   DOWNLOAD NOW ▶

3. Once the download is complete, unzip the file and extract its contents.

   The recommended practice files folder location is:
   C:\Creo Parametric Advanced Part Design Practice Files

   Note: It is recommended that you do not change the location of the practice files folder. Doing so may cause errors when completing the practices.

   Stay Informed!

   To receive information about upcoming events, promotional offers, and complimentary webcasts, visit:

   www.ASCENTed.com/updates

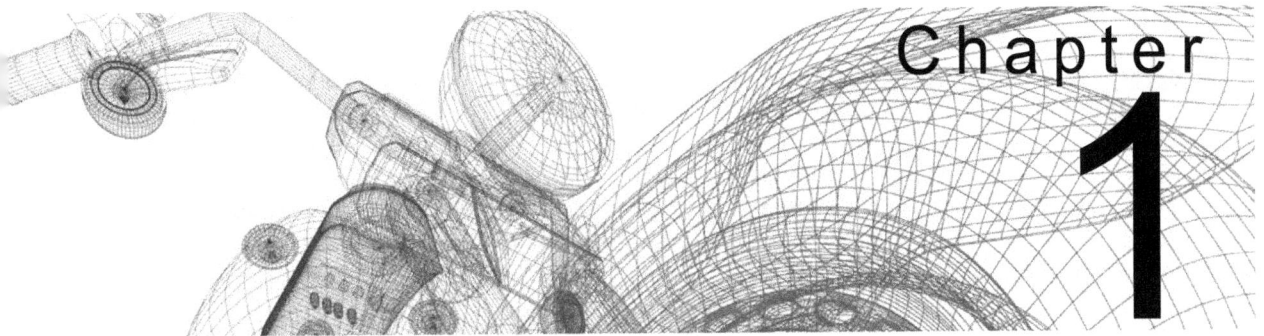

Part Design Overview

The fundamental concept in any introductory training guide is to understand that Creo Parametric is a solid modeling software package that not only enables you to create the required geometry, but also acts as a design tool. In this training guide, you will learn specialized techniques to help create and manage your part designs. Learning these techniques increases the flexibility of your part designs and enables you to create robust models.

Learning Objectives in This Chapter

- Maximize the flexibility of your models and create robust models by creating them from a solid base feature.
- Understand the importance of the sketching plane and reference selection in creating robust models.
- Identify how dimensioning and correctly setting depth options, feature order, and equations can be used to create robust models.
- Manipulate or change the design using the correct tools.
- Understand how sketching, dimensioning, referencing, and constraint techniques enable you to create a robust model that can be easily modified.

1.1 Part Design Philosophies

Before creating any part in Creo Parametric, consider the design intent of the part. By doing so, you can maximize the design flexibility. Considering *what if* scenarios that might be introduced into the part helps create a robust model that requires minimal effort to modify. Remember that Creo Parametric is a design tool. When starting a new model consider the following questions:

Default Datum Planes

Should default datum planes be used? Default datum planes are recommended in every part because they form a foundation for your model. Datum planes make an excellent selection as parents for subsequent features, thereby reducing the number of unwanted parent/child relationships. A start part should be used to ensure that your model always contains default datum planes.

Base Feature

What is the best selection for the base feature? The base feature of the part is the first geometry feature added to the part (e.g., extruded or revolved solid, datum curve, or surface). Select a form that captures the fundamental shape of the model.

Sketching Plane and Orientation References

What are the best sketching plane and sketch orientation references? These must be carefully considered because they establish parent/child relationships. Generally, you can select a sketching place and Creo Parametric will automatically select an orientation reference, but you can select a different reference if required. Whenever possible, use a default datum plane to minimize the number of unwanted parent/child relationships. The selection of these references also affects the default orientation of the model. Consider using internal datum planes as references.

If your model does not contain a planar surface that is perpendicular to the sketching plane, Creo Parametric automatically uses a projection of the X-axis belonging to the default coordinate system as the horizontal orientation for the sketch. You can change the orientation if it does not suit your design intent.

Sketcher References

Which entities should be selected as sketcher references? Sketcher references are used for dimensioning and constraining the section. They can be removed and added as required in each sketch.

When you first enter the Sketcher environment, Creo Parametric checks whether a sufficient number of sketching references have been selected. If there are enough references to locate the sketch relative to existing geometry or datum entities, you can start sketching immediately. If there are not enough references to place the sketch, you are prompted to select references for sketching.

You can use **Xsec** when defining non-perpendicular references. In the example shown in Figure 1–1, Sketcher references were created at the cross-section of the sketch plane (TOP) and two surfaces of the shell.

Sketcher references created with X sec

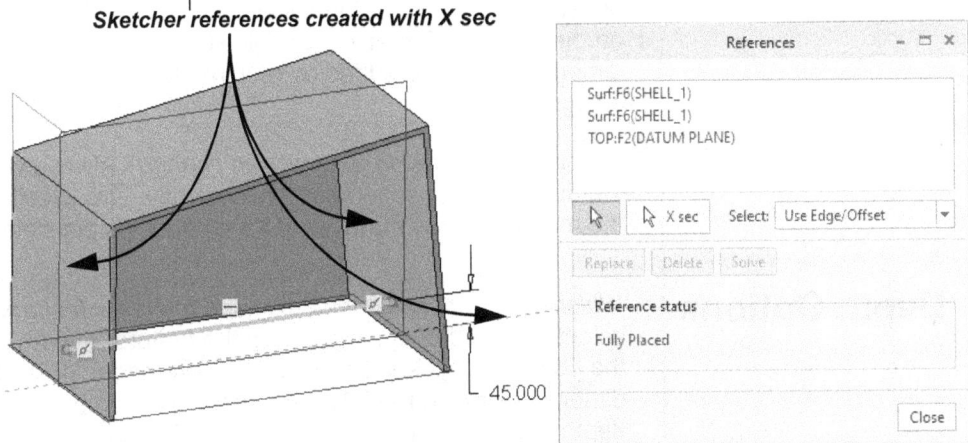

Figure 1–1

Consolidate References

You should always consider the references that are required for feature creation. Specifically, sketched references should be selected to capture design intent. When selecting references for a sketch, consider selecting a common reference for both an orientation reference and a dimensional reference.

Sketcher Tools

Which Sketcher tools should be used when creating sketches? Sketching efficiently is important. Creo Parametric offers a number of tools in the contextual menu and in the *Sketch* tab to help manipulate sketched entities. Becoming familiar with these tools is beneficial. Sketches do not need to be complex. In some situations, adding more features achieves the same result.

Parent/Child Relationships	*Which parent/child relationships are required? Which parent/child relationships should be avoided?* Parent/child relationships are established when selecting sketching planes and sketch orientation references, as well as all other references made to existing geometry throughout the feature definition (e.g., the depth option, dimensioning, or projecting or offsetting edges).
Dimensions	*Which dimensions are required to drive the design?* Use an intelligent dimensioning scheme. The dimensions should be placed so that they enable modifications. Creo Parametric is associative and you can use this to your advantage. The dimensions that are automatically added to the sketch are based on the references that were originally selected. Additional dimensions can be added as required to capture the required design intent.
	Which dimensions on the part can change? Always verify that the dimensioning scheme works correctly. This is called flexing the model. Test as many *what if* scenarios as possible.
Depth Options	*Which depth options should be used to create features?* The selection of depth options affects the feature. Always consider the possibilities if additional features are added or if other dimensions in the model are modified. Remember that some depth options result in parent/child relationships (i.e., **To Next**, **Through Until**, or **To Selected**).
Relations	*Do any relations need to be added?* Relations are user-defined mathematical equations used to capture and control design intent in a model. Creo Parametric can use relations in features, parts, and assemblies.
Feature Order	*What feature order best captures the design intent?* The feature order of a model is important. For example, should a hole be placed before or after a shell feature? Questions such as this one should be considered throughout the modeling process. The Model Tree enables you to easily review and manipulate the feature order during model creation.

1.2 Maintaining Design Intent

Realistically, not all design possibilities can be foreseen when the model is first created. Creo Parametric offers tools, which can be used to manipulate the design when a change is required.

Option	Description	Methods
Edit Dimensions	Display all dimensions associated with a selected feature.	Double-click on feature directly in graphics window or select a feature on the model or in the Model Tree, select ⟷d1 (Edit Dimensions) in the mini toolbar.
Edit Definition	Change elements (i.e., attributes, references, and sketch) used when a feature was created.	Select feature and select 🥄 (Edit Definition) in the mini toolbar.
Edit References	Select new references to replace those used to define a feature.	Select a feature and select ⚮ (Edit References) in the mini toolbar.
Reorder	Change feature order of features in the model. Consider parent/child relationships when reordering features.	Drag and drop features as required directly in Model Tree.
Insert mode	Add new a feature before any feature in model.	Drag the **green** marker to an appropriate location in Model Tree. Alternatively, select the feature in the Model Tree or Graphics window, right-click and select **Insert Here**.

1.3 Sketcher Tips

The ability to incorporate design intent in models is one of the most powerful attributes of Creo Parametric. Sketcher provides a variety of ways to incorporate design intent. Taking advantage of sketching, dimensioning, referencing, and constraint techniques enables you to combine features to create a versatile and modifiable model. Consider the following sketcher tips when creating a sketch:

Best Scheme

Sketcher ensures that the geometry is fully constrained as each entity is sketched. It does so by applying strategic dimensions, references, and sketcher constraints. The system regenerates the sketch according to your design intent. A sketch can be resolved with a variety of different dimension and reference schemes. The best scheme reflects your intent.

You can also use <Ctrl>+<T> to edit a weak dimension, making it strong.

Automatic dimensions display in light blue and are referred to as *weak* dimensions. Dimensions that you create display in dark blue and are referred to as *strong* dimensions. You cannot delete weak dimensions. You must add strong dimensions to replace them. You can make a weak dimension strong by clicking on it and selecting ⊢⊣ (Strong) in the mini toolbar, or by modifying the dimension's value. Making a weak dimension strong is recommended to ensure that the section correctly communicates the required design intent.

Simple Sketches

Try to keep sketches as simple as possible. If the sketch becomes very complex, consider whether the feature being sketched should be created as two or more simpler features. If a complex section cannot be avoided, the following techniques can help:

- Sketch a small number of entities at a time. Strengthen or create the required dimensions for the entities before proceeding with the next set. Sketching in stages makes it easier for you to achieve the dimension and reference scheme that you want to use.

- Similar to the previous technique, click ✓ (OK) after each stage of section creation. To begin the next stage of sketching, redefine the feature's section and continue sketching. If at any stage you have difficulty creating the geometry, close Sketcher and redefine the section again. This takes you back to the last stage of the section.

You can also click

☐ *(Project) to make a copy of the reference geometry.*

- Use datum curves or sketches to help define complex sections. The section can be broken into simple elements, each of which can be created as a datum curve or sketch.

  When creating the final section, ☐ (References) and

  ☐ (Project) can be used to reference this geometry. A simple set of sketches are shown in Figure 1–2.

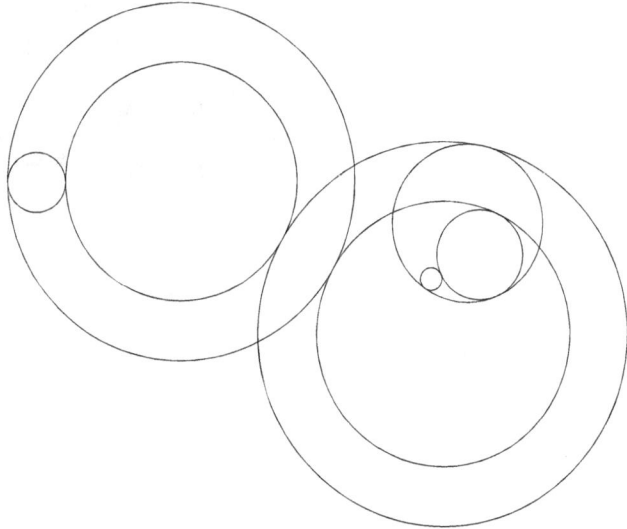

Figure 1–2

These curves can be used to create the more complex sections, as shown in Figure 1–3 and Figure 1–4.

Figure 1–3

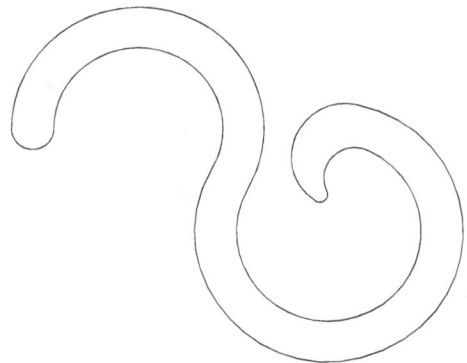

Figure 1–4

This sketch is easy to create because it references previously created datum curves. This technique is similar to the two previous techniques in that it breaks the sketching of the section into stages.

Clip Model

When creating sketched features and viewing the model in the 2D sketch orientation, it is common for the sketch to be hidden behind existing geometry, as shown in Figure 1–5.

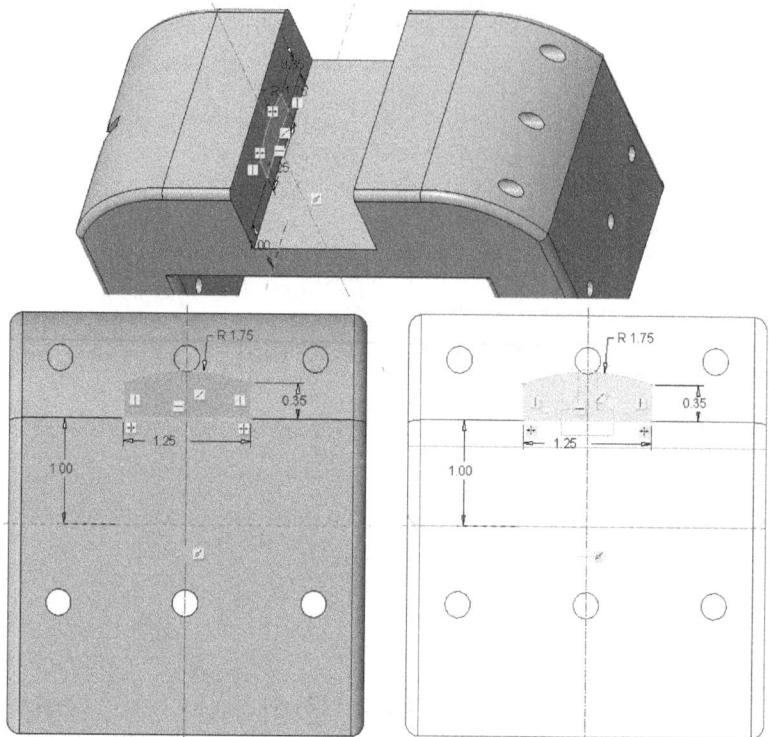

Sketch hidden by geometry. Easy to reference entities accidentally.

Even more difficult to see sketch in Hidden Line mode.

Figure 1–5

The ⬚ (Clip Model) option hides the model geometry located in front of the sketch plane, as shown in Figure 1–6.

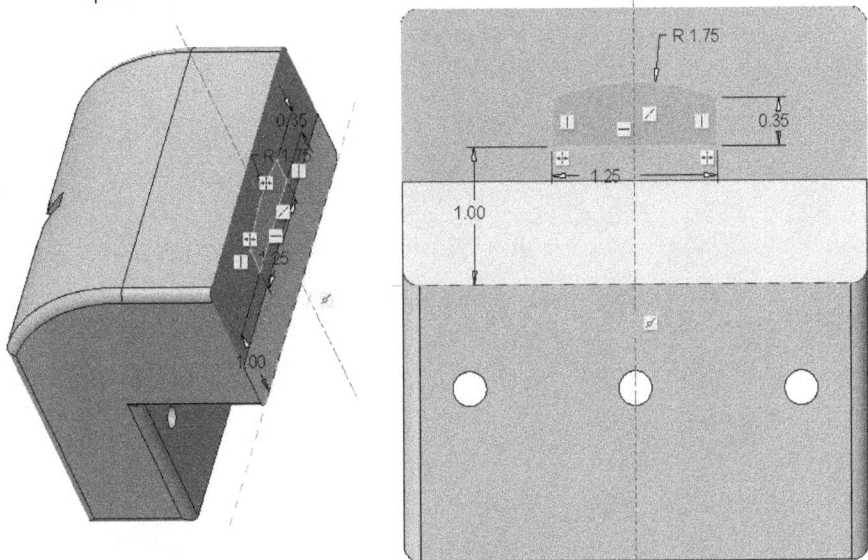

Figure 1–6

To enable clipping, click ⬚ (Clip Model) in the In-graphics toolbar. Note that if there is an active cross section when sketching, the **Clip Model** option is disabled.

The sketch view direction determines the side that is clipped.

You can click ⬚ (Sketch Setup) and then click **Flip** in the *Sketch Orientation* area in the Sketch dialog box.

Line Thickness

To help visualize the geometry that you are sketching, you can change the thickness of the sketched entities such as lines, arcs, circles, etc. Select **File>Options** to open the Creo Parametric Options dialog box.Then, select **Sketcher** and edit the *Line thickness* through the range of 1 to 3, using increments of 0.1, as shown in Figure 1–7.

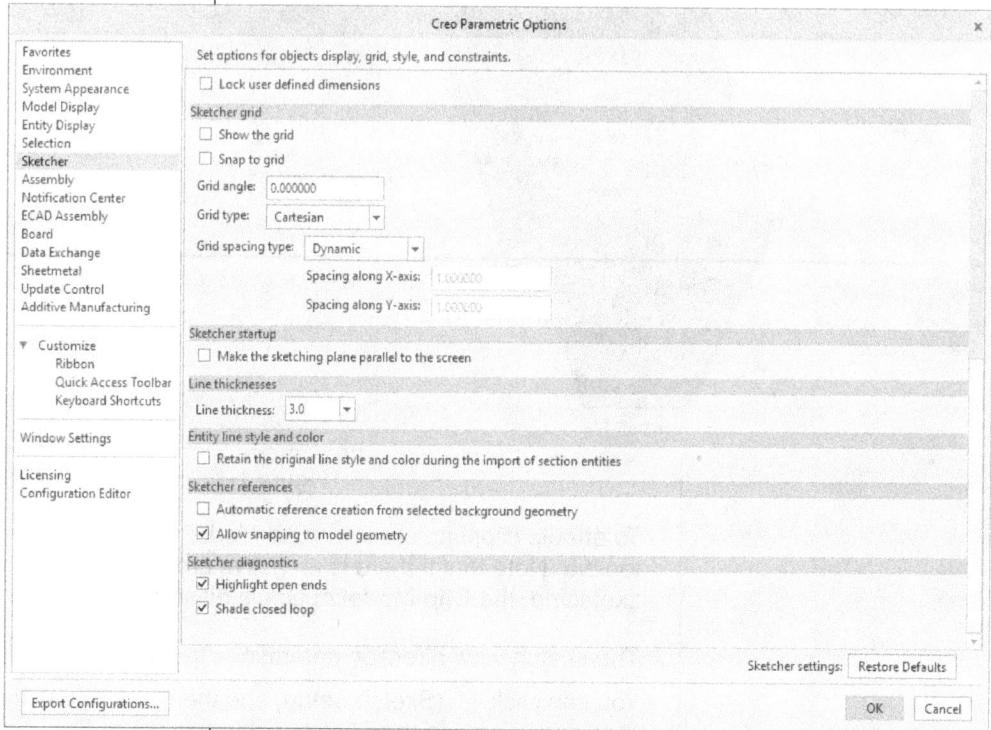

Figure 1–7

Figure 1–8 shows that changing the line thickness can make the sketched geometry clearer.

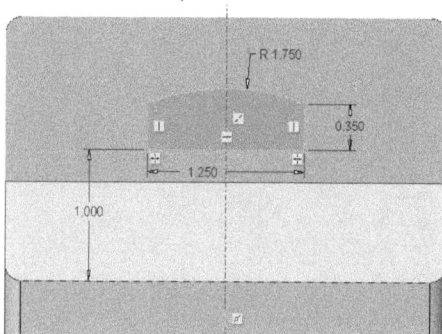

Thickness 1.0

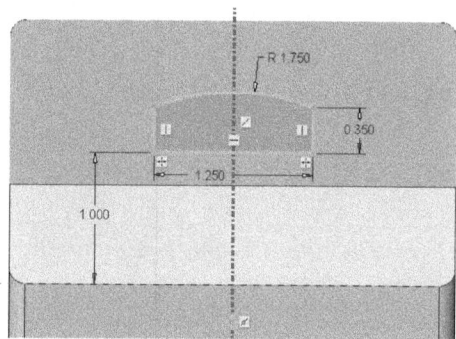

Thickness 3.0

Figure 1–8

Lock and Disable Constraints

While sketching an entity, constraint symbols automatically display next to the entities. If the constraint is not wanted, right-click twice until the constraint icon displays with a stroke through it. This disables the constraint and prevents the entity from snapping to a location as a result of the constraint.

Additionally, you can lock a required constraint while you are sketching an entity. To lock a constraint while sketching an entity, right-click or press <Shift>. The constraint highlights with an enclosed green circle. The constraint is now locked.

If a constraint is applied that you do not want to use, you can delete or override that constraint.

Sketch References and Constraints

When sketching entities, the system dynamically snaps the sketched entities to existing geometry as you hover the cursor over them. In addition to snapping to free locations along the entities, mid-line and end-line snap locations also display, as shown in Figure 1–9.

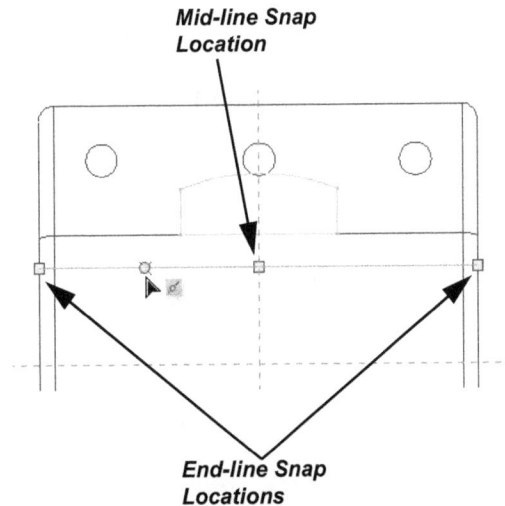

Mid-line Snap Location

End-line Snap Locations

Figure 1–9

When you select existing geometry, it is automatically turned into a sketcher reference, as shown in Figure 1–10.

Selected entity immediately turned into a sketcher reference

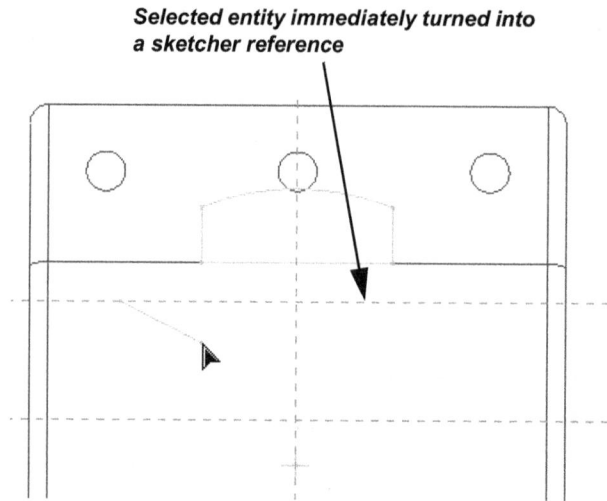

Figure 1–10

When sketching entities, the system displays a dotted line as a guide in circumstances where entities align, as shown in Figure 1–11.

Dotted line used as guide

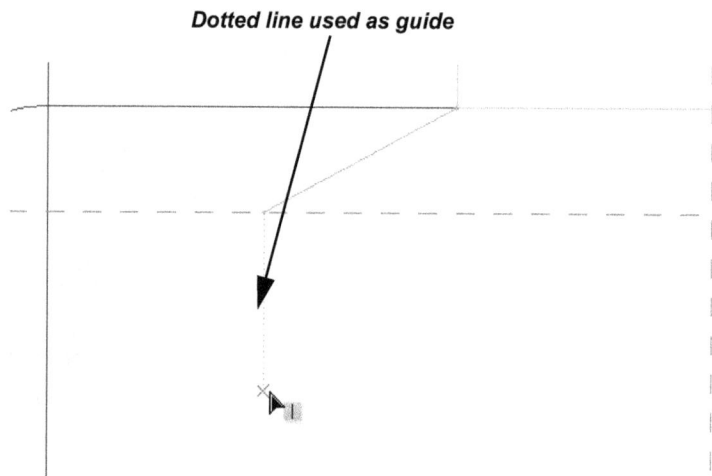

Figure 1–11

The sketch constraints are highlighted by green boxes to make them stand out visually. The color of closed sections has also been updated as shown in Figure 1–12.

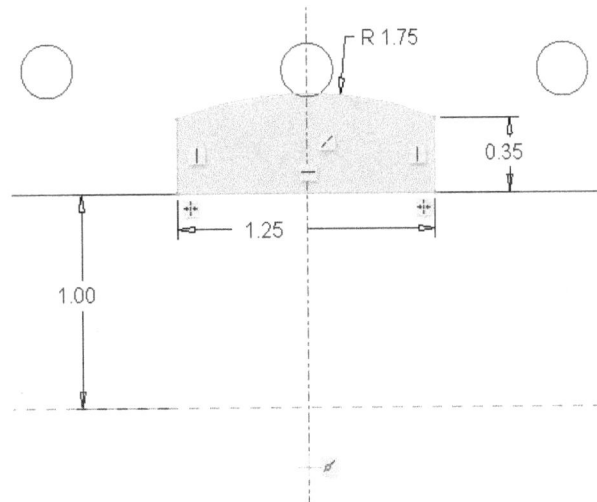

Figure 1–12

Reference in 3D

When assigning references, spin the part into a 3D view. You can then be certain of the references you are selecting. Always remember that referencing these entities results in parent/child relationships and that you need to select appropriately.

Dimension in 3D

When dimensioning a section to existing geometry, note the edges or surfaces that are being selected. Spin the model into a 3D view to be certain of what you are selecting. Dimensions result in parent/child relationships. Avoid dimensioning or aligning to edges created from rounds, drafts, and chamfers.

Rounds and Chamfers

Create rounds and chamfers as separate features instead of sketching them in a feature. This helps simplify sketches and makes the model more robust.

Construction Entities

Understand and use Sketcher centerlines, construction circles, and points to create geometry or a required dimension scheme. All solid sketched entities can be converted to construction entities and vice-versa.

You can create construction entities by clicking ▯ (Construction Mode) and creating the geometry. To toggle between solid and construction geometry, select an entity and click ▯ (Toggle Construction), as shown in Figure 1–13.

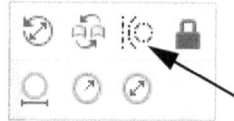

Figure 1–13

Dimension to Enable Patterns

If you plan to pattern the feature you are sketching, dimension it so that you create the required pattern dimensions.

Determine Position

When the *Sketch* tab becomes active, the model displays in the current orientation. Try spinning the model to determine the position in which the sketch is to be placed and then click ▯ (Project). Select an edge in the area in which you want to sketch. You can click ▯ (Sketch View) in the Graphics toolbar, to orient the model in a 2D view, which can make sketching easier. The **project** symbol identifies where the sketch is to be placed. The entity can be deleted once the sketch has been completed.

Sketched Section

The sketch associated with a feature is separated from the remaining elements. The feature group can be expanded in the Model Tree to display the section, as shown in Figure 1–14. This enables you to edit the sketch or its orientation references independent of the entire feature.

The 'di' (Edit Dimensions) option enables you to modify the section dimensions.

The ▱ (Edit Definition) option enables you to redefine the section in the Sketch tab.

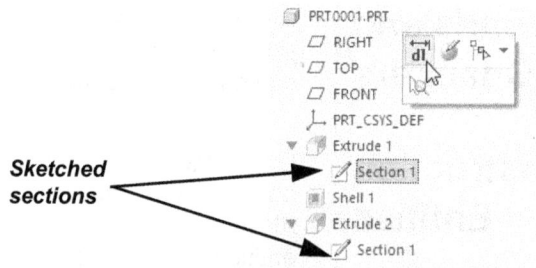

Figure 1–14

Practice 1a

Dimensioning for Design Intent

Practice Objective

- Understand how sketching, dimensioning, and constraint techniques enable you to capture specific motion and design intent.

You might need to dimension to centerlines, disable constraints, and/or lock dimensions to incorporate the design intent.

In this practice, you will create three-member linkages with two fixed end points. The end points are created for you in a single sketch. Your task will be to select the appropriate sketcher references, and then sketch and dimension to capture the design intent based on the motion depicted in the associated images. Figure 1–15 shows an example of the design intent that must be captured and the resulting sketch.

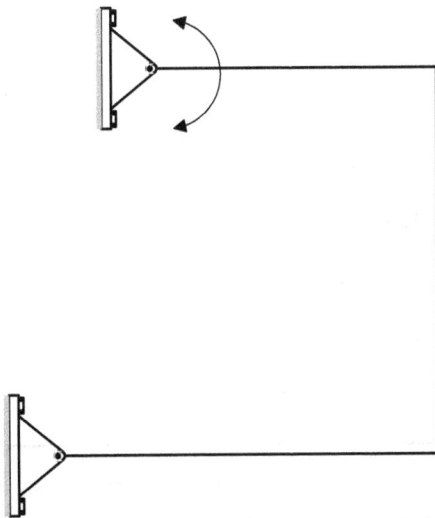

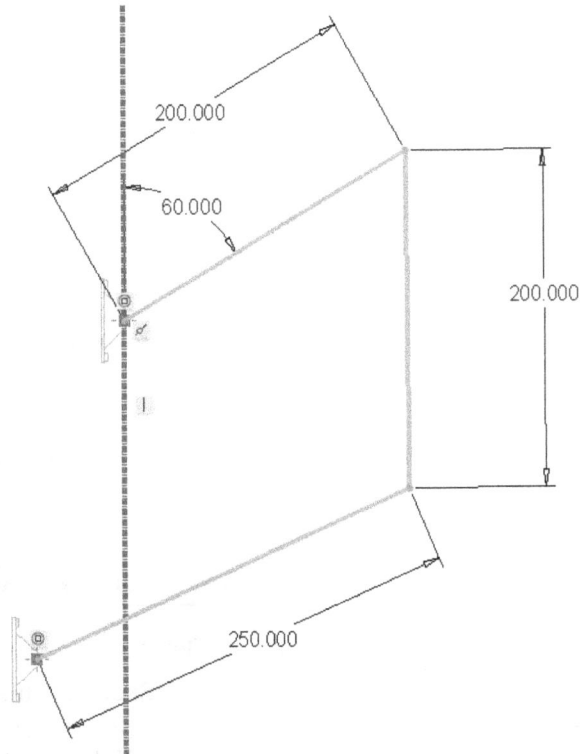

Figure 1–15

Task 1 - Open a part file.

1. Set the working directory to the *Design_Intent* folder.

2. Open **design_intent_1.prt**. The part has a single sketch and displays as shown in Figure 1–16.

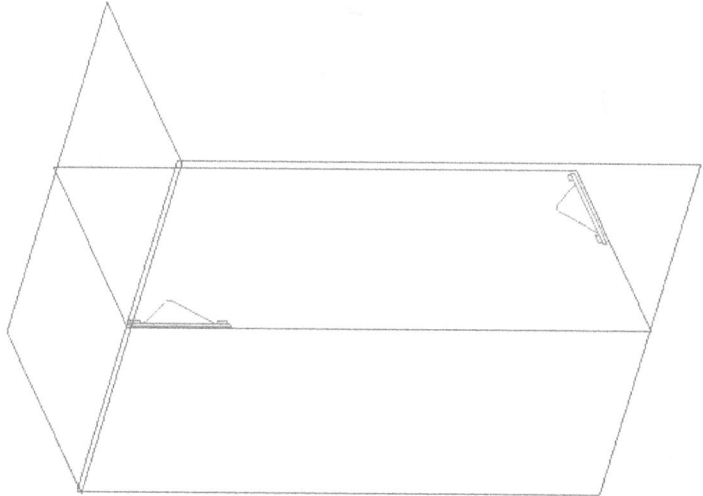

Figure 1–16

3. Set the model display as follows:

- ⚬ *(Datum Display Filters)*: Only 🔲 (Plane Display)

- ⚭ *(Spin Center)*: Off

- 🔲 *(Display Style)*: 🔲 (No Hidden)

Task 2 - Create a sketch.

1. Select datum plane **FRONT** from the Model Tree and click ⚬ (Sketch) in the mini toolbar.

2. In the Setup group in the *Sketch* tab, click 🔲 (Sketch View).

3. Click 🔲 (References).

4. Zoom in and select the arced curve shown in Figure 1–17.

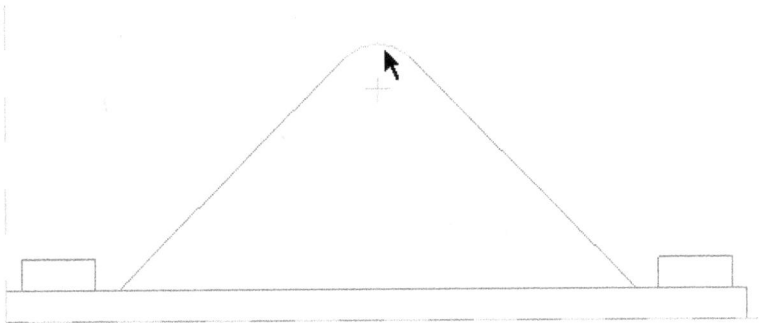

Figure 1–17

5. Pan to the other anchor and select the arced curve shown in Figure 1–18.

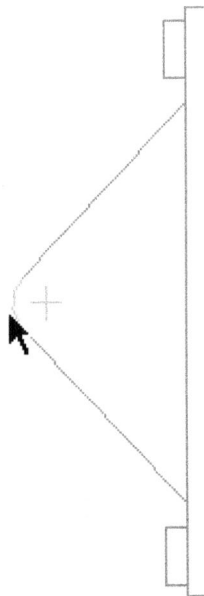

Figure 1–18

6. Click **Close** in the References dialog box.

7. Sketch the entities and dimension the sketch to capture the design intent indicated by the range of motion, as shown in Figure 1–19.

To display the full range of motion of each linkage, click

⇗ (Modify), select the driving angular dimension, and drag the dimension wheel.

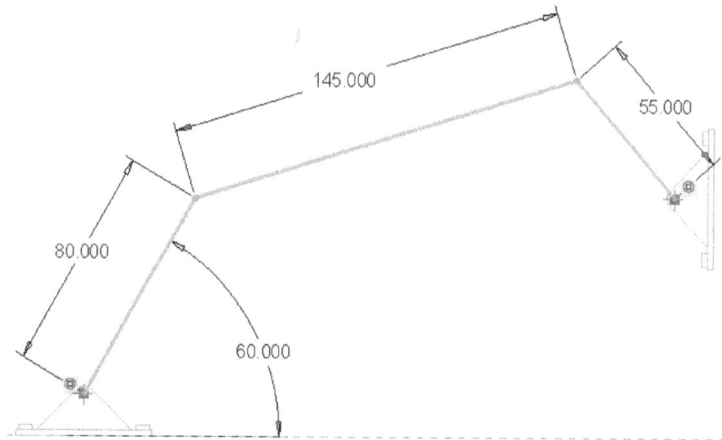

Figure 1–19

8. Save the part and erase it from memory.

Task 3 - Open a part file.

1. Open **design_intent_2.prt**. The part has a single sketch and displays as shown in Figure 1–20.

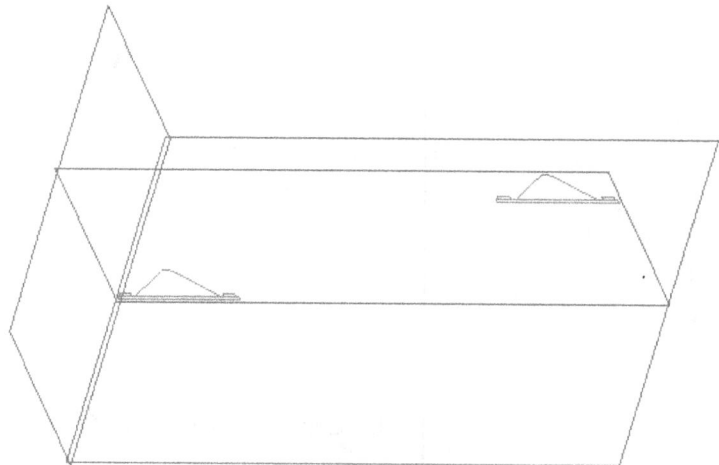

Figure 1–20

Task 4 - Create a sketch.

1. Select datum plane **FRONT** from the Model Tree and click ☒ (Sketch) in the mini toolbar.

2. In the Setup group in the *Sketch* tab, click ☒ (Sketch View).

3. As in Task 1, select the arced curves as sketcher references.

4. Sketch the entities and dimension the sketch to capture the design intent, indicated by the range of motion, as shown in Figure 1–21.

To display the full range of motion of each linkage, click ☒ (Modify), select the driving angular dimension, and drag the dimension wheel.

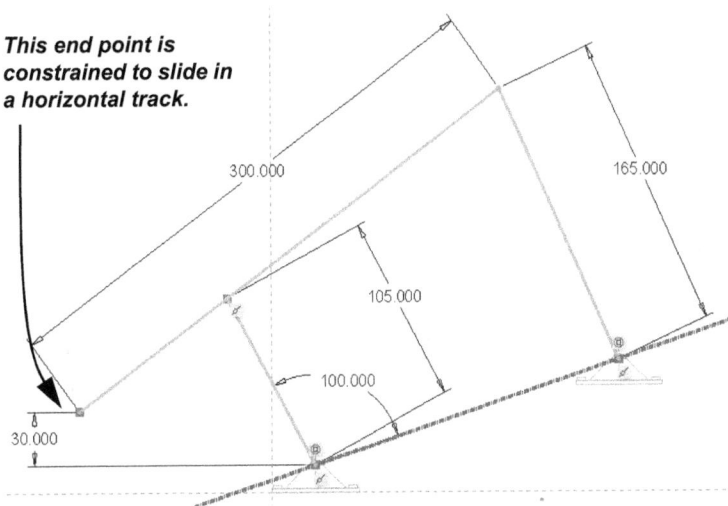

This end point is constrained to slide in a horizontal track.

300.000   165.000

105.000

100.000

30.000

Figure 1–21

5. Save the part and erase it from memory.

Task 5 - Open a part file.

1. Open **design_intent_3.prt**. The part has a single sketch and displays as shown in Figure 1–22.

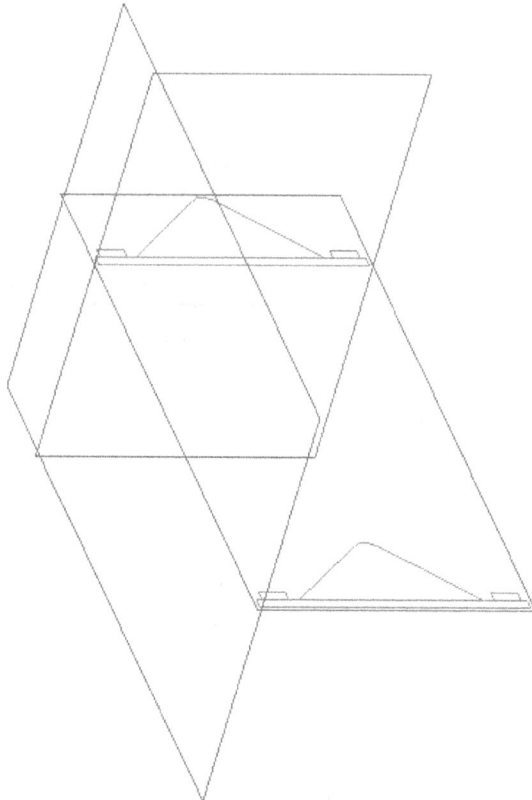

Figure 1–22

Task 6 - Create a sketch.

1. Select datum plane **FRONT** from the Model Tree and click ⬚ (Sketch) in the mini toolbar.

2. In the Setup group in the *Sketch* tab, click 🗗 (Sketch View).

3. As in Task 2, select the arced curves as sketcher references.

4. Sketch the entities and dimension the sketch to capture the design intent indicated by the range of motion, as shown in Figure 1–23.

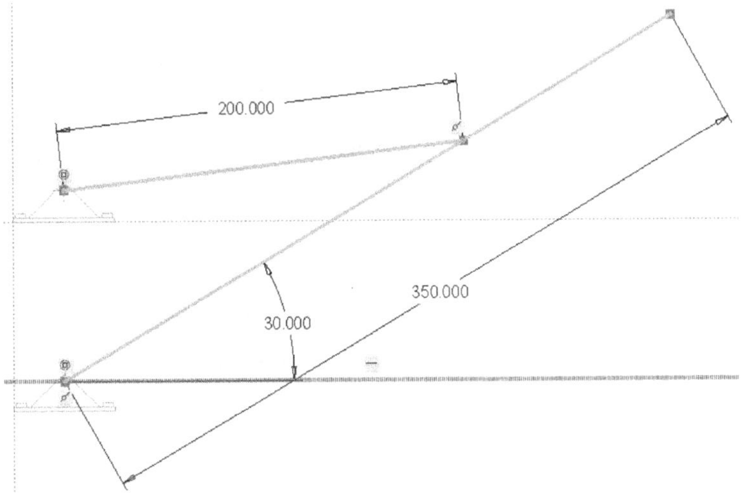

To display the full range of motion of each linkage, click

(Modify), select the driving angular dimension, and drag the dimension wheel.

Figure 1–23

5. Save the part and erase it from memory.

Practice 1b

Effective Part Design

Practice Objectives

- Compare the creation methods of two different parts and how the design techniques can affect future model changes.
- Discuss and understand design techniques.

In this practice you will open two existing parts. They parts look the same but have been modeled differently. It is an injection molded plastic part, which is a key from a keyboard.

Task 1 - Open and review a part.

1. Set the working directory to the *Effective_Design* folder.

2. Open **key_a.prt**.

3. Set the model display as follows:

   - ⚓ *(Datum Display Filters)*: All Off

   - ⤬ *(Spin Center)*: Off

   - ▢ *(Display Style)*: ▢ (Shading With Edges)

4. Spin the part around to display all of its features, as shown in Figure 1–24.

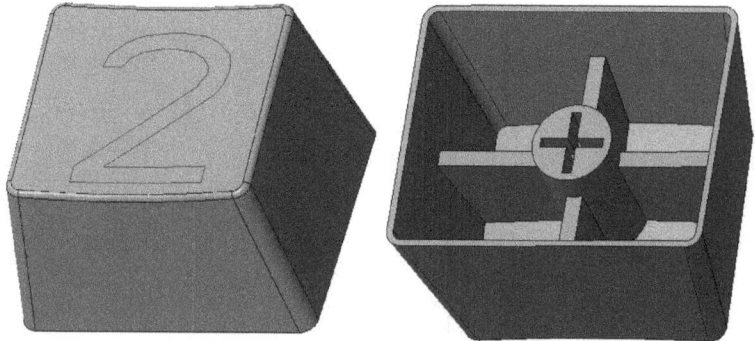

Figure 1–24

5. Press <Ctrl>+<D> to return to the default orientation.

6. Open **key_b.prt**. It displays identical to the **key_a** part, but it has been modeled differently.

7. Use ⊞ ▾ (Windows) in the Quick Access Toolbar, to toggle window activation between the two parts and compare the features listed in the Model Tree, as shown in Figure 1–25.

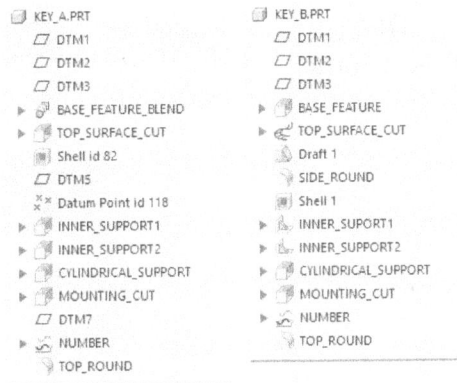

KEY_A.PRT	KEY_B.PRT
▱ DTM1	▱ DTM1
▱ DTM2	▱ DTM2
▱ DTM3	▱ DTM3
▶ ⬡ BASE_FEATURE_BLEND	▶ ⬡ BASE_FEATURE
▶ ⬡ TOP_SURFACE_CUT	▶ ⬡ TOP_SURFACE_CUT
⬡ Shell id 82	⬡ Draft 1
▱ DTM5	⬡ SIDE_ROUND
✕✕ Datum Point id 118	⬡ Shell 1
▶ ⬡ INNER_SUPPORT1	▶ ⬡ INNER_SUPORT1
▶ ⬡ INNER_SUPPORT2	▶ ⬡ INNER_SUPPORT2
▶ ⬡ CYLINDRICAL_SUPPORT	▶ ⬡ CYLINDRICAL_SUPPORT
▶ ⬡ MOUNTING_CUT	▶ ⬡ MOUNTING_CUT
▱ DTM7	▶ ⬡ NUMBER
▶ ⬡ NUMBER	⬡ TOP_ROUND
⬡ TOP_ROUND	

Figure 1–25

Design Considerations

In the following tasks, you will make the same changes to both parts and discover how the different modeling techniques and feature selections provide different results.

Task 2 - Incorporate first design change.

---

1. Ensure that the **key_a.prt** window is active.

Design Considerations

A design change requires that the offset dimension that controls **INNER_SUPPORT1** is to be changed from *0.2* to **0.25**, as shown in Figure 1–26.

*The offset dimension for **key_a.prt** is located by editing **DTM5**. The offset dimension for **key_b.prt** is located by editing **INNER_SUPPORT1**.*

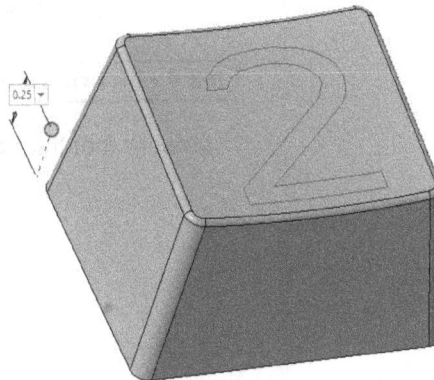

Figure 1–26

2. Incorporate this dimensional change in both **key_a.prt** and **key_b.prt**.

Design Considerations

Task 3 - Incorporate second design change.

1. Activate the **key_a.prt** window.

A second design change requires that the radius dimension of **TOP_ROUND** be changed from *0.02* to **0.05**, as shown in Figure 1–27.

Figure 1–27

2. Incorporate this dimensional change in both **key_a.prt** and **key_b.prt**. Did the geometry of both parts behave in the same way after the last dimensional change?

3. Activate **key_a.prt** window and note the interaction between the **TOP_ROUND** and the other round geometry.

Task 4 - Incorporate third design change.

1. Ensure that the **key_a.prt** window is active.

Design Considerations

A third design change requires that the radius dimension of the round geometry shown in Figure 1–28 be changed from *0.05* to **0.063**.

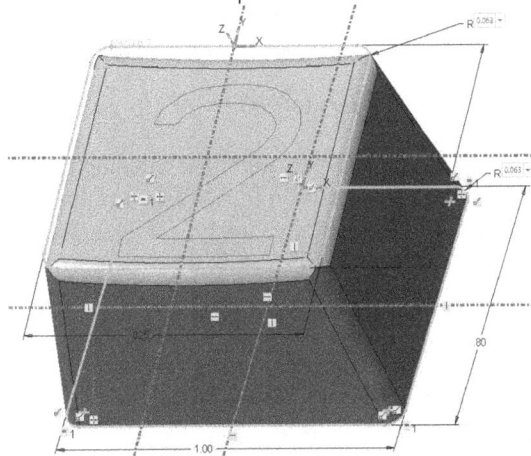

Edit the BASE_FEATURE_BLEND in key_a

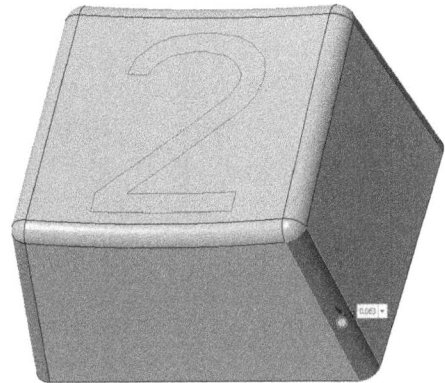

Edit the SIDE_ROUND in key_b

Figure 1–28

2. Incorporate this dimensional change in both **key_a.prt** and **key_b.prt**. Which part is easier to change?

Task 5 - Incorporate fourth design change.

---

1. Ensure that the **key_b.prt** window is active.

Design Considerations

A structural analysis must be performed on the part. Before sending the part to the analysis department, all of the rounds must be suppressed, as shown in Figure 1–29.

Figure 1–29

2. Incorporate the suppression of all of the rounds in both **key_a.prt** and **key_b.prt**. You will find that suppression of all of the rounds is only possible in **key_b.prt**.

Task 6 - Incorporate fifth design change.

1. Ensure that the **key_b.prt** window is active.

Design Considerations

Since this part is manufactured by injection molding it must have some form of draft so that it can be removed from the mold. The tooling department has asked for a design change that requires the draft angle be edited from *8.5* to **8.0**, as shown in Figure 1–30.

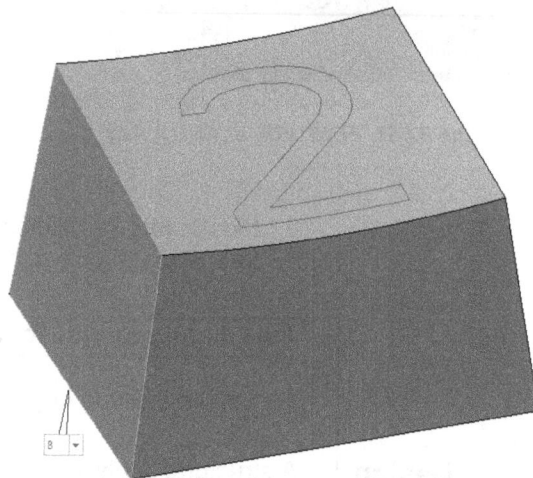

Figure 1–30

2. Incorporate this dimensional change in both **key_a.prt** and **key_b.prt**. You will find that a dimensional change request to the draft angle is only possible in **key_b.prt**. Which part would you rather work with?

3. Save both parts and erase them from memory.

Task 7 - Points for consideration.

1. Consider the following points:
    - What is the best base feature for this part?
    - Does the feature count differ between the two models? Why?
    - What feature order should be used to capture the design intent?
    - Which dimensions are required to drive the design?
    - Discuss the best practices when designing with rounds.
    - Which parent/child relationships are required?
    - Which parent/child relationships should be avoided?
    - Can any relations be added?

Chapter Review Questions

1. Which depth option creates a parent/child relationship.
   (Select all that apply.)

   a. ⊥ (Blind)

   b. ≡ (To Next)

   c. ⊣⊢ (Through All)

   d. ⊥ (Through Until)

   e. ⊥ (To Selected)

2. A parent/child relationship is established when any solid
   feature is created in the model.

   a. True

   b. False

3. If a parent feature must be deleted, which of the following
   options can be used to change the references to the child
   feature? (Select all that apply.)

   a. $\overrightarrow{d1}$ (Edit Dimensions)

   b. ✎ (Edit Definition)

   c. ✐ (Edit References)

   d. **Insert Mode**

4. Which of the following actions creates a parent/child relationship when sketching a feature? (Select all that apply.)

   a. Selecting the sketching plane.

   b. Selecting the orientation plane.

   c. Maintaining the default orientation plane.

   d. Selecting sketching references.

   e. Creating an offset entity.

   f. Projecting an existing edge to create a new entity.

   g. Dimensioning the length of a line.

   h. Aligning a new entity with an existing entity.

   i. Extruding to a Blind depth.

   j. Extruding through all surfaces.

   k. Extruding to Intersect with a selected surface or plane.

Answers: 1bde, 2a, 3bc, 4abcdefhk

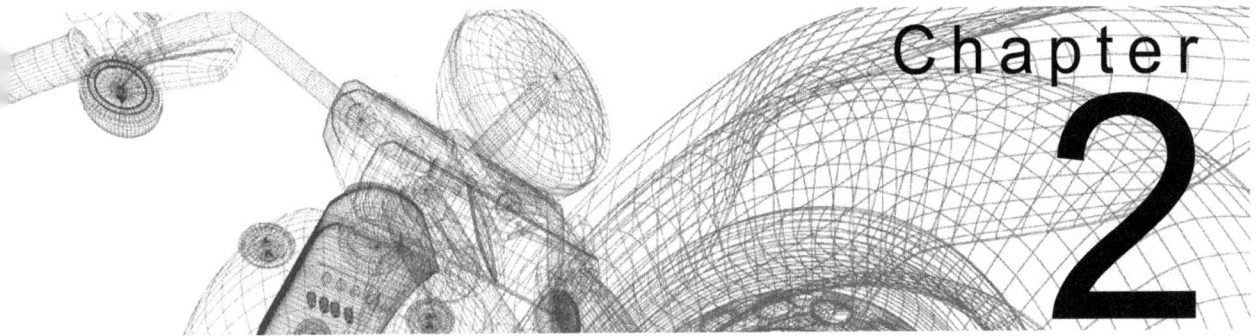

Advanced Bends

You have previously worked with basic Engineering features such as holes, rounds and blends. In this chapter, you will investigate Toroidal Bends and Spinal Bends.

Learning Objectives in This Chapter

- Learn how to create Toroidal Bend features.
- Learn how to create Spinal Bend Features.

2.1 Toroidal Bends

Toroidal Bends are used to transform solids, surfaces, or datum curves into revolved shapes. For example, you can use this functionality to transform the flat geometry shown on the left in Figure 2–1 into a tire.

Figure 2–1

To create the bend, you must specify the geometry to be bent, the profile for the geometry to wrap around, and the bend radius.

To create a Toroidal Bend feature, in the *Model* tab, click

Engineering> ◌ (Toroidal Bend). The *Toroidal Bend* dashboard displays as shown in Figure 2–2.

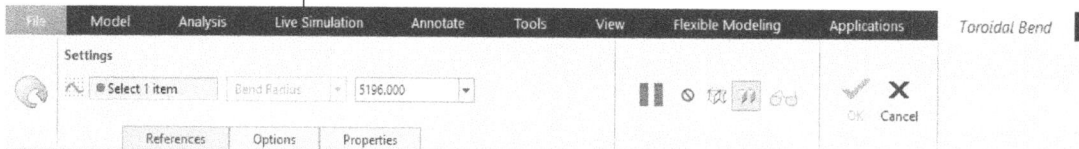

Figure 2–2

To create a toroidal bend, select the geometry you want to bend, sketch or select a profile to bend the geometry around, and define the radius of the bend. The system then wraps the geometry around the profile and rotates the geometry through the bend radius.

References

The References panel enables you to select any **Quilts** or **Curves** that you want to bend. You can also select **Solid Geometry** to automatically include all solid geometry in the model, as shown in Figure 2–3.

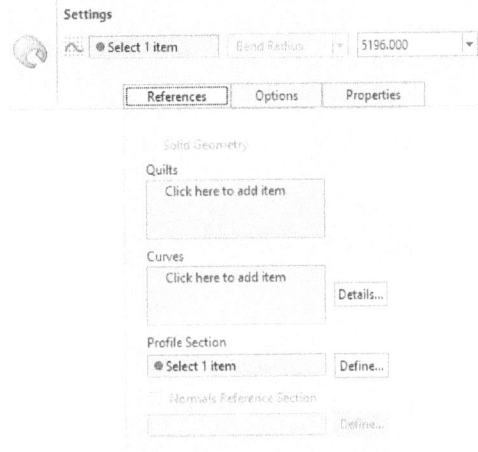

Figure 2–3

You can also right-click to access the options, as shown in Figure 2–4.

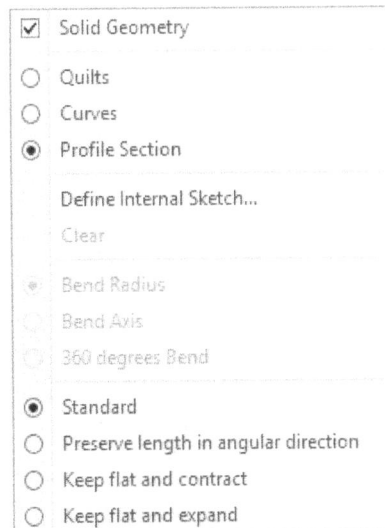

Figure 2–4

Bend Profile

The Profile Section collector is used to select an existing profile. Alternatively, click **Define** or right-click and select **Define Internal Sketch**, and sketch the required profile. The profile requires a sketched datum coordinate system, as shown in Figure 2–5.

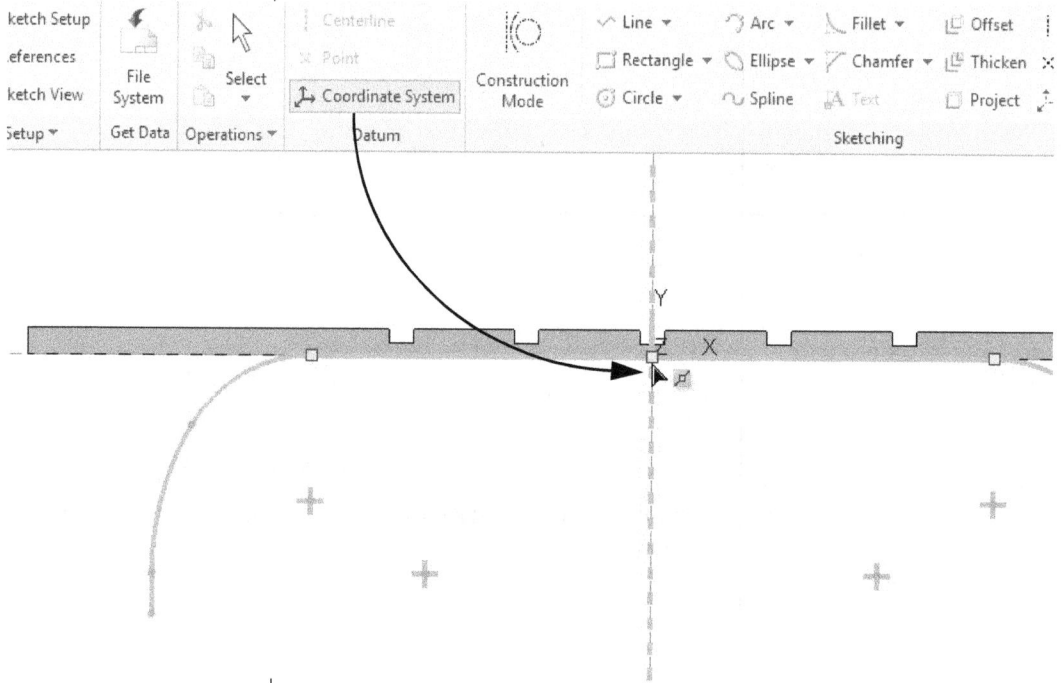

Figure 2–5

Once the profile has been established, the **Normals Reference Section** option becomes available. You can then select or sketch a reference for the normal vector direction of the bend. By default, the normals of the sketched entities follow the profile curve. Using the **Normals Reference Section**, the normals of the sketched entities follow the reference curve, as shown in Figure 2–6.

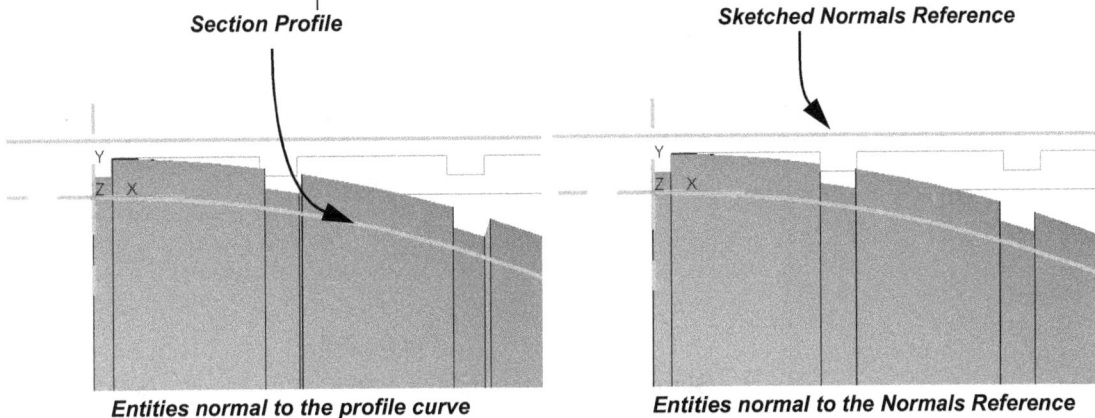

Section Profile

Sketched Normals Reference

Entities normal to the profile curve

Entities normal to the Normals Reference

Figure 2–6

Bend Radius

The Bend Radius is specified in one of three ways:

- **Bend Radius:** Set the distance between the origin of the coordinate system and the bend axis.
- **Bend Axis:** Lies on the profile section plane.
- **360 degrees Bend:** Sets two planes to define the geometry and the length of the bend, based on a full 360° rotation.

These options are set in the dashboard, as shown in Figure 2–7.

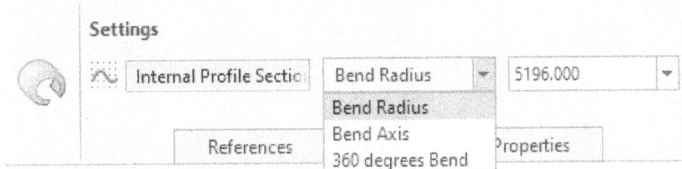

Figure 2–7

Options Panel

The Options panel controls the bending options for all curves in the curves collector, as shown in Figure 2–8.

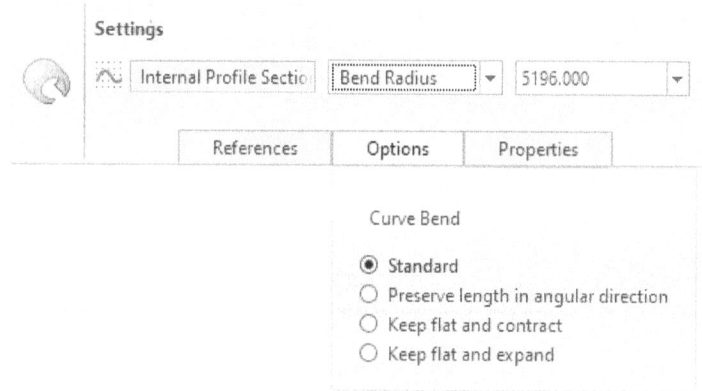

Figure 2–8

- **Standard:** Use the default algorithm for toroidal bends.

- **Preserve length in angular direction:** Bend the curve chains while maintaining a constant distance from points on the curves to the plane of the profile section, along the angular direction.

- **Keep flat and contract:** Shorten the distance from the points on the curves to the plane of the profile section, while the curve chains stay flat and in the neutral plane.

- **Keep flat and expand:** Lengthen the distance from points on the curves to the plane of the profile section, while the curve chains stay flat and in the neutral plane.

2.2 Spinal Bends

The ⌀ (Spinal Bend) tool is used to bend a solid or quilt about a curved spine. The system repositions cross sections of the model along the curve, as shown in Figure 2–9.

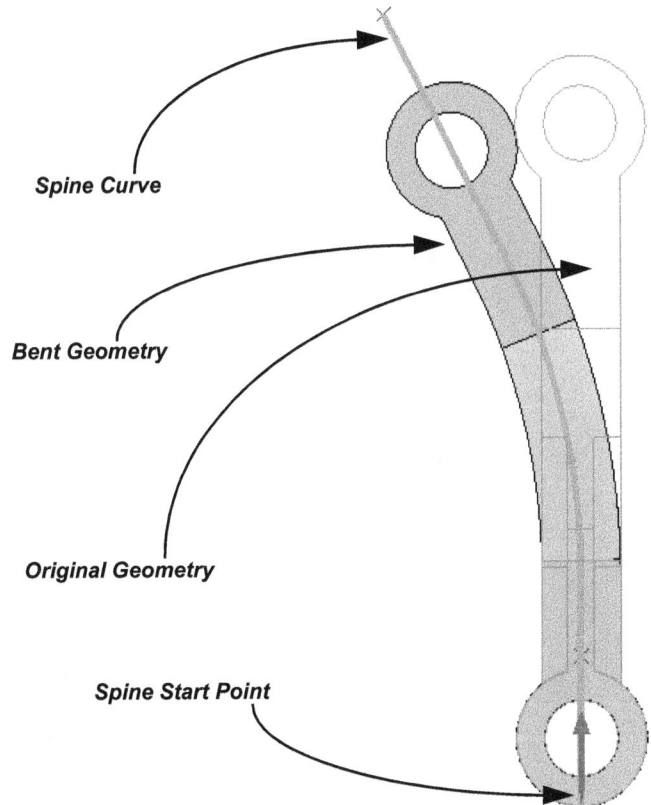

Spine Curve

Bent Geometry

Original Geometry

Spine Start Point

Figure 2–9

You can create a spinal bend by either selecting a spine for the bend, and clicking **Engineering>** ✐ (Spinal Bend) or by clicking **Engineering>** ✐ (Spinal Bend) and then selecting a spine. If using the later approach, in the *Spinal Bend* dashboard, expand the References panel, click in the *Spine* field and select the appropriate spline curve, as shown in Figure 2–10.

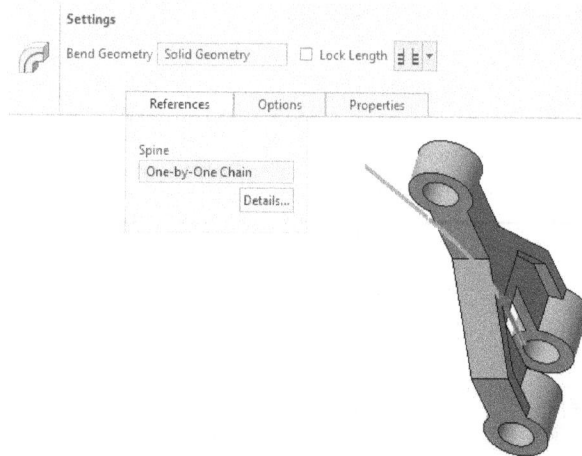

Figure 2–10

In the *Spinal Bend* dashboard, click in the Bend Geometry collector and select the geometry. The system previews the bend as shown in Figure 2–11.

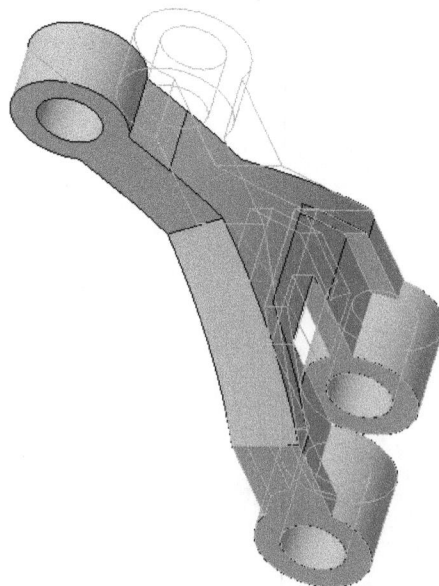

Figure 2–11

Notes on the Spine Curve:

- You can reverse the start point by clicking the arrow head.

- The spine must be C1 continuous (tangent). To ensure that the resulting surfaces are tangent, the spine should also be C2 continuous (curvature continuous).

- The geometry is created by taking an imaginary plane that passes through the start point of the spine, normal to it, and projecting the geometry onto that plane as it moves along the spine. The plane running through the start point must intersect the original quilt or solid feature.

The bend region is defined relative to an axis that is tangent to the spine at the start point of the spine. You can control the region of the bend by selecting the appropriate option in the dashboard, as shown in Figure 2–12.

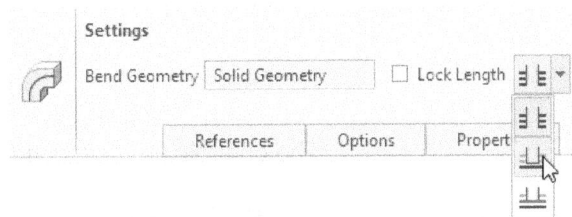

Figure 2–12

The depth options are described as follows:

- ⧩⧨ (Bend All): Bend the geometry from the start of the spine to the farthest point along the geometry to bend, in the direction of the axis.

- ⊥ (Bend to Depth): Bend the geometry from the start of the spine to a specified depth, in the direction of the axis. You can enter a depth value or use the drag handle.

- ⊥ (Bend To Selected): Bend the geometry up to a selected reference. You can use a plane that is perpendicular to the axis, or a point or vertex.

- Additionally, you can select the **Lock Length** option. By default, the bend region extends the entire length of the spine. However, if you enable the **Lock Length** checkbox, the bend region maintains its original length after it is bent.

Options Panel

The Options panel is used to control the distribution of the mass properties of the cross section along the spine, using the options in the X-Section Property Control drop-down list, as shown in Figure 2–13.

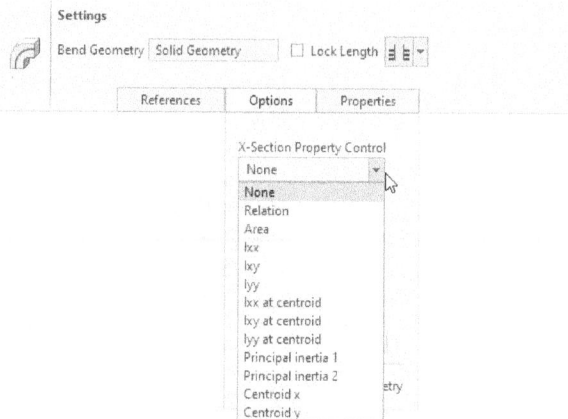

Figure 2–13

The controls are described as follows:

- **Relation:** Write a relation between the cross section properties.

- **Area:** Use cross sectional area.

- **Ixx, Ixy, or Iyy:** Planar moments of inertia of the cross section in relation to the sketched coordinate system.

- **Ixx at centroid, Ixy at centroid, or Iyy at centroid:** Planar moments of inertia of the cross section in relation to a coordinate system at the centroid and with axes parallel to the specified coordinate system.

- **Principal inertia 1:** Greater planar principal moment of inertia.

- **Principal inertia 2:** Lesser planar principal moment of inertia.

- **Centroid x:** X-coordinate of the center of area of the cross section in relation to the sketched coordinate system.

- **Centroid y:** Y-coordinate of the center of area of the cross section in relation to the sketched coordinate system.

You can further control the cross section property using one of the following types:

- **Linear:** The section property varies linearly between the values at the start and end points of the spine.

- **Graph:** The section property varies by a graph feature that determines values between the spine start and end points.

Finally, you can select the **Remove unbent geometry** checkbox to remove geometry that is not influenced by the spine, as shown in Figure 2–14.

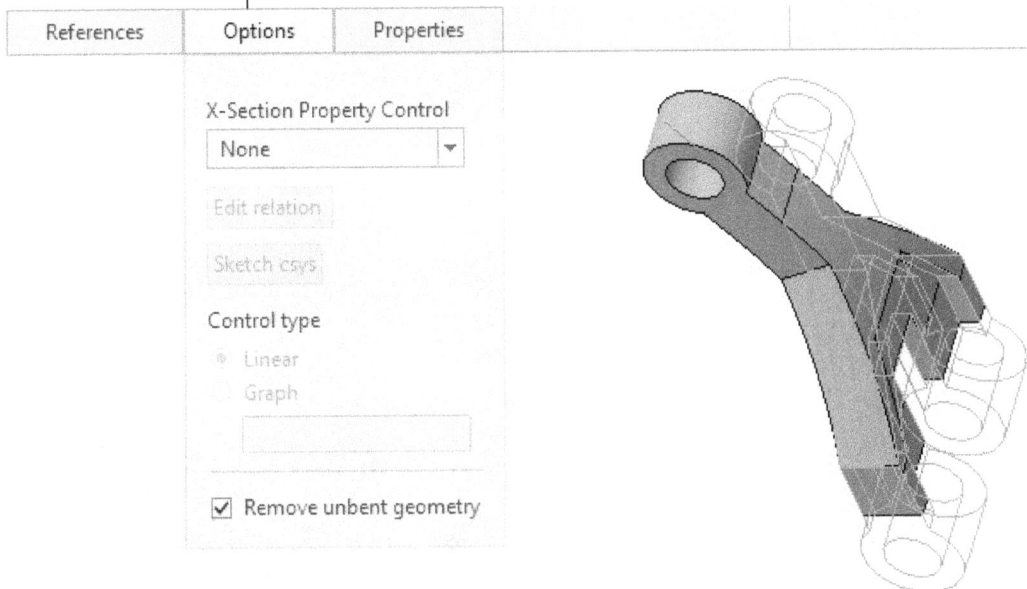

Figure 2–14

Practice 2a | Tire

Practice Objective

- Create a tire using a Toroidal Bend.

In this practice, you will use the Toroidal Bend feature to model a tire. The finished model is shown in Figure 2–15.

Figure 2–15

Task 1 - Open the tire.prt model and set the initial display.

1. Set the working directory to the *Toroidal_Bend* folder.

2. Open **tire.prt.**

3. Set the model display as follows:

    - ⚒ *(Datum Display Filters)*: All Off

    - ⤸ *(Spin Center)*: Off

    - ▢ *(Display Style)*: ▢ (Shading With Edges)

Task 2 - Add treads to the model.

1. Zoom in on the cut shown in Figure 2–16.

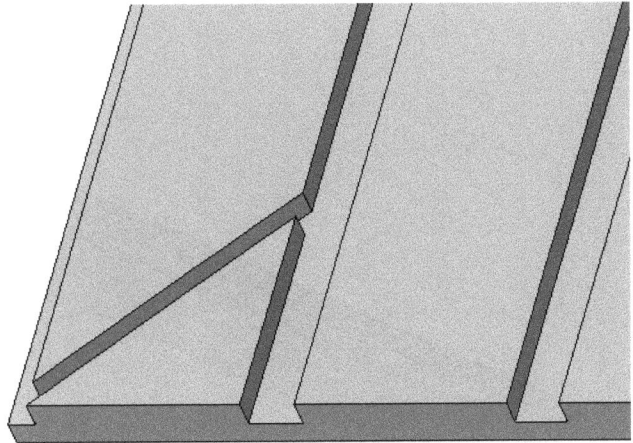

Figure 2–16

2. In the Model Tree, select **Extrude 3** and click ⊞ (Pattern) in the mini toolbar.

3. Select the *1.00* dimension and enter **1.125** as shown in Figure 2–17.

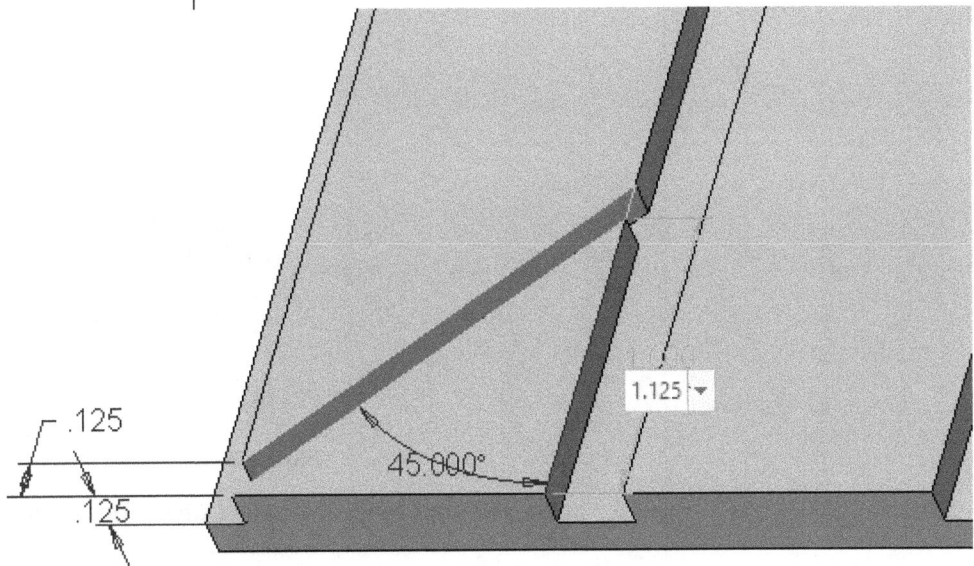

Figure 2–17

4. Enter **59** for the number of instances and complete the pattern. The resulting geometry displays as shown in Figure 2–18.

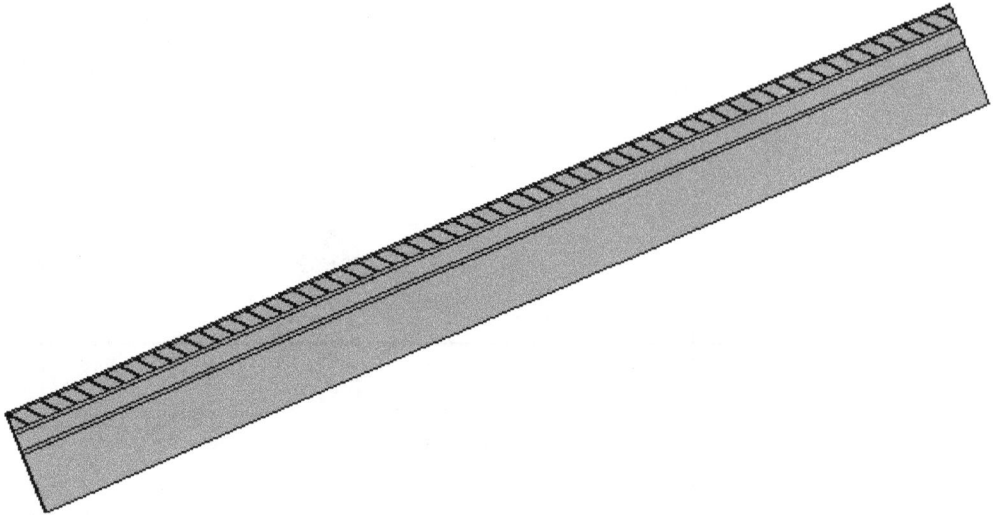

Figure 2–18

5. To pattern the original pattern, in the Model Tree, select the pattern and click ⊞ (Pattern) in the mini toolbar, as shown in Figure 2–19.

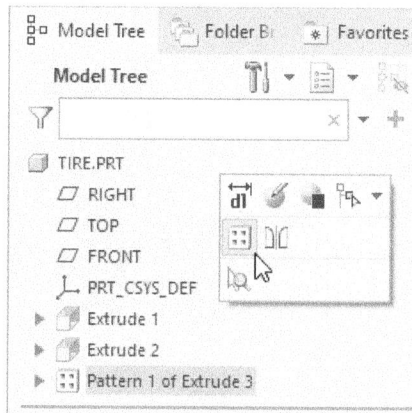

Figure 2–19

6. In the *Pattern* dashboard, select **Direction** as the pattern type.

7. Select the edge shown in Figure 2–20 to set the direction and enter **1.25** for the increment.

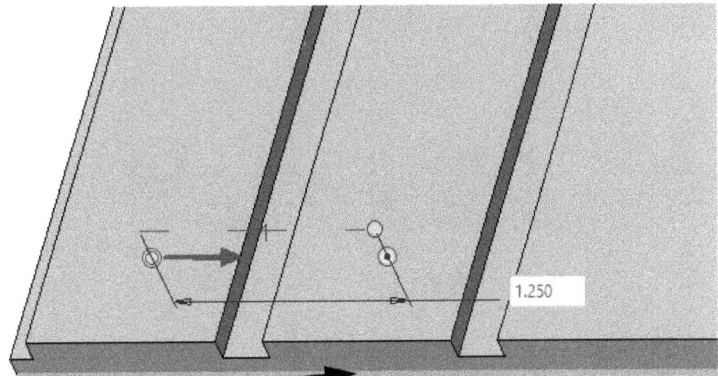

Select this edge

Figure 2–20

8. Complete the pattern. The resulting geometry displays as shown in Figure 2–21.

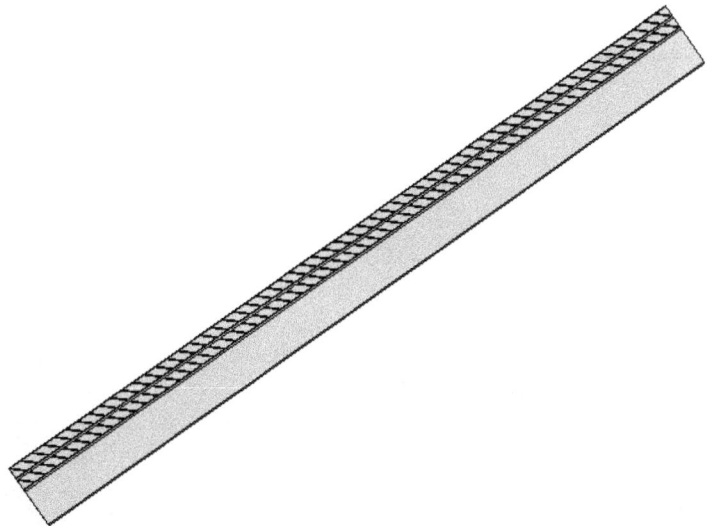

Figure 2–21

9. Create an extruded cut to a depth of **0.125** using the sketch shown in Figure 2–22.

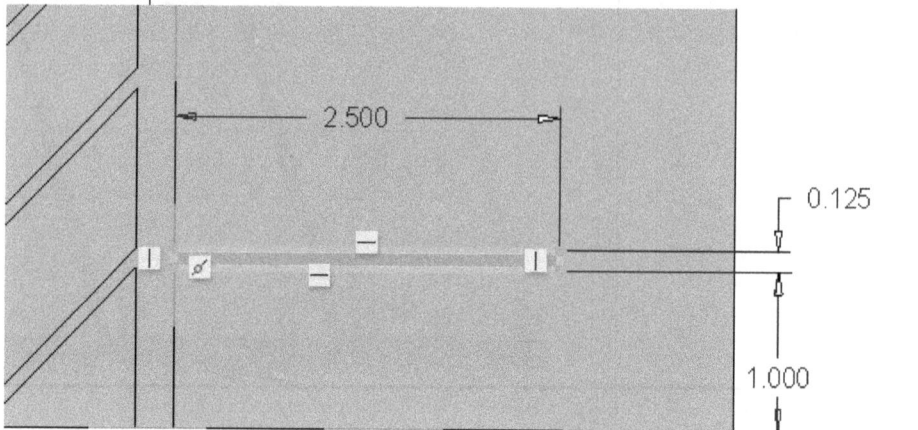

Figure 2–22

10. Select the cut and click ⊞ (Pattern).

11. Select the *1.00* dimension and enter **1.125** for the increment and **59** for the number of instances. Complete the pattern and the geometry updates as shown in Figure 2–23.

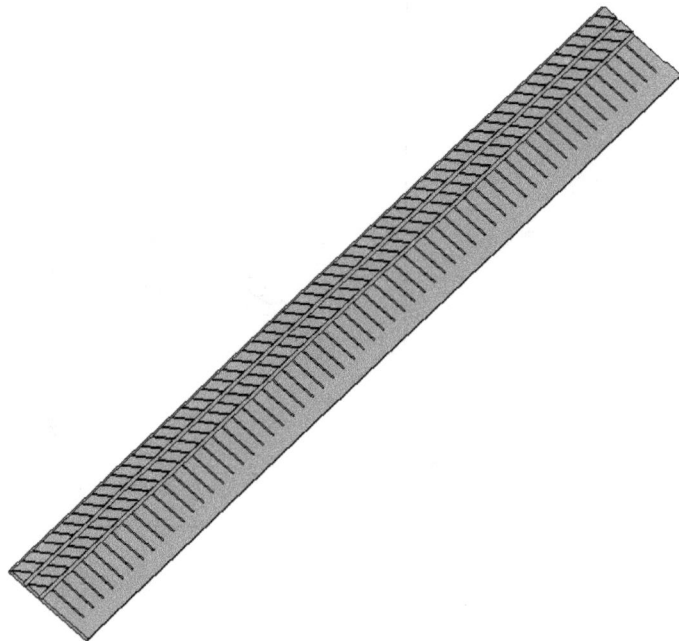

Figure 2–23

Task 3 - Mirror the geometry.

1. In the Model Tree, select the first extruded feature, press and hold <Shift>, and select the pattern you just created, then click ⟆ (Mirror) from the mini toolbar, as shown in Figure 2–24.

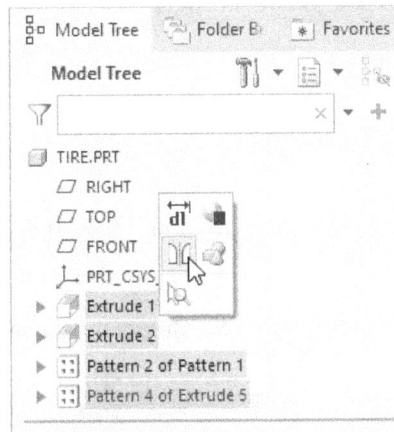

Figure 2–24

2. In the Model Tree, select datum plane **RIGHT** as the mirror plane.

3. Complete the mirror and the geometry displays as shown in Figure 2–25.

Figure 2–25

Task 4 - Create a toroidal bend to complete the tire.

1. In the *Model* tab, click **Engineering>** ◌ (Toroidal Bend).

2. The *Toroidal Bend* dashboard displays as shown in Figure 2–26.

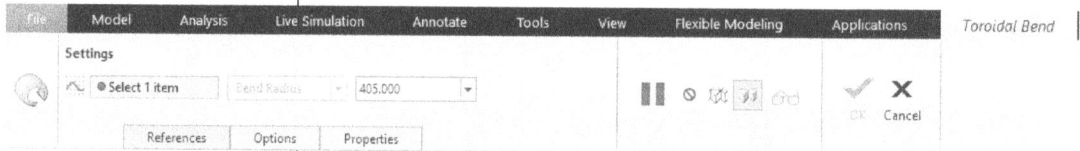

Figure 2–26

3. Right-click and select **Solid Geometry**.

4. Right-click and select **Define Internal Sketch.**

5. Select the surface shown in Figure 2–27 as the sketch plane.

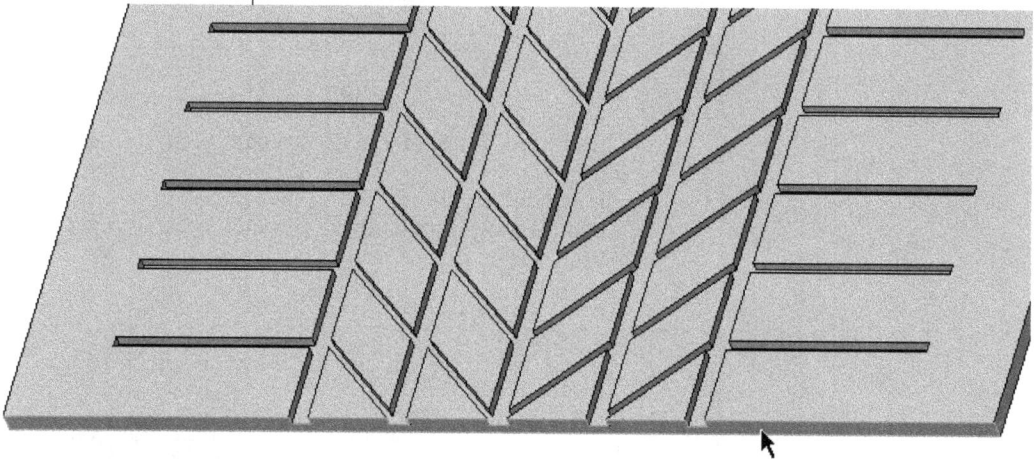

Figure 2–27

6. In the Sketch dialog box, click **Sketch**.

7. In the In-graphics toolbar, click 🖫 (Sketch View).

A profile sketch was created for you.

8. In the *Sketch* tab, click 📂 (File System), and open **profile.sec**.

9. Click on the screen to temporarily locate the section.

10. Edit the *Scale* to **1.00**, and move the section approximately to the location shown in Figure 2–28.

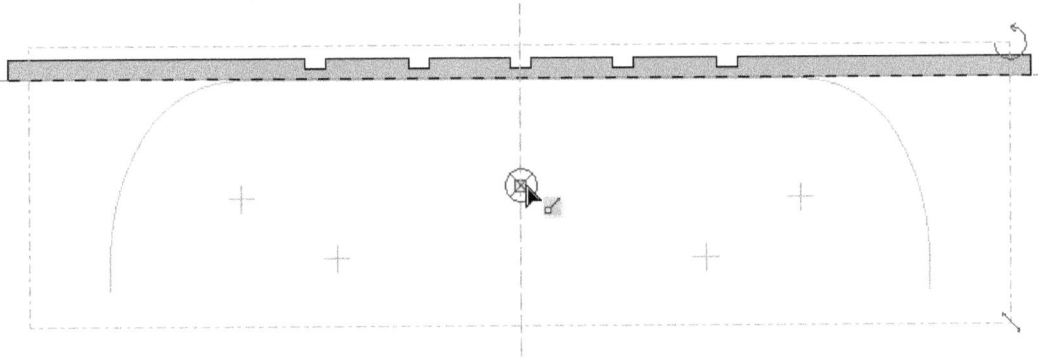

Figure 2–28

11. In the *Import Section* dashboard, click ✔ (Done).

12. Add ⌐ (Coincident) constraints between the horizontal line and bottom surface of the model, and the centerline and datum **RIGHT**, as shown in Figure 2–29.

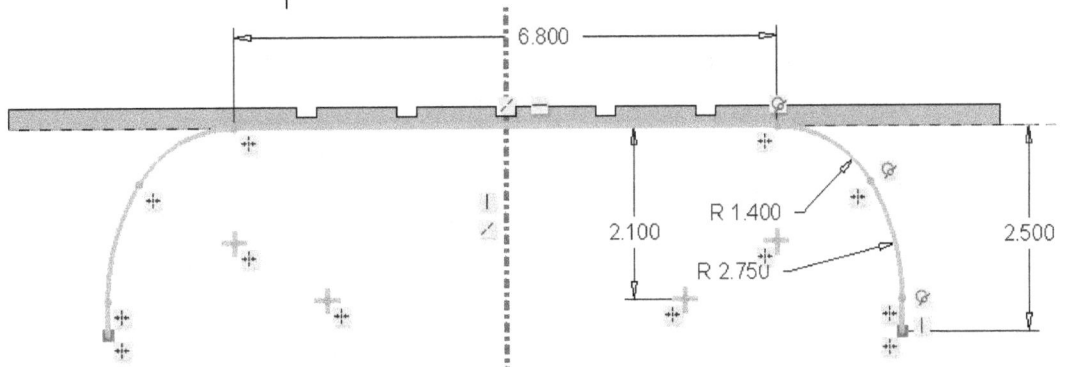

Figure 2–29

13. In the Datum group in the *Sketch* tab, click ⌖ (Coordinate System) and click to place it at the intersection of the centerline and the horizontal sketched line, as shown in Figure 2–30.

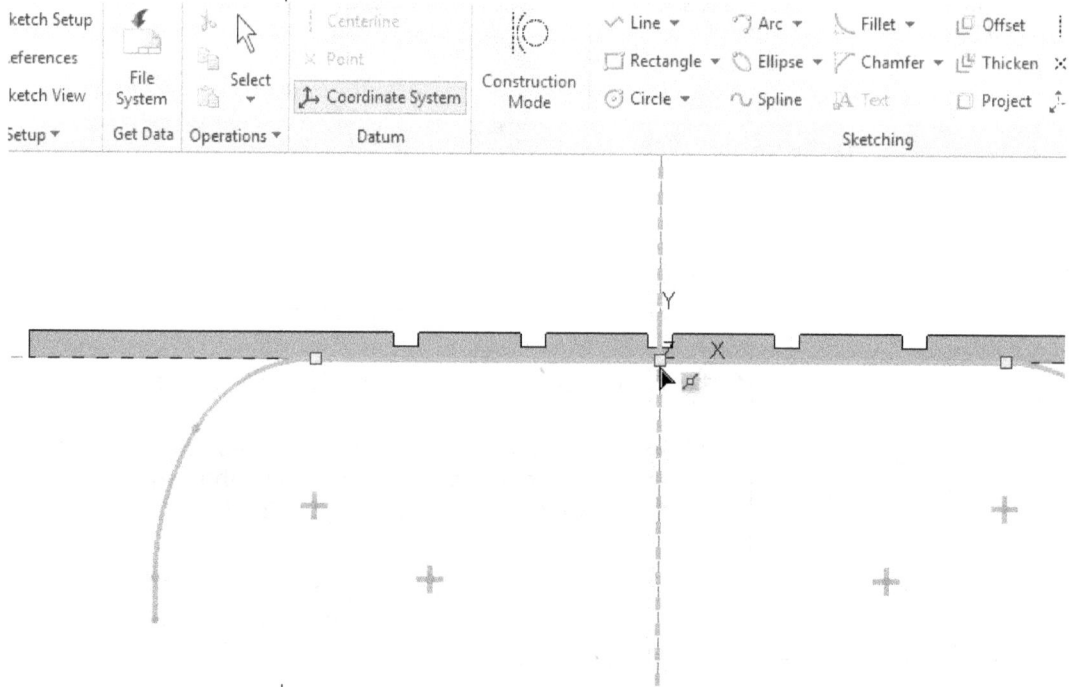

Figure 2–30

14. Complete the sketch. The model previews as shown in Figure 2–31.

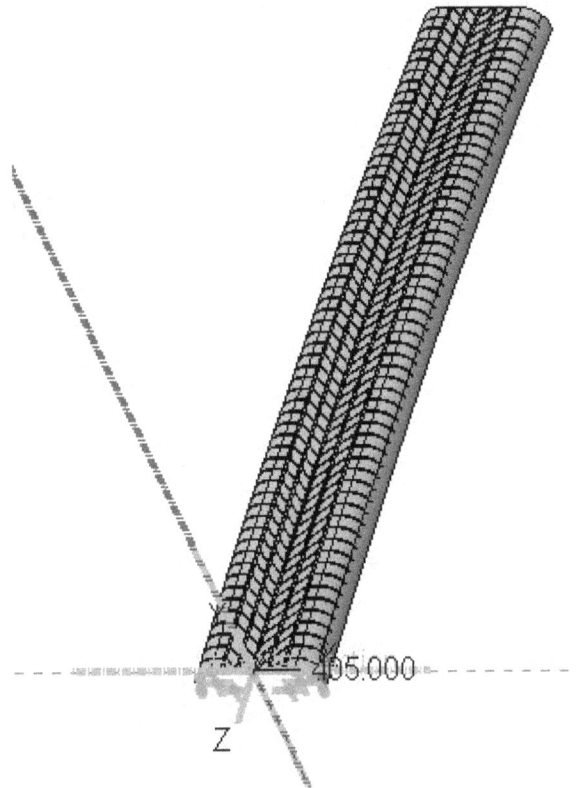

Figure 2–31

15. Select **360 degree Bend** from the Bend Radius drop-down list, as shown in Figure 2–32.

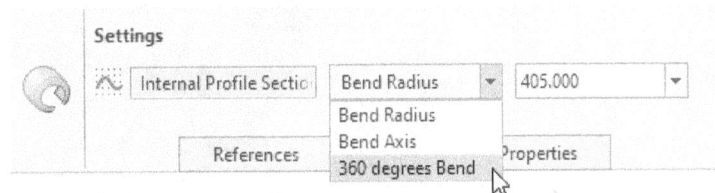

Figure 2–32

16. Select each end of the model, as shown in Figure 2–33.

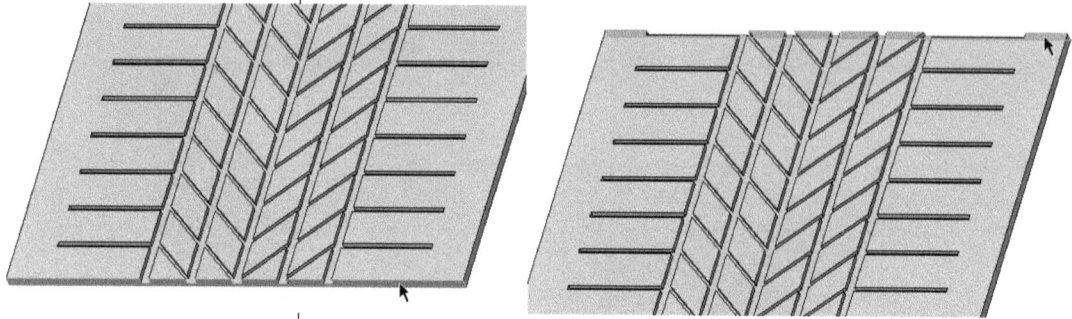

Figure 2–33

17. Complete the feature.

18. The completed model displays as shown in Figure 2–34.

Figure 2–34

19. Close the part and erase it from memory.

Practice 2b | Bent Linkage

Practice Objective

- Use a Spinal Bend to close a plastic sandwich holder.

In this practice, you use a spinal bend to create a bend in a straight linkage. The finished model is shown in Figure 2–35.

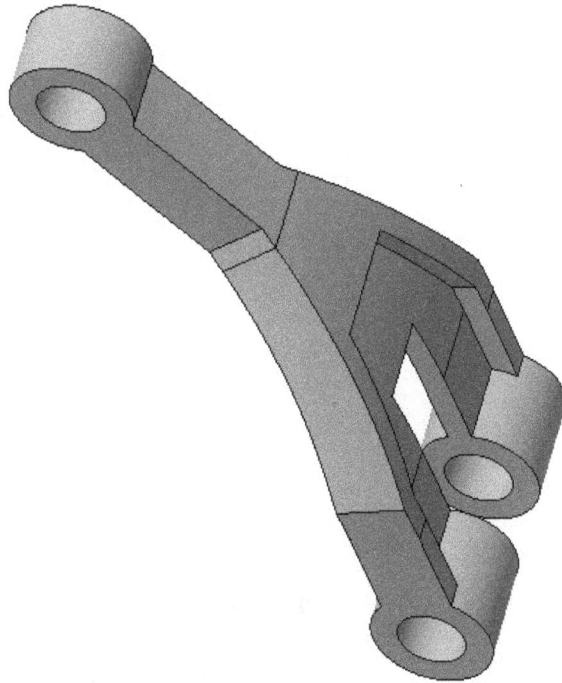

Figure 2–35

Task 1 - Open the link.prt model and set the initial display.

1. Set the working directory to the *Spinal_Bend* folder.

2. Open **link.prt.**

3. Set the model display as follows:

   - *(Datum Display Filters)*: (Point Display) Only
   - *(Spin Center)*: Off
   - *(Display Style)*: (Shading With Edges)

The model displays as shown in Figure 2–36.

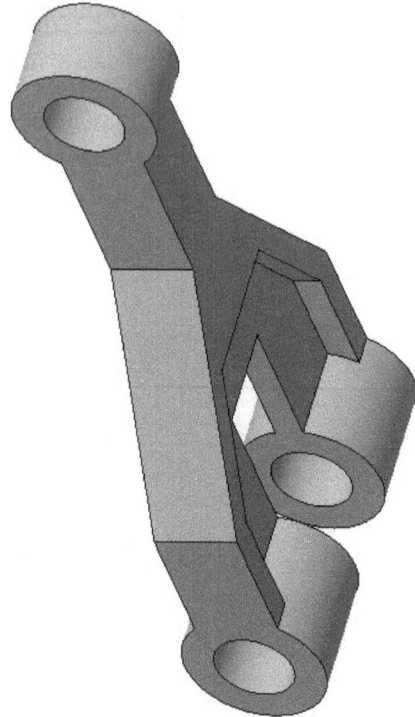

Figure 2–36

Task 2 - Create a sketch for the spine of the bend.

1. Select datum plane **FRONT** and in the mini toolbar, click
   ⬚ (Sketch).

2. In the In-graphics toolbar, click ⬚ (Sketch View).

3. Create the sketch shown in Figure 2–37.

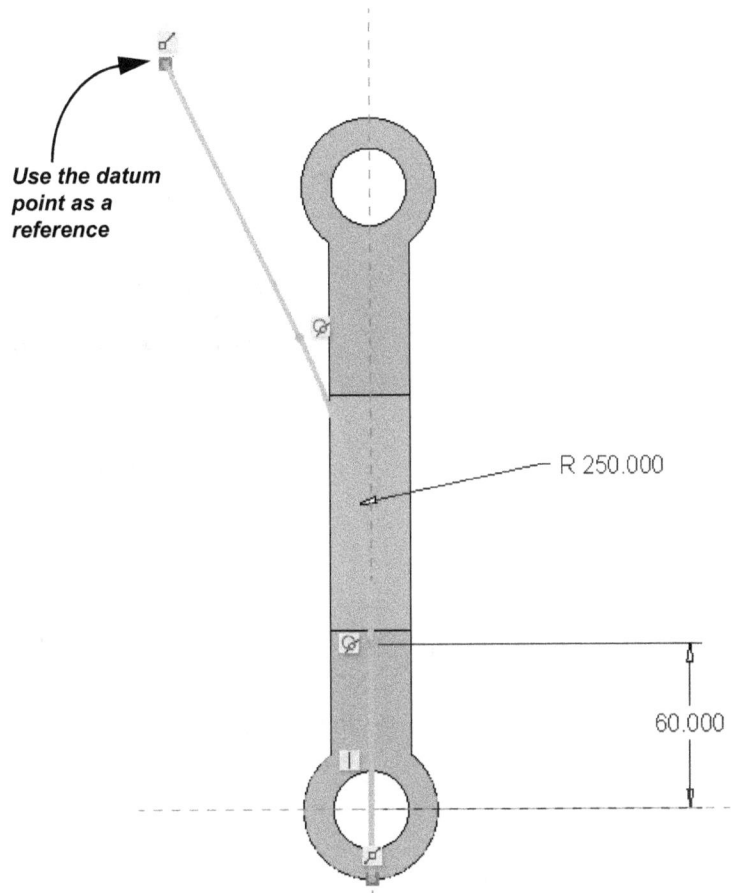

Use the datum point as a reference

R 250.000

60.000

Figure 2–37

4. Click ✓ (OK) to complete the sketch.

5. In the *Model* tab, click **Engineering>** (Spinal Bend).

6. If not already selected, select the datum curve.

7. In the *Spinal Bend* dashboard, click in the **Bend Geometry** field and select anywhere on the model. The geometry updates as shown in Figure 2–38.

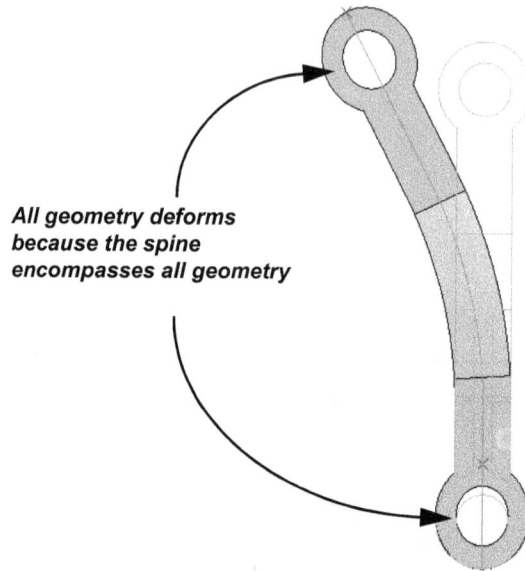

All geometry deforms because the spine encompasses all geometry

Figure 2–38

8. In the dashboard, click **Lock Length**. The model updates as shown in Figure 2–39.

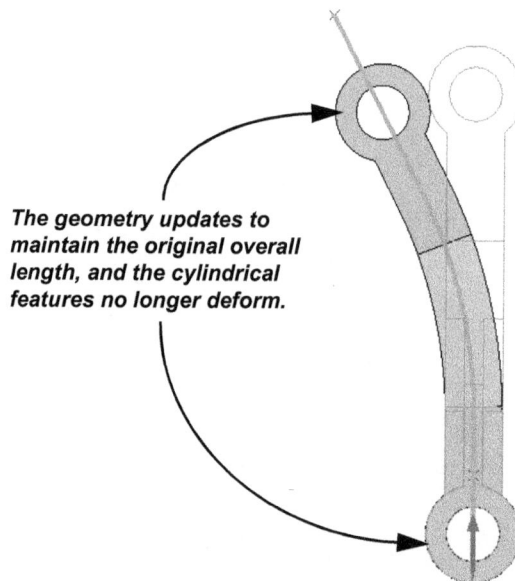

The geometry updates to maintain the original overall length, and the cylindrical features no longer deform.

Figure 2–39

9. The sketch is not sufficient for your requirements, so cancel the spinal bend.

Task 3 - Edit the Sketch 1 feature.

1. Select the **Sketch 1** feature and click ✐ (Edit Definition) from the mini toolbar.

2. In the In-graphics toolbar, click ⌸ (Sketch View).

3. In the Editing group, click ⌸ (Divide) and select the angled line approximately in the position shown in Figure 2–40.

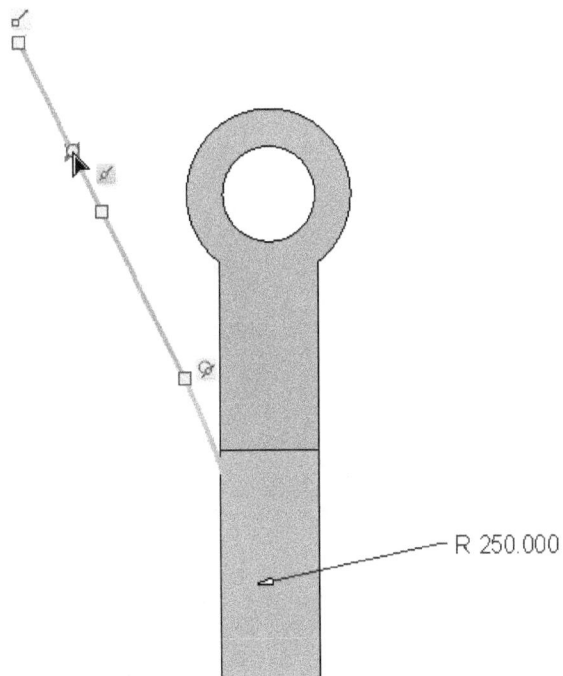

Figure 2–40

4. In the *Sketch* tab, click ⌸ (Select).

5. Select the top segment of the straight line and press <Delete> to remove it.

6. Sketch a centerline through the datum point and the line as shown in Figure 2–41.

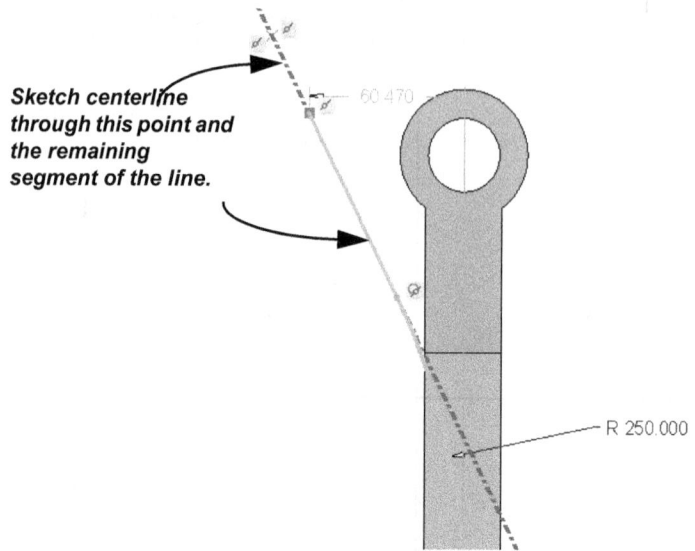

Sketch centerline through this point and the remaining segment of the line.

60.470

R 250.000

Figure 2–41

7. Sketch a centerline through the datum point and perpendicular to the first centerline for dimensioning purposes.

8. Add the **30** dimension shown in Figure 2–42.

You want the spline to not intersect the cylindrical shape (50 diameter), so the dimension of 30 will ensure it is clear when the final geometry is established.

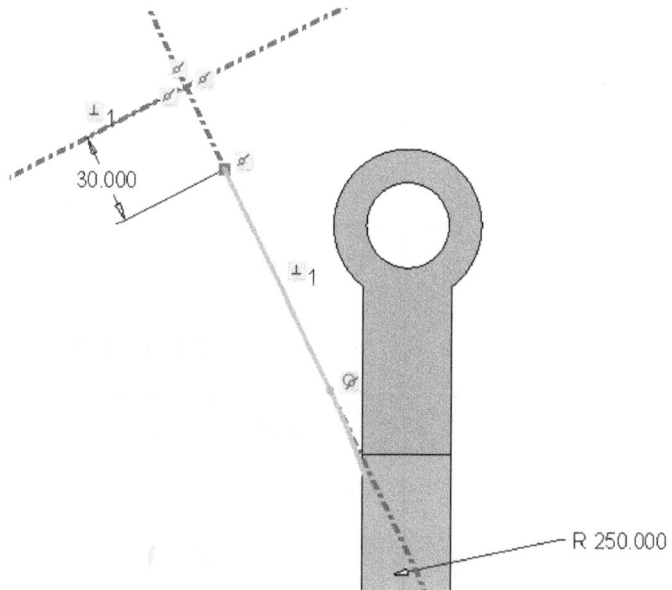

30.000

R 250.000

Figure 2–42

9. Repeat the previous steps to trim the vertical line, then dimension and constrain the sketch as shown in Figure 2–43.

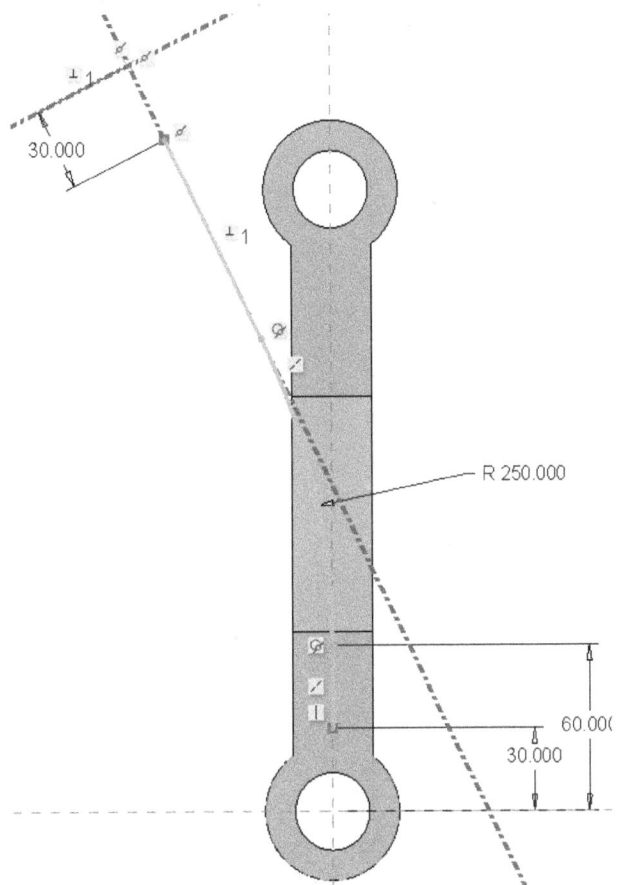

Figure 2–43

10. Click ✓ (OK) to complete the sketch.

Task 4 - Create the spinal bend.

1. In the *Model* tab, click **Engineering>** 🖉 (Spinal Bend).

2. If not already selected, select the datum curve.

3. In the *Spinal Bend* dashboard, click in the **Bend Geometry** field and select anywhere on the model. The geometry updates as shown in Figure 2–44.

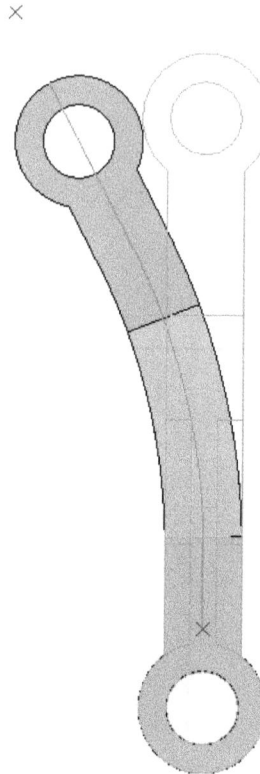

Figure 2–44

4. In the *Spinal Bend* dashboard, select ⬐ (Bend to Depth), as shown in Figure 2–45.

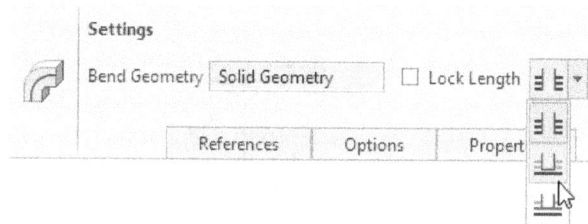

Figure 2–45

5. Use the drag handle or edit the depth to approximately **165** as shown in Figure 2–46. Note that the cylindrical entities do not distort.

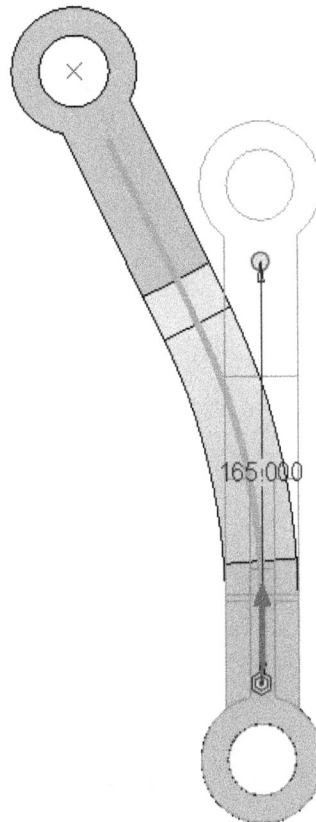

Figure 2–46

6. Click ✓ (OK) to complete the feature.

7. The completed model displays as shown in Figure 2–47.

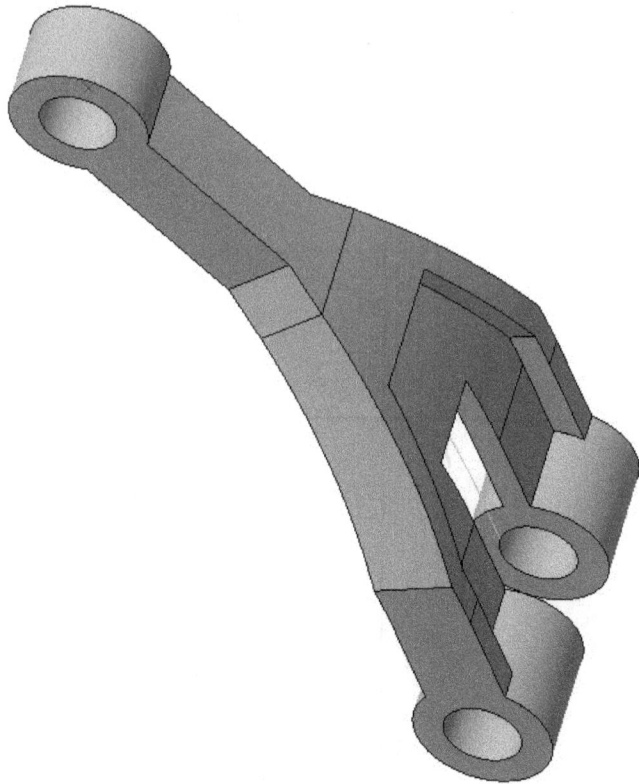

Figure 2–47

8. Close the part and erase it from memory.

Practice 2c | Plastic Case

Practice Objective

- Use a Spinal Bend to close a plastic sandwich holder.

In this practice, you use a spinal bend to close the hinge on a plastic sandwich holder. The finished model is shown in Figure 2–48.

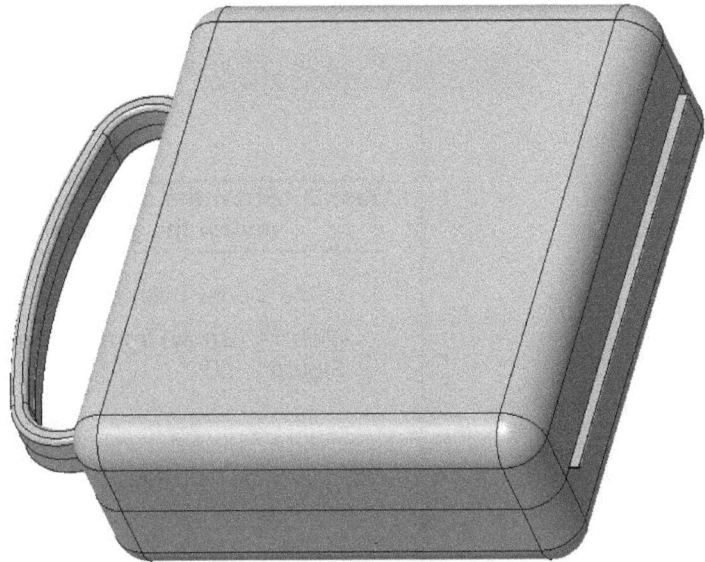

Figure 2–48

Task 1 - Open the holder.prt model and set the initial display.

1. Set the working directory to the *Plastic_Case* folder.

2. Open **holder.prt.**

3. Set the model display as follows:

    - *(Datum Display Filters)*: All Off
    - *(Spin Center)*: Off
    - *(Display Style)*: (Shading With Edges)

The model displays as shown in Figure 2–49.

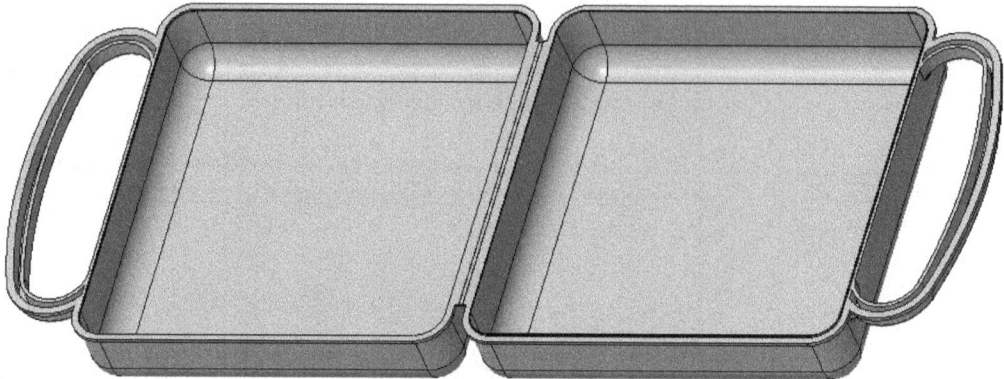

Figure 2–49

Task 2 - Show the curve for the spine of the bend, and review the geometry.

---

1. In the Model Tree, select the hidden sketch **Sketch 1** and click ◉ (Show) from the mini toolbar, as shown in Figure 2–50.

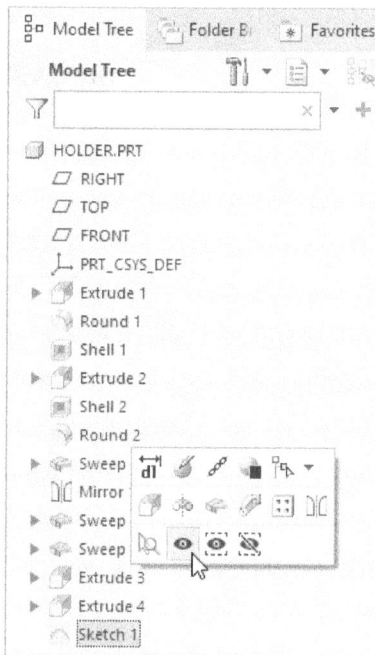

Figure 2–50

The model displays as shown in Figure 2–51.

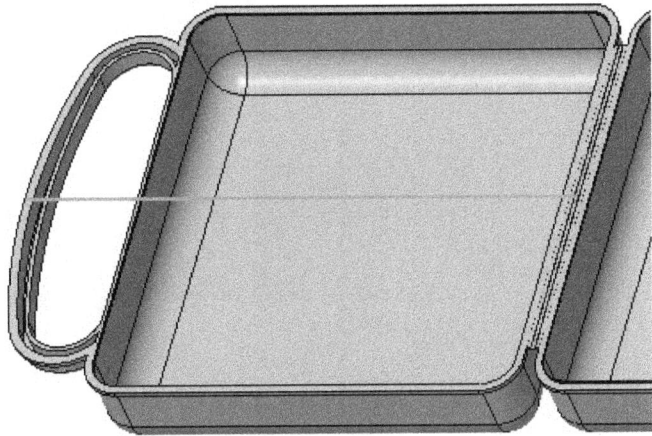

Figure 2–51

2. In the In-graphics toolbar, expand ▭ (Saved Orientations) and select **RIGHT SIDE**.

3. Select the curve and the model displays as shown in Figure 2–52.

Datum curve extends to the middle of the model, then returns

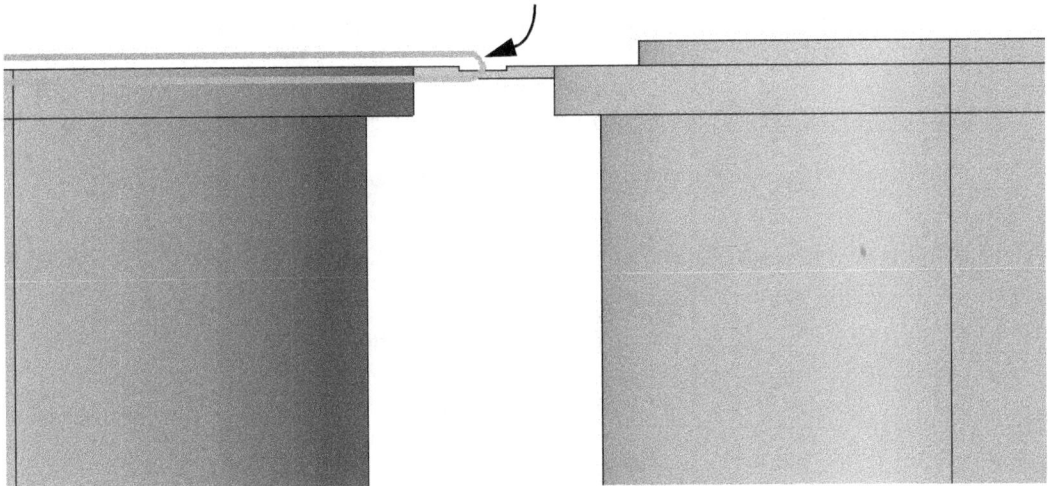

Figure 2–52

4. In the In-graphics toolbar, expand 🖺 (Saved Orientations) and select **LEFT SIDE**. The model displays as shown in Figure 2–53.

Datum curve begins at one end of the model and returns to the same end

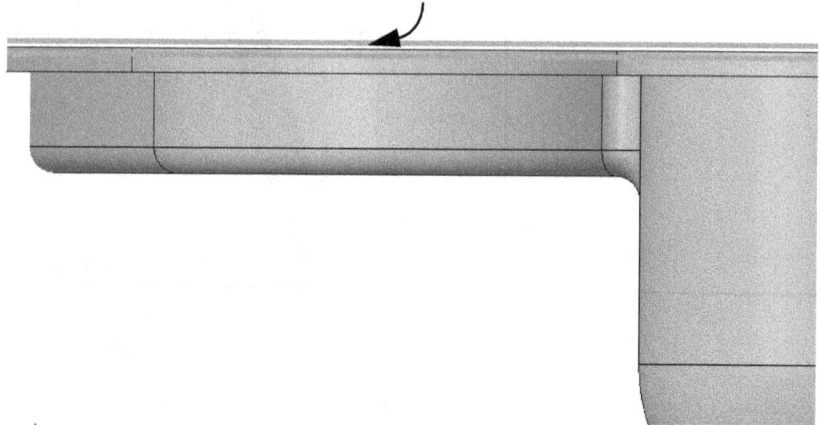

Figure 2–53

5. Press <Ctrl>+<D> to return to default orientation.

Task 3 - Create the Spinal Bend.

1. Ensure the datum curve is still selected.

2. In the *Model* tab, click **Engineering>** 🔗 (Spinal Bend). The *Spinal Bend* dashboard displays as shown in Figure 2–54.

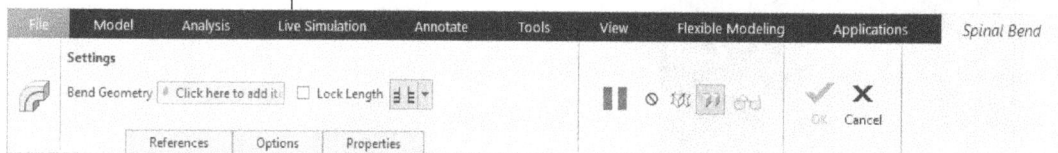

Figure 2–54

3. Expand the *References* tab and note that the *Spine* is selected as a **One-by-One Chain**, as shown in Figure 2–55.

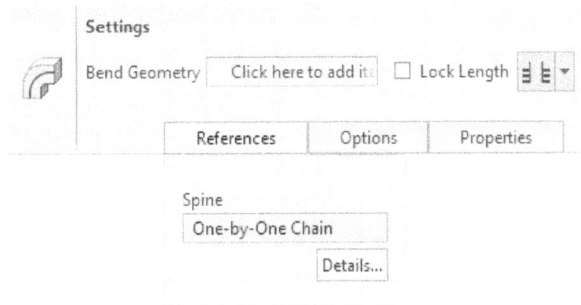

Figure 2–55

4. Click in the *Bend Geometry* field and select the model as shown in Figure 2–56.

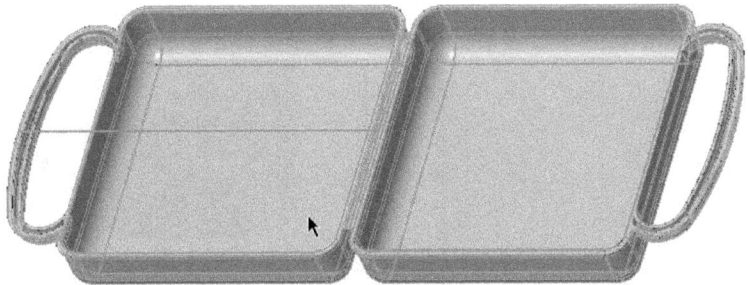

Figure 2–56

5. Click ✔ (OK). The model displays as shown in Figure 2–57.

Figure 2–57

Task 4 - Review the geometry.

1. In the Model Tree, select **Sketch 1** and click ✎ (Hide) in the mini toolbar.

2. In the In-graphics toolbar, expand 📷 (Saved Orientations) and select **LEFT SIDE**. The model displays as shown in Figure 2–58.

Figure 2–58

3. In the In-graphics toolbar, expand 📷 (Saved Orientations) and select **RIGHT SIDE**. Zoom in on the model so it displays as shown in Figure 2–59.

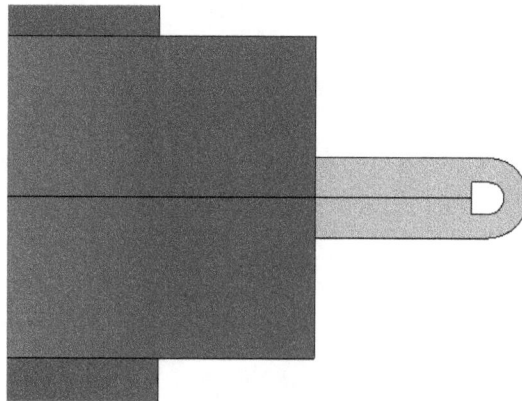

Figure 2–59

4. Close the part and erase it from memory.

Chapter Review Questions

1. Toroidal Bend features can only transform surface features.

    a. True

    b. False

2. You can sketch a new profile or select an existing profile when created a Toroidal Bend feature.

    a. True

    b. False

3. Within the profile sketch for a Toroidal Bend, you must have a sketched _____:

    a. Datum Centerline

    b. Datum Axis

    c. Datum Coordinate System

    d. Sketched Centerline

4. You can sketch a new spine or select an existing curve when creating a Spinal Bend feature.

    a. True

    b. False

5. The **Lock Length** option for a Spinal Bend ensures that the bent geometry has the same overall length as the original unbent geometry.

    a. True

    b. False

Advanced Datum Features

You have previously learned how to create datum planes and datum axes, and their use in creating geometry. In this chapter, you will learn to refine and add detail to a geometry using additional datum features.

Learning Objectives in This Chapter

- Create sketches and use the curves to create various surface features.
- Learn the different types of datum curves and the general steps to create them.
- Learn to create a 3D spline entity by selecting points that control the location and radius conditions for the curve.
- Create a datum curve that is based on a created cross-section.
- Create a datum curve by entering an equation that defines the X-, Y-, and Z-coordinates over a specified range.
- Create a datum curve that is based on the intersections of two entities.
- Use the **Copy** and **Paste** commands to create a datum curve using the various options.
- Project and wrap a 2D sketch on a surface in a selected direction, and learn the differences between the two methods.
- Use the **Trim** command to split an existing curve at a selected position.
- Create a datum curve offset a specified distance from a selected reference.
- Create a datum graph to use in a relation to control various curve features.
- Understand how to create a parameter and a relation using a datum analysis feature.
- Learn how to create a datum analysis feature in the Measure group using the Measure dialog box.
- Learn how to use the Analysis feature in the Manage group using the Analysis dialog box.

3.1 Sketched Curves

Sketches can be used to define 2D planar curves. The tools used to create a sketch are the same as those available when sketching sections for any solid geometry. Sketches are used in models for many purposes, such as sweep trajectories, parting lines for split drafts, and as a basis for creating surface and solid features.

In the example shown on the right in Figure 3–1, a sweep is the first solid feature for the part. A sketch is used to define the trajectory of the sweep, as shown on the left in Figure 3–1. The sketch is planar and the dimension scheme can be applied as required, to capture the required design intent for the trajectory.

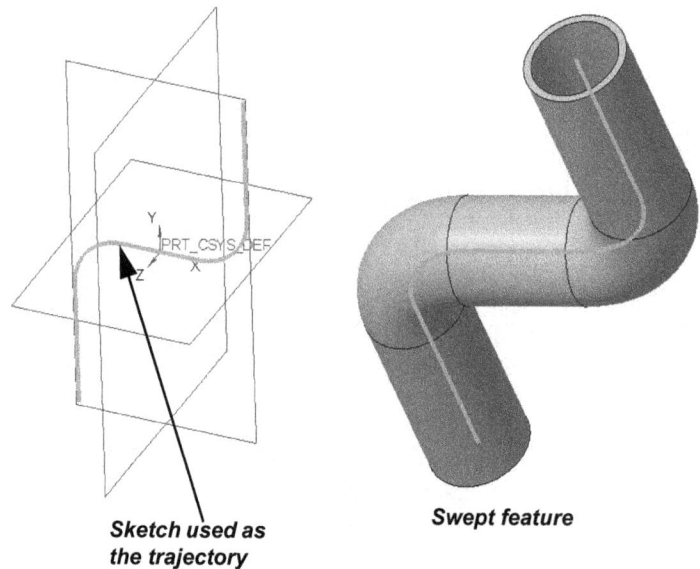

Sketch used as the trajectory

Swept feature

Figure 3–1

How To: Create Sketches

1. Select the sketch plane reference, then click ⬚ (Sketch) in the mini toolbar. Creo parametric will select an orientation reference and open the *Sketch* tab.
2. Alternatively, if you want to control the sketch orientation, click ⬚ (Sketch) in the *Model* tab. The Sketch dialog box opens as shown in Figure 3–2.

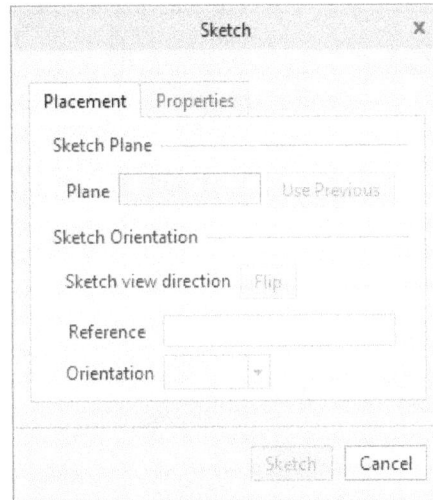

Sketch	X

Placement   Properties

Sketch Plane

Plane [ ]   Use Previous

Sketch Orientation

Sketch view direction Flip

Reference [ ]

Orientation [▾]

Sketch   Cancel

Figure 3–2

Once you select the sketching plane, Creo Parametric automatically selects the orientation reference for you if one is available. You can change it as required to control the orientation. To select a new reference, select the *Reference* field and select a new reference, then select an appropriate orientation.

If the model does not contain a planar surface that is perpendicular to the sketching plane, Creo Parametric uses a projection of the X-axis belonging to the default coordinate system for the horizontal orientation of the sketch.

To begin sketching, click **Sketch** to activate the *Sketch* tab. Create the sketch using all of the familiar sketcher tools.

3. To complete the sketch, click ✓ (OK).

3.2 Datum Curves

Datum curves, similar to sketches, are used in models for geometry creation. For example, they are used for sweep trajectories, parting lines for split drafts, and as a basis for creating surface and solid features.

Sketches are used when the entities can be created on a planar surface and are best defined with a dimensioning scheme. Datum curves can be created using different techniques. Selecting the correct technique depends on the required geometry and your design intent. The available creation options include the following:

- Curve Through points

- Data from a file

- Using a cross-section

- From an equation

- Intersecting geometry

- Copy of another feature

- Projection onto other features

- Wrap onto other features

- Trimming an existing curve

- Offsetting an existing curve/surface

All curves and sketches require references to place them in the model. These references vary depending on the type of entity you are creating. References can be datum points for the curve to pass through or previously created geometry.

Once the references have been selected, the curve or sketch can be created and used as references to create other features.

3.3 Datum Curve Techniques

Three curve options are created using the **Curve** options in the Datum group in the *Model* tab. To access these options, expand **Datum**, then hover the cursor over **Curve**, and when the menu expands, select the appropriate datum curve option, as shown in

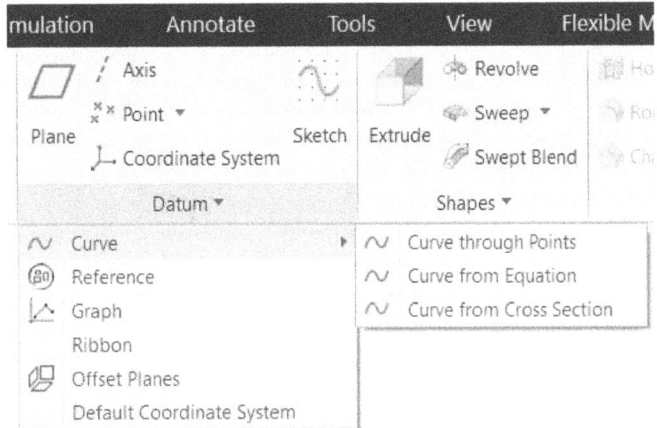

Figure 3–3

Curve Through Points

The **Curve Through Points** option enables you to create a datum curve through a series of points or vertices.

How To: Create a Curve Through Points Datum Curve

1. Select **Datum>Curve>Curve through Points** in the *Model* tab. The *Curve: Through Points* dashboard becomes active, as shown in Figure 3–4.

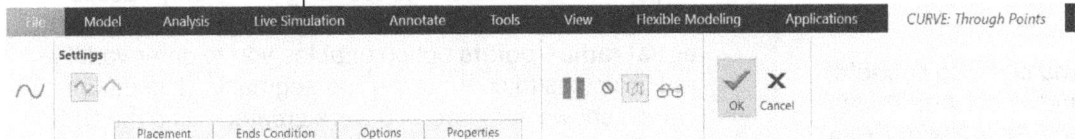

Figure 3–4

2. Select the points on the model for the curve to pass through. You can add, delete, or insert points, as required. To define the curve you can select datum points, vertices, or the endpoints of curves.

3. The Placement panel (shown in Figure 3–5), contains options to define how the points are to be connected. They can be connected by a spline or by a straight line. Click ⌇ (Spline) in the dashboard to create a spline between the points or click ⌒ (Straight Line) to create a straight line between the points. The contextual menu can also be used to specify **Connect by Spline** or **Connect by Straight Line**.

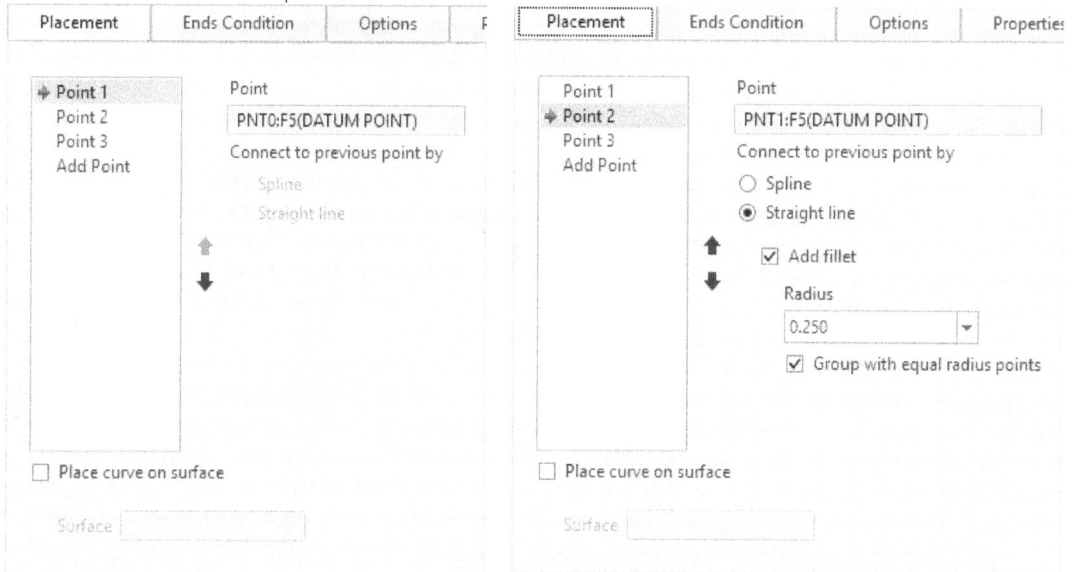

Placement	Ends Condition	Options	F

	Point
✛ Point 1	
Point 2	PNT0:F5(DATUM POINT)
Point 3	
Add Point	Connect to previous point by
	⬜ Spline
	⬜ Straight line
⬆ ⬇	

⬜ Place curve on surface

Surface [   ]

Placement	Ends Condition	Options	Propertie:

	Point
Point 1	
✛ Point 2	PNT1:F5(DATUM POINT)
Point 3	
Add Point	Connect to previous point by
	⭕ Spline
	⦿ Straight line
⬆ ⬇	☑ Add fillet
	Radius
	[0.250 ▾]
	☑ Group with equal radius points

⬜ Place curve on surface

Surface [   ]

Figure 3–5

4. The **Spline** option creates datum curves through a set of points. If points are created as a straight line, ⌄ (Add Fillet) becomes available. You can also select the **Add Fillet** option in the Placement panel. The **Group with equal radius points** option is automatically selected in the Placement panel. It creates a series of line segments that are filleted with a specified arc radius. The resulting curve only passes through the first and last points. Clearing the **Group with equal radius points** option enables you to enter variable radius values to connect the line segments. The datum curves shown in Figure 3–6 were created using the **Spline** and **Straight line** with **Add fillet** options.

*You can also right-click and select **Add Fillet** and **Group with Equal Radius Points**.*

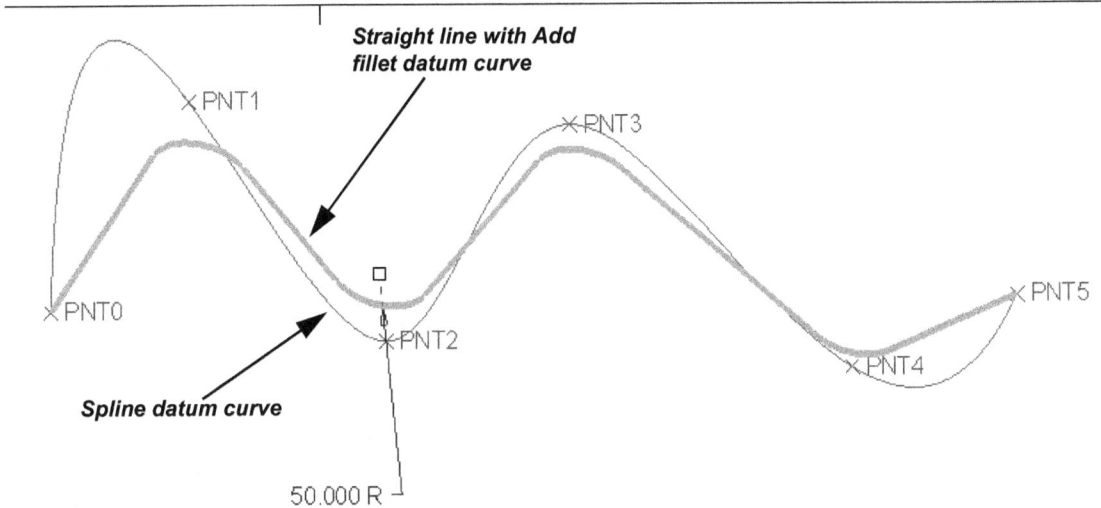

Straight line with Add fillet datum curve

PNT1

PNT3

PNT0

PNT5

PNT2

PNT4

Spline datum curve

50.000 R

Figure 3–6

To define the curve you can select datum points, vertices, or the end points of curves.

5. The datum curve can also be created through the selected points and made to lie on a selected surface. The two datum curves shown in Figure 3–7 are created through the same points. One is created without the **Place curve on surface** option, while the other is set to **Place curve on surface**.

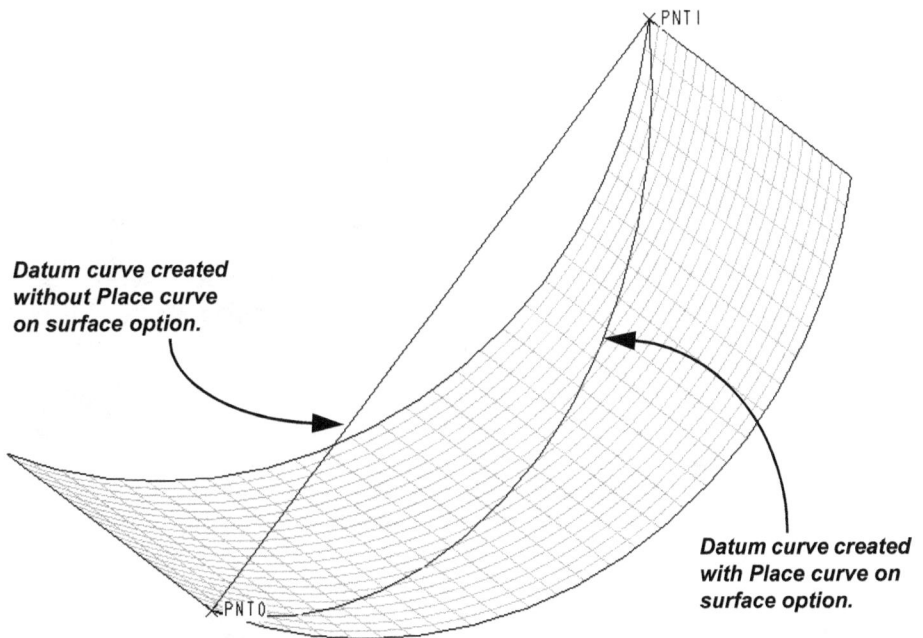

PNT1

Datum curve created without Place curve on surface option.

Datum curve created with Place curve on surface option.

PNT0

Figure 3–7

6. Set the End Conditions if required. When creating a datum curve through points, you can define the tangency direction at the start and end points of the curve. Specifying tangency direction changes the shape of the curve. To define a tangent, normal, or curvature continuous direction, select the Ends Condition panel. You can then select **Start Point** or **End Point** to define the condition (**Free, Tangency, Normal**, or **Curvature Continuous**) and the reference entity to which it is applied. The reference for the End condition can be a curve, edge, axis, or surface.

7. Tweak the curve in the Options panel, if required. This element can be defined for a curve created through two points. It enables you to add control points by selecting the curve. The control points can then be used to manipulate the shape of the curve while maintaining tangency conditions. When you select the **Tweak** option and click **Tweak Curve Settings**, the Modify Curve dialog box opens as shown in Figure 3–8.

Curves that are curvature continuous (C2) are tangent to each other. The curvature at the end of the created curve is equal to the tangent end of the connecting entity.

Curvature can be displayed for the curve while it is being manipulated by using the Diagnostics area in the Modify Curve dialog box.

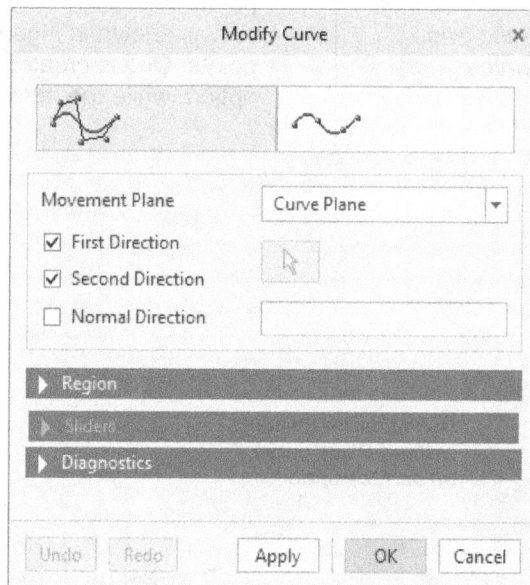

Figure 3–8

Figure 3–9 shows curves with **Tangency**, **Curvature Continuous**, and **Tweak** options applied.

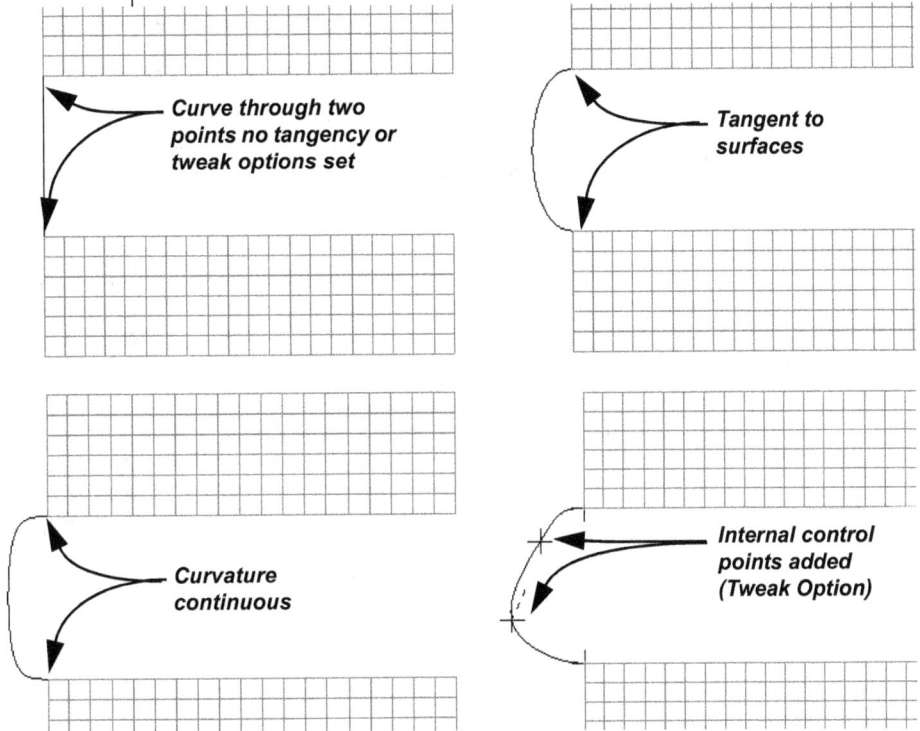

Figure 3–9

Curve through two points no tangency or tweak options set

Tangent to surfaces

Curvature continuous

Internal control points added (Tweak Option)

Import

The **Import** curve option enables you to read point data from a file to create a curve.

How To: Create a Curve from Imported Data

1. Select **Get Data>Import** in the *Model* tab.
2. Select the point data file in the Open dialog box. The curve shown in Figure 3–10 is created from a sample .IBL file. The permitted file formats include IBL, IGES, and VDA.

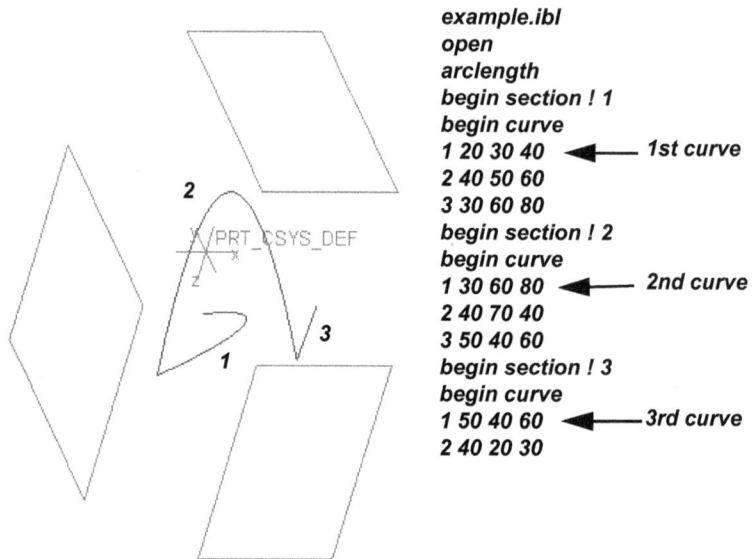

```
example.ibl
open
arclength
begin section ! 1
begin curve
1 20 30 40          ◄──── 1st curve
2 40 50 60
3 30 60 80
begin section ! 2
begin curve
1 30 60 80          ◄──── 2nd curve
2 40 70 40
3 50 40 60
begin section ! 3
begin curve
1 50 40 60          ◄──── 3rd curve
2 40 20 30
```

Figure 3–10

Curve from Cross Section

The **Curve from Cross Section** option enables you to create a datum curve based on a cross-section. The curve is created on all edges of the cross-section.

How To: Create a Curve from Cross Section

1. Select **Datum>Curve>Curve from Cross Section**.
2. Select a cross-section from the list of created sections in the *CURVE* dashboard as shown in Figure 3–11. The cross-section must already exist.

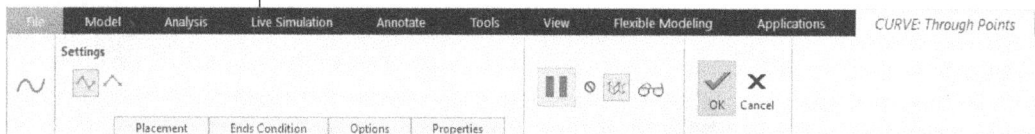

Figure 3–11

An example of a curve created from a cross-section is shown in Figure 3–12.

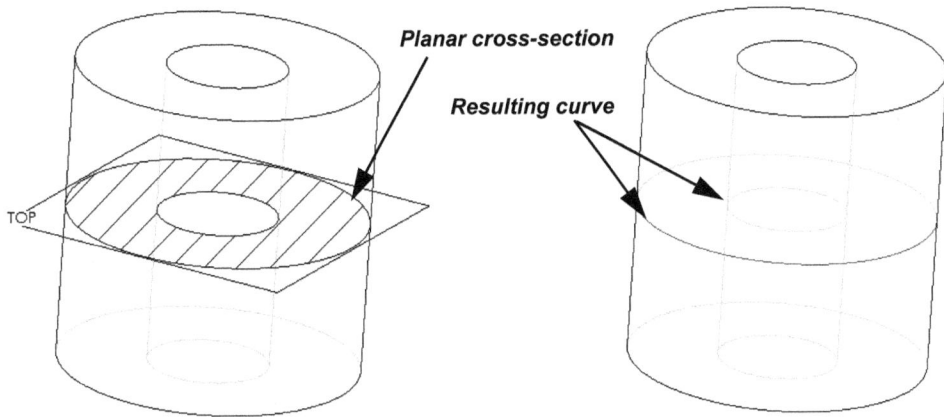

Figure 3–12

From Equation

The **Curve From Equation** option enables you to use a mathematical equation to accurately define the datum curve.

How To: Create a Datum Curve from Equation

1. Select **Datum>Curve>Curve from Equation**. The *CURVE: From Equation* dashboard becomes active as shown in Figure 3–13.

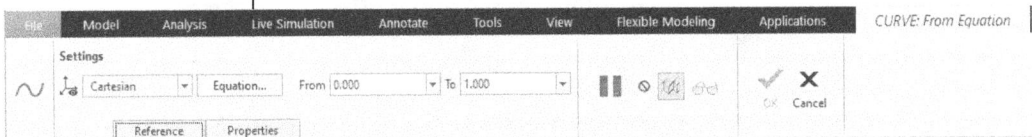

Figure 3–13

2. Select a coordinate system. It acts as the origin for the curve location.
3. Specify the coordinate type in the dashboard (**Cartesian, Cylindrical**, or **Spherical**).
4. Click **Equation** and specify the equation. The equation requires values for *x, y, z,* or *r, theta, z,* or *rho, theta, phi,* (depending on the type of coordinate system). The equation is written in terms of a **t** parameter, which ranges in value from 0 to 1. Click **OK** in the Equation dialog box.

5. Click ✔ (OK) in the *CURVE: From Equation* dashboard to complete the curve. The curve shown in Figure 3–14 follows a sine wave defined by equations.

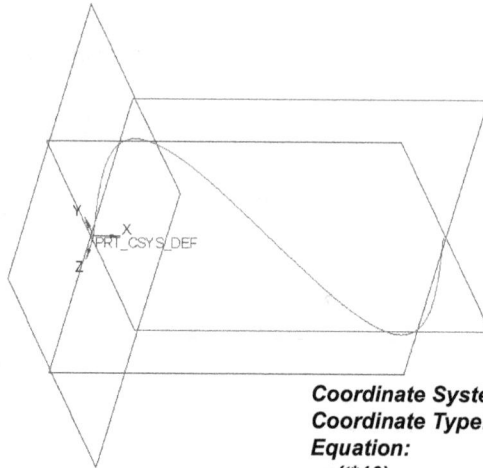

Coordinate System: PRT_CSYS_DEF
Coordinate Type: Cartesian
Equation:
x=(t*10)
y=4*sin(t*360)
z=0

Figure 3–14

Intersect

The **Intersect** option is used to create a curve at the intersection of two references. You can use the following reference combinations:

*   Two surfaces.

*   A surface and a solid surface.

*   A surface and a datum plane.

*   A solid surface and a datum plane.

*   Intersection of two sketches. The curve is created at the virtual intersection as if the sketches were extruded surfaces.

How To: Create a Datum Curve Using the Intersect Option

1. Select two references, as shown in Figure 3–15.

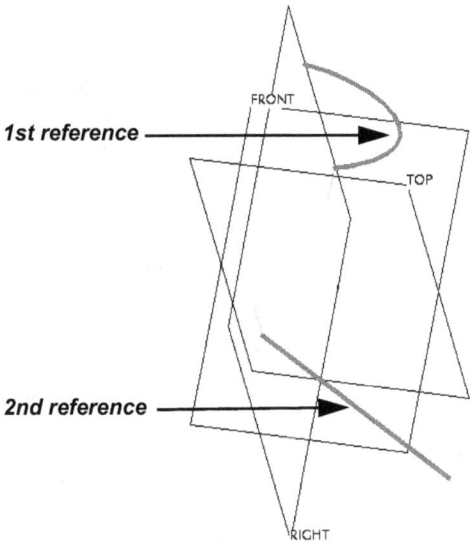

Figure 3–15

2. Click ⟳ (Intersect) in the *Model* tab. The resulting curve displays as shown in Figure 3–16.

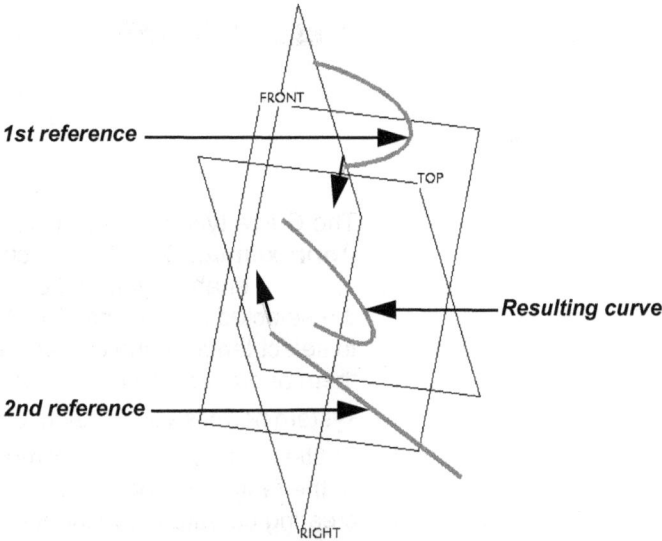

Figure 3–16

Composite Curves

The **Copy** option enables you to select edges and curves from which to create a single composite curve on top of the individual references. The referenced edges and curves must form a continuous chain or closed loop.

Composite curves can be used in the following situations:

- To create an analysis feature that measures a number of curves simultaneously.

- In situations where a pattern is required along a non-linear edge. The curve can be created using all of the edges and the pattern dimension can be driven using a datum point created on the curve using the **Length Ratio** option.

How To: Create a Copied Datum Curve

Do not select multiple references by pressing and holding <Ctrl> since that does not form a chain, and is therefore not suitable for the creation of a composite curve.

1. Select the references (i.e., curves, solid edges, and surface edges). Multiple references must be selected as a chain. Select the first reference in the chain, press and hold <Shift>, then select adjacent edges using **One-by-one** or query-select to establish an **Intent Chain**, **Surface loop from to**, or **Surface loop** chain.

You can also press <Ctrl>+<C> and <Ctrl>+ <V> to copy and paste.

2. Click 📄 (Copy) and 📋 (Paste) in the *Model* tab. The *CURVE: Composite* dashboard displays as shown in Figure 3–17.

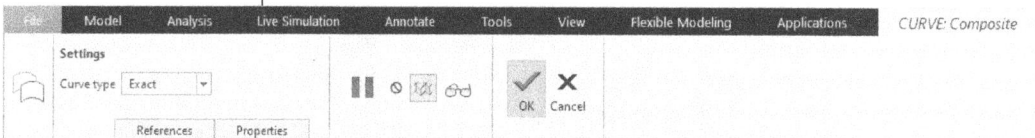

Figure 3–17

The Curve type drop-down list contains two options: **Exact** and **Approximate**. By default, a curve is copied using the **Exact** option. It enables you to create a datum curve exactly on top of the selected references. The **Approximate** option enables you to select tangent and curvature continuous entities and have them approximated by a curvature continuous datum curve. The system permits you to select entities that are within 5° of tangent. Entities that are beyond 5° must be removed from the selection, or the feature is aborted. Approximate curves are useful for creating curvature continuous surfaces.

Project

The **Project** option enables you to project datum curves onto non-planar surfaces to form a 3D datum curve.

How To: Create a Projected Datum Curve

1. Click ≲ (Project) in the *Model* tab. The *Projected Curve* dashboard displays as shown in Figure 3–18.

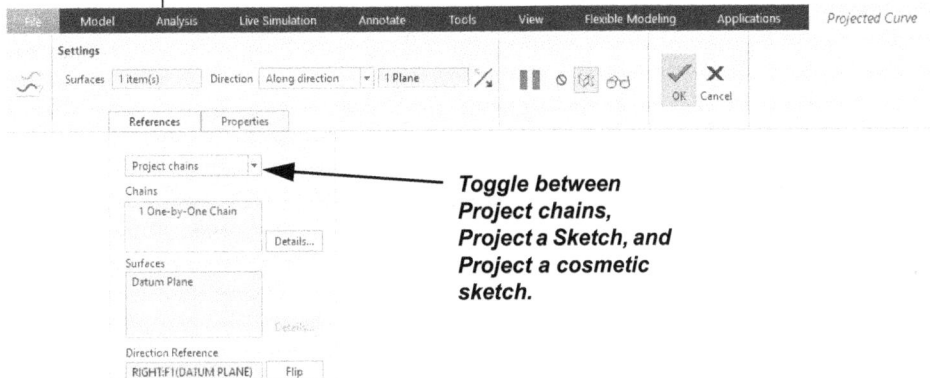

Toggle between
Project chains,
Project a Sketch, and
*Project a cosmetic
sketch.*

Figure 3–18

You can also select the reference curve before you click ≲ (Project).

To select multiple surfaces, press and hold <Ctrl> while selecting.

The projection surface and reference direction can also be defined in the References panel.

2. Select the curve or edge chains to project. By default, the curve is created using the **Project chains** option. To sketch the curve to be projected, select **Project a Sketch** in the References panel.
3. Right-click and select **Select Surfaces**. Select the surface(s) or datum plane on which to project the curve.
4. Right-click and select **Select Direction Reference**. Select a plane, axis, straight edge, or coordinate system as the projection direction. By default, **Along direction** is selected in the Direction drop-down list. This option can be changed to **Normal to Surface**, if required.

5. Complete the feature. The curves shown in Figure 3–19 are projected **Along direction** and **Normal to surface**.

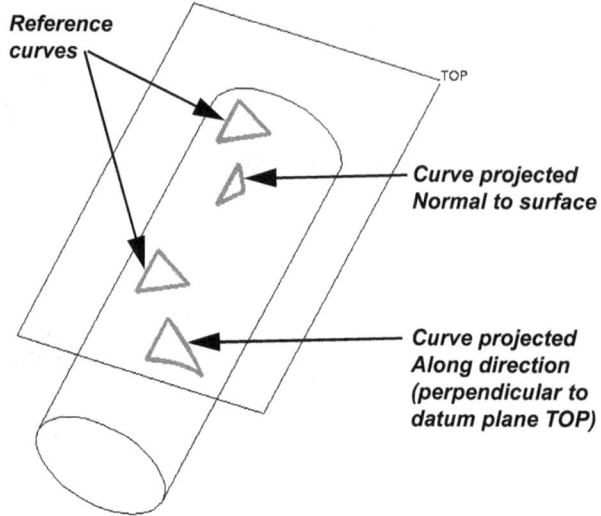

Reference curves

TOP

Curve projected Normal to surface

Curve projected Along direction (perpendicular to datum plane TOP)

Figure 3–19

Wrap

The **Wrap** option enables you to project datum curves onto non-planar surfaces to form a 3D datum curve, similar to transferring a decal to a surface. Wrapped (formed) datum curves are created in the same manner as projected datum curves, except that wrapped datum curves preserve the length of the original curve. An origin must be specified to determine the curve reference point as the starting point for the curve projection.

How To: Create a Wrapped Datum Curve

1. Select **Editing>Wrap** in the *Model* tab. The *Wrap* dashboard displays as shown in Figure 3–20.

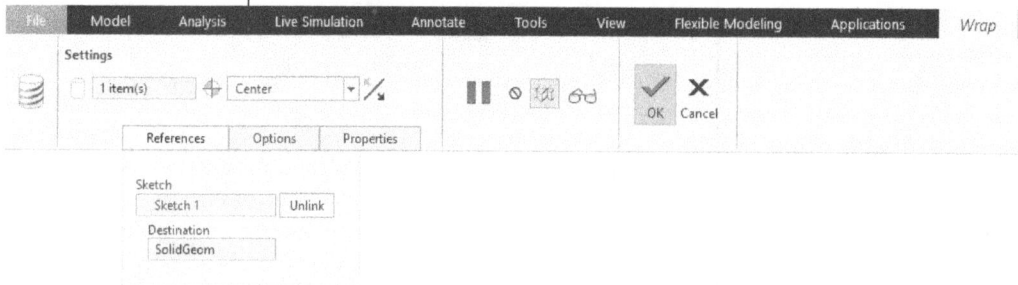

Figure 3–20

*You can also select the reference sketch before you select **Editing> Wrap**.*

2. Select the existing sketch to wrap or sketch the curve by selecting a plane on which to sketch. You can also right-click and select **Define Internal Sketch**.
3. Select the surface onto which to project the wrapped curve. In some cases, Creo Parametric automatically selects the surface, but you can select another one if required.
4. Specify the origin in the *Wrap* dashboard. The default option is **Center**. Alternatively, you can select **Sketcher CSYS** if you have placed a sketcher coordinate system in the sketch.
5. If the sketch is disconnected, you can select **Ignore intersection surface** in the Options panel, to prevent the sketch from wrapping onto intersecting surfaces. The **Trim at boundary** option in the Options panel can also be used to trim the curve.

In Figure 3–21, the same sketch is used to create a projected and a wrapped datum curve. The length of the wrapped curve is the same as the sketched one, but the length of the projected curve is different from the original one.

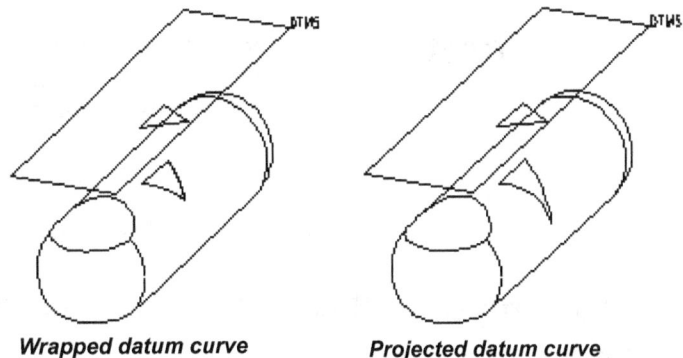

Wrapped datum curve   *Projected datum curve*

Figure 3–21

Trim

The **Trim** option enables you to split an existing curve at a selected position.

How To: Create a Trimmed Datum Curve

1. Select the reference curve.
2. Click ⬚ (Trim) in the *Model* tab.

3. Select the split reference (point, curve, plane, or surface). The trimmed curve and object display in the References panel, as shown in Figure 3–22.

Figure 3–22

The trimming object and curve can be defined in the References panel.

4. Click (Flip Trimmed Curve) in the *Curve Trim* dashboard to select the side of the curve that you want to keep. You can toggle between keeping **one side** or the **other**, or **both sides**.
5. Complete the feature. The original curve is not displayed, but is kept in case the trim feature is deleted.

Offset

The **Offset** option enables you to create a datum curve by offsetting it a specified distance from a reference. You can create an offset datum curve using any of the following:

- Offset from an existing curve, along or normal to a surface.

- Offset from a surface boundary.

Offset Along or Normal to a Surface

How To: Create a Datum Curve at an Offset from an Existing Curve, Along the Surface, Normal to Curve

1. Select a curve.
2. Click (Offset) in the *Model* tab. The *Offset* dashboard displays as shown in Figure 3–23.

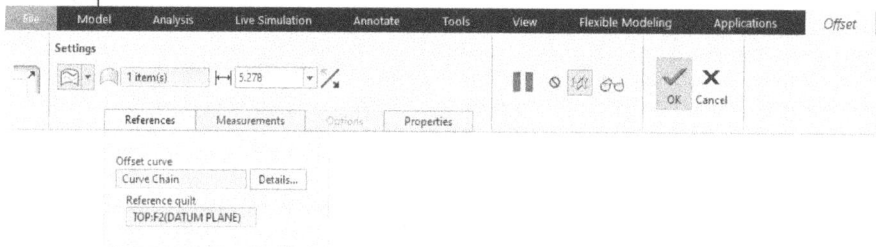

Figure 3–23

3. Click (Along Surface) or (Normal to Surface) in the menu to define the offset along a reference surface or normal to a reference surface, respectively.
4. Select the reference surface along which the offset is measured.
5. Enter an offset value. If you are offsetting using (Normal to Surface) you can also select a graph feature to drive the offset values. This is done using the Options panel.
6. Complete the feature. The datum curve shown in Figure 3–24 is created at an offset from an existing curve, along surface, normal to curve.

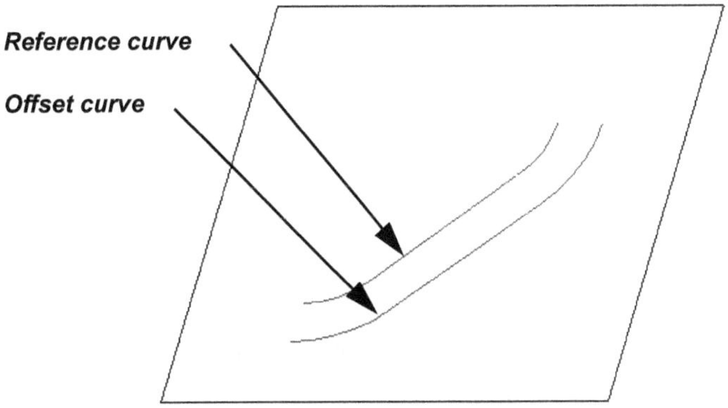

Figure 3–24

If you do use a graph to define the offset values, the following restrictions apply:

- The reference curve must lie on a reference surface or plane.
- This offset method is only able to offset one line, arc, or spline curve segment.
- The graph curve can consist of only one entity.
- Graph X-values must range from 0 to 1. A value of 0 on the graph causes the curve to touch the surface.

The datum curve shown on the right in Figure 3–25 is created at an offset normal to surface using the graph shown on the left.

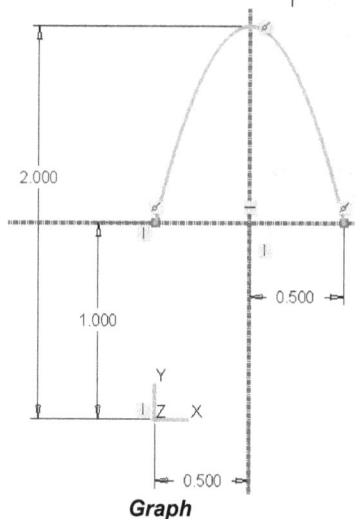

Graph

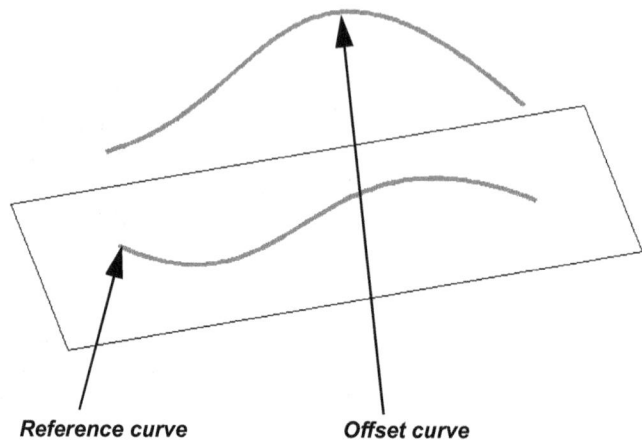

Reference curve   *Offset curve*

Figure 3–25

Offset from a Surface Boundary

How To: Create a Datum Curve at an Offset from a Surface Boundary

1. Select the surface boundary.
2. Click ⌐ (Offset) in the *Model* tab.
3. By default, a single offset value is assigned along the entire edge. To add extra points on the curve, hover the cursor over the circular handle of the existing point, right-click, and select **Add**.
4. Change position and offset values for each point directly in the Graphics window or by using the Measurements panel.

5. The *Offset* dashboard displays as shown in Figure 3–26.

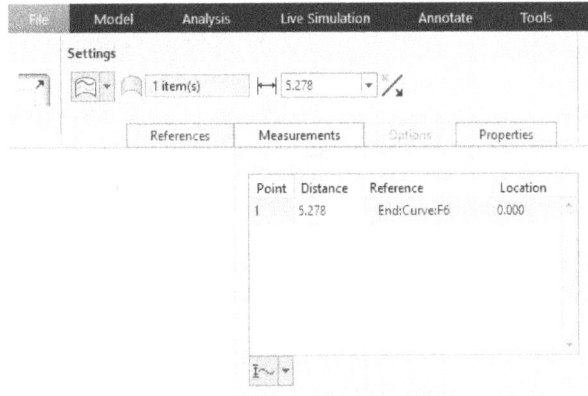

Figure 3–26

*You can also right-click on the Measurements panel and select **Add**.*

6. Complete the feature. The datum curve shown in Figure 3–27 was created at an offset from a surface boundary.

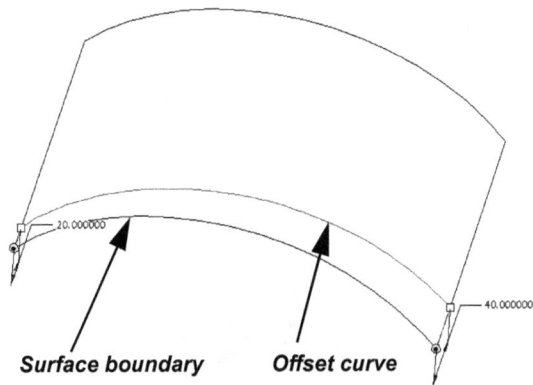

Surface boundary   Offset curve

Figure 3–27

3.4 Datum Graphs

Using relations, a datum graph feature can be used to associate a graphical XY function to control part geometry. In the feature list, the graph feature must display before the feature it controls.

Figure 3–28 shows an example of a datum graph sketch. It can be used in a relation to create the model shown in Figure 3–29.

Datum graphs must have only one X value for each Y value.

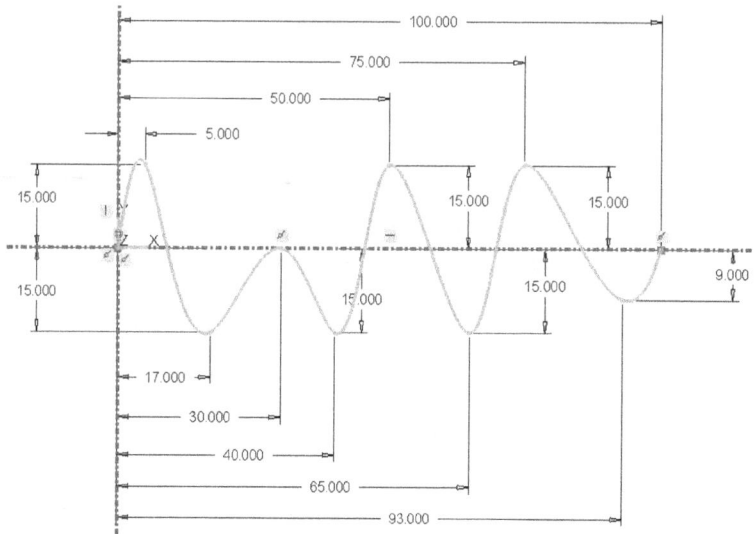

Figure 3–28

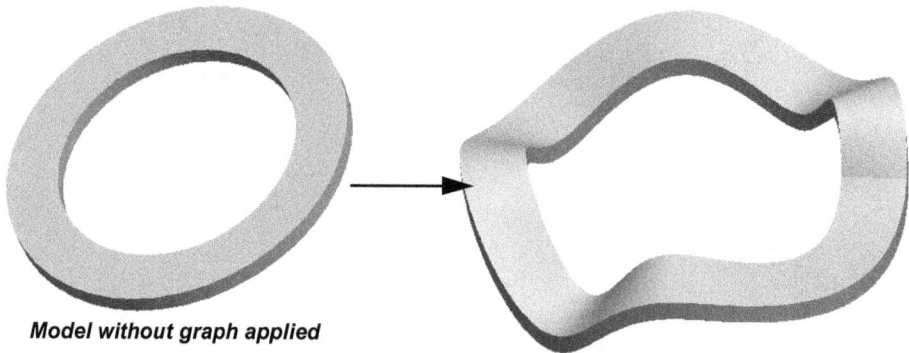

Model without graph applied

Figure 3–29

To create a datum graph, select **Datum>Graph** in the *Model* tab and enter a name for the graph. Creo Parametric opens another window and activates the *Sketch* tab.

A datum graph is stored with the model and can be used in any relation.

Datum graph sketches require the following information:

- A sketcher coordinate system.

- Sketched entities to represent the function.

- An appropriate dimensioning scheme (consider design intent).

- An horizontal and vertical centerline (recommended but not required).

Use the following syntax to reference the datum graph in a relation:

evalgraph ("graph_name", x)

Where:

- **evalgraph =** A system function that evaluates a datum graph feature.

- **graph_name =** The name of the graph referenced in the relation.

- **x =** The value along the X-axis for which the Y value is returned.

Consider the graph shown in Figure 3–30.

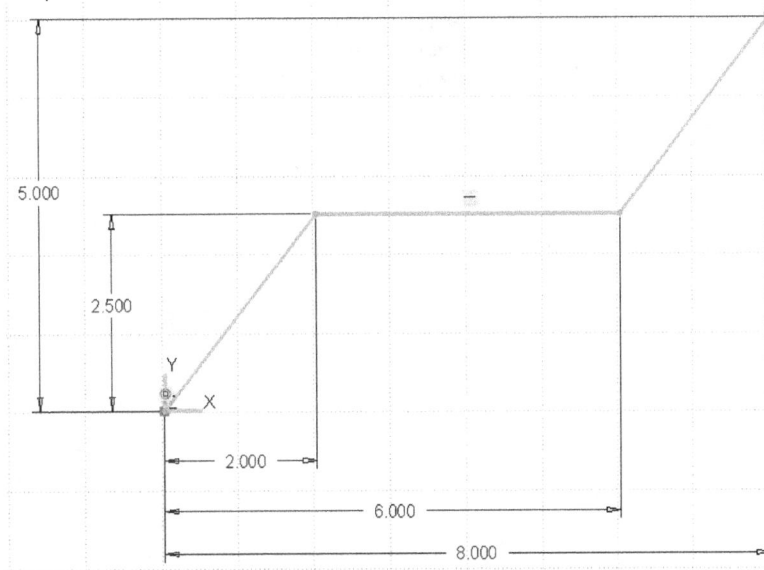

Figure 3–30

In the examples shown in Figure 3–31, a relation referencing the datum graph shown in Figure 3–30 is added to change the part. A relation can also include functions that are performed on the evalgraph portion of the relation. For example, d5 = evalgraph ("diameter",7) * 2.

Before Relation:

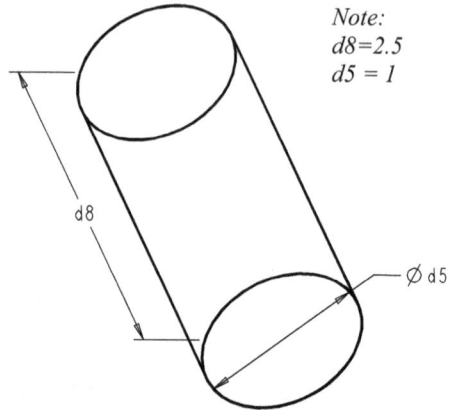

Note:
d8=2.5
d5 = 1

After Relation:

(Refer to graph in Figure 3–30 to verify the value for d5 at x=7 is 3.75.)

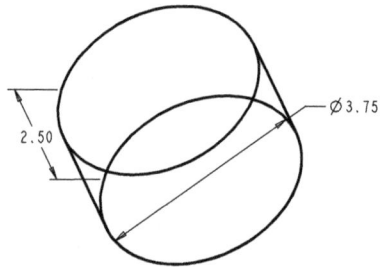

Relation:
d5 = evalgraph ("diameter", 7)

Figure 3–31

3.5 Datum Analysis

*To create an analysis feature you must have the **Behavioral Modeler** option available with the Creo Parametric license.*

A datum analysis feature can be used to generate parameters and datum features based on an analysis calculation on the part geometry. An analysis feature, plus any dependent features and relations, update automatically when changes are made to the design.

Once the analysis feature has been defined, the resulting parameters can be used in a relation. The relation can be written in the following way:

result_parameter_name: fid_analysis_feature_name

Where:

result_parameter_name = The name of the results parameter created as a result of the analysis.

analysis_feature_name = The name of the analysis feature.

In the example shown in Figure 3–32 and Figure 3–33, sweeping a section along a datum curve creates the solid geometry and the dimension d14 drives the height of the section of the geometry. The design intent of the part is to have the height of the protrusion equal to 50% of the distance around the trajectory. To accomplish this, a datum analysis feature is created to measure the distance around the trajectory. The analysis feature is then used in a relation to capture the design intent.

Before Analysis:

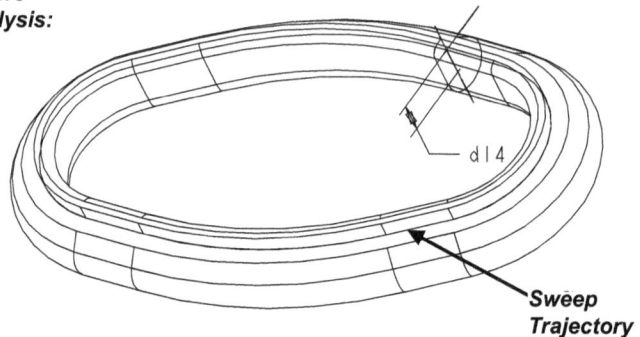

Figure 3–32

After Analysis:

Analysis Information:
analysis_feature_name = ANALYSIS_LENGTH_1
results_parameter_name = LENGTH

Analysis created using the Length dialog box.
A measurement of the sweep trajectory length is generated.

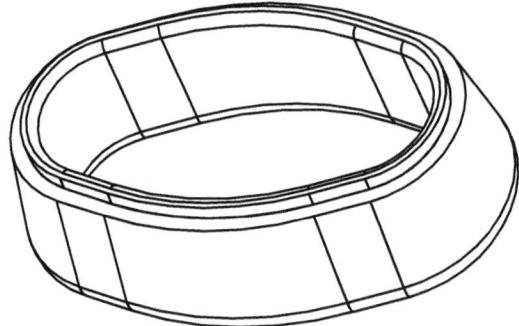

Relation:
*d14 = 0.5 * LENGTH:fid_ANALYSIS_LENGTH_1*

Figure 3–33

If parameters are defined in a part or assembly, they can be inserted directly into a relation. To insert a parameter into a relation, expand the *Local Parameters* area in the Relations dialog box and select the parameter name. Right-click and select **Insert to Relations**, as shown in Figure 3–34.

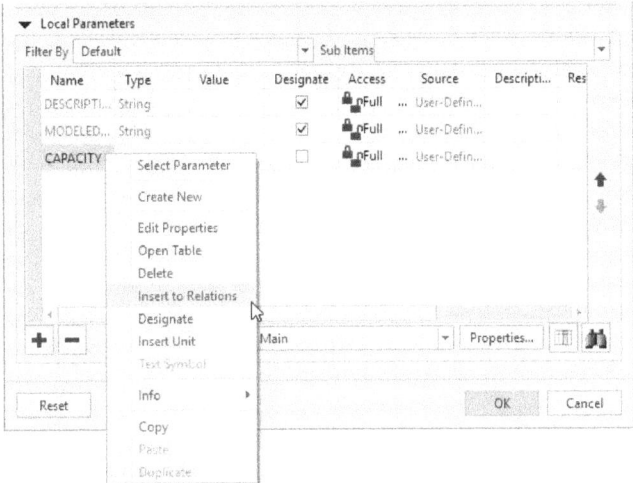

Figure 3–34

Creo Parametric enables you to create the analysis types as follows:

Analysis Type	Description
Measure	Measures distance, length, angle, area, volume or diameter of selected references. To create this type of analysis, select the *Analysis* tab, click (Measure), and select the appropriate option from the Measure Summary dialog box as shown below.

Model Report	Calculates model mass properties, finds short edges, or measures thickness of selected entities. To create this type of analysis, select the *Analysis* tab, and select the appropriate option as shown below.

Inspect Geometry	Measures radius, curvature, dihedral angle, deviation, and slope of selected references. To create this type of analysis, select the *Analysis* tab, and select the appropriate option as shown below.

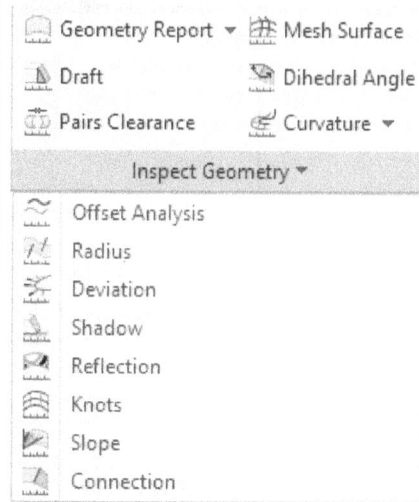

Custom	This group contains **User-Defined**, **Excel**, **External**, **Mathcad**, and **Prime** as shown below. The analysis available depends on the license available. Some of the more commonly used analysis in this group are **Excel** and **User-Defined**.

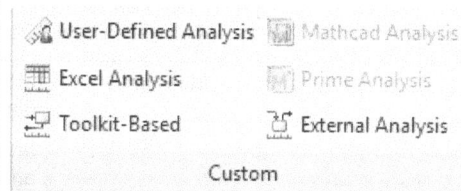

Relation	This type of the analysis feature is defined by means of a relation(s). Relations enable you to define analysis feature parameters. To create this type of analysis, select the *Tools* tab and click $d=$ (Relations).

3.6 Analysis Feature Techniques

All the analysis features are created in the *Analysis* tab. Depending on the type of analysis feature required, they are created using one of two dialog boxes.

How To: Create a Datum Analysis Feature

1. Select the *Analysis* tab, which activates as shown in Figure 3–35.

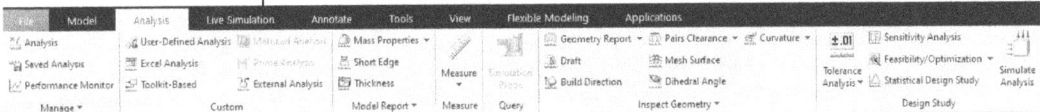

Figure 3–35

2. Select the type of analysis from the groups that you want to add to your model. A dialog box opens corresponding to the analysis type.

   For example, if you click ✎ (Measure), the Measure Summary dialog box opens, as shown in Figure 3–36.

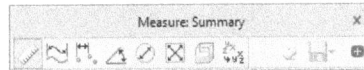

Figure 3–36

3. When the Measure dialog box opens you can select the type of measurement that you want to create and then click

   ⊕ (Expand The Dialog) to expand the dialog box, as shown in Figure 3–37.

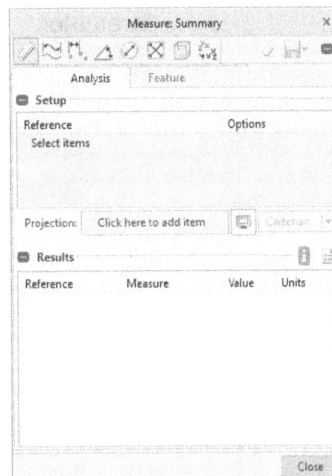

Figure 3–37

The item to measure can be preselected or selected when the *Analysis* tab is active and displays in the Measure dialog box. The results also display in the View window.

4. Click ⊟ (Open Options) in the Measurement dialog box to set various options. For example, you can toggle the **Show Feature Tab** option, as shown in Figure 3–38. This will show or remove the *Feature* tab in the dialog box.

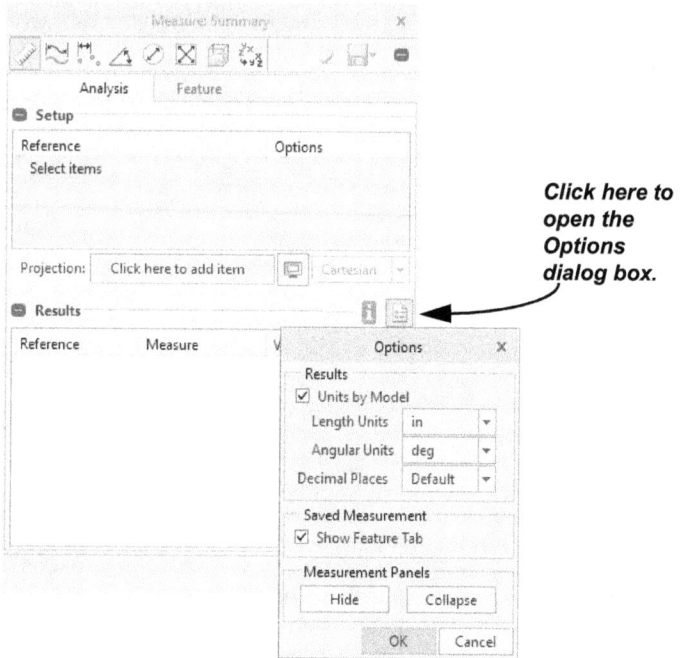

Click here to open the Options dialog box.

Figure 3–38

Select the *Feature* tab shown in Figure 3–39 to display the parameter.

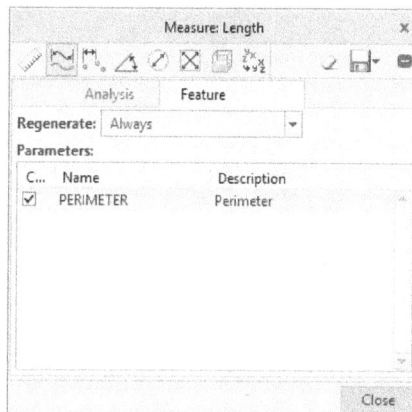

Figure 3–39

The Regenerate drop-down list enables you to assign when the analysis feature regenerates. The menu options include the following:

- **Always:** Regenerates the analysis feature during model regeneration.

- **Read Only:** Excludes the analysis feature from the model regeneration.

- **Design Study:** Only regenerates the analysis feature when it is used by a design study.

In the *Parameters* area, you can specify whether you want to create displayed parameters.

5. By default, the **Make Feature** option is preselected in the Measure dialog box. The **Feature** option creates an analysis feature. Enter an appropriate name for the analysis feature. By default, the default name identifies the analysis type (e.g., **MEASURE_LENGTH_#** for length analysis feature). The updated dialog box opens as shown in Figure 3–40.

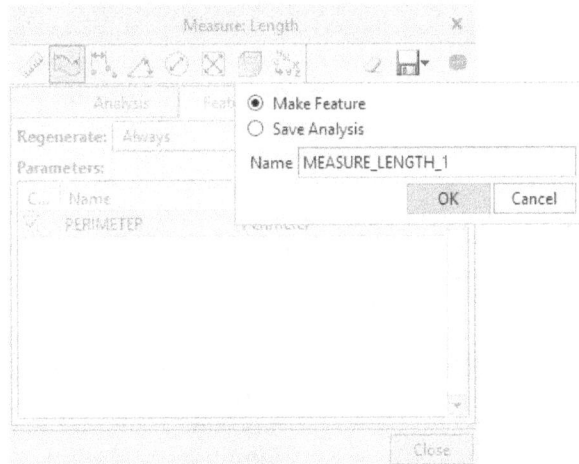

Figure 3–40

6. Click **OK** and then **Close** in the Measure dialog box to complete the feature.

How To: Create a Datum Analysis Feature in the Manage Group in the Analysis tab

1. To create an analysis feature, click (Analysis). The ANALYSIS dialog box opens as shown in Figure 3–41. Enter a name for the Analysis feature and press <Enter>. The default name is **Analysis#**.

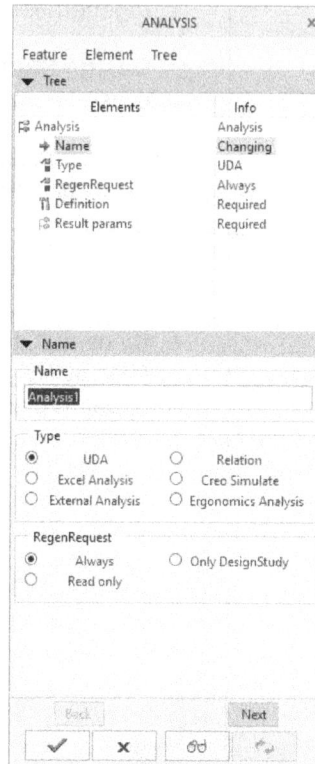

Figure 3–41

2. Select the type of analysis that you want to add to your model: **UDA**, **Excel Analysis**, **Relation**, **Prime**, **Creo Simulate**, or **Motion**.

    Regeneration options enable you to assign when the analysis feature regenerates. To define a regeneration option, select an option in the *RegenRequest* area in the ANALYSIS dialog box. The options include the following:

    - **Always:** Regenerates the analysis feature during model regeneration.
    - **Read Only:** Excludes the analysis feature from the model regeneration.
    - **Only Design Study:** Only regenerates the analysis feature when it is used by a design study.

3. Click **Next** at the bottom of the dialog box to continue. The appropriate dialog box opens so that you can define the required analysis.

4. Once the analysis has been defined, click ✔ (OK) to complete the analysis feature.

Practice 3a | Curve Network

Practice Objectives

- Create sketched curves using the Spline command in the Sketch tab.
- Create and locate points using the Ratio option.
- Create a 3D datum curve using the Curve through Points command.

In this practice, you will create a network of curves that form the outline of a car bumper. When designing complex surfaces, curves are generally created in this way to form the shape and are subsequently used to create surface geometry. The top of Figure 3–42 shows the datum curves that you will create while the bottom shows how the curves can be used to create the surface geometry for the bumper.

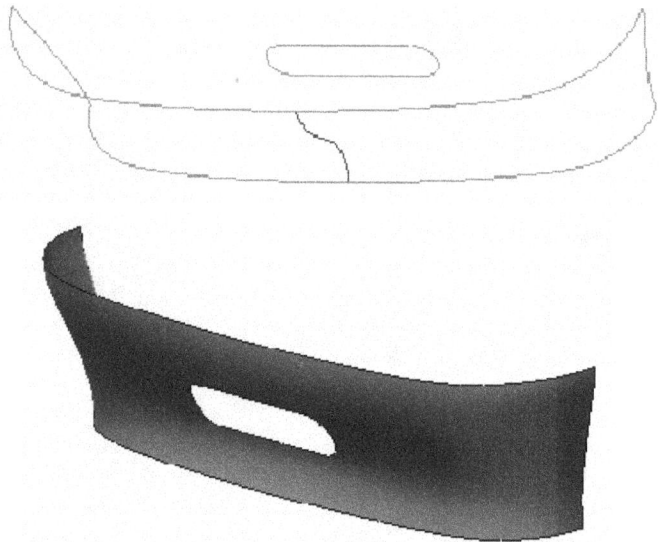

Figure 3–42

Task 1 - Create a new part.

1. Set the working directory to the *Curve_Network* folder.

2. Create a new part called **bumper** using the default template.

3. Set the model display as follows:

   - ⅍ *(Datum Display Filters)*: All Off

   - ⋙ *(Spin Center)*: Off

   - ▢ *(Display Style)*: ▢ (Shading With Edges)

Task 2 - Create the profile by creating a sketch.

Design Considerations

In this task, you will create a single sketched feature. This sketch will be used to define the bottom of the bumper geometry. It will be mirrored so that any change made to one side of the curve reflects on the mirrored side.

1. Select datum plane **TOP** from the Model Tree and click

   ▦ (Sketch) in the mini toolbar, to sketch a curve using datum plane TOP as the sketching plane. The system automatically assigns an orientation reference and the *Sketch* tab becomes active.

2. If required, click 🗗 (Sketch View) to orient the sketch in the 2D view.

3. Sketch and dimension the section shown in Figure 3–43. It consists of a vertical centerline on datum plane **RIGHT** and a seven-point spline. Add the symmetry constraints prior to adding any dimensions.

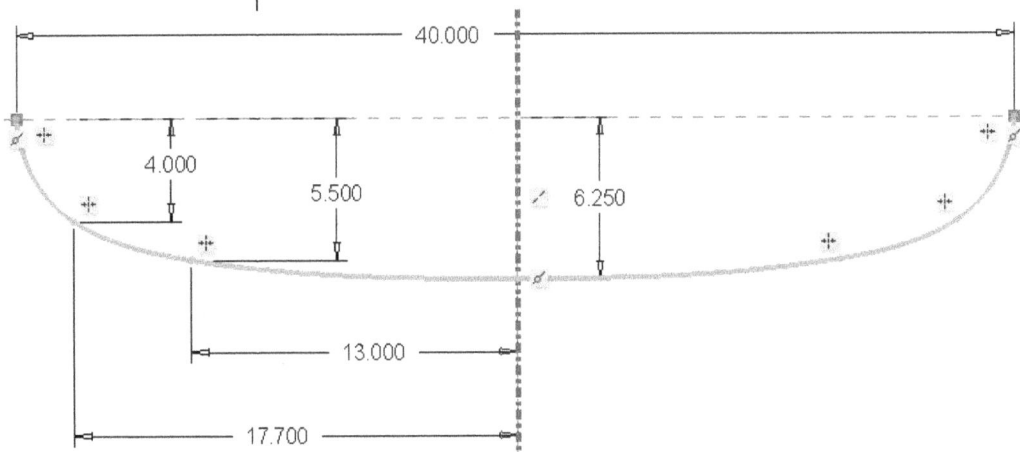

Figure 3–43

4. Drive the end points and center point of the spline with 90° dimensions, as shown in Figure 3–44. To create the angular dimensions at the end points, click ⊢⁺⊣ (Dimension) in the *Sketch* tab, select the spline, select the end point of the spline, select the reference, and place the dimension by pressing the middle mouse button.

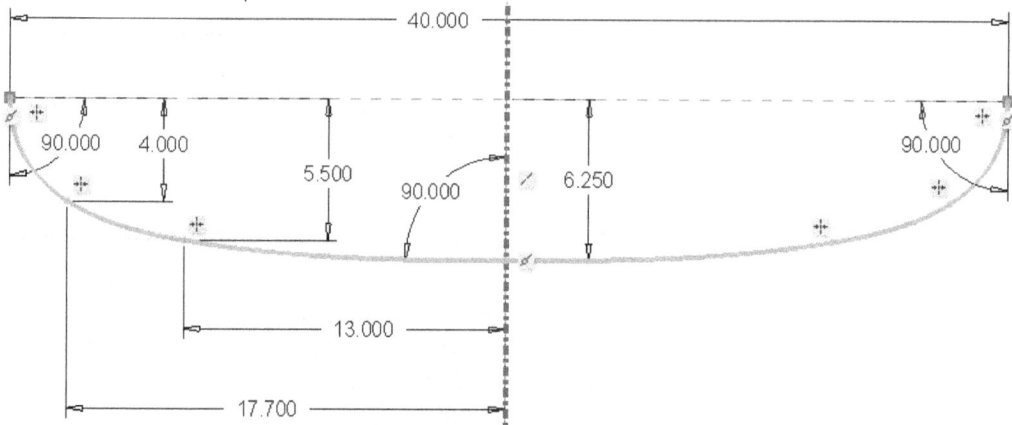

Figure 3–44

5. Click ✓ (OK) to complete the curve. The curve displays as shown in Figure 3–45.

Datum planes are toggled on for clarity.

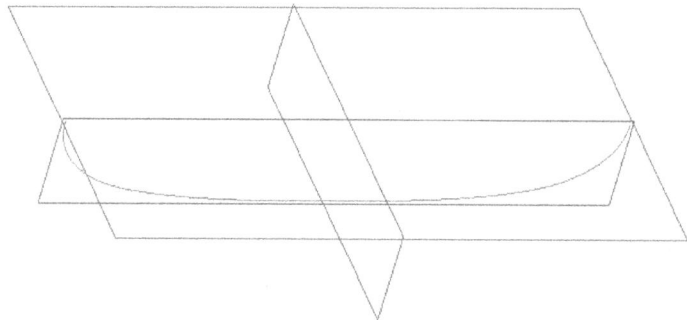

Figure 3–45

6. Click anywhere on the screen to clear the curve selection.

Task 3 - Create a second sketch.

Design Considerations

In this task, you will create a second sketched feature. This sketch will be used to define the top of the bumper geometry. It is created so that it offsets the previous sketch. This relationship is required so that if any changes are made to the first sketch, the second sketch updates.

1. Click ⁑ (Sketch) to sketch a curve.

2. Click ▱ (Plane) in the *Model* tab, to create a new plane to use for the sketching plane.

3. Select datum plane **TOP** and set the *Translation* value to **10**. Click **OK** to complete the datum plane.

4. Maintain the default orientation selection of datum plane **RIGHT**.

5. Click **Sketch**.

6. Click ⊡ (Sketch View.

7. Click ⌐ (Offset) to create an offset entity. Select the **Loop** option and select the first curve from which to offset. Set the Offset Distance to **2.20**, as shown in Figure 3–46.

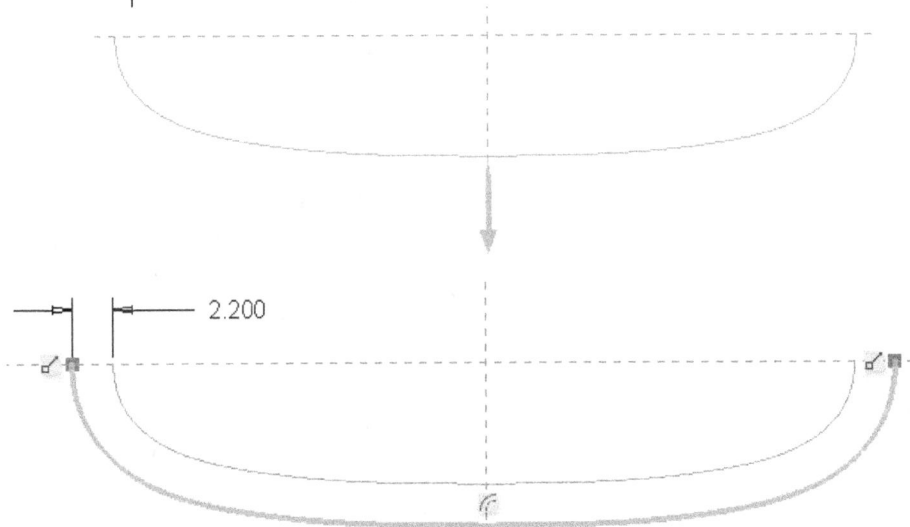

2.200

Figure 3–46

8. Click ✓ (OK) to complete the datum curve.

Task 4 - Create datum points.

In this task, you will create a datum point on the two sketches that have been created. These points will be created using the **Ratio** option to ensure that they are at the midpoint of both curves. The **Ratio** option is used so that if the design intent changes, the point locations can easily be changed by editing the ratio value. These points are placed so that they can be used to create a datum curve in the next task.

1. In the In-graphics toolbar, enable ⁂ (Point Display).

2. Click ⁂ (Point) to create datum points.

3. Select on the top datum curve near the center. A datum point displays with a *Ratio* value that positions the point along the curve. Change the value to **0.50**, as shown in Figure 3–47.

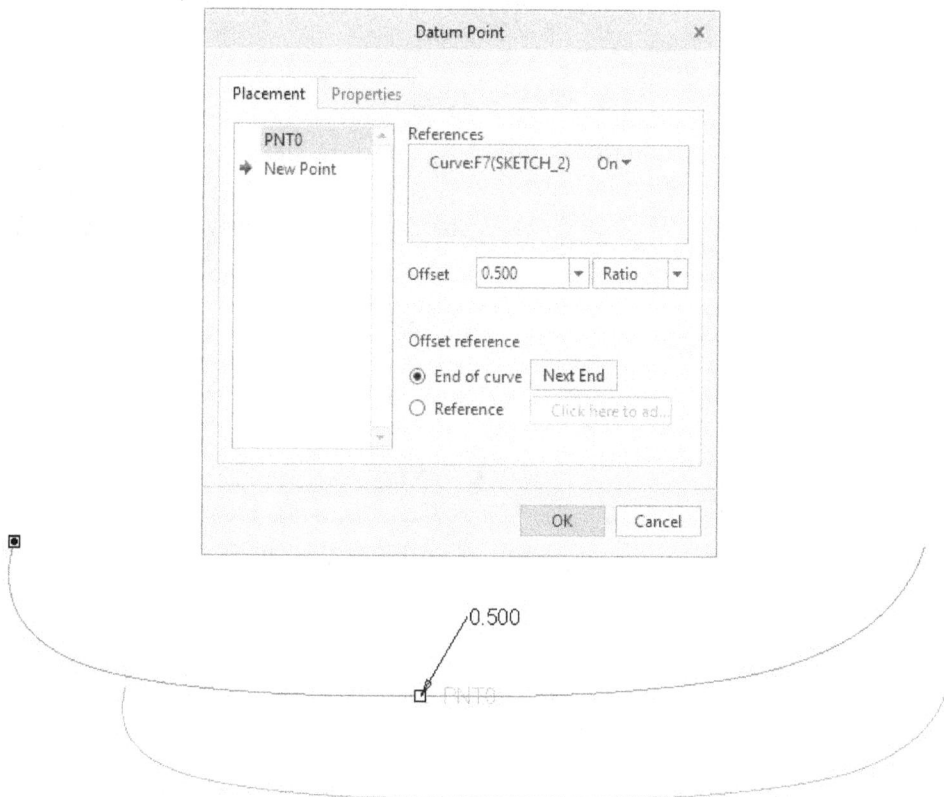

Figure 3–47

4. Select **New Point** in the left pane in the Datum Point dialog box.

5. Select on the bottom datum curve near the center. A datum point displays. Change the value to **0.50**. The datum points display, as shown in Figure 3–48.

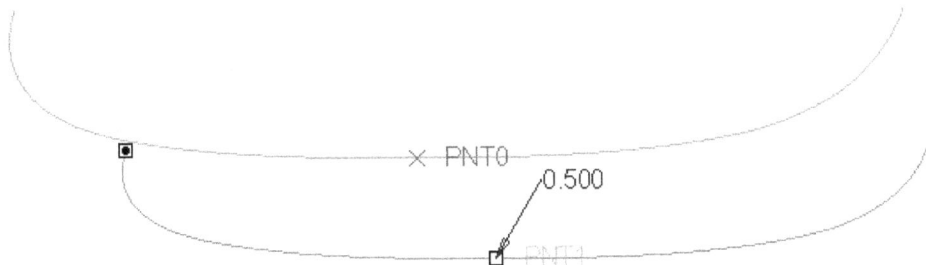

Figure 3–48

6. Click **OK** to complete the datum points.

Task 5 - Create a Curve through Points datum curve.

Design Considerations

In this task, you will create a datum curve through the two points that you created in the last task. This datum curve is created using the **Curve Through Points** option. Although the curve is created using only two points, you can further refine the shape of the curve using the optional **Tweak** element.

1. To create a Curve through Points curve, select **Datum>Curve>Curve through Points** in the Datum group in the *Model* tab, as shown in Figure 3–49.

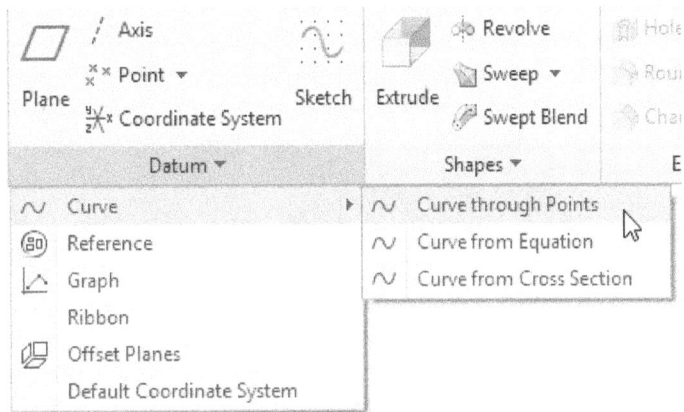

Figure 3–49

2. The *Curve: Through Points* dashboard becomes active. Select the two points that you just created, if required.

3. In the In-graphics toolbar, click 🗔 (Saved Orientations) and select **RIGHT**.

4. Select the Options panel. Select the **Tweak curve** option and click **Tweak Curve Settings**.

5. The Modify Curve dialog box opens. Move the two control points to modify the shape of the curve to look similar to that shown in Figure 3–50.

Additional control points can be added to increase control of the shape of the curve.

Click ⌒, *verify that* **Add** *is selected, and select the curve. Click*

⤳ *and move the points.*

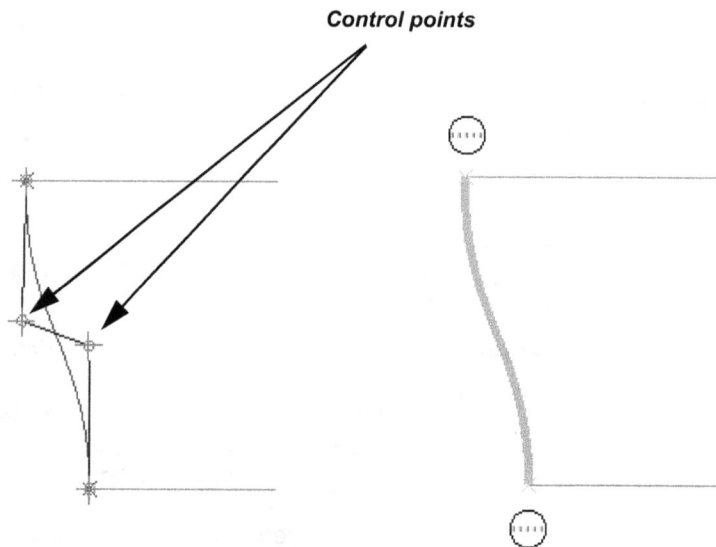

Control points

Figure 3–50

6. Click **OK** in the Modify Curve dialog box. Click ✔ (OK) in the *CURVE: Through Points* dashboard to complete the datum curve.

7. Press <Ctrl>+<D> to return to default orientation.

Task 6 - Create three additional sketches.

Design Considerations

In this task, you will create three additional sketches to complete the bumper's curve network. The first curve is created by sketching a spline between end points. Once this is created, it will be mirrored to ensure that the same shape is obtained for the second curve. The final curve in this task represents the license plate area on the bumper and will be created using lines and arcs. The three datum curves are shown in Figure 3–51.

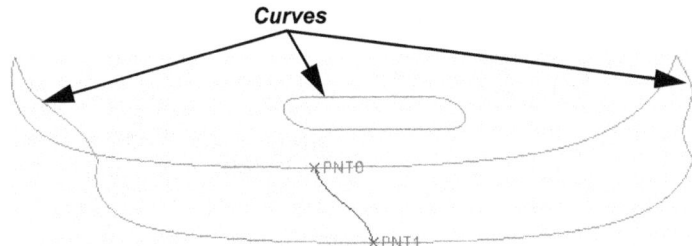

Figure 3–51

1. Select datum plane **FRONT** and click ⟨Sketch⟩ in the mini toolbar to sketch a datum curve.

2. Click ⟨Sketch View⟩.

3. Click ⟨Spline⟩ in the Sketching group. Sketch and dimension the spline as shown in Figure 3–52.

Four points are used to define the spline. Your spline might vary from that shown in the image because the shape is dependent on the precise location of the spline points.

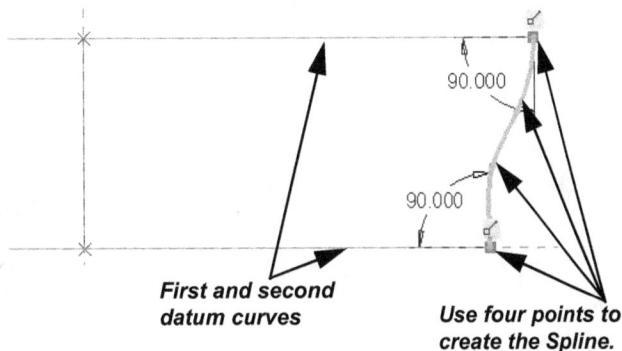

Figure 3–52

4. Click ⟨OK⟩ to exit the sketcher and complete the curve.

5. Create the second datum curve by mirroring the curve that was just created. Select the curve and click ⬚⬚ (Mirror). Select datum plane **RIGHT** from the Model Tree to mirror about, then complete the feature. The part displays as shown in Figure 3–53.

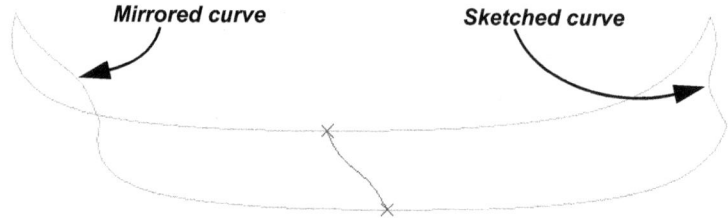

Mirrored curve   *Sketched curve*

Figure 3–53

6. Create a sketched datum curve on datum plane **FRONT**. Use the **Palette** command and drag the **Racetrack** shape to the position shown in Figure 3–54. Dimension the curve as shown in Figure 3–54.

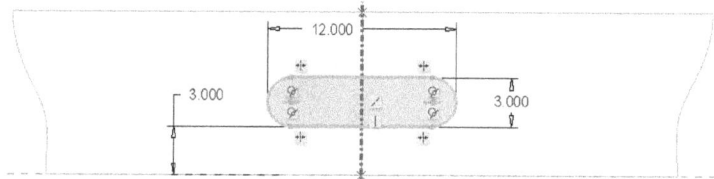

12.000

3.000

3.000

Figure 3–54

The completed part displays as shown in Figure 3–55.

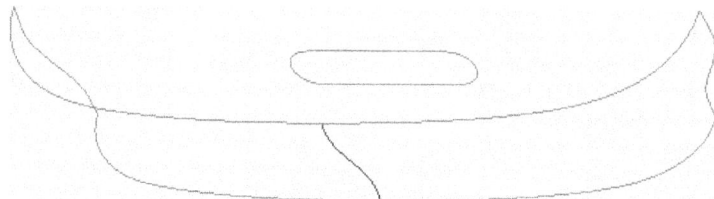

Figure 3–55

7. Save the part and erase it from memory. This curve network could be used to further define a part using Boundary Blend surfaces, as shown in Figure 3–56.

Boundary Blend surfaces are covered in the Creo Parametric: Surface Design guide.

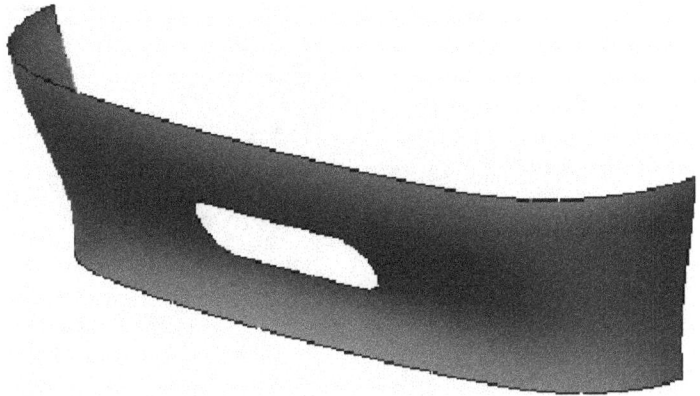

Figure 3–56

Practice 3b | Wrapped Datum Curves

Practice Objectives

- Create a new offset coordinate system.
- Create a datum curve from an equation using the newly created coordinate system.
- Wrap a datum curve around a surface.

In this practice, you will create a sinusoidal curve on the surface of a barrel cam as shown in Figure 3–57.

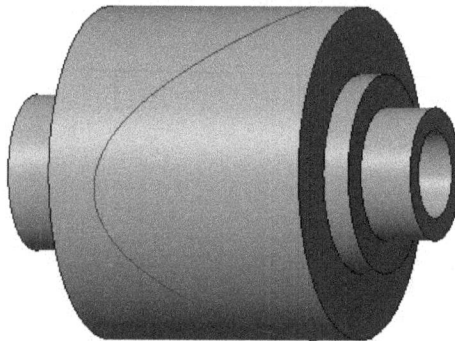

Figure 3–57

Task 1 - Open a part file.

1. Set the working directory to the *Wrapped_Curve* folder.

2. Open **barrel_cam.prt**.

3. Set the model display as follows:

   - ⁀⁄ꜞ. *(Datum Display Filters)*: All Off

   - ⋟ *(Spin Center)*: Off

   - ▢. *(Display Style)*: ▢ (Shading With Edges)

Task 2 - Create an offset datum coordinate system.

Design Considerations

In this task, you will create a new coordinate system that is offset from the default coordinate system created with the default template. This coordinate system is required for a future task in which it will be used as a reference for creating a datum curve.

Click ⊥ *(Coordinate System) in the Model tab to create a coordinate system.*

1. Create a datum coordinate system offset from the default coordinate system (select **PRT_CSYS_DEF** in the Model Tree). Translate the new coordinate system relative to the Y-axis by a value of **-15**.

The model displays as shown in Figure 3–58. The datum coordinate system sits on the outside surface of the part because the outside diameter is 30.

*Alternatively, the second coordinate system could have been created by selecting **3 planes**. A datum plane created on the fly, tangent to the surface of the part, would be required for this.*

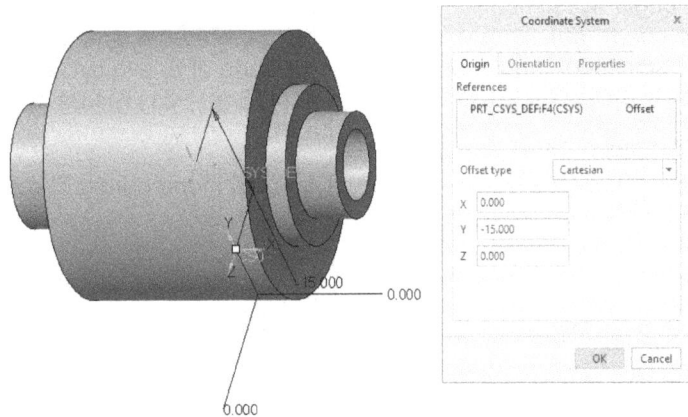

Figure 3–58

Hint: A relation should be added to ensure that this position is always maintained, regardless of the diameter ($d13=-d1/2$) where d13 is the offset dimension for the coordinate system, and d1 is the diameter of the cylinder. The $ symbol will allow for a negative value).

Task 3 - Create a curve from an equation.

Design Considerations

In this task, you will create a datum curve by entering an equation. The equation is based on Cartesian coordinates and defines a sine curve. The curve is created relative to the coordinate system that you created in the previous task. In the following task, the curve will be wrapped onto the cylindrical surface of the model for use as a trajectory for a cut.

1. Select **Datum>Curve>Curve from Equation** in the *Model* tab.

2. Select **CS0** as the *Coordinate system*.

3. Select **Cartesian** as the *Coordinate type*.

*For a Cartesian coordinate system, equations for X, Y, and Z are entered in terms of the **t** variable, which varies from 0 to 1. The equations for a circle of radius 4 and centered at the origin would be x=4*cos(t*360), y=4*sin(t*360), and z=0.*

4. Click **Equation** in the dashboard. Enter the following three equations in the editor. The equations create a sine curve that is used later in the practice.

   x = 8 * sin (t * 720)

   y = (t * pi * d1) (where d1 is the diameter dimension of the cylinder)

   z = 0

   This generates a sine curve in the X-Y plane with an amplitude of 8, two cycles (hence, t*720), and a period of 94.2478 (pi * d1) (94.2478 is the circumference of the barrel cam).

5. Click **OK** in the editor. The curve displays as shown in Figure 3–59.

Figure 3–59

6. Complete the curve.

7. Save the part.

Task 4 - Wrap the datum curve onto the model.

Design Considerations

In this task, you will wrap the datum curve onto the cylindrical surface of the model. Once it has been wrapped, the original datum curve is no longer required and will be hidden from the display. In a future practice, this curve will be used as the trajectory for a cut.

1. Select **Editing>Wrap** in the *Model* tab.

2. For the sketching plane, select datum plane **FRONT** and maintain the default orientation reference.

3. Select **CS0** as an additional sketcher reference.

4. Click ⤴ (Coordinate System) and create a geometry coordinate system aligned to **CS0**.

5. Click ▢ (Project).

6. Select **Single** and select the datum curve that was created using the equation.

7. Close the Type dialog box.

8. Click ✓ (OK) to complete the sketch.

9. Maintain **SolidGeom** as the *Destination* in the References panel. This creates the curve by forming the curve to all surfaces of the part.

10. Complete the feature.

11. Select the datum curve created by equation and select ▨ (Hide) in the mini toolbar to hide the curve from the display. The model displays as shown in Figure 3–60.

*You can also click **Define** in the References panel in the Wrap dashboard.*

*To display a hidden curve, right-click and select **Unhide**.*

As an alternative to hiding the curve, you can add it to a layer and blank it.

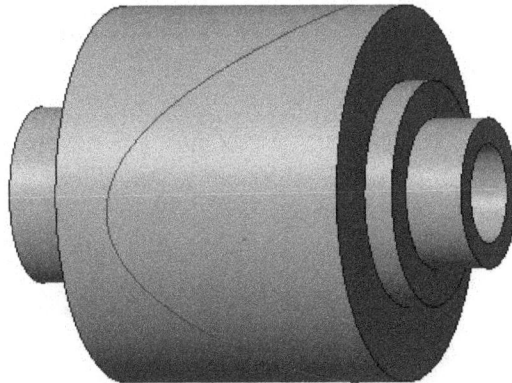

Figure 3–60

12. Save the part and erase it from memory.

Practice 3c	# Analysis Features

Practice Objectives

- Create an analysis feature to measure the volume of the solid tank.
- Create an analysis feature to measure the volume of the shelled tank and compare two volume values.
- Create a user-defined parameter and use it in a relation to display the difference between the two analysis features.
- Add a column to the Model Tree to display the values for the user-defined parameter and the two analysis features.

In this practice, you will create analysis features to determine the inside volume of a model.

Task 1 - Open a part file.

1. Set the working directory to the *Analysis_Feature* folder.

2. Open **tank.prt**.

3. Set the model display as follows:

    - ⅍ *(Datum Display Filters)*: All Off

    - ⌖ *(Spin Center)*: Off

    - ▯ *(Display Style)*: ▯ (Shading With Edges)

Task 2 - Create analysis features to measure volumes in the tank.

Design Considerations

In this task, you will create a volume measurement feature that measures the volume of the entire model. While creating the feature, you will create a parameter that you can use in a future relation to calculate the hollow volume.

1. Select the *Analysis* tab, expand the ✐ (Measure) fly-out and select ▯ (Volume) in the Measure group. The Measure: Volume dialog box opens.

2. Note that the volume measurement is automatically calculated, as shown in Figure 3–61. Click ⊕ (Expand The Dialog) and then ⊕ (Expand Results), if required, to view the *Results* field. The volume displays in the *Results* area as **39.4618 in^3**.

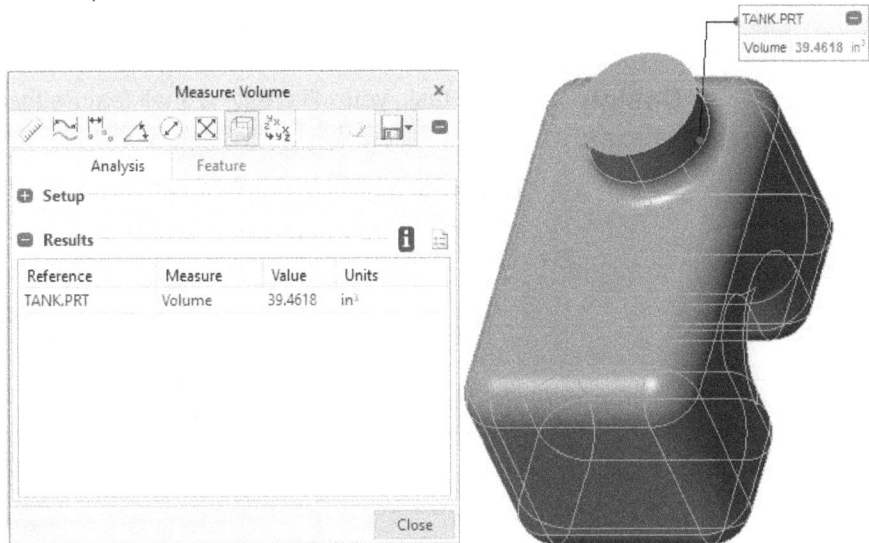

Figure 3–61

3. In the Volume dialog box, expand ▣▾ (Save Analysis). The **Make Feature** option is selected. Set the *Name* of the analysis feature to **vol_solid**, as shown in Figure 3–62. This helps to easily identify the feature once you have added multiple analysis features to the model.

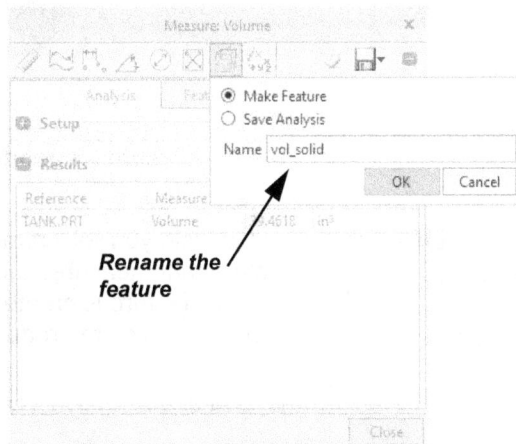

Rename the feature

Figure 3–62

4. Click **OK**.

5. Click **Close** in the Measure dialog box.

6. The analysis feature now displays in the Model Tree.

Task 3 - Create a shell feature.

Design Considerations

In this task, you will create a shell feature that hollows out the model, leaving a **0.1** thickness on all but the top opening.

1. Create a shell feature with a *Thickness* of **0.1**, as shown in Figure 3–63.

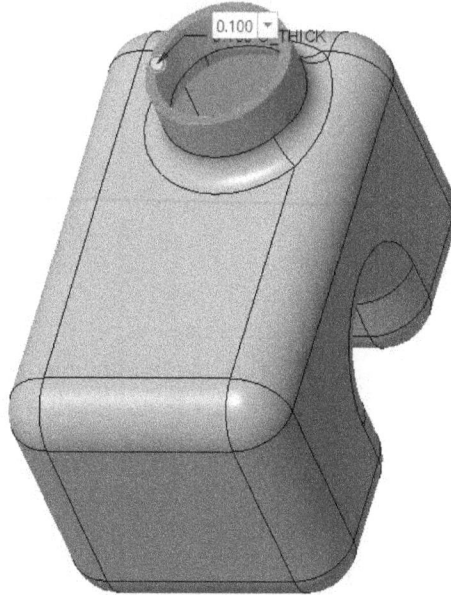

Figure 3–63

Task 4 - Create a second analysis feature.

Design Considerations

In this task, you will create a second volume measurement feature that measures the volume of the entire model. This analysis feature is created after the shell so it will take into account the volume reduction.

1. Select the *Analysis* tab and click ✐ (Measure).

2. Click 🖹 (Volume) in the Measure dialog box. Measure the volume of the shelled model. Use the options that you used in Task 2.

3. Rename the feature to **vol_shelled**.

Task 5 - Create a parameter and write a relation.

1. Select the *Tools* tab and click ᵈ= (Relations) to open the Relations editor.

2. Expand the *Local Parameter* area and click ✚ (Add New Parameter) to add a parameter.

3. Set the parameter *Name* to **Capacity** and select the **Designate** option, as shown in Figure 3–64.

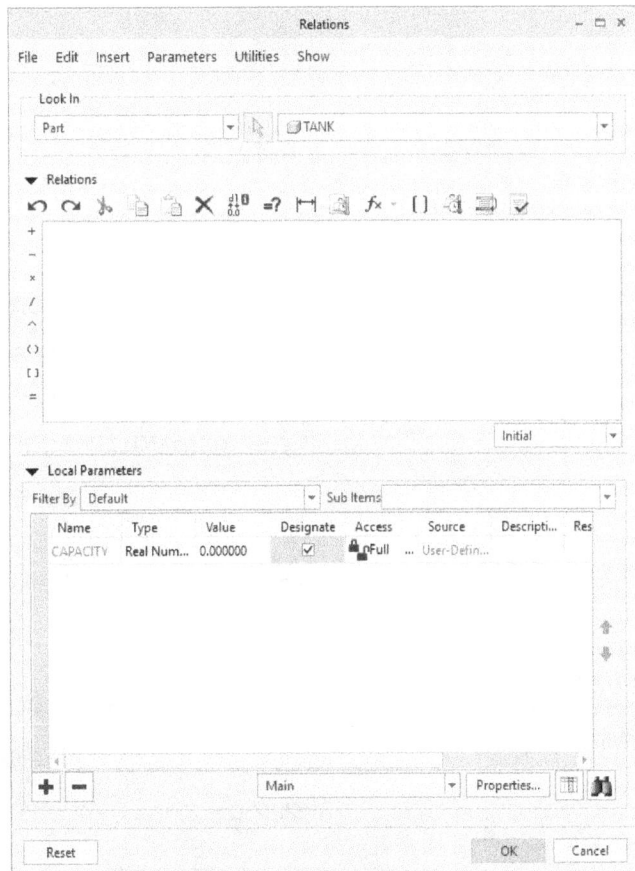

Figure 3–64

4. In the Filter By drop-down list, select **Current and all sublevels**.

5. Select the **Capacity** parameter in the *Name* column, right-click, and select **Insert to Relations**, as shown in Figure 3–65.

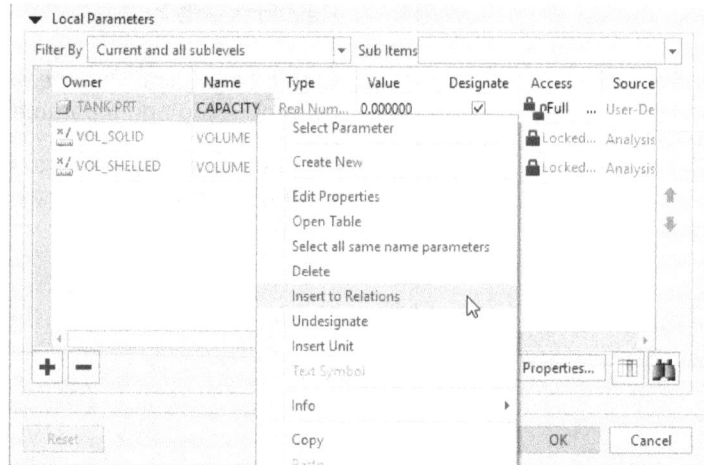

Figure 3–65

6. Type = after the **CAPACITY** parameter.

7. Select the **VOL_SOLID** parameter in the *Name* column, right-click, and select **Insert to Relations**,

8. Type - after **VOLUME:FID_1142**.

9. Select the **VOL_SHELLED** parameter in the *Name* column, right-click, and select **Insert to Relations**,

10. The relation should display as follows:

    CAPACITY = VOLUME:FID_1142 - VOLUME:FID_1310

11. Click ☑ (Verify Relations).

12. Click **OK** in the Verify Relations dialog box.

13. Click **OK** in the Relations dialog box.

Task 6 - Add columns to the Model Tree to display the parameter value.

The relation could also be manually typed (on one line) as ***capacity=volume:fid_ vol_solid-volume:fid_ vol_shelled.***

Design Considerations

In this task, you will customize the Model Tree to display the parameter and analysis values. By doing so, you can quickly identify the volume changes if any dimension on the model changes.

1. In the Model Tree, click ⊤↓ ▾ (Settings)>**Tree Columns**.

2. Select **Model Params** in the Type drop-down list.

3. Select the **CAPACITY** parameter and move it to the *Displayed* area, as shown in Figure 3–66.

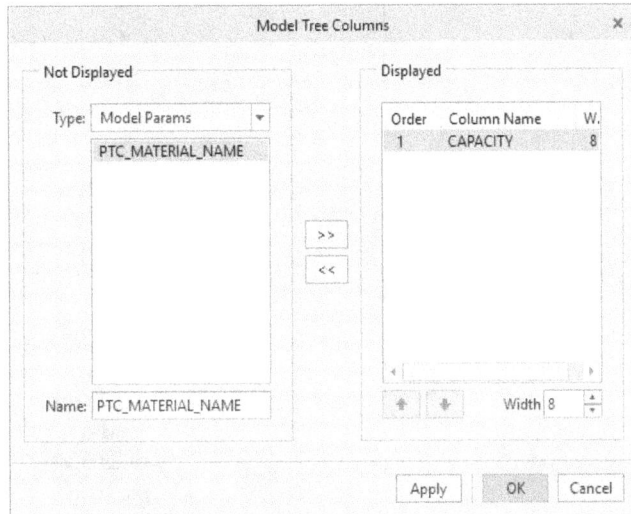

Figure 3–66

4. Select **Feat Params** in the Type drop-down list.

5. Type **volume** in the *Name* field, as shown Figure 3–67. Press <Enter>.

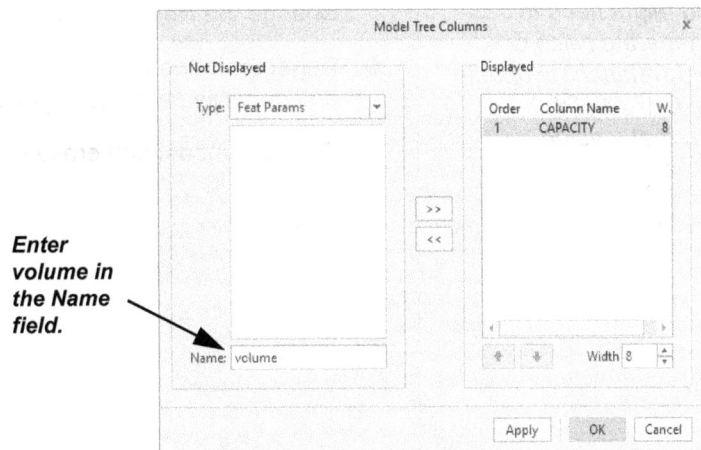

Figure 3–67

6. Click **OK**.

7. Adjust the size of the Model Tree window and columns, as shown in Figure 3–68. Click ⬛ (Regenerate) to update the values if required.

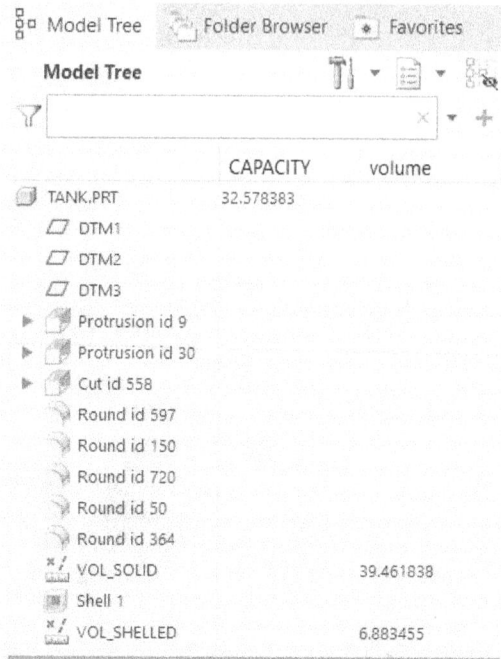

Figure 3–68

8. Edit the first protrusion listed in the Model Tree (**id 9**). Change the *Height* of the tank from *3* to **6**.

9. Regenerate the model. Note that the values of the volume and capacity parameters update in the Model Tree.

10. Save the model and erase it from memory.

*You might need to regenerate twice or verify relations to update the **CAPACITY** parameter value.*

Chapter Review Questions

1. Which End Condition options are available for a **Curve through Points**? (Select all that apply.)

   a. **Free**

   b. **Tangency**

   c. **Curvature Continuous**

   d. **Normal**

2. Which references for the End condition can be selected? (Select all that apply.)

   a. Edge

   b. Axis

   c. Surface

   d. Point

3. Which curve is an example of a Wrap curve as shown in Figure 3–69?

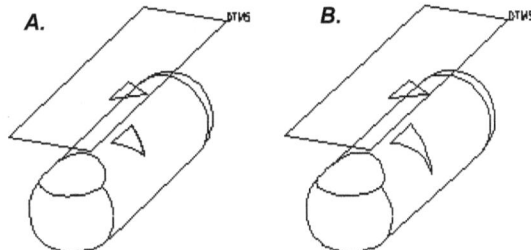

Figure 3–69

   a. A

   b. B

4. Which icon can be used to display a saved measurement in the *Analysis* tab?

   a.

   b.

   c.

5. If the analysis feature name is **ANALYSIS_LENGTH_1** and the results parameter name is **LENGTH**, what is the correct way to write a relation to control the length using the analysis?

   a. d14 = 0.5 * ANALYSIS_LENGTH_1:fid_LENGTH

   b. d14 = 0.5 * LENGTH:fid_ANALSIS_LENGTH_1

   c. d14 = 0.5 * ANALYSIS_LENGTH

   d. d14 = 0.5 * LENGTH

6. Datum graphs require which of the following items?

   a. A sketcher coordinate system.

   b. Horizontal and Vertical centerlines.

   c. Datum points.

   d. Construction entities.

Answers: 1abcd, 2abc 3a, 4b, 5b, 6a, 7b, 8a

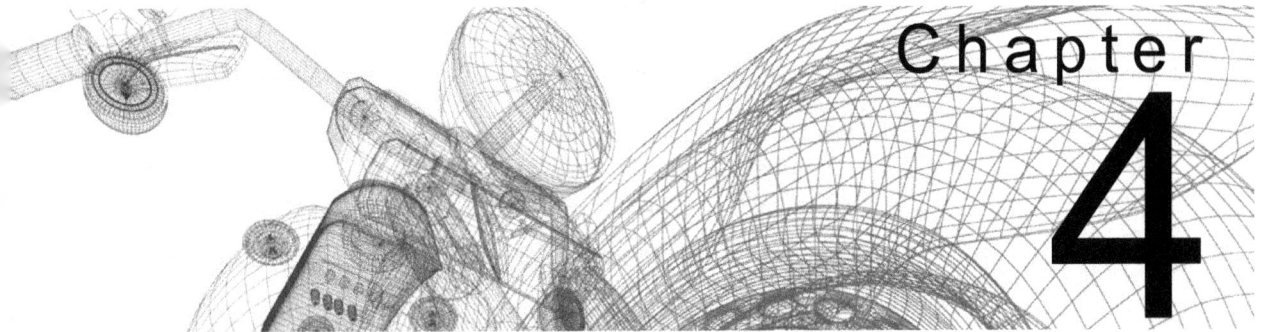

Relations

Capturing design intent is an important part of modeling in Creo Parametric. You have already learned the benefits of building models with the appropriate references and how to make them modifiable. Creo Parametric enables you to automate the control of the design intent in a model by using relations. This chapter covers why relations are useful for capturing intent between features.

Learning Objectives in This Chapter

- Learn how to create equality or conditional relations for a part, assembly, or section.
- Learn the operators, parameters, and functions available in the Relation dialog box.

4.1 Part Relations

Part relations are user-defined mathematical equations that can be used to control geometry in a model. All dimensions in a Creo Parametric model contain a symbolic dimension. An example of a symbolic dimension in a part is d6. The symbolic dimension is used in relations to reference part dimensions.

Relations can be equality or conditional statements, as follows:

- Equality statements equate one side of the equation to the other.

  d36 = 2.75 + d20 * (1 - d42)

- Conditional statements use If/Else/Endif statements to equate a value based on a specified condition.

  If (d12 + d16) <= 10
  d3 = d6
  Else
  d4=d6
  Endif

A relation can use any combination of dimension symbols, parameters, and numerical values. Relations can be written at the part level using the **Part**, **Feature** or **Section** options in the Relations dialog box, as shown in Figure 4–1.

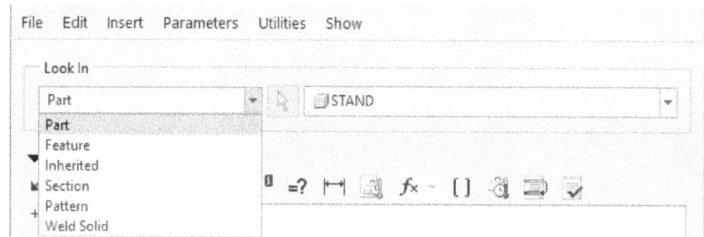

Figure 4–1

Part relations are added to the model and divided into two portions. The first portion, known as the *Initial* relation, is calculated before features are regenerated. The second portion, known as the *Post Regeneration* relation, is calculated after features have been regenerated.

- Feature relations are added to the model and regenerated at the time of feature regeneration and follow the same rules as part relations.

- Section relations are added to the model and regenerated at the time of section regeneration and follow the same rules as part relations.

General Steps

Use the following general steps to create a part relation:

1. Start the creation of the relation.
2. Specify the geometry to be referenced.
3. Enter a comment statement.
4. Enter the relation.
5. Complete the relation.
6. Flex the model.

Step 1 - Start the creation of the relation.

Click d= (Relations) in the *Tools* tab to open the Relation dialog box, as shown in Figure 4–2.

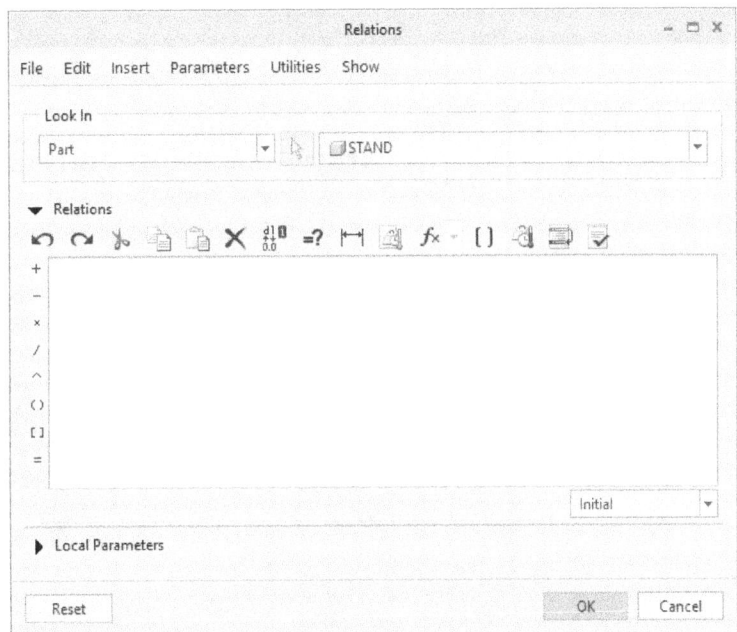

Figure 4–2

Step 2 - Specify the geometry to be referenced.

To select the type of geometry referenced by the relation, expand the drop-down list in the *Look In* area, as shown in Figure 4–3. The option also determines where the relation is written.

*For example, if **Feature** is specified as the **Look In** option, select a feature in a part and enter the relation. The relation is created in and calculated with the feature.*

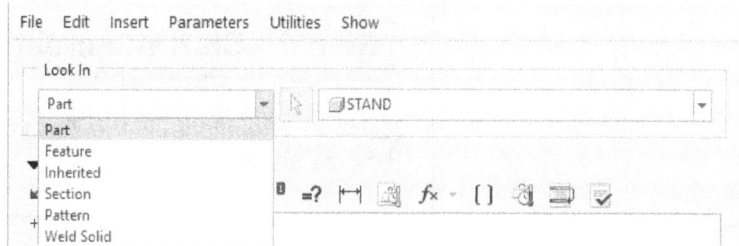

Figure 4–3

Step 3 - Enter a comment statement.

Comment lines are useful for describing and organizing relations. They are also valuable for downstream users of the model who do not know its original design intent. Comment lines display before a relation and must be preceded with /*, as shown in Figure 4–4.

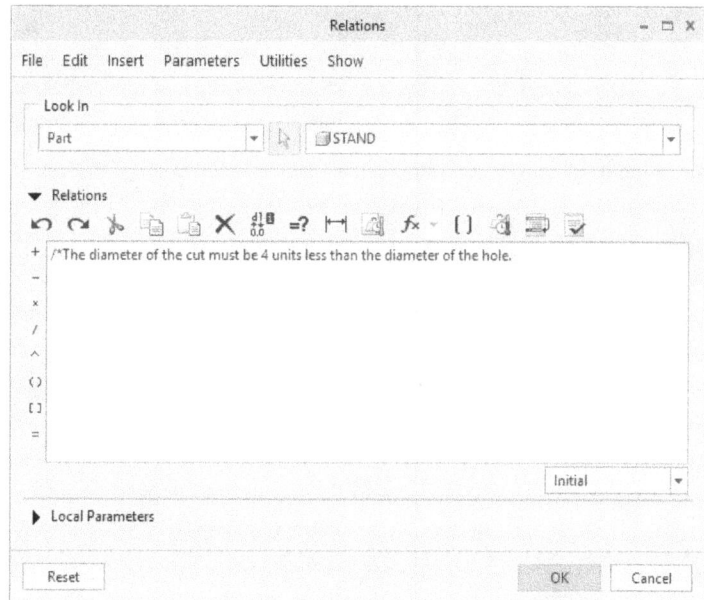

Figure 4–4

Step 4 - Enter the relation.

Equations can be entered manually or inserted from the model. To manually enter the relation, enter the operators, symbolic dimensions and numerical values using the keyboard.

To insert a dimension into a relation, select the dimension on the model. The selected symbolic dimension displays in the *Relations* area in the Relations dialog box, as shown in Figure 4–5.

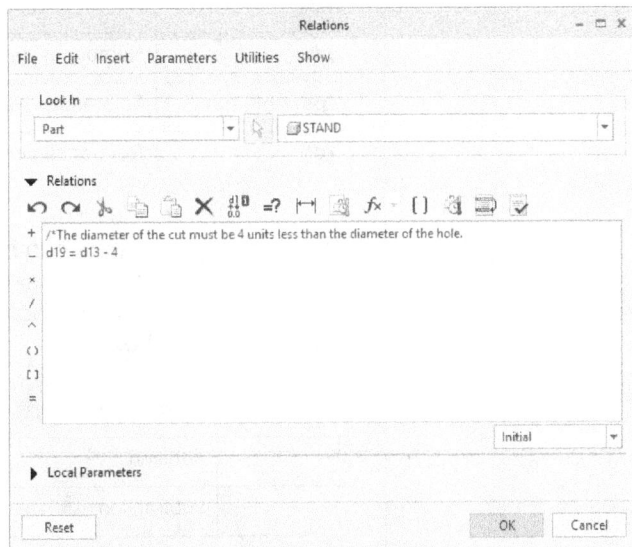

Figure 4–5

The following can be included when entering a relation:

- Symbols

- Operators

- Functions

Symbols

The following symbols can be used when writing a relation. The number (#) sign represents the dimension symbol number (e.g., d3).

Symbol	Description
d#	Part dimensions.
d#:#	Dimensions in assemblies. The second # is the session ID.
sd#	Sketcher dimensions (Feat Rel).
kd#	Known dimensions in Sketcher (Feat Rel).
p#	Number of instances in a pattern.
tp#, tm#, tpm#	Tolerance values.
rd#	Reference dimensions.

Operators

The following operators can be used in relations. The operators can be manually entered using keyboard icons, or for those available, you can select the required icon in the left side of the Relations dialog box.

Operator	Description	Operator	Description
+	addition	<	less than
-	subtraction	<=	less than or equal
/	division	==	equal to
*	multiplication	!=	not equal to
^	exponentiation	&	and
( )	grouping	|	or
>	greater than	!	not
>=	greater than or equal		

Functions

The following functions can be used in relations.

Mathematical Function

Sin ()	tanh ()
cos ( )	sqrt ( )

tan ( )	log ( )
asin ( )	ln ( )
acos ( )	exp ( )
atan ( )	abs ( )
sinh ( )	ceil ( ) Smallest integer not less then the real value.
cosh ( )	floor ( ) Largest integer not greater then the real value.

Parameters

The following parameters can be used in relations. User-defined parameters can also be used.

Predefined parameters

PI (= 3.1415...) Mathematical constant, π

G (= 9.8 m/sec2) Gravity constant

C1,C2,C3,C4 (= 1.0, 2.0, 3.0, 4.0) Common parameters for all models in current session can be modified by relations.

Mass Property	Description
mp_mass	Mass
mp_volume	Volume
mp_surf_area	Surface area
mp_cg_x	X of center gravity
mp_cg_y	Y of center gravity
mp_cg_z	Z of center gravity

Step 5 - Complete the relation.

When all of the relations and their comments have been added to the Relations dialog box, click (Verify Relations) to verify that all of the relations can be executed. Once you have been prompted that all of the relations have been successfully verified you can complete the relations by clicking **OK**.

Step 6 - Flex the model.

Once relations have been added to the model it is recommended that you make changes to the model to ensure that the model relations work correctly. Doing so is called *flexing the model* and it can help save valuable design time downstream by resolving any issues that might occur due to the most recently added relation as soon as possible before additional features or relations are added.

Practice 4a | Conditional Relations

Practice Objectives

- Open and investigate a part that contains two datum analysis features.
- Create a conditional statement and relations for a part in the Relation dialog box to capture the required design intent.
- Edit and create equations between the model and the user-defined parameters.
- Create user-defined parameters in a model for driving the model geometry or providing additional model information.
- Edit model dimensions that drive the geometry to ensure that the model updates as required.

In this practice, you will create part relations using conditional statements. You will create an analysis feature on an existing part and use the conditional relations to control its dimension values. The model shown on the left in Figure 4–6 is the model that you will begin working with. When you have completed the practice, the model will display as shown on the right.

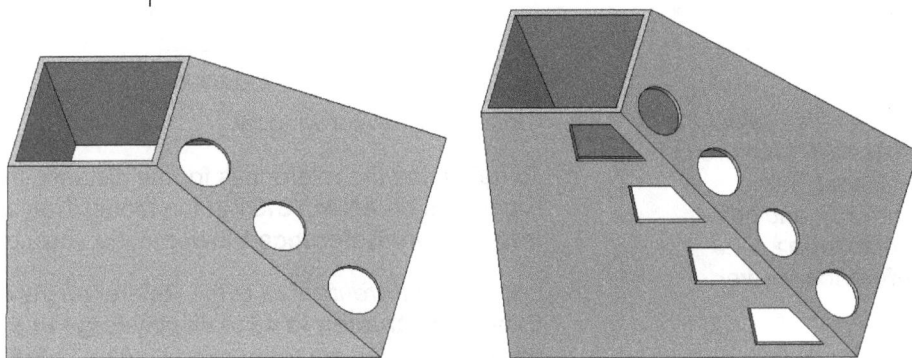

Figure 4–6

Task 1 - Open and investigate the part called stand.prt.

Design Considerations

It is recommended that you investigate the model before working on it. This involves reviewing the features so that you understand the feature order, reviewing feature information on key features in the model and reviewing the relations and parent/child relationships that exist between features in the model. Once you have a basic understanding of this information it will help you to work more efficiently with the model to meet your required design changes and intent.

1. Set the working directory to the *Conditional_Relations* folder.

---

2. Open **stand.prt**.

3. Set the model display as follows:

- ⚙ *(Datum Display Filters)*: All Off

- ↗ *(Spin Center)*: Off

- ⬜ *(Display Style)*: ⬜ (Shading With Edges)

4. Use the Model Player to become familiar with the feature sequence. What are the fifth and sixth features?

*You can also select the **ANALYSIS1** feature in the Model Tree, right-click, and select **Information>Feature Information**.*

5. Right-click the analysis feature **ANALYSIS1** in the Model Tree, and select **Information>Feature Information**. In the Browser window, you can determine that the analysis feature contains a distance measurement. A parameter called **DIST** is present and is equal to 20, as shown in Figure 4–7.

Local Parameters						
Symbolic constant ▶	Current value ▶	TYPE ▶	SOURCE ▶	ACCESS ▶	DESIGNATED ▶	DESCRIPTION ▶
DIST	2.000000e+01	Real Number	Analysis feature	Locked	NO	

Figure 4–7

*You can also select the **ANALYSIS1** feature in the Model Tree, right-click, and select **Information> Reference Viewer**.*

6. Close the Browser window.

7. To determine the references for the distance measurement, Right-click on **ANALYSIS1** in the Model Tree and select **Information>Reference Viewer** in the *Tools* tab.

8. Look at the *Parents* area in the Reference Viewer dialog box. Expand **Protrusion id 45** to display **Edge id 51** and **Edge id 60**. These edges are referenced by **ANALYSIS1**. Select each of them to highlight them on the model.

9. Use the same technique to investigate the **ANALYSIS2** analysis feature.

10. In the *Model* tab, expand **Model Intent** and click

    d= (Relations). The Relations dialog box opens containing the following relations:

    / Number of holes and spacing based on angle.*
    if angle:FID_ANALYSIS2 > 45
       P2 = 4
    else
       P2 = 3
    endif
    D38 = dist:FID_ANALYSIS1/P2
    D34 = D38/2

11. In the Relations dialog box, select **Show>Info**. The Browser window opens containing the information shown in Figure 4–8.

Relation Table		
Relation	Parameter	New Value
Relations for STAND:		
Initial Relations		
/* Number of holes and spacing based on angle.		
if angle:FID_ANALYSIS2>45		
P2 =4		
else		
P2 =3	P2	3.000000e+00
endif		
D38 =dist.FID_ANALYSIS1/P2	D38	6.666667e+00
D34 =D38 /2	D34	3.333333e+00

Figure 4–8

12. Close the Browser window.

13. In the Relations dialog box, click ⊢⊣ (Display Specified Dimension) and enter **d38**. This is an easy way to verify the dimension symbols used in the part.

14. Repeat the previous step for **d34**.

15. **P2** represents the number of holes in the pattern. According to the relation and the current value for the angle, how many holes should there be?

16. Close the Relations dialog box.

You can also select the dimension symbol name in the Relations area

and click ⊢⊣ (Display Specified Dimension) to display the dimension in the Graphics window.

Task 2 - Modify the part to verify the relation.

1. Edit the *Height* of the blended protrusion, from *12* to **18**. Note that the part automatically regenerates to the new height. However, the number of holes does not appear to change.

2. Regenerate the model by clicking 🔀 (Regenerate) in the Quick Access toolbar. What values do the analysis features have now?

Task 3 - Create an analysis feature.

Design Considerations

In this task, you will create an analysis feature that measures the distance between the two edges shown in Figure 4–9. This value will be used in a future relation to equally space a cut along this front surface.

1. Select the *Analysis* tab.

2. Create an analysis feature named **ANALYSIS3** by expanding ✏ (Measure) and selecting ⬑ (Distance).

3. Press and hold <Ctrl> and select the two edges shown in Figure 4–9. The current value for this analysis feature is **19.6977**.

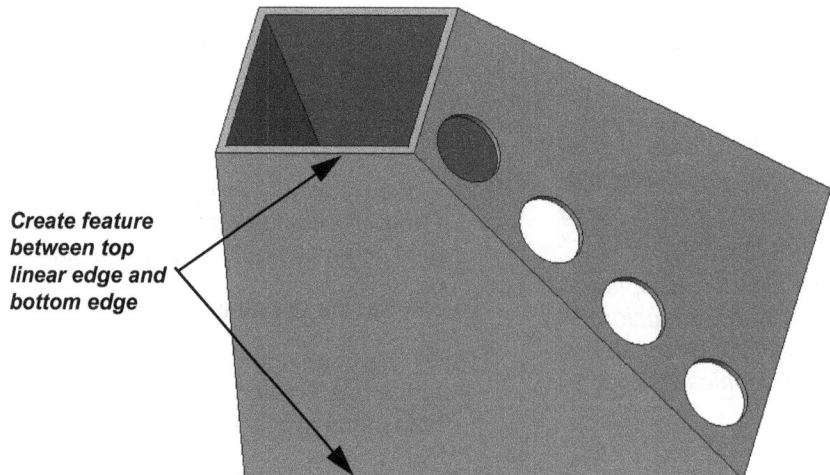

Create feature between top linear edge and bottom edge

Figure 4–9

4. In the Measure Distance dialog box, click 🖫▾ (Save Analysis).

5. Edit the name to **ANALYSIS3** and press <Enter>.

Task 4 - Create a cut feature on the front blend face.

1. Create an extruded cut in the lower right corner, as shown in Figure 4–10. Select the sketch plane shown in Figure 4–10.

2. When prompted for references, select the edge between the angled surface and the sketch plane surface, and click **Close**.

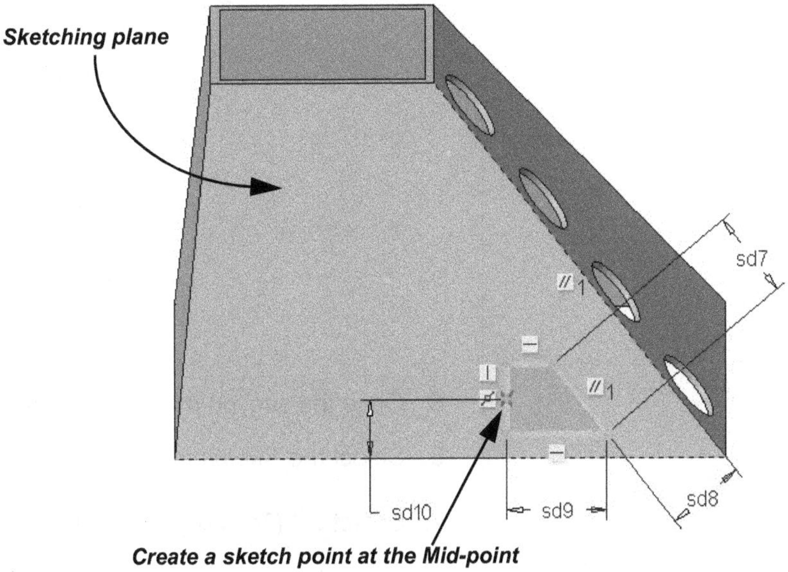

Create a sketch point at the Mid-point

Figure 4–10

3. Before completing the sketch, select the *Tools* tab and click

   d= (Relations) to add relations for the sketch. Section relations are added to the model and regenerated at the time of section regeneration to ensure that the relation is calculated when the feature is regenerated.

4. Enter the relations shown in Figure 4–11. Note that the sd# symbols might differ from the symbols shown in Figure 4–11. Dimension symbol **d37** is the diameter of the hole.

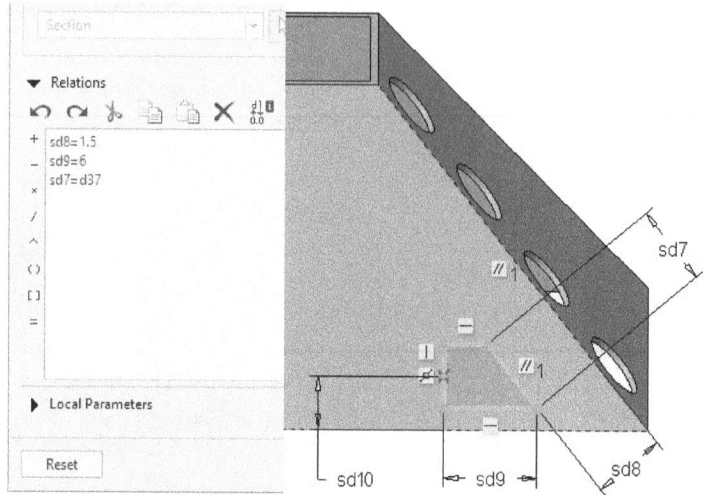

Figure 4–11

5. Once the section has regenerated, modify *sd10* to **2.45**.

6. Select the *Sketch* tab and complete the section.

7. Select ≣ (To Next) for the depth option in the dashboard.

8. Click on the screen and select ◢ (Remove Material) in the mini toolbar.

9. If required, click ⚹ (Change Depth Direction).

10. Complete the cut.

Task 5 - Pattern the cut.

1. Pattern the cut using a **Direction** pattern. Select **d50** shown in Figure 4–12 to set the direction.

2. Set the *Dimension* increment to **4**. Set the number of *Instances* to **3**. Relations added later in this practice control this value.

The dimension symbols shown in Figure 4–12 might differ from symbols in your current model.

3. In the Options panel, select **Variable** for the Regeneration option, the click ✓ (OK). The pattern displays as shown in Figure 4–12.

Instance 2 is highlighted to display all pattern dimensions.

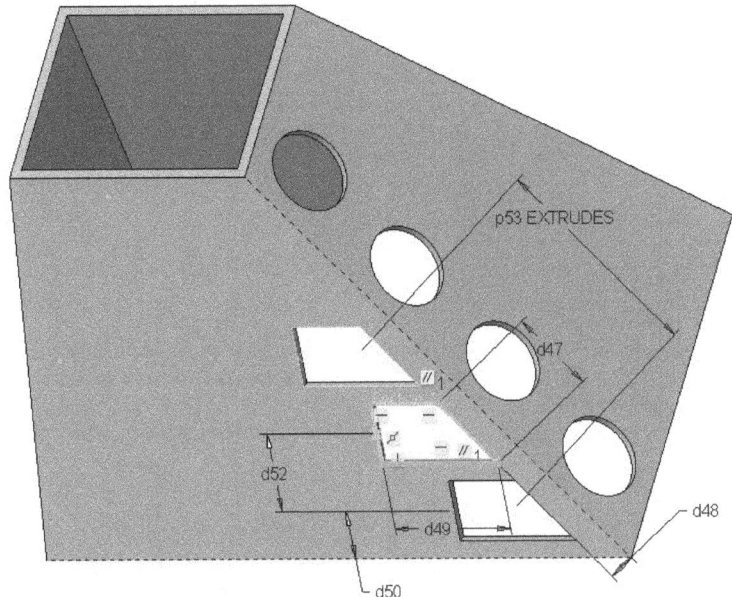

Figure 4–12

Task 6 - Add relations.

Design Considerations

In this task, you will add relations to drive the cut pattern using an analysis feature to ensure that the cuts are evenly spaced regardless of changes to the model's height. If you add relations at the Part level, they will be evaluated before the regeneration of any feature in the model, including the analysis feature. In that case you will have to regenerate the model twice to incorporate relations into the model correctly (as discussed in Task 2). To avoid having to regenerate twice you will add the relations at the Feature level instead. Feature relations are evaluated when the feature is regenerated.

1. To add the relation, click d= (Relations) in the *Tools* tab.

2. The Relations dialog box opens. Select **Feature** in the Look In drop-down list.

3. Select the cut feature that you created in Task 5. Ensure you select the pattern leader (the original cut) and not a pattern instance, as shown in Figure 4–13.

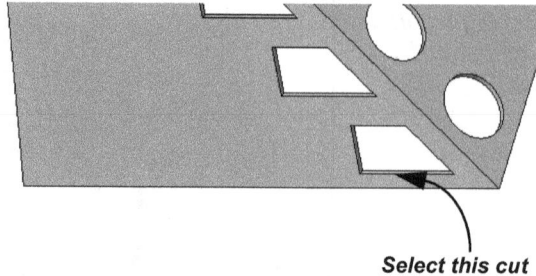

Select this cut

Figure 4–13

Dimension symbols shown in Figure 4–12 might differ from symbols in your current model.

4. Add a relation that equates the number of cut pattern instances to the number of hole pattern instances, as follows:

/* **Relations driving the cut feature.**

p53 = p2

5. Add a relation that drives the value of **d52** (refer to Figure 4–12 for the pattern increment) that ensures the cuts are evenly spaced. Use the distance measurement of the **ANALYSIS3** analysis feature, as follows:

d52 = distance:FID_ANALYSIS3 / p53

6. Add the relation **d50 = d52/2** to position the cut according to the value for **d52**.

7. Verify the relations then click **OK** in the Relations dialog box.

8. Modify the blend *Height* to **20** and regenerate. The model updates as shown in Figure 4–14.

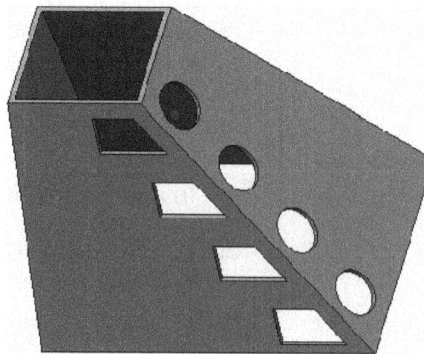

Figure 4–14

9. Save the part and erase it from memory.

Chapter Review Questions

1. Which of the following statements are true regarding relations? (Select all that apply.)

    a. Dimensions and parameters can be used in a relation to drive a value.

    b. Equations can be manually entered in the Relations dialog box.

    c. Equations can be created using a combination of manual entry and selecting dimensions directly from the model.

    d. Creo Parametric enables you to create both equality and conditional relations.

2. Which of the following is the correct syntax that must be used to precede a comment statement for a relation?

    a. */

    b. !

    c. /*

    d. #

3. Which of the following icons enables you to select a function from a predefined list?

    a. d=

    b. $f_\times$

    c. [ ]

    d.

4. Relations can be added to the model by entering an equation in the main graphic window when modifying a dimension.

    a. True

    b. False

5. Which of the following are valid operators that can be used in a relation? (Select all that apply.)

    a. ^

    b. !

    c. ( )

    d. #

6. Feature relations are added to the model and regenerated at the time of feature regeneration and follow the same rules as part relations.

   a. True

   b. False

7. Section relations are added to the model and regenerated at the time of section regeneration and follow the same rules as part relations.

   a. True

   b. False

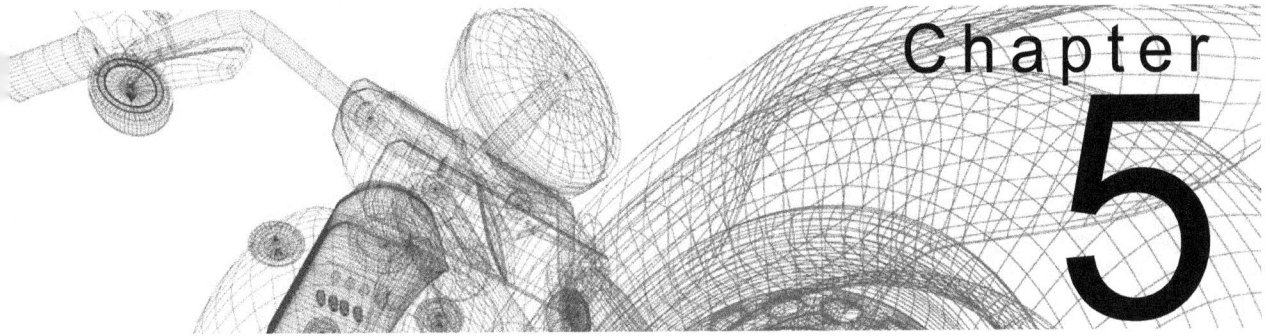

Sweeps with Variable Sections

Basic sweep features enable you to create geometry by sweeping a cross-section along a single trajectory. This chapter introduces variable section sweeps. Variable section sweeps enable you to select multiple trajectories that the cross-section follows, giving you greater control over the geometry of the cross-section.

Learning Objectives in This Chapter

- Create a Variable Section Sweep by selecting a trajectory and type, and sketching the cross-section.
- Learn the differences between the Normal to Origin, Normal to Trajectory, and Constant Normal Direction sweeps.
- Learn the differences between Automatic, Normal to Surface, and X-Trajectory to control the cross-section.
- Learn how to use the trajpar parameter and the evalgraph to change the cross-section of the sweep.

5.1 Sweeps with Variable Sections

The ☞ (Sweep) tool enables you to sweep along multiple curves, giving you greater control over the geometry of the cross-section. You can control the shape and size of the section by its interaction with the trajectories or using relations.

Some examples of Variable Section Sweeps are shown in Figure 5–1.

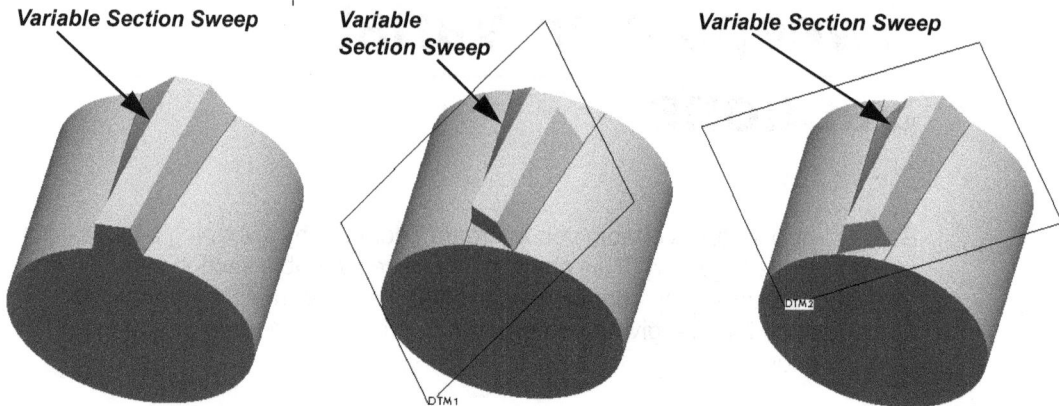

Variable Section Sweep

Variable Section Sweep

Variable Section Sweep

Figure 5–1

General Steps

Use the following general steps to create a Variable Section Sweep:

1. Start the creation of the feature.
2. Select the trajectories.
3. Define the section plane control.
4. Define the attributes for the feature.
5. Sketch the cross-section.
6. (Optional) Control the sweep using relations.
7. Complete the feature.

Step 1 - Start the creation of the feature.

Click ☜ (Sweep) in the *Model* tab. The *Sweep* dashboard becomes active, as shown in Figure 5–2.

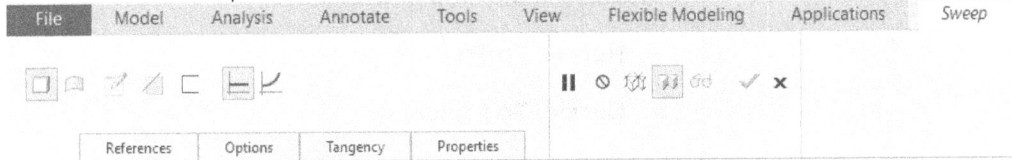

| File | Model | Analysis | Annotate | Tools | View | Flexible Modeling | Applications | *Sweep* |

References   Options   Tangency   Properties

Figure 5–2

Step 2 - Select the trajectories.

When the *Sweep* dashboard is available you can immediately begin selecting the trajectories for the sweep. The trajectories define how the geometry of the feature is created. Trajectories can be a selected edge, curve, or sketch that exists in the model.

The first trajectory that is selected is the Origin trajectory. To select any additional curves, press and hold <Ctrl> and select them on the model. Additional trajectories display as **Chain 1**, **Chain 2**, etc. Once selected, the trajectories display on the model and in the References panel, as shown in Figure 5–3.

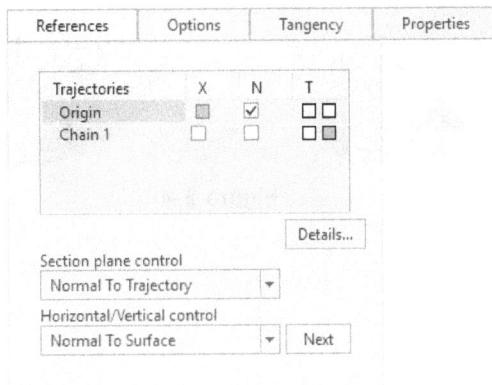

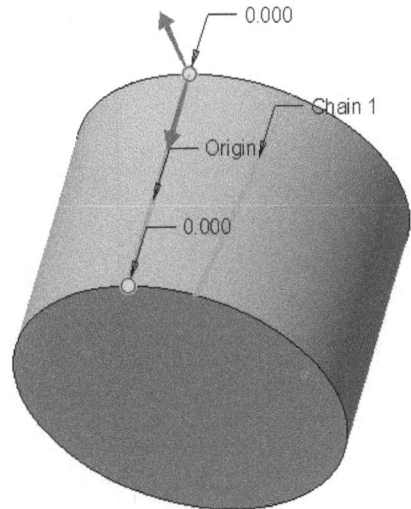

Figure 5–3

Step 3 - Define the section plane control.

In the References panel, you can define how the sketch of the section is oriented with respect to the trajectories. It is defined using the section plane control options. The following options are available in the drop-down list:

- **Normal To Trajectory**

- **Normal To Projection**

- **Constant Normal Direction**

Normal To Trajectory

The **Normal To Trajectory** option enables you to create a sweep where the cross-section remains perpendicular to the selected trajectory. By default, this is the Origin trajectory. Additional trajectories can be defined to further control the size and shape of the feature.

The model shown on the left in Figure 5–4 displays the two curves that were selected as the origin and Chain 1 trajectories. The final geometry for the sweep is shown on the right.

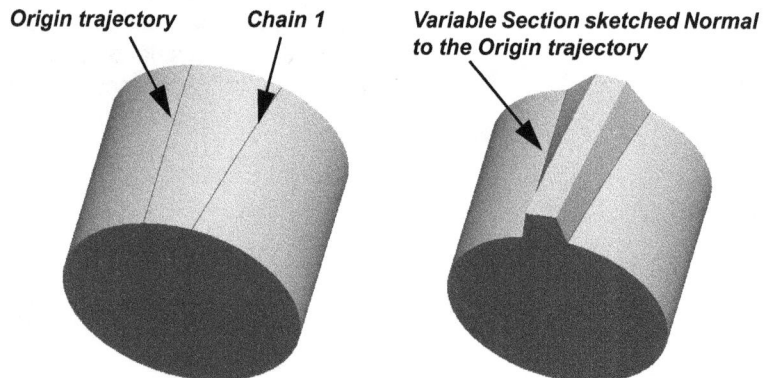

Figure 5–4

You can also use the **Normal To Trajectory** option to create a sweep in which the cross-section remains normal to any of the additional chains that were selected. With this option, the Origin trajectory defines the origin of the section while a second trajectory, called the *Normal trajectory*, is the trajectory to which the section remains normal. To create a sweep in which the cross-section remains normal to one of the additional selected curves, place a checkmark in the *N* column of the required normal trajectory in the References panel, as shown in Figure 5–5.

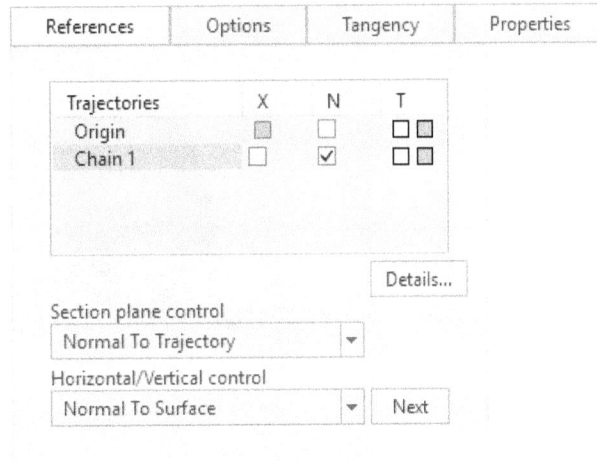

Figure 5–5

Figure 5–6 shows the protrusion created with the **Normal To Trajectory** option set to **Chain 1**.

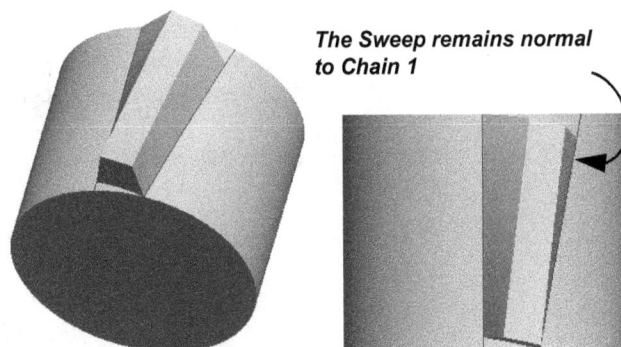

The Sweep remains normal to Chain 1

Figure 5–6

Normal To Projection

The **Normal To Projection** option enables you to create a sweep in which the cross-section remains normal to a specific feature or surface of a feature. With this option, a projection reference (plane, edge, curve, axis, or coord sys) is required to define orientation of the sketching plane. The section remains normal to the projection reference as it moves along the trajectories. Additional trajectories can also be used to further control the feature, as shown in Figure 5–7.

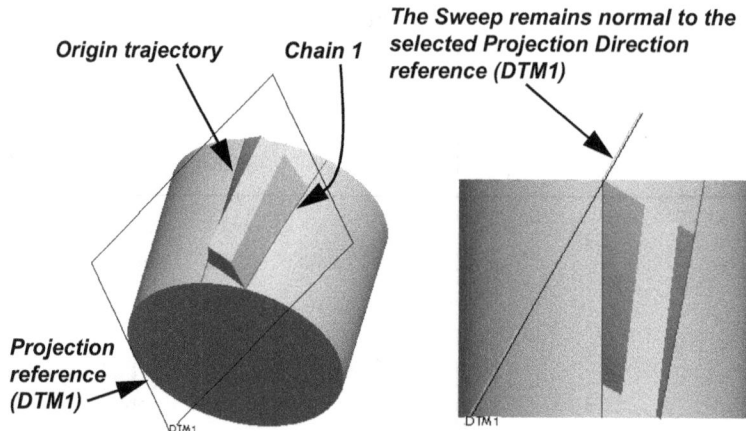

Figure 5–7

Constant Normal Direction

The **Constant Normal Direction** option enables you to create a sweep where the cross-section remains parallel to a specific feature or surface of a feature. With this option, a normal reference (plane, edge, curve, axis, or coord sys) is required to define the orientation of the sketching plane. The section remains parallel to the normal reference as it moves along the trajectories. Additional trajectories can also be used to further control the feature, as shown in Figure 5–8.

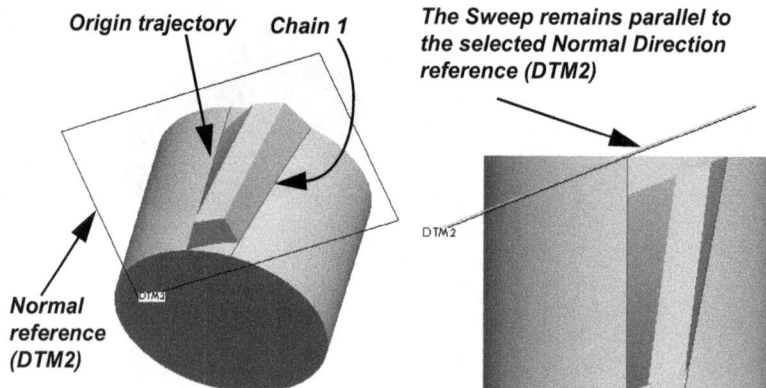

Figure 5–8

Horizontal/ Vertical Control

The cross-section can be further controlled by changing its angular rotation on the section plane as it sweeps. This is done using the **Horizontal/Vertical Control** options. Depending on the type of selected sweep trajectories, there are three options:

- **Automatic:** The default option if the selected Origin trajectory does not have associated surfaces. Creo Parametric assumes a sketch orientation that minimizes the overall twist of the sweep.

- **Normal To Surface:** The default option if the selected Origin trajectory is associated with a surface. For example, it could be a curve on a surface, the edge of a surface or solid, or a curve created from the intersection of two surfaces. It continuously reorients the sketch along the sweep by keeping the vertical, Y-axis of the sketch perpendicular to the selected surface.

- **X-Trajectory:** This option enables you to select a trajectory to control the orientation of the section as it sweeps along the Origin trajectory. It continuously reorients the sketch along the sweep by aligning the horizontal, X-axis of the sketch with the intersection of the section plane and the selected X-trajectory as shown in Figure 5–9.

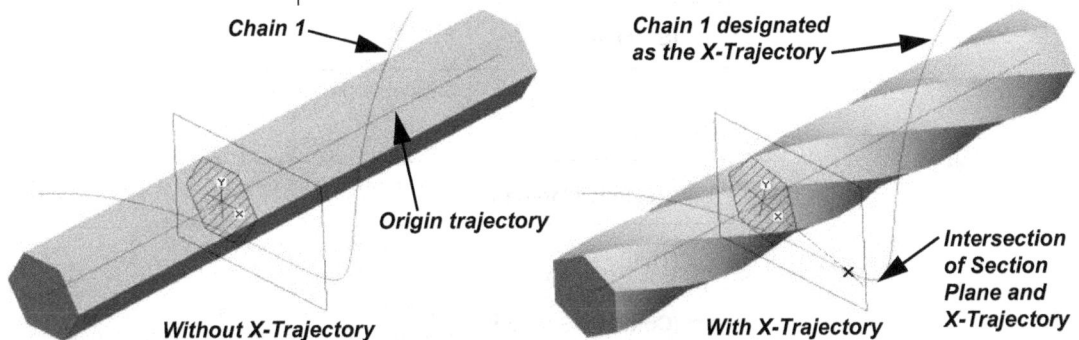

Chain 1

Origin trajectory

Without X-Trajectory

Chain 1 designated as the X-Trajectory

Intersection of Section Plane and X-Trajectory

With X-Trajectory

Figure 5–9

Step 4 - Define the attributes for the feature.

You can create a Variable Section Sweep as a protrusion, thin protrusion, cut, thin cut, surface, or surface trim. All of the icons and their descriptions are shown in Figure 5–10. All of these options are available in the *Sweep* dashboard as shown in Figure 5–10.

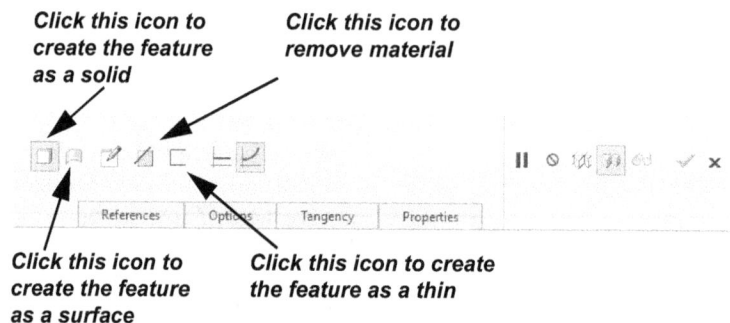

Click this icon to create the feature as a solid

Click this icon to remove material

Click this icon to create the feature as a surface

Click this icon to create the feature as a thin

Figure 5–10

Icon	Description
(Solid)	Creates the feature as a solid.
(Surface)	Creates the feature as a surface.
(Create or Edit Section)	Creates a sketch for the cross section.
(Remove Material)	Creates the feature as a cut.
(Thin)	Creates the feature as a thin.
(Constant Section)	Sweeps a constant cross section along the trajectory. This icon is selected by default.
(Variable Section)	Sweeps a cross section along the trajectory, but enables the section to vary based on the selection of secondary trajectories.

Step 5 - Sketch the cross-section.

Once you select whether to create the Variable Section Sweep as a solid or surface, you can sketch the cross-section. The cross-section is created at the start point. The start point is indicated by an arrow. You can change the default start point by selecting the References panel and clicking **Details**. The Chain dialog box opens. Select the *Options* tab and click **Flip** to move the startpoint to the other end, as shown in Figure 5–11.

The Chain dialog box can also be used to select multiple curves to define as one trajectory.

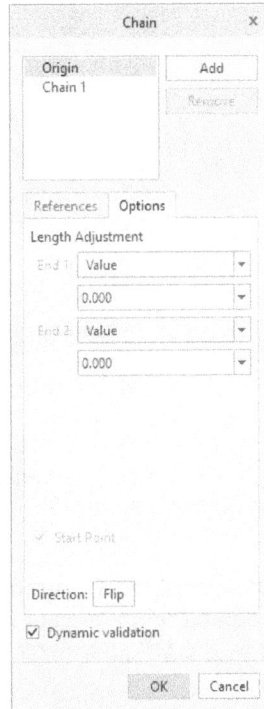

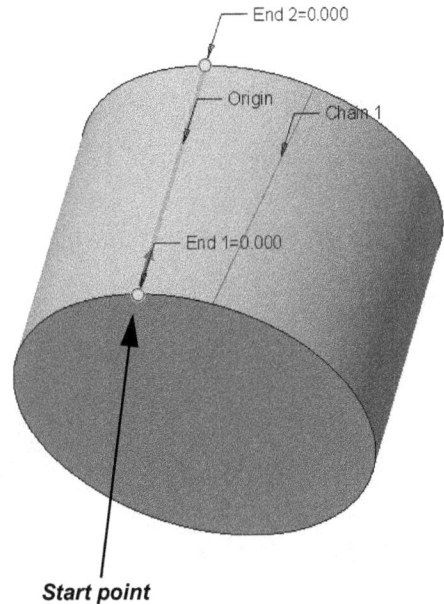

Figure 5–11

You can also flip the start point by right-clicking on the arrow and selecting **Flip** as shown in Figure 5–12.

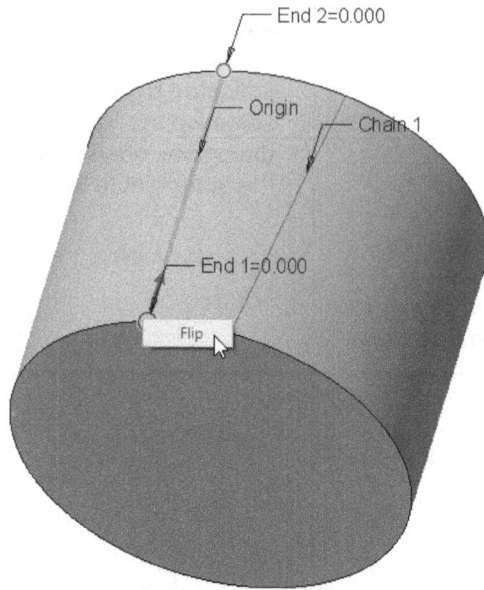

Figure 5–12

Click ✎ (Create or Edit Section) to activate the *Sketch* tab. The orientation of the sketch is dependent on the section plane control option that was selected.

Normal To Trajectory

If you select **Normal To Trajectory** as the section plane control option, the default orientation of the model in Sketcher is determined by the Origin trajectory, as shown in Figure 5–13.

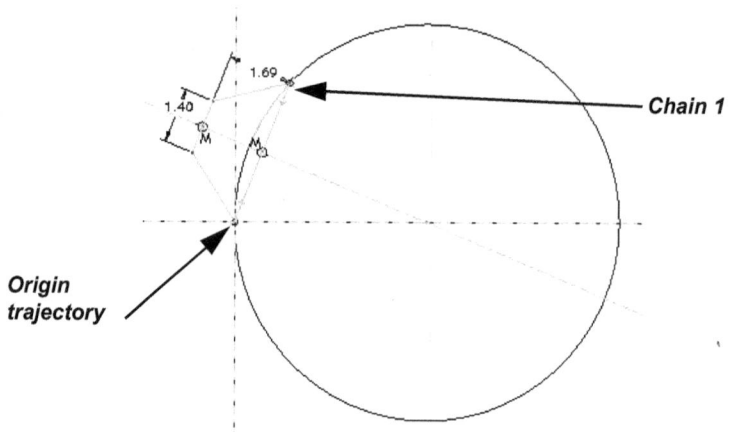

Figure 5–13

Normal To Projection

If you select **Normal To Projection** as the section plane control option, the orientation is determined by the projection reference and the Origin trajectory, as shown in Figure 5–14.

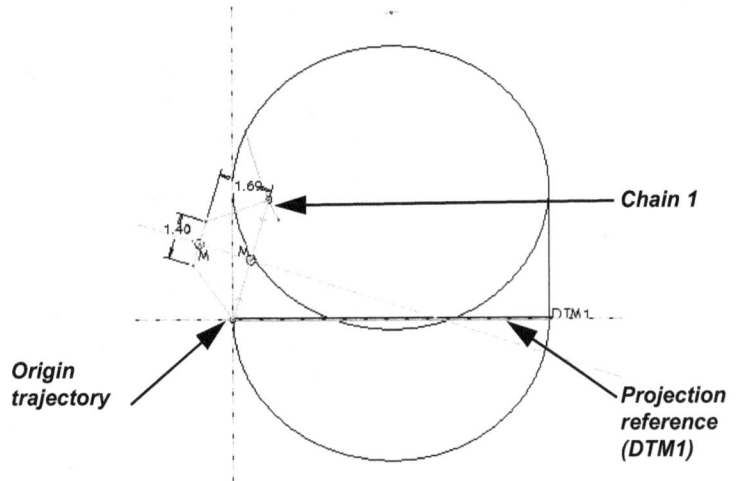

Figure 5–14

Constant Normal Direction

If you select **Constant Normal Direction** as the section plane control option, the orientation is determined by the normal reference and the Origin trajectory, as shown in Figure 5–15.

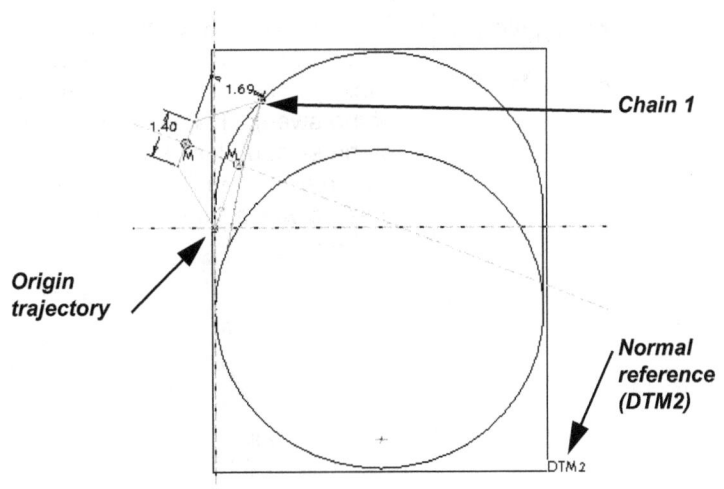

Figure 5–15

Regardless of its orientation, the sketch must be created relative to the origin and any additional chains. It might help to orient the model into 3D to display the orientation of the trajectories.

Restrictions for Variable Section Sweeps

The following are some restrictions for Variable Section Sweeps:

- For Variable Section Sweeps using the **Normal To Trajectory** option, the Origin trajectory can only consist of tangent entities.

- For Variable Section Sweeps using the **Normal To Projection** option, the projection of the Origin trajectory entities in the projection reference direction must be tangent.

- The Chains cannot cross the Origin trajectory, but its end points can lie on the Origin trajectory.

- All additional trajectories must intersect the sketching plane of the sweep, but do not need to be the same length as the Origin trajectory. The length of the sweep is as long as the shortest trajectory.

- The sketching plane can only intersect any trajectory once at any given location along the sweep.

Step 6 - (Optional) Control the sweep using relations.

Trajectory Parameter

Every Variable Section Sweep includes a trajectory parameter called *trajpar*. Trajpar is a parameter, the value of which varies linearly between 0 and 1 along the Origin trajectory for the length of the sweep. Trajpar equals 0 at the beginning and 1 at the end of the sweep. It is used frequently in relations to further control Variable Section Sweeps. The part shown in Figure 5–16 is created with a Variable Section Sweep. No relations were added to the part.

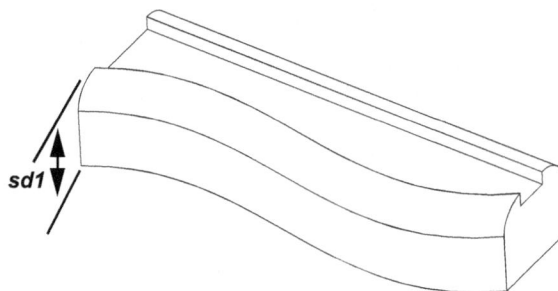

sd1

Figure 5–16

The following relation, which includes trajpar, can be added to
the part to control the value of a Sketcher dimension (height of
the model):

   sd1 = trajpar * 2 + 2

This relation forces the value of sd1 to vary between 2 at the
beginning of the sweep and 4 at the end of the sweep. The
resulting part displays as shown in Figure 5–17.

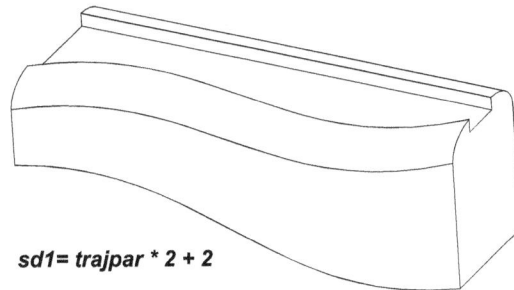

sd1= trajpar * 2 + 2

Figure 5–17

Evalgraph

The Evalgraph function enables you to use a datum graph in a
relation to control a section of the feature.

The graph must exist in the model before the feature that uses it.
To create a graph, select **Datum>Graph** in the *Model* tab, enter
a name, and sketch the section. An example of a datum graph is
shown in Figure 5–18. Along with the entities capturing the intent
of the graph, it must include a sketcher coordinate system. Using
horizontal and vertical centerlines, and displaying the sketcher
grid is also recommended.

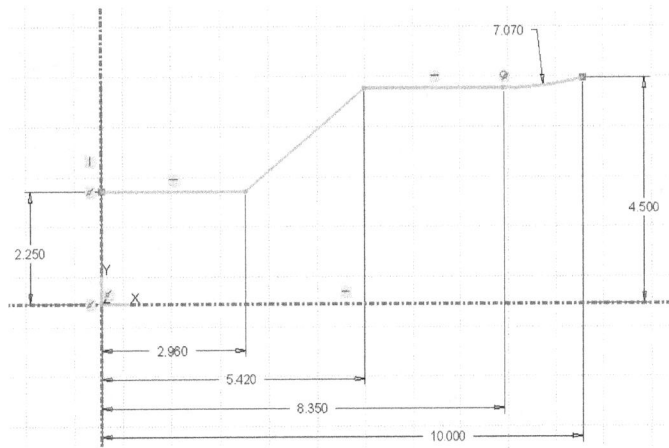

Figure 5–18

The following relation can be added to the part shown in Figure 5–16 to control the value of the sketcher dimension. The Evalgraph function can also be used in conjunction with trajpar.

sd1 = evalgraph("length", trajpar*10)

Where:

- Length is the name of the graph feature.

- Trajpar*10 obtains corresponding values for X-coordinates of 0 to 10.

The resulting model displays as shown in Figure 5–19.

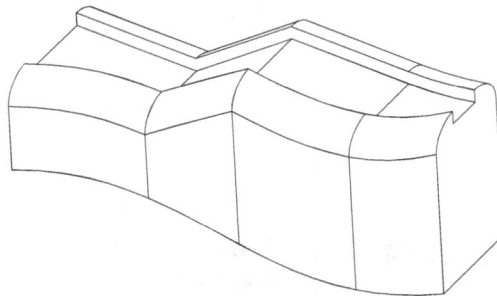

Figure 5–19

Step 7 - Complete the feature.

To complete the feature, click ✔ (OK) in the *Sweep* dashboard.

Practice 5a | Variable Section Sweep - Normal To Trajectory

Practice Objectives

- Create two sketches to represent the trajectories for the Sweep feature.
- Create a Sweep feature using the Normal to Trajectory option and selecting two trajectories.
- Edit the section of the sweep and add a relation for the height dimension using the trajpar parameter.
- Edit the section of the sweep and add a relation using a known dimension and the height of the section.
- Create a datum graph, edit the section of the sweep, and add a relation using the datum graph to vary the height of the section.

In this practice, you will create a basic sweep feature that is driven by an origin and one additional trajectory, as shown in Figure 5–20. To begin you will create a simple sketch that will be driven along both trajectories to create the required geometry. You will then further customize the shape of the geometry using relations to control the height using trajpar and a graph feature.

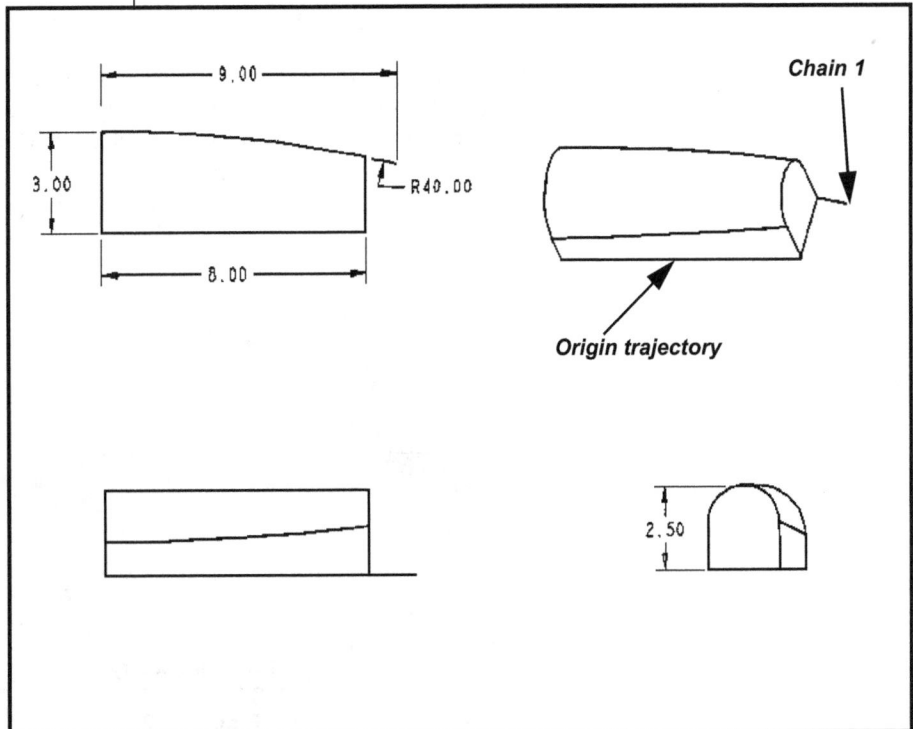

Figure 5–20

Task 3 - Create the Variable Section Sweep protrusion.

Design Considerations

In this task, you will select the previously created curves as the Origin and Chain 1 trajectories. These curves will control the width of the section as it sweeps along them. The feature only progresses as far as the shortest trajectory. In this case, the Origin trajectory defines the length. The height of the feature is not driven by a trajectory. In this task, the height is based on the sketched geometry for the feature.

1. In the In-Graphics toolbar, expand ⁺⁄₂ (Datum Display Filters) and toggle off ⬚ (Plane Display).

2. Click ⬡ (Sweep).

3. Select the first datum curve (straight line) as the Origin trajectory.

4. Press and hold <Ctrl> and select the second datum curve (arc) as **Chain 1**.

5. Click **References** in the *Sweep* dashboard to display the default feature settings, as shown in Figure 5–22.

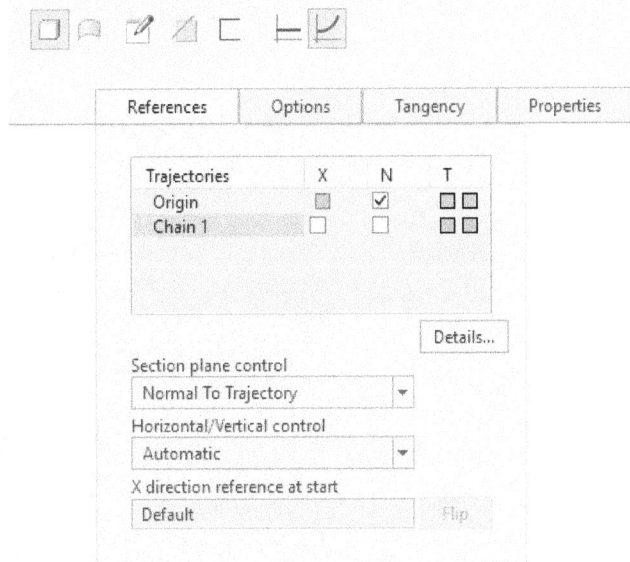

Figure 5–22

*Click 🖼 (Sketch View)
to orient the sketch to
the sketch view.*

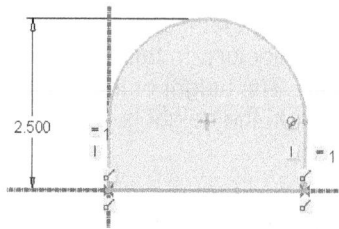

6. The section for the protrusion can now be sketched. Click
🖉 (Create or Edit Section) and sketch the section, as shown
in Figure 5–23.

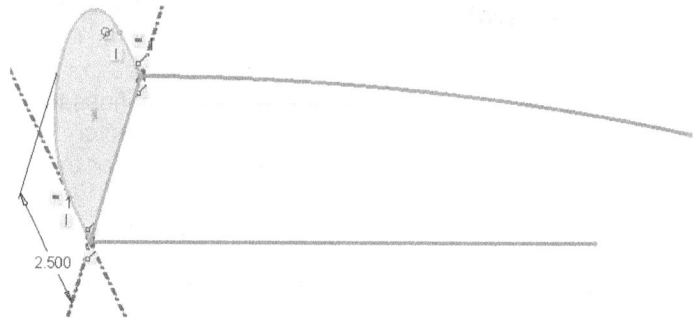

Sketch view

Figure 5–23

7. Complete the sketch and the feature. The completed feature
displays as shown in Figure 5–24.

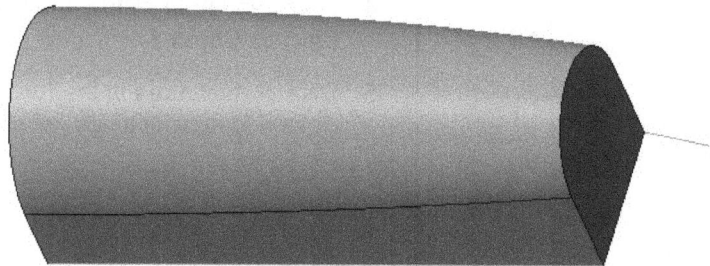

Figure 5–24

Task 4 - Redefine the sweep feature.

**Design
Considerations**

In this task, you will edit the definition of the sweep to include
trajpar in a sketcher relation. Trajpar is a trajectory parameter. Its
value varies between 0 and 1 as the section is swept along the
Origin trajectory. Trajpar equals 0 at the beginning of the sweep
and 1 at the end of the sweep. It is frequently used in relations to
further control Variable Section Sweeps. In this situation, trajpar
will be used to control the feature's height.

1. Select the sweep feature and click 🖋 (Edit Definition) in the
mini toolbar.

2. Click 🖉 (Create or Edit Section) in the *Sweep* dashboard.

Trajpar varies between 0 at the beginning of the sweep and 1 at the end of the sweep.

3. Select the *Tools* tab, click d= (Relations), and enter the following relations (where sd# is the Sketcher dimension symbol in your section):

   /* Relations to control section height along trajectory

   min_height = 2.50

   *sd# = (1 + trajpar) * min_height*

   With this relation, trajpar linearly increases the height of the feature between 2.5 and 5 as it sweeps along the trajectory.

4. Click **OK** to close the Relations dialog box.

5. Select the *Sketch* tab and click ✓ (OK) to exit Sketcher.

6. Click ✔ (OK) to complete the feature. The feature displays as shown in Figure 5–25.

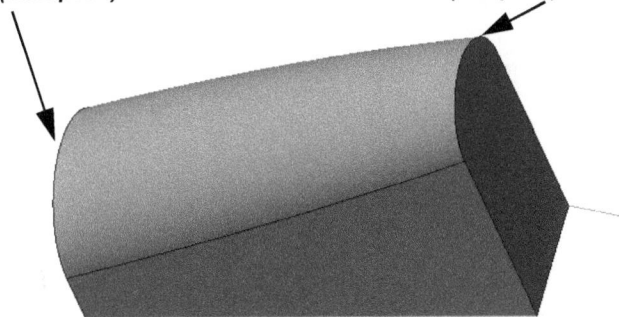

Figure 5–25

Task 5 - Redefine the sweep feature so that the area of its section is always equal to 7.

Design Considerations

In this task, you will edit the definition of the sweep again. This time, a relation is created in the sketch that changes the height as required to maintain a constant cross-sectional area of 7 at all locations along the sweep. To accomplish this you need to create a known dimension. This is a dimension created in a sketch which measures a known distance (e.g., the distance between two fixed points in the model). It is not possible to modify the value of a known dimension directly, but it can be used in a Sketcher relation. In this example, you will use a known dimension to measure the width of the section as it sweeps along the trajectories. You can then determine the required height of the section for the duration of the sweep to maintain a constant area.

1. Redefine the section for the feature so that it has the dimension scheme shown in Figure 5–26.

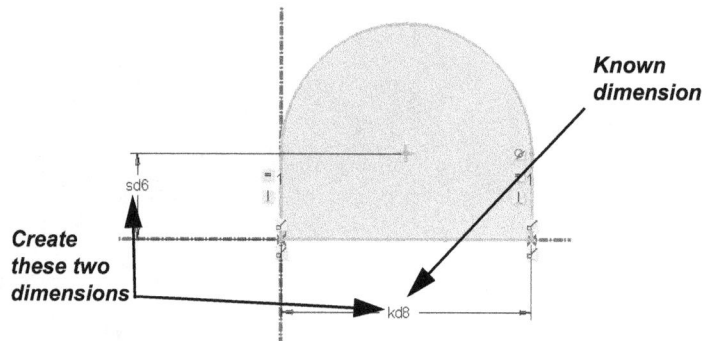

Known dimension

Create these two dimensions

Figure 5–26

Note: Create the **kd#** dimension between points that will be swept along the trajectory. In the Dimension group, click ⟷ (Dimension), then to select the correct point, place the cursor on the curve end point, right-click and select **Pick From List**. Select **Point (Reference)** in the Pick From List dialog box and click **OK**. Use this selection method for both points and then place the known dimension.

2. Select the *Tools* tab and click (Switch Dimensions) to display the dimension symbols. Known dimension symbols are shown as kd#.

3. Click d= (Relations) to open the Relations editor.

4. Change the previous relations to comments in the Relation editor to remove them from regeneration, as follows:

   /* Relations to control section height along trajectory

   /*min_height = 2.50

   /*sd# = (1 + trajpar) * min_height

5. Add new relations using the sd# and kd# dimensions applicable to your sketch:

   /* Relations to control section area

   x_sec = 7

   r = kd# / 2

   sd# = (x_sec - 0.5 * PI * r * r) / kd#

   The relations are based on the following formula to calculate the rectangular and semi-circular areas:

$$xsec = (sd\#)(kd\#) + \frac{\pi(kd\#/2)^2}{2}$$

6. Close the Relations dialog box.

7. Select the *Sketch* tab and complete the sketch.

8. Click ✔ (OK) to complete the feature. The feature displays as shown in Figure 5–27.

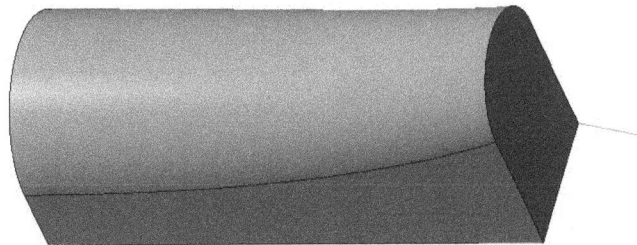

Constant Cross-Sectional Area

Figure 5–27

PI = π = 3.14159
(geometric constant)

Task 6 - Redefine the sweep feature so that the section height is driven by a graph.

Design Considerations

In this task you will edit the definition of the sweep to drive the height of the feature using a graph feature. To use a graph feature, it must exist in the Model Tree list before the feature that will reference it. Therefore, you will first insert the graph before the sweep. Once created, you will edit the sketcher relation for the sweep and make changes to the relation.

1. In the Model Tree, place the feature insertion point after the second datum curve feature, as shown in Figure 5–28. This activates Insert mode.

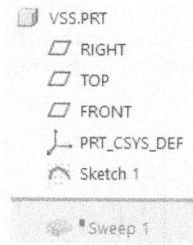

Figure 5–28

2. Select **Datum>Graph** in the *Model* tab to create a graph to drive the height of the feature along the trajectory.

3. Name the graph **height** and sketch the section shown in Figure 5–29 using a spline. Ensure that you have used a sketcher coordinate system for the graph origin.

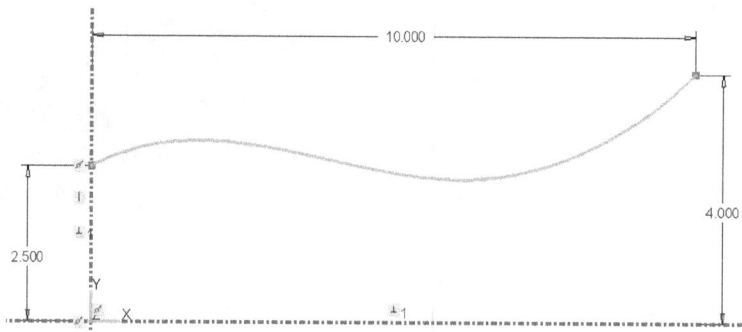

Click ▲ *(Select) and double-click on a dimension to modify it.*

Figure 5–29

4. Complete the feature.

5. In the Model Tree, place the feature insertion point at the end of the feature list to cancel Insert mode.

6. Edit the definition of the section for the Variable Section Sweep. Comment the relations used to control the section area.

7. Replace the existing relations with the following:

   /* Relations to control the section height with the height graph

   sd# = evalgraph("height", trajpar*10)

Design Considerations

In this relation, trajpar was multiplied by ten to enable the feature to use the full extent of the graph. Without this, the feature would only use values from the graph in the range of 0 to 1 in the X-axis. By scaling the X-axis of the graph in this way, it enables greater detail in sketching the curve and makes the graph easier to view.

8. Close the Relations dialog box.

9. Select the *Sketch* tab and complete the sketch.

10. Click ✔ (OK) to complete the feature. The feature displays as shown in Figure 5–30.

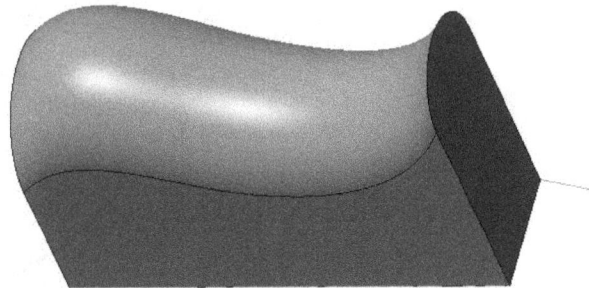

Section height controlled by datum graph
Figure 5–30

11. Save the part and erase it from memory.

Practice 5b | Tire

Practice Objectives

- Create a Sweep feature using the Normal to Projection option and selecting two trajectories.
- Edit the section of the sweep and add a relation for the height dimension using the trajpar parameter.
- Edit the Sweep feature and change the type to Constant Normal Direction.
- Pattern the feature using an Axis pattern type and mirror the entire model.

In this practice, you will create a sweep feature that is driven by an origin and one additional trajectory, as shown in Figure 5–31. Both of these trajectories exist in the model. You will then customize the shape of the geometry using relations to control the height using trajpar. Finally, you will pattern the Variable Section Sweep feature and mirror the model geometry to complete the geometry as shown in Figure 5–31.

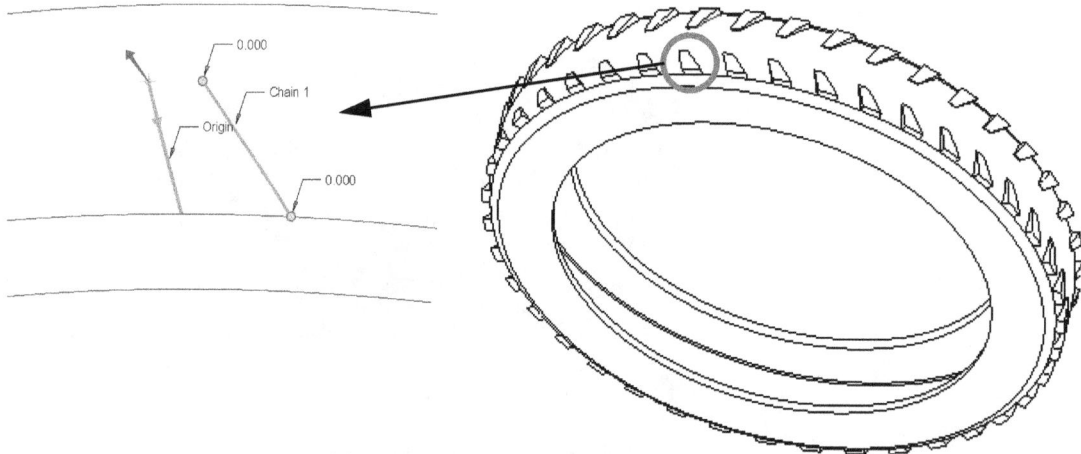

Figure 5–31

Task 1 - Open a part file.

1. Set the working directory to the *VSS_Tire* folder.

2. Open **tire.prt**.

3. Set the model display as follows:

- *(Datum Display Filters)*: All Off

- *(Spin Center)*: Off

- *(Display Style)*: (No Hidden)

Task 2 - Create the Variable Section Sweep protrusion.

Design Considerations

In this task you will select existing curves as the Origin and **Chain 1** trajectories. These curves help define the shape of the feature as the section progresses along them. The height of the feature is not driven by a trajectory. In this task the height will be based on sketched geometry.

1. Click (Sweep) in the *Model* tab.

2. Zoom in on the curves and select the first projected curve as the Origin trajectory, then press and hold <Ctrl> and select the second projected curve as **Chain 1**, as shown in Figure 5–32.

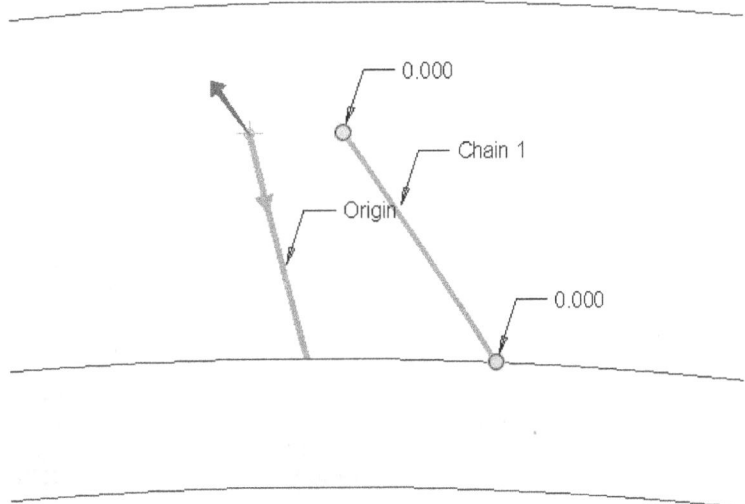

Figure 5–32

3. Click **References** in the *Sweep* dashboard to display the default feature settings, as shown in Figure 5–33.

Figure 5–33

4. In the Section plane control drop-down list, select the **Normal To Projection** option. The Reference panel displays as shown in Figure 5–34.

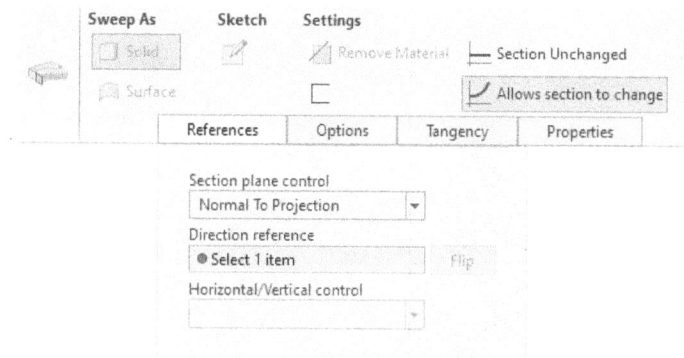

Figure 5–34

5. In the Model Tree, select datum plane **RIGHT** as the Direction reference.

6. The section for the protrusion can now be sketched. Click

   (Create or Edit Section) and sketch the section as shown in Figure 5–35. Sketch a rectangle between the trajectory endpoints.

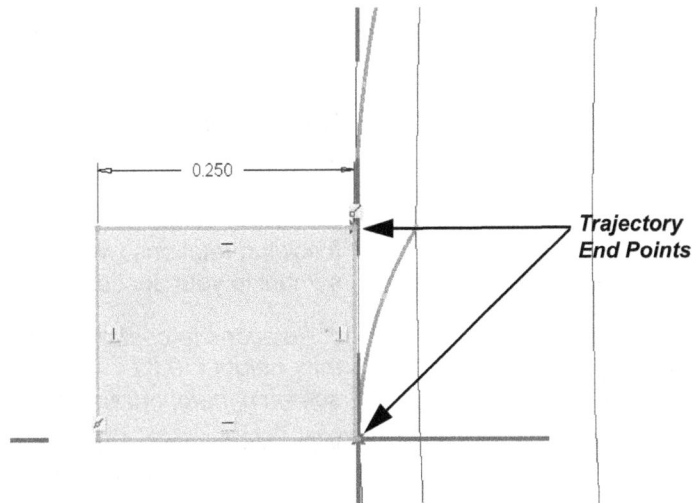

Figure 5–35

7. Complete the sketch and the feature. The completed feature displays as shown in Figure 5–36, when you use predefined views.

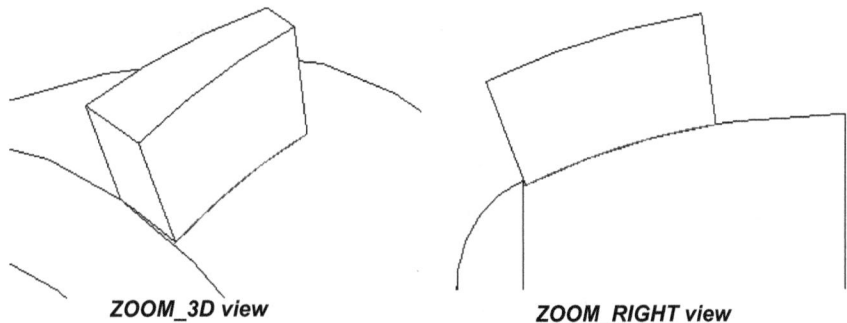

ZOOM_3D view   *ZOOM_RIGHT view*

Figure 5–36

Task 3 - Redefine the sweep feature.

Design Considerations

In this task, you will edit the definition of the sweep to include trajpar in a sketcher relation. Trajpar is a trajectory parameter. Its value varies between 0 and 1 as the section is swept along the Origin trajectory. Trajpar equals 0 at the beginning of the sweep and 1 at the end of the sweep. It is frequently used in relations to further control Variable Section Sweeps. In this situation, trajpar is used to control the feature's height.

1. Select the sweep feature and click 🖌 (Edit Definition) in the mini toolbar.

2. Click on the screen and select 📝 (Create or Edit Section) in the mini toolbar.

3. Select the *Tools* tab, click d= (Relations), and enter the following relations (where sd# is the Sketcher dimension symbol in your section):

/* Relations to control section height along trajectory
min_height = 0.02
sd#=min_height+trajpar/6

With this relation, trajpar linearly increases the height of the feature as it sweeps along the trajectory.

4. Click **OK** to close the Relations dialog box.

5. Select the *Sketch* tab and click ✓ (OK) to exit Sketcher.

6. Click ✓ (OK) to complete the feature. The completed feature displays as shown in Figure 5–37, when you use the predefined named views.

Trajpar varies between 0 at the beginning of the sweep and 1 at the end of the sweep.

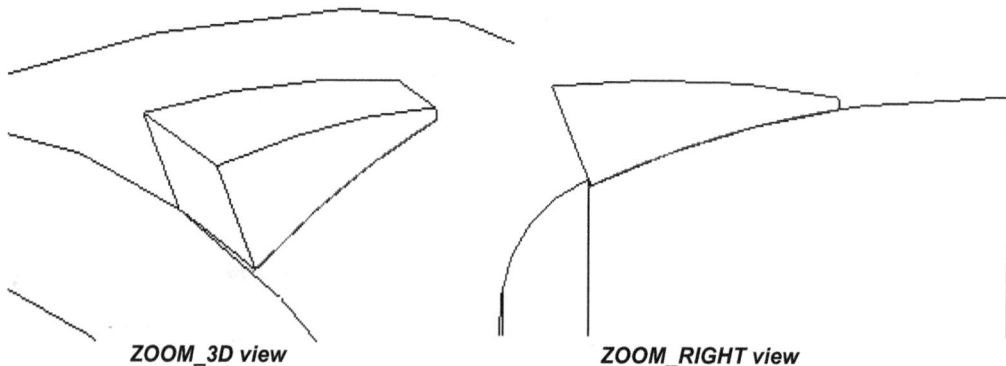

ZOOM_3D view   *ZOOM_RIGHT view*

Figure 5–37

Task 4 - Redefine the sweep feature.

Design Considerations

In this task, you will change the **Section plane control** option and note the affect of this option.

1. Select the sweep feature and click 🖌 (Edit Definition) in the mini toolbar.

2. Select the References panel in the *Sweep* dashboard to display the feature settings.

3. In the Section plane control drop-down list, select the **Constant Normal Direction** option. The References panel displays as shown in Figure 5–38.

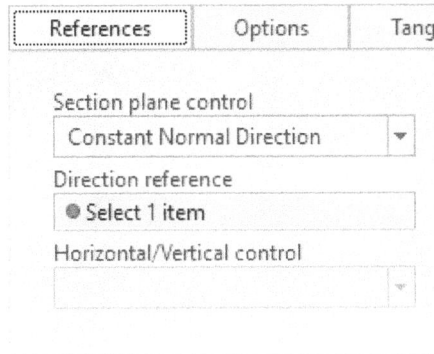

References	Options	Tang

Section plane control

Constant Normal Direction	▾

Direction reference

⦿ Select 1 item

Horizontal/Vertical control

	▾

Figure 5–38

4. Select datum plane **FRONT** as the direction reference.

5. Click ✔ (OK) to complete the feature. The completed feature displays as shown in Figure 5–39, when you use the predefined named views.

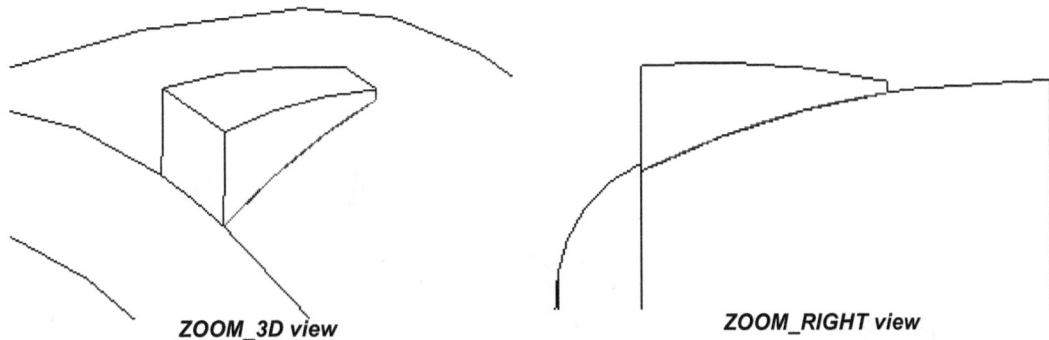

ZOOM_3D view

ZOOM_RIGHT view

Figure 5–39

Task 5 - Pattern the sweep feature.

1. Pattern the sweep feature 40 times using an **Axis** pattern. Ensure that instances are equally distributed. The model displays as shown in Figure 5–40.

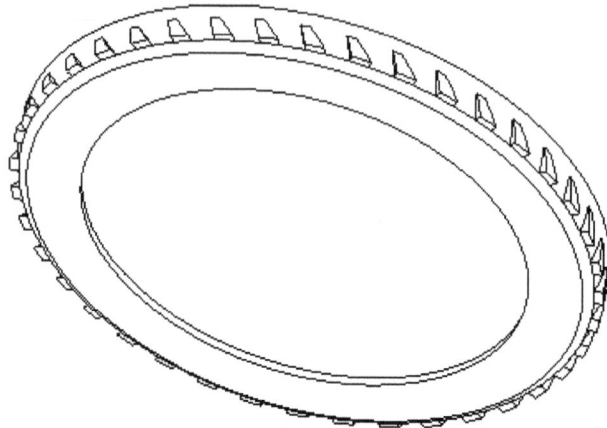

Figure 5–40

Task 6 - Mirror the model geometry.

1. Mirror the entire model geometry by selecting **TIRE.PRT** in the Model Tree and clicking ⬗ (Mirror). Mirror about datum plane **FRONT**. The model displays as shown in Figure 5–41.

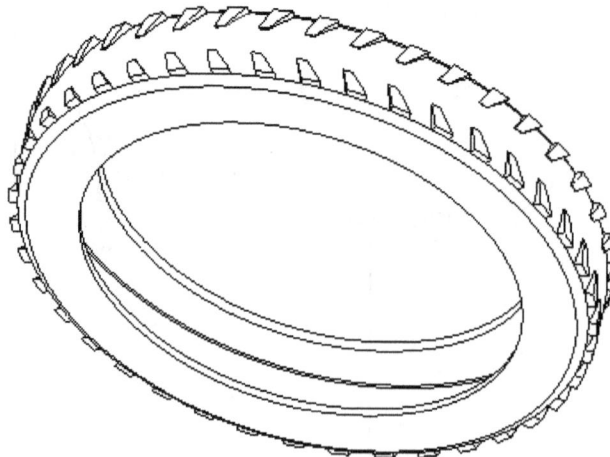

Figure 5–41

2. Save the part and erase it from memory.

Practice 5c | (Optional) Bottle

Practice Objectives

- Create a Sweep feature using multiple trajectories and a datum graph to control the cross-section.
- Add additional features to complete the model.

In this practice, you will create the triangular shaped bottle shown in Figure 5–42 using a variable section sweep.

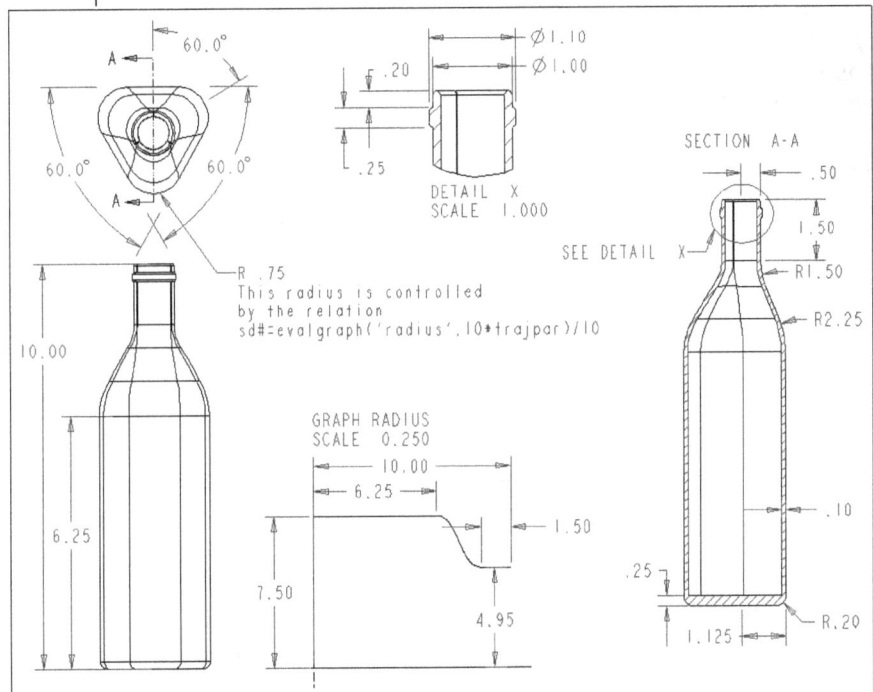

Figure 5–42

Task 1 - Create a new part.

1. Set the working directory to the *VSS_Bottle* folder.

2. Create a new part and set the *Name* to **bottle**.

3. Set the model display as follows:

   - ⅍ *(Datum Display Filters)*: ⬡ (Plane Display) only

   - ⊱ *(Spin Center)*: Off

   - ▢ *(Display Style)*: ▢ (Shading With Edges)

Task 2 - Create a datum curve.

1. In the Model Tree, select datum plane **FRONT** and click
   ⬚ (Sketch) in the mini toolbar.

2. Sketch and dimension the vertical line shown in Figure 5–43.

You can modify a dimension in Sketcher mode by clicking the middle mouse button to activate the selection option, and double-clicking on the dimension. The new value can be entered in the input panel in the Graphic window.

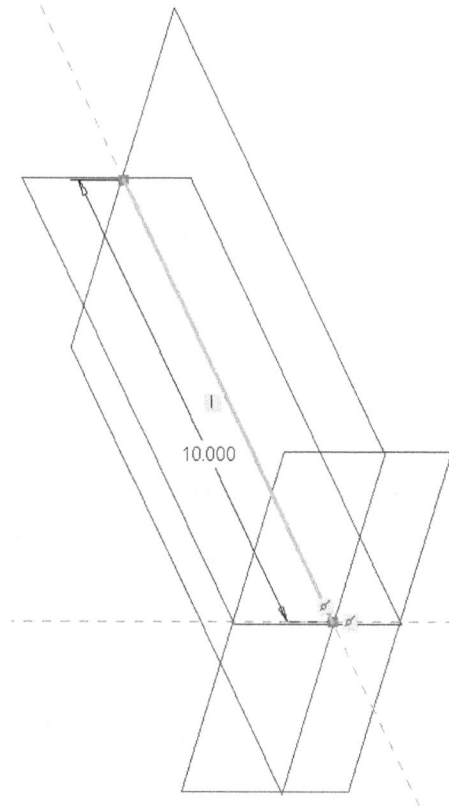

10.000

Figure 5–43

Task 3 - Create a second datum curve.

1. Select **FRONT** and click ⬚ (Sketch) in the mini toolbar.

2. Click 🔲 (Sketch View) from the In-graphics toolbar.

3. Disable datum plane display.

4. Sketch and dimension the curve shown in Figure 5–44.

Note that the top horizontal centerline runs through the endpoint of the first curve.

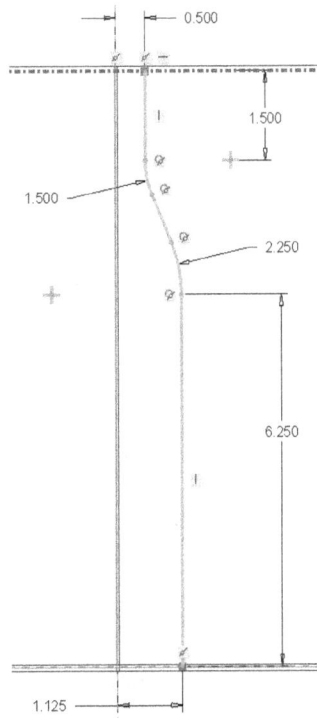

0.500

1.500

1.500

2.250

6.250

1.125

Figure 5–44

Task 4 - Create two additional curves using the Pattern command.

1. In the Model Tree, select the new **Sketch 2** that you just created and click ⠿ (Pattern) in the mini toolbar.

2. Select **Axis** from the pattern type drop-down list, as shown in Figure 5–45.

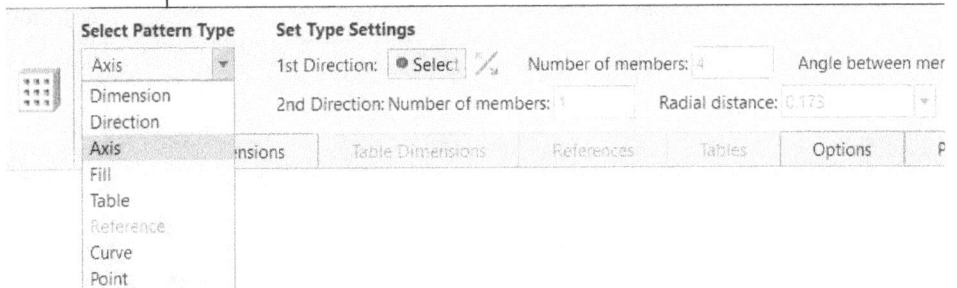

Select Pattern Type | Set Type Settings

Axis
Dimension
Direction
Axis
Fill
Table
Reference
Curve
Point

1st Direction: ● Select — Number of members: 4 — Angle between mer

2nd Direction: Number of members: 1 — Radial distance: 0.173

nsions | Table Dimensions | References | Tables | Options | P

Figure 5–45

3. In the dashboard, expand the ⚙ (Datum) flyout and select ╱ (Axis), as shown in Figure 5–46.

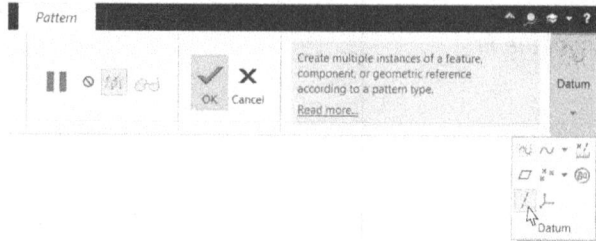

Figure 5–46

4. In the Model Tree, select **RIGHT**, then hold <Ctrl> and select **FRONT**.

5. Click **OK** in the Datum Axis dialog box.

6. Click ▶ (Resume) in the dashboard.

7. If not already selected, select the axis.

8. Set the number of *Instances* to **3**.

9. Set the *Angular* increment to **120**.

10. Click ✔ (OK).

11. In the In-graphics toolbar, disable ▱ (Plane Display). Figure 5–47 shows the resulting four datum curves.

Curves are selected for clarity. Refer to this image for the next task.

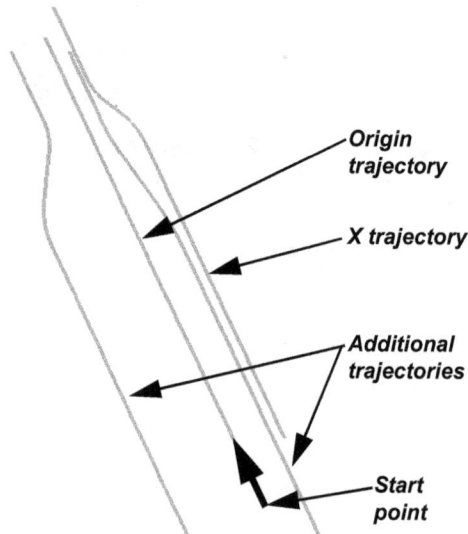

Figure 5–47

12. Save the part.

Task 5 - Create a variable section sweep protrusion.

1. Click 🐝 (Sweep).

2. Select the first datum curve (**Sketch 1**) as the Origin trajectory shown in Figure 5–47.

3. Hold <Ctrl> and select the second datum curve shown as the X trajectory in Figure 5–47. The model displays as shown in Figure 5–48.

Model is rotated slightly in this image.

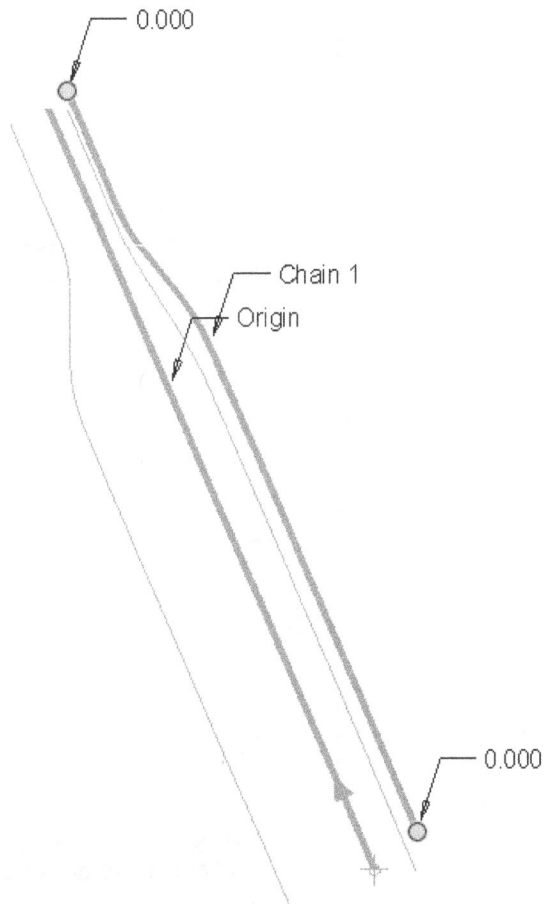

Figure 5–48

4. Click **References** in the *Sweep* dashboard.

5. Change the value of the **Horizontal/Vertical control** option from *Automatic* to **X-Trajectory**. The reference settings in the *Sweep* dashboard correspond to Figure 5–49.

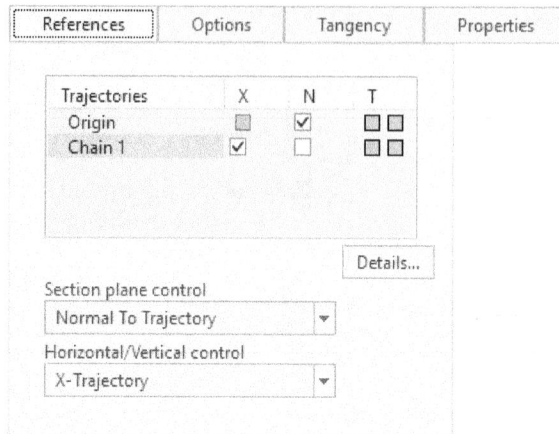

References	Options	Tangency	Properties

Trajectories	X	N	T	
Origin	☐	☑	☐	☐
Chain 1	☑	☐	☐	☐

Details...

Section plane control
Normal To Trajectory ▼

Horizontal/Vertical control
X-Trajectory ▼

Figure 5–49

6. Hold <Ctrl> and select the additional datum curves shown in Figure 5–47. The reference settings in the *Sweep* dashboard correspond to Figure 5–50.

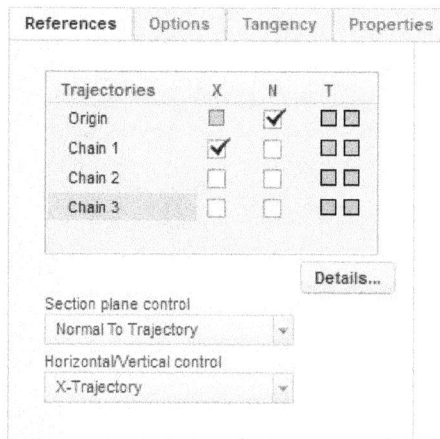

References	Options	Tangency	Properties

Trajectories	X	N	T	
Origin	☐	☑	☐	☐
Chain 1	☑	☐	☐	☐
Chain 2	☐	☐	☐	☐
Chain 3	☐	☐	☐	☐

Details...

Section plane control
Normal To Trajectory ▼

Horizontal/Vertical control
X-Trajectory ▼

Figure 5–50

7. Accept the placement of the start point at the Origin trajectory end closest to datum plane **TOP**, as shown in Figure 5–47.

8. The section for the sweep can now be sketched. Click on the screen and select ✎ (Create or Edit Section) in the mini toolbar.

Task 1 - Create a new part.

1. Set the working directory to the *VSS_Normal_Trajectory* folder.

2. Using the default template, create a new part and set the *Name* to **vss**.

3. Set the model display as follows:

   - *(Datum Display Filters)*: *(Plane Display) Only*

   - *(Spin Center)*: Off

   - *(Display Style)*: *(Shading With Edges)*

Task 2 - Create the origin and X trajectories.

1. Select datum plane **TOP** as the sketching plane and click (Sketch) in the mini toolbar.

2. Sketch the Origin trajectory (straight line) as shown in Figure 5–21.

3. Complete the sketch.

4. Create a second sketch with the same references as the first curve. Sketch the arc as shown in Figure 5–21. Align the center point of the arc with datum plane **RIGHT**. This curve represents the first additional chain.

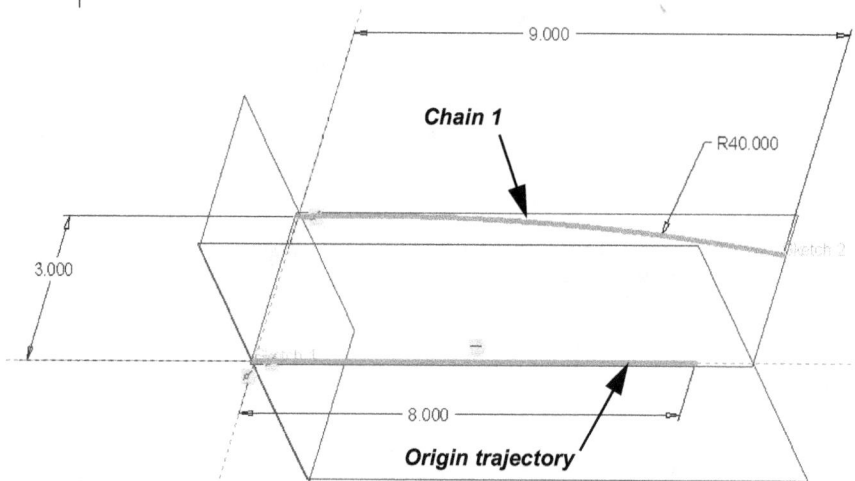

Figure 5–21

9. Click (Sketch View) from the In-graphics toolbar and sketch the section, as shown in Figure 5–51.

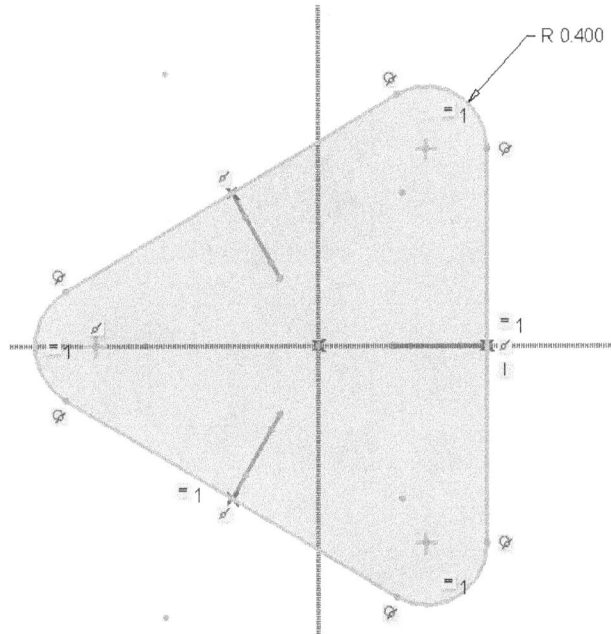

Figure 5–51

The completed feature is shown in Figure 5–52.

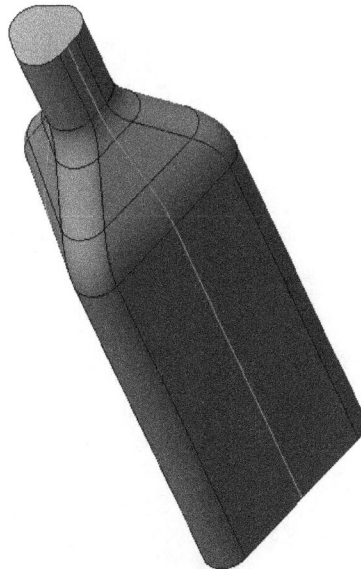

Figure 5–52

Task 6 - Insert a datum graph feature before the base feature.

This datum graph feature is used to control the value of the filleted corners of the base feature.

1. Use Insert mode to insert the graph just before the sweep.

2. Select **Datum>Graph** in the *Model* tab to create the graph.

3. Name the graph **radius** and sketch the graph shown in Figure 5–53.

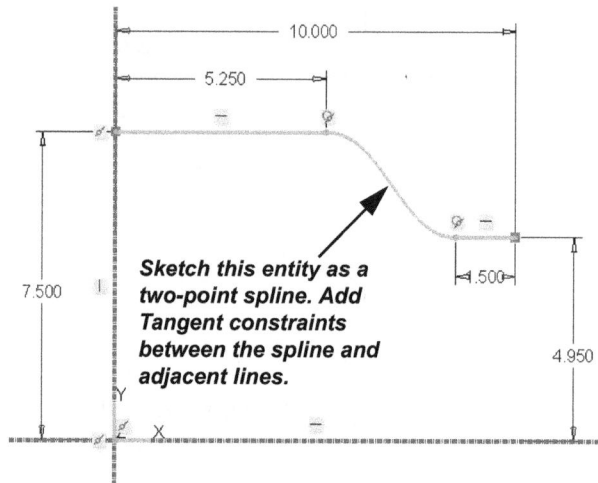

Sketch this entity as a two-point spline. Add Tangent constraints between the spline and adjacent lines.

Figure 5–53

4. Complete the sketch and cancel Insert mode by dragging the **Insert Here** marker to the end of the feature list.

Task 7 - Redefine the base feature section so that the radial dimension is driven by the radius graph.

1. In the Model Tree, select **Sweep 1** and click 🥄 (Edit Definition) in the mini toolbar.

2. Click on the screen and select 📝 (Create or Edit Section) in the mini toolbar.

3. Select the *Tools* tab and click d= (Relations).

4. In the Look In drop-down list, select **Section**. Add the following relation for the dimension driving the radius of the sketch (use the appropriate sd#):

    sd# = evalgraph('radius', 10 * trajpar)/10

    Why is trajpar multiplied by 10? Why is the function value divided by 10? The values along the Y-axis of the radius datum graph were multiplied by a factor of 10 to simplify the sketch and modification of the graph. The redefined protrusion is shown in Figure 5–54.

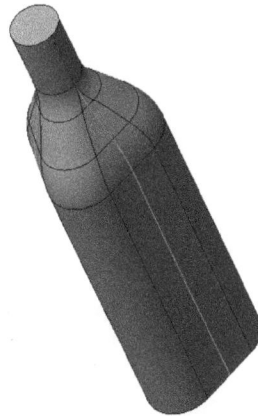

Figure 5–54

Task 8 - Create a shell feature with varying wall thickness.

---

1. Click ▣ (Shell) in the *Model* tab.

2. Select the top circular surface as the surface to remove as shown in Figure 5–55. Set the shell *Thickness* to **0.1** and press <Enter>.

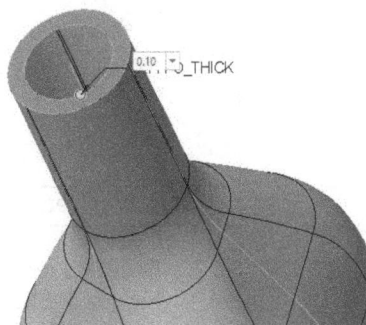

Figure 5–55

3. Right-click and select **Non Default Thickness**.

4. Select the bottom rounded triangular surface to have a
   different thickness as shown in Figure 5–56. Set the
   Thickness for this surface to **0.25**.

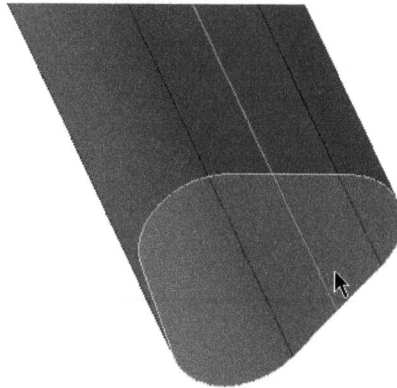

Figure 5–56

5. In the *Shell* dashboard, click ✓ (OK). The completed feature
   is shown in Figure 5–57.

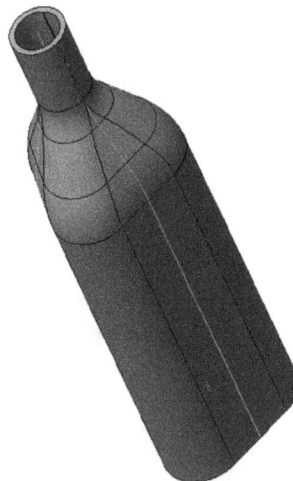

Figure 5–57

Task 9 - Create a neck of the bottle.

---

1. Create a revolved feature using the section shown in
   Figure 5–58.

2. Use datum plane **FRONT** as the sketching plane.

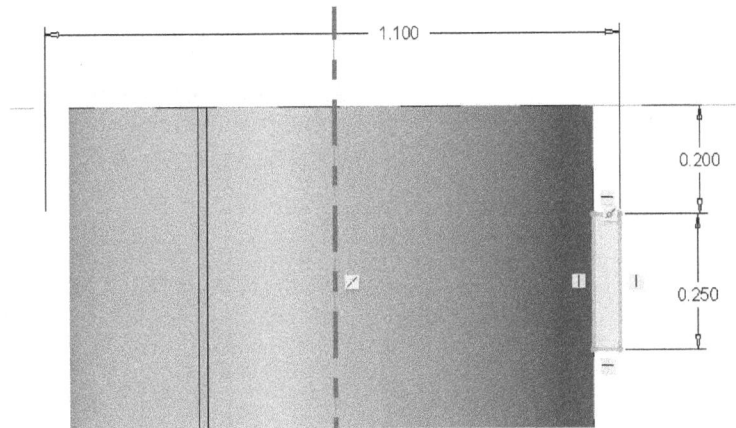

Figure 5–58

Task 10 - Create rounds on the edges of the neck.

1. Click (Round).

2. Select the cylindrical surface generated by the revolved feature you just created, hold <Ctrl> and select an inner circular edge created by neck, as shown in Figure 5–59.

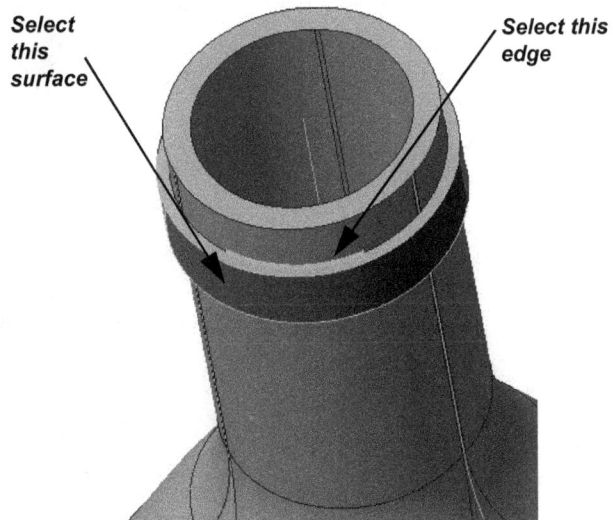

Figure 5–59

3. Set the *Radius* value to **0.07**.

4. Finish the round.

5. Repeat the Steps to create a round on the bottom of the neck.

Task 11 - Create a full round on the top bottle surface.

1. Select an inner circular edge of the top surface. Hold <Ctrl> and select the corresponding outer circular edge of the top surface, as shown in Figure 5–60.

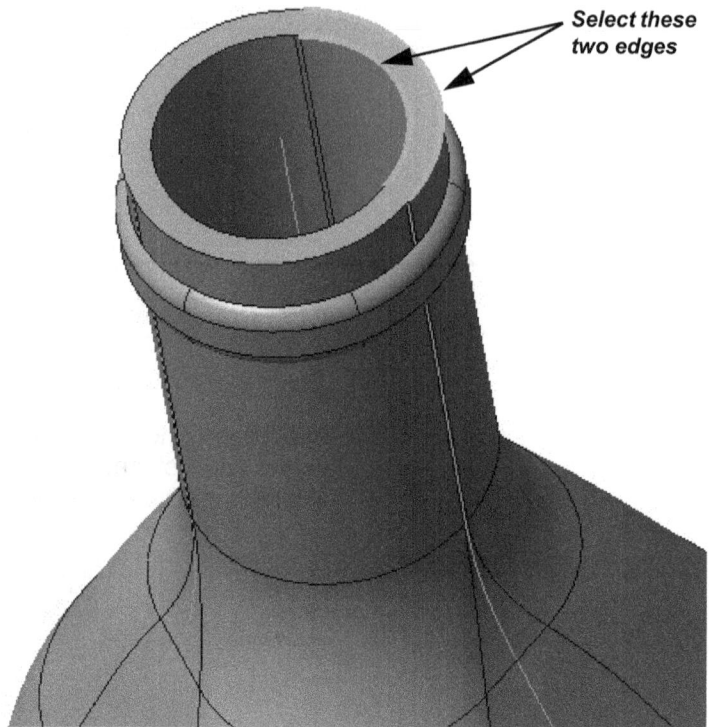

Select these two edges

Figure 5–60

2. Click ⟲ (Round) in the mini toolbar.

3. Click on the screen and select ⟲ (Full Round) in the mini toolbar.

4. Click ✓ (OK).

Task 12 - Create a round on the bottom edge of the bottle.

1. Select the edge of the bottom bottle surface.

2. Click ⟲ (Round) in the mini toolbar. The initial geometry of the round displays on all of the edges of the bottom bottle surface.

3. Double-click on the radial dimension and set it to **0.2**.

4. Complete the feature.

5. Hide the datum curves. The completed model is shown in Figure 5–61.

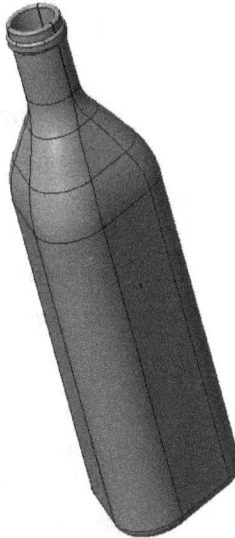

Figure 5–61

6. Save the layer status to save the hidden status of the datum curves.

7. Save the part and erase it from memory.

Chapter Review Questions

1. Which option enables you to create a sweep in which the cross-section remains normal to a specific feature or surface of a feature?

   a. **Normal To Trajectory**

   b. **Normal To Projection**

   c. **Constant Normal Direction**

2. Which option enables you to create a sweep where the cross-section remains perpendicular to the selected trajectory?

   a. **Normal To Trajectory**

   b. **Normal To Projection**

   c. **Constant Normal Direction**

3. Which option enables you to create a sweep where the cross-section remains parallel to a specific feature or surface of a feature?

   a. **Normal To Trajectory**

   b. **Normal To Projection**

   c. **Constant Normal Direction**

4. The length of the sweep is as long as the shortest trajectory.

   a. True

   b. False

5. The **trajpar** is a parameter, the value of which varies linearly between which values along the Origin trajectory for the length of the sweep?

   a. 0 to 10

   b. 1 to 10

   c. 0 to 1

   d. The user sets the value.

6. Given the current Model Tree, the graph feature named **RADIUS** shown in Figure 5–62, can be used to control the **Sweep 1** profile.

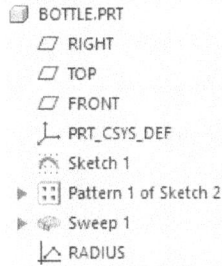

> BOTTLE.PRT
>   RIGHT
>   TOP
>   FRONT
>   PRT_CSYS_DEF
>   Sketch 1
> ▶ Pattern 1 of Sketch 2
> ▶ Sweep 1
>   RADIUS

Figure 5–62

a. True

b. False

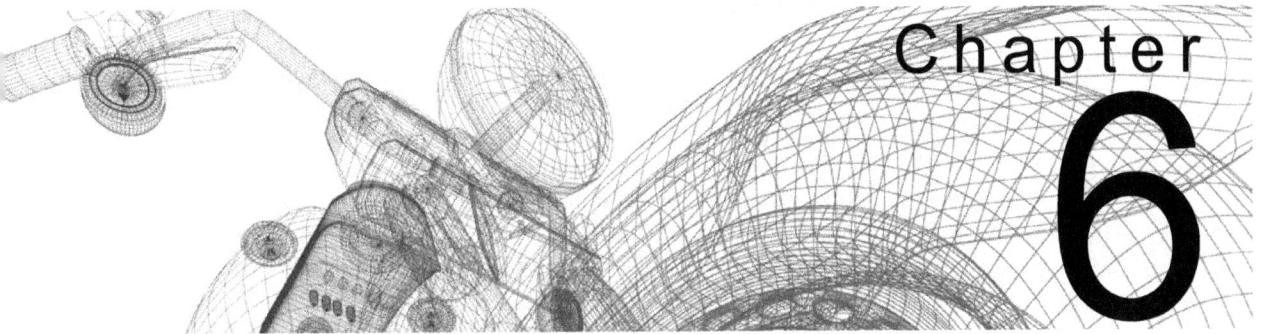

Helical Sweeps

Helical sweeps are a specific Creo Parametric feature that enable you to create spring and thread geometry. A helical sweep is defined by specifying a profile, pitch, and cross-section.

Learning Objectives in This Chapter

- Create a Helical Sweep feature by creating a trajectory and cross-section, and entering a pitch value.
- Learn the different options that can be used to change the shape of a Helical Sweep.
- Learn about Volume-based Helical Sweeps.

6.1 Helical Sweeps

A spring, thread, or any other spiral form can be created using the **Helical Sweep** command. The profile and pitch define the trajectory of a Helical Sweep. The section represents the shape that is going to be swept along the helical path. For example, it could be a circular section to form a spring or a triangular section to generate a v-form thread. When a section is revolved, its radial distance from the center of the helix is defined by the section origin and the axis of revolution. The pitch represents the distance between the coils of the helical feature. An example of a Helical Sweep displays as shown in Figure 6–1.

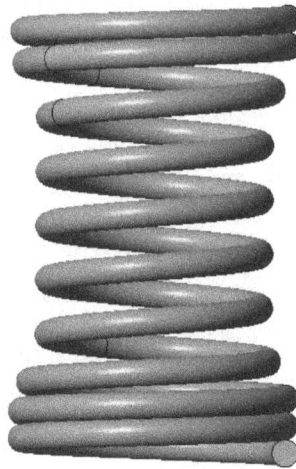

Figure 6–1

Expand ⟐ (Sweep) in the *Model* tab and click ⟐ (Helical Sweep) to start the creation of the Helical Sweep. The *Helical Sweep* tab becomes active as shown in Figure 6–2.

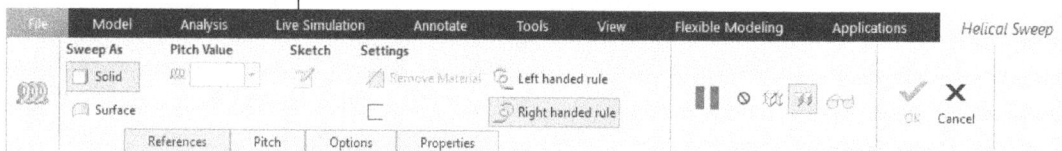

Figure 6–2

Select the appropriate options to create a solid or surface, remove material, and so on.

The profile defines the trajectory of a Helical Sweep and can be linear or non-linear.

How To: Sketch the profile

1. Click on the screen and select ⚙ (Define Internal Helix Profile) in the mini toolbar.
2. Define the sketching plane and orientation plane.
3. Select the sketcher references (if the default references are not suitable).
4. Create an axis of revolution using a centerline in the Datum group.
5. Sketch the profile.
6. Click ✓ (OK) to complete the sketch and exit Sketcher.

After defining the helical profile you can define additional options in the Reference panel or mini toolbar, as shown in Figure 6–3.

*You can also click References and click **Define**.*

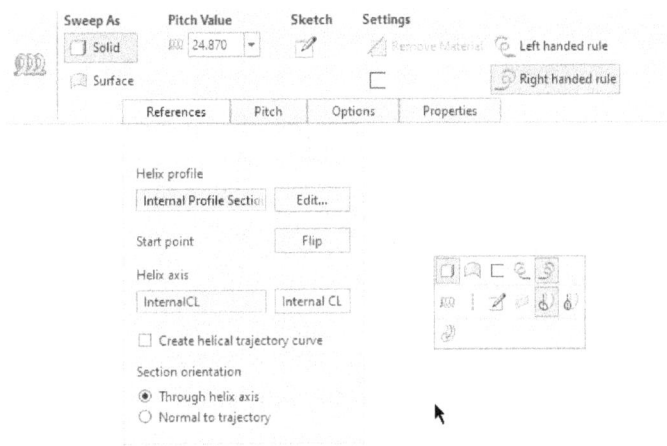

Figure 6–3

Start Point

Once the profile has been sketched you can change the start point in the References panel by clicking **Flip** or by clicking the arrow head in the graphics area.

Axis of Revolution

When you create the Helical Sweep feature, you must specify an axis of revolution. This can be included in the sketch or you can assign it outside the sketch. To clear the internal centerline, click **Internal CL** in the Placement panel or ⁝ (Internal CL) in the mini toolbar, select **Axis of revolution collector**, and then select a new reference. The internal centerline in the sketch can be reused at any time by clicking **Internal CL** or ⁝ (Internal CL) again.

If the axis of revolution is not included in the sketch (selected or created), the *Axis of revolution collector* field indicates that you must select a reference: an existing straight curve, edge, axis, or the axis of a coordinate system that lies on the sketching plane.

Create Helical Trajectory Curve

You can create a curve that maps to the helix by enabling the **Create helical trajectory curve** option in the References panel or ✐ (Create Helical Trajectory Curve) in the mini toolbar. You can then use the resulting curve as a reference for other features.

Section Orientation

The default option, **Through helix axis** in the References panel, or ✐ (Through Helix Axis) in the mini toolbar, creates a plane that passes through the axis of revolution to orient the profile.

The **Normal to trajectory** option in the References panel or ✐ (Normal to Trajectory) in the mini toolbar creates the cross-section normal to the helical trajectory.

The pitch represents the distance between the coils of the helical feature. When you finish sketching the profile of the Helical Sweep, you must define the pitch.

You can enter the pitch value in the *Helical Sweep* tab or in the Pitch panel as shown in Figure 6–4.

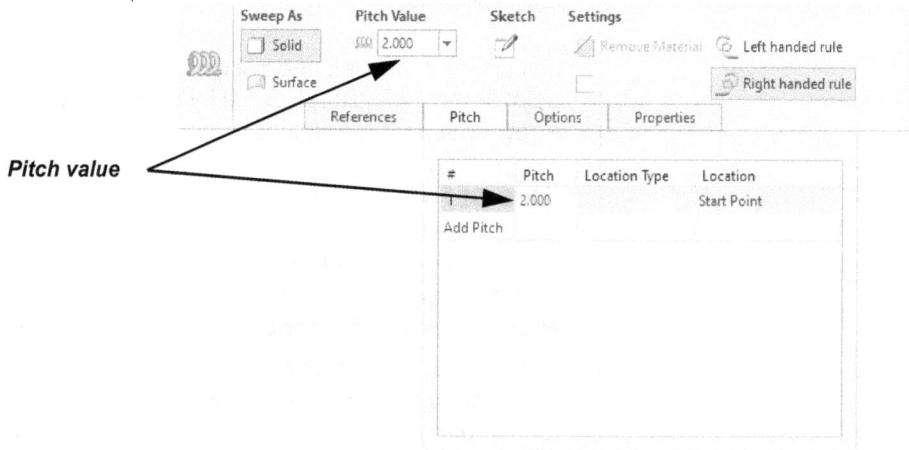

Pitch value

Figure 6–4

You can also add pitch
values by right-clicking
on the model and
selecting **Add Pitch
Point**

The pitch value can be constant or vary across the helical profile. To add additional values, select the Pitch panel and select **Add Pitch**. Change the location and value of the pitch as shown in Figure 6–5.

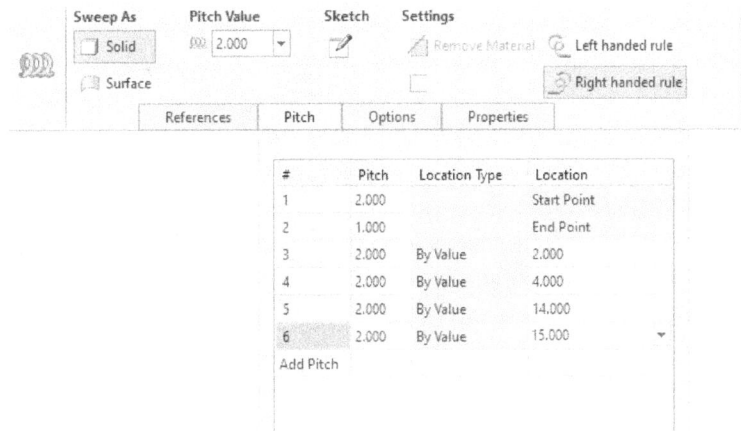

	Pitch	Location Type	Location
1	2.000		Start Point
2	1.000		End Point
3	2.000	By Value	2.000
4	2.000	By Value	4.000
5	2.000	By Value	14.000
6	2.000	By Value	15.000
Add Pitch			

Figure 6–5

The cross-section for the Helical Sweep automatically uses the sketching plane that was defined for the profile created in Step 3.

How To: Sketch the Cross-section for the Helical Sweep

1. Click ✐ (Create or Edit Section) in the *Helical Sweep* tab or mini toolbar to sketch the cross-section.
2. Select the sketcher references (if the default references are not suitable).
3. Sketch the profile relative to the start point of the profile. This location is indicated by intersecting hash lines.
4. Click ✓ (OK) to complete the sketch.

5. Click ✔ (OK) to complete the feature. Some examples of Helical Sweeps are shown in Figure 6–6.

Example 1
Linear Profile
Constant Pitch

Example 2
Linear Profile
Variable Pitch

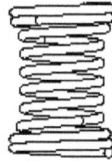

Example 3
Non-Linear Profile
Variable Pitch

Example 4
Non-Linear Profile
Variable Pitch

Figure 6–6

6.2 Volume Helical Sweep

Volume Helical Sweeps enable you to model geometry that results from the cutting tools used in manufacturing. Creo Parametric uses an axis-symmetric revolved geometry to represent the cutting tool that follows a helical path, as shown in an example in Figure 6–7.

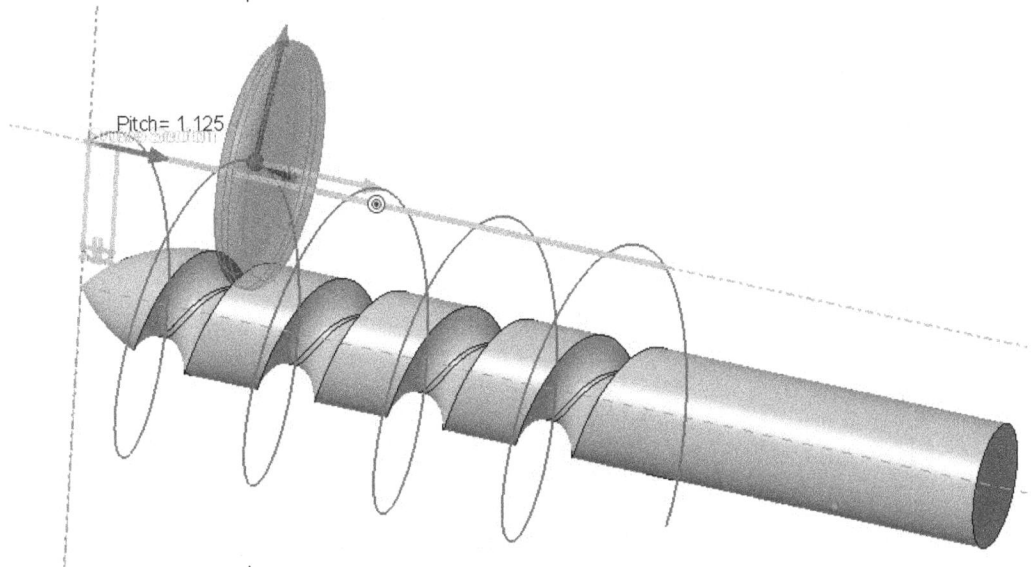

Figure 6–7

To create a volume helical sweep, in the *Model* tab, expand
(Sweep) and select (Volume Helical Sweep). The Volume Helical Sweep dashboard opens as shown in Figure 6–8.

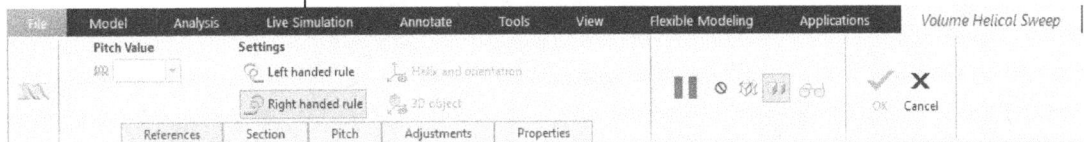

Figure 6–8

The required references are a sketched Helical sweep profile as well as a helix axis. The sweep rotates around the helix axis. You can select an existing sketch for the helix profile or you can sketch one by clicking **Define** in the References panel or by clicking and selecting 𝕞𝕞 (Define Internal Helix Profile), as shown in Figure 6–9.

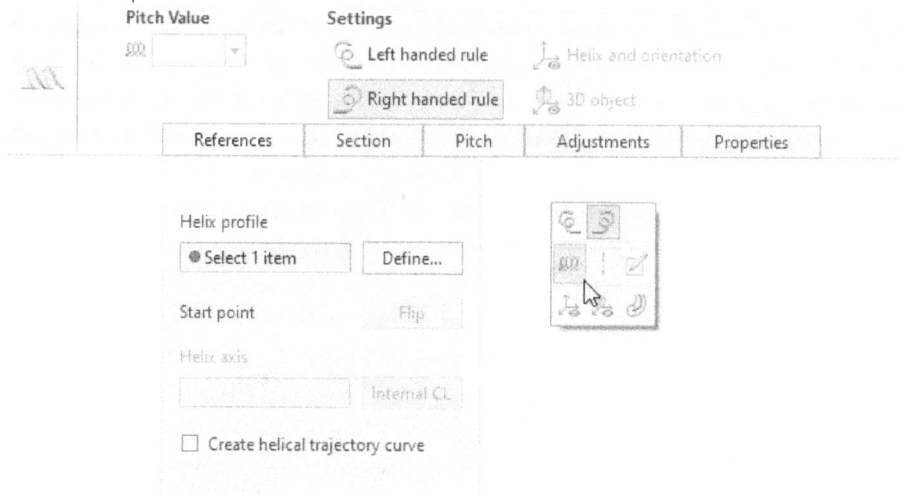

Figure 6–9

The sketch for the helix profile consists of the profile curve but can also include a centerline, which will automatically be used as the Helix axis, as shown in Figure 6–10. Alternatively, if you have an existing axis you want to revolve around, that can be selected instead of including the centerline.

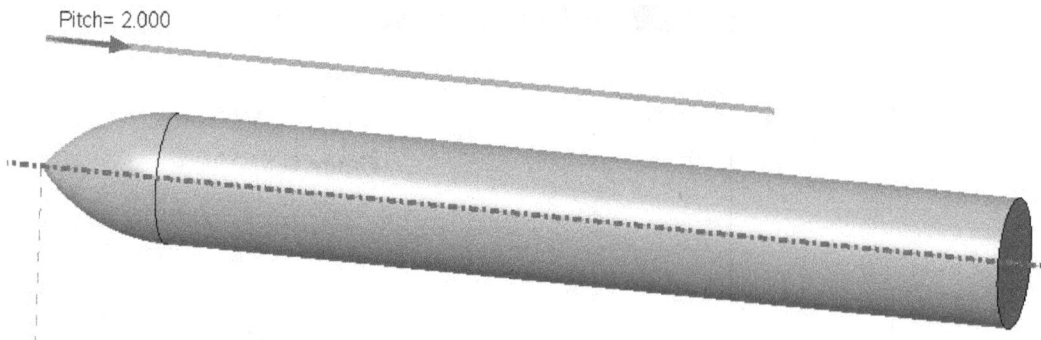

Figure 6–10

You edit the pitch value to control the spacing between rotations.

The section profile, which represents the profile of the tool, can either be sketched or selected from an existing sketch in the model. To sketch a section, select **Create/Edit section** from the Section panel or ✎ (Create/Edit Section) in the mini toolbar, as shown in Figure 6–11.

Figure 6–11

The section profile can only consist of lines and arcs that result in a convex shape, as shown in the example in Figure 6–12.

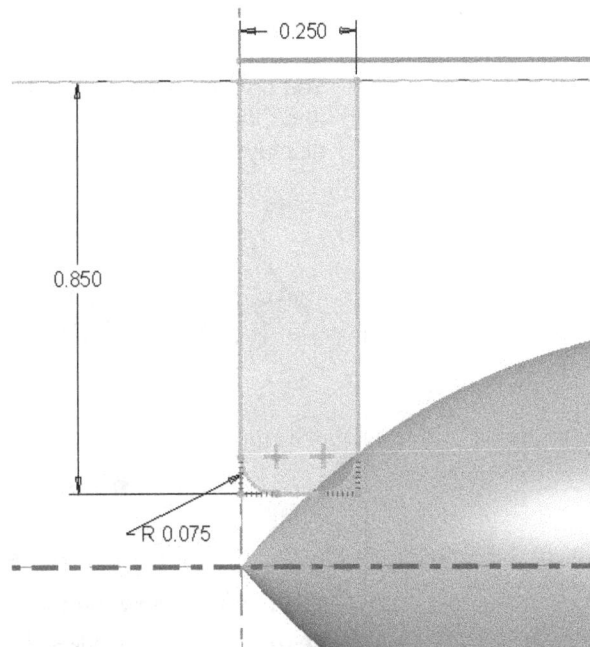

Figure 6–12

As the section revolves around the profile axis, any existing geometry intersected by the section is removed, as shown in Figure 6–13.

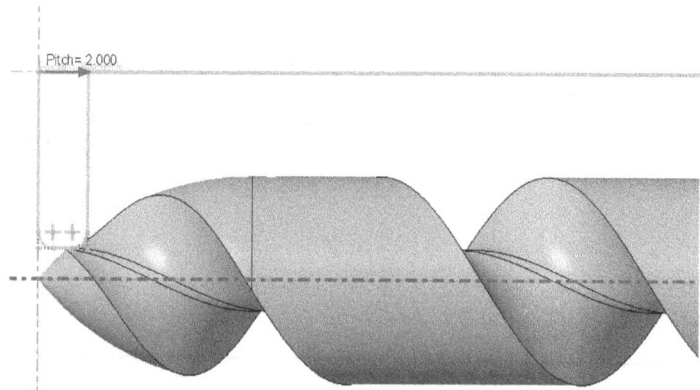

Pitch= 2.000

Figure 6–13

Note that since the section can only consist of lines and arcs that form a convex shape, the section and helical geometry must not create situations where the geometry is self intersecting.

You can review the resulting cutting path by clicking ↱ (Helix and Orientation) in the dashboard or mini toolbar. The path displays as shown in Figure 6–14.

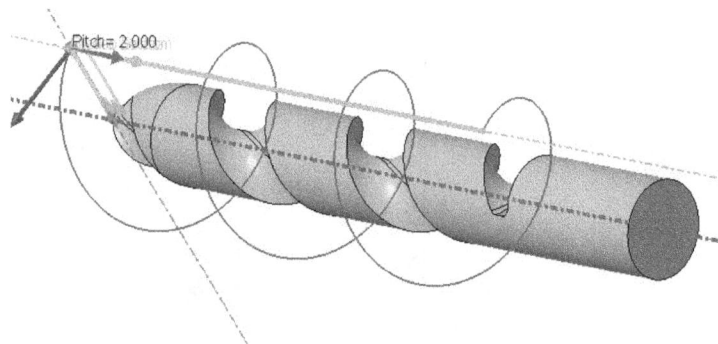

Pitch= 2.000

Figure 6–14

You can also view the tool created by the section (shown in Figure 6–15) by clicking ↱ (3D Object). Note that this option is only available once ↱ (Helix and Orientation) is selected.

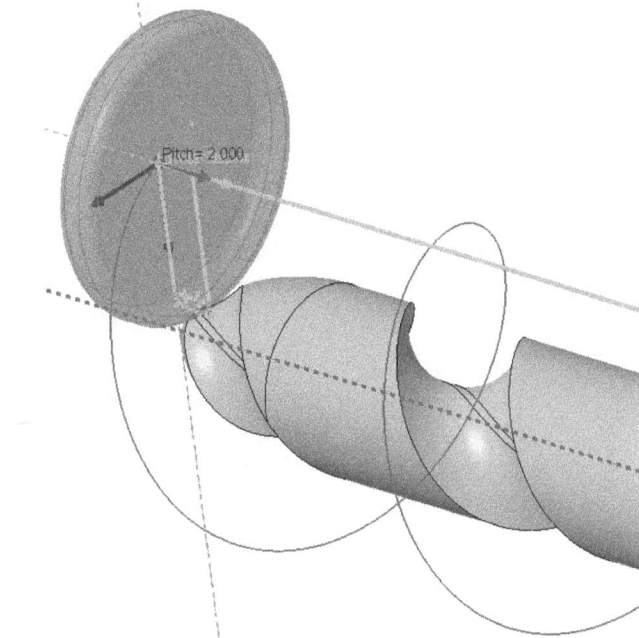

Figure 6–15

You can review the path of the tool by dragging it along the helix. Select the drag handle at the center of the section and drag the tool as shown in Figure 6–16.

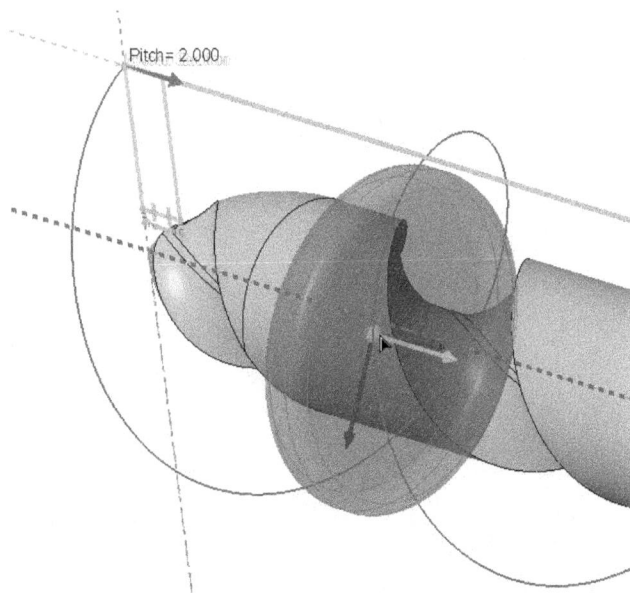

Figure 6–16

The section rotates by following a right-hand thread by default. You can reverse the direction by toggling between ⟳ (By Right-Hand Rule) and ⟲ (By Left-Hand Rule) in the dashboard or mini toolbar.

You have control over the angle at which the profile section enters the geometry. You can enter an angle to rotate about the X-axis (red axis) or Z-axis (blue axis) using the Adjustment panel, as shown in Figure 6–17.

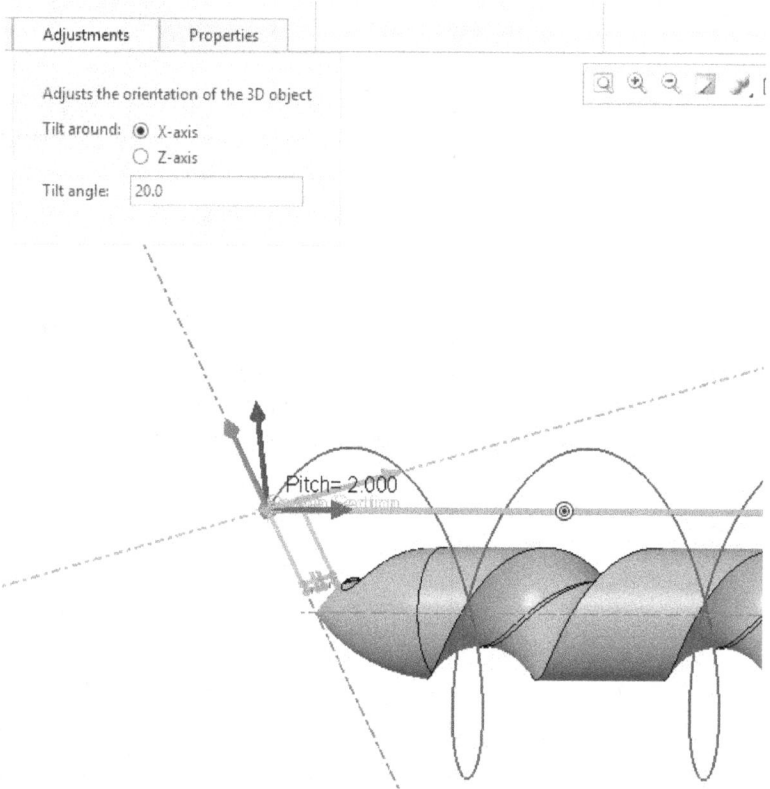

Figure 6–17

If you want to model a screw conveyor scenario, edit the X-axis Tilt angle to **90.0**, as shown in Figure 6–18.

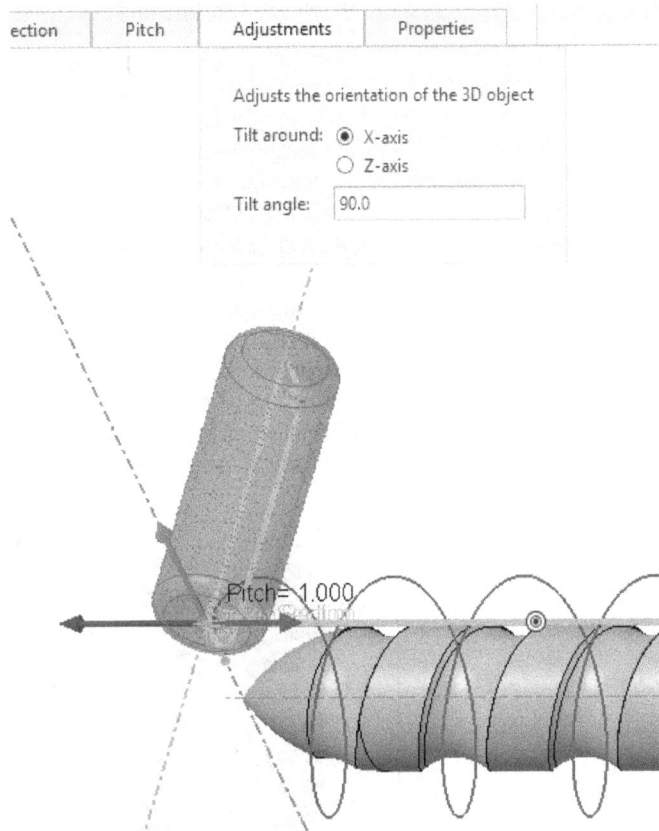

Figure 6–18

Finally, you can create a curve that maps to the helix by enabling the **Create helical trajectory curve** option in the References panel or ✏ (Create Helical Trajectory Curve) in the mini toolbar. You can then use the resulting curve as a reference for other features.

Practice 6a

Springs Using a Helical Sweep

Practice Objectives

- Create a Helical Sweep feature using a circle for the cross-section.
- Edit the Helical Sweep to add multiple pitch values to the spring.
- Edit the Helical Sweep feature to add multiple vertices to the profile to change the shape of the spring.

In this practice you will create a model of a spring. To create the geometry you will use the **Helical Sweep** option. This feature is created by sketching a sweep profile and axis of revolution and is completed by defining the pitch and the spring section. The pitch represents the distance between the coils of the helical feature. In this practice you will create the initial constant pitch spring, as shown on the left in Figure 6–19. You will then edit the definition of this spring to vary the pitch for two different scenarios, as shown in the center and right in Figure 6–19.

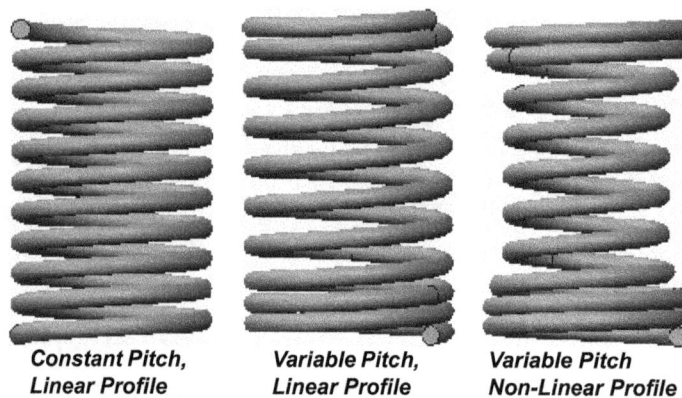

| Constant Pitch, Linear Profile | Variable Pitch, Linear Profile | Variable Pitch Non-Linear Profile |

Figure 6–19

Task 1 - Create a new part.

1. Set the working directory to the *Helical_Sweep* folder.

2. Create a new part called **helical_spring**.

3. Set the model display as follows:

   - *(Datum Display Filters)*: All Off

   - *(Spin Center)*: Off

   - *(Display Style)*: (Shading With Edges)

Task 2 - Create the constant pitch, linear profile Helical Sweep.

1. Expand ☞ (Sweep) in the *Model* tab and click ꙮ (Helical Sweep). The *Helical Sweep* tab displays as shown in Figure 6–20.

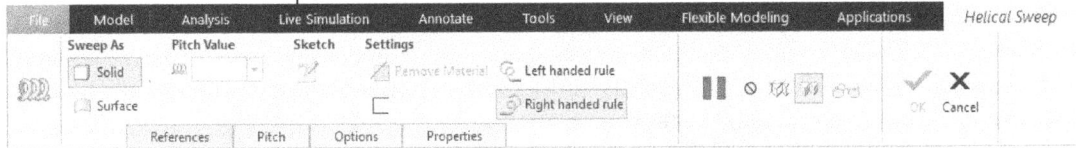

| File | Model | Analysis | Live Simulation | Annotate | Tools | View | Flexible Modeling | Applications | *Helical Sweep* |

Sweep As   Pitch Value   Sketch   Settings

☐ Solid   ⏚   ✎   ☒ Remove Material   ⟳ Left handed rule

☐ Surface   ☐   ⟳ Right handed rule   ▮▮ ⊘ ⟲ ⤢ ✓ ✗
                                                          OK Cancel

References   Pitch   Options   Properties

Figure 6–20

2. To sketch the sweep profile, click on the screen and select ꙮ (Define Internal Helix Profile) in the mini toolbar. In the Model Tree, select datum plane **FRONT** as the sketching plane and click **Sketch**.

3. In the *Sketch* tab, click ⋮ (Centerline) in the Sketching group and sketch a centerline on datum plane **RIGHT**. Sketch a vertical line that represents the revolved surface on which the wire is rolled, as shown in Figure 6–21. The arrow indicates the start point for the sweep.

*If the start point in your sketch is on the other end of the line, select the correct endpoint, right-click and select **Start Point**. This will move it to the correct location.*

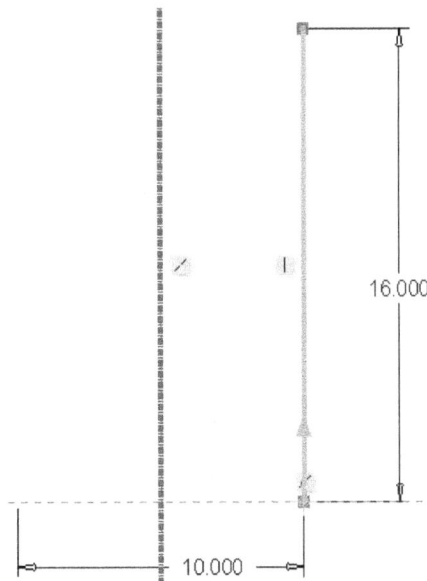

16.000

10.000

Figure 6–21

4. Complete the sketch.

5. Set the *Pitch* value to **2**, as shown in Figure 6–22.

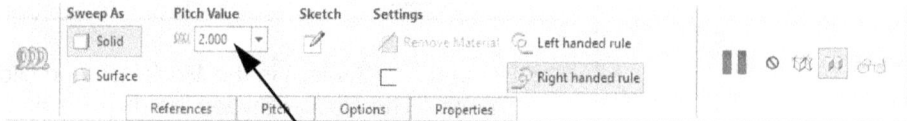

Enter pitch value

Figure 6–22

6. Click on the screen and select ✎ (Create or Edit Sweep Section) and sketch the spring cross-section as a circle, as shown in Figure 6–23.

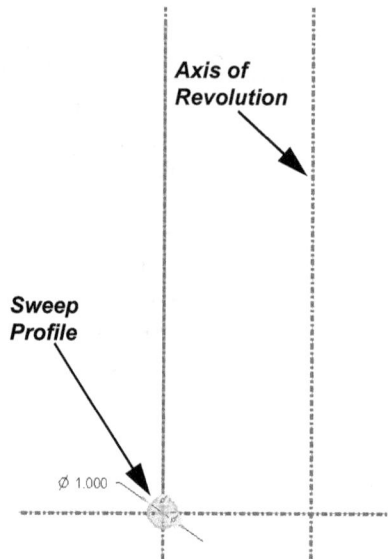

Axis of Revolution

Sweep Profile

Ø 1.000

Figure 6–23

7. Complete the sketch and the feature. The model displays as shown in Figure 6–24.

Figure 6–24

Task 3 - Redefine the Helical Sweep to define a variable pitch.

Design Considerations

The design intent for the Helical Sweep has changed. It is now required that the pitch vary over its length. This can be accomplished by editing the original feature's definition and adding pitch points. The new pitch values and the location can be entered for each point in the Pitch panel.

1. Select the helical sweep and click ![edit] (Edit Definition).

2. Select the Pitch panel. Select **Add Pitch**, as shown in Figure 6–25.

*You can also right-click on the helix profile in the view window and select **Add Pitch Point**.*

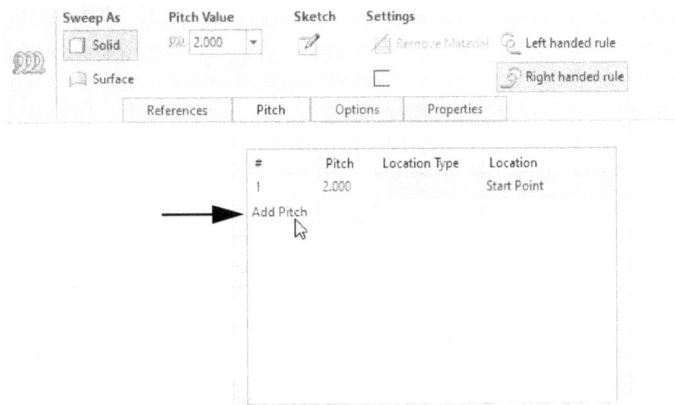

Figure 6–25

3. Continue to add pitch points and modify the location and values as shown in Figure 6–26.

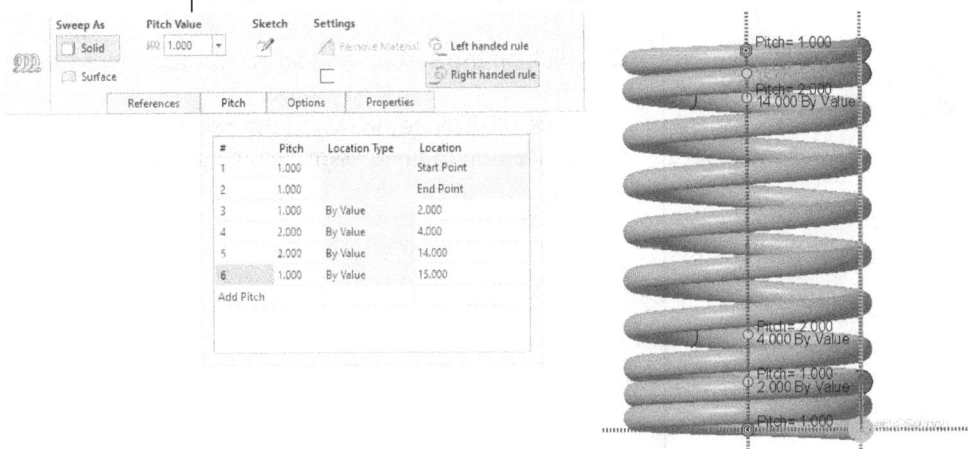

Figure 6–26

---

4. Complete the feature. Note the varying pitch values as shown in Figure 6–27.

Figure 6–27

Task 4 - Redefine the Helical Sweep to define a non-linear, variable pitch profile.

Design Considerations

The design intent for the Helical Sweep has changed again. You now need to change the profile from linear to non-linear, but the variable pitch values will remain the same. This can be done by editing the original feature's definition. The sketch of the linear profile must be edited to divide the linear profile and remove the constraints so that the non-linear profile can be created.

1. Edit the definition of the helical sweep.

You can also click **References** *and click* **Edit***.*

2. Click on the screen and select ⚙ (Edit Internal Helix Profile).

3. Click ⟋ (Divide) to divide the profile into five linear entities. Dimension the line segments as shown in Figure 6–28.

Constraints and dimensions turned off for clarity.

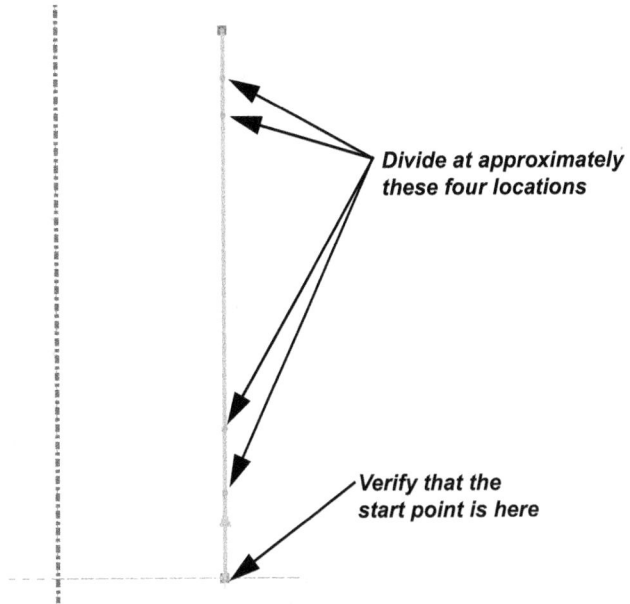

Divide at approximately these four locations

Verify that the start point is here

Figure 6–28

To remove the constraint you can also select the constraint symbol and press <Delete>.

4. Modify the sweep profile as shown in Figure 6–29. To remove assigned constraints, right-click on the constraint symbol and select **Delete**.

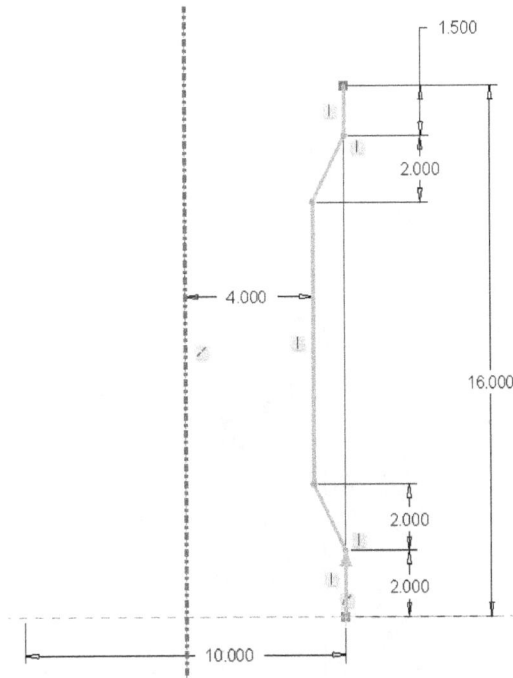

1.500

2.000

4.000

16.000

2.000

2.000

10.000

Figure 6–29

5. Complete the sketch.

6. Complete the feature. The model displays as shown in Figure 6–30.

Figure 6–30

7. Save the part and erase it from memory.

Practice 6b

Volume Helical Sweep

Practice Objective

- Create a Volume Helical Sweep feature.

In this practice, you will review the Volume Helical Sweep feature.

Task 1 - Open the baseplate.prt model.

1. Set the Working Directory to *Volume_Helical_Sweep*.

2. Open **bit.prt**.

3. Set the model display as follows:

   - ⁎ *(Datum Display Filters)*: All Off

   - ⤷ *(Spin Center)*: Off

   - ▢ *(Display Style)*: ▢ (Shading With Edges)

   The model displays as shown in Figure 6–31.

Figure 6–31

Task 2 - Begin the creation of a Volume Helical Sweep and create the sweep profile.

1. In the *Model* tab, in the Shapes group, expand ⬙ (Sweep) and select ⬙ (Volume Helical Sweep), as shown in Figure 6–32.

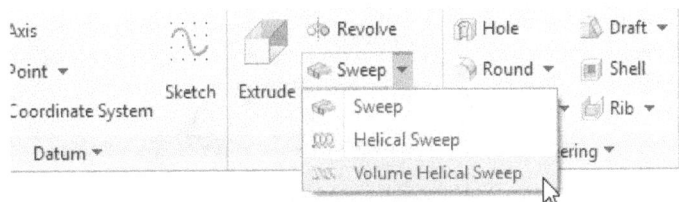

Figure 6–32

2. Expand the References panel in the ribbon and note that Helix sweep profile collector is active, as shown in Figure 6–33.

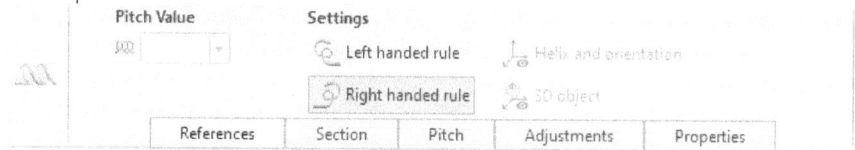

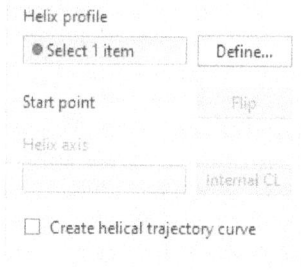

Pitch Value	Settings		
	Left handed rule	Helix and orientation	
	Right handed rule	3D object	
References	Section	Pitch	Adjustments	Properties

Helix profile
Select 1 item   Define...

Start point   Flip

Helix axis

Internal CL

☐ Create helical trajectory curve

Figure 6–33

You can also click **Define** *in the References tab.*

3. Click on the screen and select ≋ (Define Internal Helix Profile) in the mini toolbar.

4. In the Model Tree, select **FRONT** as the sketch plane.

5. In the Sketch dialog box, click **Sketch**.

6. In the In-graphics toolbar, click ≋ (Sketch View).

7. Sketch and dimension the line and centerline shown in Figure 6–34.

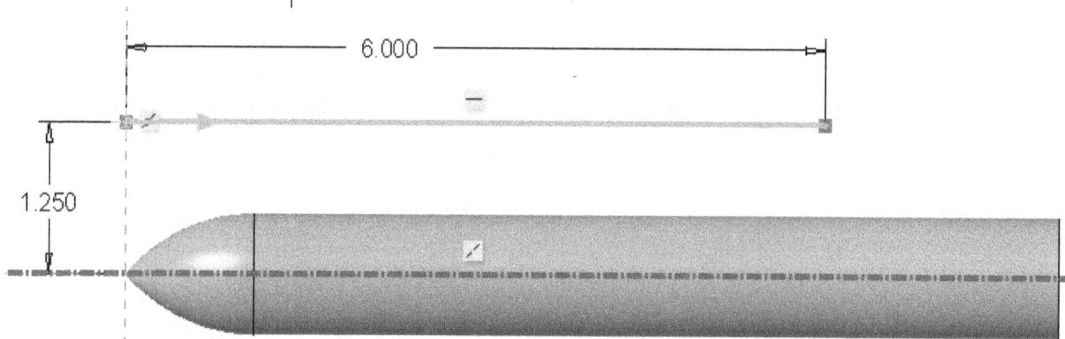

6.000

1.250

Figure 6–34

8. In the *Sketch* tab, click ✓ (OK).

Task 3 - Sketch the section profile which represents the tool.

1. Click on the screen and select ✎ (Create/Edit Section) in the mini toolbar.

2. Sketch and dimension the geometry shown in Figure 6–35.

Note that the constraints are turned off in this image for clarity. Sketch a rectangle, then use fillet arcs to create the radii. Use the Equal constraint so you can drive the radii with a single dimension.

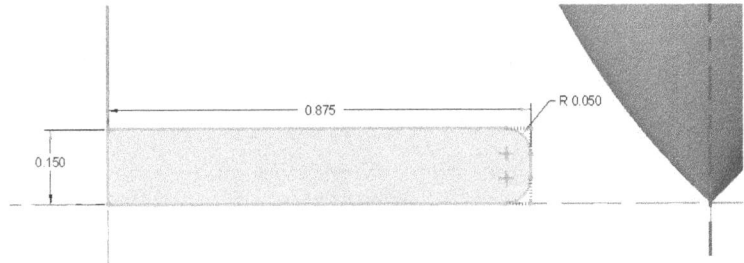

Figure 6–35

3. Set the orientation to **FRONT**.

4. In the *Sketch* tab, click ✓ (OK). The geometry previews as shown in Figure 6–36.

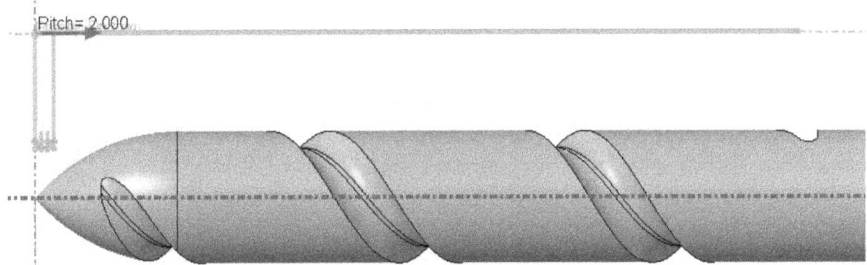

Figure 6–36

Task 4 - Edit the pitch value to see the impact on the geometry.

1. Double-click on the pitch value on the screen and edit it to **0.50**. The preview updates, as shown in Figure 6–37.

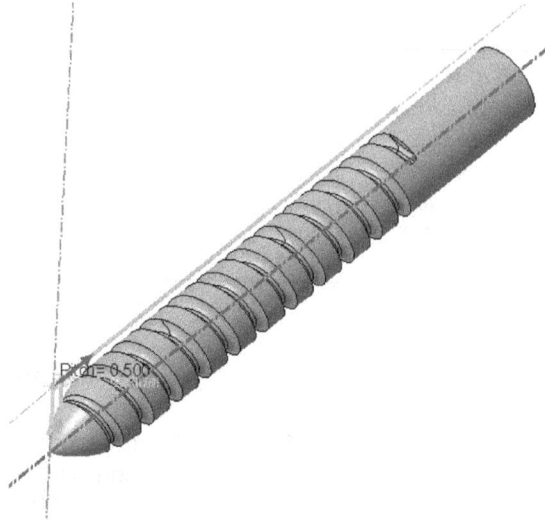

Figure 6–37

2. Edit the pitch to **1.00** and the preview updates as shown in Figure 6–38.

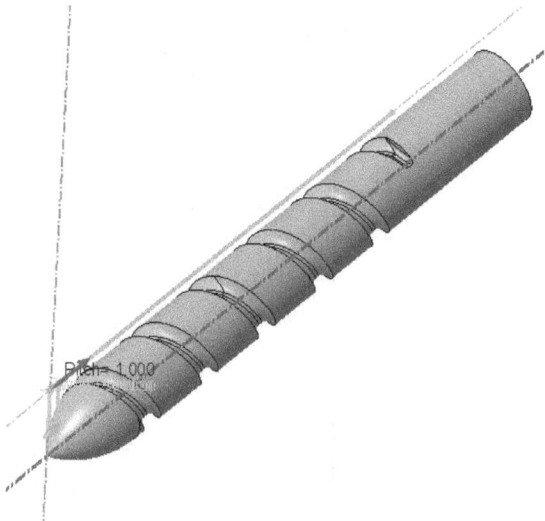

Figure 6–38

Task 5 - Change the cutting angle of the tool.

1. Click on the screen and select ⌲ (Helix and Orientation) in the mini toolbar to enable the display of the helical path, as shown in Figure 6–39.

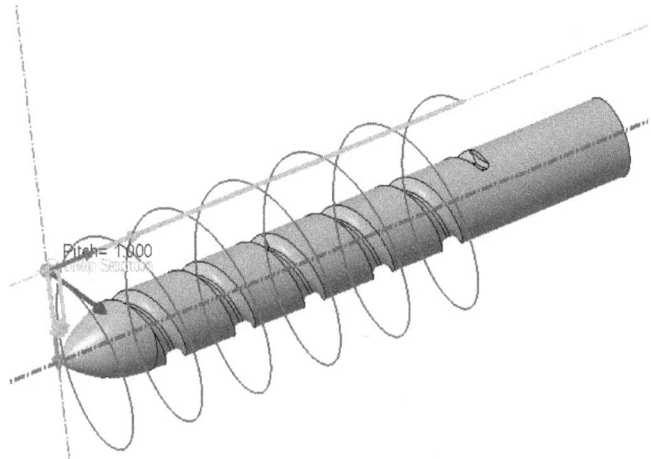

Figure 6–39

2. Click on the screen and select ⌲ (3D Object) to view the 3D model of the tool, as shown in Figure 6–40.

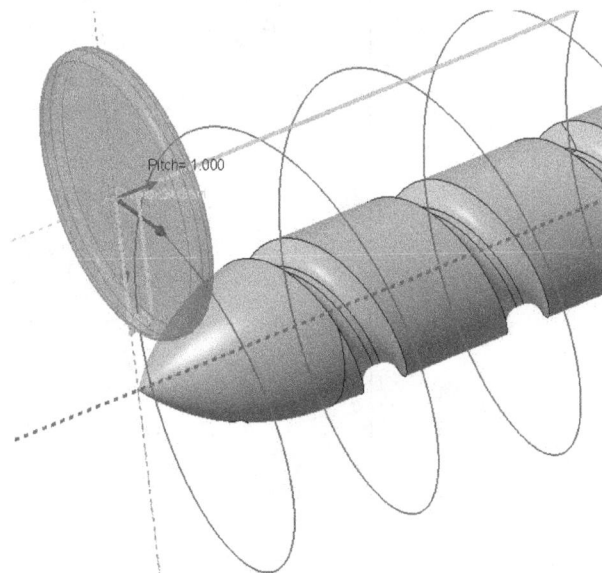

Figure 6–40

3. Click the Adjustments panel in the dashboard.

4. Enable the Z-axis option and edit the tilt angle to **10**.

5. In the In-graphics toolbar, expand (Saved Orientations) and select **FRONT**. The model displays as shown in Figure 6–41.

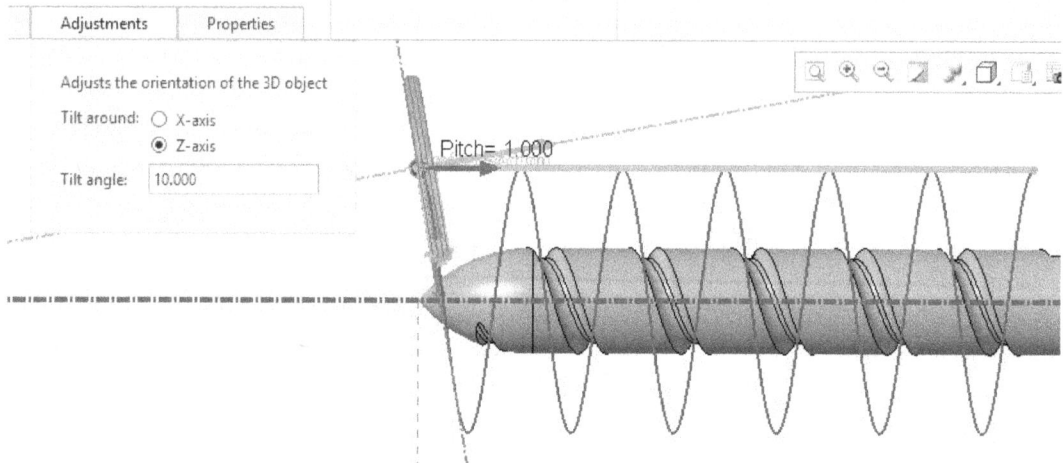

Adjustments | Properties

Adjusts the orientation of the 3D object

Tilt around: ○ X-axis
● Z-axis

Tilt angle: 10.000

Pitch= 1.000

Figure 6–41

6. Return to default orientation.

7. Review the path and orientation of the tool by clicking and holding the handle at the center of the tool, then dragging it along the path, as shown in Figure 6–42.

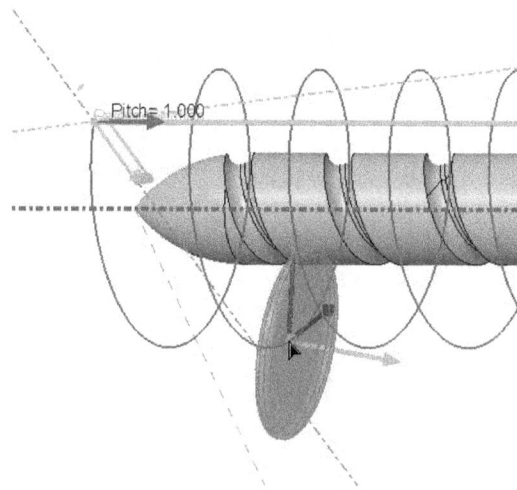

Pitch= 1.000

Figure 6–42

8. Edit the *Tilt angle* back to **0**.

Task 6 - Change the model to represent a screw conveyor scenario.

1. Click the References panel and click **Edit** next to the *Helix sweep profile* collector.

2. Edit the *1.25* dimension to **0.75** and click ✓ (OK).

3. Click on the screen and select 🖊 (Create/Edit Section) in the mini toolbar.

4. Edit the dimensions as shown in Figure 6–43.

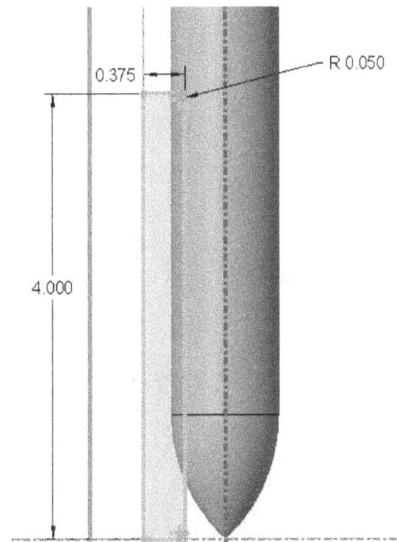

Figure 6–43

5. Click ✓ (OK).

6. Select the *Adjustments* panel and enable **X-axis**.

7. Edit the *Tilt angle* to **90**, which turns the tool perpendicular to the helix, as shown in Figure 6–44.

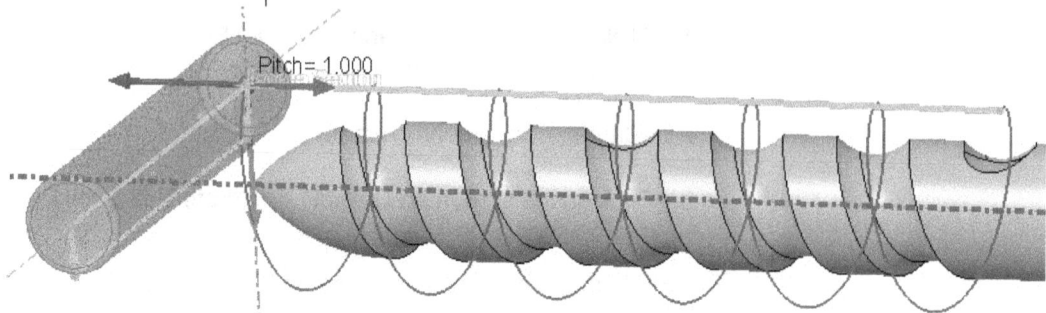

Pitch= 1.000

Figure 6–44

8. Click ✔ (OK). The completed model displays as shown in Figure 6–45.

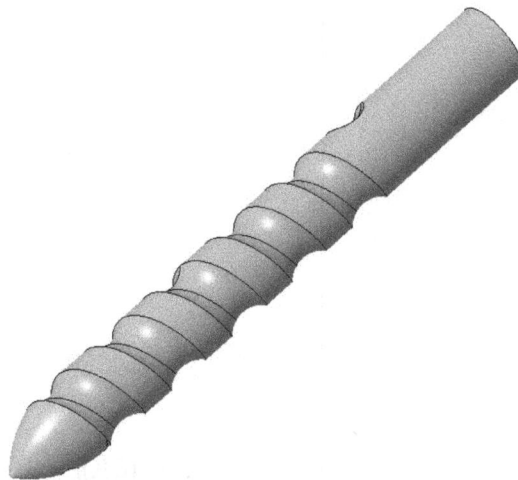

Figure 6–45

9. Close the file and erase it from memory.

Chapter Review Questions

1. When you create the Helical Sweep feature, you need to specify an axis of revolution. Which icon in the *Sketch* tab can be used to create an internal centerline?

   a.　┊　(Centerline) in the Sketching group

   b.　┊　(Centerline) in the Datum group

   c.　⌄　(Line)

2. Which section orientation option in the References panel creates the cross-section normal to the helical trajectory?

   a.　**Normal to trajectory**

   b.　**Through axis of revolution**

3. Which section orientation option in the References panel creates a plane that passes through the axis of revolution to orient the profile?

   a.　**Normal to trajectory**

   b.　**Through axis of revolution**

4. What is the maximum number of pitch values that can be added to a linear helical sweep?

   a.　1

   b.　2

   c.　3

   d.　There is no maximum.

5. For a Volume Helical Sweep, the **Internal Helix Profile** defines the geometric shape of the manufacturing tool.

   a.　True

   b.　False

6. You are creating a Volume Helical Sweep, and after completing the section, you want to preview the tool but the 🏀 (Show 3D Object) option is unavailable. What is the likely issue?

   a. The section is sketched such that it does not intersect any solid geometry.

   b. The section is sketched such that it will remove all geometry.

   c. The helical path resulting from the sweep must first be shown.

   d. The section is tilted 90 degrees about the X Axis.

Advanced Blends

A Blend is a feature that has varied cross-sections over a specified length. This chapter introduces advanced blends that provide further control when creating complex geometry. A Swept Blend is a combination of a blended feature and a swept feature. This feature type permits advanced cross-section control such as specifying area at a specific point on the trajectory, as well as tangency options.

Learning Objectives in This Chapter

- Learn to create a Rotational Blend by sketching or selecting multiple sections and defining an angle of rotation.
- Learn the various options that can be used to create a Rotational Blend.
- Learn to create a Swept Blend feature by selecting one or multiple trajectories to define the path and by sketching multiple sections.
- Use the Section Control plane options to define the orientation of the section with respect to the trajectory.
- Select or sketch the sections for the Swept Blend feature.
- Define the tangency and blend control options to control the shape of the blend.

7.1 Rotational Blend

A Rotational Blend creates geometry in which all of the planar sections intersect at a common axis. Rotational bends can be closed, open, smooth, or straight as shown in Figure 7–1. Closed Blends are created with the first and last sections blended together.

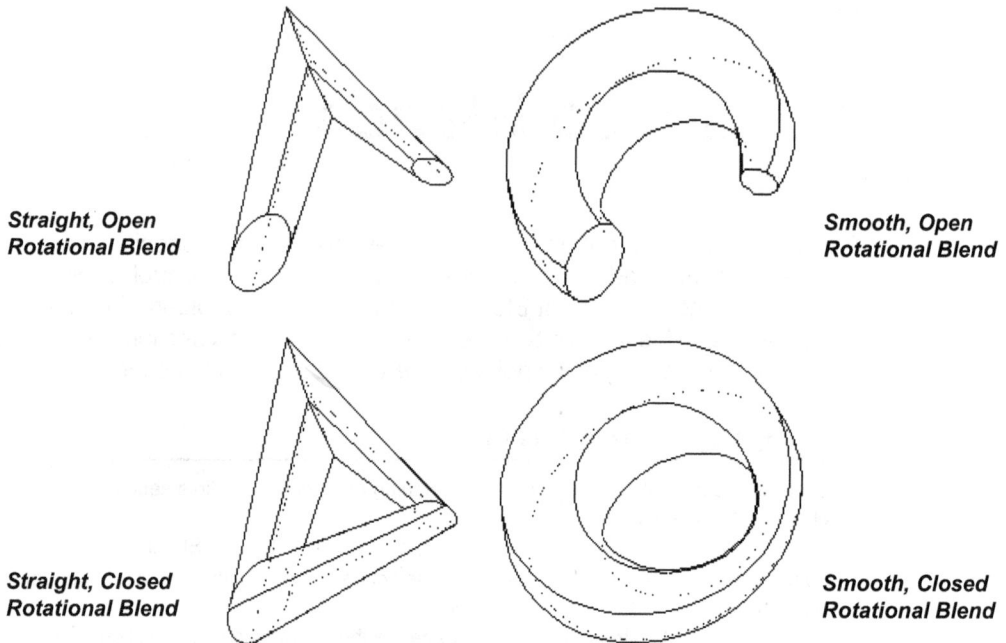

**Straight, Open
Rotational Blend**

**Smooth, Open
Rotational Blend**

**Straight, Closed
Rotational Blend**

**Smooth, Closed
Rotational Blend**

Figure 7–1

To create a Rotational Blend, select **Shapes>Rotational Blend**. The *Rotational Blend* tab activates as shown in Figure 7–2.

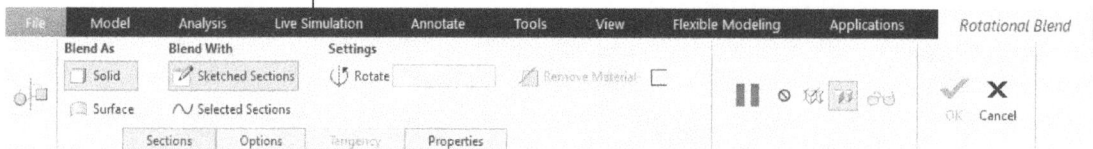

Figure 7–2

You can select or sketch the sections for the blend. The various methods for choosing to sketch or select the sections are shown in Figure 7–3.

Click here to sketch the section

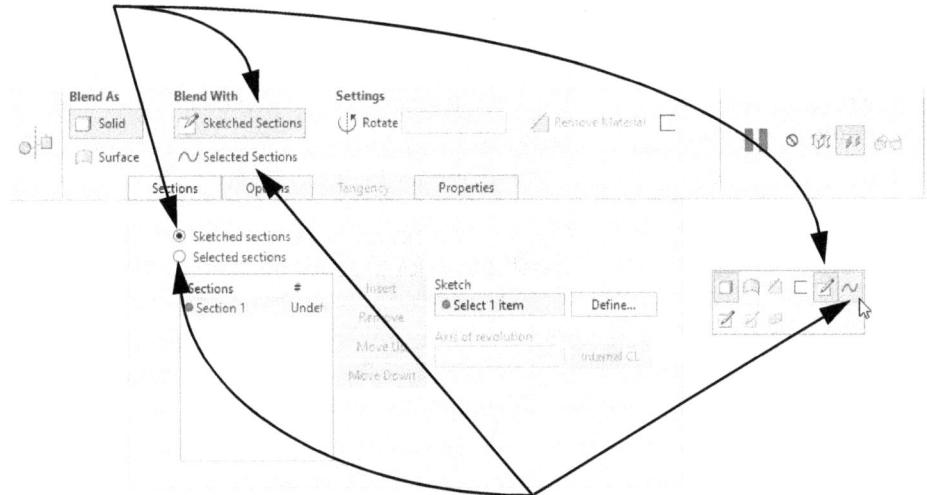

Click here to select the section

Figure 7–3

A selected section requires you to select the entities to make up the section. A sketched section requires you click **Define** or

(Sketch) in the mini toolbar, select a sketching plane and orientation plane, and sketch the section.

A sketched section also requires an axis of revolution for the rotational direction. This can be a centerline in a sketch, as shown in Figure 7–4, or a selected entity such as a datum axis.

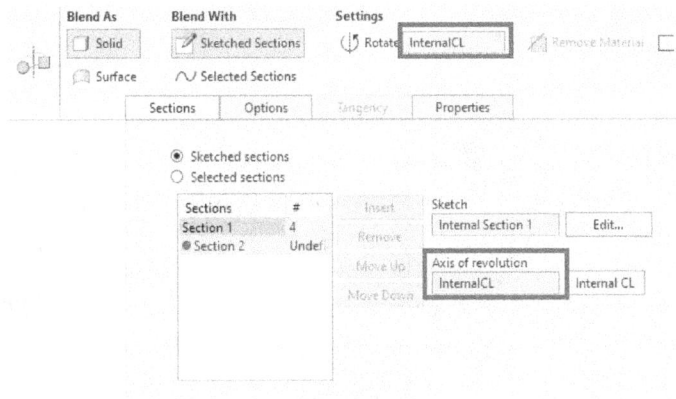

Figure 7–4

Rotational Blends rotate each section about the axis to a maximum rotational angle of 120°.

Click **Insert** in the Sections panel to select or sketch additional sections.

You can also drag the angle rotation value in the graphics window.

A sketched section requires an angle rotation value or a reference to specify the distance between the sections. In the dashboard you can click Click ⟂ (Reference) to specify a sketch plane for the next section.

You can also select **Reference** in the Section panel to define the sketch plane for the next section as shown in Figure 7–5.

Click here to specify an offset value

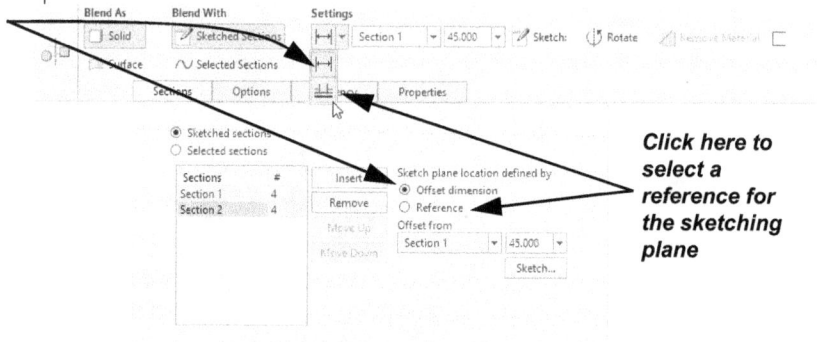

Click here to select a reference for the sketching plane

Figure 7–5

Select the Options panel to specify a **Straight** or **Smooth** blend as shown in Figure 7–6. You can create a closed rotational blend by selecting **Connect end and start sections**.

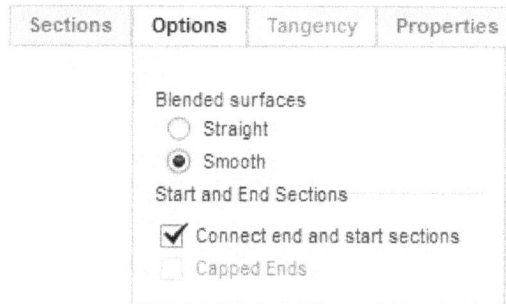

Figure 7–6

Select the Tangency panel to define tangency requirements as shown in Figure 7–7. The tangency can be set at the start and end section using **Free**, **Tangent**, or **Normal**.

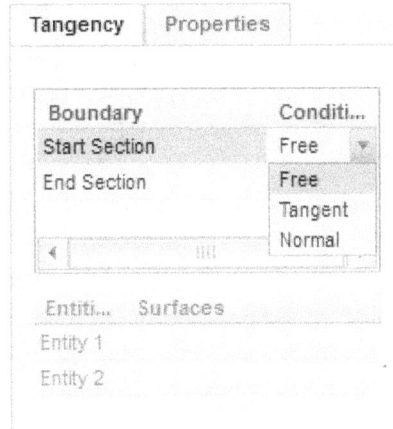

You can also right-click on a Boundary Condition marker to set the tangency.

Tangency	Properties

Boundary	Conditi...
Start Section	Free
End Section	Free
	Tangent
	Normal

Entiti...	Surfaces
Entity 1	
Entity 2	

Figure 7–7

Click ✔ (OK) to complete the blend.

To change the definition of the Blend, select it and click (Edit Definition) in the mini toolbar. Each section can be changed, added, and removed in the Sections panel. Select the section that you want to change and click **Edit** or (Edit Internal Sketch) from the mini toolbar. Sections can also be reordered in the Sections panel by selecting the section and clicking **Move Up** or **Move Down**.

7.2 Swept Blends

A Swept Blend is a combination of a blended feature and a swept feature. This type of Blend enables you to sketch multiple sections at specified points along a trajectory called the Origin trajectory. Each of the sections are then blended together. The main body of the faucet shown in Figure 7–8 was created using a Swept Blend.

Figure 7–8

General Steps

Use the following general steps to create a Swept Blend:

1. Start the creation of the feature.
2. Select the trajectory.
3. Define the section plane control.
4. Define the sections for the feature.
5. Define tangency, if required.
6. Define blend control, if required.
7. Complete the feature.

Step 1 - Start the creation of the feature.

Click ✐ (Swept Blend) in the *Model* tab. The *Swept Blend* tab activates as shown in Figure 7–9.

Click this icon to create the feature as a solid

Click this icon to create the feature as a cut

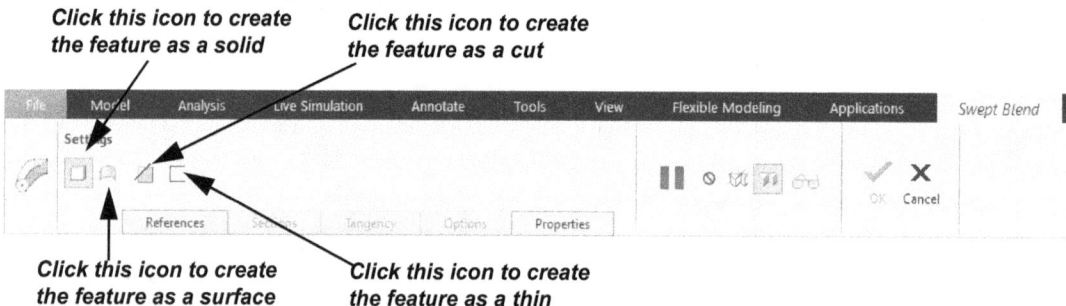

Click this icon to create the feature as a surface

Click this icon to create the feature as a thin

Figure 7–9

To begin, define the feature as a ▢ (Solid) or ◠ (Surface) by selecting the appropriate icon in the dashboard or the mini toolbar. When creating the Swept Blend as a solid feature, you can also specify whether the feature removes material or is created as a thin feature.

Step 2 - Select the trajectory.

Next, you must define a trajectory for the feature. The Origin trajectory defines how the geometry of the feature is going to be created. The Origin trajectory can be a selected edge, curve, or sketch that exists in the model.

There is one special case in which you can select two trajectories. The first trajectory is the Origin trajectory. The second trajectory is used to specify the orientation of the Swept Blend feature's cross-section as the section is swept along the Origin trajectory. To select a second trajectory, press and hold <Ctrl> and select it in the model.

Once selected, the trajectory is indicated in the model and in the References panel, as shown in Figure 7–10.

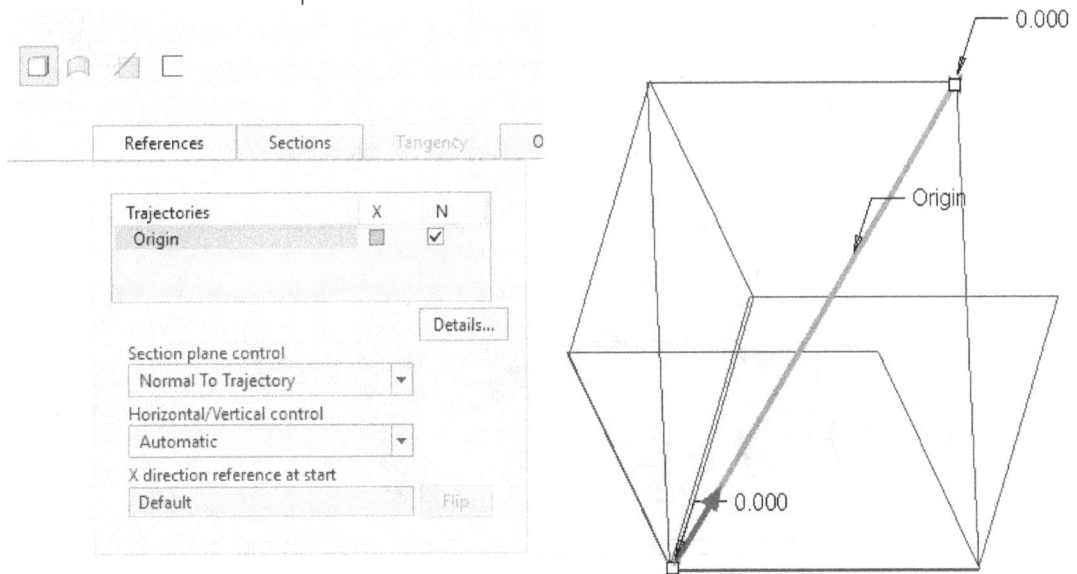

Figure 7–10

Step 3 - Define the section plane control.

In the References panel you can define how the section of the Swept Blend feature is oriented with respect to the trajectory. This is defined using the Section plane control options. The following options are available in the drop-down list:

- **Normal To Trajectory**
- **Normal To Projection**
- **Constant Normal Direction**

Figure 7–11 shows examples of four simple features that were created using different types of section plane control.

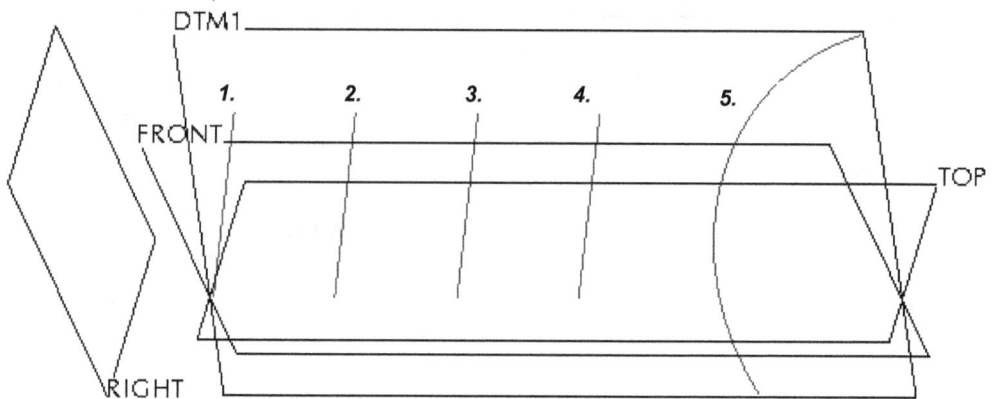

All trajectories (lines and arc) are sketched on datum plane DTM1

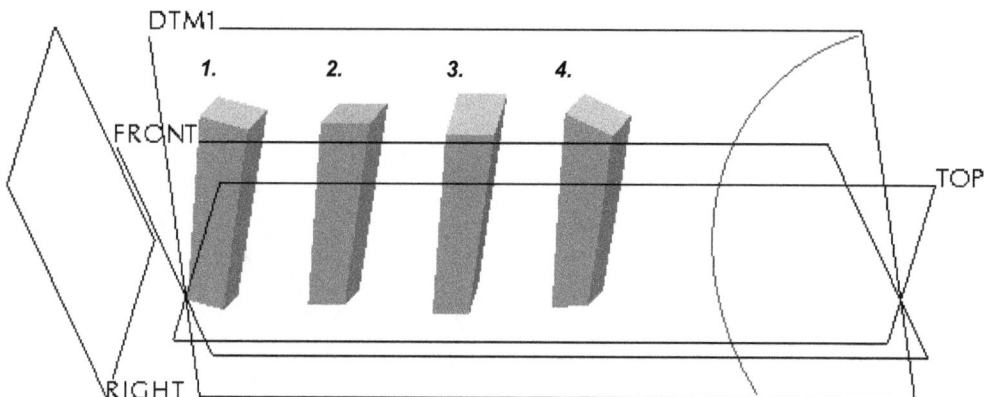

1. *Normal To Trajectory (1 trajectory, 1)*
2. *Normal To Projection (datum plane RIGHT)*
3. *Constant Normal Direction (datum plane TOP)*
4. *Normal To Trajectory (2 trajectories, 4 and 5)*

Figure 7–11

Normal To Trajectory

The **Normal To Trajectory** option enables you to create a Swept Blend where the cross-section remains perpendicular to the specific trajectory. You can select one or two trajectories if the **Normal To Trajectory** option is set.

One Trajectory

Figure 7–12 shows the *Swept Blend* tab and the model with one trajectory selected.

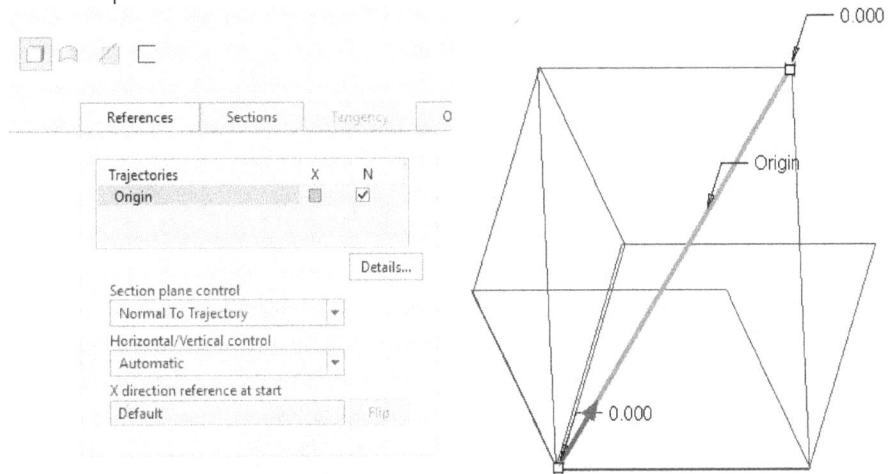

The Origin trajectory is a line sketched on the angled datum plane

Figure 7–12

The final geometry for the feature is shown in Figure 7–13.

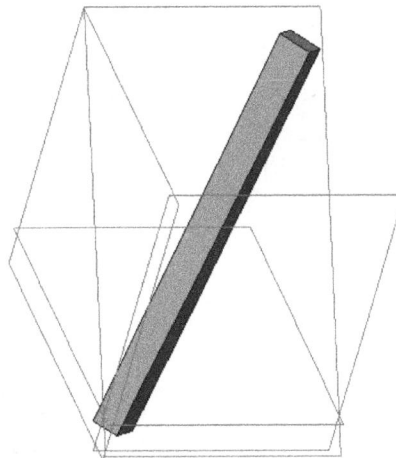

Figure 7–13

Two Trajectories

Figure 7–14 shows the *Swept Blend* tab and the model with two trajectories selected. To drive the section orientation by the secondary trajectory, you must place a checkmark in the *N* column of the Secondary trajectory in the References panel, as shown in Figure 7–14.

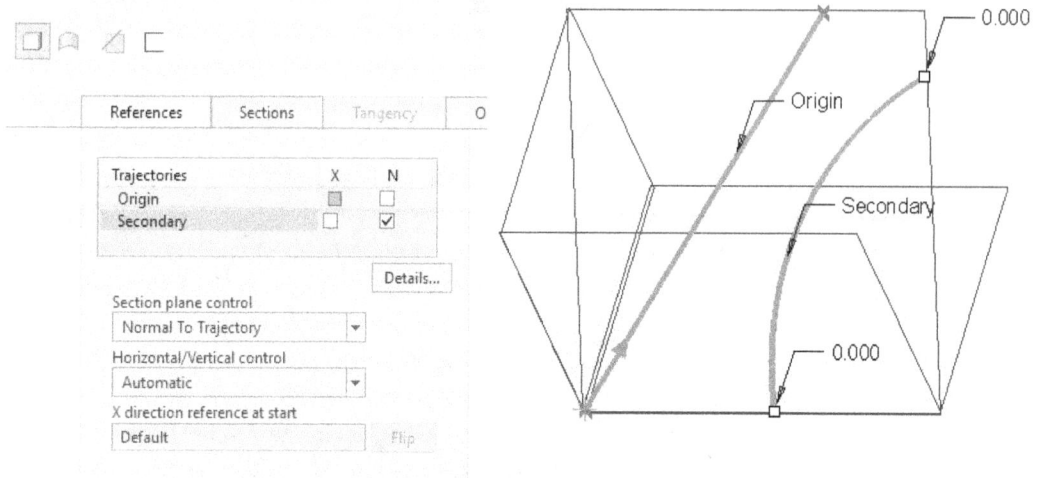

The Origin trajectory is a line sketched on the angled datum plane

The secondary trajectory is an arc sketched on the angled datum plane

Figure 7–14

The final geometry for the feature is shown in Figure 7–15.

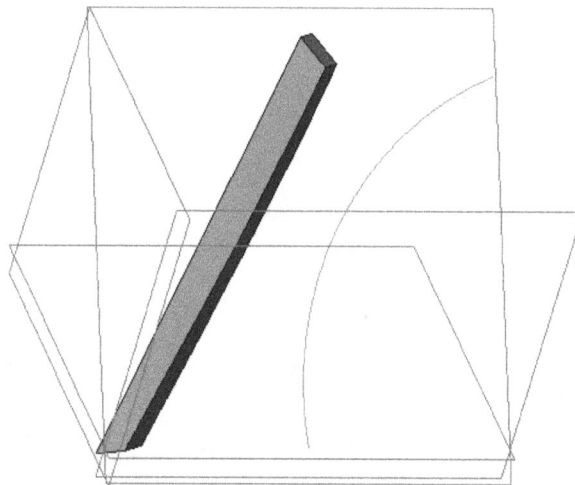

Figure 7–15

Normal To Projection

The **Normal To Projection** option enables you to create a Swept Blend where the cross-section remains normal to a specific feature or surface of a feature. With this option, a projection reference (plane, edge, curve, axis, or coord sys) is required to define the orientation of the sketching plane. The section remains normal to the projection reference as it moves along the trajectory. Figure 7–16 shows the *Swept Blend* tab and the model with the trajectory selected.

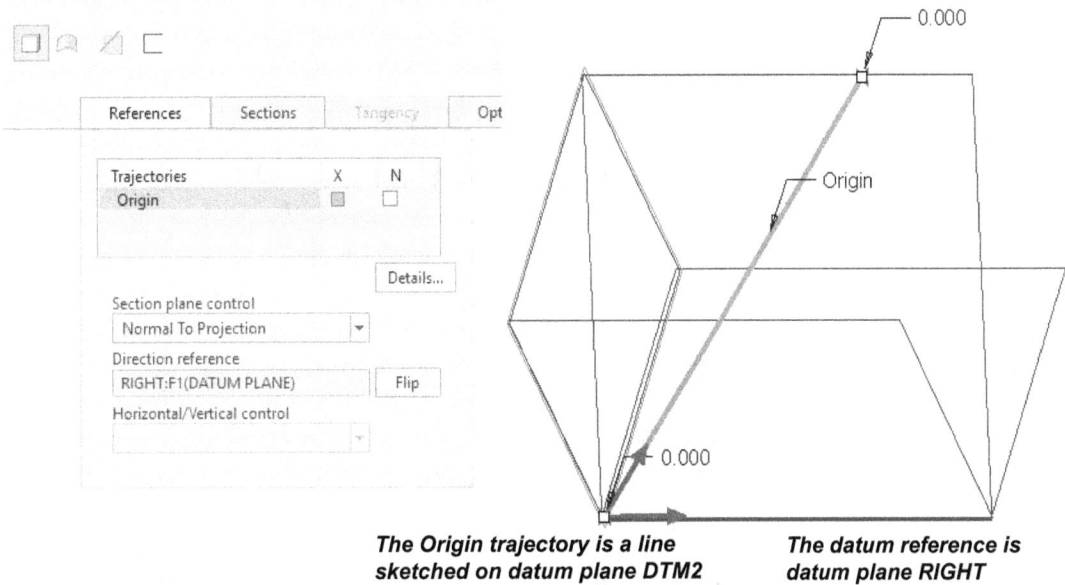

The Origin trajectory is a line sketched on datum plane DTM2

The datum reference is datum plane RIGHT

Figure 7–16

The final geometry for the feature is shown in Figure 7–17.

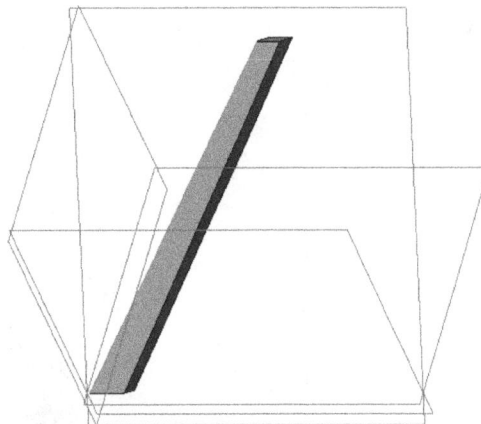

Figure 7–17

Constant Normal Direction

The **Constant Normal Direction** option enables you to create a Swept Blend where the cross-section remains parallel to a specific feature or surface of a feature. With this option, a normal reference (plane, edge, curve, axis, or coord sys) is required to define the orientation of the sketching plane. The section remains parallel to the normal reference as it moves along the trajectory. Figure 7–18 shows the dashboard and the selected references.

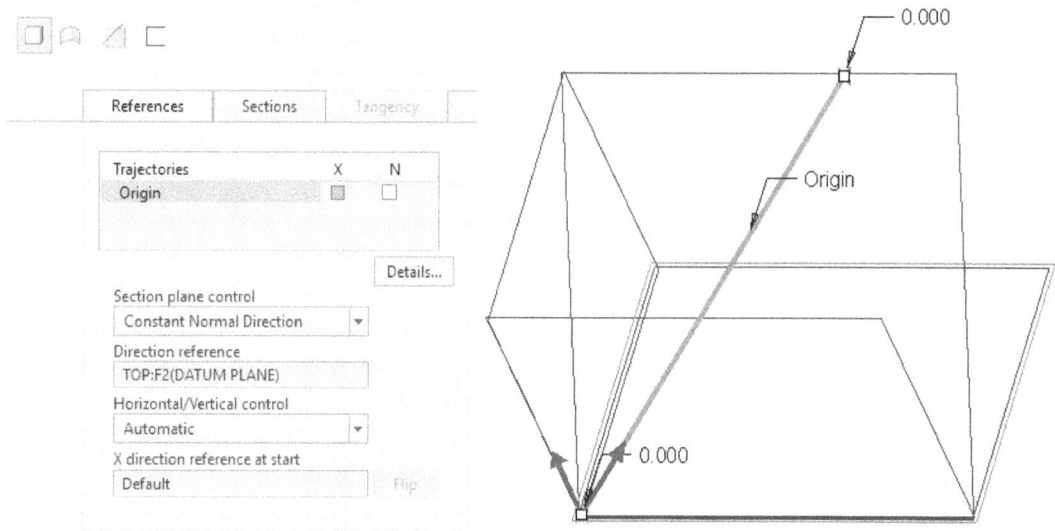

The Origin trajectory is a line sketched on datum plane DTM2

The datum reference is datum plane TOP

Figure 7–18

The final geometry for the feature is shown in Figure 7–19.

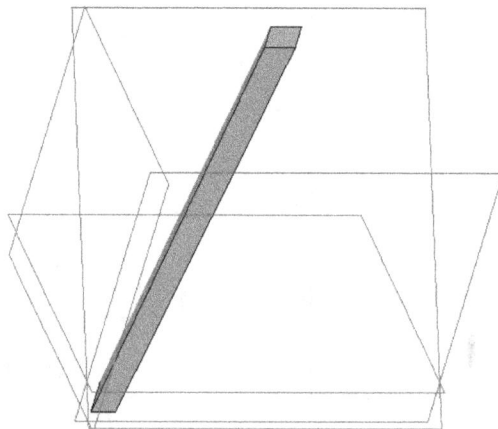

Figure 7–19

Step 4 - Define the sections for the feature.

Once the trajectory has been defined, you need to define the sections for the feature. One of two methods can be used to define sections: you can sketch the sections (default) or you can select the sections from existing geometry.

Consider the following tips when creating sections:

- A minimum of two sections are required for a Swept Blend feature (at any two points for an open trajectory, or at the start point and any other point for a closed trajectory).

- Sections cannot be sketched at sharp points on the Origin trajectory.

- The same number of vertices are required in each section (blend vertex can be used).

- Verify that the start points for each section are in the correct location to prevent twisting of the feature.

- Sections can be created or selected in any order.

Sketched Sections

Define the location of the first sketched section by right-clicking and selecting **Section Location**, as shown in Figure 7–20.

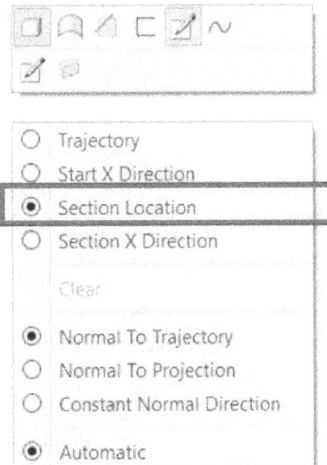

Figure 7–20

Alternatively, you can define the location for a section in the Sections panel in the tab, as shown in Figure 7–21.

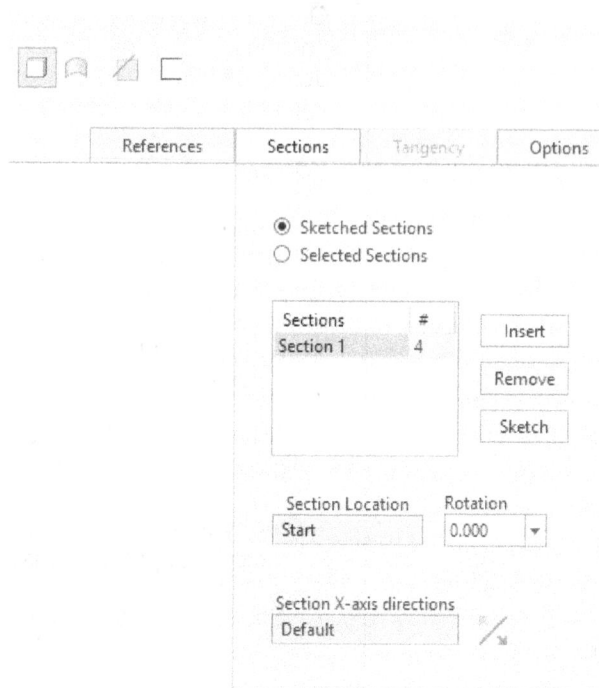

Figure 7–21

You can select the start or end point of the trajectory, an inner point along the trajectory (i.e., a point where two adjacent entities of the trajectory are connected), or a datum point lying on the trajectory. If required, the *Rotation* field in the Sections panel enables you to specify the section rotation about the Z-axis.

*You can also click the **Sketch** button in the Sections panel in the tab.*

To sketch the first section, right-click and select **Sketch**. Creo Parametric activates the *Sketch* tab without prompting for a sketch plane or orientation reference plane. The sketching plane is identified by an orange coordinate system lying on the trajectory and two centerlines (X- and Y-axes). Sketch the section according to your needs. An arrow indicating the start point of the section is also displayed. Verify that the start point is in the correct location to prevent twisting of the feature. To change the start point position, right-click on the section vertex where the start point should be and select **Start Point**.

*You can also click the **Insert** button in the Sections panel in the tab.*

Additional sections can be added to the feature by right-clicking and selecting **Insert Section**. Repeat the process used for the first section (i.e., select the section location and sketch the section).

When two or more sections are defined, a geometry preview displays as shown in Figure 7–22. Section names are attached to individual sections. To redefine a section, right-click on its name and select **Sketch**. To remove a section, right-click on its name and select **Remove Section**.

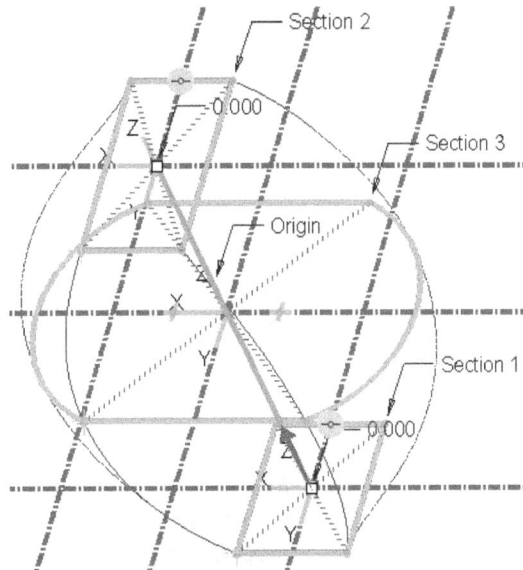

Figure 7–22

The list of sections is also displayed in the Sections panel, as shown in Figure 7–23. You can also modify or remove a section by selecting the section name in the list and clicking the appropriate button.

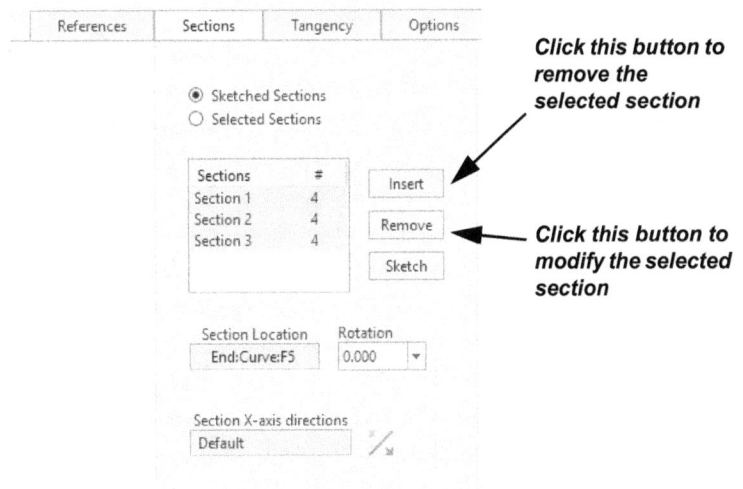

Figure 7–23

Selected Sections

Sections can also be created before you access the Swept Blend feature. To select sections, right-click and select **Selected Sections**, as shown in Figure 7–24.

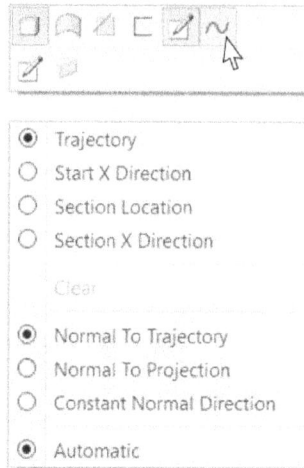

Figure 7–24

Alternatively, you can select the sections using the Sections panel in the tab by selecting **Selected Sections** in the drop-down list, as shown in Figure 7–25.

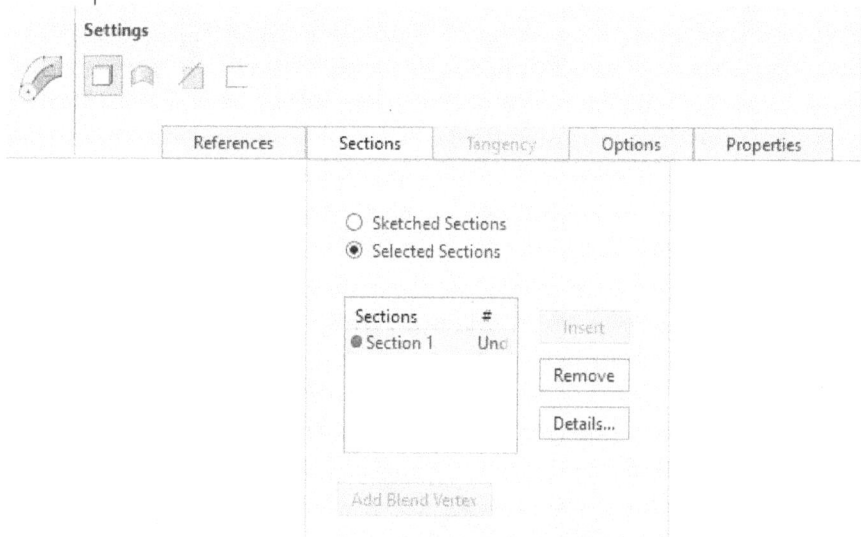

Figure 7–25

Once the first section has been selected, a circular handle and an arrow display indicating the start point of the section, as shown in Figure 7–26. Verify that the start point is in the correct location compared to the other sections, to prevent twisting of the feature. To change the start point position, drag the circular handle to another section vertex.

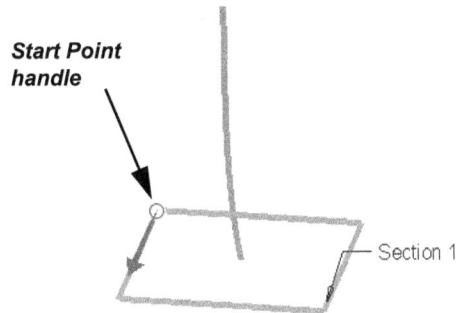

Figure 7–26

Add additional sections if required, by clicking **Insert** in the Sections panel before selecting the next section.

When two or more sections are selected, a geometry preview displays. To remove a section, right-click on its name and select **Remove Section,** as shown in Figure 7–27. Alternatively, a section can be removed by selecting its name in the list and clicking the **Remove** button in the Sections panel in the tab.

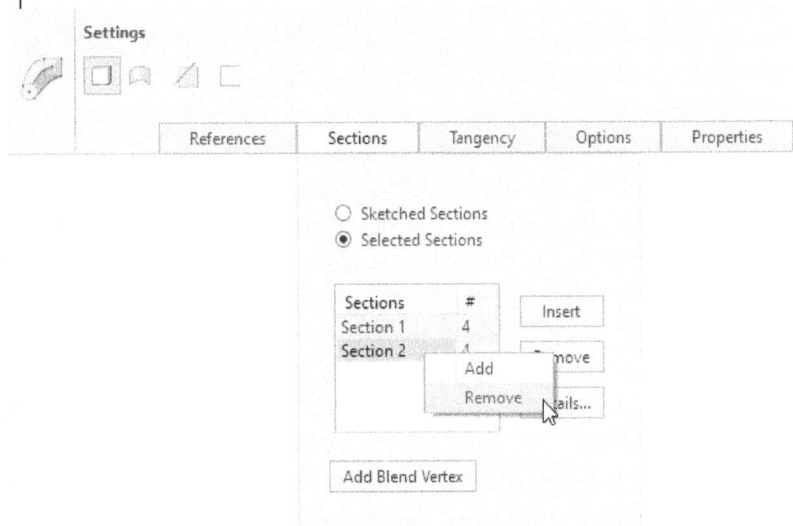

Figure 7–27

Step 5 - Define tangency, if required.

*Alternatively, you can right-click on the **Tangency** icon in the model and select **Tangent**.*

The Tangency panel shown in Figure 7–28 enables you to establish tangency between the Swept Blend and existing geometry. To define a tangent transition between geometry, change the **Free** option to the **Tangent** option and select a surface adjacent to the highlighted boundary.

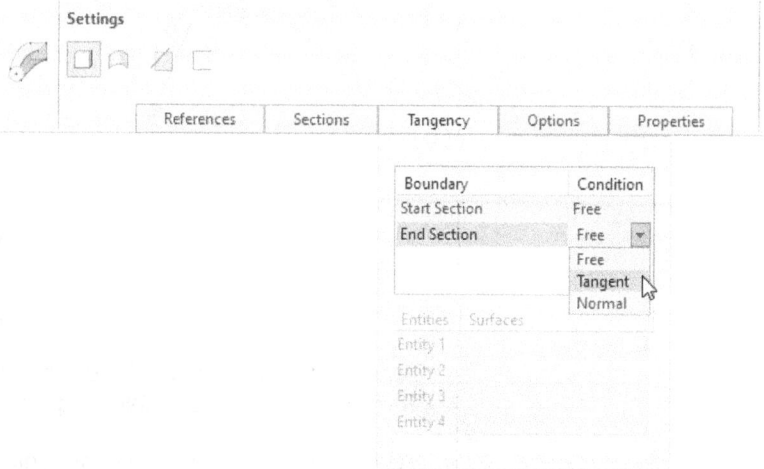

Settings

Boundary	Condition
Start Section	Free
End Section	Free

Free
Tangent
Normal

Entities | Surfaces
Entity 1
Entity 2
Entity 3
Entity 4

References   Sections   Tangency   Options   Properties

Figure 7–28

Step 6 - Define blend control, if required.

The Options panel shown in Figure 7–29 enables you to control the shape of the Swept Blend between the sections using a perimeter or area graph.

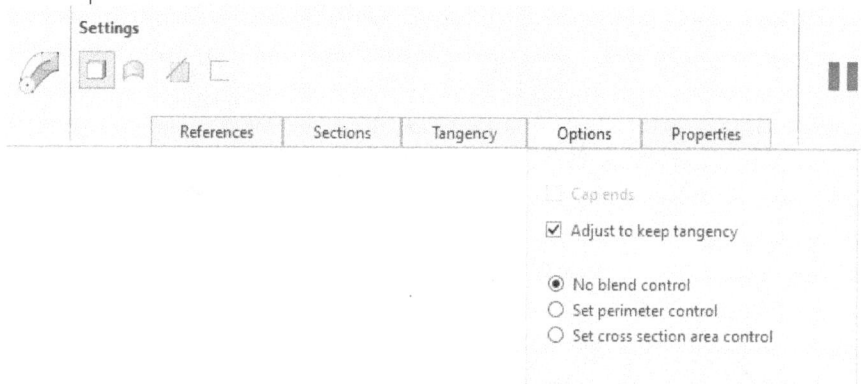

Settings

References   Sections   Tangency   Options   Properties

☐ Cap ends

☑ Adjust to keep tangency

◉ No blend control
○ Set perimeter control
○ Set cross section area control

Figure 7–29

The **Adjust to keep tangency** option can be used so that, if the origin trajectory is almost tangent, or tangent but not curvature continuous, the blend is adjusted to create tangent surfaces.

The **Set perimeter control** option uses the perimeter of the sections to control the shape of the feature. If the sections have different perimeters, Creo Parametric uses linear interpolation to determine the perimeter of the feature section between the defined sections.

The **Set cross-section area control** option enables you to specify the cross-section area of the section at specified points lying on the trajectory, as shown in Figure 7–30. You can use natural breaks in the trajectory or create datum points along the trajectory. Press and hold <Ctrl> to select two or more datum points.

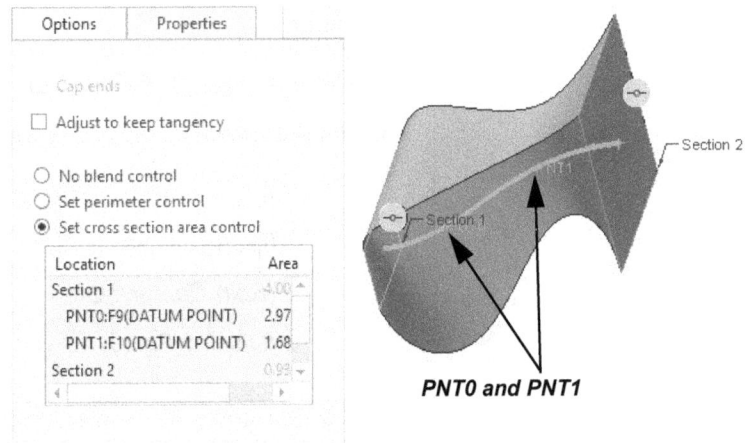

Figure 7–30

Step 7 - Complete the feature.

To complete the feature, click ✔ (OK) in the *Swept Blend* dashboard.

Practice 7a

Rotational Blend with Sketched Sections

Practice Objectives

- Create a Rotational Blend by sketching multiple sections and moving the start point locations.
- Define tangency between existing geometry and the Rotational Blend.

In this practice, you will create a drawer handle using a Rotational Blend created by sketching the various sections.

Task 1 - Open an existing part.

1. Set the working directory to the *Rotational_Blend_Sketched* folder.

2. Open **drawer_handle.prt**.

3. Set the model display as follows:

    - ⁎⁄⁎ *(Datum Display Filters)*: ⌁ (Csys Display) and ⌁ (Plane Display) only

    - ⋋ *(Spin Center)*: Off

    - ⬚, *(Display Style)*: ⬚ (Shading With Edges)

Task 2 - Create a Rotational Blend.

1. Select **Shapes>Rotational Blend** in the *Model* tab. The *Rotational Blend* dashboard activates, as shown in Figure 7–31.

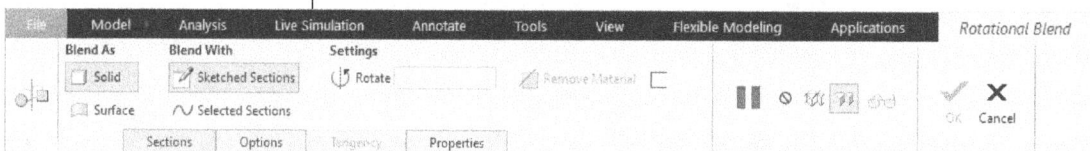

Figure 7–31

2. Click **Sections** in the *Rotational Blend* dashboard.

3. Ensure **Sketched sections** is selected and click **Define**, as shown in Figure 7–32.

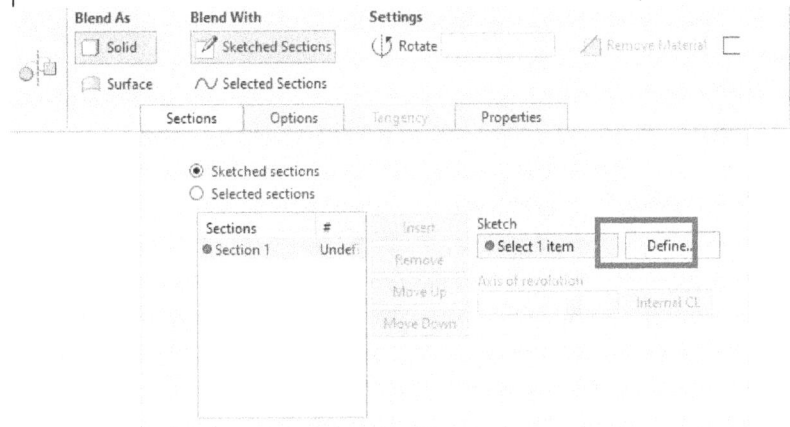

Figure 7–32

4. Select datum plane **FRONT** for the Sketch Plane and click **Sketch**.

5. Click (Sketch View).

6. Create the sketch shown in Figure 7–33.

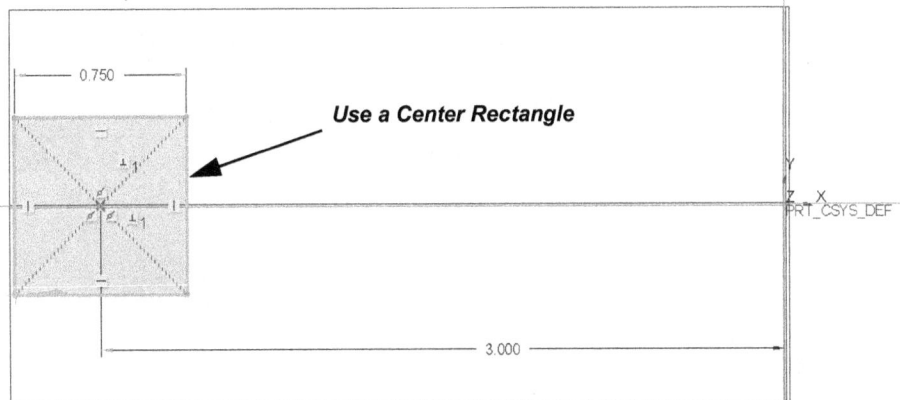

Figure 7–33

7. Complete the sketch.

8. Select the **Y-Axis** of the Coordinate system as the rotation axis.

9. In the Sections tab, click **Insert** to add a second section.

10. Click on the screen and select (Sketch) in the mini toolbar.

11. Click 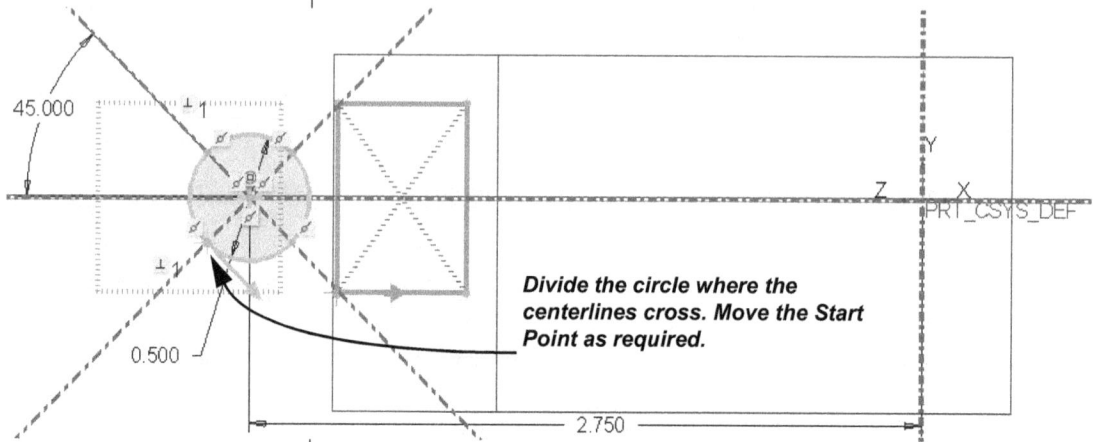 (Sketch View).

12. Create the sketch shown in Figure 7–34.

Divide the circle where the centerlines cross. Move the Start Point as required.

Figure 7–34

13. If required, select the appropriate vertex to align with the previous section, right-click and select **Start Point**.

14. Complete the sketch.

15. In the Section tab, click **Insert** to add a third section.

16. Click on the screen and select ✎ (Sketch) in the mini toolbar.

17. Click 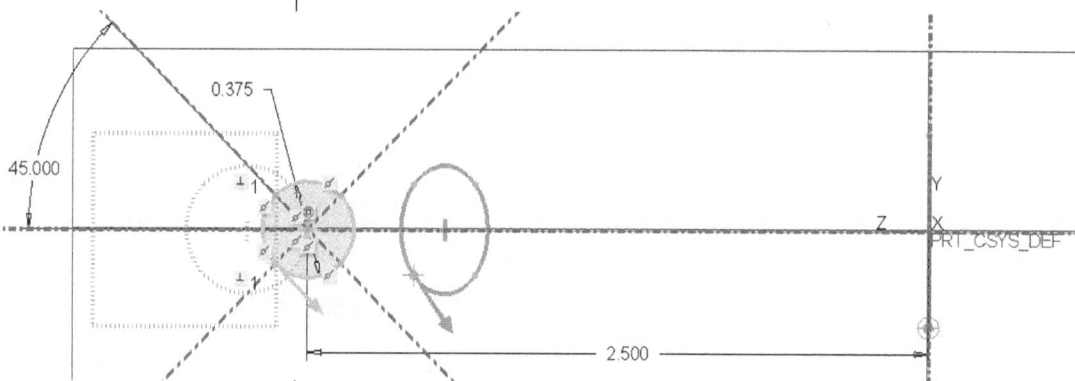 (Sketch View).

18. Create the sketch shown in Figure 7–35. Remember to divide the circle at the intersections with the centerline.

Figure 7–35

19. If the diameter dimension displays as **0.38**, you can select it, right-click and select disable the **Round Display Value** option.

20. Click ✓ (OK) to complete the sketch.

21. Click ✓ (OK).

22. Toggle off the display of datum features, and the model displays as shown in Figure 7–36.

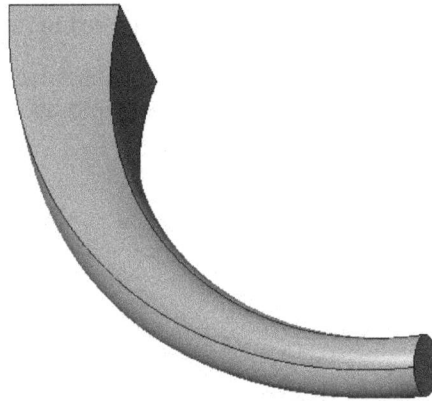

Figure 7–36

23. In the Model Tree, select the rotational blend and click ⭧ (Mirror) in the mini toolbar.

24. Select datum **RIGHT** in the Model Tree and click ✓ (OK).

25. The model displays as shown in Figure 7–37. Note the discontinuity between the mirrored sections.

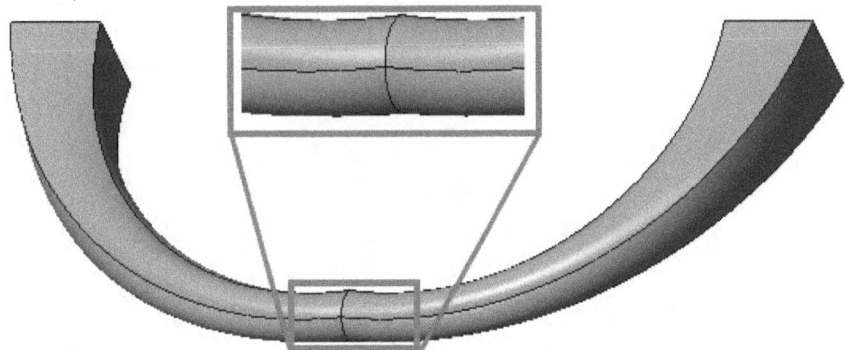

Figure 7–37

26. Delete the mirror feature.

Task 3 - Add a section to the handle.

Design Considerations

To further refine the geometry, an additional section will be added.

1. In the Model Tree, select the rotational blend and click 🖱 (Edit Definition) in the mini toolbar.

2. Select the **Sections** tab.

3. Click **Insert** to add a section.

4. In the *Offset from* drop-down list, select **Section 2**, and edit the angle to **30**, as shown in Figure 7–38.

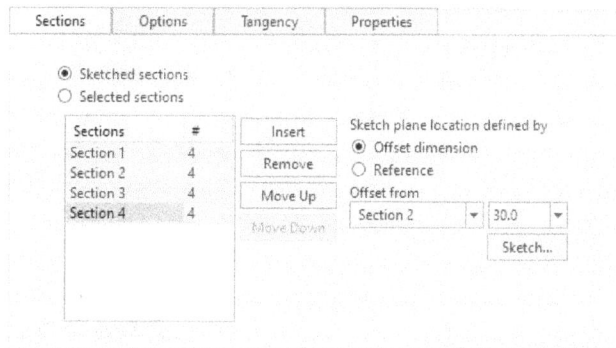

Figure 7–38

5. Click **Sketch**.

6. Click 📐 (Sketch View).

7. Create the sketch shown in Figure 7–39. Remember to divide the circle.

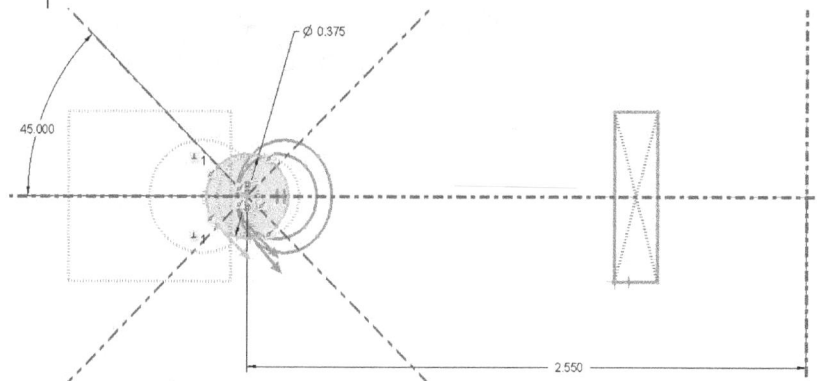

Figure 7–39

8. Click ✓ (OK) to complete the sketch.

9. Select the Sections panel.

10. Select Section 4, and click **Move Up** once.

11. Click ✓ (OK). The model displays as shown in Figure 7–40.

The geometry cannot be created because the sections are out of order.

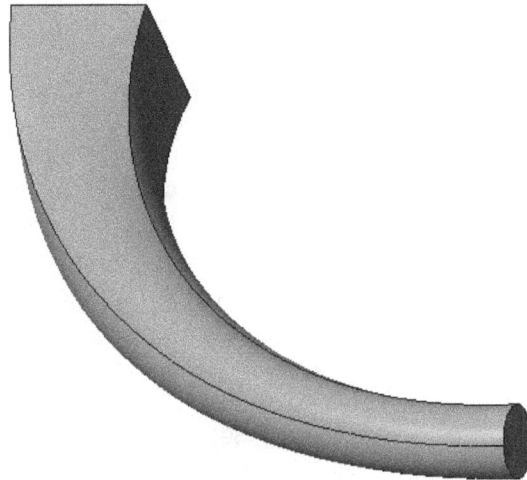

Figure 7–40

12. Select the blend and click ⫛ (Mirror).

13. Select datum **RIGHT** in the Model Tree and click ✓ (OK).

14. The model displays as shown in Figure 7–41. Note the discontinuity between the mirrored sections is less pronounced.

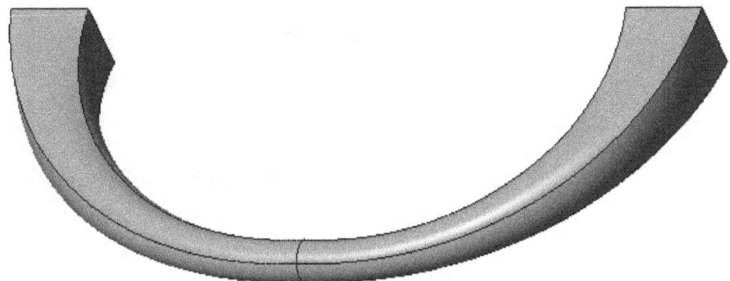

Figure 7–41

Task 4 - Control the tangency at the ends of the handle.

1. In the Model Tree, select the rotational blend and click 🥄 (Edit Definition) in the mini toolbar.

2. Select the Tangency control point, right-click and select **Normal**, as shown in Figure 7–42.

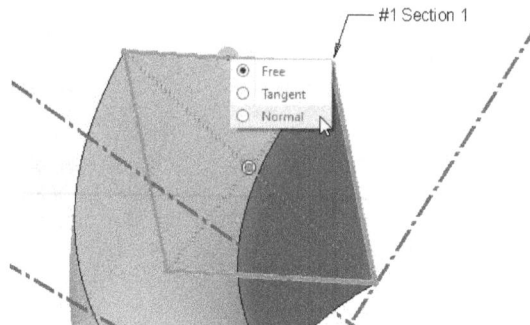

Figure 7–42

3. Set the tangency control at the other end to **Normal**.

4. Click ✔ (OK). The model displays as shown in Figure 7–43.

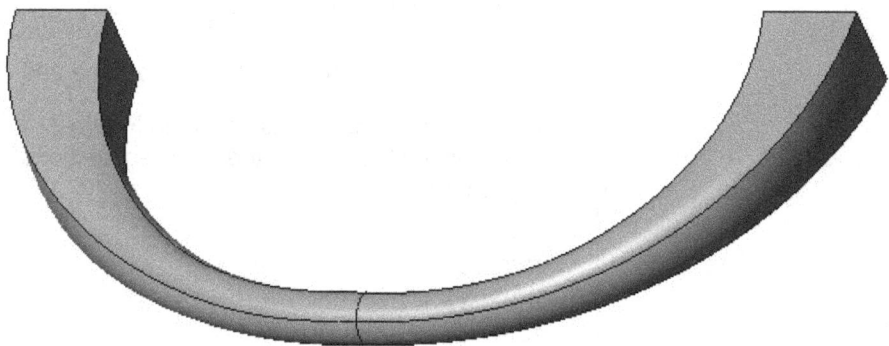

Figure 7–43

5. Save the part and erase it from memory.

Practice 7b

Rotational Blend with Selected Sections

Practice Objective

- Create a Rotational Blend by selecting multiple sections.

In this practice, you will create a door handle using a Rotational Blend created by selecting existing sections.

Task 1 - Open a part containing sketched sections.

1. Set the working directory to the *Rotational_Blends_Selected* folder.

2. Open **door_handle.prt**.

3. Set the model display as follows:

    - ⁺⁄ₓ *(Datum Display Filters)*: All Off

    - ⤝ *(Spin Center)*: Off

    - ▢ *(Display Style)*: ▢ (Shading With Edges)

Task 2 - Create a Rotational Blend feature.

1. Click **Shapes>Rotational Blend** in the *Model* tab.

2. In the *Rotational Blend* dashboard, click ∿ (Selected Sections).

3. Select the rectangular section shown in Figure 7–44.

Note the location of the start point.

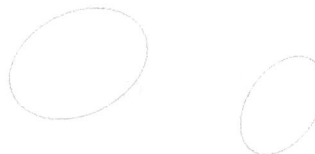

Figure 7–44

4. Right-click and select **Insert**.

5. Select the circular section shown in Figure 7–45.

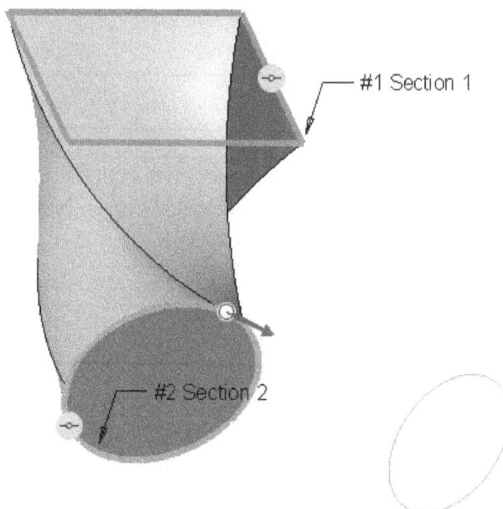

Figure 7–45

6. Select the start point and drag it along the sketched curve to the position shown in Figure 7–46, so that it matches with the first section.

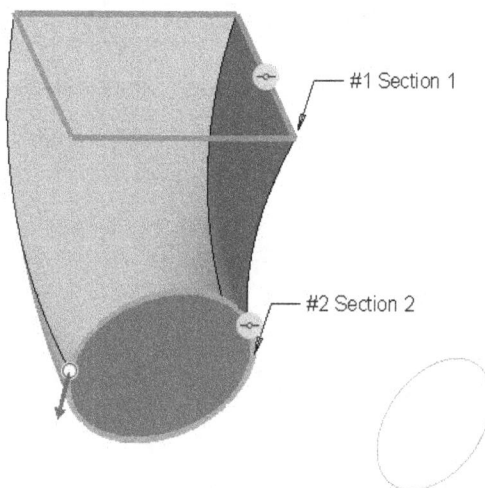

Figure 7–46

7. Right-click and select **Insert**.

8. Select the small circular section shown in Figure 7–47.

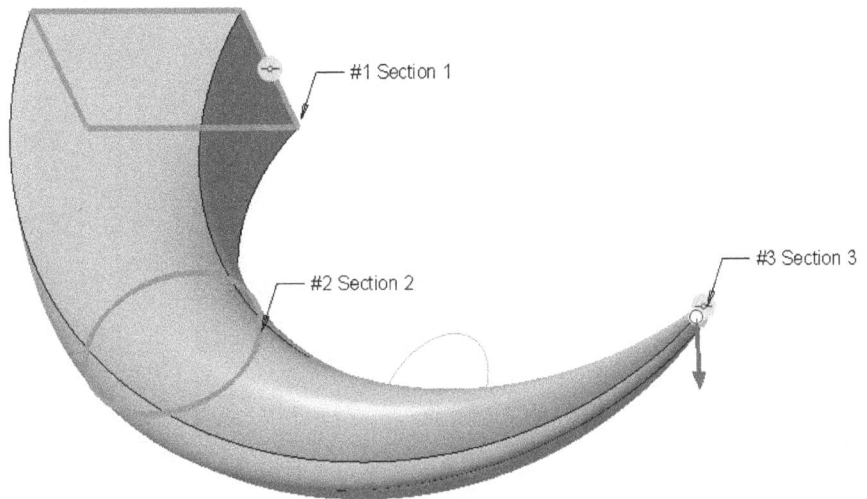

#1 Section 1

#3 Section 3

#2 Section 2

Figure 7–47

9. Click ✔ (OK).

Task 3 - Edit the definition of the sweep to insert a section.

1. Select the blend and click 🖌 (Edit Definition) in the mini toolbar.

2. In the dashboard, click the Sections panel as shown in Figure 7–48.

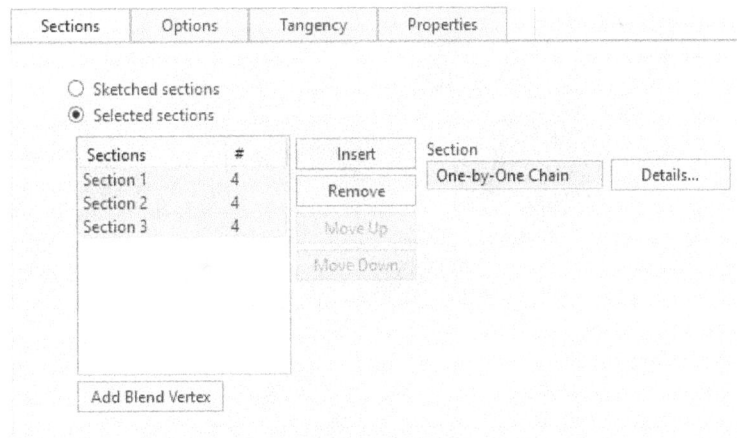

Sections	Options	Tangency	Properties

○ Sketched sections
◉ Selected sections

Sections	#		Section	
Section 1	4	Insert	One-by-One Chain	Details...
Section 2	4	Remove		
Section 3	4	Move Up		
		Move Down		

Add Blend Vertex

Figure 7–48

3. Click **Insert** in the Sections panel.

4. Select the curve shown in Figure 7–49.

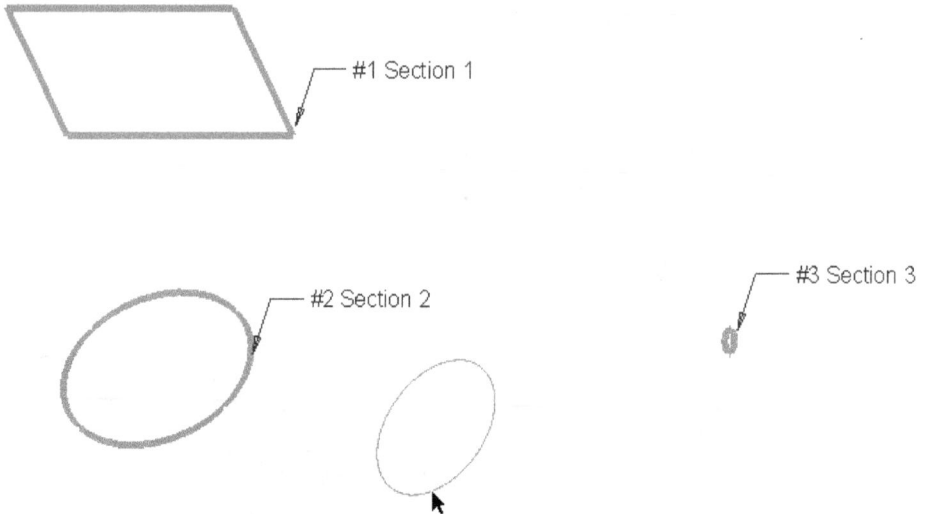

Figure 7–49

5. Click **Move Up** and the blend previews as shown in Figure 7–50.

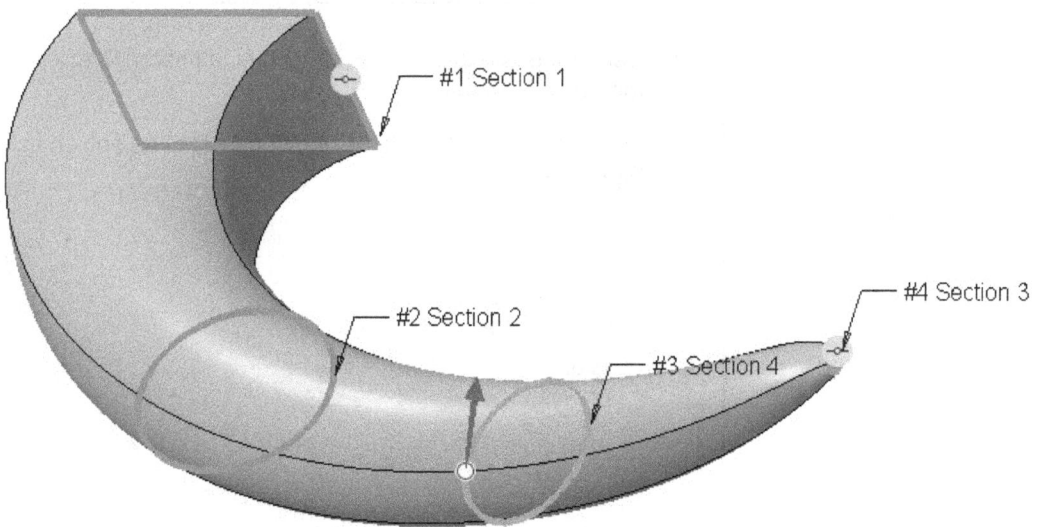

Figure 7–50

Task 4 - Change the boundary influence of the start section

1. Select the boundary influence marker, right-click and select **Normal**, as shown in Figure 7–51.

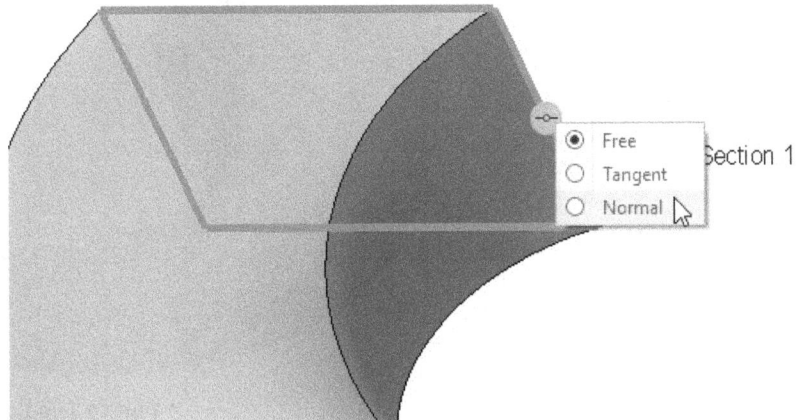

Figure 7–51

2. The model updates as shown in Figure 7–52.

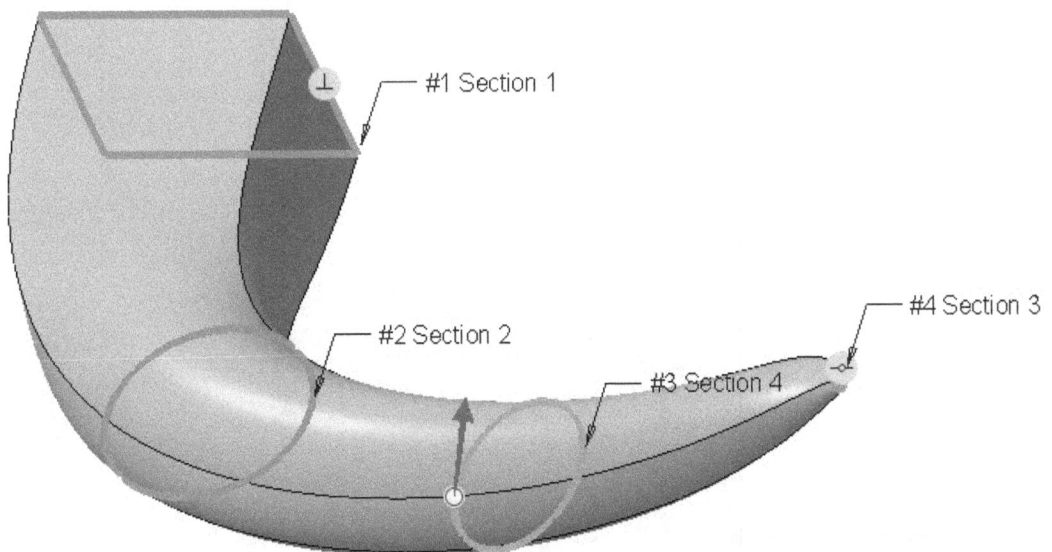

Figure 7–52

3. Click ✓ (OK).

4. Hide all of the datum curves, and the completed model displays as shown in Figure 7–53.

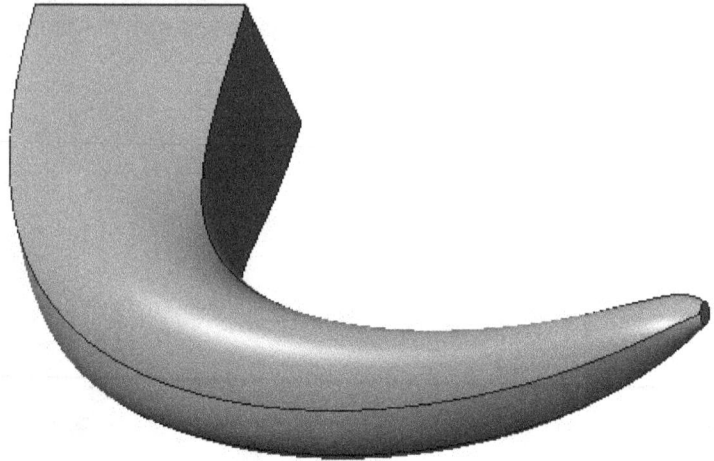

Figure 7–53

5. Save the part and erase it from memory.

Practice 7c | Swept Blend

Practice Objectives

- Create a Swept Blend feature by selecting a trajectory to define the path and sketching two sections.
- Define the tangency option as Normal to further control the shape of the swept blend feature.

In this practice, you will create a swept blend feature by selecting a trajectory and two sections. You will also set tangency conditions for the swept blend. The finished model displays as shown in Figure 7–54.

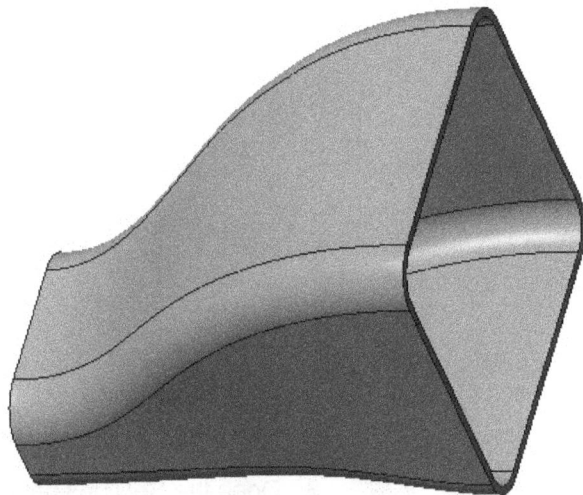

Figure 7–54

Task 1 - Open a part file.

1. Set the working directory to the *Swept_Blend* folder.

2. Open **transition_tube.prt**.

3. Set the model display as follows:

   - ⅍ *(Datum Display Filters)*: All Off

   - ⅌ *(Spin Center)*: Off

   - ◻ *(Display Style)*: ◻ (Shading With Edges)

Task 2 - Create a swept blend.

1. Click ✐ (Swept Blend) in the Shapes group. The *Swept Blend* dashboard becomes active.

2. Select the curve shown in Figure 7–55.

This is the trajectory for the swept blend.

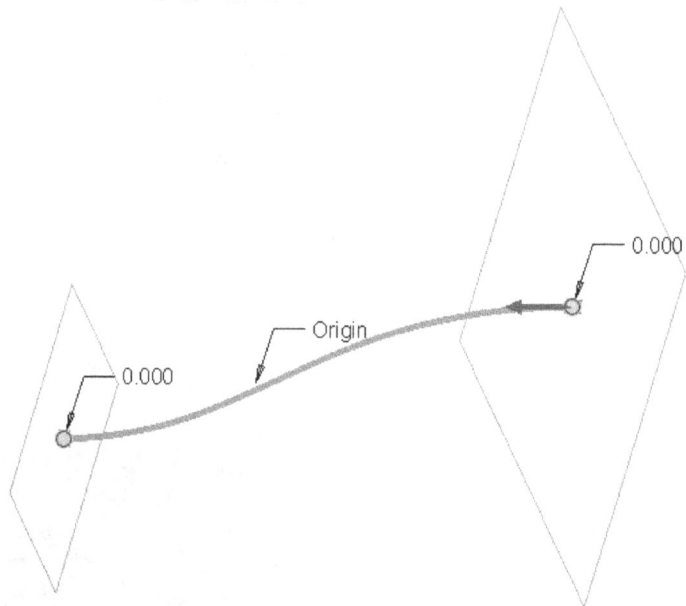

Figure 7–55

3. Open the Sections panel in the *Swept Blend* dashboard.

4. Select the **Selected Sections** option as shown in Figure 7–56.

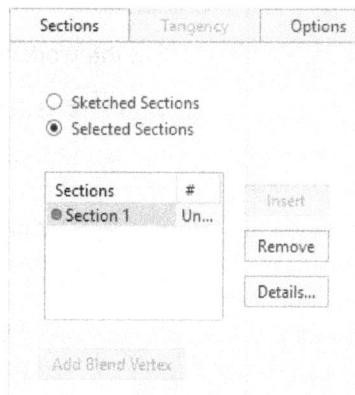

Figure 7–56

5. Select the large square section.

6. Right-click and select **Insert Section** and select the second section. The part displays as shown in Figure 7–57.

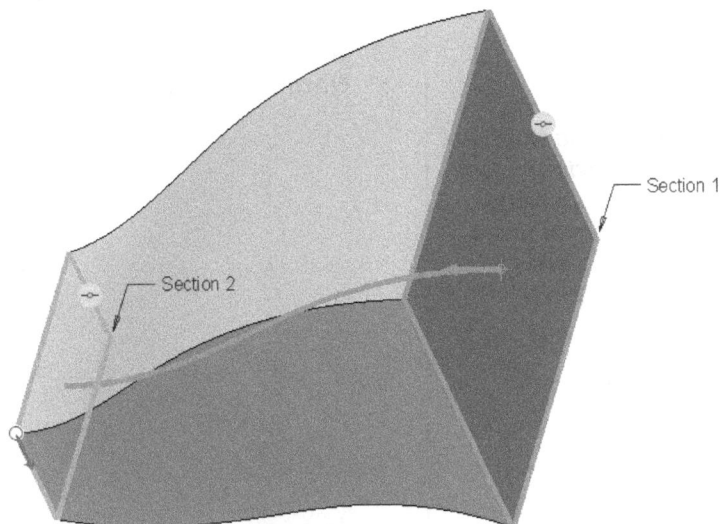

Section 1

Section 2

Figure 7–57

7. Complete the swept blend. The part displays as shown in Figure 7–58.

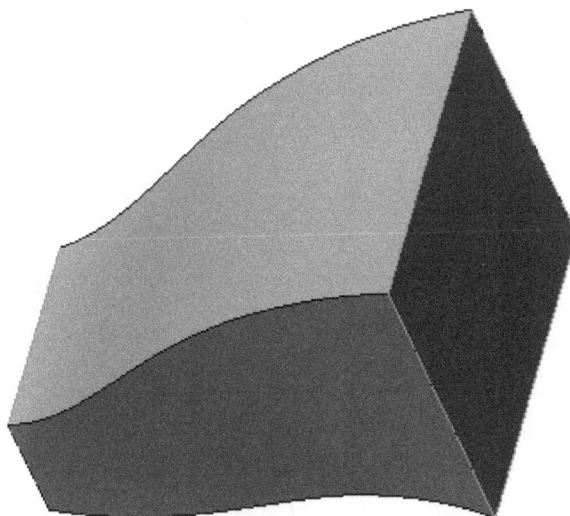

Figure 7–58

Task 3 - Apply tangency conditions to the swept blend.

1. Set the orientation to the saved orientation **FRONT**.

2. Edit the definition of the **Swept Blend 1** feature.

3. Right-click each end-point and set the *Boundary Control* to **Normal**, as shown in Figure 7–59.

By selecting the Normal tangency condition, you make the swept blend geometry normal to the sketch plane used to create the sections.

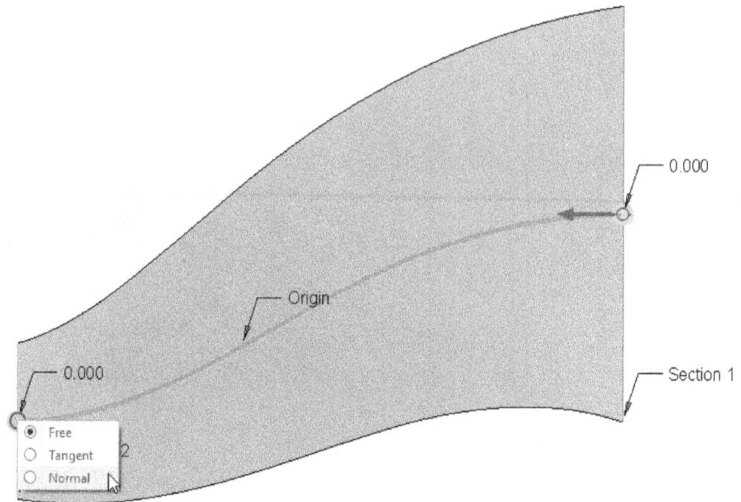

Figure 7–59

The swept blend geometry updates, as shown in Figure 7–60.

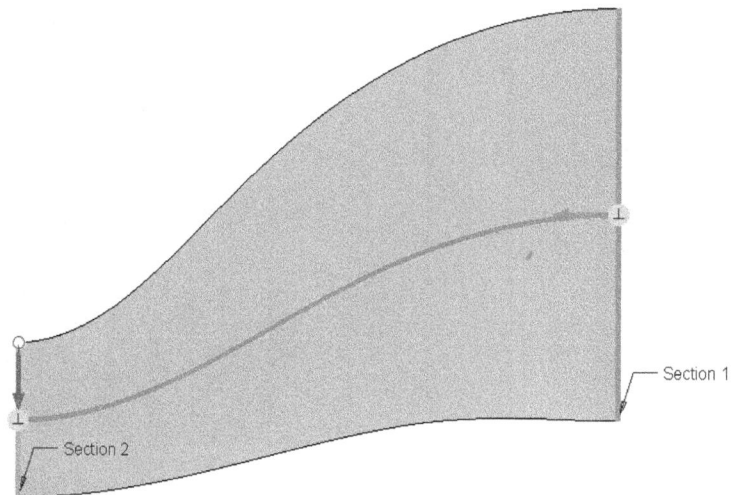

Figure 7–60

4. Click ✓ (OK).

5. Hide **Sketch 1**, **Sketch 2**, and **Sketch 3**.

Task 4 - Complete the part.

In this task, you will complete the part by adding rounds and then shelling the part.

1. Create a round with a *Radius* of **0.25** on the four edges shown in Figure 7–61.

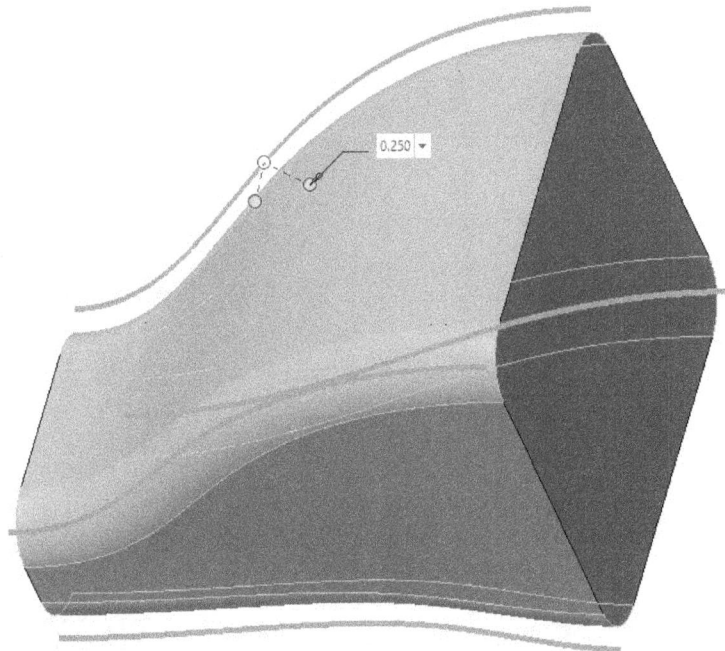

Figure 7–61

2. Shell the part to a *Thickness* of **0.063** and remove the two planar surfaces, as shown in Figure 7–62.

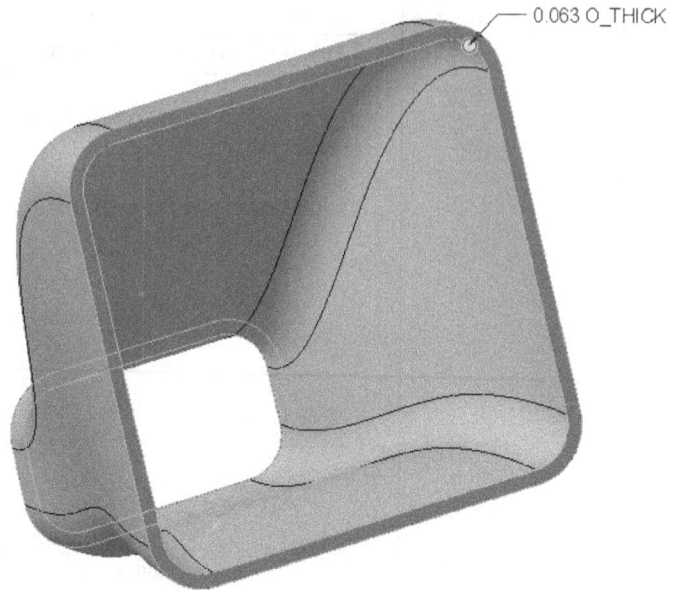

Remember to press <Ctrl> when selecting the surfaces to remove.

0.063 O_THICK

Figure 7–62

The completed part displays as shown in Figure 7–63.

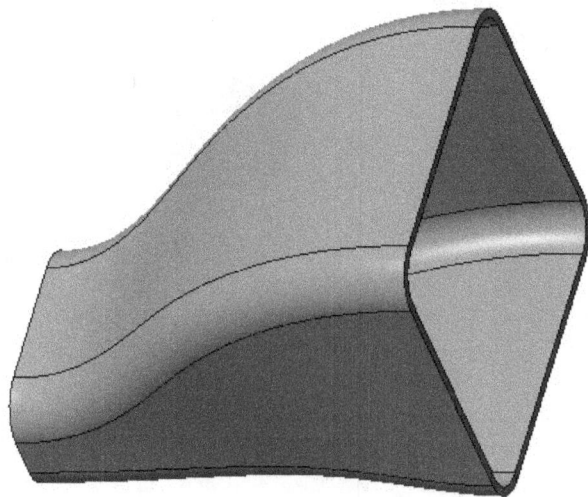

Figure 7–63

3. Save the part and erase it from memory.

Practice 7d | Coat Hook

Practice Objectives

- Create a sketch and create datum points to define the section locations for the swept blend feature.
- Select the sketch for the trajectory and create a section at each datum point location.
- Create a swept blend cut and additional geometry to complete the part.

In this practice, you will create a coat hook part. The coat hook is designed with a hook on both ends so that it can be hung in either direction. To easily obtain the base geometry for this model, you will be using a Swept Blend. Additional features including a cut and some rounds will be added to complete the part so that it displays as shown in Figure 7–64.

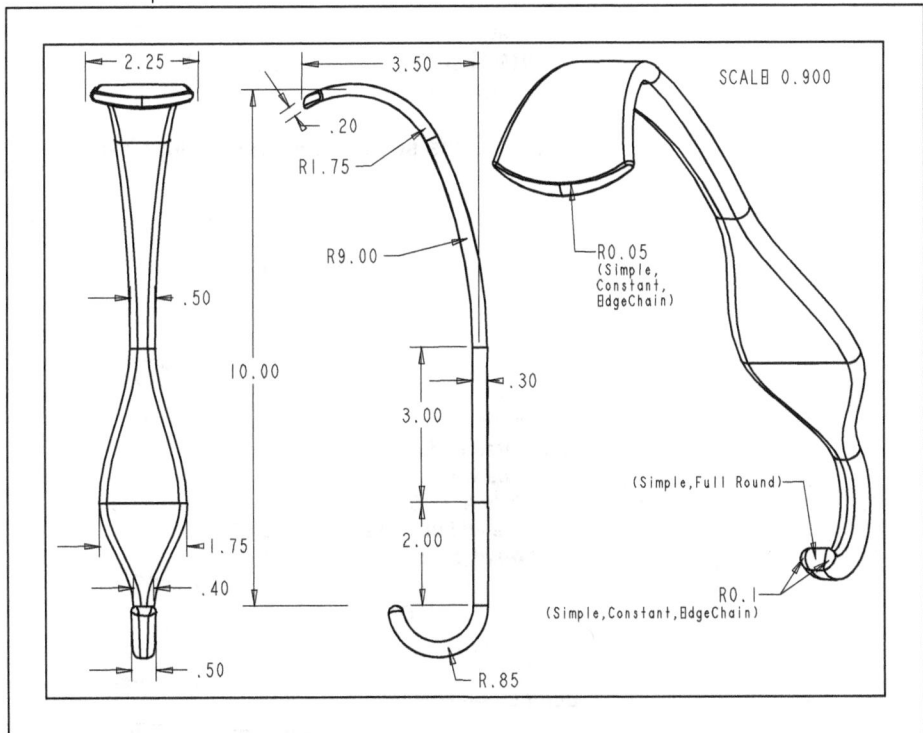

Figure 7–64

Task 1 - Create a new part.

1. Set the working directory to the Coat_Hook folder.

2. Create a new part called **coat_hook** using the default template.

3. Set the model display as follows:

   - *(Datum Display Filters)*: (Point Display), (Plane Display) Only

   - *(Spin Center)*: Off

   - *(Display Style)*: (Shading With Edges)

Task 2 - Create a trajectory for a Swept Blend.

Design Considerations

In this task, you will create a sketch, which is used later as a trajectory for a Swept Blend. The trajectory must be divided to provide locations for placing sections of the Swept Blend.

1. Click (Sketch) to create a sketch. Select datum plane **RIGHT** as the sketching plane and datum plane **TOP** as the Top reference.

2. Create the section shown in Figure 7–65.

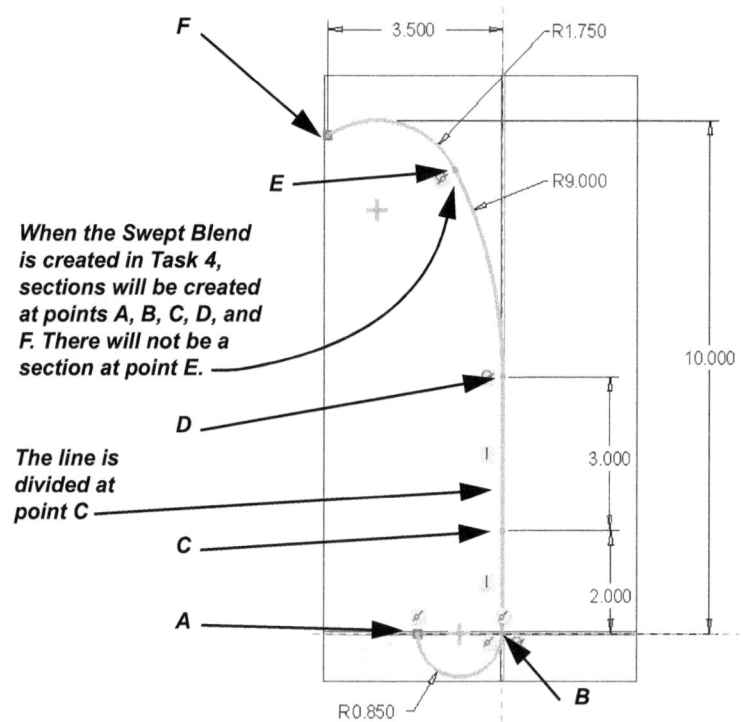

When the Swept Blend is created in Task 4, sections will be created at points A, B, C, D, and F. There will not be a section at point E.

The line is divided at point C

Figure 7–65

3. Divide the vertical line into two segments at point **C**. A section is required at Point **C**, therefore it must be the start/end of an entity.

4. Complete the sketch.

Task 3 - Create datum points.

In this task, you will create datum points, which are used later when selecting locations for the Swept Blend sections.

1. Create five separate datum points **A**, **B**, **C**, **D**, and **F**, as shown in Figure 7–65. The model displays as shown in Figure 7–66. The datum points are in the same locations as the end points of each of the sketched entities created in the Task 2.

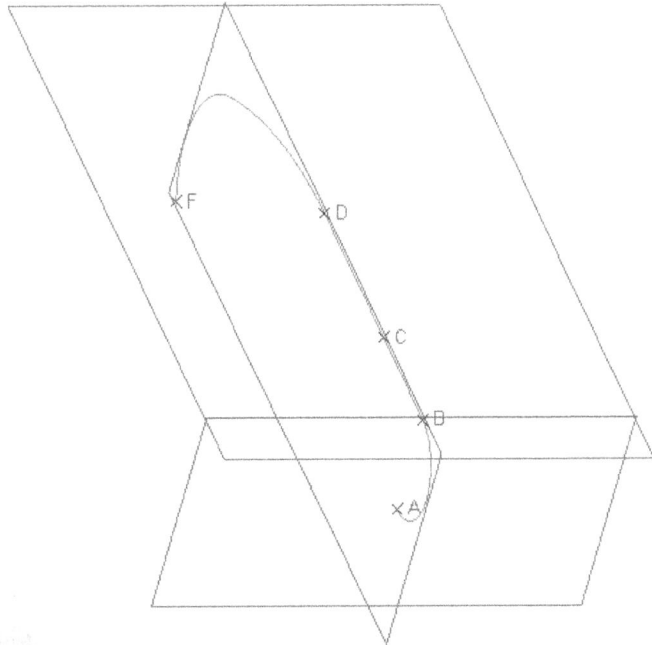

Figure 7–66

2. Change the name of each point to the appropriate letter in the Datum Point dialog box.

Task 4 - Create a Swept Blend protrusion.

Design Considerations

In this task, you will create the coat hook using a Swept Blend protrusion. All of the sections are created on the trajectory that was created in the previous tasks. The geometry for a Swept Blend is created by blending defined sections along the trajectory. Each section is blended based on its start point. Therefore, it is important that the start points in each section are consistent with the way you want the sections to blend together. In this design, you will sketch a total of five sections to create the geometry.

1. Click ✎ (Swept Blend) in the *Model* tab.

2. Select the sketch created in the Task 2 as the trajectory for the Swept Blend. The model displays as shown in Figure 7–67.

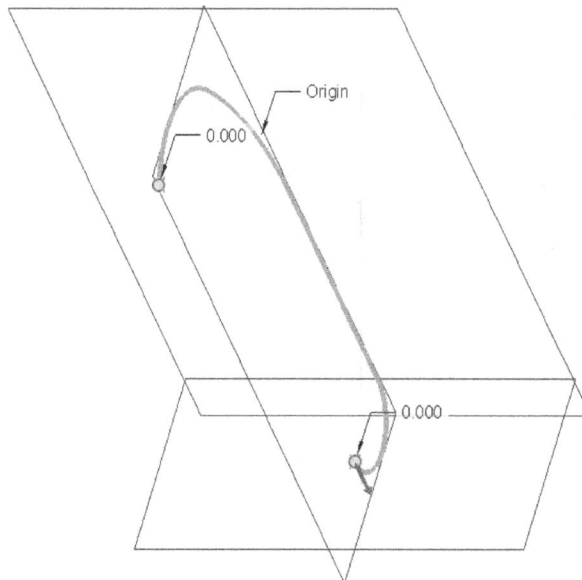

Figure 7–67

By default, all of the sections are placed normal to the trajectory, so you do not have to change the default settings of the Section plane control in the References panel.

3. To start sketching a section, select the Sections panel, click Point **A**, and select ✎ (Sketch) in the mini toolbar.

4. Toggle off the display of datum planes.

Tip: Use the racetrack profile in the Sketcher Palette dialog box or create a centered rectangle and add arcs.

*To relocate the start point, right-click on the required vertex and select **Start Point**.*

5. Sketch the first section at point **A** as shown in Figure 7–68. An easy way to recognize the point on the trajectory for the current section is by locating the coordinate system on the sketch. The coordinate system is located on the trajectory. Note the start point. The point location is important, but the direction is not.

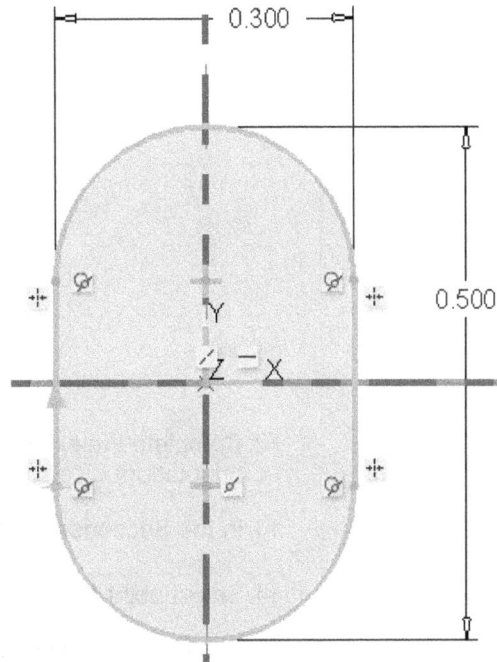

Figure 7–68

You can select all of the section entities and press <Ctrl>+<C> to copy, followed by <Ctrl>+<V> to paste this section into Sketcher for points B, C, D, and F.

6. Complete the sketch and reorient the model to the default orientation.

7. Select **Insert** in the Sections panel.

8. Select the *View* tab and click (Point Tag Display).

9. Select the *Swept Blend* tab.

10. Select point **B** and select (Sketch) in the mini toolbar.

11. Sketch the second section at point B as shown in Figure 7–69. Verify that the start point matches that of the first section.

*To relocate the start point, select the required vertex, right-click and select **Start Point**.*

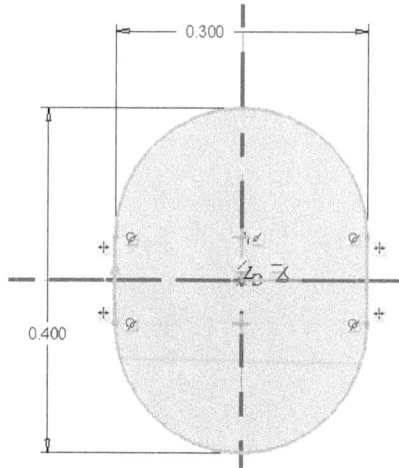

Figure 7–69

12. Complete the sketch and reorient the model to the default orientation.

13. In the Sections panel, click **Insert**.

14. Select point **C** and select ✎ (Sketch) in the mini toolbar.

15. Sketch the third section as shown in Figure 7–70.

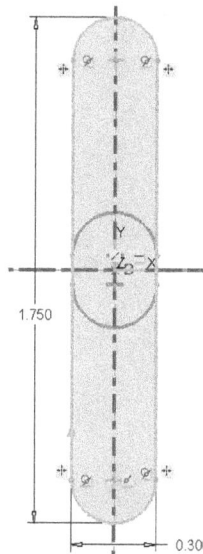

Figure 7–70

16. Complete the sketch and reorient the model to the default orientation.

17. In the Sections panel, click **Insert**.

18. Select point **D** and select ✏ (Sketch) in the mini toolbar.

19. Sketch the fourth section as shown in Figure 7–71.

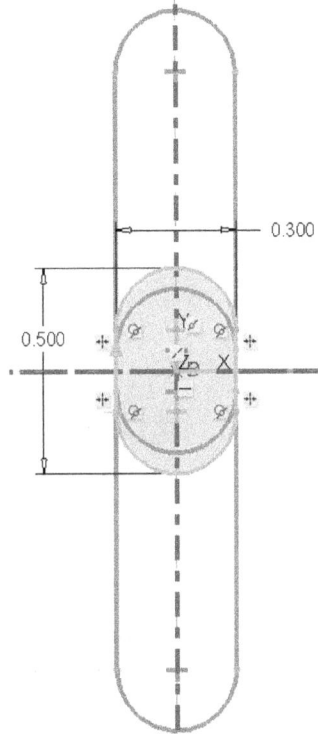

Figure 7–71

20. Complete the sketch and reorient the model to the default orientation.

21. In the Sections panel, click **Insert**.

22. Select point **F** and select ✏ (Sketch) in the mini toolbar. Ensure that you select the point at the end of the curve.

23. Sketch the fifth section as shown in Figure 7–72.

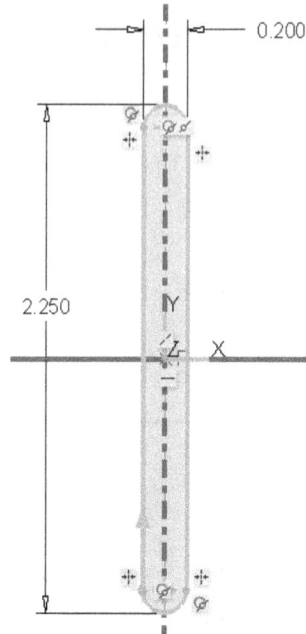

Figure 7–72

24. Complete the sketch and reorient the model to the default orientation.

25. Toggle off the display of datum points.

26. Complete the feature. The completed protrusion displays as shown in Figure 7–73. If any of the sections looks twisted, it is because the start points for that section were not correctly set. To change them, right-click on the section name and select **Sketch**. Change the start point and complete the sketch and the feature.

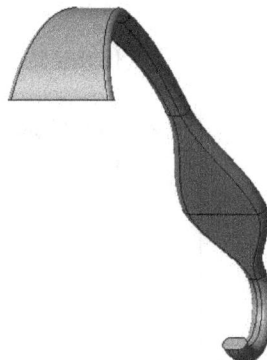

Figure 7–73

Task 5 - Create a trajectory for the Swept Blend cut.

Design Considerations

In this task, you will create a sketch, which is used later as a trajectory for a Swept Blend cut. The trajectory must be divided to provide locations for placing sections of the Swept Blend cut.

1. Toggle off the display of datum points.

2. Click ▧ (Sketch) to create a sketch.

3. Create a datum plane on the fly through the edge shown in Figure 7–74 and normal to the top, thin surface. This datum plane will be used as sketching plane for the new sketch.

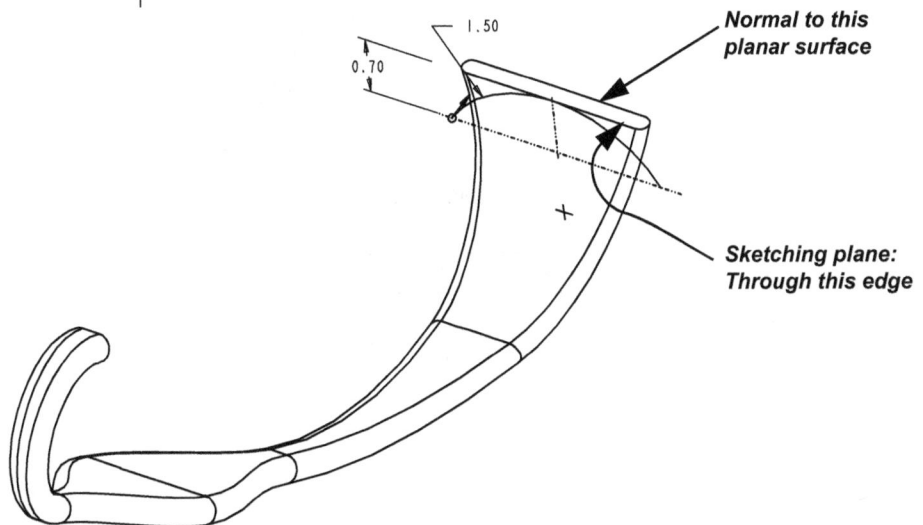

Figure 7–74

4. Select datum plane **RIGHT** as the right orientation reference and activate the *Sketch* tab.

5. Sketch the Origin trajectory as an arc, tangent to the top edge.

6. Sketch a centerline through the end points of the arc.

7. Divide the arc into two segments to create an additional vertex lying on datum plane **RIGHT**. The sketch is shown in Figure 7–75.

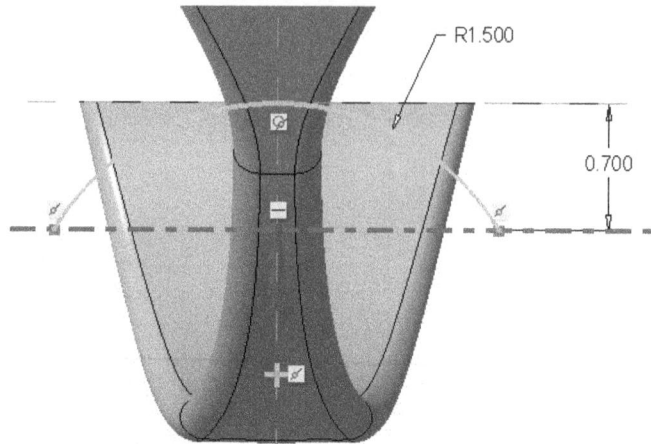

Figure 7–75

8. Complete the sketch.

Task 6 - Create an extruded cut.

1. Create the extruded cut, as shown in Figure 7–76.

Depth

Side 1   ⟂ To Next   ▼   [   ]

Side 2   ⟂ To Next   ▼   [   ]

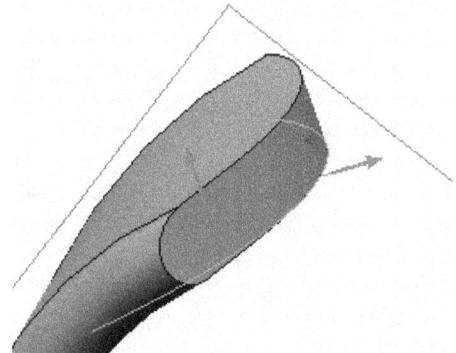

Figure 7–76

2. Complete the feature and reorient the model to the default orientation. The part displays as shown in Figure 7–77.

Figure 7–77

Task 7 - Create simple round edges.

In the remaining three tasks, you will create rounds to complete the part.

To select multiple edges, press and hold <Ctrl> while selecting the edges.

1. Select the chain of edges created by the extruded cut feature and click ⬙ (Round) in the mini toolbar. Set the *Radius* in the *Round* tab to **0.05**.

2. Click ✔ (OK) to complete the round feature. The completed model displays as shown in Figure 7–78.

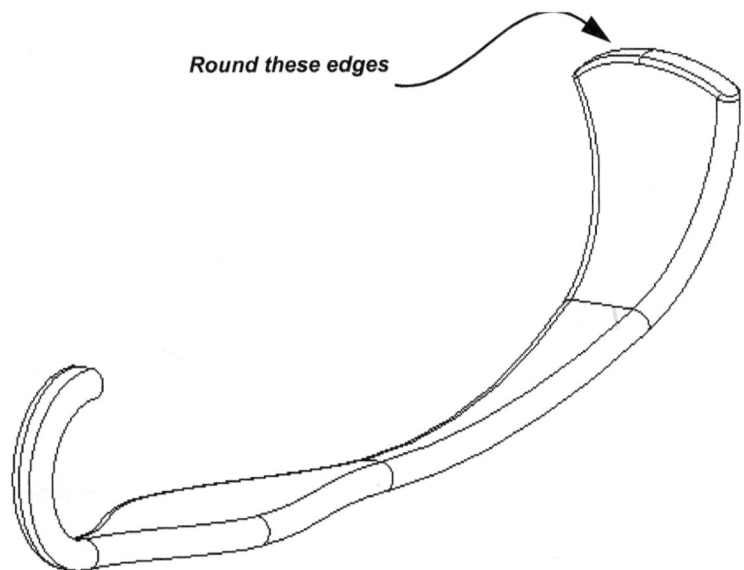

Round these edges

Figure 7–78

Task 8 - Create a full round.

1. While holding <Ctrl>, select the two straight edges on the thin end of the base feature, as shown in Figure 7–79.

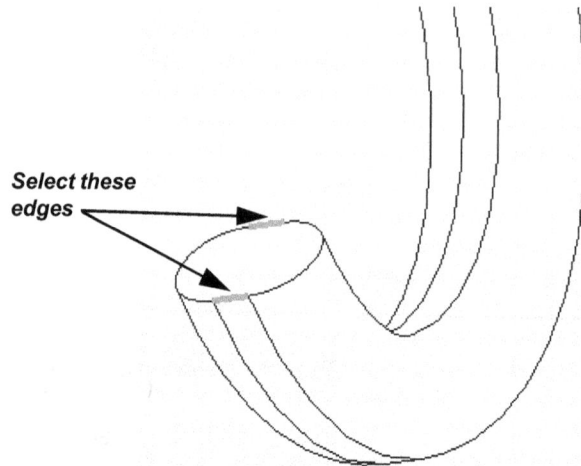

Select these edges

Figure 7–79

2. Click (Round) in the mini toolbar.

3. Click on the screen and select (Full Round) in the mini toolbar.

4. Click (OK) to complete the round feature. The model displays as shown in Figure 7–80.

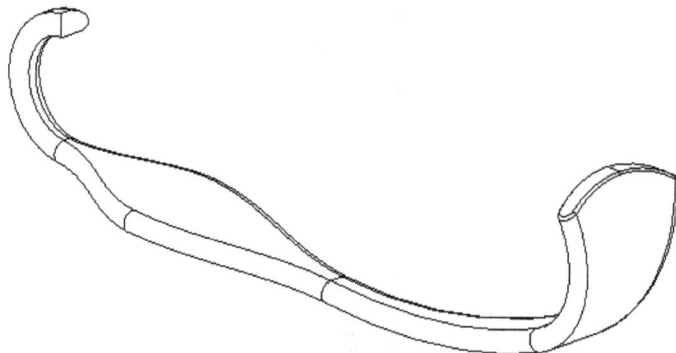

Figure 7–80

5. While holding <Ctrl>, select the edges generated by the full round on the thin end of the base feature to be rounded, as shown in Figure 7–81.

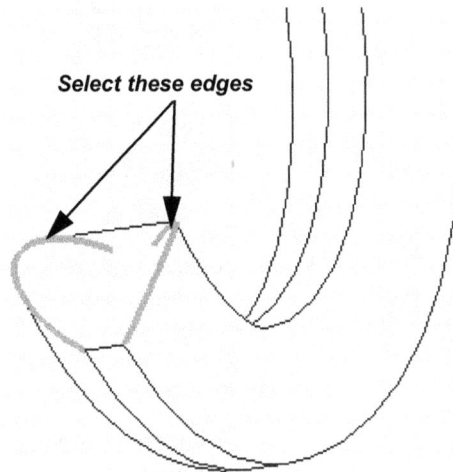

Select these edges

Figure 7–81

6. Click ⬙ (Round) from the mini toolbar.

7. Once the round displays, double-click on the *Radius* value in the Graphics window and set it to **0.05**.

You can also click the middle mouse button to accept the value and complete the feature.

8. Complete the feature. The completed part is shown in Figure 7–82.

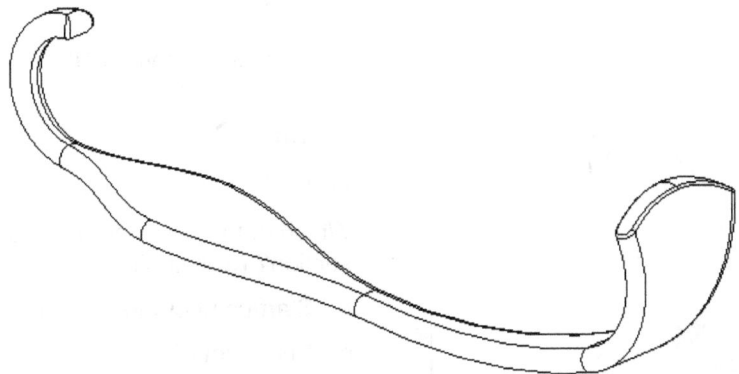

Figure 7–82

9. Save the part and erase it from memory.

Chapter Review Questions

1. Which of the following options are available in the Sections panel for a Rotational blend? (Select all that apply.)

    a. Reorder

    b. Insert

    c. Remove

    d. Rename

2. A sketched section of a rotational blend requires an axis of revolution for the rotational direction.

    a. True

    b. False

3. Rotational Blends rotate each section about an axis. What is the maximum rotational angle?

    a. 120°

    b. 90°

    c. 180°

    d. There is no maximum.

4. The **Tangency** option for Rotational blends must be defined.

    a. True

    b. False

5. Sections for a Rotational blend do not require the same number of entities.

    a. True

    b. False

6. Which of the following entities can be selected to specify a section? (Select all that apply.)

    a. Start point of the trajectory.

    b. End point of the trajectory.

    c. Inner point along the trajectory.

    d. Datum point lying on the trajectory.

7. A Swept Blend feature can only contain one trajectory.

    a. True

    b. False

8. Which statement is false for a Swept Bend?

   a. A minimum of two sections are required.

   b. Sections cannot be sketched at sharp points on the Origin trajectory.

   c. The same number of vertices are required in each section.

   d. Tangency options must be specified.

9. Which option enables you to control the shape of the Swept Blend between sections using a perimeter of the sections?

   a. No bend control.

   b. Set perimeter control.

   c. Set cross-section area control.

Designing with Rounds

Round features are known as pick-and-place features. You select placement locations for the feature and the predefined geometry is placed without needing to sketch any geometry. A variety of references and placement methods can be used and result in different parent/child relationships and design intent.

Learning Objectives in This Chapter

- Learn the four types of rounds.
- Learn the different selection techniques for an Edge Chain round using the Chain dialog box.
- Create different types of rounds using either the Surface to Surface method, or the Edge to Surface method.
- Learn to use the Pieces panel to exclude pieces and remove ambiguity.
- Learn the placement methods of Edge to Surface, Surface to Surface, and Edge Chain rounds and how parent/child relationships are established.
- Learn the advantages of using the Intent Chain selection technique and how it affects the model.
- Create a round by selecting placement references and using the different selection techniques.
- Specify to create a round using a dimension or reference.
- Learn the difference between Rolling Ball and Normal to Spine.
- Learn the differences between a Conic, C2 Continuous, or D1 X D2 Conic cross-section.
- Learn how to create a transition and the types available.

8.1 Round Types and References

Simple round geometry and advanced round geometry use the same round set attributes during creation.

Round Types

The four round types available are described as follows:

Type	Description
Constant	Enables you to set the radius of the round at the same value along the selected references.
Variable	Enables you to specify radii at the end points and at intermediate vertices and datum points along the edges being rounded.
Full Round	Enables you to replace a whole surface with a rounded surface. The round radius is automatically calculated to replace the bounded surface while maintaining tangency to the adjacent surfaces.
Through Curve	Enables you to control the radius of the round using a selected edge or datum curve that falls on one of the adjacent surfaces to the edge that is being rounded.

Examples of the Constant, Variable, Full, and Through Curve rounds are shown in Figure 8–1 and Figure 8–2.

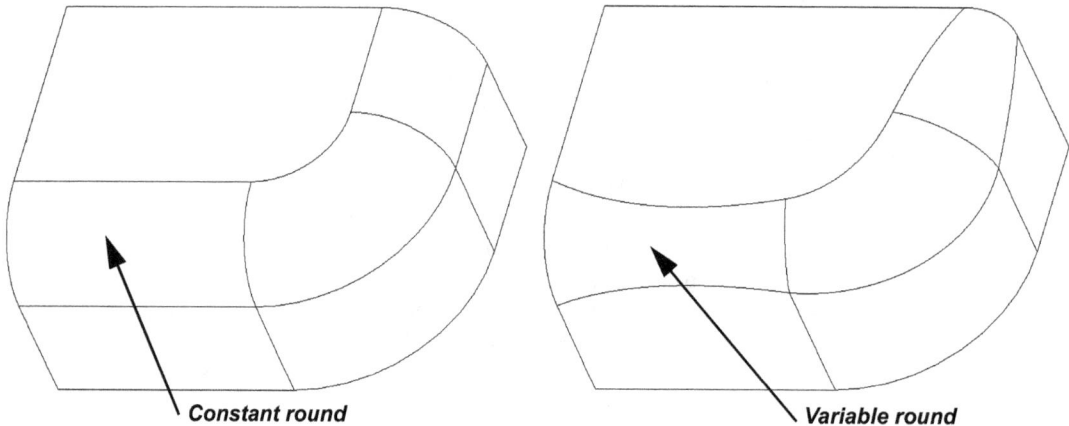

Constant round

Variable round

Figure 8–1

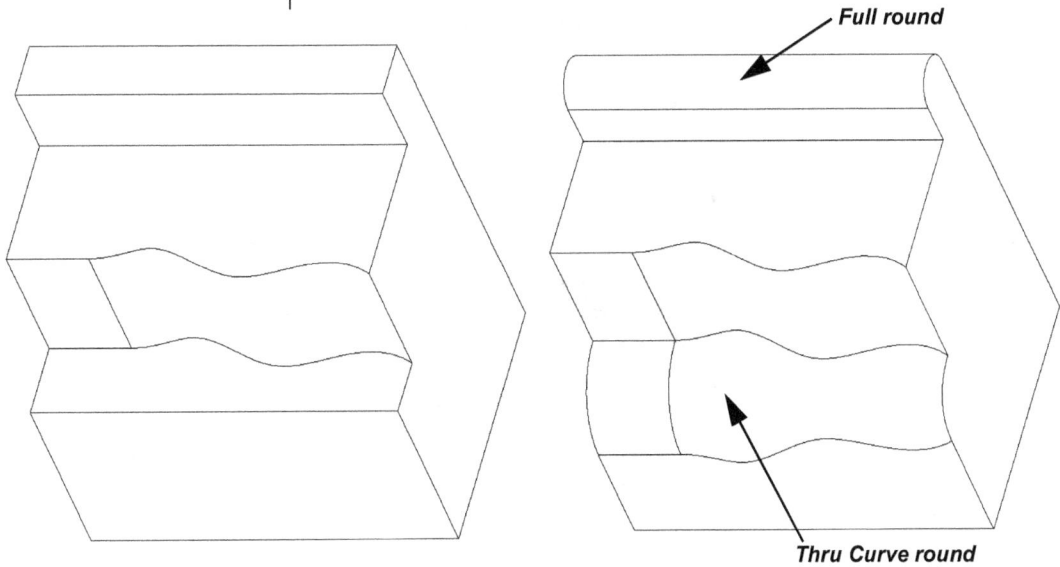

Full round

Thru Curve round

Figure 8–2

When two adjacent points have the same radius, the resulting round between the points has a constant radius.

To create the Variable round shown in Figure 8–1, additional locations were required to vary the radius. In addition to the end points, you can select vertices, datum points, or right-click and select **Add Radius**. The additional locations used to create the Variable round are shown in Figure 8–3. Each additional radius location displays its own radius value, which can be modified.

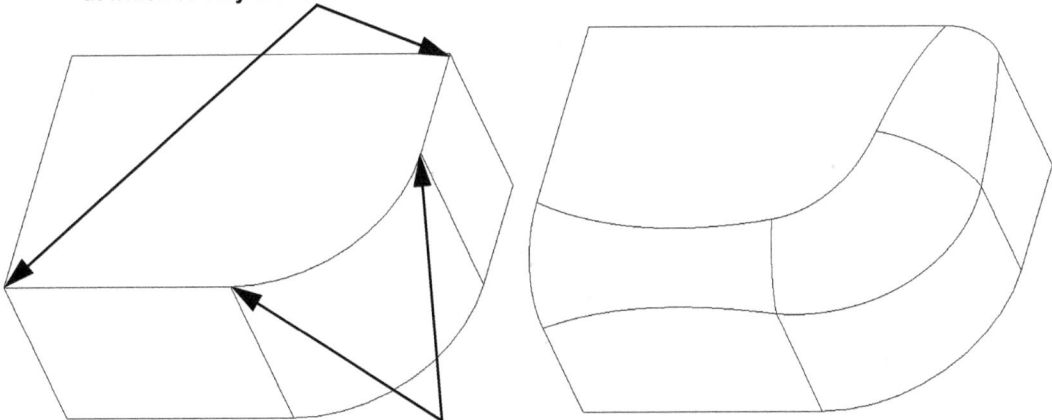

Creo Parametric default locations at which to vary the radius

Vertices selected at which to vary the radius

Figure 8–3

8.2 Placement Methods

Each placement method creates rounds with different behavior and parent/child relationships. The option that you use should be the one that maintains your design intent.

Edge Chain Round

An Edge Chain round builds a round tangent to two surfaces by removing the selected common edge. Constant, Variable, and Thru Curve rounds can be created when selecting an edge as a reference for a round.

References for a round display in the *References* field in the Sets panel in the *Round* dashboard, as shown in Figure 8–4.

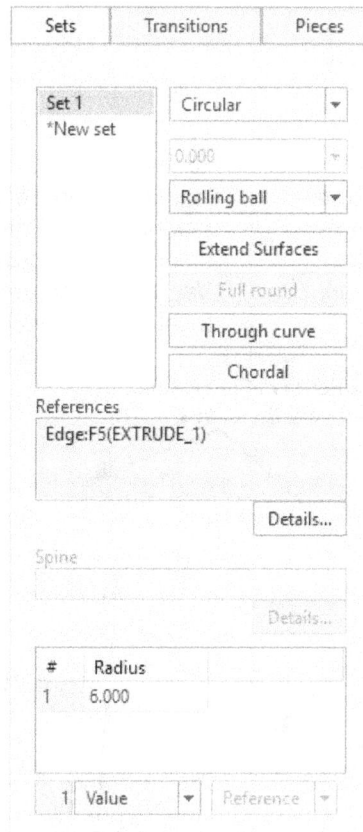

Figure 8–4

Click **Details** to open the Chain dialog box. This dialog box enables you to view, add, or remove references. Figure 8–5 shows the Chain dialog box after a single edge was selected.

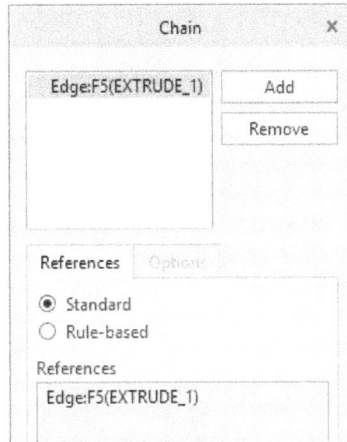

Figure 8–5

The **Standard** rule is the **Tangent** chain, in which all of the edges that are tangent to the selected edge are selected, as shown in Figure 8–6.

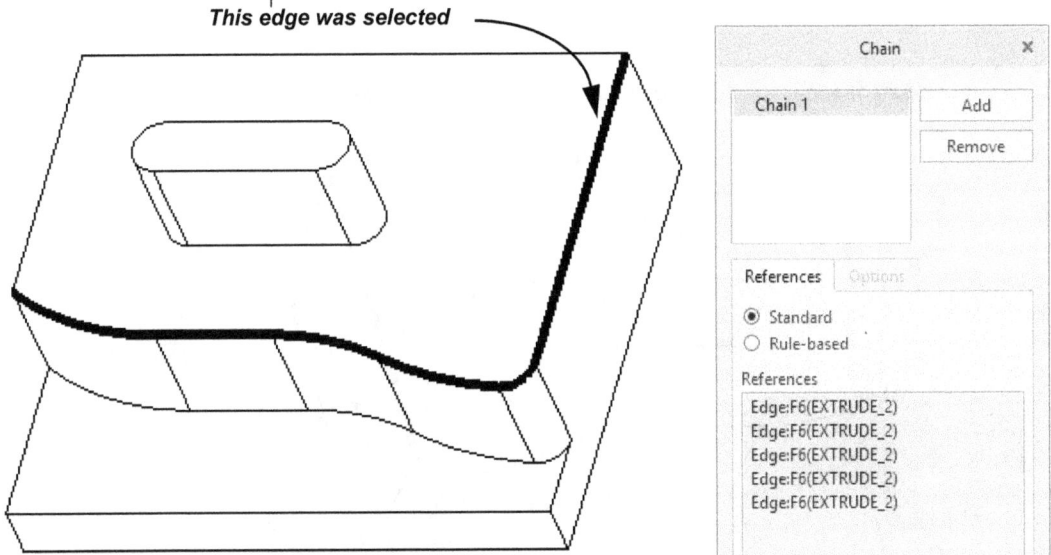

Figure 8–6

Select the **Rule-based** option to change the rule from *Tangent* to **Partial loop** or **Complete loop**, as shown in Figure 8–7.

Figure 8–7

The **Partial loop** rule keeps the initially selected edge as the *Anchor* and prompts for an *Extent Reference*. This permits *from-to* selection, as shown in Figure 8–8. Click **Flip** to flip the direction of the loop.

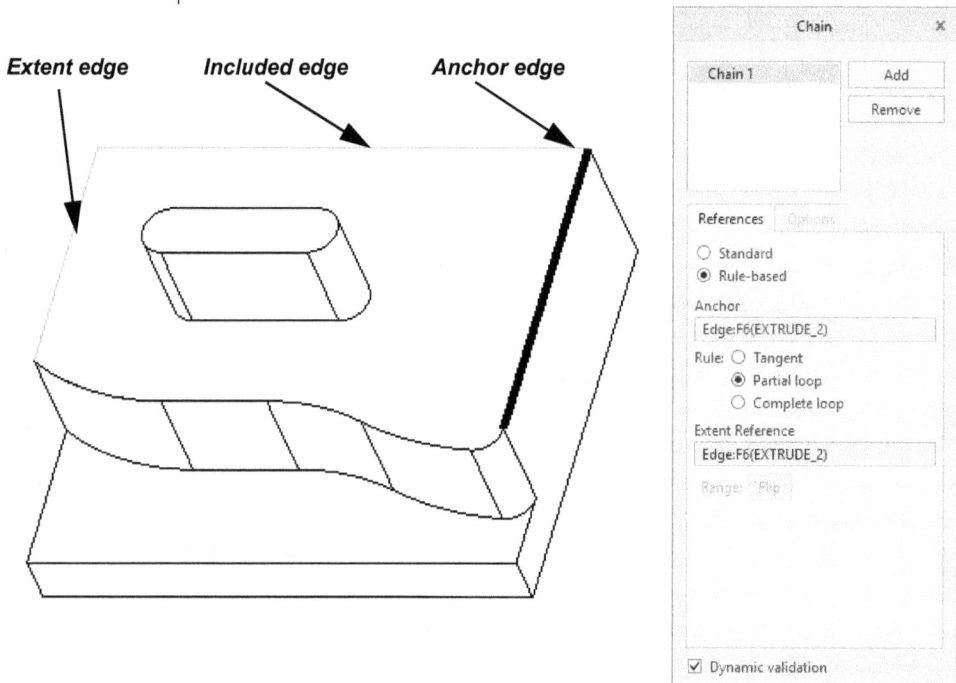

Figure 8–8

The **Complete loop** rule selects all of the edges that bound the surface of the selected edge, as shown in Figure 8–9.

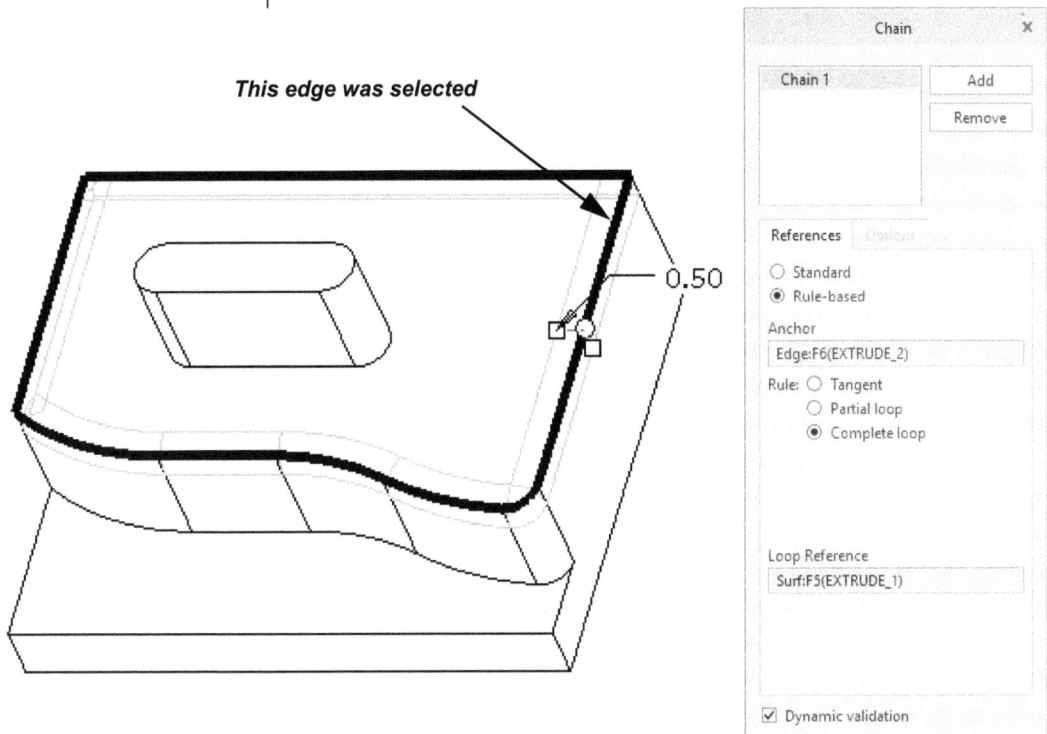

Figure 8–9

Surface to Surface Round

Two surfaces can be selected as references for round creation. This placement method results in a smooth transition between two surfaces that might or might not have a common edge.

A round that references surfaces can be created as a Constant, Variable, Full, or Thru Curve round. An example of a Constant round using two surfaces as references is shown in Figure 8–10.

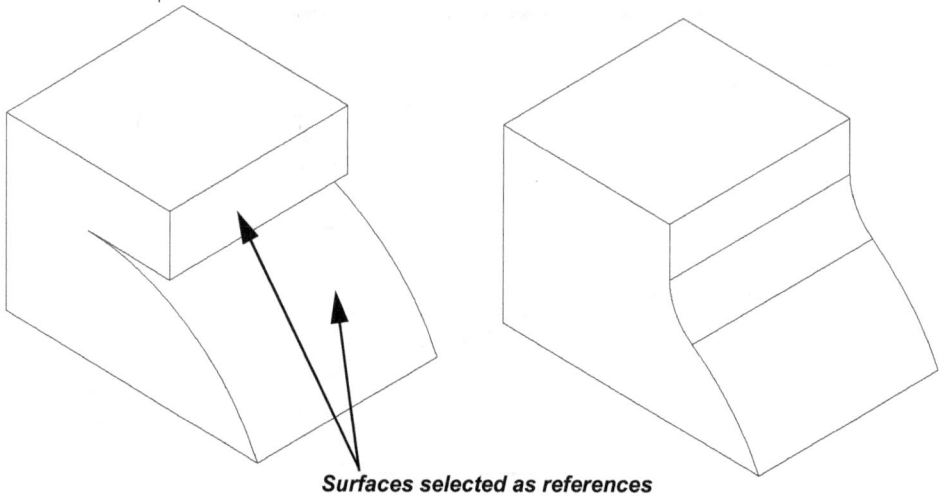

Surfaces selected as references

Figure 8–10

An example of a **Full** round using two surface references is shown in Figure 8–11. This round type requires a third surface selection to define the Driving surface.

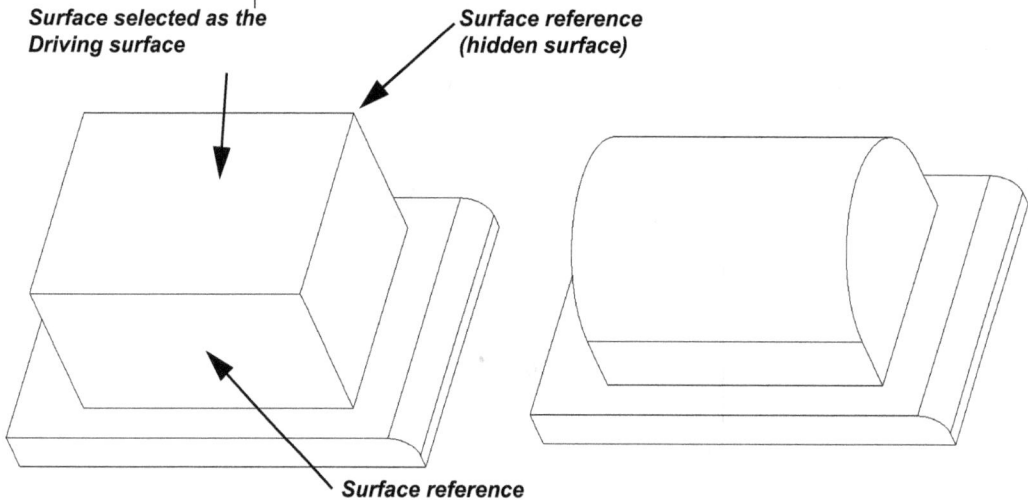

Surface selected as the Driving surface

Surface reference (hidden surface)

Surface reference

Figure 8–11

An example of a **Through Curve** round using two surface references is shown in Figure 8–12.

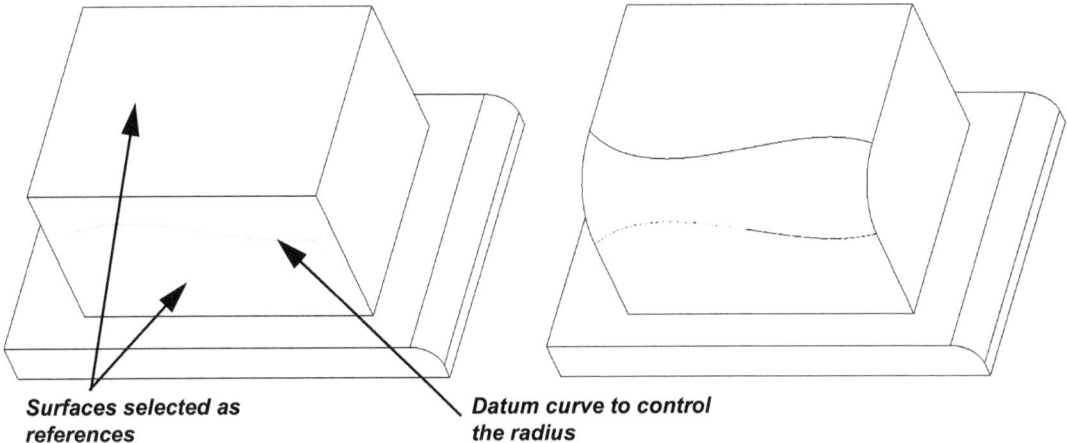

Surfaces selected as references

Datum curve to control the radius

Figure 8–12

Edge to Surface Round

A round created using an edge and a surface creates a round between a selected edge and a selected surface to which it is tangent. A round created using this placement method can be created with a Constant or Variable round.

The round feature does not have to be tangent to any of the adjacent surfaces of the selected edge. An example of a Constant round using an edge and surface reference is shown in Figure 8–13.

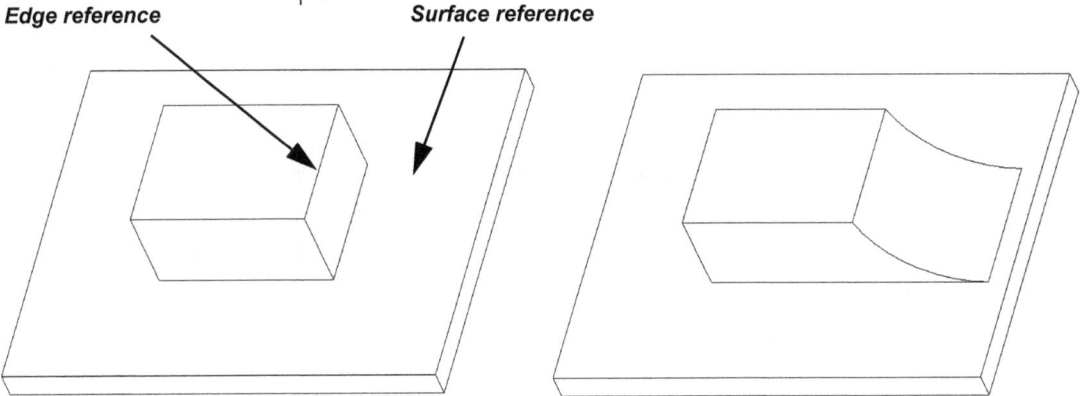

Edge reference

Surface reference

Figure 8–13

Round Placement Ambiguity

Occasionally, the placement of a round is ambiguous. This occurs when the references used for the placement of the round might result in more than one possible solution. For example, the model shown in Figure 8–14 shows a surface to surface round being constructed.

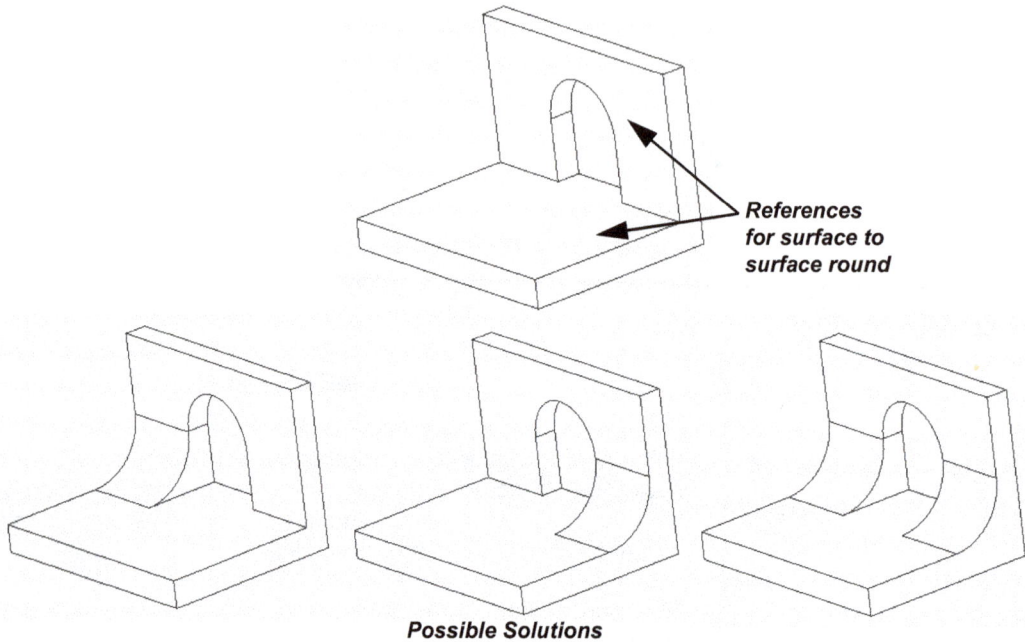

References for surface to surface round

Possible Solutions

Figure 8–14

If a round ambiguity condition exists, the Pieces panel can be opened and a piece can be **Excluded**, as shown in Figure 8–15.

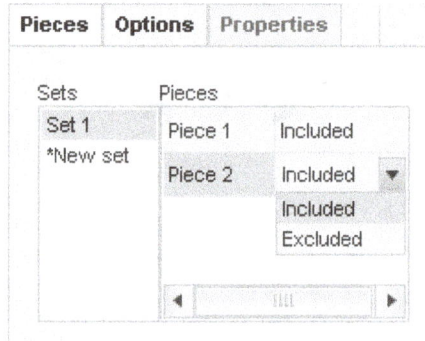

Figure 8–15

8.3 Parent/Child Relationships

The references selected during the creation of a round establish parent/child relationships and determine the subsequent behavior of the round as the part is modified. Using the correct placement method and references to capture your design intent is important.

Edge to Surface Rounds

When selecting an edge and a surface to define a round, the round is dependent on the edge and surface selected to locate it. The round must touch the reference edge at some point along its course and the tangency point of the round must be inside the selected reference surface.

In the example shown in Figure 8–16, the round was created between edge A and reference surface B with a radius of 1. If the round was modified to be less than the distance between edge A and surface B, it would fail because it could no longer contact the reference edge. If the features that created edge A or surface B were deleted, the round would also fail because of missing references used to locate the round on the model.

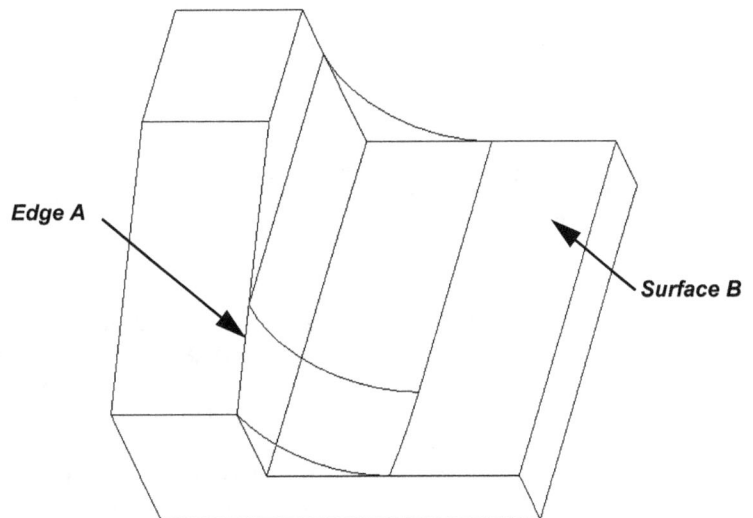

Figure 8–16

Surface to Surface Rounds

When selecting two surfaces to define a round, the round is dependent on the two surfaces selected to locate it. If these surfaces cannot be found or the round cannot fit between them, the round fails.

In the example shown in Figure 8–17, the round was created between surfaces A and B with a radius of 1. If the round was modified to a radius smaller than the distance between surfaces A and B, it would fail because it could no longer contact its placement references. If the features that created surface A or surface B were deleted, the round would also fail because of missing references used to locate the round on the model.

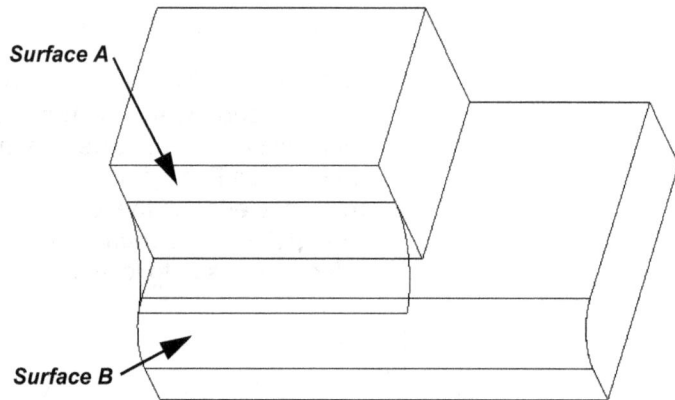

Surface A

Surface B

Figure 8–17

Edge Chain Rounds

When using edge chain rounds, the round is dependent on the edges that were selected during creation. If a selected reference cannot be found, the round fails because of missing references. Consider the following selection methods:

- When selecting edges using <Ctrl>, you are selecting references one by one. The round is dependent on every edge that is selected. The removal of any edge would cause the round to fail because of missing references.

- Using the **Tangent** rule, the round is only dependent on the edge used to start the chain. The removal of one of the automatically selected tangent edges would not cause the round to fail because of missing references.

- Using the **Partial loop** rule, the round is dependent on the reference surface used to start the round as well as the edges used to define the *from-to* for the round.

- Using the **Complete loop** rule, the round selects one of the edges as the start of the chain and it becomes dependent on that edge.

Note that an edge is defined as the interaction between two surfaces. Therefore, modifying the model might cause one surface to interact with a different surface, creating a completely new edge as shown in Figure 8–18. This can also result in failure of the round.

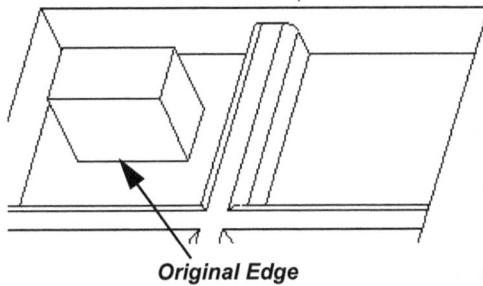

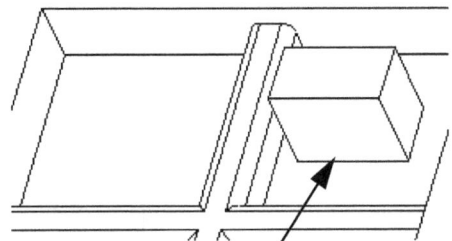

Original Edge

If the model is modified to produce this result, this edge is a completely new edge

Figure 8–18

8.4 Intent Chain

An edge selection technique called **Intent Chain** provides more flexibility in capturing your design intent. It processes information differently than other edge techniques. When using **Intent Chain**, explicit edges are not selected. Instead, the interaction between two features or between a feature and the entire part is selected. This makes the round more flexible, but can also cause the round to be more difficult to limit.

To use **Intent Chain** when selecting references for a round, you can right-click to step through the possible edge options, or use the 🔲 (Pick From List) option, as shown in Figure 8–19.

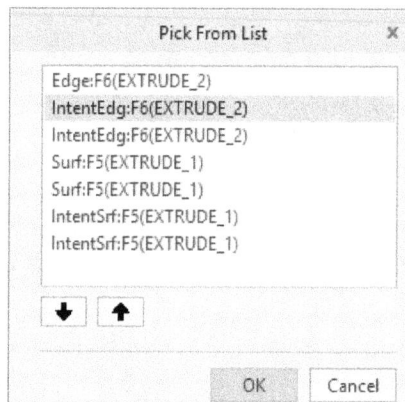

Pick From List	✕
Edge:F6(EXTRUDE_2)	
IntentEdg:F6(EXTRUDE_2)	
IntentEdg:F6(EXTRUDE_2)	
Surf:F5(EXTRUDE_1)	
Surf:F5(EXTRUDE_1)	
IntentSrf:F5(EXTRUDE_1)	
IntentSrf:F5(EXTRUDE_1)	

↓ ↑

OK   Cancel

Figure 8–19

When you set the configuration option **provide_pick_message_always** to **yes**, the message area provides a description of how the intent chain is defined. The intent chain is defined as either *feature X part* or *side srfs X end srfs*. This enables you to consider the possible intended interactions that Creo Parametric recognizes.

The selections made sometimes look the same at the time of creation, but might behave differently when the part is changed. In the example shown in Figure 8–20, an **Intent Chain** round was created around the bottom of the protrusion. The initial result displays the same whether the round is created with *feature X part* or *side surfs X end surfs*.

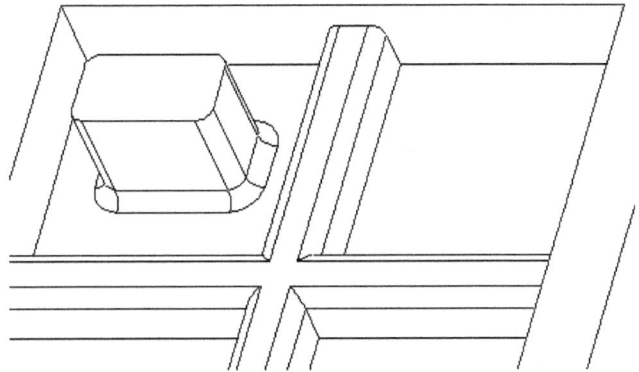

Figure 8–20

If the protrusion is modified so that it intersects the rib, the result is different. The result of using *feature X part* is shown in Figure 8–21. The round is created based on the interaction of the feature with the entire part. Therefore, the round extends across the rib by default.

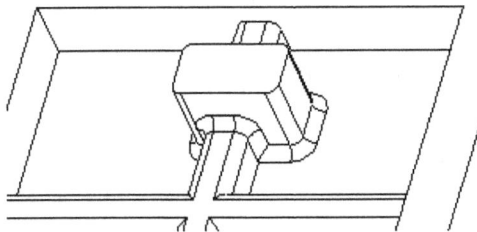

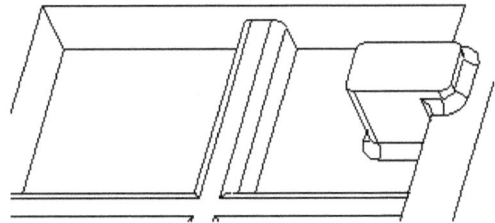

Figure 8–21

The result of using *side surfaces X end surfaces* is shown in Figure 8–22. The round is only created between the side surfaces of the protrusion and the surfaces that contact the end of the protrusion. As a result, a round that does not consider the rib to be generated. Both of these rounds could fail if created using other **Edge Chain** option.

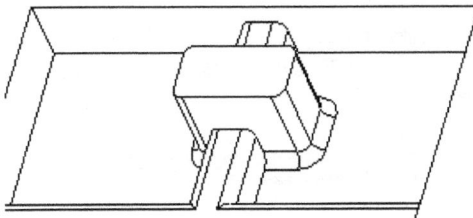

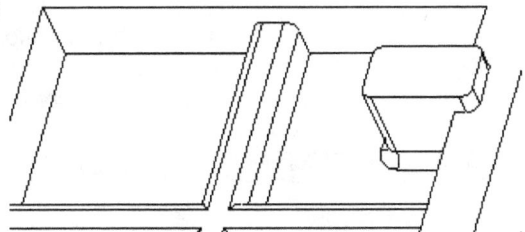

Figure 8–22

8.5 Creating Rounds

Unless the required geometry dictates otherwise, create round features as late as possible in the feature regeneration sequence. Rounds add complex geometry to the model requiring longer regeneration time. Additionally, avoid using them as parents for subsequent features. Figure 8–23 shows an example of how a simple part can be made to look complex by adding rounds.

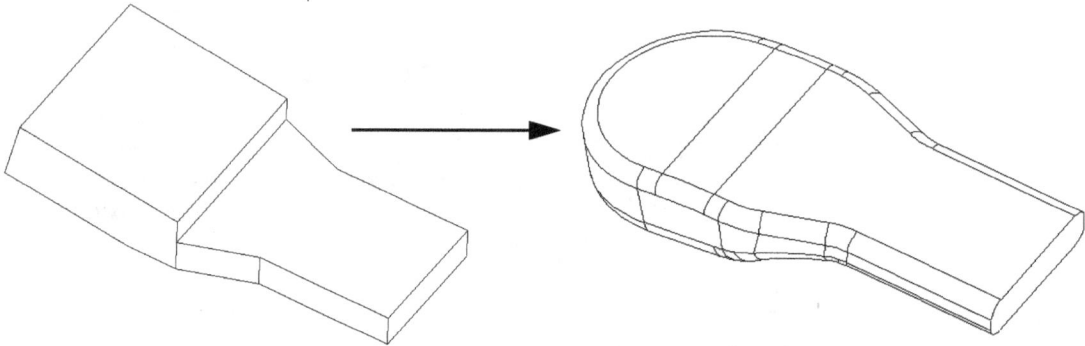

Figure 8–23

General Steps

Use the following general steps to create a round:

1. Start the creation of the feature.
2. Select the placement references.
3. Define the dimensions of the feature.
4. Select the round creation method.
5. Define the cross-section.
6. Define the transitions, as required.

Step 1 - Start the creation of the feature.

To start the creation of a round, click ⌐ (Round) in the *Round* dashboard or mini toolbar. The *Round* dashboard activates as shown in Figure 8–24.

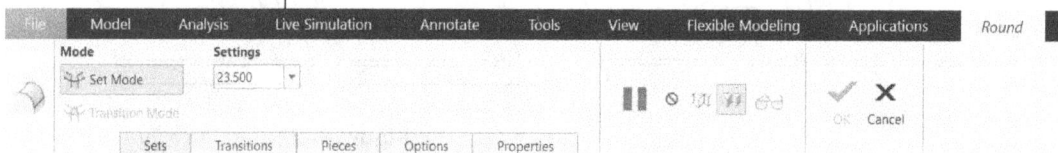

Figure 8–24

Step 2 - Select the placement references.

You can select the reference(s) before or after starting the creation of the round feature. References can be surfaces or edges depending on the type of round that you want to create (i.e., Constant, Variable, Full, or Through Curve round). Figure 8–25 shows examples of the various round types on simple block-shaped protrusions.

You can change the round type by right-clicking and selecting the required option. The types of rounds available depend on the selected references.

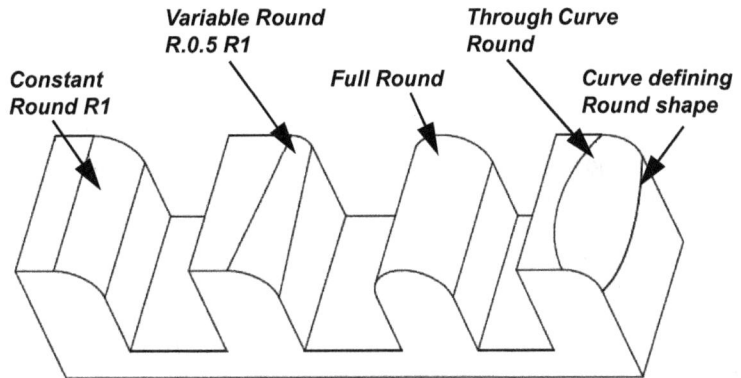

Variable Round R.0.5 R1

Through Curve Round

Constant Round R1

Full Round

Curve defining Round shape

Figure 8–25

Each round reference and the round types that you can create using each reference are described as follows:

Reference Type	Definition	Round Type
Edges or edge chains	Places a round by selecting one or more edges or edge chains.	Constant, Variable, Through Curve, or Full
Surface to Edge	Places a round by selecting a surface first and then an edge.	Constant, or Variable
Surface to Surface	Places a round by selecting two surfaces.	Constant, Variable, Through Curve, or Full

Selection Techniques

Knowing the selection techniques helps you to efficiently select edges to add to a round. The following selection types are available for selecting edges:

- One-by-one
- Tangent
- Partial loop
- Surface loop
- Intent edges

Tangent edges are automatically selected once an adjacent edge has been selected, as shown in Figure 8–26.

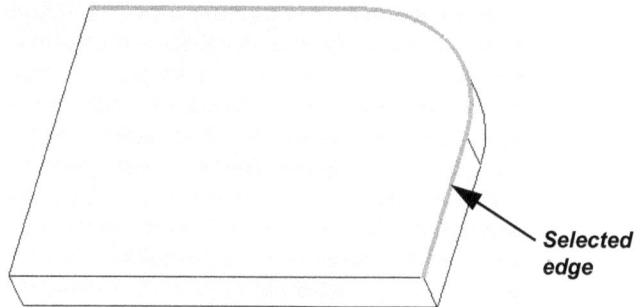

Selected edge

Figure 8–26

*You can remove all of the round references in the Graphics window by right-clicking and selecting **Clear**.*

*You can remove all of the round references from the Sets panel by right-clicking and selecting **Remove All**.*

*You can remove an individual reference from the Sets panel by right-clicking on the reference and selecting **Remove**.*

To use the Surface Loop technique, select an edge, press <Shift> and move the cursor onto the required surface. The Surface Loop tag displays as shown in Figure 8–27. Click the left mouse button and release <Shift>. Creo Parametric selects the edges that form a loop around the selected surface.

Initial edge selected

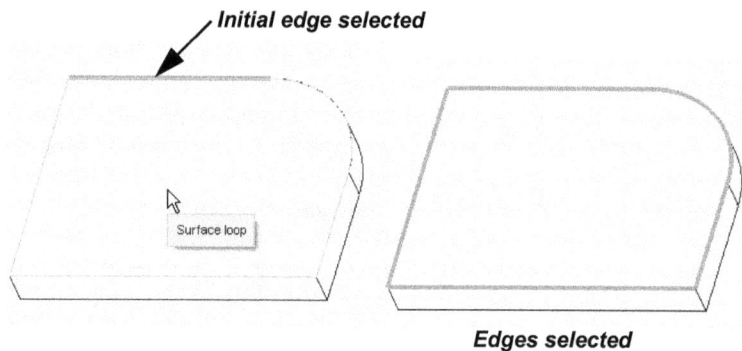

Surface loop

Edges selected

Figure 8–27

The **Intent edges** option selects edges based on their inclusion in an intent group. When you create a feature, such as an extruded protrusion, the resulting edges form intent groups. There are three basic intent groups:

- Start edges (edges contained in the original sketched section).

- End edges (edges contained in the section at the end of its path).

- Side edges (all of the side edges of the protrusion).

To select the entities using the **Intent edges** option, hover the cursor over an edge as shown in Figure 8–28, and right-click.

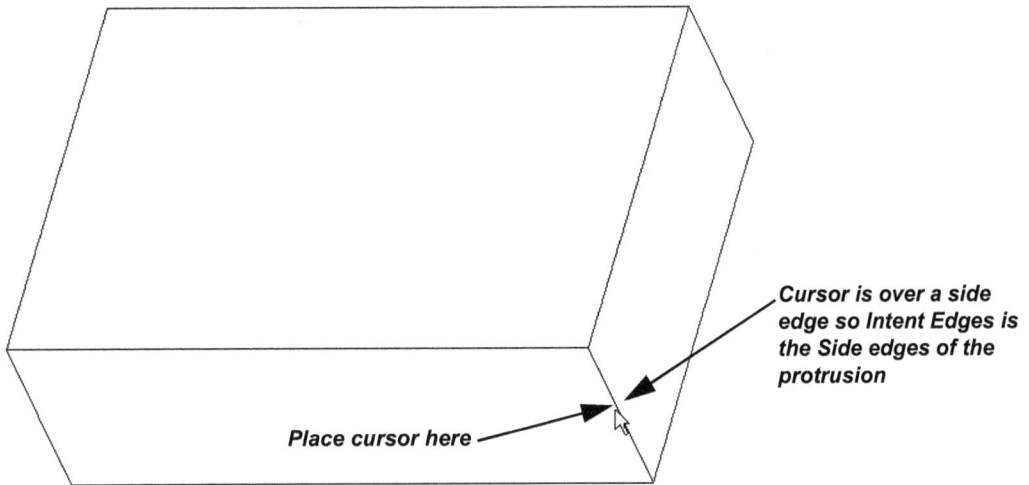

Cursor is over a side edge so Intent Edges is the Side edges of the protrusion

Place cursor here

Figure 8–28

Select (Pick From List) in the menu. The Pick From List dialog box opens as shown on the left in Figure 8–29. Select **IntentEdg** in the dialog box and click **OK**. The four edges forming the Intent Edges highlight and the round is created on them, as shown in the model on the right in Figure 8–29.

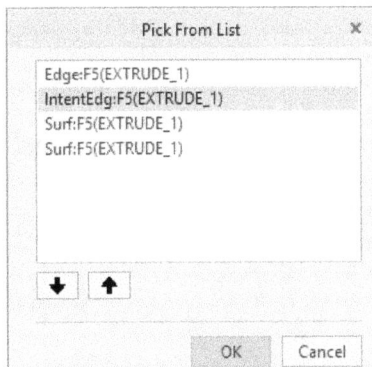

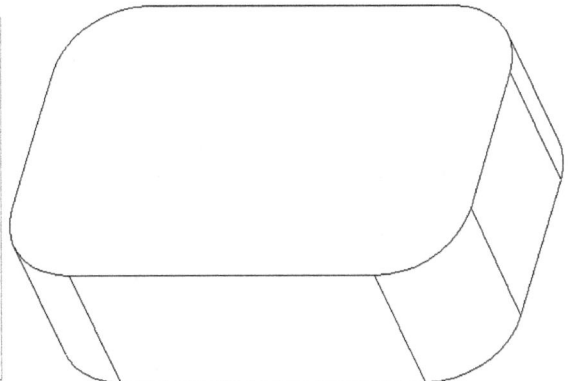

Pick From List

Edge:F5(EXTRUDE_1)
IntentEdg:F5(EXTRUDE_1)
Surf:F5(EXTRUDE_1)
Surf:F5(EXTRUDE_1)

OK   Cancel

Figure 8–29

If you redefine the shape of the protrusion's section from the rectangle to a triangle, the result displays as shown in Figure 8–30 (three rounds).

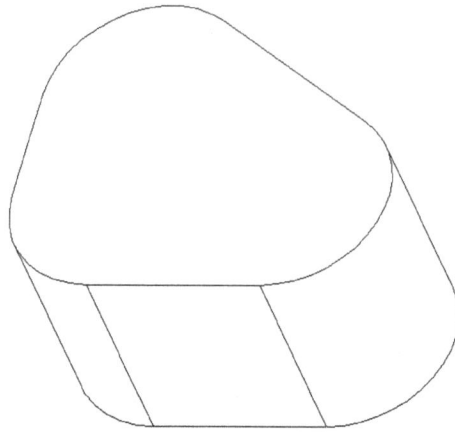

Figure 8–30

Step 3 - Define the dimensions of the feature.

The dimensions of the radii can be changed by dragging the handles on the model, as shown in Figure 8–31. Alternatively, you can change the round radii directly in the tab or by double-clicking on the radius value in the Graphics window.

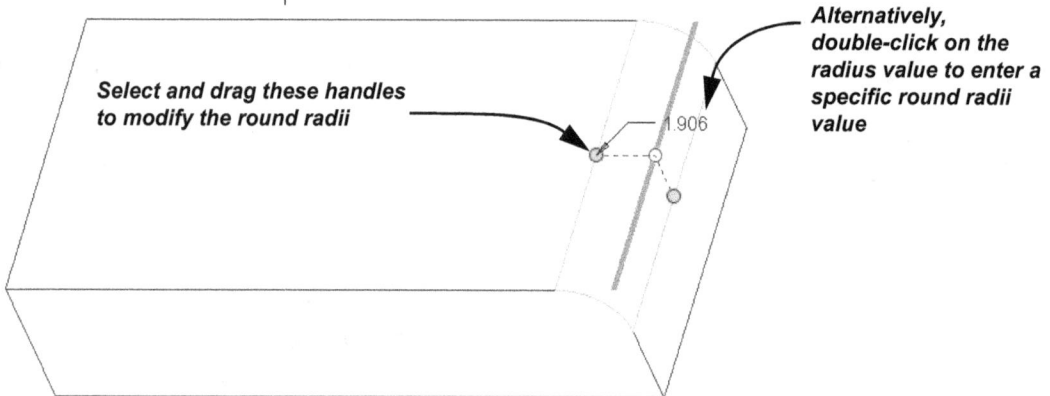

Select and drag these handles to modify the round radii

Alternatively, double-click on the radius value to enter a specific round radii value

1.906

Figure 8–31

Alternatively, you can press <Shift> while dragging the dimension handle onto a selected reference.

The radius value can also be driven by a reference and therefore no radius value assigned to it. To use a reference, select **Reference** in the drop-down list in the Sets panel (as shown in Figure 8–32), and select a reference that the round must pass through. The reference used can be a point or vertex.

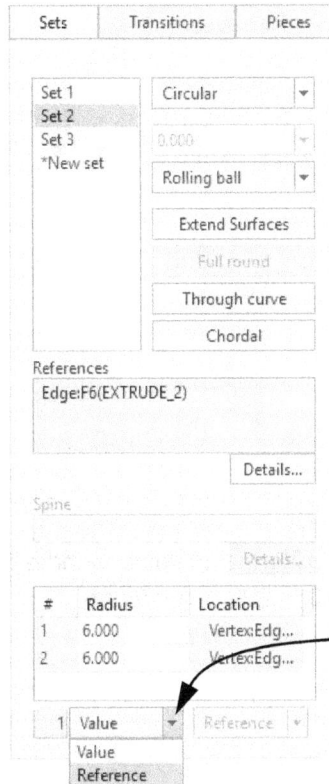

Radius value can be driven by value or reference

Figure 8–32

Step 4 - Select the round creation method.

By default, all of the rounds are created using the **Rolling ball** option. With this option, the round is created by rolling a spherical ball along the surfaces to which it would naturally stay tangent. You can also create the round using the **Normal to spine** option. In this method the round is created by sweeping an arc or conic cross-section normal to a spine.

To change the round creation method use the drop-down list in the Sets panel, as shown in Figure 8–33.

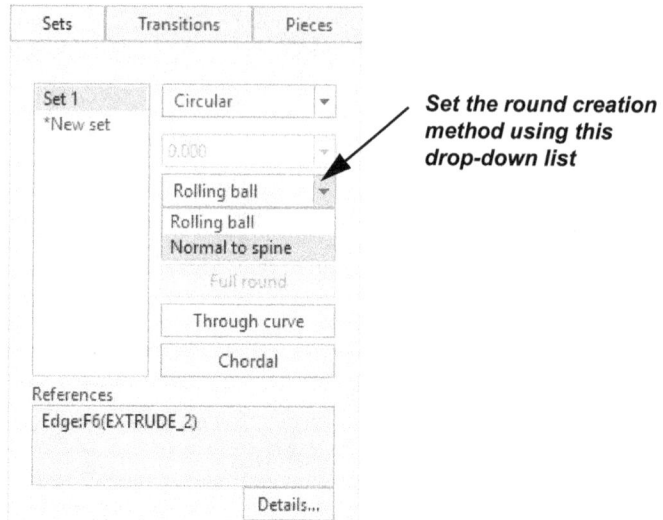

Set the round creation method using this drop-down list

Figure 8–33

Consider the rounds in Figure 8–34. Note the unique behavior of the tangent lines. The main difference between a Rolling ball and a Normal to spine round is the behavior of the cross-section from one end to the other.

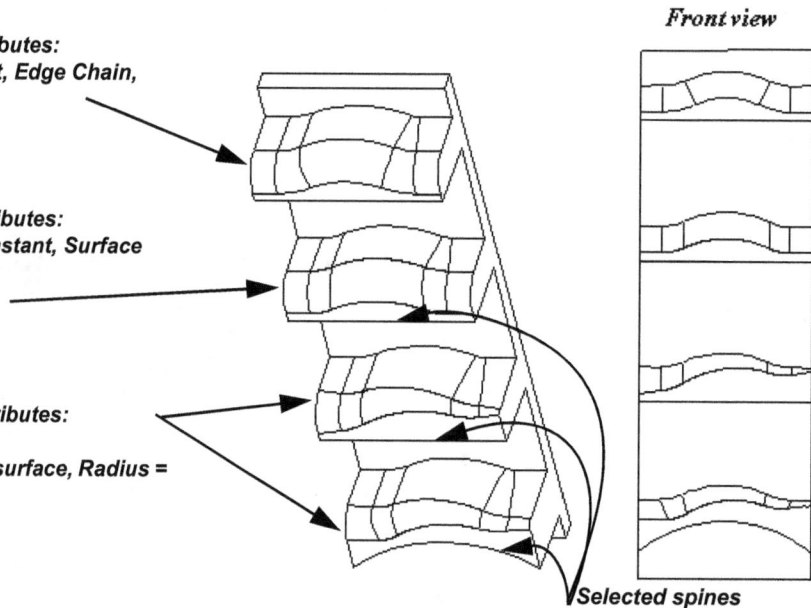

1 round set with Attributes:
Rolling ball, Constant, Edge Chain,
Radius = 1.5

1 round set with Attributes:
Normal to spine, Constant, Surface
to surface,
Radius = 1.5

1 round set with Attributes:
Normal to spine,
Variable, Surface to surface, Radius =
1.5 and 0.25

Front view

Selected spines

Figure 8–34

Step 5 - Define the cross-section.

By default, rounds are constructed with a circular cross-section, as shown in Figure 8–35. You can also change the shape of the cross- section to **Conic**, **C2 Continuous**, or **D1 X D2 Conic**.

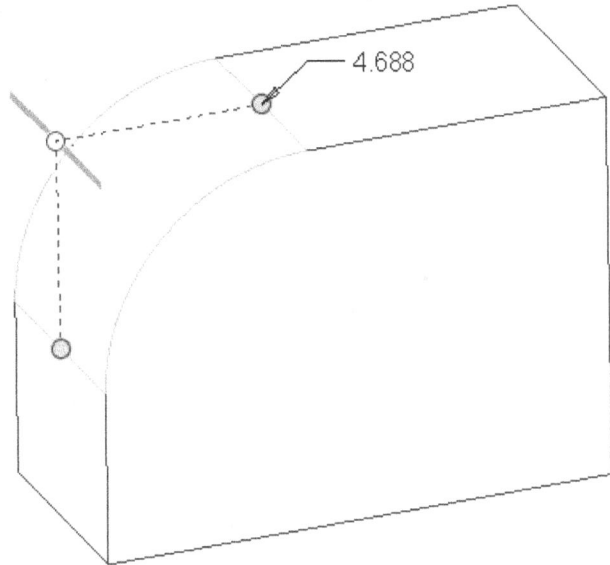

4.688

Figure 8–35

To change the cross-section of the round, use the drop-down list in the Sets panel, as shown in Figure 8–36.

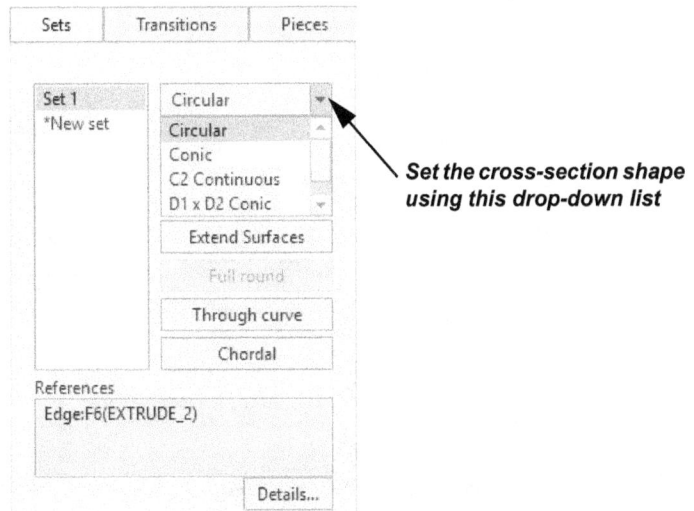

Set the cross-section shape using this drop-down list

Figure 8–36

A conic cross-section is defined with a user-specified conic parameter (rho) value. Varying the value of Rho changes the shape of the cross-section. You can also modify the distance (D), of the round from the selected edge. For a Conic round, the distance is equal on both sides. Figure 8–37 shows an example of a Conic round.

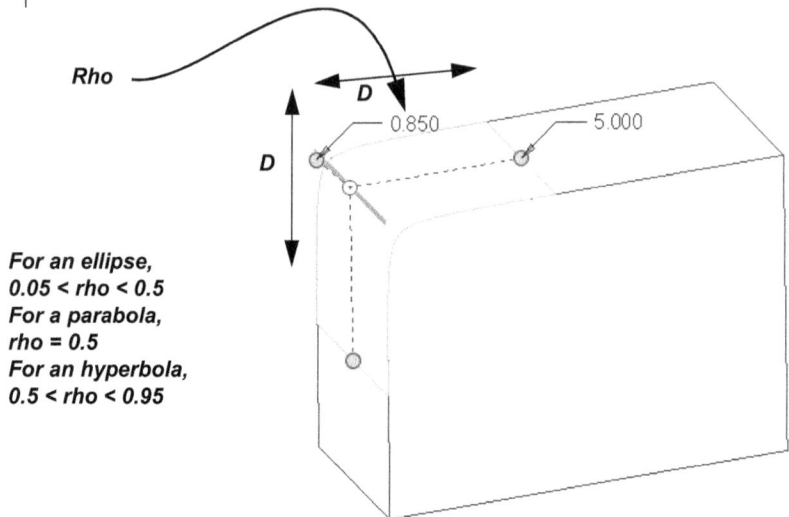

Rho

D

D

0.850

5.000

For an ellipse,
0.05 < rho < 0.5
For a parabola,
rho = 0.5
For an hyperbola,
0.5 < rho < 0.95

Figure 8–37

A **C2 Continuous** round is created with a spline cross-section that has curvature continuity with the adjoining surfaces. This round can be both a constant and variable radius. The shape of the spline can be adjusted to obtain the required curvature, as shown in Figure 8–38.

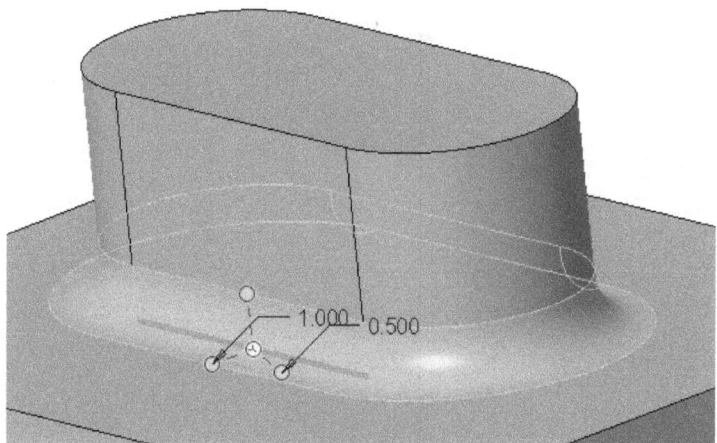

1.000 0.500

C2 Continuous
Figure 8–38

A round can also be curvature continuous by defining it as a **D1 x D2 Conic** cross-section, as shown in Figure 8–39. This option can only be used with a constant round set.

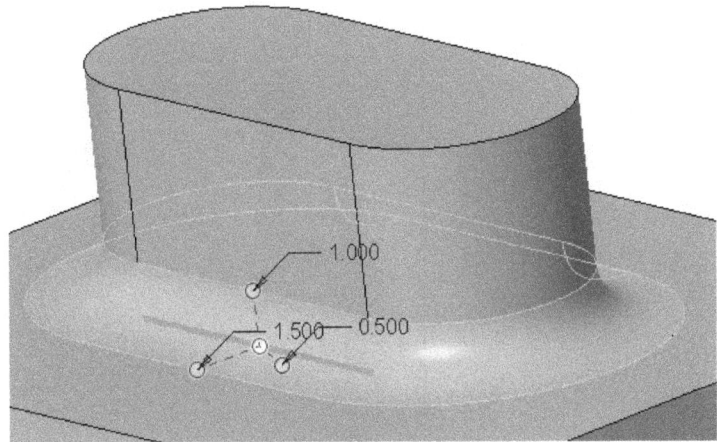

D1 x D2 Conic
Figure 8–39

The D1 x D2 Conic round is created with independent distances for each side of the round and a user-specified conic parameter (rho) value, as shown in Figure 8–40.

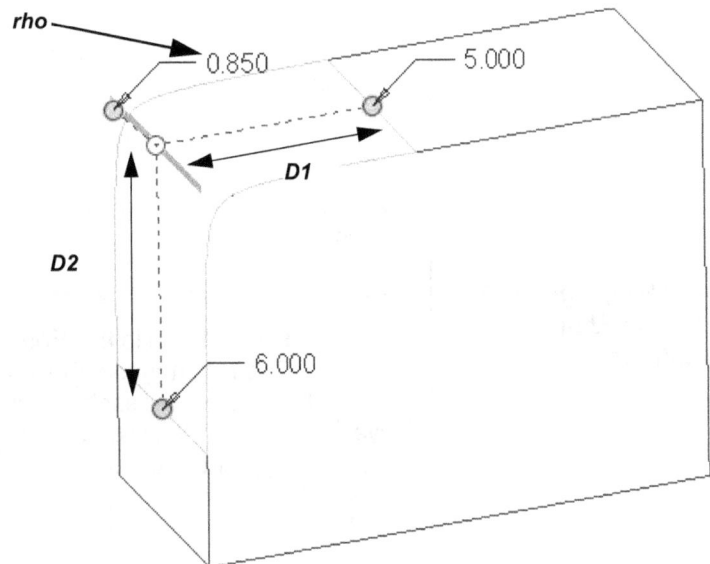

Figure 8–40

Finally, a round can be curvature continuous by defining it as a **D1 x D2 C2** cross-section which uses a spline cross-section and independent lengths. The three cross-section types for curvature continuous rounds display as shown in Figure 8–41.

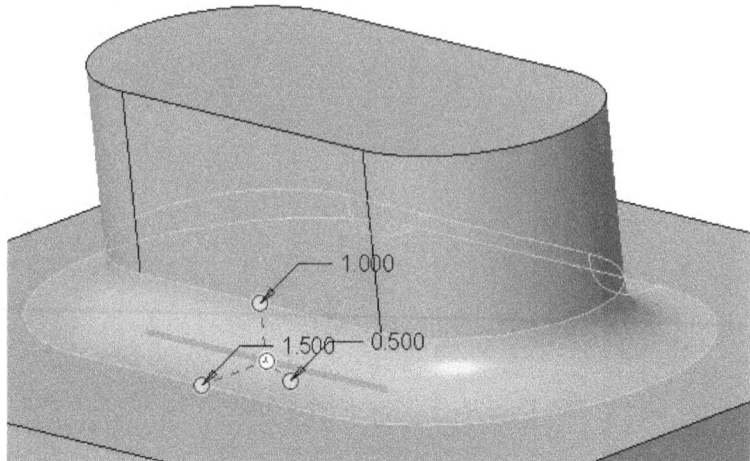

D1 x D2 Conic
Figure 8–41

Step 6 - Define the transitions, as required.

A transition is filler geometry that connects round sets. Transitions are located where round sets meet or terminate.

Creo Parametric uses default transitions during the initial round creation and provides many alternative transition types, enabling you to create and modify transitions to obtain the required geometry.

Alternatively, right-click and select **Show transitions***.*

To define a transition between sets of rounds, click

✦ (Transition Mode) in the *Round* dashboard or mini toolbar, to switch to Transition mode. Once in Transition mode, you can hover the cursor over each transition area to highlight them in cyan. Select the transition area on the model to change the transition type from the system assigned default.

Once a transition has been selected, all of the possible transition types for the selected item display in the drop-down list in the dashboard. You can also change the type of transition by right-clicking on the transition area and selecting the appropriate option, as shown in Figure 8–42.

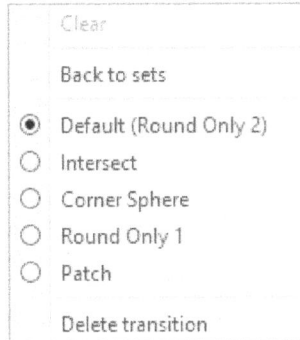

Clear

Back to sets

◉ Default (Round Only 2)
○ Intersect
○ Corner Sphere
○ Round Only 1
○ Patch

This section lists the available transitions

Delete transition

Figure 8–42

Practice 8a

Designing With Rounds

Practice Objectives

- Use the Surface to Edge selection technique to create a round, and use a reference to define the radius value.
- Create variable, constant, and full rounds using the appropriate selection techniques.
- Create a round using the C2 Continuous cross-section type.

In this practice, you will complete the geometry for a telephone handset. The only geometry that is required is a variety of rounds. The original and completed models are shown in Figure 8–43. To create the geometry, you will create constant, full, and variable rounds. While creating the rounds, note that the interaction of round features with each another enables you to achieve the required geometry. At the end of feature creation, consider reordering the round features to test how the geometry changes if the feature order of the rounds changes.

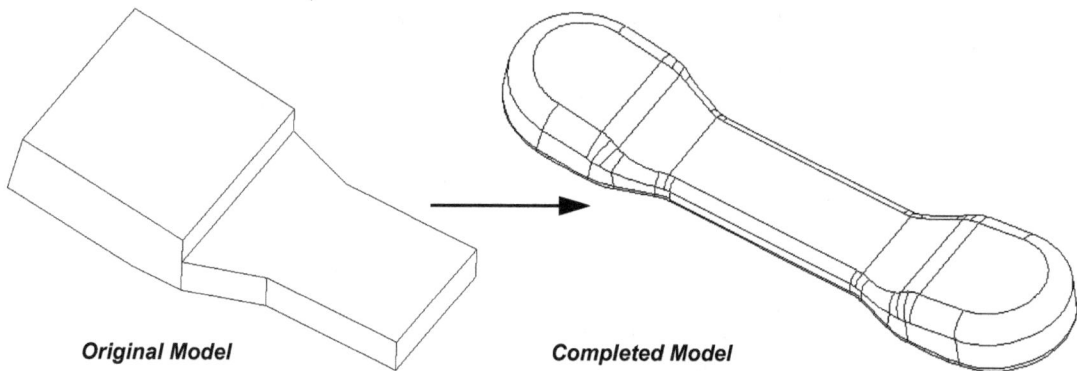

Original Model

Completed Model

Figure 8–43

Task 1 - Open a part file.

1. Set the working directory to the *Designing_With_Rounds* folder.

2. Open **phone.prt**.

3. Set the model display as follows:

   - ⚙ *(Datum Display Filters)*: All Off

   - ☞ *(Spin Center)*: Off

   - ▢ *(Display Style)*: ▢ (No Hidden)

Task 2 - Create a constant round between the surface and edge.

To include more then one reference in a round set, press and hold <Ctrl> while selecting.

1. Click 🎗 (Round) to create a round.

2. Select the surface shown in Figure 8–44 first, press and hold <Ctrl> and then select the edge. The surface must be selected first, otherwise the round is only added to the edge.

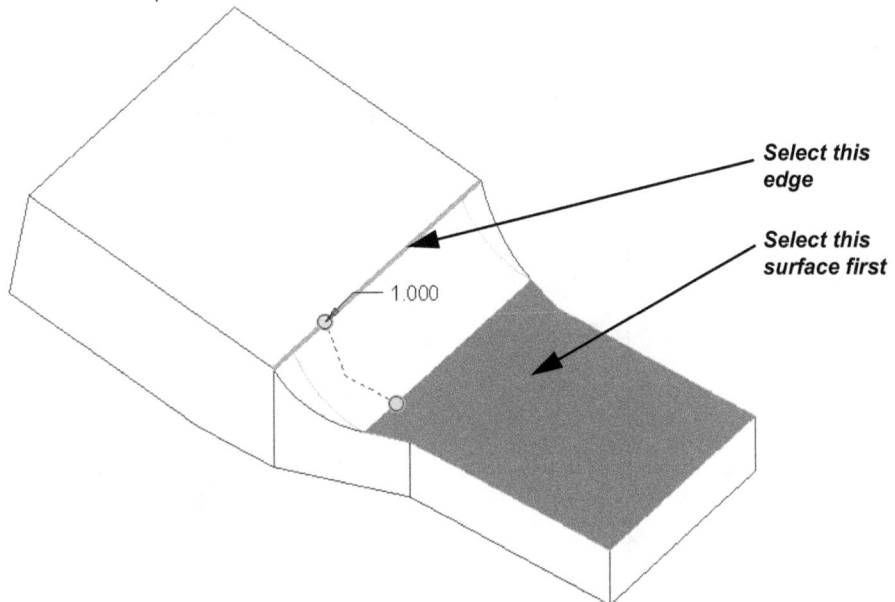

Select this edge

Select this surface first

1.000

Figure 8–44

3. Click **Sets** in the *Round* dashboard to display the Sets panel.

4. Change the distance specification from *Value* to **Reference, as shown in Figure 8–45.**

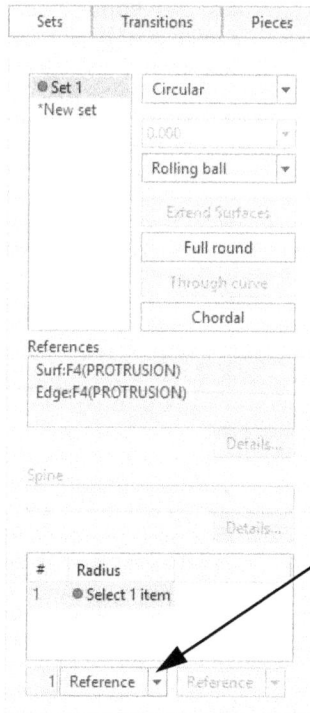

Set option to
Reference

Figure 8–45

5. Select the vertex shown in Figure 8–46.

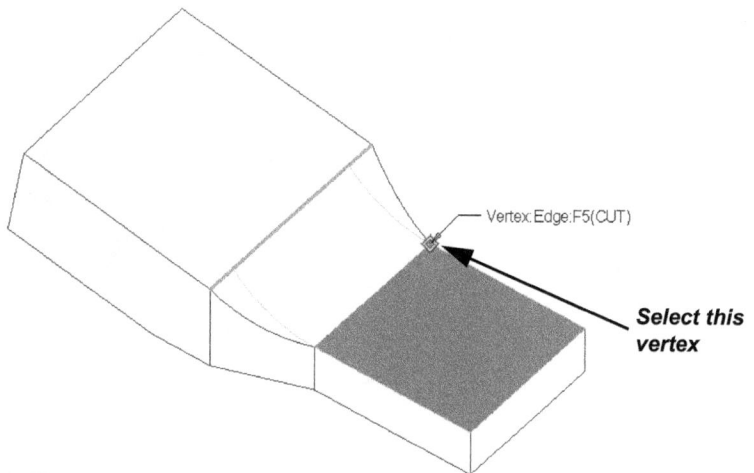

Vertex:Edge:F5(CUT)

Select this
vertex

Figure 8–46

6. Click ✓ (OK) to complete the round.

Task 3 - Create a variable round on three edges.

1. Hold <Ctrl> and select the three edges shown in Figure 8–47. In the mini toolbar, click 🖉 (Round).

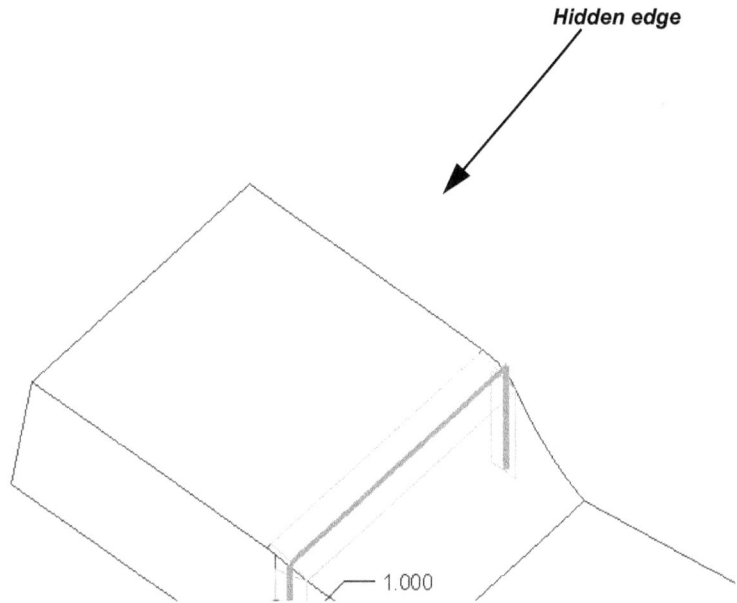

Hidden edge

— 1.000

Figure 8–47

2. Drag the round radius handle to change the radius to approximately **1.0**.

3. Click on the screen and select 🖋 (Make Variable) in the mini toolbar.

4. Enter **2**, **1**, **1**, and **2** for the four points, as shown in Figure 8–48.

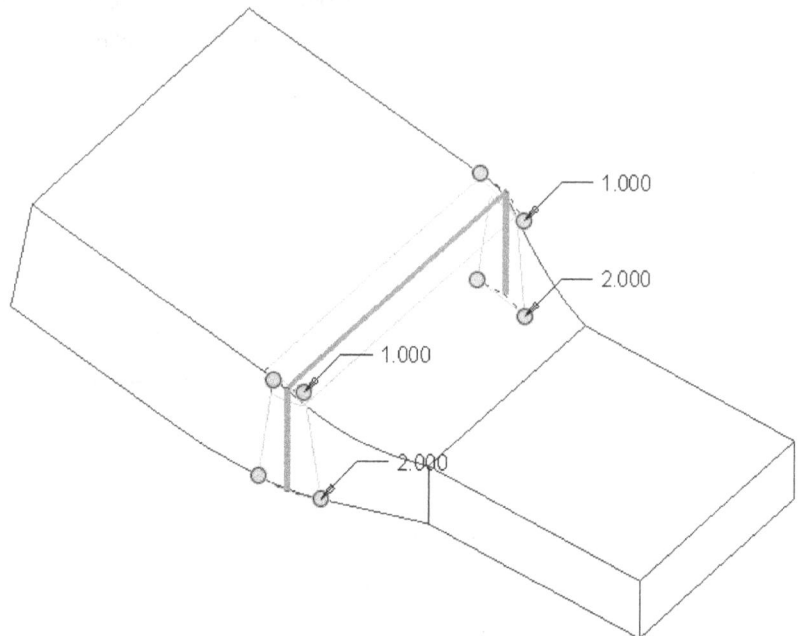

Figure 8–48

5. Click ✓ (OK) to complete the round.

Task 4 - Create a constant round on two edges.

Design Considerations

In the previous tasks, rounds were created by first selecting the feature toolbar icon, and then selecting the references and specific options for the round. In this task, you will reverse this order by first selecting the edges, and then selecting the feature toolbar icon. This technique is called the object-action technique for feature creation. Many features in Creo Parametric can be created in this way. Using this technique enables you to quickly create basic features.

1. Select the two edges shown in Figure 8–49.

*If you are having trouble selecting the edges, try changing the selection filter from **Geometry** to **Edge**.*

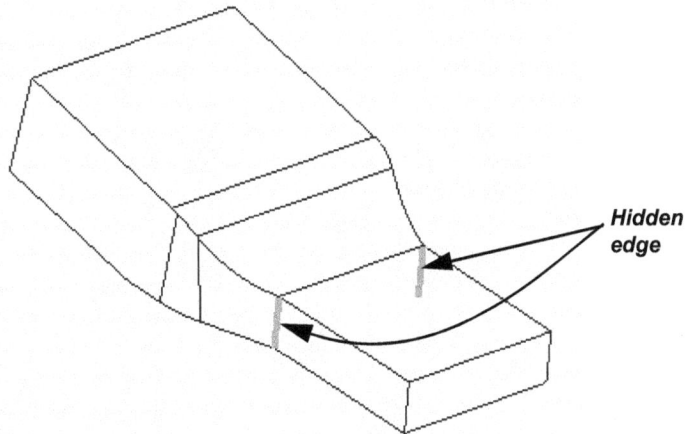

Figure 8–49

2. In the mini toolbar, click ⮑ (Round).

3. Edit the *Radius* to **1**.

4. Complete the round.

Task 5 - Create a full round.

1. Select the two edges shown in Figure 8–50 and click ⮑ (Round) in the mini toolbar.

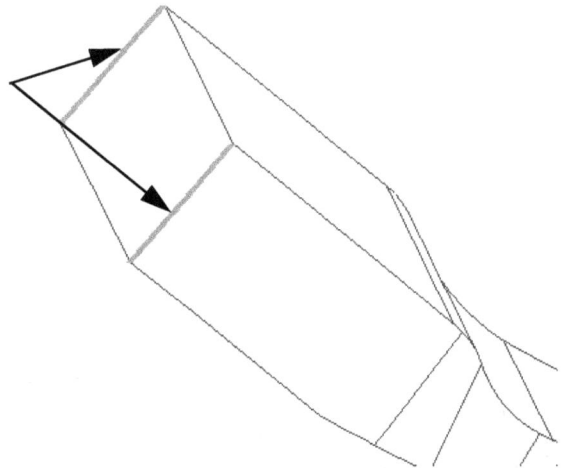

Select these edges

Figure 8–50

2. Click on the screen and select ⮑ (Full Round).

---

3. Complete the feature. The full round is created as shown in Figure 8–51.

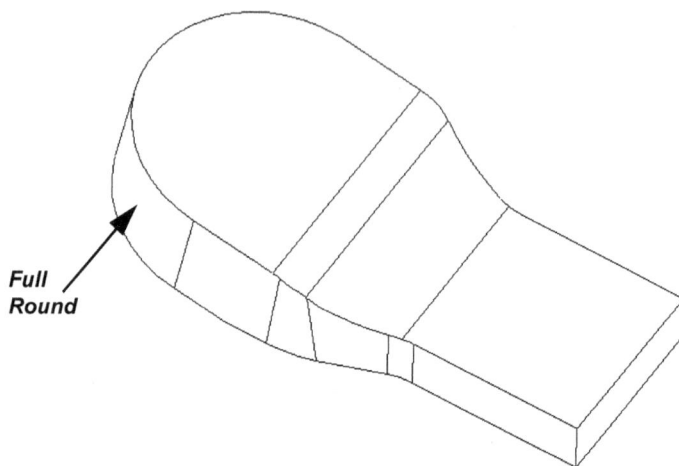

Figure 8–51

Task 6 - Create a constant round.

1. Rotate the model and select the edge shown in Figure 8–52, then click ⌖ (Round) in the mini toolbar.

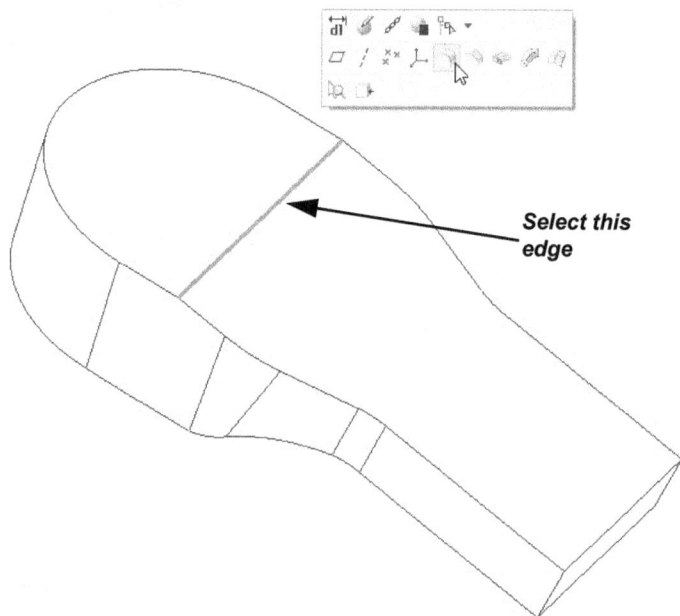

Figure 8–52

2. Edit the radius to **4.00**.

3. Complete the round.

Task 7 - Create a variable round.

---

1. Rotate the model and select the edge shown in Figure 8–53.

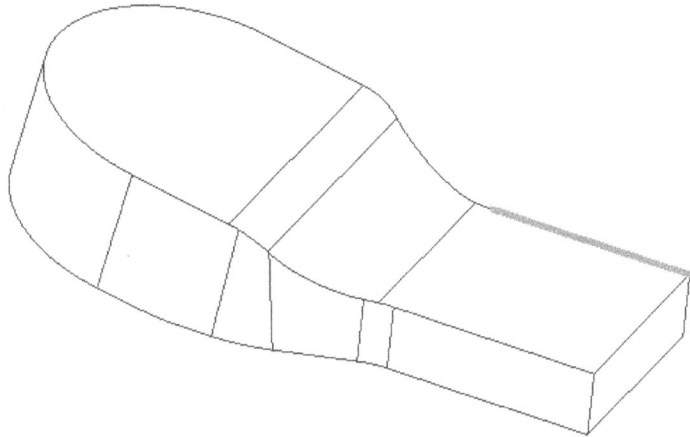

Figure 8–53

2. Hold <Shift> and select the edge shown in Figure 8–54 to select the chain. In the mini toolbar, click (Round).

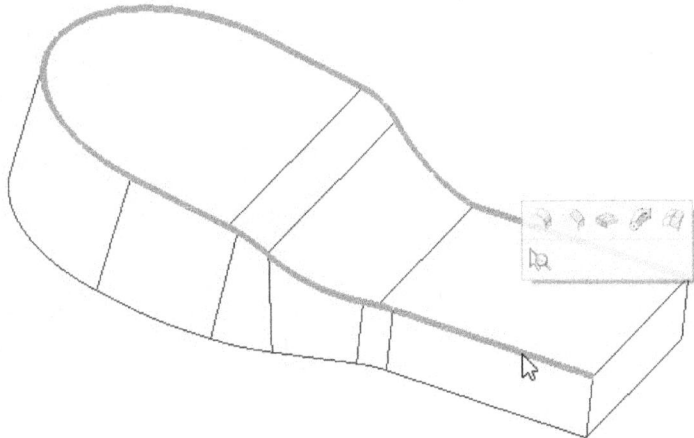

Figure 8–54

3. Click on the screen and select (Make Variable) in the mini toolbar.

4. Edit the two radii to **0.4**.

---

5. Place the cursor on the handle of an existing radius, right-click and select **Add radius**, as shown in Figure 8–55. Note that the new radius entry is added to the Sets panel in the *Round* dashboard.

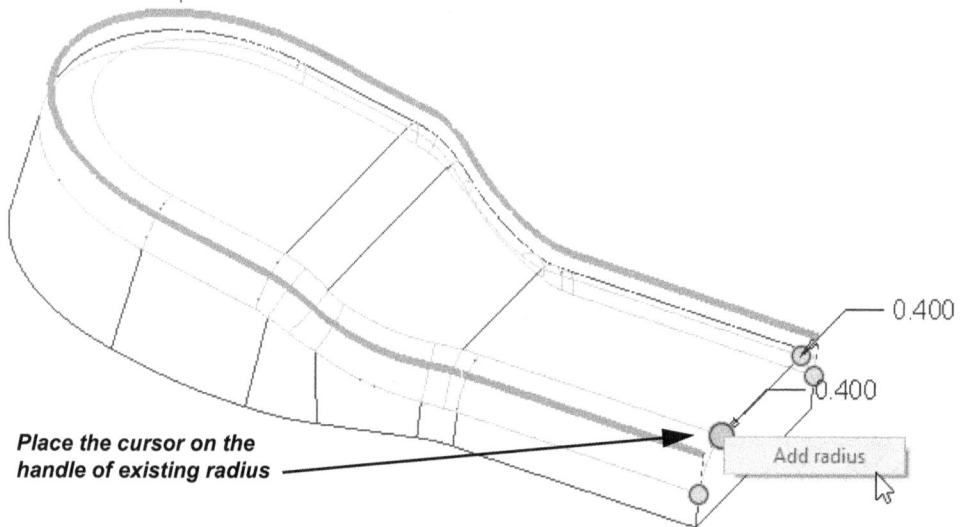

Place the cursor on the handle of existing radius

0.400

0.400

Add radius

Figure 8–55

6. Repeat Step 3 four more times to create a total of six radii.

Design Considerations

By default, the intermediate points that are added for a variable round are added using the **Ratio** option. This enables you to enter a value between 0 and 1 to place the point exactly at a location on the entity. In some situations, assigning a value that changes does not meet the design intent. Therefore, the placement type can be changed so that it lies exactly on a selected reference. It is recommended that if the location is not going to change, you should use the **Reference** option instead of ratio values.

7. Click ⊘ (No Preview) to toggle off the **Preview**. This will make it easier to select the vertices in the next step. The part displays as shown in Figure 8–56.

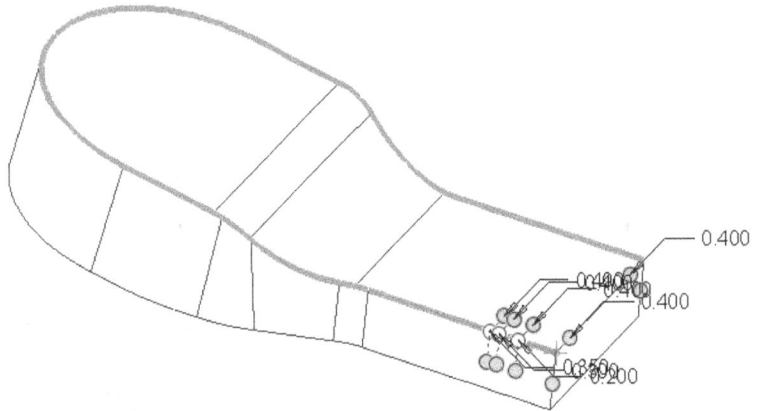

Figure 8–56

8. In the Sets panel, select the 3rd entry and change the type of radius placement from *Ratio* to **Reference**, as shown in Figure 8–57.

The first radii you need to change is radii #3. The first two radii are the end points of the round.

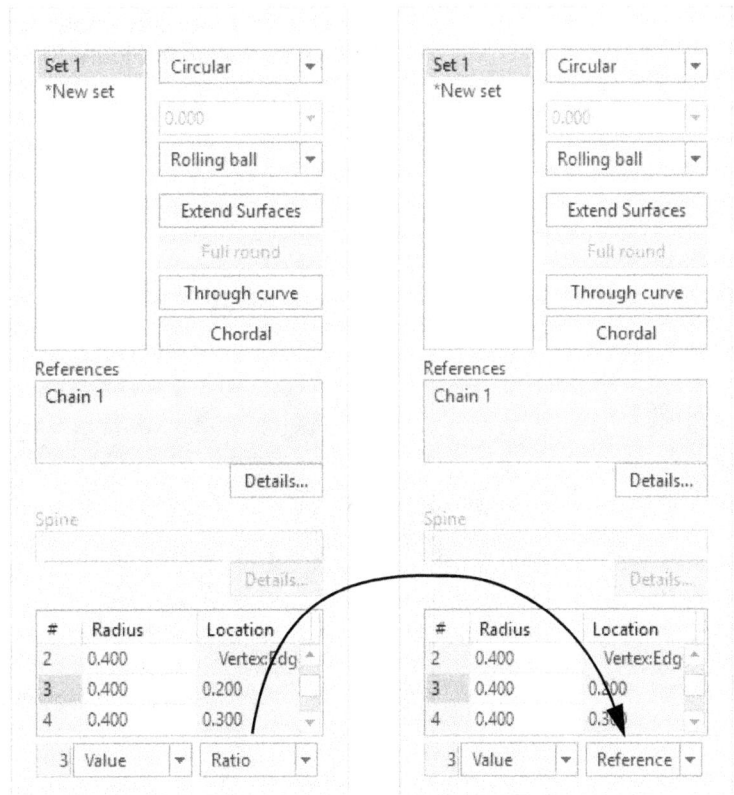

Figure 8–57

9. Select a vertex on the model.

10. Move all of the radii to the locations shown in Figure 8–58 using the technique used in Steps 5 and 6.

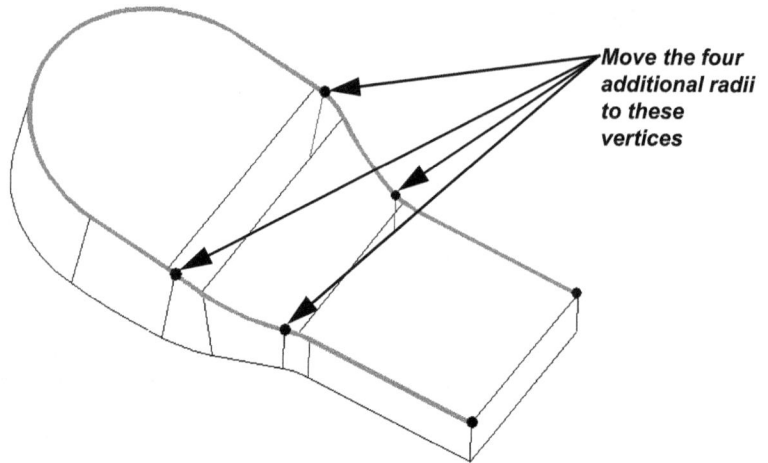

Move the four additional radii to these vertices

Figure 8–58

When the four radii have been moved to four vertices, the part displays as shown in Figure 8–59.

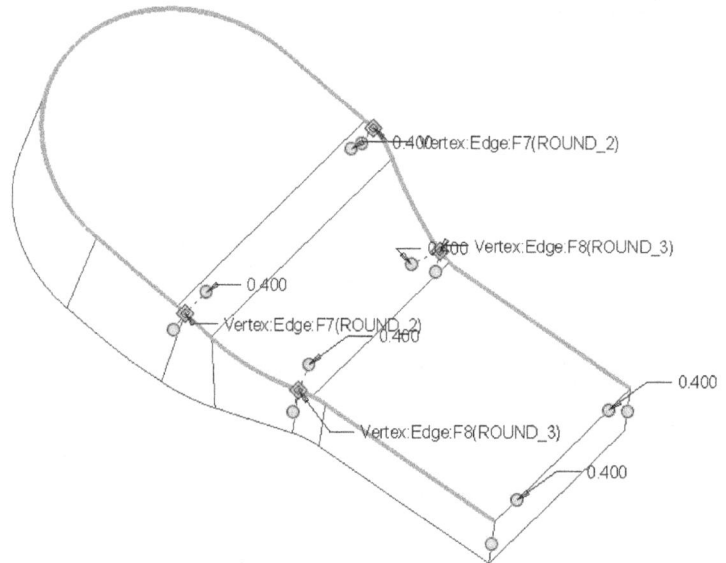

Figure 8–59

11. Click ▨ (Attached) to toggle on the **Preview** and edit the radius values shown in Figure 8–60.

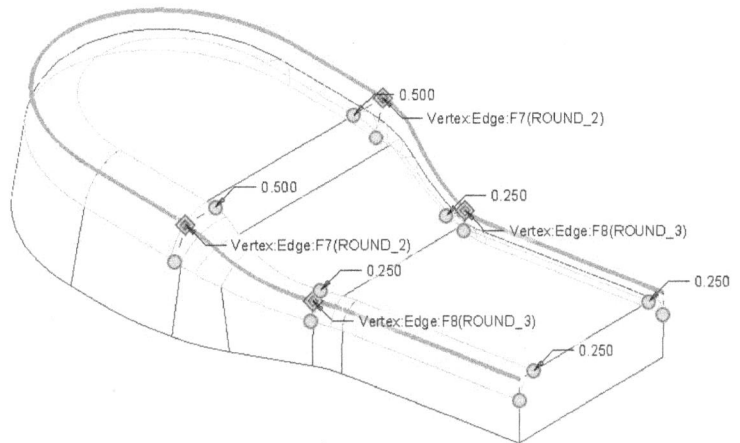

Figure 8–60

12. Complete the round.

Task 8 - Create a constant round.

---

1. Create a constant round with a *Radius* of **0.25** on the back edge of the part, as shown in Figure 8–61.

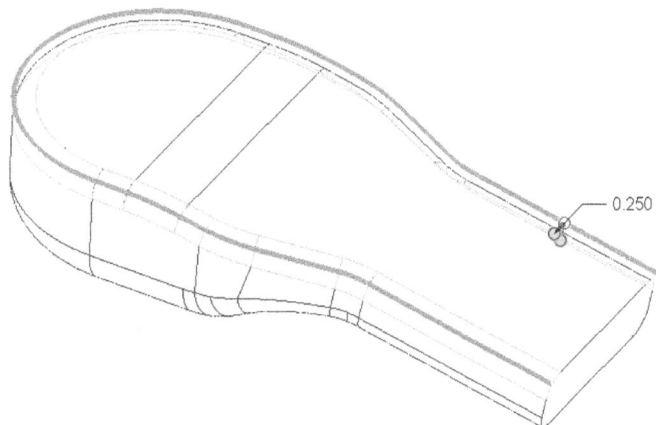

Figure 8–61

2. Complete the feature.

Task 9 - Mirror the whole geometry.

Design Considerations

To complete the headset geometry, you will mirror the entire model. Mirroring ensures that both sides of the model are identical and that any changes made to one side are reflected in the other.

1. Select the part name in the Model Tree. In the ribbon, in the Editing group, click ⎅⎆ (Mirror).

2. Select the planar surface as the plane to mirror about, as shown in Figure 8–62.

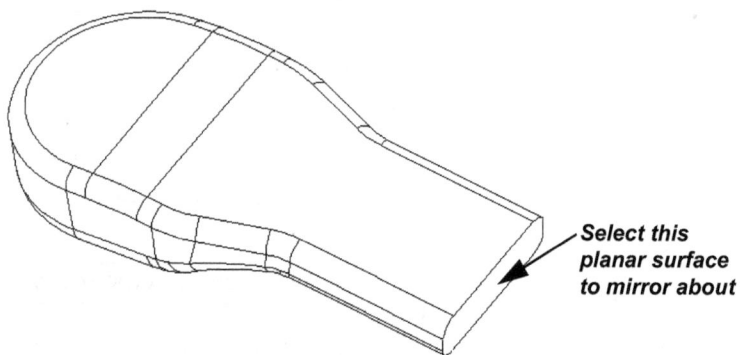

Select this planar surface to mirror about

Figure 8–62

3. Complete the feature. The part displays as shown in Figure 8–63.

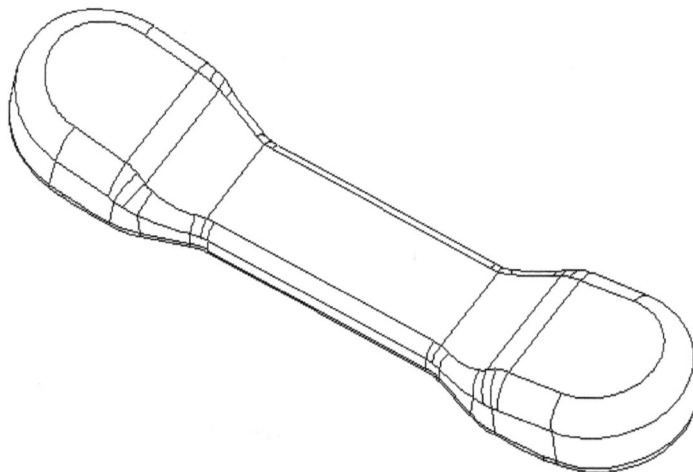

Figure 8–63

4. Save the part and erase it from memory.

Practice 8b | Through Curve Rounds

Practice Objective

- Create a round using the **Through curve** option for the value.

Task 1 - Open a part file.

1. Set the working directory to the *Through_Curve_Rounds* folder.

2. Open **thru_curve.prt**.

3. Set the model display as follows:

    - $\overset{x}{\nearrow}$ *(Datum Display Filters)*: All Off

    - $\searrow$ *(Spin Center)*: Off

    - $\square$ *(Display Style)*: No Hidden)

Task 2 - Create a Through Curve, edge chain round.

1. Create a round on the edge shown in Figure 8–64.

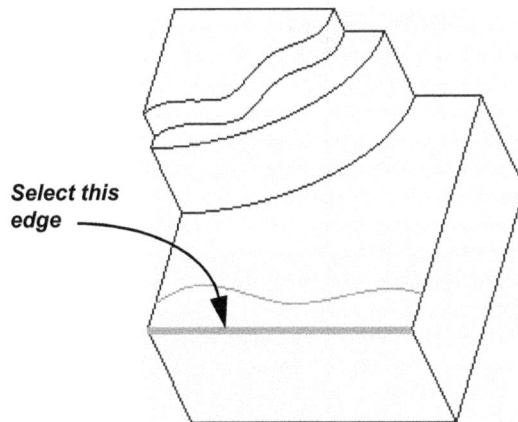

Select this edge

Figure 8–64

2. Click on the screen and select $\heartsuit$ (Through Curve) in the mini toolbar.

3. Select the curve shown in Figure 8–65.

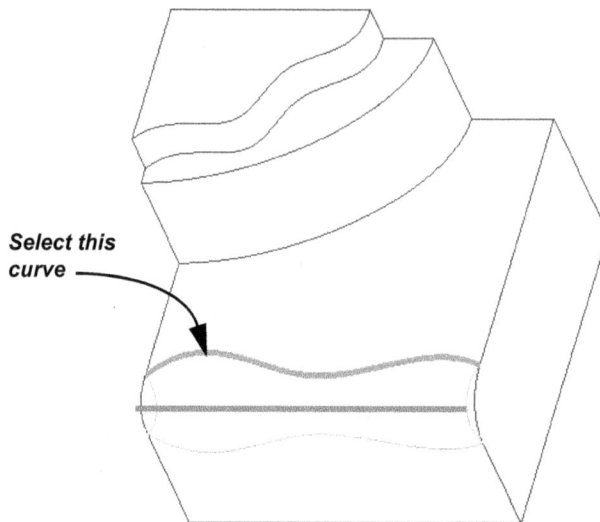

Select this
curve

Figure 8–65

4. Complete the round. The part displays as shown in Figure 8–66.

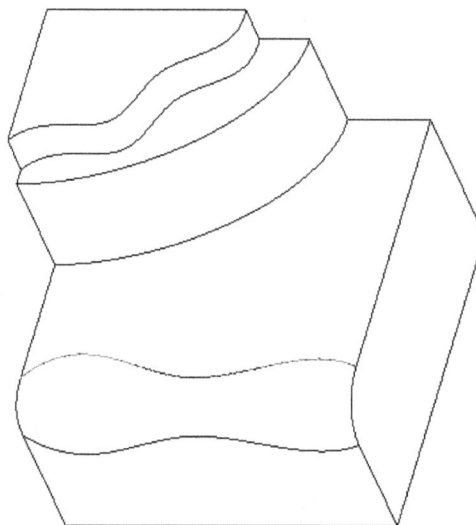

Figure 8–66

Task 3 - Create a Thru Curve, surface to surface round.

1. Hold <Ctrl> and select the two surfaces shown in Figure 8–67 and select 🔾 (Round).

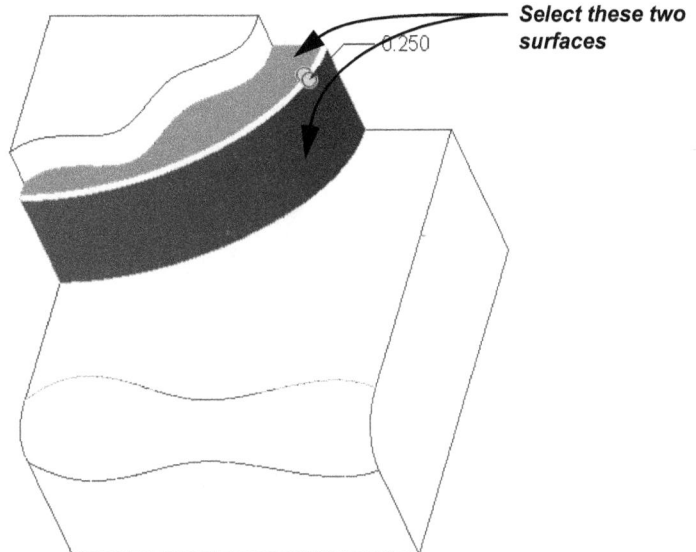

Select these two surfaces

0.250

Figure 8–67

2. Click on the screen and select 🔾 (Through Curve) in the mini toolbar.

3. Select the edge shown in Figure 8–68.

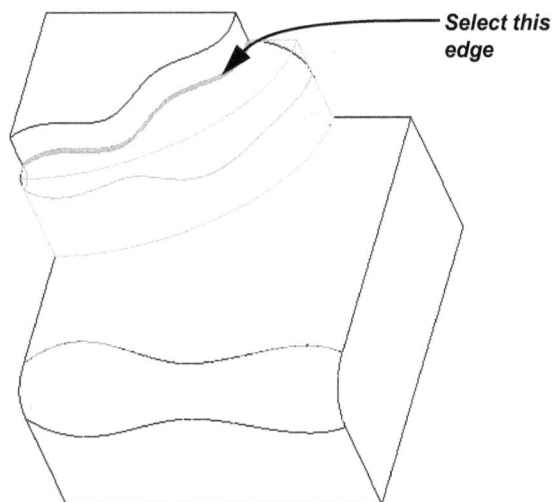

Select this edge

Figure 8–68

4. Complete the round. The finished part displays as shown in Figure 8–69.

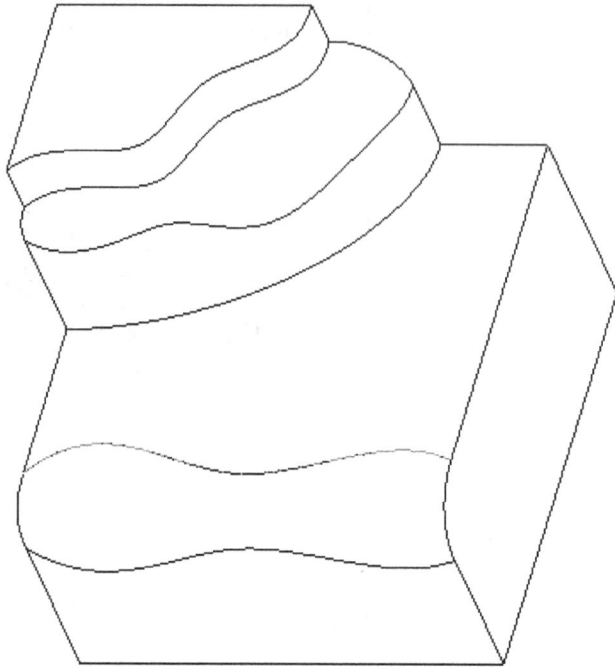

Figure 8–69

5. Save the part and erase it from memory.

Practice 8c

Intent Chain Rounds

Practice Objective

- Learn the advantages of using the Intent Chain selection technique and how it affects the model.

Task 1 - Open a part file.

1. Set the working directory to the *Intent_Chain_Rounds* folder.

2. Open **intent_chain.prt**.

3. Set the model display as follows:

   - ×⁄⁄. *(Datum Display Filters)*: All Off

   - ⁓ *(Spin Center)*: Off

   - ▢. *(Display Style)*: No Hidden

Task 2 - Ensure the message area displays the intent chain type.

1. Click **File>Options>Configuration Editor**.

2. Click **Add**.

3. In the Add Option dialog box, type **provide_pick_message_always** in the *Option name* field.

4. Select **Yes** for the *Option value* field and click **OK**.

5. Click **OK**, then click **No** when prompted to save the setting.

Task 3 - Create a round.

1. Create a round with a *Radius* of **0.125** using the edge shown in Figure 8–70.

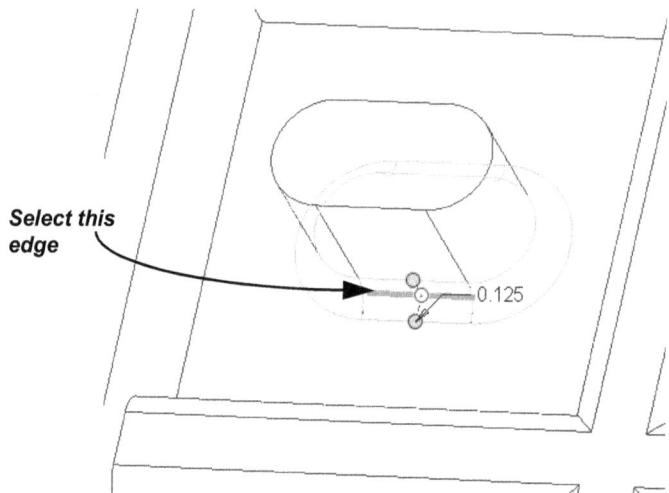

Figure 8–70

2. Complete the round.

3. The design intent has changed and the protrusion with the round must be moved to a new location. Modify the location of the protrusion from *0.75* to **2.0**, as shown in Figure 8–71.

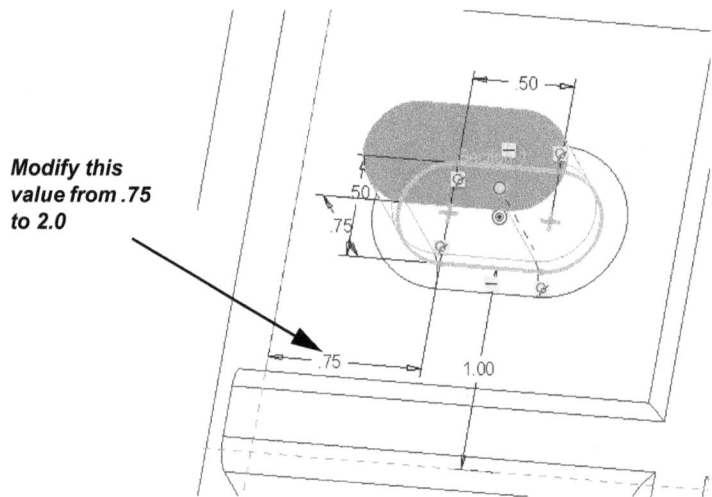

Figure 8–71

4. Regenerate the part.

Design Considerations

The round fails because the protrusion now intersects the rib and some of the edges that the round references no longer exist.

*If the config option **regen_failure_ handling** is set to **Resolve_mode** and the resolve environment displays, select **Undo Changes**.*

5. In the Quick Access toolbar, click (Undo) to undo the changes.

Task 4 - Redefine the round so that the protrusion can intersect the rib and the round does not fail.

1. Edit the definition of the round.
2. Click **Sets** in the *Round* dashboard and click **Details**. The Chain dialog box opens.
3. Select the **Rule-based** option. Note that the rule is set to **Tangent**. Select the **Standard** option. Four edges are shown as the round references, as shown in Figure 8–72.

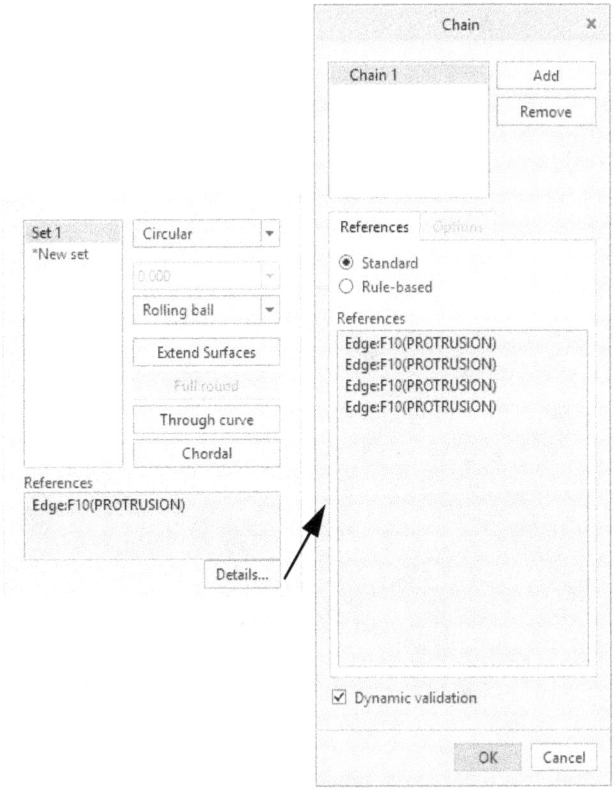

Figure 8–72

4. Click **Remove** to remove all four edge references.

5. Select the same edge, but this time right-click and select
   ⬚ (Pick From List). Select the first instance of
   IntentEdg:F10 as shown in Figure 8–73.

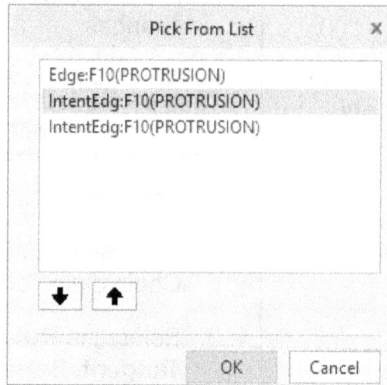

Pick From List ✕

Edge:F10(PROTRUSION)
IntentEdg:F10(PROTRUSION)
IntentEdg:F10(PROTRUSION)

⬇ ⬆

OK   Cancel

Figure 8–73

6. Note that the message area indicates this edge is created as
   feature x part, as shown in Figure 8–74.

➡ Showing Intent Chain (F10 X PART) created by feature 10 (PROTRUSION), model INTENT_CHAIN. Confirm selection.

Figure 8–74

7. Click **OK**. The intent edge is now listed in the *References*
   area as shown in Figure 8–75.

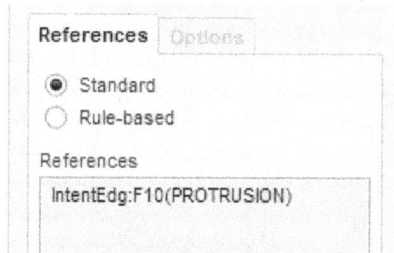

References Options

⦿ Standard
◯ Rule-based

References

IntentEdg:F10(PROTRUSION)

Figure 8–75

8. Click **OK** in the Chain dialog box.

9. Complete the round.

10. Modify the location of the protrusion from *0.75* to **2.0**, as shown in Figure 8–76.

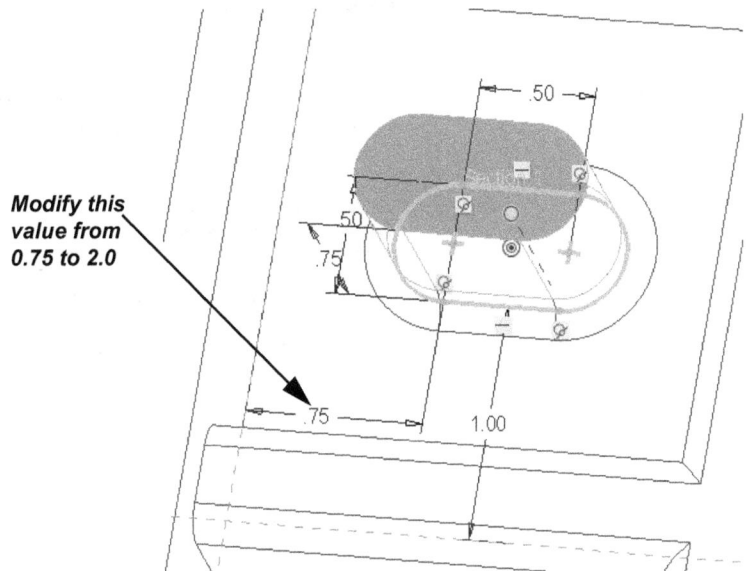

Modify this value from 0.75 to 2.0

Figure 8–76

11. Regenerate the part as shown in Figure 8–77. The round updates according to your design intent.

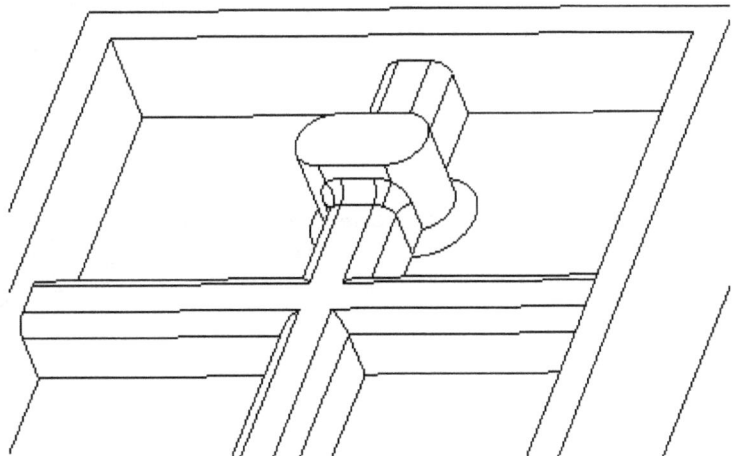

Figure 8–77

12. Save the part and erase it from memory.

Practice 8d

Parent/Child Relationships in Rounds

Practice Objective

- Learn how different selection techniques can affect the parent/child relationships between the features.

Task 1 - Open a part file.

1. Set the working directory to the *PCR_In_Rounds* folder.

2. Open **rounds_pc.prt**.

3. Set the model display as follows:

    - *(Datum Display Filters)*: All Off

    - *(Spin Center)*: Off

    - *(Display Style)*: No Hidden)

Task 2 - Create rounds on the cylindrical protrusions.

1. Create a round with a *Radius* of **0.5** on the edge shown in Figure 8–78. Select the back side of the circular curve.

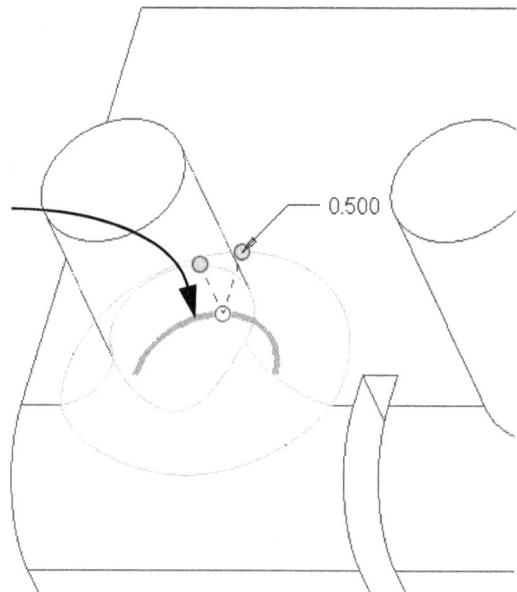

Select the back side of this edge

0.500

Figure 8–78

The resulting round displays as shown in Figure 8–79.

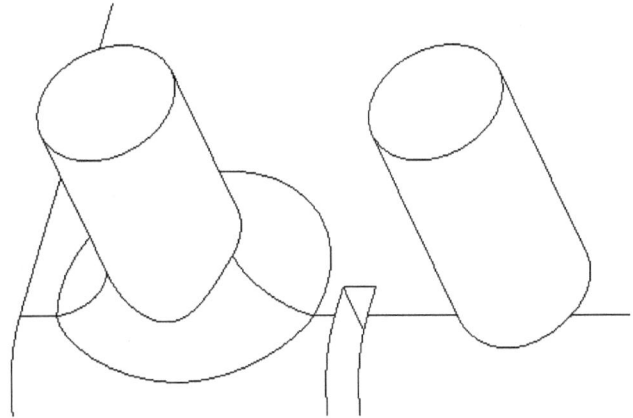

Figure 8–79

2. Create a second round with a *Radius* of **0.5** on the front cylindrical edge on the right side cylinder, as shown in Figure 8–80.

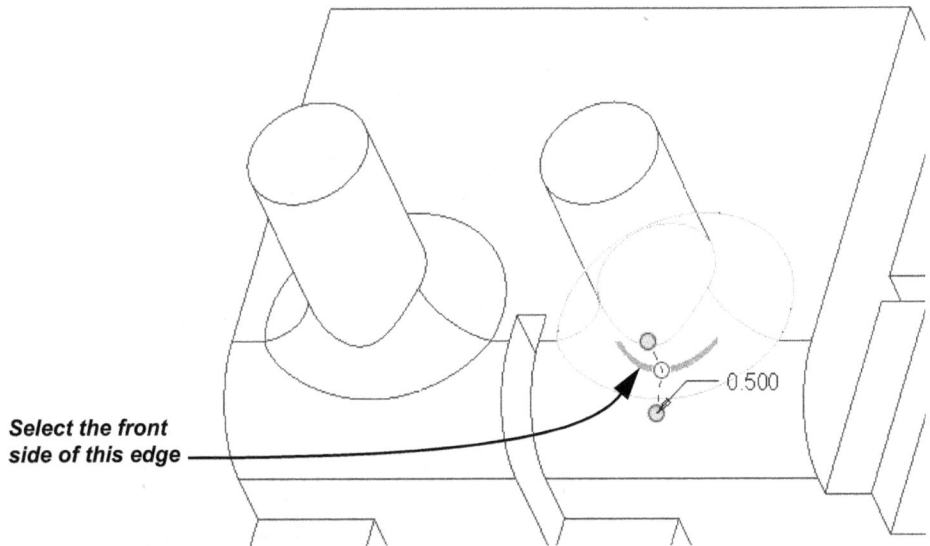

Select the front side of this edge

0.500

Figure 8–80

- The resulting round displays as shown in Figure 8–81.

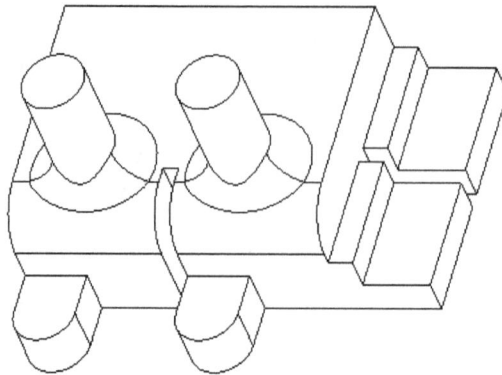

Figure 8–81

Design Considerations

The two rounds look identical. How does the selection of two different references (back edge versus front edge) affect the round? Are both rounds equally flexible to changes made to the model?

Task 3 - Change the model by deleting an existing round feature.

1. Select the round feature shown in Figure 8–82. Right-click on the feature and select **Delete**. Click **OK** to delete the feature.

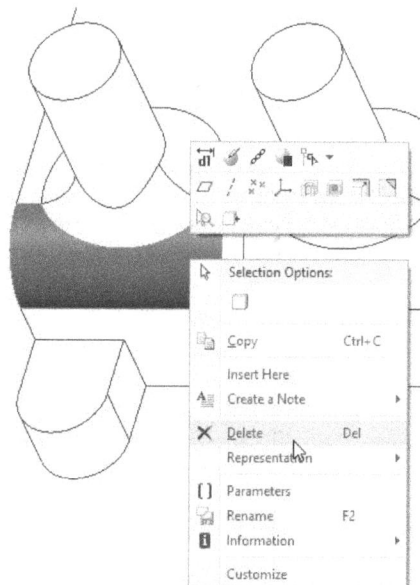

Figure 8–82

2. The feature is successfully deleted without affecting the model. Delete the other round feature that is shaded in Figure 8–83. The Delete dialog box opens.

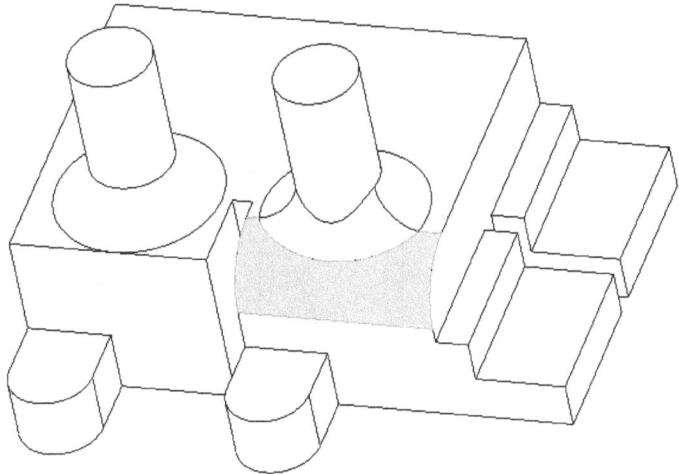

Figure 8–83

Design Considerations

The second round feature is a child of the feature being deleted. The edge reference selected to create the round was created by the intersection of the cylinder and the feature being deleted.

3. Click **Options** and select **Suspend**, as shown in Figure 8–84.

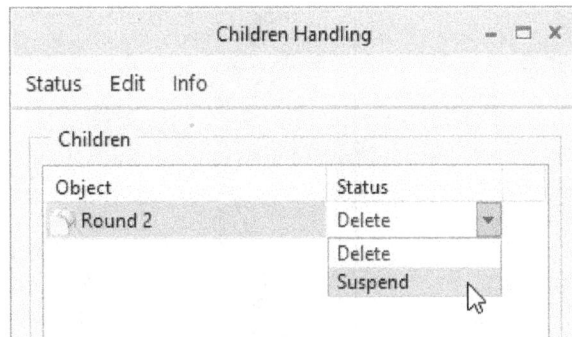

Figure 8–84

4. Click **OK**.

5. Select **Round 2** in the Model Tree. In the mini toolbar, click (Edit Definition).

*If the **Resolve** menu displays, select **Quick Fix>Redefine> Confirm**.*

6. Remove the original edge reference and select the back edge, as you did for the left side round.

7. Complete the round. The part displays as shown in Figure 8–85. The failure would not have occurred if the correct reference was originally selected.

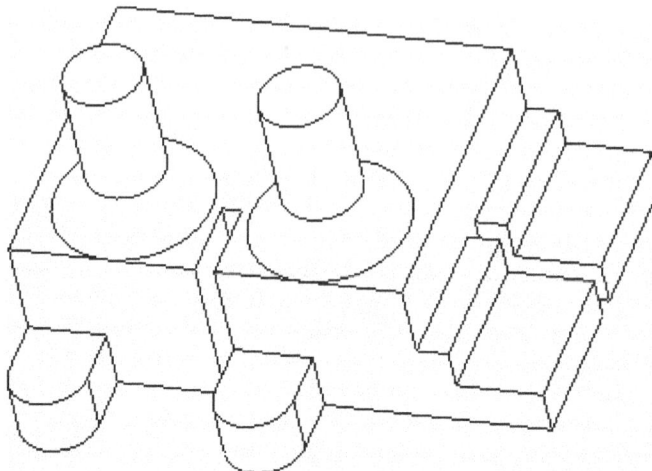

Figure 8–85

Task 4 - Create rounds on the two front bosses.

1. Create a round with a *Radius* of **0.5** on the left boss. Select the edge shown in Figure 8–86.

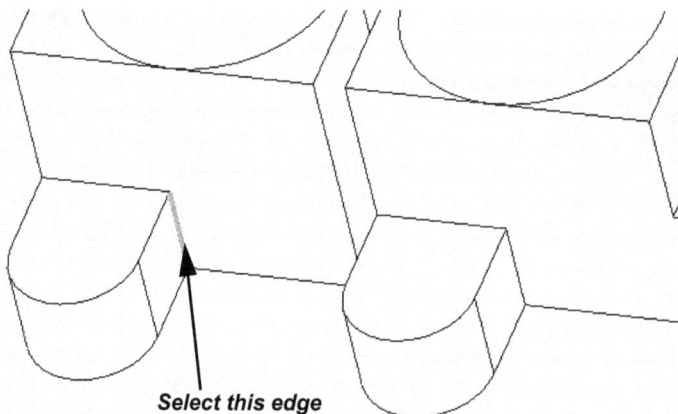

Select this edge

Figure 8–86

2. Create a round by selecting the two surfaces shown in Figure 8–87. Set the *Radius* to **0.5**.

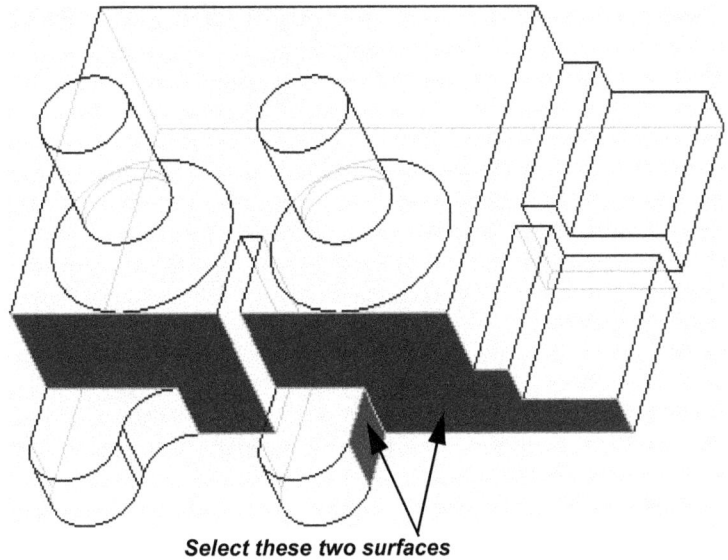

Select these two surfaces

Figure 8–87

The part displays as shown in Figure 8–88.

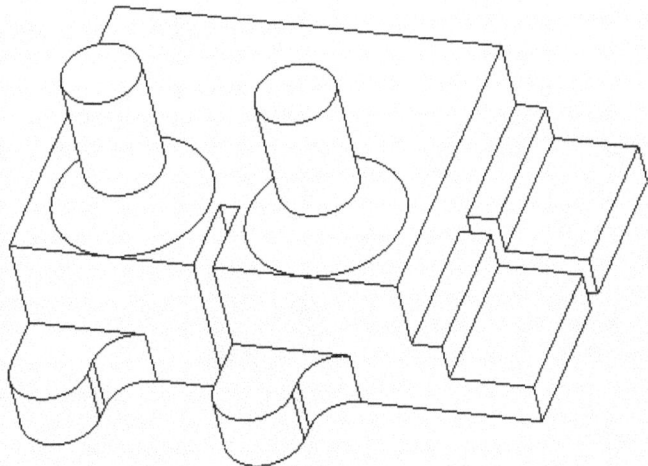

Figure 8–88

Again the two rounds look identical, but how will they react to design changes?

Task 5 - Modify the radii of the rounds on the bosses.

1. Edit the *Radius* of the round on the left side boss to **0.75**.

2. Regenerate the model. The round updates as shown in Figure 8–89.

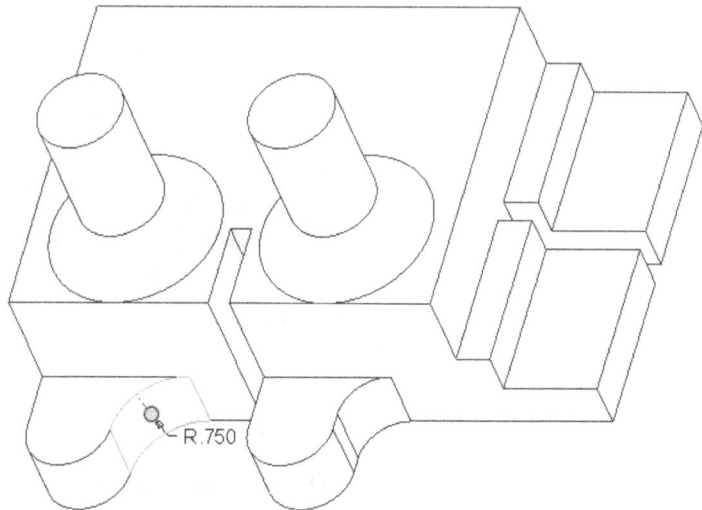

Figure 8–89

3. Edit the *Radius* of the round on the right side boss to **0.75**.

4. Regenerate the model. The part displays as shown in Figure 8–90.

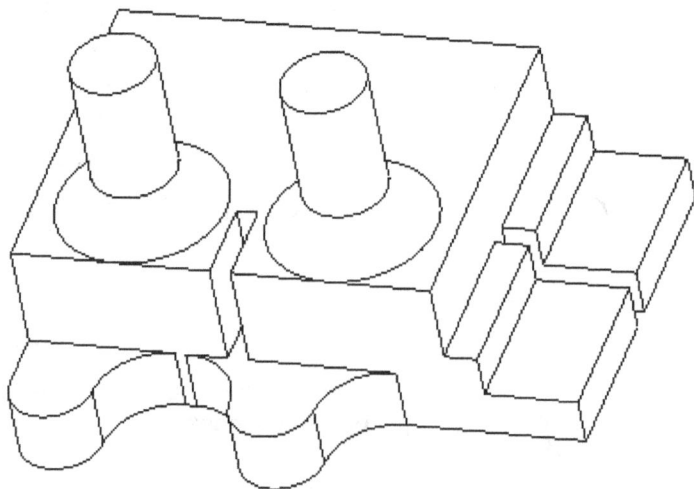

Figure 8–90

Design Considerations

The larger radius has caused the round surface to extend past the surface reference selected from the side of the boss. If this type of modification is required, a different type of reference should be used.

5. Edit the definition of the round. Remove both surface references and select the edge shown in Figure 8–91.

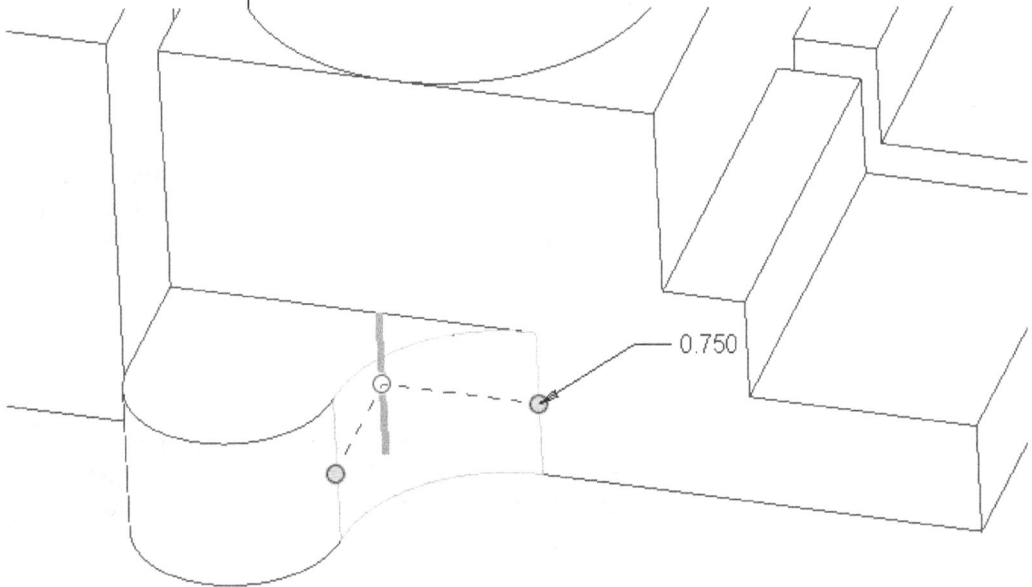

0.750

Figure 8–91

6. Complete the round.

7. Save the part and erase it from memory.

Chapter Review Questions

1. To select edges using the **Intent Chain** option, which type of selection tool must be used?

   a. **Pick from List**

   b. **Next**

   c. **Select references**

   d. **Chain**

2. When selecting edges using the Tangent rule, the round is only dependent on the edge used to start the chain. The removal of one of the automatically selected tangent edges would not cause the round to fail because of missing references.

   a. True

   b. False

3. When selecting edges using <Ctrl>, you are selecting references one by one. The round is not dependent on every edge that is selected. The removal of any edge would not cause the round to fail because of missing references.

   a. True

   b. False

4. A round that is created by selecting three surfaces for references can be created using which of the following round types? (Select all that apply.)

   a. **Constant Round**

   b. **Variable Round**

   c. **Full Round**

   d. **Thru Curve Round**

5. A round created using an edge and a surface creates a round between a selected edge and a selected surface to which it is tangent. A round created using this placement method can be created using which of the following round types? (Select all that apply.)

   a. **Constant Round**

   b. **Variable Round**

   c. **Full Round**

   d. **Thru Curve Round**

6. Which of the following selection types are available for selecting edges? (Select all that apply.)

   a. One-by-one

   b. Tangent

   c. Partial loop

   d. Surface loop

   e. Intent edges

7. Which icon is used to specify transitions?

   a.

   b.

   c.

   d.

Advanced Rounds

Advanced functionality and techniques can be applied to rounds to control their shape. You can also determine how they interface with each other by using transitions. Advanced round functionality enables you to handle complex rounding problems.

Learning Objectives in This Chapter

- Learn to create a round with multiple sets into one feature and to control the shape, spine, and transitions.
- Create a conic shaped round and specify the rho value to create an elliptical, parabolic, or hyperbolic shape.
- Learn the difference between using the Rolling Ball and Normal to Spine options to control the cross-sectional shape of the round.
- Add transitions to the Round feature to control the extent of the round or how two rounds come together at a corner.
- Use different techniques to manipulate or create a Round feature.
- Study the different round shapes and how they were created.

9.1 Introduction to Advanced Rounds

During round creation, additional options provide more control over the final geometry of a round feature.

The Sets panel enables you to define several sets of rounds into one feature and to specify the shape, spine, and transitions of the round to handle complex rounding problems.

The advanced round options enable you to:

- Create a round with a conic shape.

- Create a Normal to Spine round.

- Create a single round feature with different types of references (e.g., edge chain, surface to surface, etc.).

- Create a surface to surface round that uses more than one pair of reference surfaces.

- Create a single round feature that has both a constant radius and a variable radius.

- Create a single constant radius round feature that has multiple edges, each with different radii values.

- Control the shape of transitions between rounds.

- Prevent regeneration failure.

Round Sets

A round set is a subset of a round feature that contains the information required to create the envelope surfaces. This information includes the round style, shape, placement references, and radius definition. A new set is added by selecting ***New set** in the Sets panel, as shown in Figure 9–1.

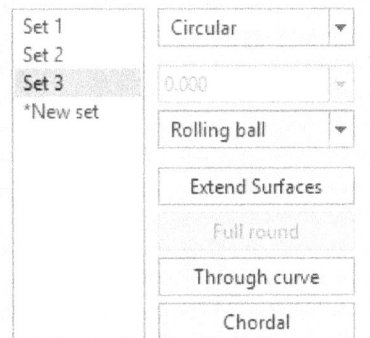

Set 1	Circular ▼
Set 2	
Set 3	0.000 ▼
*New set	Rolling ball ▼
	Extend Surfaces
	Full round
	Through curve
	Chordal

Figure 9–1

Each round set must be of a single style, radius, shape, and placement method. Advanced techniques enable you to create multiple round sets in a single feature.

Advanced round techniques combine multiple round sets into a single round feature. One set of a round can be a constant radius edge chain round, while the second set can be a variable surface to surface round, as shown in Figure 9–2.

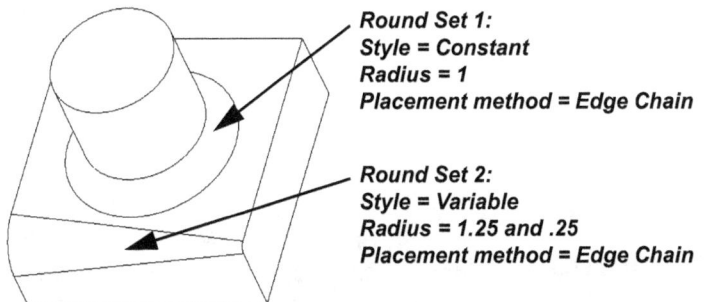

Round Set 1:
Style = Constant
Radius = 1
Placement method = Edge Chain

Round Set 2:
Style = Variable
Radius = 1.25 and .25
Placement method = Edge Chain

Figure 9–2

9.2 Round Shapes

Advanced round options can be defined in the Sets panel, as shown in Figure 9–3.

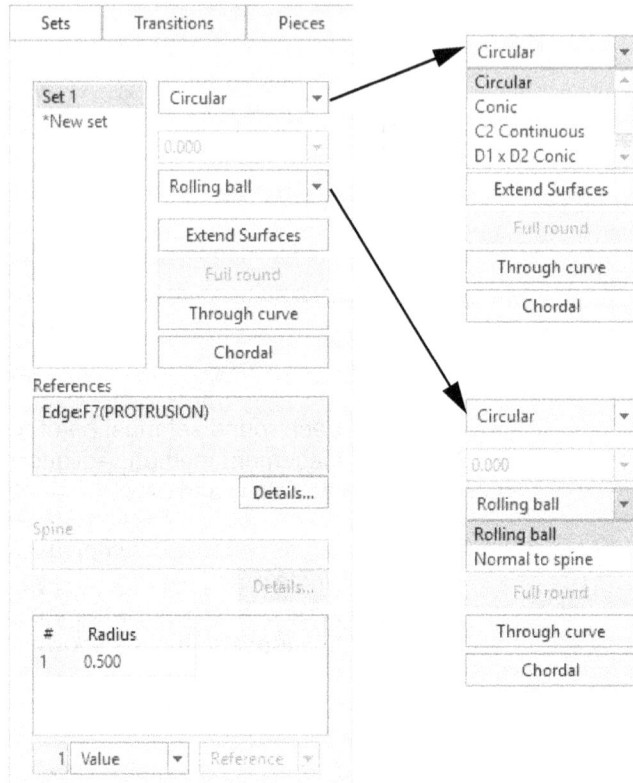

Figure 9–3

Circular versus Conic

The **Circular** and **Conic** options enable you to control the shape of the round. With a circular-shaped round, a circular cross-section is used between the placement references defined by the rolling ball or spine to generate envelope surfaces. The **Circular** option is the default option for all rounds. All simple rounds use the circular shape.

With a conic-shaped round, a conic cross-section is created between the placement references. Unlike a circular round, the conic's shape is not only controlled by a radius value. The radius value that is assigned only determines the tangency point for the rolling ball or spine. The conic is driven by a parameter called *Rho*.

The **Conic** parameter controls the sharpness of the conic cross-sectional shape of the round feature. Different values assigned to Rho create different shapes. The following ranges are used for the different shapes:

- **Elliptical:** 05 < Rho < .5

- **Parabolic:** Rho = .5

- **Hyperbolic:** 5 < Rho < .95

The difference between a circular round with a *Radius* of **2** and two conic rounds with *Rho* values of **.25** and **.75** is shown in Figure 9–4.

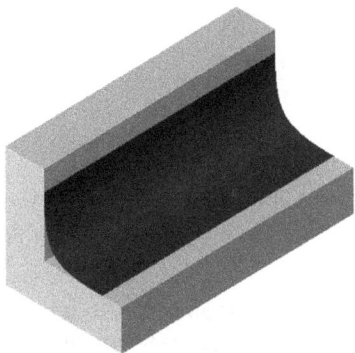

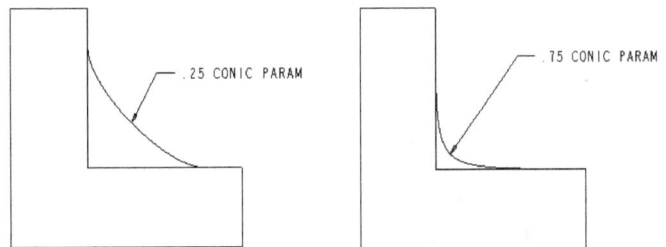

Figure 9–4

The **D1xD2 Conic** option results in a dimensioning scheme, as shown in Figure 9–5.

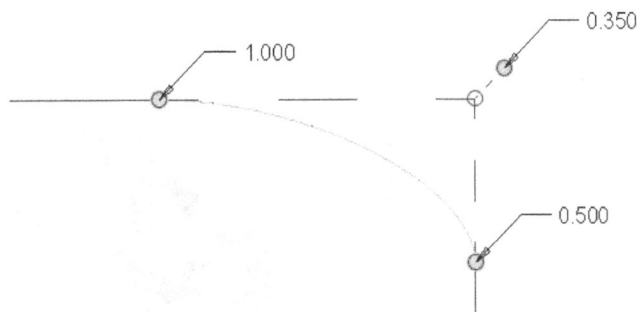

Figure 9–5

The default conic parameter is **0.5**. This can be changed with the **ratio_grid_interval** config.pro option, which can be set to a value within a range between 0 and 1.

The **C2 Continuous** option creates a round with a spline cross-section that has curvature continuity with the adjoining surfaces. This round can be both a constant and variable radius. The shape factor of the spline can be adjusted to obtain the required curvature. You can also create this round with two leg lengths. This option can only be used with a constant round set. The shape factor must be between 0.05 and 0.95, as shown in Figure 9–6.

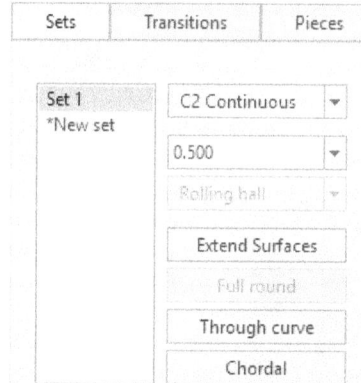

Figure 9–6

Rolling Ball versus Normal to Spine

The **Rolling ball** option defines the round geometry with a ball of a specific radius as it rolls along the placement references. The point at which the rolling ball touches the model becomes the locating point for the cross-sectional shape of the round. The placement references for placing the rolling ball can be edges, surfaces, or a combination of the two. The **Rolling ball** option is the default for all rounds. Examples of rounds being located with a rolling ball are shown in Figure 9–7.

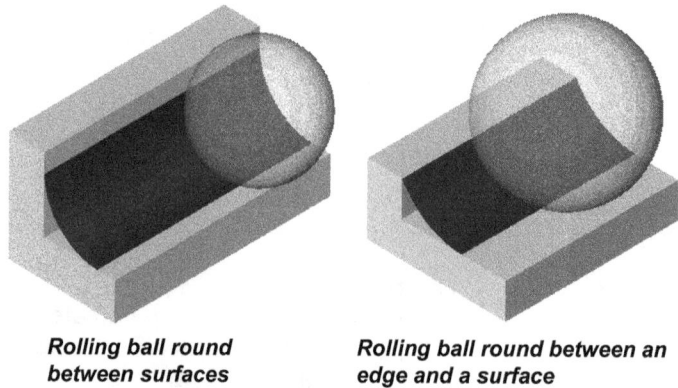

Rolling ball round
between surfaces

Rolling ball round between an
edge and a surface

Figure 9–7

The **Normal to spine** option sweeps an arc-shaped cross-section along a spine trajectory to create the round. As the arc is swept across the spine trajectory, it remains perpendicular at all points. The spine required as the perpendicular reference depends on the selection method. These methods are as follows.

Method	Description
Edge Chain	Creo Parametric uses the selected edge(s) as the spine trajectory. As the arc sweeps along the edge, it remains tangent to both adjacent surfaces.
Surf to Surf	Specify the edge or datum curve to use as the spine trajectory. The arc remains tangent to the selected surfaces at all points along the sweep.
Edge to Surf	Specify the edge or datum curve to use as the spine trajectory. The arc remains tangent to the selected surface and touches the selected edge.

The **Normal to spine** option might work when the **Rolling ball** option fails. A Rolling Ball round can fail if the curvature of the surfaces or the radius (of a variable round) changes too quickly. When the surface of the Rolling Ball intersects itself, it can also fail. If any of these situations occur, the **Normal to spine** option might be able to create the required round geometry where the **Rolling ball** option cannot do so.

An attempt to place a surface to surface round between the top and front surfaces of a model is shown in Figure 9–8. If created as a Rolling Ball round, the round cannot be created at the specified size due to the tight curvature on the front surface. This causes the Rolling Ball to self-intersect and fail. By using the **Normal to spine** option and the back edge of the model as the spine, the round can be created with the required size.

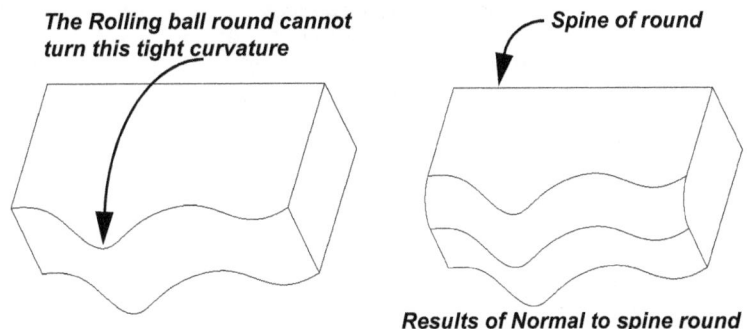

The Rolling ball round cannot turn this tight curvature

Spine of round

Results of Normal to spine round

Figure 9–8

When defining a surface to surface variable radius round, the **Spline** option becomes available in the Sets panel. Figure 9–9 shows a spine reference with three radius locations.

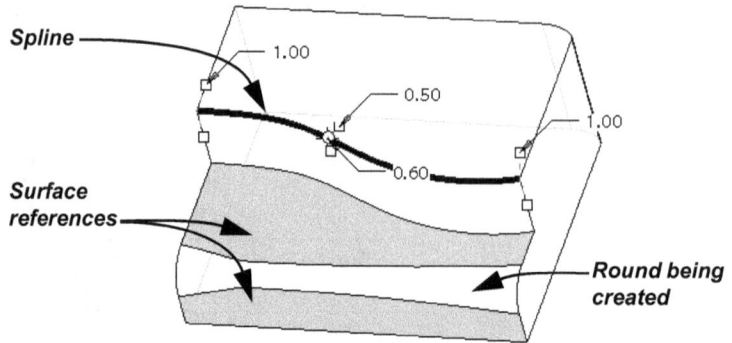

Figure 9–9

Consider the rounds in Figure 9–10. Note the unique behavior of the tangent lines. The main difference between a **Rolling ball** and a **Normal to spine** round is the behavior of the cross-section from one end to the other.

1 round set with Attributes:
Rolling ball, Constant,
Edge Chain, Radius = 1.5

1 round set with Attributes:
Normal to spine, Constant,
Surface to surface,
Radius = 1.5

1 round set with Attributes:
Normal to spine, Variable,
Surface to surface,
Radius = 1.5 and 0.25

Front view

Selected spines

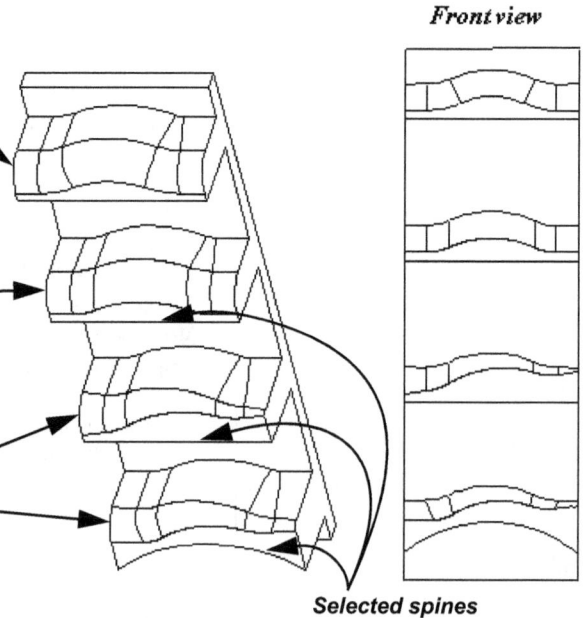

Figure 9–10

9.3 Transitions

A transition is geometry that is added to round pieces to join them together and attach them to existing geometry at their loose ends. Transitions can only be applied at the ends of round pieces as shown in Figure 9–11.

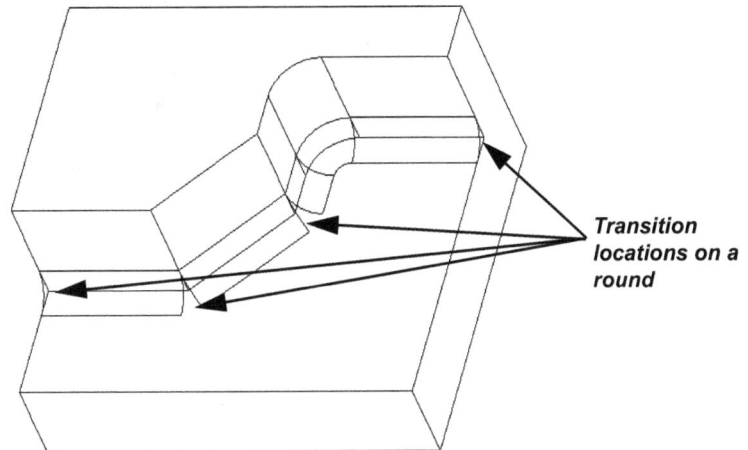

Transition locations on a round

Figure 9–11

Default and User-Defined Transitions

Creo Parametric automatically adds transitions by extending the round envelope and existing part surfaces, and then creating new geometry as required. In most cases, Creo Parametric adds the appropriate transition to the round based on the selected references. No action is required by you. These transitions are called default transitions. However, in some instances the system might not be able to create a transition or produce the required shape. In these cases, you can manually add the transitions.

To define a transition between sets of rounds, click

⌇ (Transition Mode) in the *Round* dashboard to switch to Transition mode. Once in Transition mode, you can hover the cursor over each transition area to highlight it in cyan. Select the transition area on the model to change the transition type from the default. Once a transition has been selected, all of the possible transition types for the selected item display in the drop-down list in the *Round* dashboard. You can also change the type of transition by right-clicking on the transition area and selecting the appropriate option.

Figure 9–12 shows examples of the default and user-defined transitions.

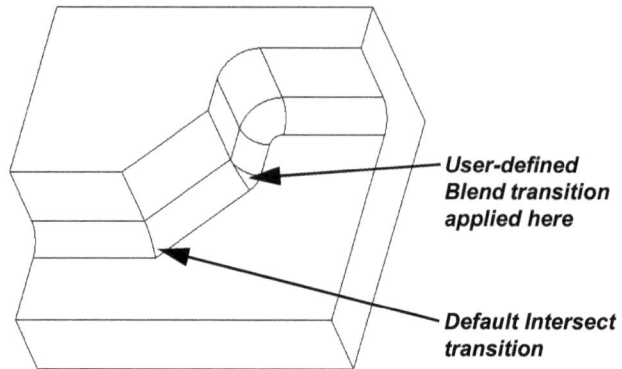

Figure 9–12

Four types of user-defined transitions are available:

- Stop

- Blend

- Continue

- Corner

Each transition has differing options based on the geometry you are working with.

Stop Transitions

The **Stop** transition enables you to attach open-ended pieces of a round to the model. It can only be used on the ends of a single round object. Figure 9–13 shows the available **Stop transition** options.

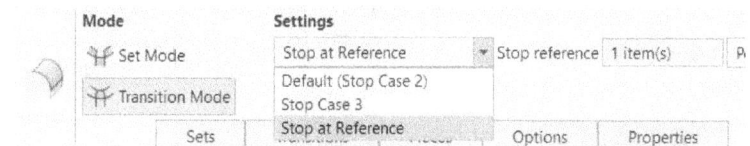

Figure 9–13

The exact attachment of a default Stop transition depends on the geometry that is encountered. In some cases, the system might not be able to interpret which surfaces to extend to close off the round. In these cases, a **Stop at Reference** transition can be applied to the surfaces to close the round.

Figure 9–14 shows examples of a **Stop at Reference** transition.

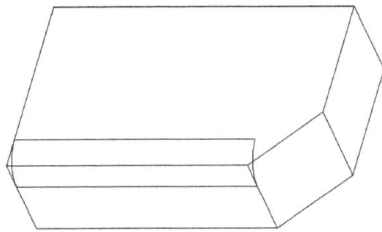

Initial envelope surface

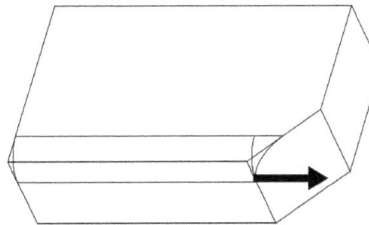

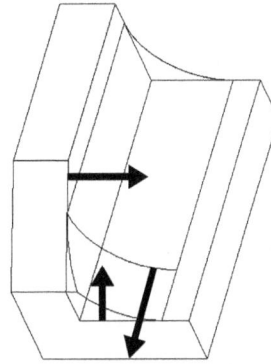

Envelope surface extended complete the round

Round attached to model after Stop at reference transition is applied

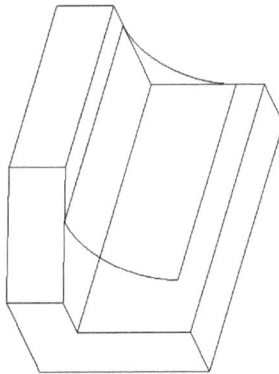

Initial envelope surface

Round attached to model with Stop at Reference transition applied

Figure 9–14

The Stop reference can be a point, vertex, surface, or plane, as shown in Figure 9–15.

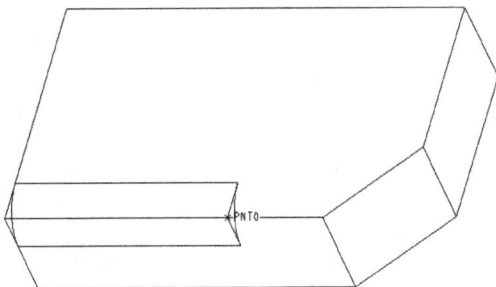

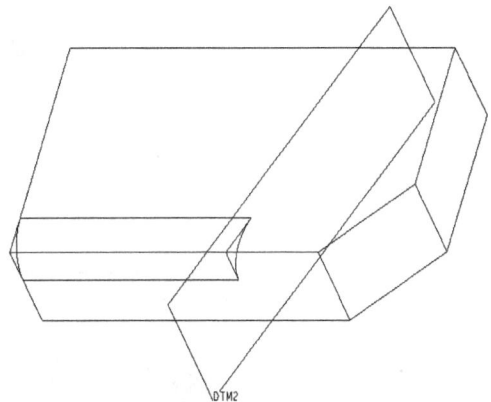

Figure 9–15

The **Stop Case 1**, **Stop Case 2**, and **Stop Case 3** transition types assign stop references generated by Creo Parametric to the selected transition. Figure 9–16 shows examples of the stop transition types.

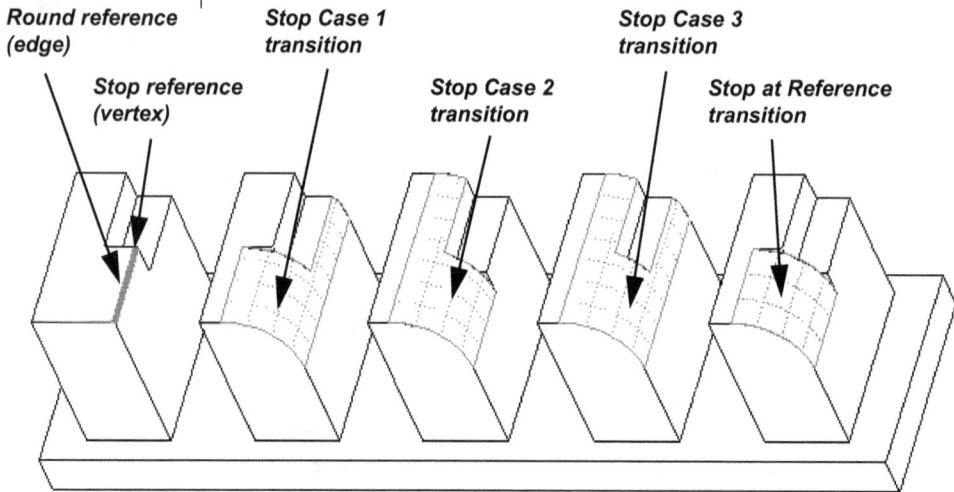

Round reference (edge)
Stop reference (vertex)
Stop Case 1 transition
Stop Case 2 transition
Stop Case 3 transition
Stop at Reference transition

Figure 9–16

Blend and Continue Transitions

A **Blend** transition blends by creating a fillet surface between adjacent surfaces to the selected edge. A **Continue** transition continues the round geometry. In a Continue transition, the surfaces about the round are extended to meet it, if applicable. Figure 9–17 shows examples of blend and continue transitions.

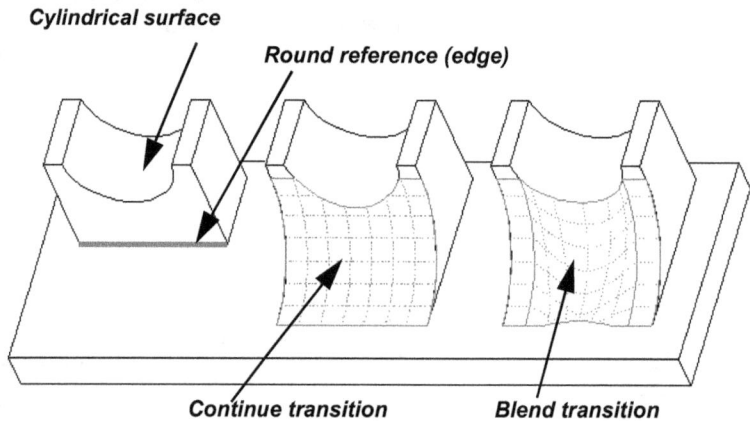

Cylindrical surface
Round reference (edge)
Continue transition
Blend transition

Figure 9–17

Corner Transitions

Several types of transitions can be used at a corner where two or more round sets meet. Along with the **Blend** and **Stop** transitions, the **Intersect**, **Corner Sphere**, **Round Only 1,** and **Round Only 2** transitions can be used, as shown in Figure 9–18.

Figure 9–18

An **Intersect** transition extends the round set until it intersects with adjacent round sets and forms a sharp edge. This command is only available if the active round set intersects another round set. Figure 9–19 shows an example of a corner with **Intersect**, **Blend**, and **Stop** transitions applied.

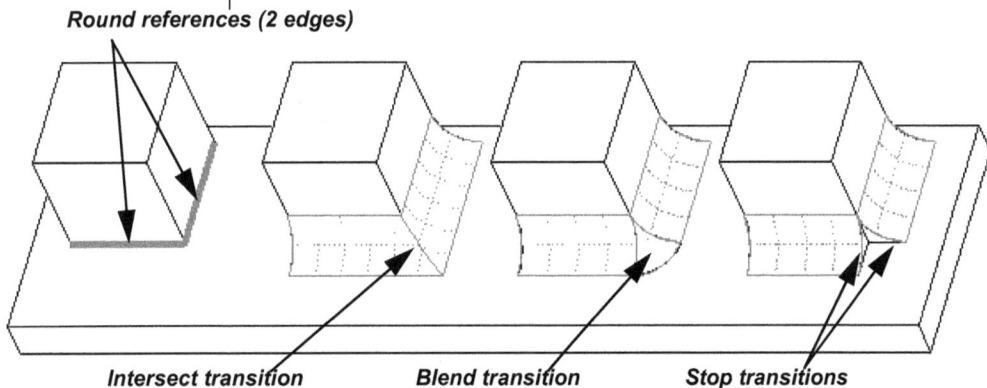

Figure 9–19

Corner Sphere and **Round Only 1** or **2** are similar transitions. A **Corner Sphere** transition rounds the corner where there are three intersecting round sets. By default, the created sphere is the same radius as the largest round involved in the intersection. You can modify the radius and the distance back from the corner where the blend starts, if required.

A **Round Only 1** or **2** transition also rounds the corner where there are three intersecting round sets. However, it creates the geometry with compounded rounds, which are wrapped around the corner using the radius of the largest intersecting round.

Figure 9–20 shows the different types of corner transitions.

**Round references
(3 sets, each set contains 1 edge)**

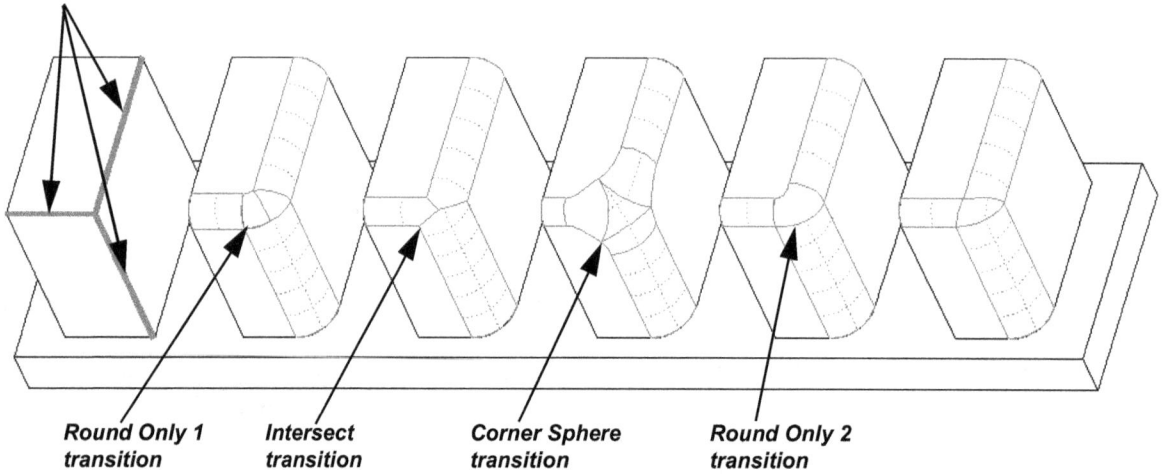

**Round Only 1
transition**

**Intersect
transition**

**Corner Sphere
transition**

**Round Only 2
transition**

Figure 9–20

9.4 Tips for Creating Rounds

Use the following tips and techniques when creating a round:

- Manipulate the type, references, shape, cross-section, or transition of the round to create the required round geometry.

- If round geometry cannot be created, try breaking the single round into separate rounds.

- Try using a sweep, blend, or extruded protrusion to create a round if the geometry cannot be created using a round feature.

- If the round cannot be created as a solid, create it as a surface and click 🗹 (Solidify) in the *Model* tab to create the solid geometry.

- If you are creating a Full round, the edge references must share a common surface.

- If you are selecting two surfaces to create a Full round, you must also select a Driving Surface reference.

9.5 Case Studies

Figure 9–21 shows round shapes that have been created using the following transitions types:

- The first series (1 - 5) displays rounds with one or two sets.

- The second series (6 -10) displays rounds with three sets and constant radii.

- The third series (11 - 14) displays rounds with three sets and variable radii.

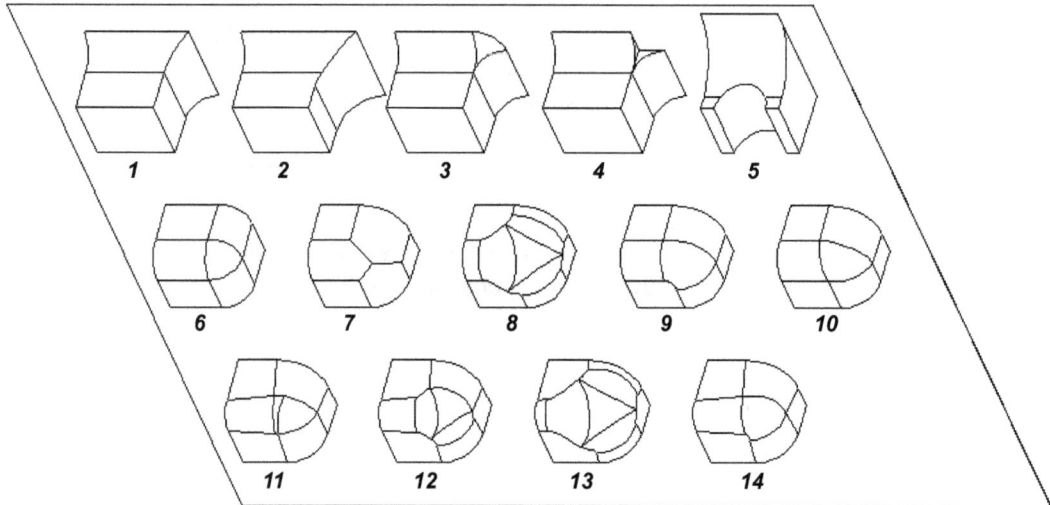

Figure 9–21

These rounds are described as follows:

Round	Description
1	1 Set: [2 edges, Constant, R = 1] Transition: Intersect (default)
2	2 Sets: [1 edge, Constant, R = 1], [1 edge, Constant, R = 1.5] Transition: Intersect (default)
3	1 Set: [2 edges, Constant, R = 1] Transition: Blend
4	1 Set: [2 edges, Constant, R = 1] Transition: Stop at Reference (twice)

5	1 Set: [1 edge, Constant, R = 2] Transition: Continue
6	3 Sets: [1 edge, Constant, R = 1], [1 edge, Constant, R = 1], [1 edge, Constant, R = 1] Transition: Round Only
7	3 Sets: [1 edge, Constant, R = 1], [1 edge, Constant, R = 1.2], [1 edge, Constant, R = 1.5] Transition: Intersect
8	3 Sets: [1 edge, Constant, R = 1], [1 edge, Constant, R = 1.2], [1 edge, Constant, R = 1.5] Transition: Corner Sphere [R = 1.65, L1 = 0.75, L2 = 0.15, L3 = 0.4]
9	3 Sets: [1 edge, Constant, R = 1], [1 edge, Constant, R = 1.2], [1 edge, Constant, R = 1.5] Transition: Round Only
10	3 Sets: [1 edge, Constant, R = 1], [1 edge, Constant, R = 1.2], [1 edge, Constant, R = 1.5] Transition: Patch
11	3 Sets: [1 edge, Variable, R = 0.75, R = 1], [1 edge, Variable, R = 1.25, R = 1], [1 edge, Variable, R = 1.5, R = 1] Transition: Round Only
12	3 Sets: [1 edge, Variable, R = 0.75, R = 1], [1 edge, Variable, R = 1.25, R = 1], [1 edge, Variable, R = 1.5, R = 1] Transition: Corner Sphere [default values]
13	3 Sets: [1 edge, Variable, R = 0.75, R = 1], [1 edge, Variable, R = 1.25, R = 1], [1 edge, Variable, R = 1.5, R = 1] Transition: Corner Sphere [R = 1.65, L1 = 1.2, L2 = 0.05, L3 = 0.05]
14	3 Sets: [1 edge, Variable, R = 0.75, R = 1], [1 edge, Variable, R = 1.25, R = 1], [1 edge, Variable, R = 1.5, R = 1] Transition: Round Only

Practice 9a | Advanced Rounds

Practice Objective

- Create multiple round sets and define their transition types.

In this practice, you will complete the geometry for a plastic molded part. The original and completed models are shown in Figure 9–22. To create all of the geometry, you will create constant rounds that contain multiple round sets. Because each round has multiple sets, you can further customize the geometry at the intersections of these sets using various transition options. If each set was created as an independent round, you would not be able to access any options to control these intersections.

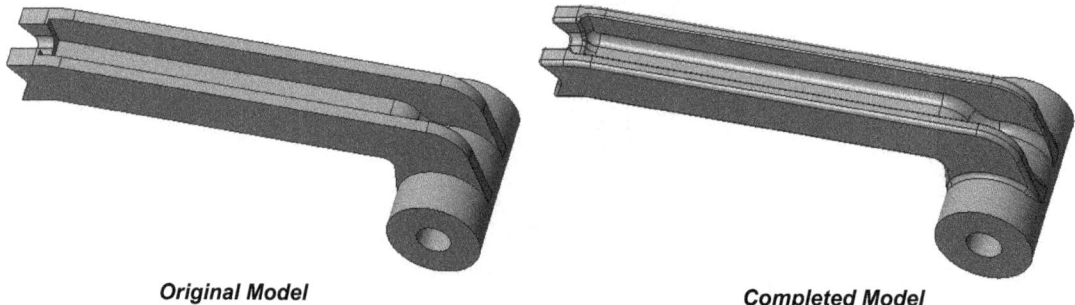

Original Model

Completed Model

Figure 9–22

Task 1 - Open a part file.

1. Set the working directory to the *Advanced_Rounds* folder.

2. Open **lever.prt**.

3. Set the model display as follows:

   - ⌖ *(Datum Display Filters)*: All Off

   - ⊱ *(Spin Center)*: Off

   - ▢ *(Display Style)*: ▢ (No Hidden)

Task 2 - Create a five-set round with two transitions.

Design Considerations

You are required to round the edges of the plastic part. The five sets of edges rounded in this task all intersect one another. You will customize the intersection of these rounds to simplify the shape of the round and more easily create the mold.

1. Select the edge reference shown in Figure 9–23 and click
   (Round) in the mini toolbar.

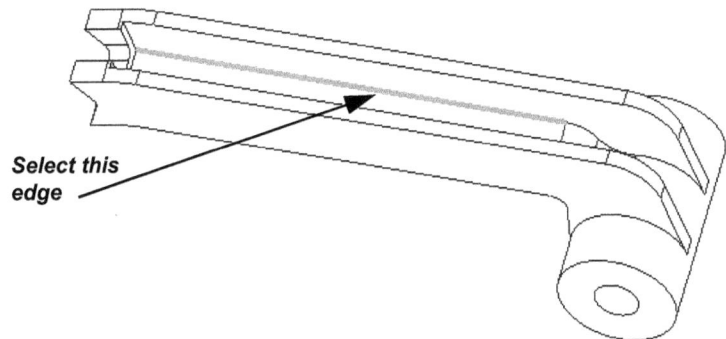

Select this edge

Figure 9–23

2. Edit the *Radius* value to **1**. Note that a surface displays on the model representing the round set geometry.

3. Select the opposite edge as a reference, as shown in Figure 9–24. DO NOT hold <Ctrl> while selecting.

By adding this second edge without using <Ctrl>, Creo Parametric automatically adds a second set to the same round feature.

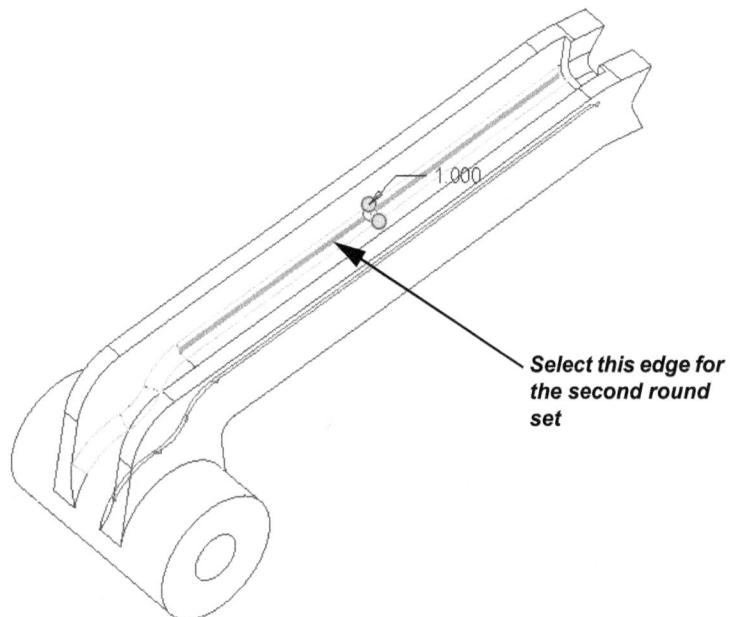

1.000

Select this edge for the second round set

Figure 9–24

4. Select the short vertical edge reference shown in Figure 9–25, and set the *Radius* to **0.90**.

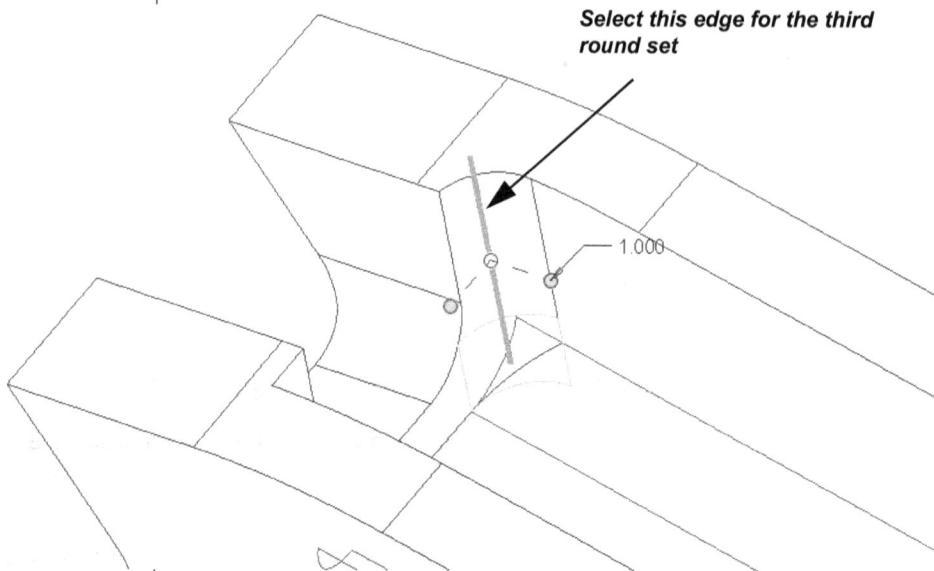

Select this edge for the third round set

— 1.000

Figure 9–25

5. Select the opposite edge to create a fourth round, with a *Radius* of **0.9**, as shown in Figure 9–26.

Select this edge for the fourth round set

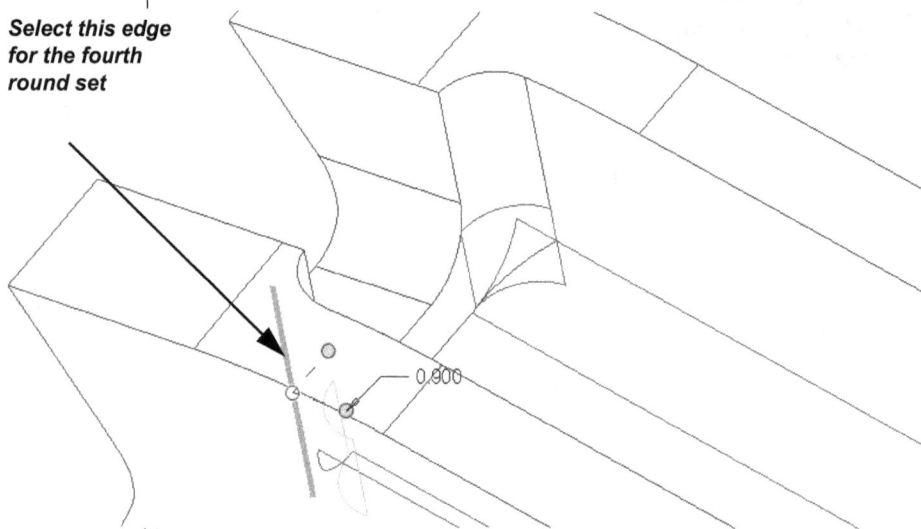

— 0.900

Figure 9–26

6. Select the surface reference shown in Figure 9–27, press <Ctrl>, and select the edge. Set the *Radius* value to **1.5**.

Select this edge as the edge reference of the fifth round set

Select this surface as the surface reference of the fifth round set

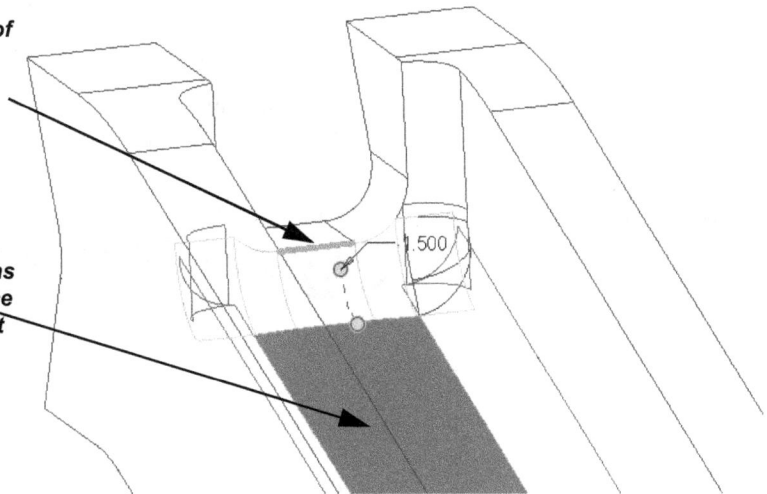

1.500

Figure 9–27

7. Review the Sets panel to verify that five sets have been created. You can select each set in the list to display the references that were assigned.

8. Click on the screen and select ⊓ (Transition Mode) in the mini toolbar.

9. Zoom to where the round sets meet.

10. Select the first transition as shown in Figure 9–28, right-click and select **Round Only 1**.

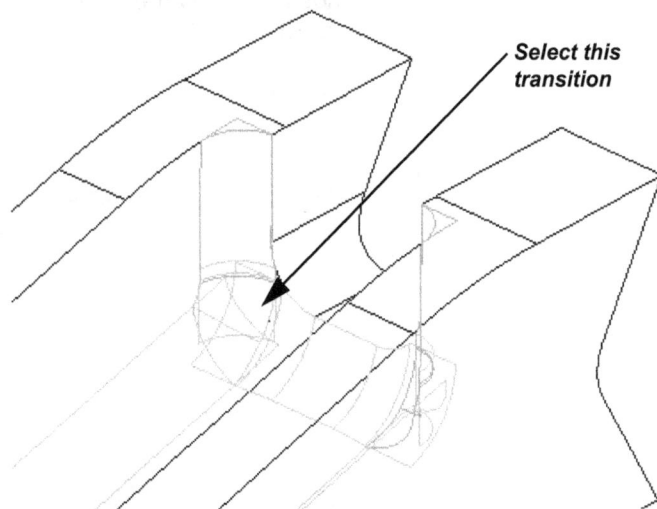

Select this transition

Figure 9–28

11. Repeat the Steps for the second transition.

12. Click ✔ (OK) in the *Round* dashboard.

13. Set the display to ⬜ (Shading With Edges). The model displays as shown in Figure 9–29.

One new round feature displays in the Model Tree.

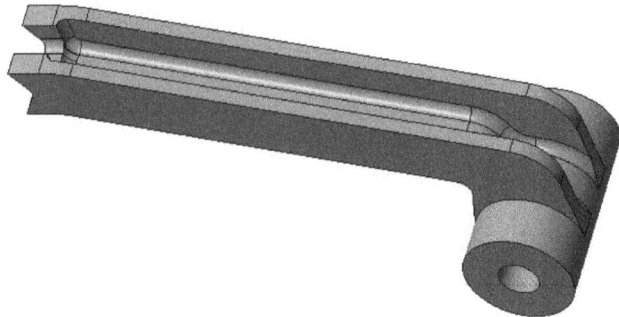

Figure 9–29

14. Set the display to ⬜ (No Hidden).

Task 3 - Create a five-set round with two Corner Sphere transitions.

Design Considerations

You are required to round the edges of the plastic model to ensure that the model does not have any sharp edges when it is handled. The five sets of edges rounded in this task all intersect with one another. You will customize the intersection of these rounds to simplify the shape of the round and more easily create the mold.

1. Create a **0.2** radius round on the edge shown in Figure 9–30.

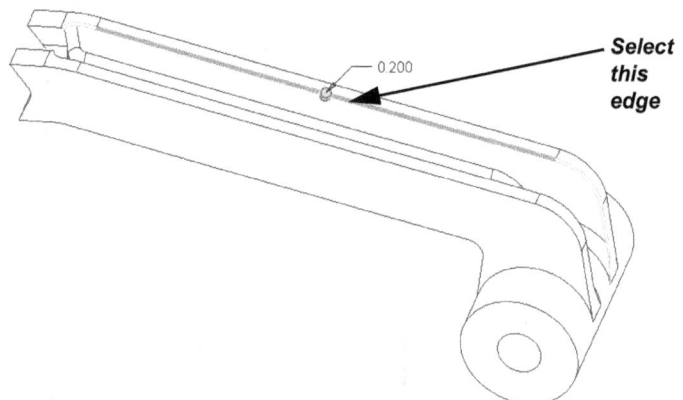

Select this edge

Figure 9–30

2. Select the edge reference shown in Figure 9–31 and use a *Radius* of **0.2**.

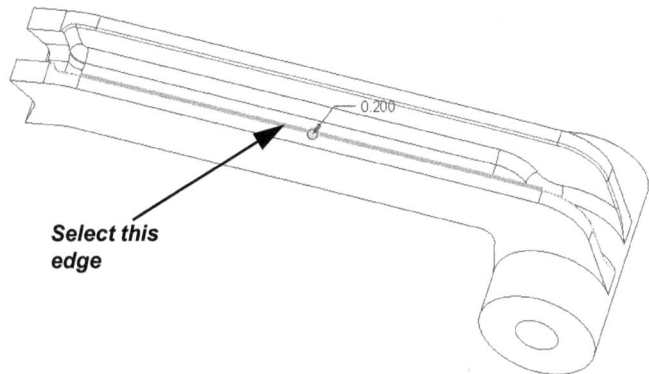

Figure 9–31

3. Select the edge shown in Figure 9–32 and set the *Radius* to **0.4**.

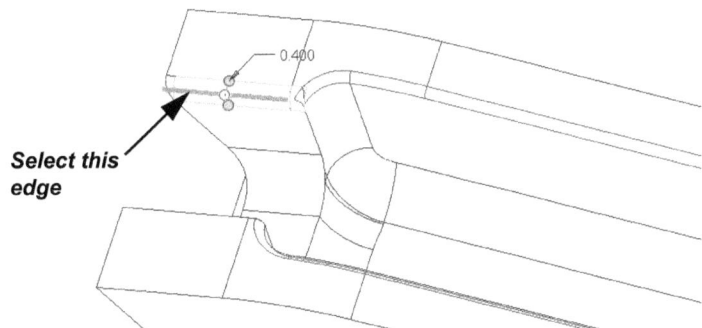

Figure 9–32

4. Select the opposite horizontal edge reference, as shown in Figure 9–33, and keep the *Radius* at **0.4**.

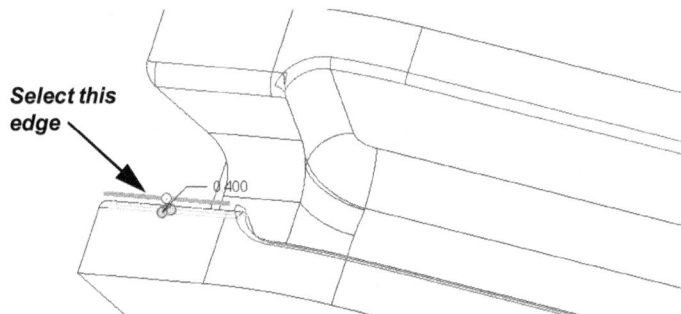

Figure 9–33

5. Select the short horizontal edge reference shown in Figure 9–34 and set the *Radius* to **0.3**.

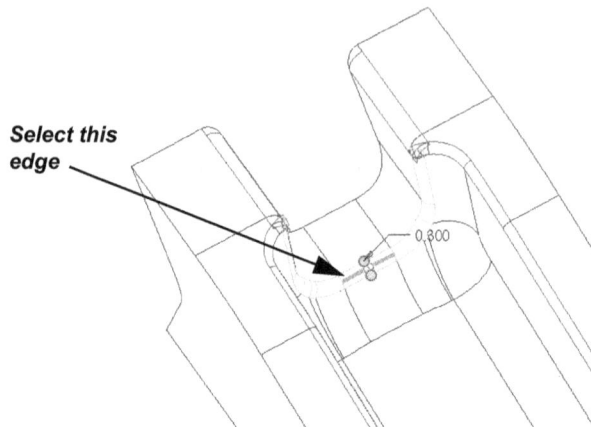

Select this edge

0.300

Figure 9–34

6. Click on the screen and select ᛨ (Transition Mode) in the mini toolbar.

7. Zoom to where the round sets meet.

8. Select the first transition as shown in Figure 9–35, right-click and select **Corner Sphere**. Maintain the default values in the *Round* dashboard.

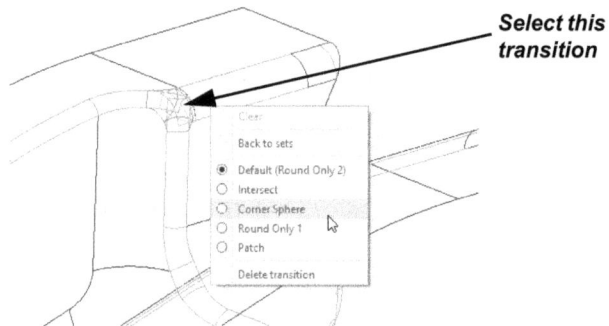

Select this transition

Clear
Back to sets
⦿ Default (Round Only 2)
○ Intersect
○ Corner Sphere
○ Round Only 1
○ Patch
Delete transition

Figure 9–35

9. Repeat the Steps for the second transition.

10. Click ✔ (OK) in the *Round* dashboard to complete the round.

11. Set the display to ⬜ (Shading With Edges). The model displays as shown in Figure 9–36.

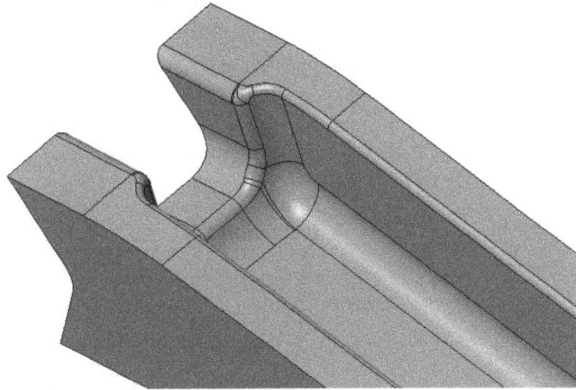

Figure 9–36

12. Set the display to 🗐 (No Hidden).

Task 4 - Create an eight-set round with four Patch transitions.

Design Considerations

Similar to the previous task, you must add rounds to the edges of the plastic model to ensure that the model does not have any sharp edges when it is handled. You will also customize the intersection of these rounds.

1. Use the techniques from the previous tasks to add eight constant round sets to the model, as shown in Figure 9–37.

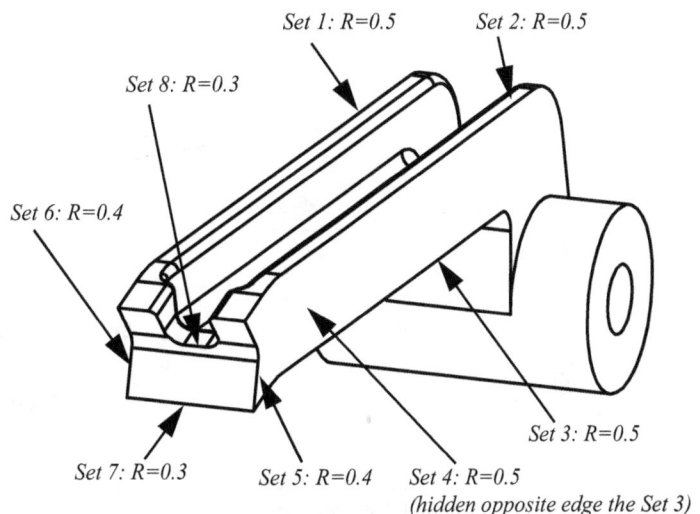

Set 1: R=0.5   *Set 2: R=0.5*
Set 8: R=0.3
Set 6: R=0.4
Set 3: R=0.5
Set 7: R=0.3   *Set 5: R=0.4*   *Set 4: R=0.5*
(hidden opposite edge the Set 3)

Figure 9–37

2. Add four **Patch** transitions where the round sets meet. The resulting model displays as shown in Figure 9–38.

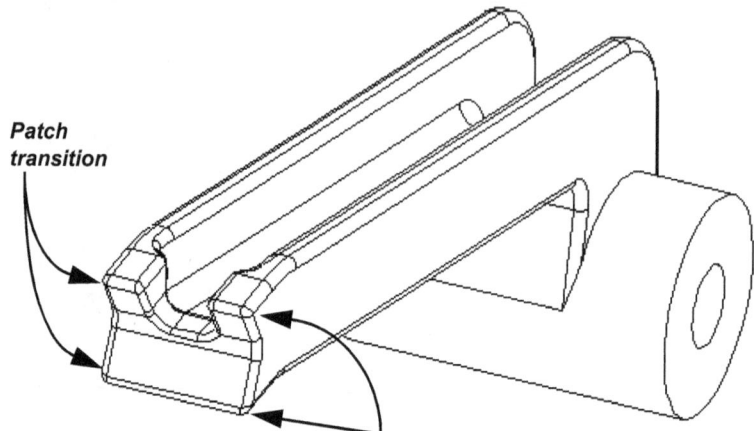

Patch transition

Patch transition

Figure 9–38

Task 5 - Create a round.

Design Considerations

The two edges that are rounded in this task do not intersect one another. Therefore, you do not need to add any transitions.

1. Add a round with a *Radius* of **0.5** to the two reference edges shown in Figure 9–39.

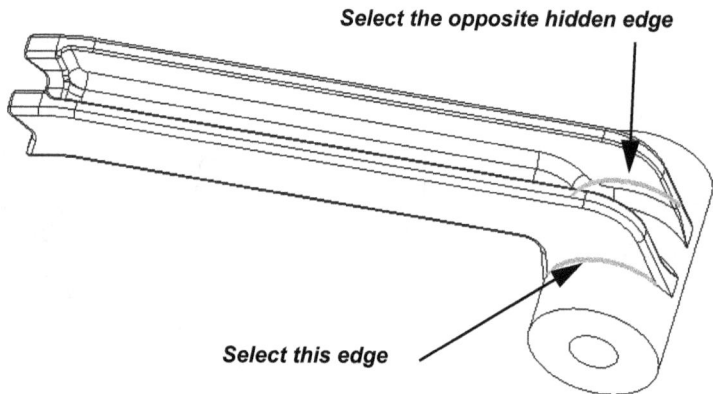

Select the opposite hidden edge

Select this edge

Figure 9–39

2. Set the display to ▢ (Shading With Edges). The resulting model displays as shown in Figure 9–40.

Figure 9–40

3. Save the part and close the window.

Practice 9b

Stop Transitions

Practice Objective

- Create rounds and change the extent of the rounds using the **Stop at Reference** transition type.

In this practice, you will create rounds that stop at a specific location using **Stop** transitions.

Task 1 - Open a part file.

1. Set the working directory to the *Stop_Transitions* folder.

2. Open **clip.prt**.

3. Set the model display as follows:

   - *⁺⁄* (Datum Display Filters): All Off

   - ⋟ (Spin Center): Off

   - ⬜ (Display Style): ⬜ (No Hidden)

4. Create a **0.5** radius round on the edge shown in Figure 9–41.

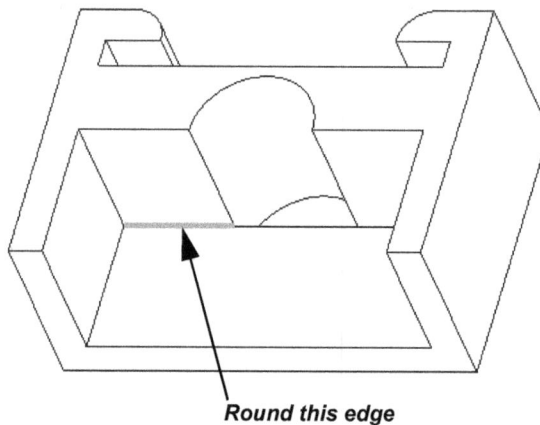

Round this edge

Figure 9–41

5. Complete the feature.

6. Set the model orientation to **TOP**.

7. Note how the system extends the cylindrical surface to close off the circular cut, as shown in Figure 9–42. This is not the required shape.

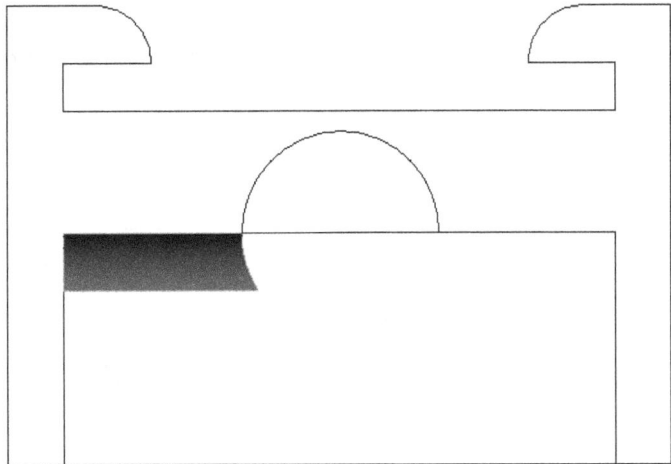

Figure 9–42

Task 2 - Prevent the system from extending the end of the round feature.

---

1. Press <Ctrl>+<D> to return to default orientation.

2. Edit the definition of the round that you just created.

3. Click on the screen and select ⊥ (Transition Mode) in the mini toolbar.

4. Select the transition shown in Figure 9–43, right-click, and select **Stop at Reference**.

5. Select the vertex shown in Figure 9–43 as the location at which the round should stop.

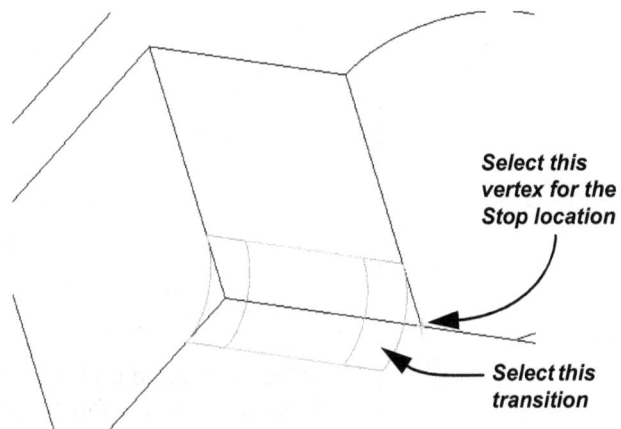

Select this vertex for the Stop location

Select this transition

Figure 9–43

---

6. Complete the feature and set the model orientation to **TOP**. Note that the round now ends with a flat surface, normal to the edge as shown in Figure 9–44.

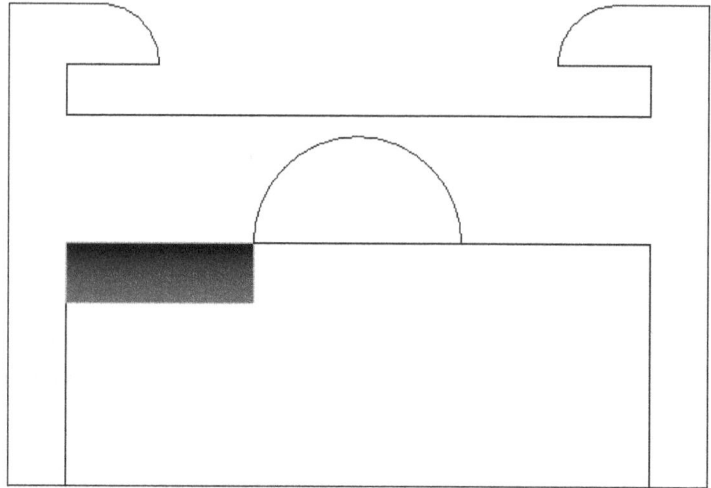

Figure 9–44

7. Create a second round on the opposite side using the same technique, as shown in Figure 9–45.

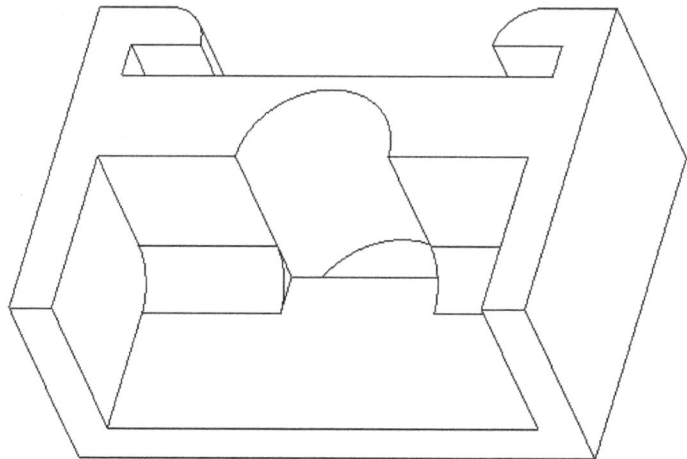

Figure 9–45

Task 3 - Round the bottom edge.

For the final round on this part, you need to round the bottom edge, but the round must stop at the midpoint of the edge at datum plane **RIGHT**.

1. Create a constant round with a *Radius* of **.375** on the edge shown in Figure 9–46.

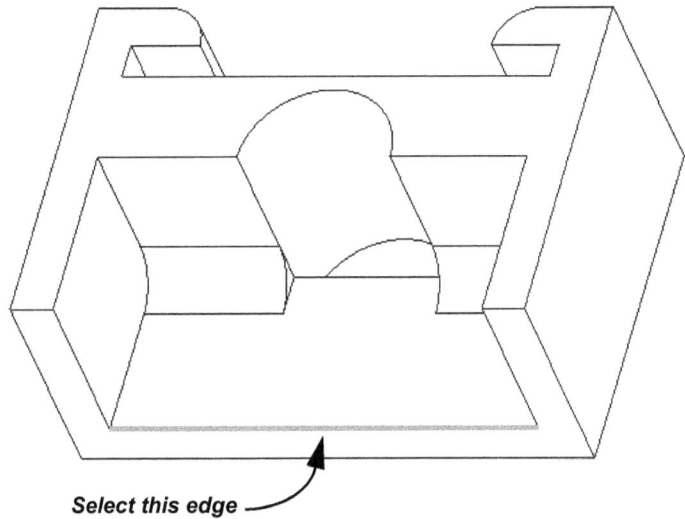

Select this edge

Figure 9–46

2. Click on the screen and select ⊹ (Transition Mode) in the mini toolbar.

3. Select the transition on the right end of the selected edge shown in Figure 9–47, right-click, and select **Stop at Reference**.

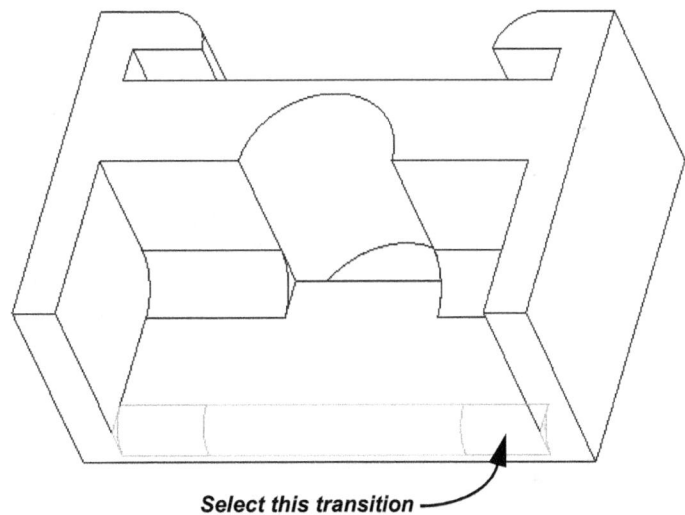

Select this transition

Figure 9–47

4. Select datum plane **RIGHT** in the Model Tree as the location at which the round should stop.

5. Complete the round feature. The model displays as shown in Figure 9–48.

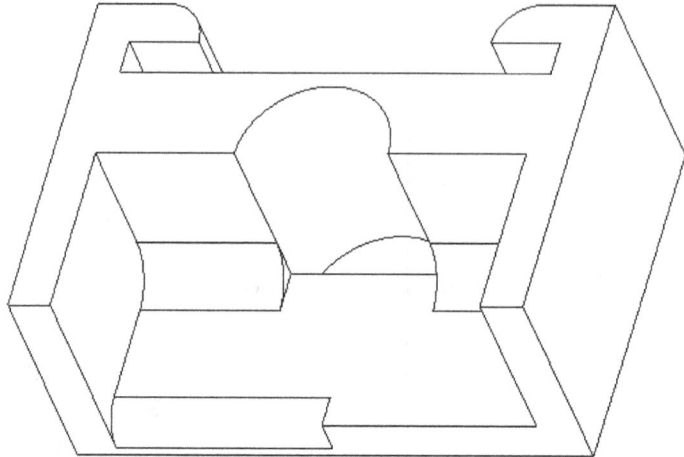

Figure 9–48

6. Save the part and close the window.

Practice 9c | Changing Round Shape

Practice Objectives

- Create a round and change the shape using the Normal to Spine option.
- Create a round with a conic cross-section and change the rho value to change the shape.

In this practice, you will create rounds by changing the round shape from *Rolling ball* to **Normal to spine**. You will also change a round so that it is in the shape of a conic.

Task 1 - Open a part file.

1. Set the working directory to the *Round_Shape* folder.

2. Open **round_shape.prt**.

3. Set the model display as follows:

   - ⁑. *(Datum Display Filters)*: All Off

   - ⸜ *(Spin Center)*: Off

   - ▢. *(Display Style)*: ▢ (Shading With Edges)

Task 2 - Create a round.

1. Create a constant round between the surfaces shown in Figure 9–49.

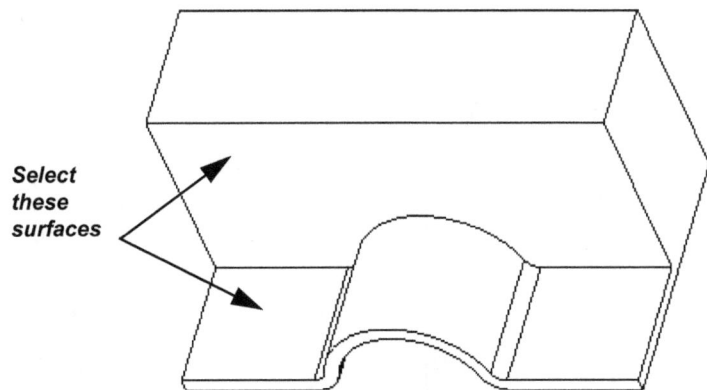

Select these surfaces

Figure 9–49

2. Set the *Radius* for the round to **5.0**.

3. Click 👓 (Verify Mode) in the *Round* dashboard to preview the model geometry. The model displays as shown in Figure 9–50. Note that the round does not account for the curved geometry.

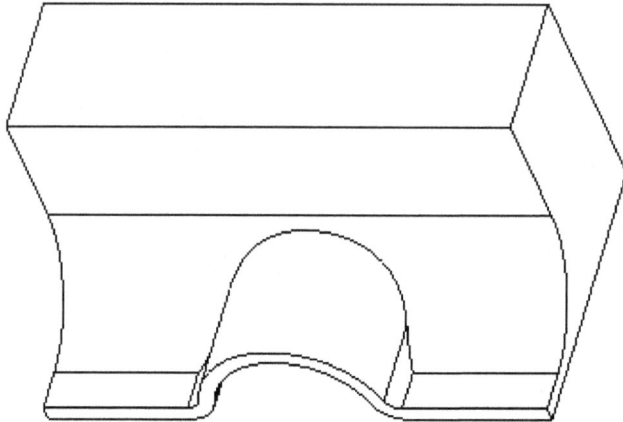

Figure 9–50

4. Click ▶ (Resume) to resume the feature creation.

5. Open the Sets panel in the *Round* dashboard and change *Rolling ball* to **Normal to spine** using the drop-down list as shown in Figure 9–51.

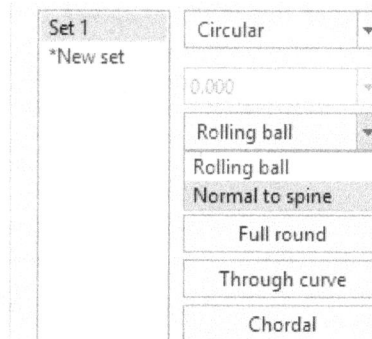

Figure 9–51

6. Select the edge shown in Figure 9–52 as the spine.

Select this edge for the spine to be normal to

5.000

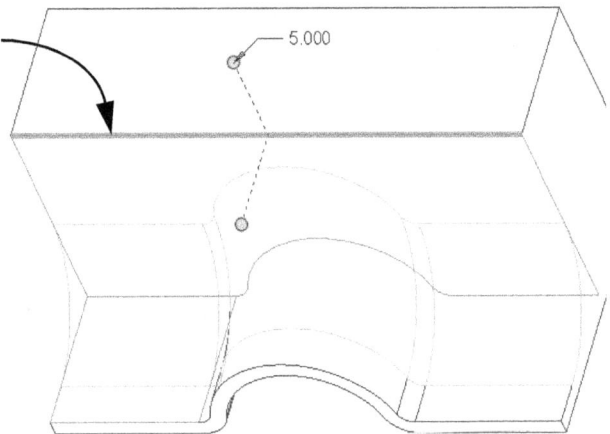

Figure 9–52

7. Complete the feature. The model displays as shown in Figure 9–53.

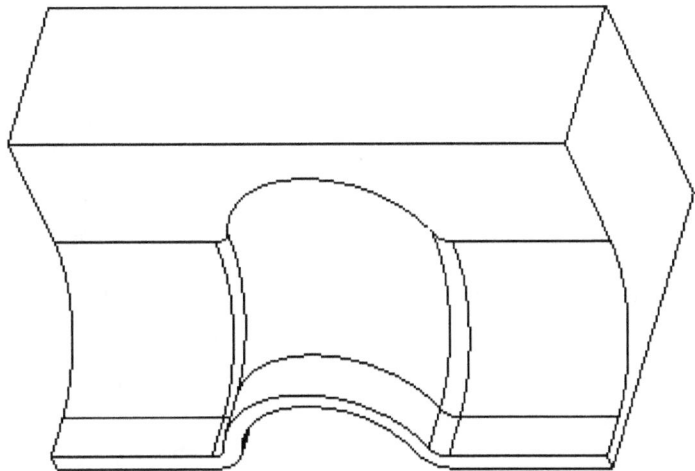

Figure 9–53

Task 3 - Create a round and change its shape from Circular to Conic.

1. Create a round with a *Radius* **1.50** on the five edges shown in Figure 9–54.

Select these five edges

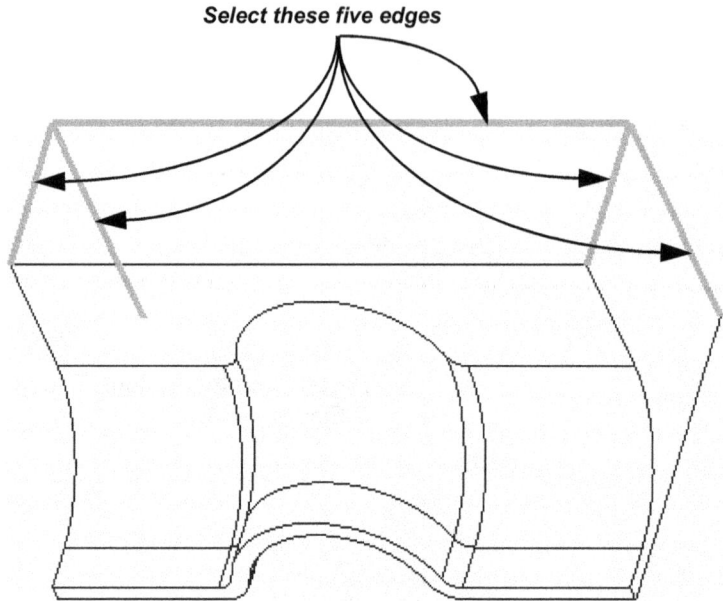

Figure 9–54

2. Open the Sets panel in the *Round* dashboard and change *Circular* to **Conic** using the drop-down list.

3. Set the *Conic* parameter to **0.2** in the Sets panel under the **Conic** option, as shown in Figure 9–55.

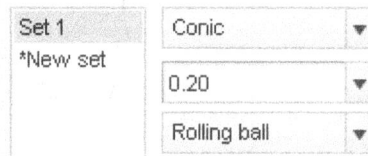

Figure 9–55

4. Complete the feature. The model displays as shown in Figure 9–56.

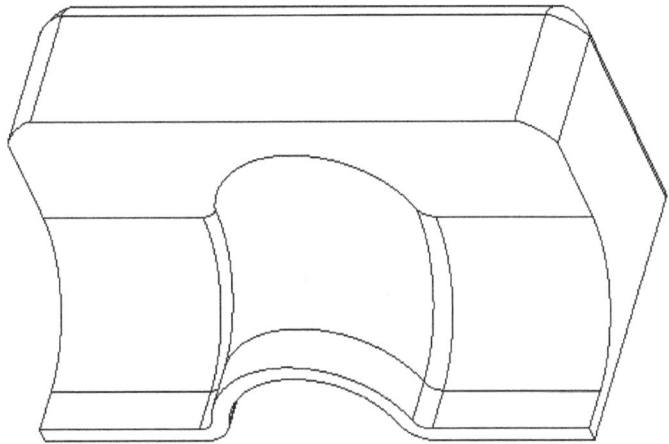

Figure 9–56

5. Reorient the model to the **FRONT** orientation. Note the shape of the round shown in Figure 9–57.

Note the shape of this silhouette

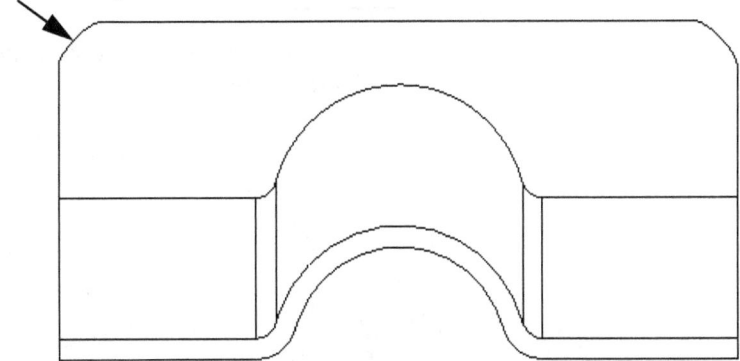

Figure 9–57

6. In the Model Tree, select **Round 2** and click
   ⟷dʼ (Edit Dimensions) in the mini toolbar.

7. Double-click the **.2 CONIC PARAM** dimension and set the new value to **0.7**.

8. Regenerate the model. The part displays as shown in Figure 9–58. Note how the round shape has changed.

Note the changed shape of this silhouette

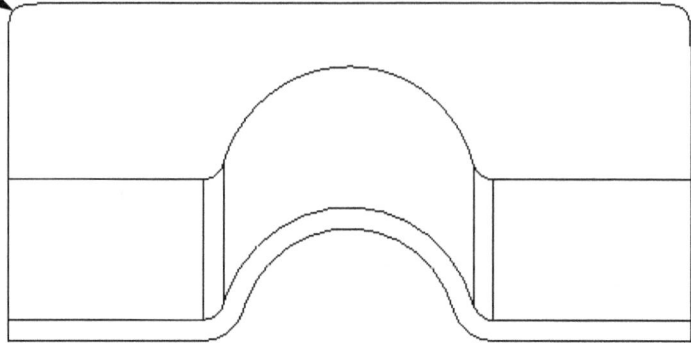

Figure 9–58

9. Return to the default view.

Task 4 - (Optional) Add transitions.

1. Add two **Patch** transitions to the conic round as shown in Figure 9–59.

Patch transitions

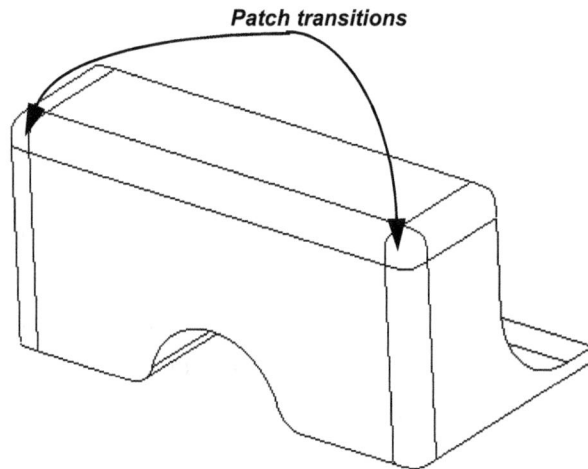

Figure 9–59

2. Save the part and erase it from memory.

Practice 9d | Blend and Continue Transitions

Practice Objective

- Create multiple rounds with different transitions.

In this practice, you will create a number of rounds with transitions to display the difference between **Blend Surface** and **Continue** transitions. The completed model is shown in Figure 9–60.

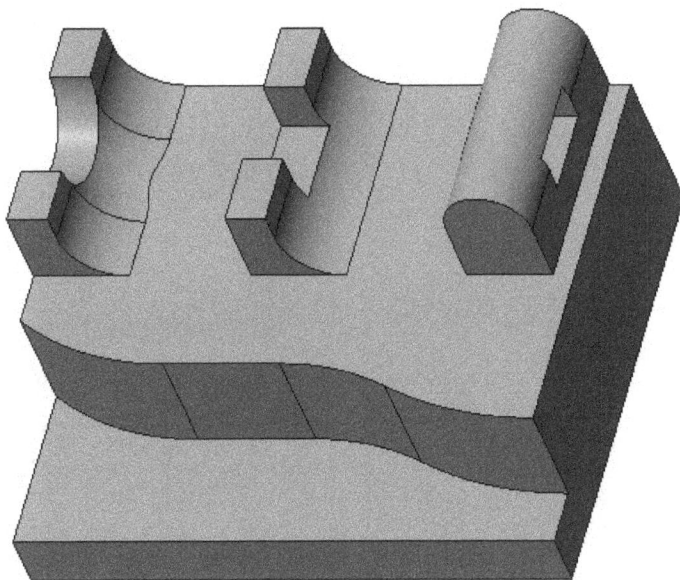

Figure 9–60

Task 1 - Open a part file.

1. Set the working directory to the *Blend_Continue_Transitions* folder.

2. Open **transition_blend_continue.prt**.

3. Set the model display as follows:

   - ⁺⁄⏚ *(Datum Display Filters)*: All Off

   - ⊱ *(Spin Center)*: Off

   - ⬛ *(Display Style)*: ⬛ (Shading With Edges)

Task 2 - Create a round.

1. Start a round with a *Radius* of **1** on the edge shown in Figure 9–61. DO NOT click ✓ (OK).

Select this edge

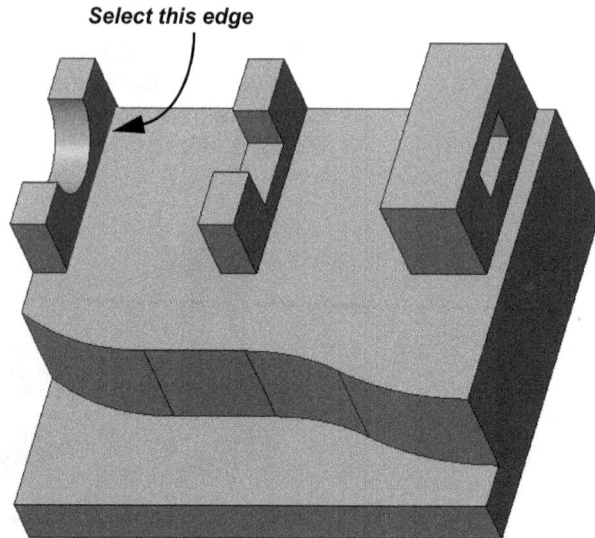

Figure 9–61

The radius previews as shown in Figure 9–62.

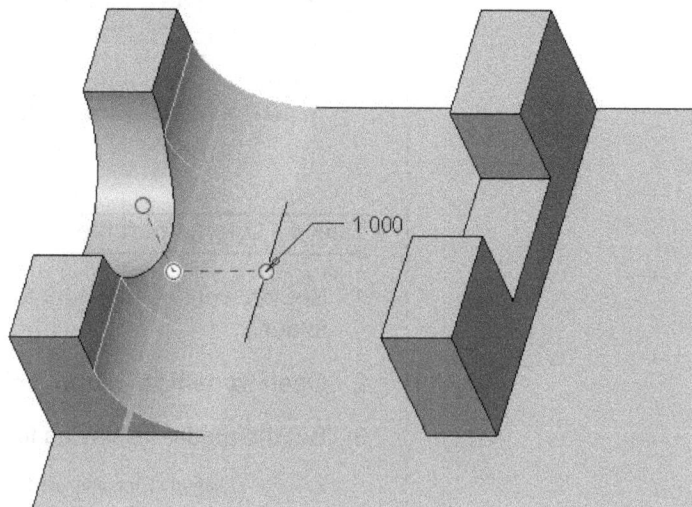

1.000

Figure 9–62

Design Considerations

The round is split by the cut in the top of the protrusion. To create the round, the system automatically adds a **Default (Continue)** transition to the round.

2. Use 👓 (Verify Mode) to preview the model geometry. Orient the model as shown in Figure 9–63.

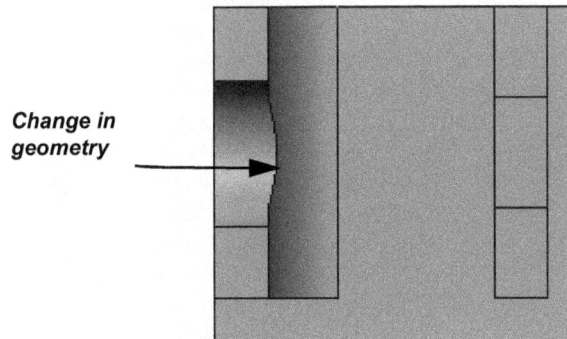

Change in geometry

Figure 9–63

Design Considerations

Note that the round has changed the geometry of the cut. This is a result of using the **Default (Continue)** transition. If this is not correct, a Blend transition must be specified.

3. Click ▶ (Resume) to resume the feature creation.

4. Click on the screen and select 🕆 (Transition Mode) in the mini toolbar, then select the transition as shown in Figure 9–64.

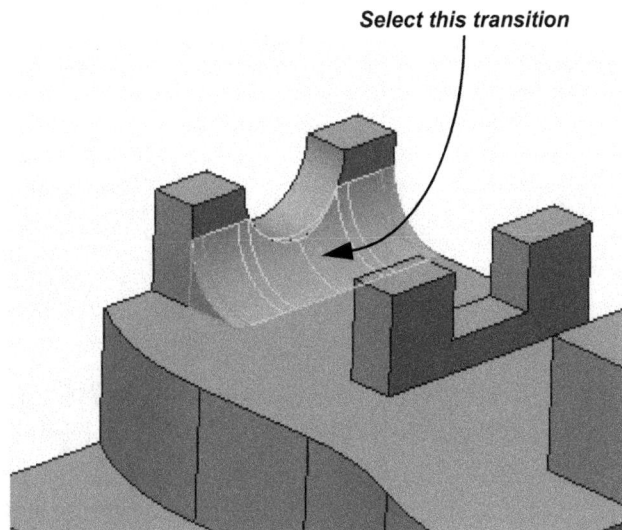

Select this transition

Figure 9–64

5. Change the transition type to **Blend**.

6. Use ᗙ (Verify Mode) to preview the model geometry. Orient the model as shown in Figure 9–65.

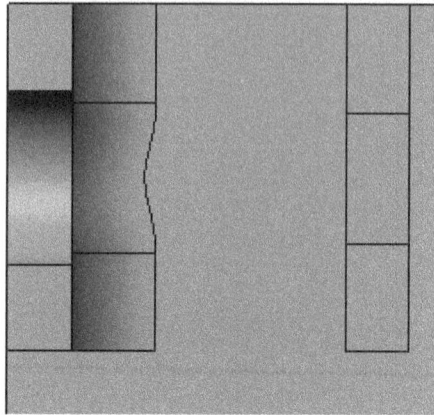

Figure 9–65

Design Considerations

By specifying a **Blend** transition, the original width of the protrusion is maintained.

7. Complete the round.

Task 3 - Create a round.

---

1. Create round with a *Radius* of **1** on the edge shown in Figure 9–66.

Select this edge

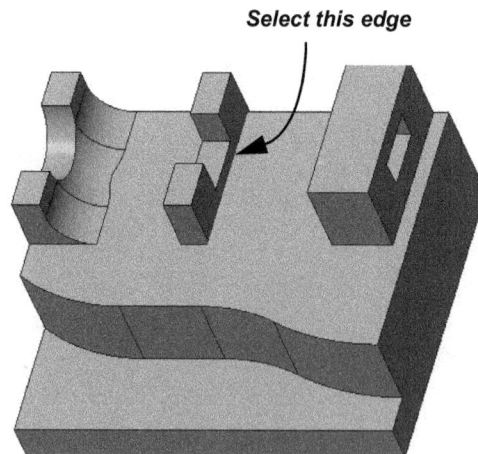

Figure 9–66

2. Use ∞ (Verify Mode) to preview the model geometry. The round is created with the **Default (Continue)** transition, enabling the round to be created, as shown in Figure 9–67.

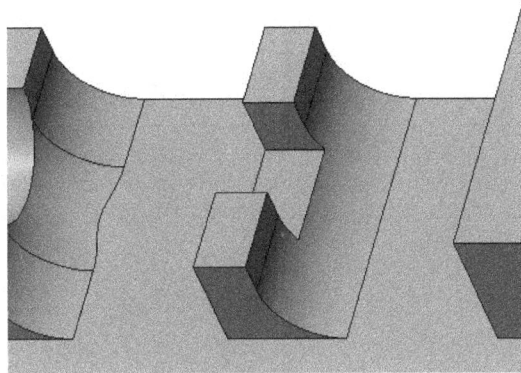

Figure 9–67

Task 4 - Change the transition type.

1. Click ▶ (Resume) to resume the feature creation.

2. Click on the screen and select ✝ (Transition Mode) in the mini toolbar.

3. Select the middle transition.

4. Expand the Transition type drop-down list.

Design Considerations

Note that there are no options. The **Default (Continue)** is the only transition type available. This is because the geometry of the cut is linear. Therefore, the system cannot blend the round geometry.

5. Complete the feature.

Task 5 - Create a full round.

1. Create a full round. Select the edges shown in Figure 9–68.

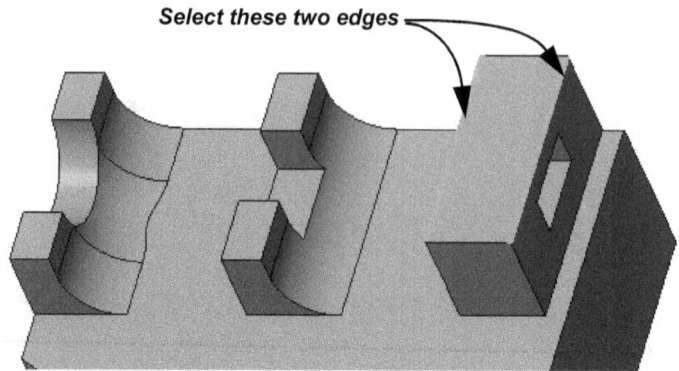

Select these two edges

Figure 9–68

2. Click on the screen and select ⌂ (Transition Mode) in the mini toolbar.

3. Select the middle transition.

4. Expand the Transition type drop-down list.

Design Considerations

Note that the only two options are **Patch** and **Default (Continue)**. This is because the geometry of the cut is linear.

5. Keep **Default (Continue)** and complete the feature. The part is shown in Figure 9–69.

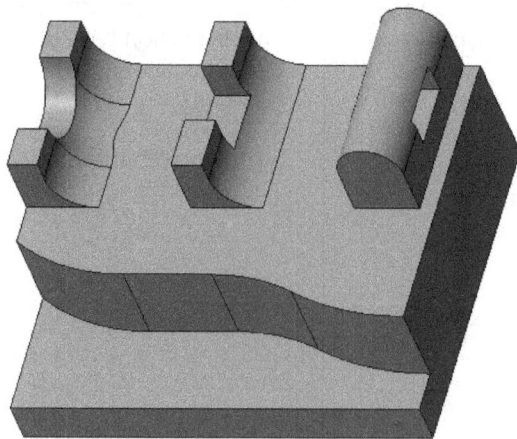

Figure 9–69

6. Save the part and erase it from memory.

Chapter Review Questions

1. Each round set must be of a single style, radius, shape, and placement method.

   a. True

   b. False

2. A transition is geometry that is added to round pieces to join them together and attach them to existing geometry at their loose ends. Transitions can only be applied at which of the location(s) shown in Figure 9–70? (Select all that apply.)

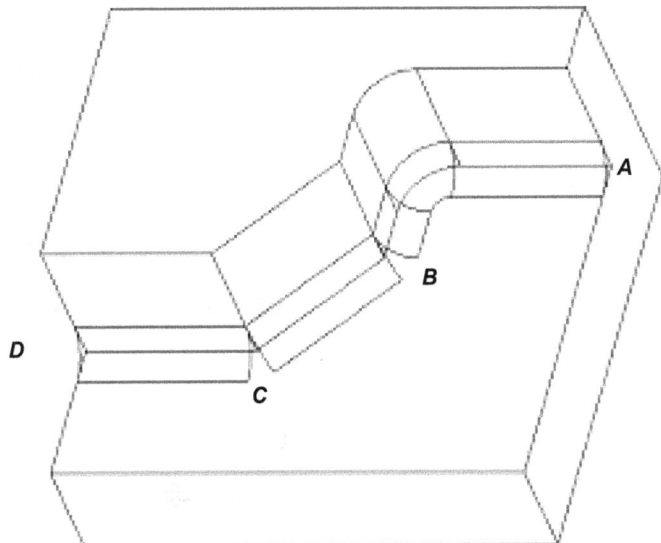

Figure 9–70

   a. A

   b. B

   c. C

   d. D

3. Which of the following can be used in a transition as a Stop reference? (Select all that apply.)

   a. Point

   b. Vertex

   c. Axis

   d. Plane

Use Figure 9–71 to answer the following three questions.

Round references (2 edges)

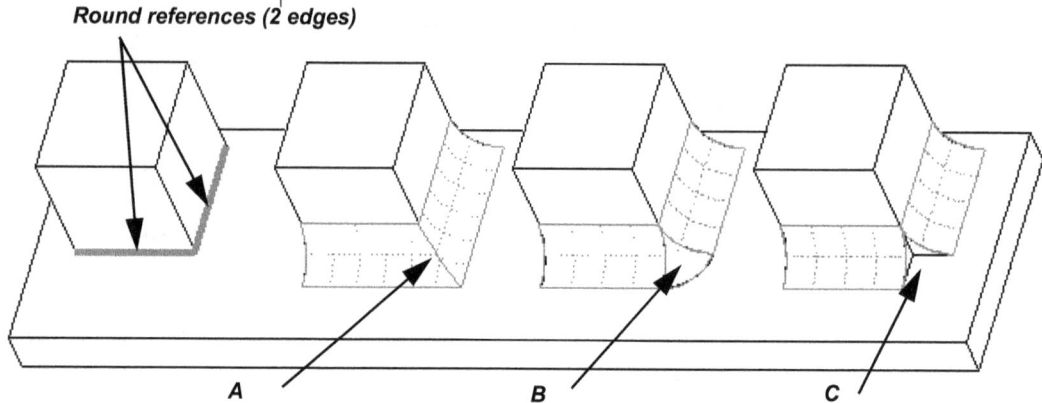

Figure 9–71

4. Identify the Blend transition.
   a. A
   b. B
   c. C

5. Identify the Intersect transition.
   a. A
   b. B
   c. C

6. Identify the Stop transition.
   a. A
   b. B
   c. C

7. Which of the following can be manipulated to create a round?
   (Select all that apply.)
   a. Type
   b. References
   c. Shape
   d. Cross-section
   e. Transition

Answers: 1a, 2abcd, 3abd, 4b, 5a, 6c, 7abcde

Advanced Drafts

Like rounds, draft features have a known geometry. You select placement references for the feature and predefined geometry is placed without needing to sketch any geometry.

Learning Objectives in This Chapter

- Learn to create a draft by specifying a draft surface, draft hinge, pull direction, and draft angle.
- Create a Variable Pull Direction Draft by selecting a pull direction, draft hinge, and draft angle.
- Specify additional sets if required, and specify additional options.
- Understand how to exclude surfaces from drafting when those surfaces already meet the required draft angle.
- Learn how to use round handling in drafts.

10.1 Drafts

A draft is a feature that tapers selected surfaces to a specified angle. Creo Parametric permits a draft angle ranging between -89.9° and $+89.9^\circ$. Draft features can be created with a constant or variable angle. When a constant angle is used, all of the selected surfaces are drafted to the same angle. When a variable angle is used, a single surface can have a variable angle. Figure 10–1 shows a preview of a simple draft on one surface of the model.

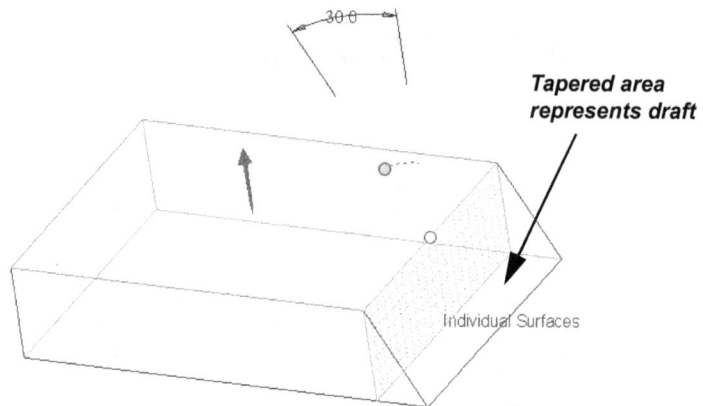

Tapered area represents draft

Individual Surfaces

Figure 10–1

As you build the features for your part, always consider whether a draft is required in the model. A draft cannot be added to a surface that has been rounded. Therefore, consider leaving the round and draft features to the end of feature creation order. Doing so also helps reduce unwanted parent/child relationships that might otherwise be established.

General Steps

Use the following general steps to create a draft.

1. Start the creation of the feature.
2. Select draft surface(s).
3. Select draft hinge.
4. Specify the pull direction.
5. Enter the draft angle.
6. Split the draft, if required.
7. Add additional draft angles, if required.
8. Set draft options, if required.

Step 1 - Start the creation of the feature.

To create a draft feature, click ✎ (Draft) in the *Model* tab.

Step 2 - Select draft surface(s).

Use <Ctrl> to select more then one reference.

When the *Draft* dashboard activates, you are prompted to select the surfaces to draft on the model. Once the draft surfaces have been selected, you can manipulate these surfaces directly in the Graphics window or in the References panel. All of the selected surfaces are listed in the *Draft surfaces* area in the References panel, as shown in Figure 10–2.

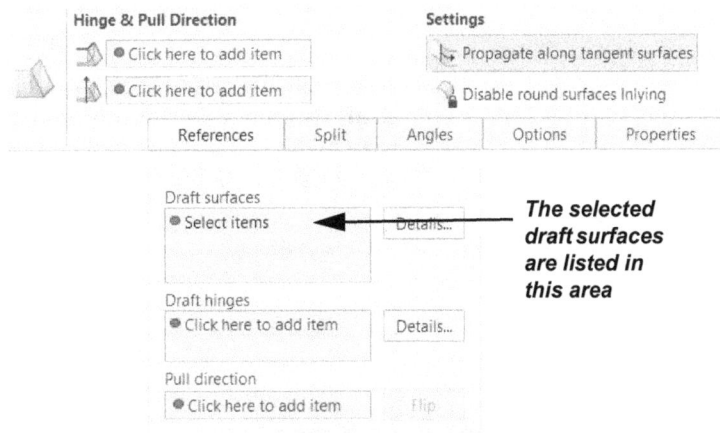

Figure 10–2

You can also activate the Draft surfaces area in the References panel.

To add a surface, activate the selection of draft surfaces by right-clicking and selecting **Draft Surfaces**. Press <Ctrl> and select any additional surfaces.

*To remove draft surfaces, you can also right-click on items in the Draft surfaces area in the References panel and select **Remove**.*

To remove draft surfaces, activate the selection of draft surfaces by right-clicking and selecting **Draft Surfaces**. Press <Ctrl> and select any previously selected surface. This action removes previously selected surfaces from the set of draft surfaces.

Step 3 - Select draft hinge.

A draft hinge is a line or curve about which the drafted surfaces are pivoted (also called neutral curves). Draft hinges can be defined by selecting a plane, in which case the draft surfaces are pivoted about their intersection with this plane, or by selecting individual curve chains on the draft surface.

Figure 10–3 shows a plane being used as a draft hinge.

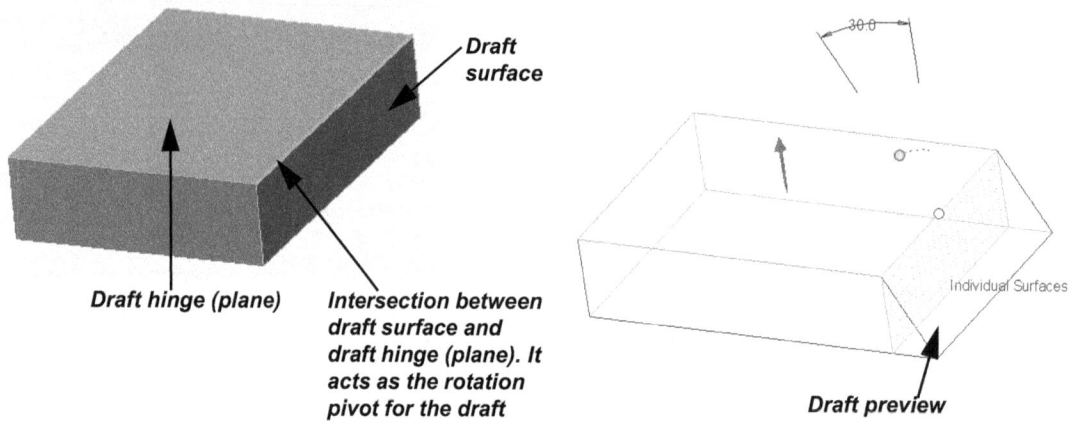

Draft surface

Draft hinge (plane)

Intersection between draft surface and draft hinge (plane). It acts as the rotation pivot for the draft

Individual Surfaces

Draft preview

Figure 10–3

To specify the draft hinge, right-click on the reference and select **Draft Hinges**. Alternatively, you can activate the *Draft hinges* area in the References panel or the *Draft hinges* field in the *Draft* dashboard, as shown in Figure 10–4.

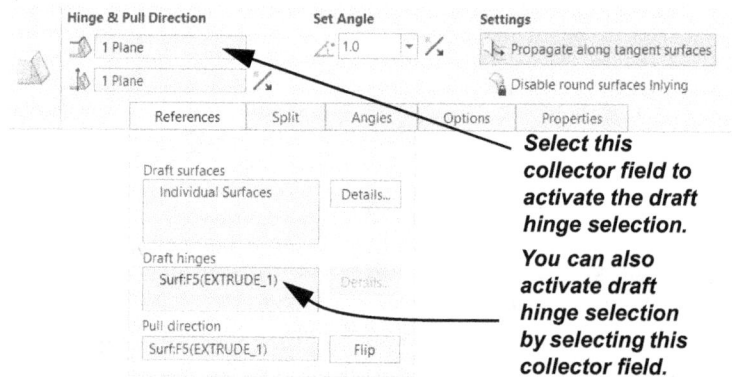

Select this collector field to activate the draft hinge selection.

You can also activate draft hinge selection by selecting this collector field.

Figure 10–4

Step 4 - Specify the pull direction.

The pull direction is the direction that is used to measure the draft angle. This is usually the direction of the mold opening. You can define it by selecting a plane (in which case the pull direction is normal to the plane), a straight edge, a datum axis, or two points (such as datum points or model vertices). The pull direction is sometimes called the draft direction.

In situations where the draft hinge is specified as a surface, the pull direction is automatically assigned the same surface reference. To specify a new or alternative pull direction, right-click and select **Pull direction**. Alternatively, you can select in the *Pull direction* area in the References panel or the *Pull direction* field in the *Draft* dashboard to activate it, as shown in Figure 10–5.

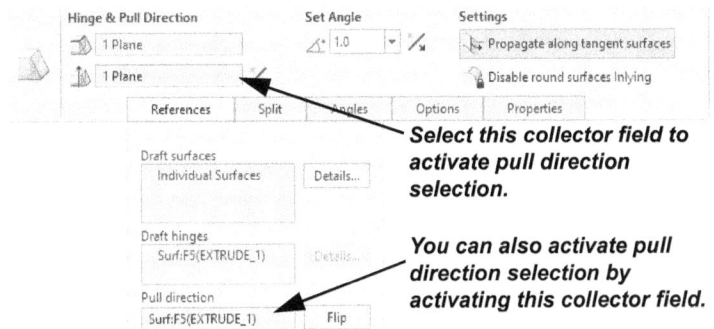

Select this collector field to activate pull direction selection.

You can also activate pull direction selection by activating this collector field.

Figure 10–5

Step 5 - Enter the draft angle.

A draft angle is the angle between the draft direction and the resulting drafted surfaces. Draft angles must be between −89.9° and +89.9°.

The draft angle can be set by entering it in the *Draft* dashboard, as shown in Figure 10–6. You can also drag the draft angle handle on the model, or double-click and enter a value on the model.

Draft angle value

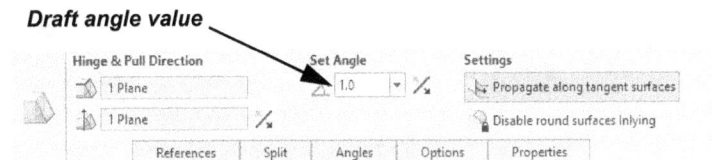

Figure 10–6

Step 6 - Split the draft, if required.

A draft can be split so that the surface can have different angles on each side of the split reference. To split the draft, select the appropriate type of draft in the Split options drop-down list in the Split panel, as shown in Figure 10–7. You can split a draft at the draft hinge or along a line or curve (object).

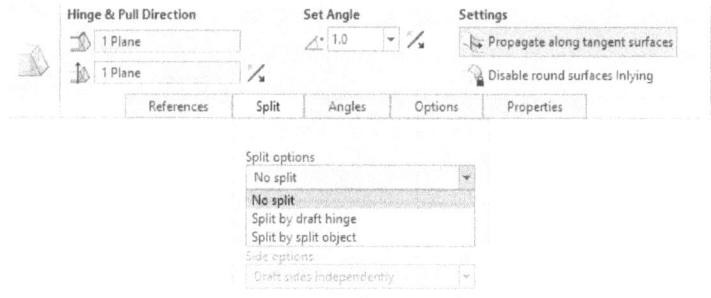

Figure 10–7

In addition to defining the split options you can also define options for each side of the split. These side options are set in the Side options drop-down list as shown in Figure 10–8.

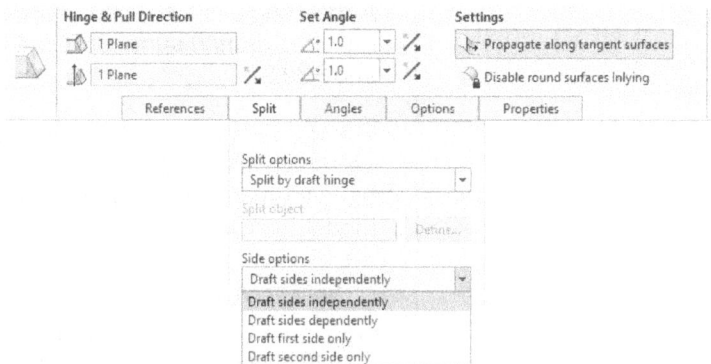

Figure 10–8

The options include the following:

- **Draft sides independently:** Draft angles for each side of the drafted surface.

- **Draft sides dependently:** Equal draft angles for both sides of the drafted surface.

- **Draft first side only** or **Draft second side only:** A draft angle for one side while the other side of the split remains not drafted.

Figure 10–9 shows examples of the different draft options.

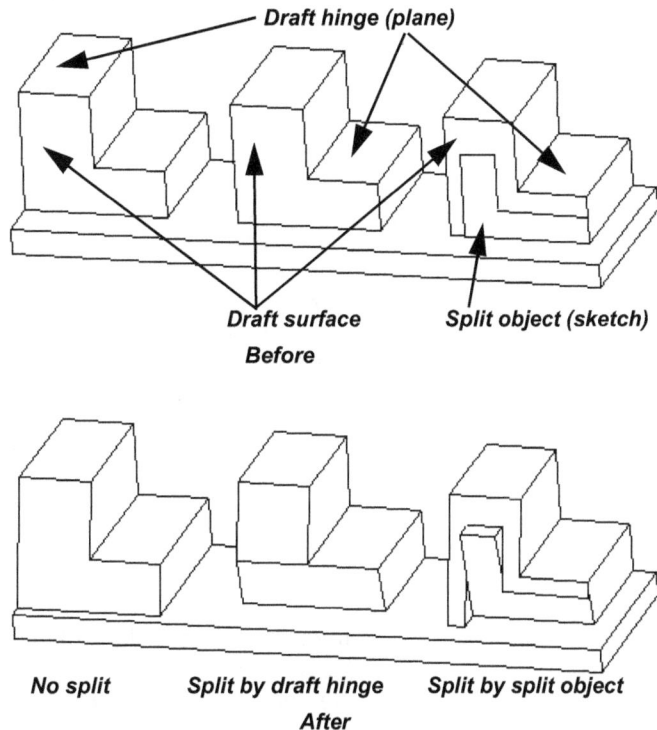

Draft hinge (plane)

Draft surface

Split object (sketch)

Before

No split   **Split by draft hinge**   **Split by split object**

After

Figure 10–9

Step 7 - Add additional draft angles, if required.

*To make a variable draft constant, right-click on it and select **Make Constant**.*

You must add additional draft angles to create a variable angle draft.

To add a draft angle, place the cursor over the circular handle shown in Figure 10–10, right-click and select **Add Angle**.

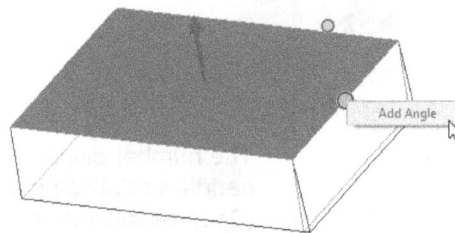

Add Angle

Figure 10–10

Alternatively, you can open the Angles panel, place the cursor as shown in Figure 10–11, right-click and select **Add Angle** to define a control point for entering another draft angle.

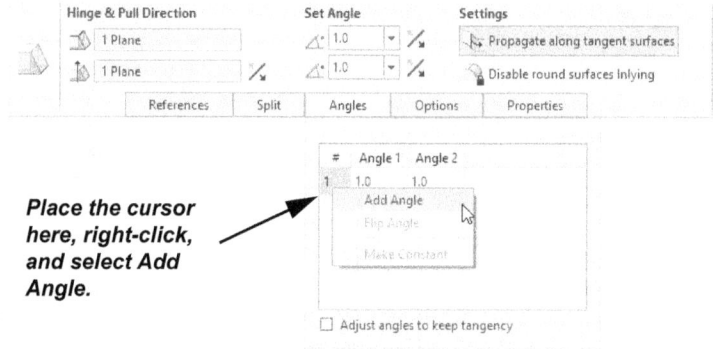

Place the cursor here, right-click, and select Add Angle.

Figure 10–11

The **Adjust angles to keep tangency** option forces the resultant draft surfaces to be tangent. This option is not available for Variable draft, as variable draft always keeps the surfaces tangent.

To move control points, place your cursor on the circular handle (as shown in Figure 10–12), click the left mouse button, and drag the handle along the draft hinge to new position.

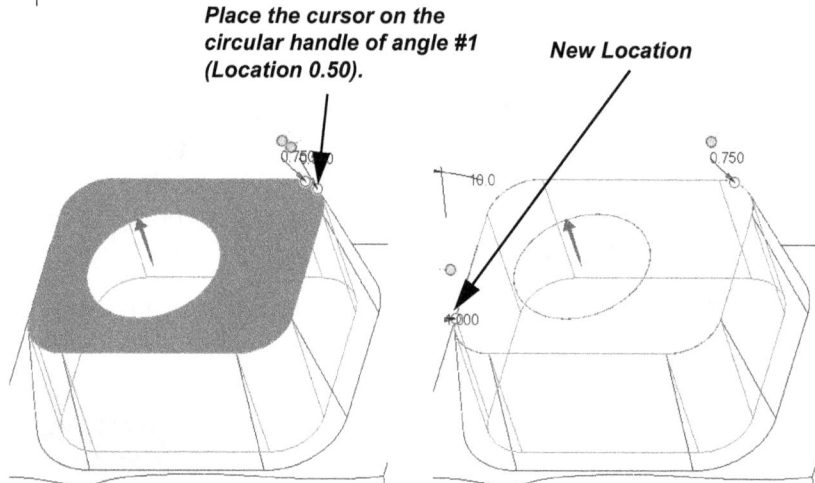

Place the cursor on the circular handle of angle #1 (Location 0.50).

New Location

Figure 10–12

The number displayed next to the circular handle indicates the handle's relative position on the draft hinge segment (0 represents one end point and 1 represents the opposite end point). Each control point is assigned its own angle entry.

Alternatively, you can press and hold <Shift> while dragging the circular handle to the required vertex.

You can also move the control point in the Angles panel. Select the *Reference* cell of draft angle entry, as shown in Figure 10–13.

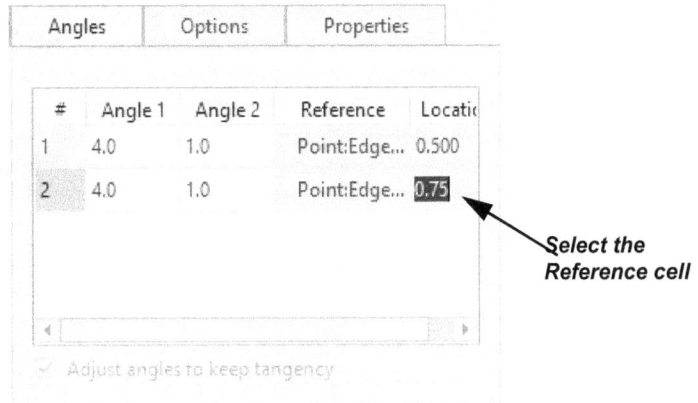

Angles	Options	Properties

#	Angle 1	Angle 2	Reference	Locatio
1	4.0	1.0	Point:Edge...	0.500
2	4.0	1.0	Point:Edge...	0.75

Select the Reference cell

Adjust angles to keep tangency

Figure 10–13

Once active, move the cursor along the draft hinge. Note that the new location of the draft angle handle is indicated by a green cross symbol. Click the left mouse button to select a new location for the selected draft angle entry. This method enables you to place the draft angle handle on the draft hinge vertex.

Step 8 - Set draft options, if required.

The Options panel enables you to customize additional options when creating a draft. These options include excluding loops in the selected surfaces, enabling or disabling draft on tangent surfaces, and extending intersected surfaces. The Options panel is shown in Figure 10–14.

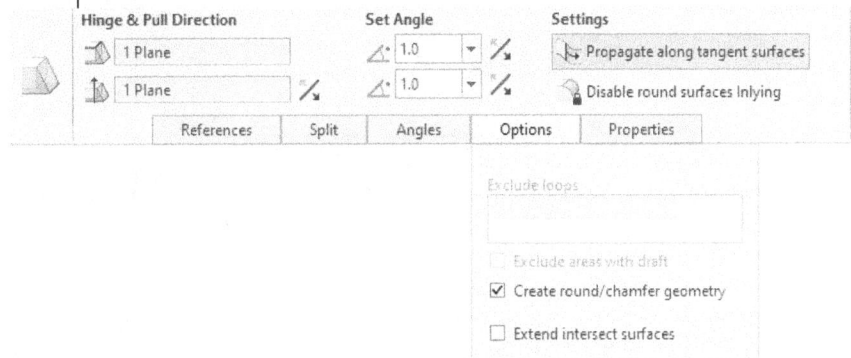

Hinge & Pull Direction | Set Angle | Settings

1 Plane — 1.0 — Propagate along tangent surfaces
1 Plane — 1.0 — Disable round surfaces Inlying

| References | Split | Angles | Options | Properties |

Exclude loops

Exclude areas with draft
☑ Create round/chamfer geometry
☐ Extend intersect surfaces

Figure 10–14

Figure 10–15 shows examples of a model with the **Extend intersect surfaces** option enabled and disabled.

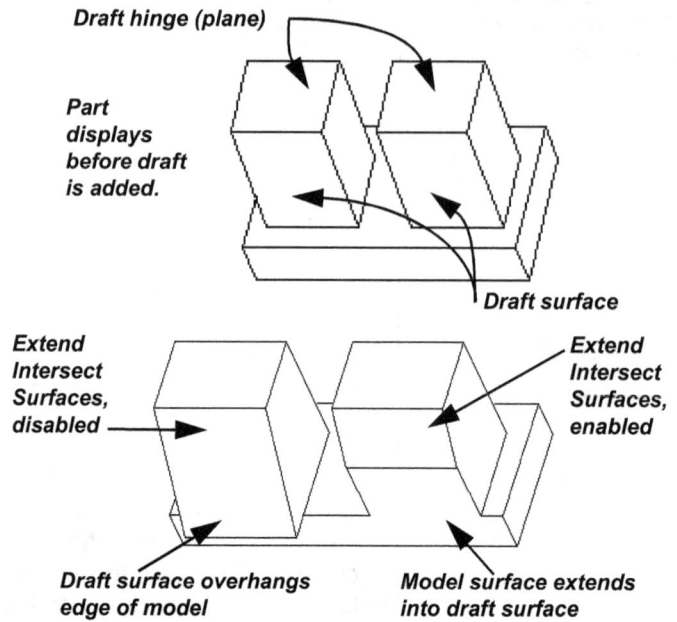

Draft hinge (plane)

Part displays before draft is added.

Draft surface

Extend Intersect Surfaces, disabled

Extend Intersect Surfaces, enabled

Draft surface overhangs edge of model

Model surface extends into draft surface

Figure 10–15

10.2 Excluded Areas

When drafting surfaces, you can exclude areas that would otherwise meet the defined draft. Consider the example shown in Figure 10–16.

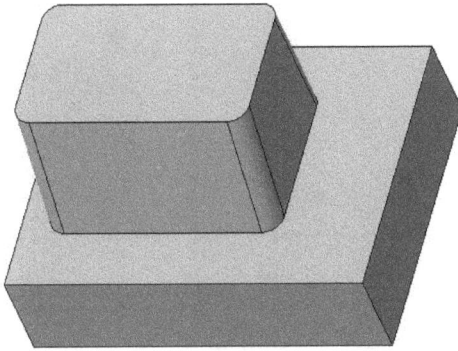

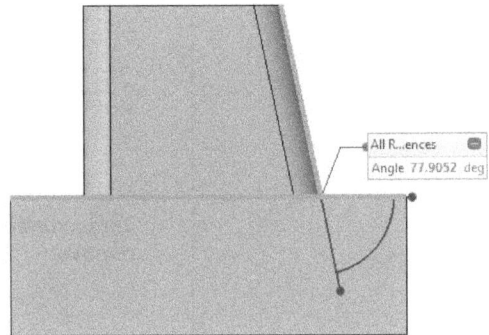

One surface is created at an angle

Figure 10–16

The boss at on the top of the model already contains an angular surface. If you apply a 2° draft to all vertical surfaces of the boss, the angled surface changes to match the draft, as shown in Figure 10–17.

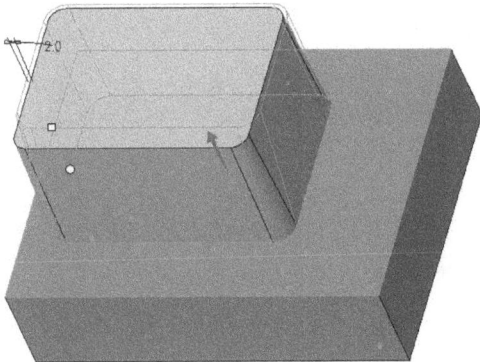

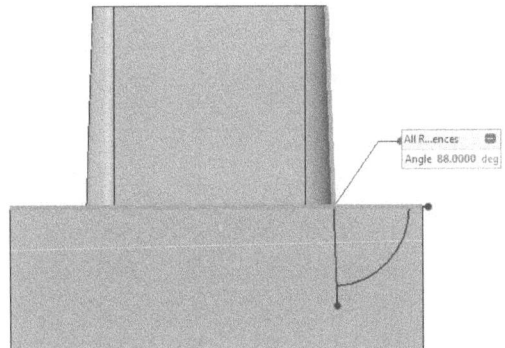

Geometry is altered to match the draft

Figure 10–17

Since the angle of the surface is actually more than enough to satisfy the draft, you can automatically remove it from the set of surfaces by enabling the **Exclude areas with draft** option, as shown in Figure 10–18.

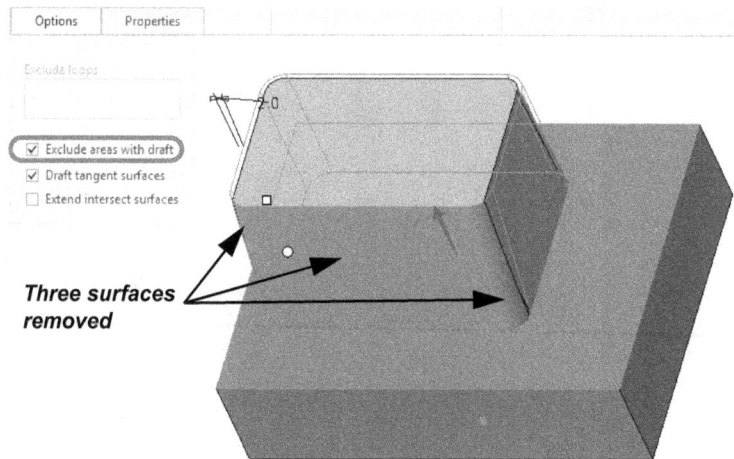

Figure 10–18

Note that a connecting surface is automatically created with tangent transitions to drafted and excluded surface areas, so always verify your results to ensure that the resulting geometry is accurate.

10.3 Variable Pull Direction Draft

A Variable Pull Direction Draft (VPDD) is a feature that tapers the geometry by sweeping a ruled surface normal to the draft hinge at a specified angle. The VPDD provides additional options for more control over the final geometry of a draft feature. The main differences between the VPDD and the Draft command are as follows:

- VPDD enables you to select a non-planer pull-direction surface.

- The surfaces to draft are determined by the draft hinge.

- The draft angle can range between -89.9° and +89.9°.

General Steps

Use the following general steps to create a draft.

1. Start the creation of the feature.
2. Specify the Pull direction
3. Select the draft hinge.
4. Enter the draft angles.
5. Add additional angles, if required.
6. Add additional sets of draft angles, if required.
7. Split the draft, if required.
8. Set the draft options, if required.

Step 1 - Start the creation of the feature.

To create a VPDD draft feature, expand 🅰 (Draft) in the *Model* tab and click 🏵 (Variable Pull Direction Draft). The *Variable Pull Direction* dashboard displays as shown in Figure 10–19.

Figure 10–19

Step 2 - Specify the pull direction.

The pull direction is the direction that is used to measure the
draft angle. You can define it by selecting a surface or plane (in
which case the pull direction is normal to the plane).

To specify a pull direction, right-click and select **Pull direction**.
Alternatively, you can select in the *Pull direction* area in the
References panel or the *Pull direction* field in the *VPDD*
dashboard, as shown in Figure 10–20.

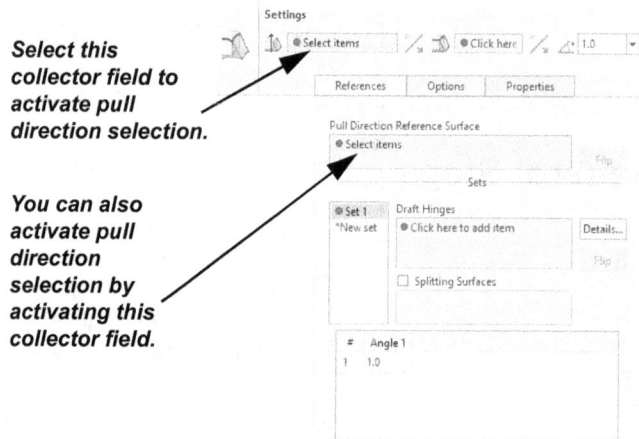

*Select this
collector field to
activate pull
direction selection.*

*You can also
activate pull
direction
selection by
activating this
collector field.*

Figure 10–20

To remove the pull direction surface, right-click on the collector
field and select **Remove**.

Step 3 - Select the draft hinge.

A draft hinge is a line or curve about which the drafted surfaces
are pivoted (also called neutral curves). Draft hinges can be
defined by selecting a curve or edge, in which case the draft
surfaces are pivoted about their intersection. The surfaces to
draft are defined by the draft hinge.

To specify the draft hinge, right-click and select **Draft Hinges**.
Alternatively, you can also activate the *Draft hinges* area in the
References panel or the *Draft hinges* field in the *Variable Pull
Direction Draft* dashboard, as shown in Figure 10–21.

Figure 10–21

Step 4 - Enter the draft angles.

The VPDD can be created with a constant or variable angle. When a constant angle is used, all of the selected surfaces are drafted to the same angle. When a variable angle is used, a single surface can have a variable angle.

The VPDD angles must be between –89.9° and +89.9°. Enter the draft angle in the References panel or the *angle* field in the *Variable Pull Direction Draft* dashboard, as shown in Figure 10–22.

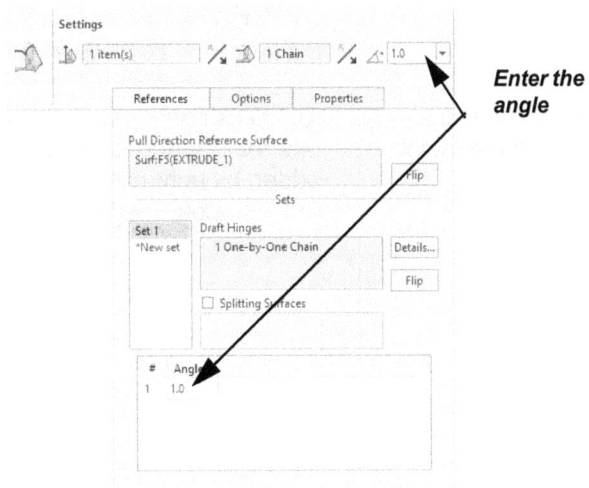

Figure 10–22

Step 5 - Add additional angles, if required.

The **Sets** option in the References panel enables you to define several sets of draft angles into one feature to handle complex draft problems.

To add an additional draft angle, place the cursor over the circular handle, right-click and select **Add Angle**. Alternatively, you can open the Angles panel, place the cursor as shown in Figure 10–23, right-click and select **Add Angle** to define a control point for entering another draft angle.

Figure 10–23

Step 6 - Add additional sets of draft angles, if required.

You can also select ***New set*** *in the Sets panel.*

The Sets panel enables you to define several sets of drafts into one feature and to specify the angle of the draft. A new set is added by right-clicking in the View window and selecting **Add set**, as shown in Figure 10–24.

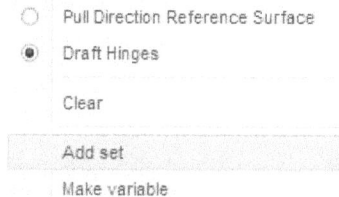

Figure 10–24

Step 7 - Split the draft, if required.

Select the References panel in the *Variable Pull Direction Draft* dashboard and select **Splitting Surfaces** to create geometry that requires a draft in two directions as shown in Figure 10–25. Select a surface or plane to split the draft.

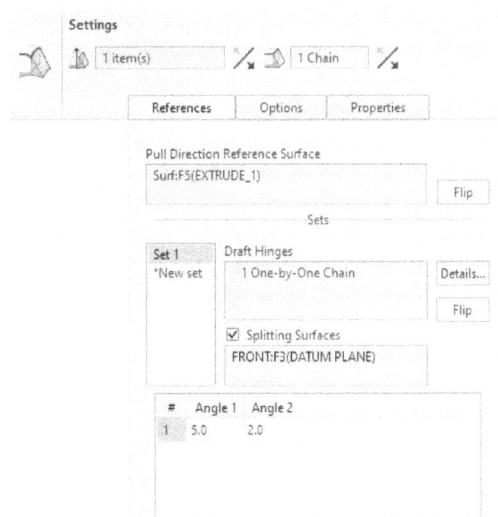

Settings

1 item(s)   1 Chain

References   Options   Properties

Pull Direction Reference Surface

Surf:F5(EXTRUDE_1)

Flip

Sets

Set 1	Draft Hinges	
*New set	1 One-by-One Chain	Details...
		Flip

☑ Splitting Surfaces

FRONT:F3(DATUM PLANE)

#	Angle 1	Angle 2
1	5.0	2.0

Figure 10–25

Step 8 - Set the draft options, if required.

The Options panel enables you to create the draft as a solid or surface as shown in Figure 10–26. The **Attach to solid or quilt** is the default option and creates the draft as a solid. The **Create new quilts** option creates the new draft as a non-solid surface and enables you to extend the geometry by selecting an **Extent** option.

Options   Properties

Attachment

◉ Attach to solid or quilt

○ Create new quilts

Extent

Specify Length   ▾

Figure 10–26

10.4 Round Handling in Draft

Draft can be applied to surfaces adjacent to rounds and
chamfers. The rounds and chamfers are highlighted in a different
color, as shown in Figure 10–27.

Figure 10–27

The rounds and chamfers are handled in the same way as they
are in Flexible Modeling, where Creo Parametric automatically
removes them, completes the modification, and then recreates
them.

Additionally, you might have a set of draft surfaces that include
rounds, referred to as inlying rounds, as shown in Figure 10–28.

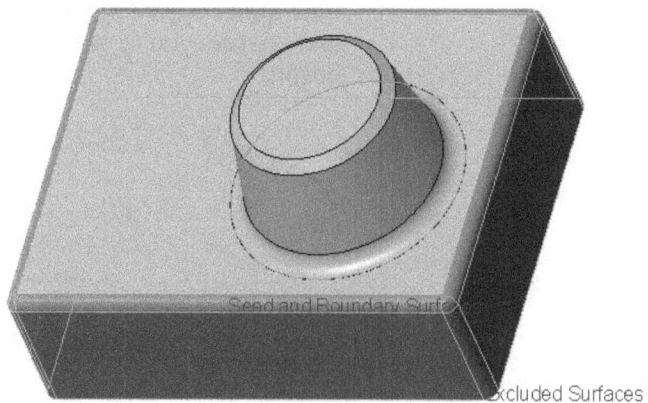

Figure 10–28

In this case, you can choose to include or exclude those rounds using the 🔒 (Exclude Inlying Rounds) option in the dashboard. If you exclude them, the rounds are created with a constant radius. If you include them, the resulting radius will not be constant, as the rounds are also drafted. Both scenarios are shown in Figure 10–29.

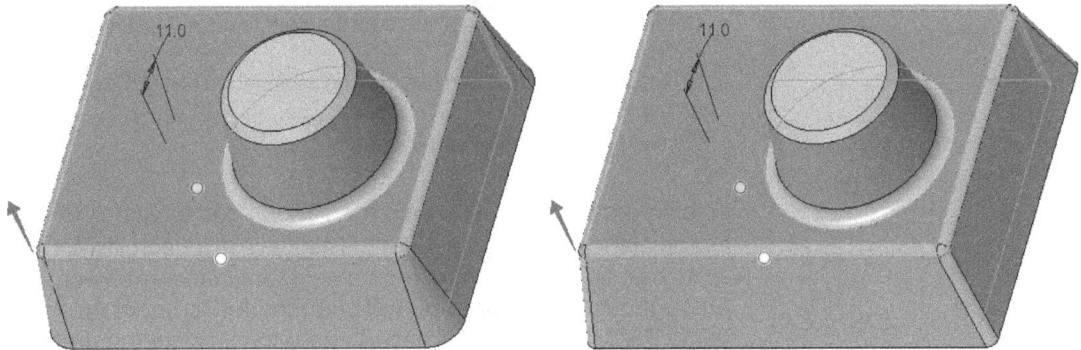

Figure 10–29

You can also choose not to recreate the round geometry after applying the draft by disabling the **Create round/chamfer geometry** option in the *Options* tab in the dashboard. The geometry that results with this option disabled displays as shown in Figure 10–30.

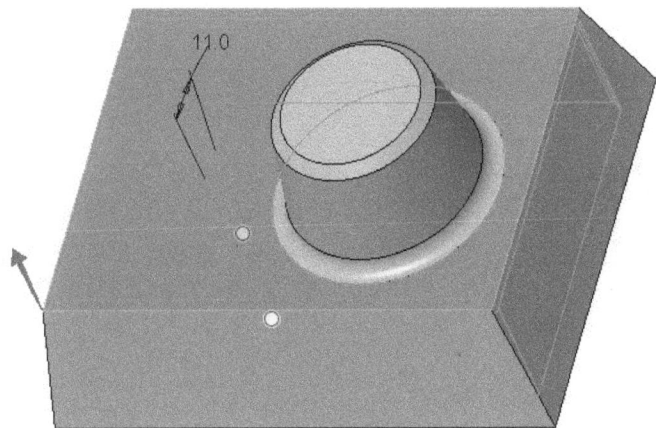

Figure 10–30

Practice 10a | Create Advanced Draft Features

Practice Objectives

- Create a No Split draft by specifying a draft surface, draft hinge, and draft angle.
- Create a Split by Split Object draft and Draft Hinge draft by using a sketched datum curve.
- Create a Split draft using a curve for the draft hinge and splitting reference.
- Create a Variable draft and use the Angles panel to specify the locations for the angle values.
- Create a No Split draft on a cylinder.

In this practice, you will create the various combinations of draft features shown in Figure 10–31. They will include splits and no splits that are created based on a selected plane or object. Throughout the practice you will be prompted to orient the model to the **FRONT** and **BACK** saved views to visualize the draft based on the provided graphics.

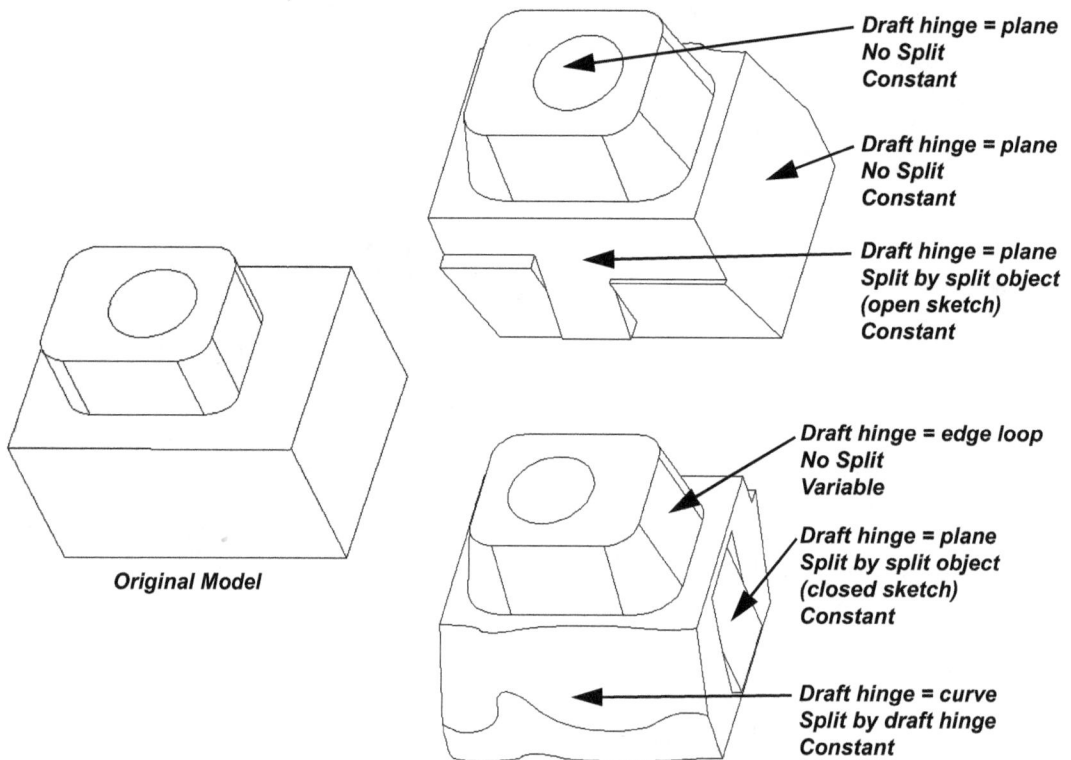

Draft hinge = plane
No Split
Constant

Draft hinge = plane
No Split
Constant

Draft hinge = plane
Split by split object
(open sketch)
Constant

Original Model

Draft hinge = edge loop
No Split
Variable

Draft hinge = plane
Split by split object
(closed sketch)
Constant

Draft hinge = curve
Split by draft hinge
Constant

Figure 10–31

Task 1 - Open a part file.

1. Set the working directory to the *Advanced_Draft* folder.

2. Open **drafts.prt**.

3. Set the model display as follows:

    - ⚡ *(Datum Display Filters)*: All Off

    - ⋟ *(Spin Center)*: Off

    - ▢ *(Display Style)*: ▢ (No Hidden)

Task 2 - Create a No split draft.

1. Click ◭ (Draft) in the *Model* tab.

2. Select the surface shown in Figure 10–32 as the surface to draft.

3. Right-click and select **Draft Hinges**.

4. Select the surface shown in Figure 10–32 as the draft hinge.

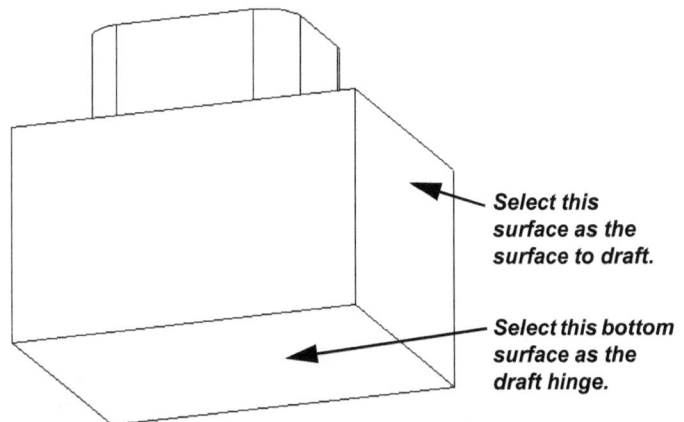

Select this surface as the surface to draft.

Select this bottom surface as the draft hinge.

Figure 10–32

5. Set the draft *Angle* to **10** to create the draft, as shown in Figure 10–33. The angle can be entered directly on the model or in the tab. Alternatively, you can drag the angle handle on the model.

You might need to enter -10 to flip the direction.

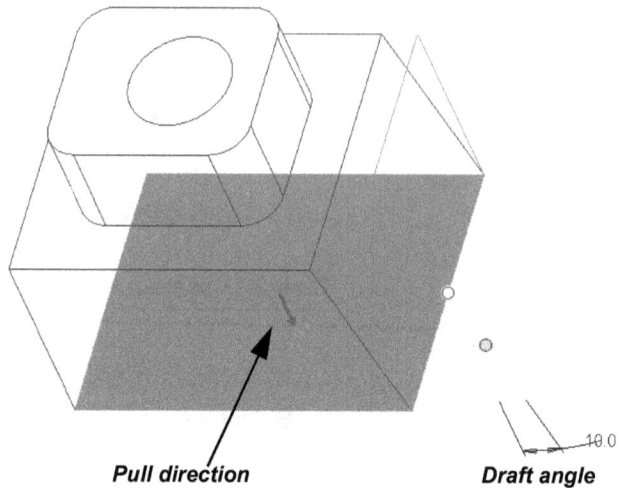

Pull direction   **Draft angle**

Figure 10–33

6. Click **References** in the *Draft* dashboard to display the References panel and compare it with Figure 10–34.

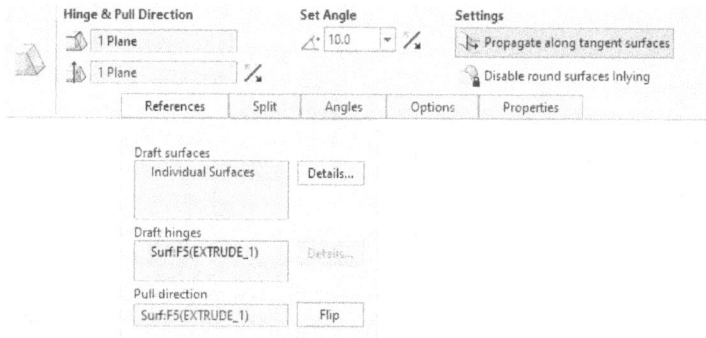

Figure 10–34

7. Click **Flip** next to the *Pull direction* field in the panel to reverse the pull direction.

8. Click (Reverse Angle) next to the *Draft angle* field in the tab to reverse the angle.

Design Considerations

Because the draft hinge and pull direction references are the same in this example, the resulting geometry is the same whether you flip directions with the pull direction or using the draft angle icons. The only thing that varies is how the dimension displays on the model.

9. Click **Split** in the dashboard to display the Split panel, as shown in Figure 10–35. You can see that the draft is created using the **No split** option by default.

Figure 10–35

10. Click ✔ (OK) to complete the Draft feature. The part displays as shown in Figure 10–36.

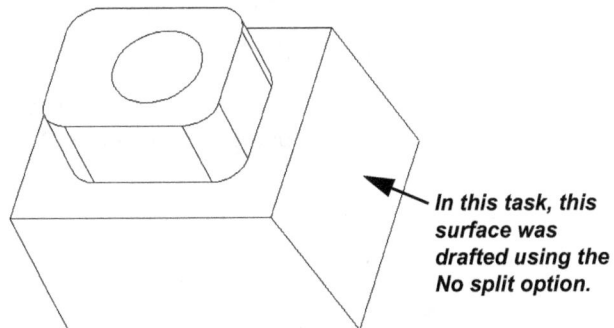

In this task, this surface was drafted using the No split option.

Figure 10–36

Task 3 - Create a Split by split object draft (section is open).

1. Click (Draft).

2. Select the surface shown in Figure 10–37 as the surface to draft.

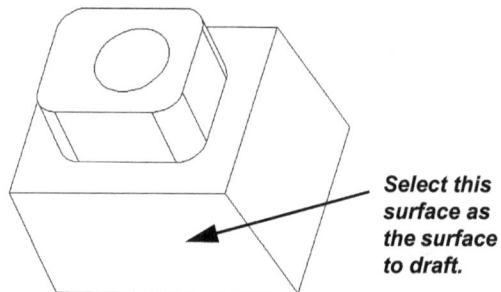

Select this surface as the surface to draft.

Figure 10–37

3. Right-click and select **Draft Hinges**.

4. Select **TOP** as the draft hinge.

5. Click **Split** in the *Draft* dashboard to display the Split panel. Select **Split by split object** in the Split options drop-down list.

6. Click **Define** in the Split panel.

7. Select the same surface that is being drafted as the sketching plane and select **TOP** as the *Top reference* to orient the model for sketching.

8. Click **Sketch**.

9. Sketch the splitting lines, as shown in Figure 10–38.

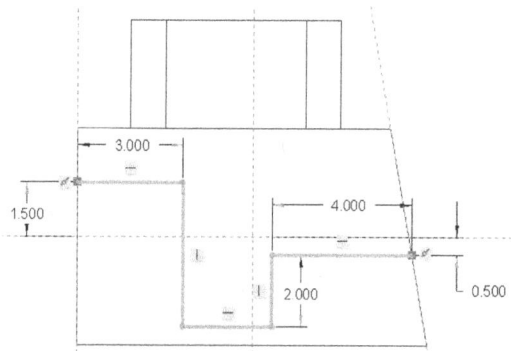

Figure 10–38

10. Complete the sketch.

11. Move the drag handles to preview the draft surfaces. Set the draft *Angle* to **10** for the first direction and **10** for the second direction.

12. Click ✎ (Reverse Angle) in the tab to reverse the angle to add or remove material for both sides as required so that the draft displays as shown in Figure 10–39.

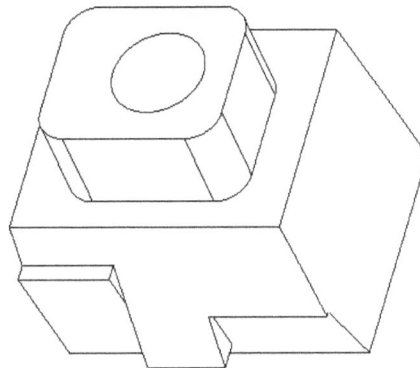

Figure 10–39

13. Click ✔ (OK) to complete the draft feature.

Task 4 - Create a Split by split object draft (section is closed).

---

1. Click ⬚ (Draft).

2. Select the surface shown in Figure 10–40 as the draft surface.

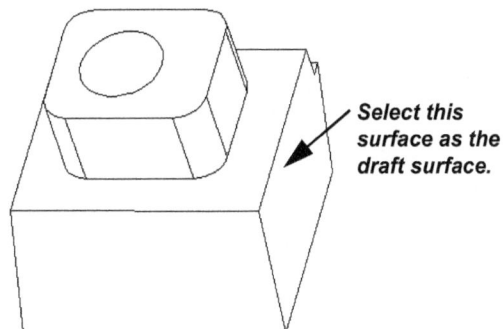

Select this surface as the draft surface.

Figure 10–40

3. Right-click and select **Draft Hinges**.

4. Select **TOP** as the draft hinge.

5. Click the Split panel. Select **Split by split object** in the Split options drop-down list.

6. Click **Define** in the panel.

7. Select the surface that is being drafted as the sketching plane and select **TOP** as the *Top reference* to orient the model for sketching.

8. Sketch the splitting lines as shown in Figure 10–41.

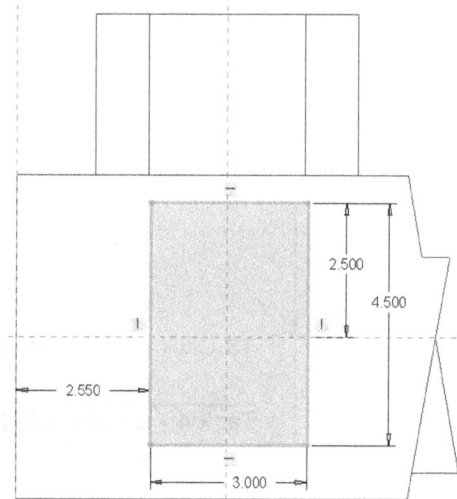

Figure 10–41

9. Complete the sketch.

10. Move the drag handles to preview the draft surfaces. Set the draft angle to **5** for the first direction and to **5** for the second direction.

11. Click ⚹ (Reverse Angle) in the *Draft* dashboard to reverse the angle to add or remove material for both sides as required, and click ✔ (OK) so that the draft displays as shown in Figure 10–42.

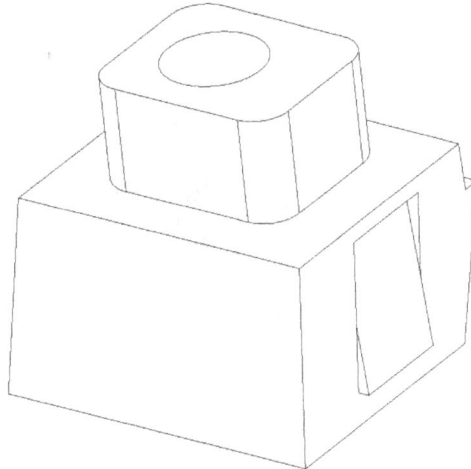

Figure 10–42

Task 5 - Create a datum curve for use a as split object.

1. Select the surface shown in Figure 10–43 as the sketch plane for a datum curve.

2. Click ⬚ (Sketch).

3. Sketch a spline similar to that shown in Figure 10–43.

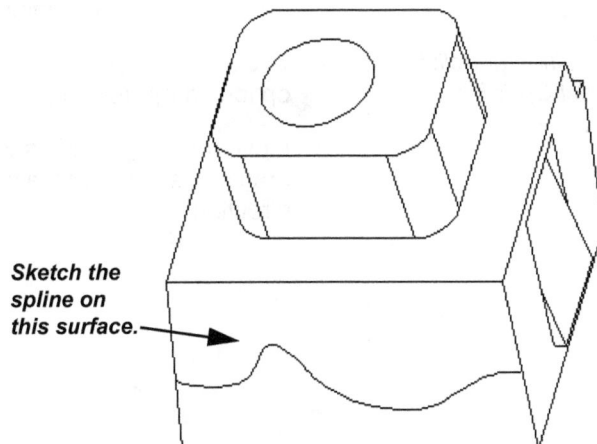

Sketch the spline on this surface.

Figure 10–43

Task 6 - Create a Split by draft hinge draft.

1. Click 🔺 (Draft).

2. Select the surface shown in Figure 10–44 to draft.

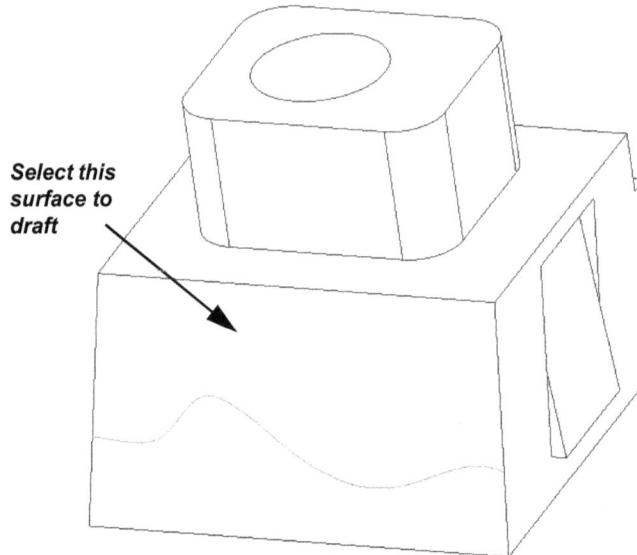

Select this surface to draft

Figure 10–44

3. Right-click and select **Draft Hinges**.

4. Select the curve as the draft hinge.

5. Right-click and select **Pull Direction**.

6. Select the bottom of the part as the reference plane to which the direction is perpendicular.

*You can also right-click and select **Split by draft hinge**.*

7. Click the Split panel. Select **Split by draft hinge** in the Split options drop-down list.

8. Move the drag handles to preview the draft surfaces. Set the draft angle to **10** for the first direction and to **10** for the second direction.

9. Click ⚒ (Reverse Angle) in the tab to reverse the angle to add or remove material for both sides as required, so that the draft displays as shown in Figure 10–45.

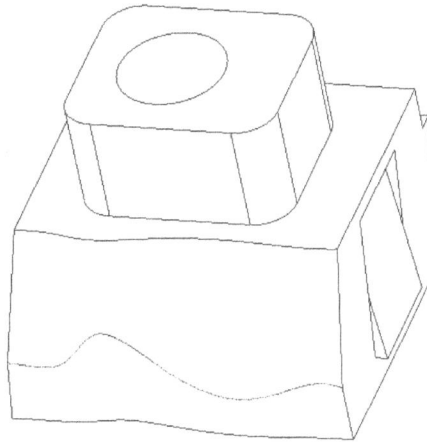

Figure 10–45

10. Click ✔ (OK) to complete the draft feature. Create a No split, Variable draft.

1. Click ◭ (Draft).

2. Select the surface shown in Figure 10–46. It is selected so that you can use the Loop selection technique to select the actual surfaces to be drafted.

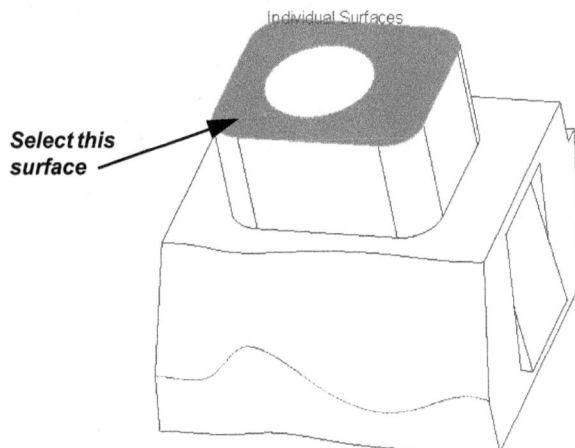

Individual Surfaces

Select this surface

Figure 10–46

3. Press and hold <Shift> and move the cursor over the outer edge of the selected surface. Click the left mouse button to select the edge. Creo Parametric clears the original surface and selects all of the neighboring surfaces that are connected to the original surface, as shown in Figure 10–47.

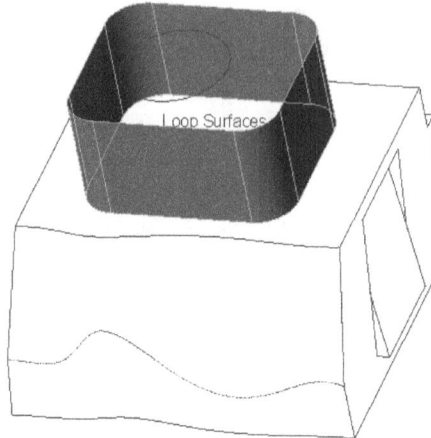

Figure 10–47

4. Right-click and select **Draft Hinges**. Select the surface shown in Figure 10–48.

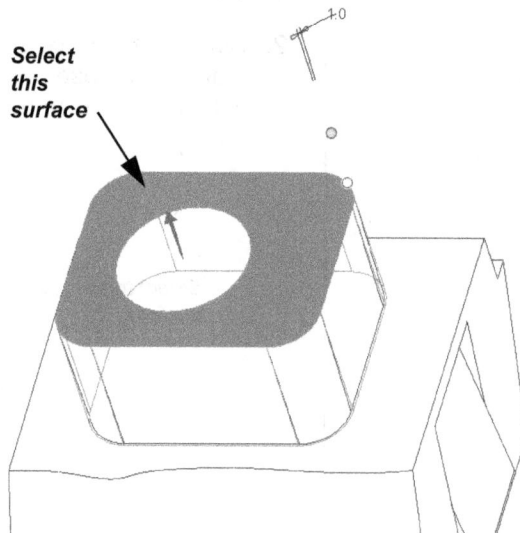

Figure 10–48

5. Set the draft angle to **10**. Click (Reverse Angle) if required, so the preview displays as shown in Figure 10–49.

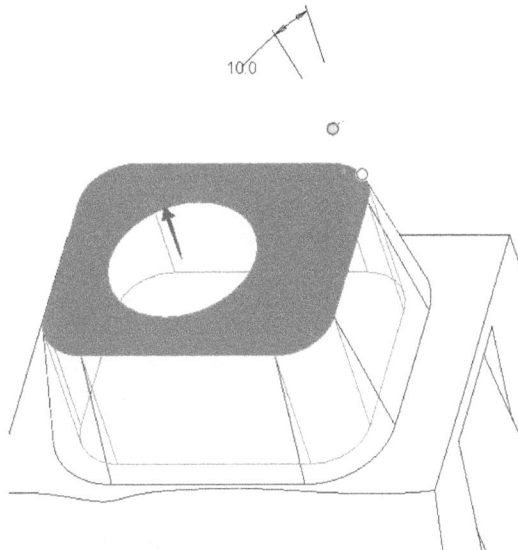

Figure 10–49

6. Click the Angles panel to create varying draft angles in the feature.

*You can also right-click on the circular draft handle and select **Add Angle**.*

7. Place your cursor on the first entry, right-click, and select **Add Angle**, as shown in Figure 10–50.

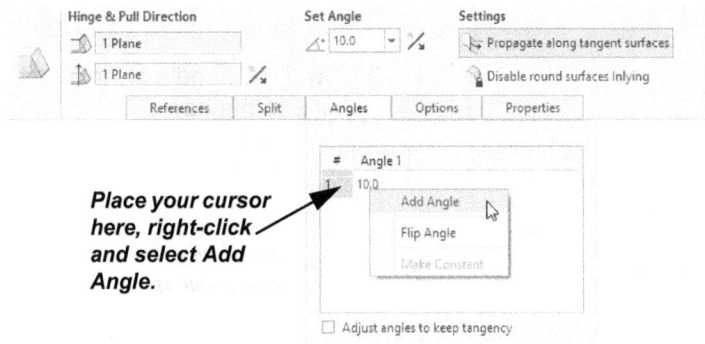

Place your cursor here, right-click and select Add Angle.

Figure 10–50

The panel now contains two angle entries, as shown in Figure 10–51.

#	Angle 1	Reference	Location
1	10.0	Point:Edge...	0.500
2	10.0	Point:Edge...	0.750

Adjust angles to keep tangency

Figure 10–51

The position of draft handles on your model might differ from the position shown in Figure 10–52.

8. Place the cursor on the circular handle of angle #1 (Location 0.50), as shown in Figure 10–52.

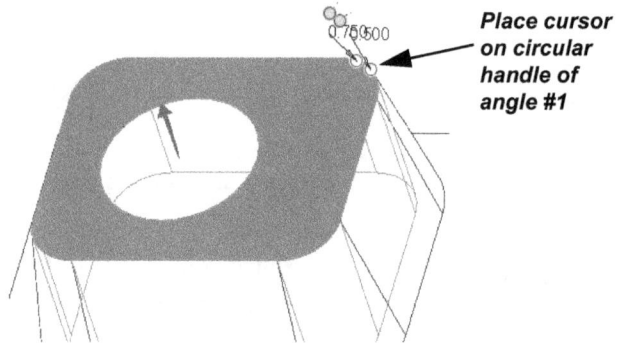

Place cursor on circular handle of angle #1

Figure 10–52

9. Drag the handle of Angle #1 and Angle #2 along the edge loop to the new positions shown in Figure 10–53.

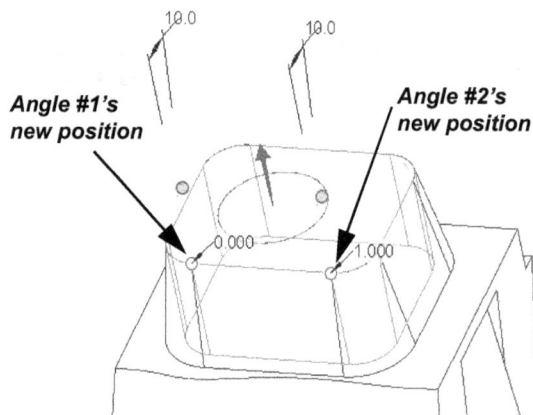

Angle #1's new position

Angle #2's new position

Figure 10–53

10. Open the Angles panel and select the *Reference* cell of draft Angle 2, as shown in Figure 10–54.

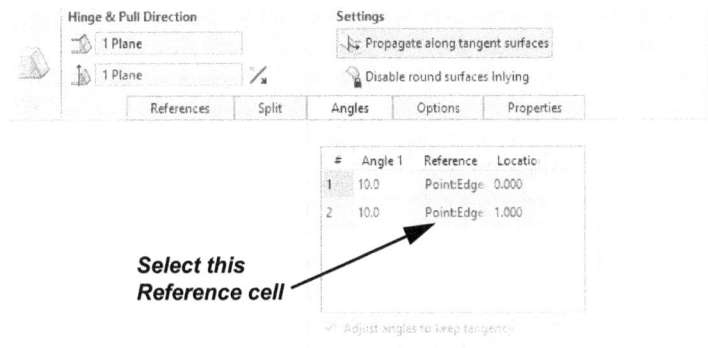

Figure 10–54

11. Right-click and select **Add Angle**. Repeat to add a total of six additional angles, and move them onto the appropriate vertices to create those shown in Figure 10–55.

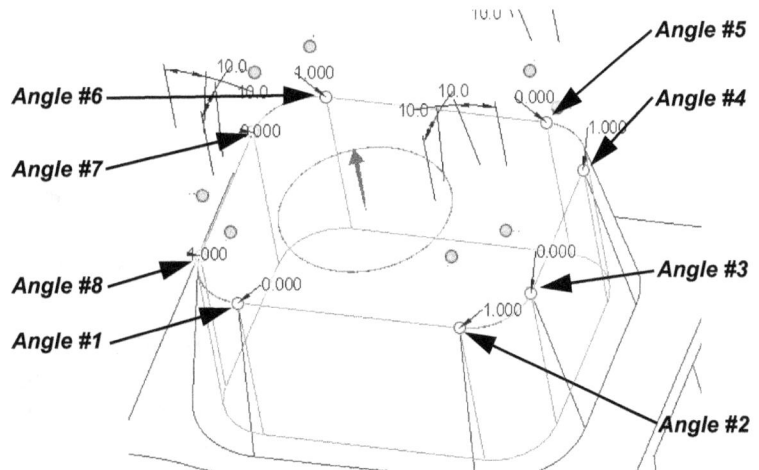

Figure 10–55

12. In the Angles panel, modify the angles shown in Figure 10–55 (above) to the following values:

- Set angles #1, #2, #5, #6 to **5**.
- Set angles #3, #4, #7, #8 to **15**.

13. Click ✔ (OK) to complete the draft feature. The part displays as shown in Figure 10–56.

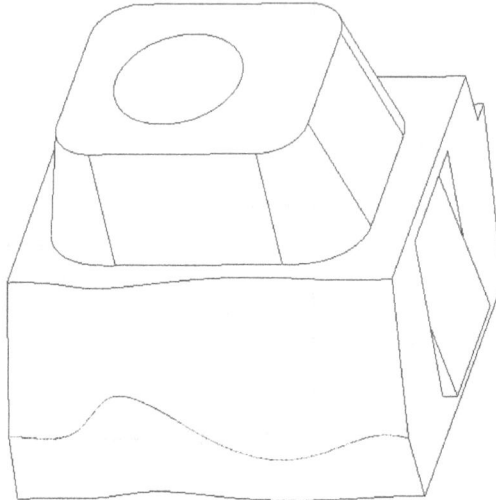

Figure 10–56

Task 7 - Create a No Split draft of the cylindrical surface.

1. Click ⬦ (Draft) and select the surface shown in Figure 10–57. It is selected so that you can use a selection technique to select the actual surfaces to be drafted.

Select this surface to draft.

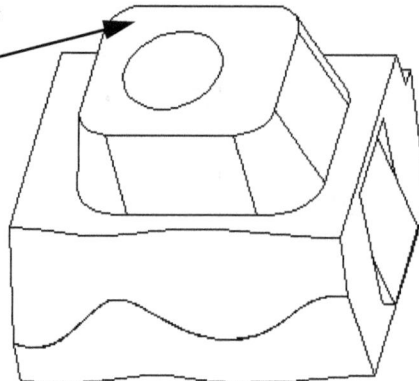

Figure 10–57

2. Hold <Shift> and move the cursor over the inner edge of the selected surface. Use the left mouse button to select the edge. Creo Parametric clears the original surface and selects all of the neighboring surfaces that are connected to the original surface, as shown in Figure 10–58.

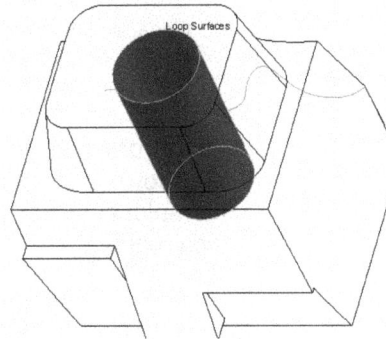

Figure 10–58

3. Right-click and select **Draft Hinges**.

4. Select an appropriate plane as the draft hinge.

5. Use the drag handle to achieve the draft shown in Figure 10–59.

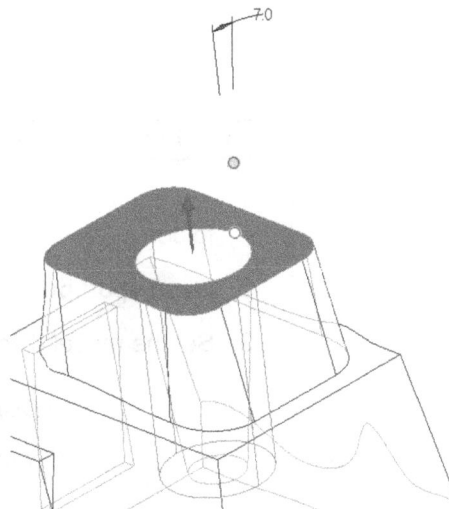

Figure 10–59

6. Set the draft *Angle* to **7**.

7. Click ✔ (OK) to complete the draft feature.

8. Save the part and erase it from memory.

Practice 10b | Creating Variable Pull Direction Drafts

Practice Objectives

- Create a Variable Pull Direction Draft by selecting a pull direction, draft hinge, and draft angle.
- Specify an additional Variable Pull Direction Draft set using the References panel and set the angle value.

In this practice, you will create a VPDD with multiple angle sets as shown in Figure 10–60. The pull direction surface is non-planar, which makes it impossible to use the regular **Draft** command.

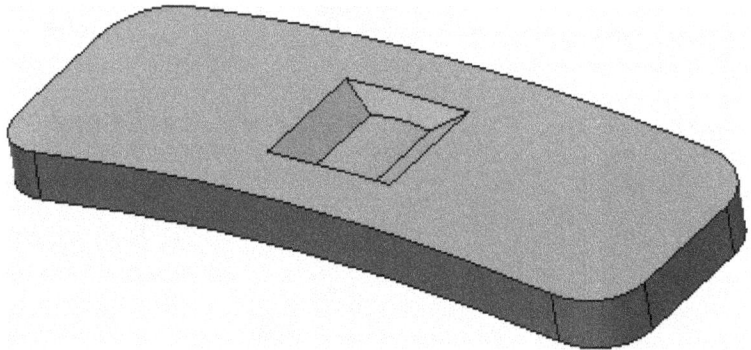

Figure 10–60

Task 1 - Open a part file.

1. Set the working directory to the *Variable_Pull_Direction* folder.

2. Open **vpdd.prt**.

3. Set the model display as follows:

   - ✴ *(Datum Display Filters)*: All Off

   - ⤳ *(Spin Center)*: Off

   - ▭ *(Display Style)*: ▱ (No Hidden)

Task 2 - Create a VPDD.

1. Expand ✎ (Draft) in the *Model* tab and click ↗ (Variable Pull Direction Draft).

2. Select the surface shown in Figure 10–61 as the *Pull Direction*.

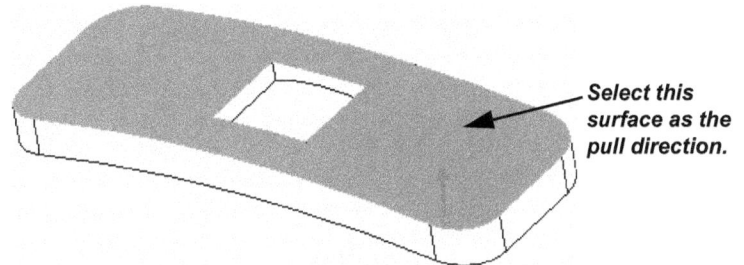

Select this surface as the pull direction.

Figure 10–61

3. Right-click and select **Draft Hinges**.

4. Select the edge shown in Figure 10–62 as the draft hinge.

You might need to enter -60 to flip the direction.

5. Set the draft angle to **60** to create the draft, as shown in Figure 10–62. The angle can be entered directly on the model or in the *Variable Pull Direction Draft* dashboard. Alternatively, you can drag the angle handle on the model.

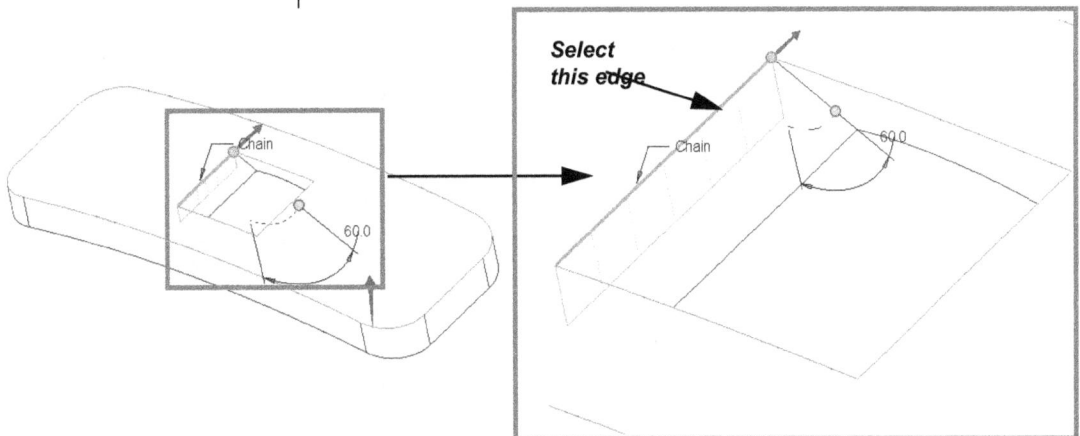

Select this edge

Figure 10–62

6. Hold <Ctrl> and select the opposite edge. This adds the selected edge to **Set 1**. The part displays as shown Figure 10–63.

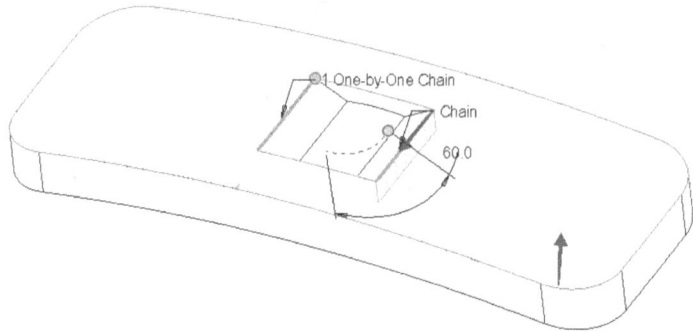

Figure 10–63

*You can also right-click and select **Add set**.*

7. Click **References** in the *Variable Pull Direction Draft* dashboard to display the References panel and select ***New set** as shown in Figure 10–64.

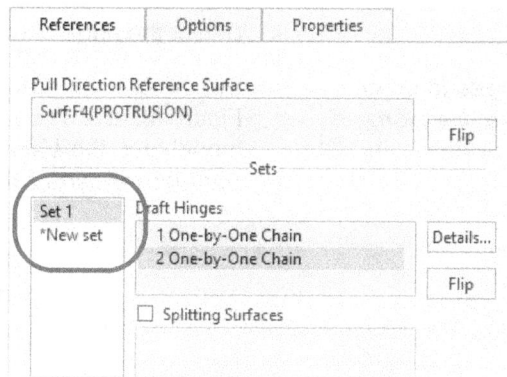

Figure 10–64

8. Select the edge shown in Figure 10–65.

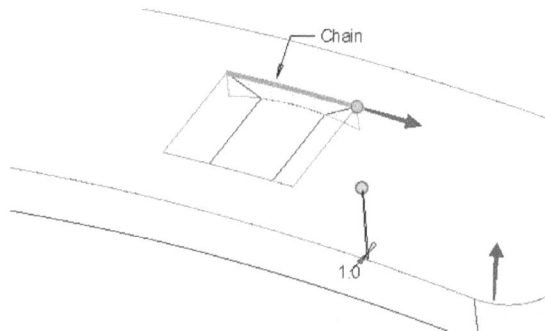

Figure 10–65

9. Set the draft angle to **40** to create the draft.

10. Hold <Ctrl> and select the opposite edge to add it to **Set 2**. The part displays as shown in Figure 10–66.

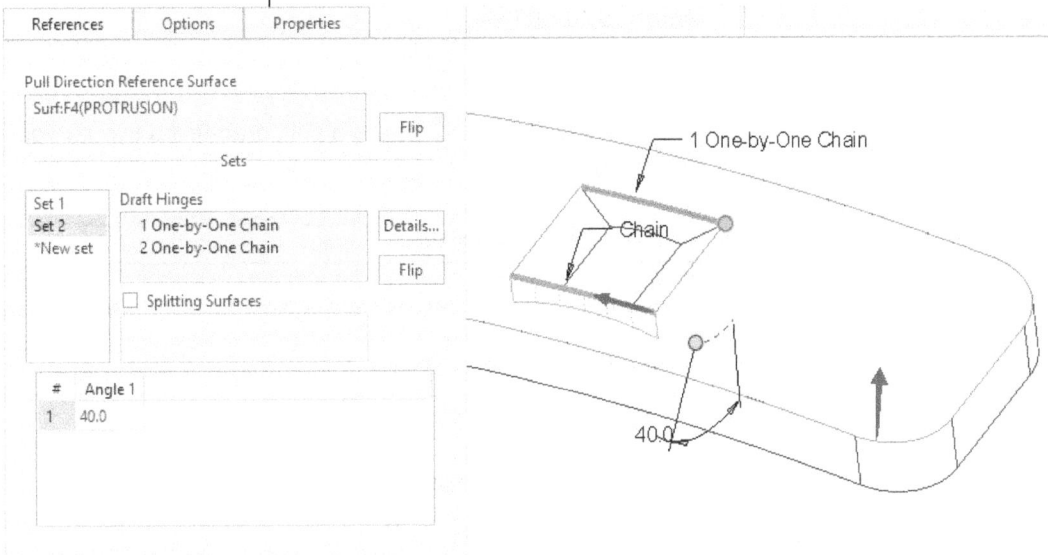

Figure 10–66

11. Complete the VPDD.

12. Set the display style to ▱ (Shading With Edges).

13. The part displays as shown in Figure 10–67.

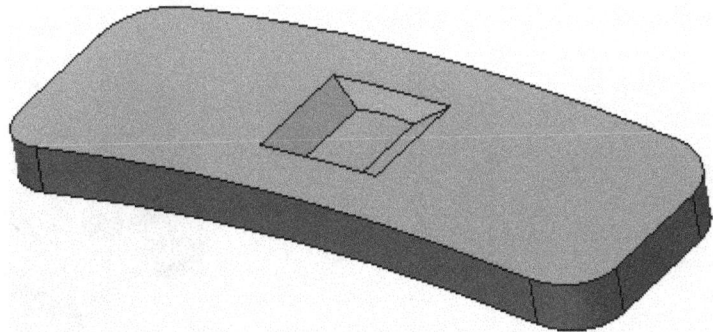

Figure 10–67

14. Save the part and erase it from memory.

Practice 10c

Split Draft with Two Chains of Edges

Practice Objective

- Create Draft split with two chains of edges.

In this practice, you will create a split draft using two curves as draft hinges.

Task 1 - Open a part file.

1. Set the working directory to the *Split_Draft_Chains* folder.

2. Open **split_draft.prt**.

3. Set the model display as follows:

   - ⅍ *(Datum Display Filters)*: All Off

   - ⁎ *(Spin Center)*: Off

   - ⬚ *(Display Style)*: ⬚ (Shading With Edges)

Task 2 - Create a draft feature.

1. Click ⬛ (Draft) in the *Model* tab.

2. Select the surface shown in Figure 10–68.

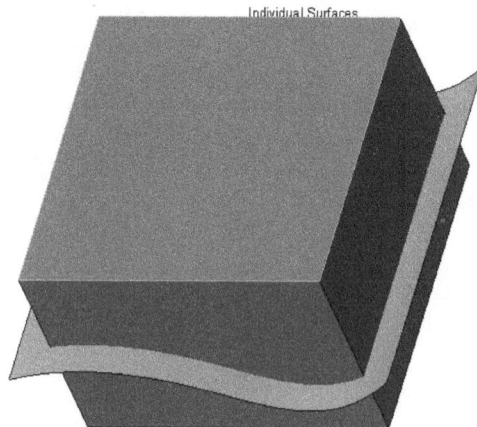

Figure 10–68

3. Press and hold <Shift> and select the edge shown in Figure 10–69 to select the surface loop.

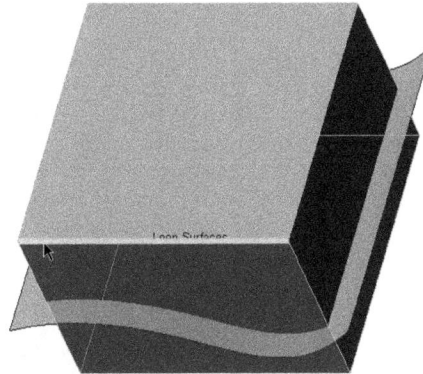

Figure 10–69

4. Select the Split panel.

5. Select **Split by split object**.

6. Select the extruded surface as the splitting object.

Task 3 - Define the Draft hinges.

---

1. Select the References panel.

2. Click **Details** next to the *Draft hinges* field. The Chain dialog box opens, as shown in Figure 10–70.

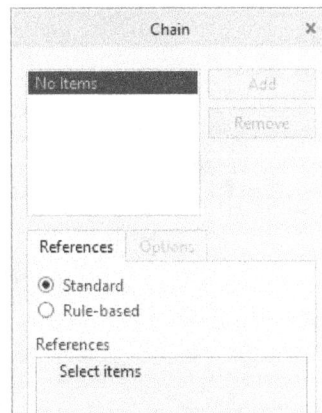

Figure 10–70

3. Select **Rule-based** and then select **Complete loop**.

4. Select the edge shown in Figure 10–71.

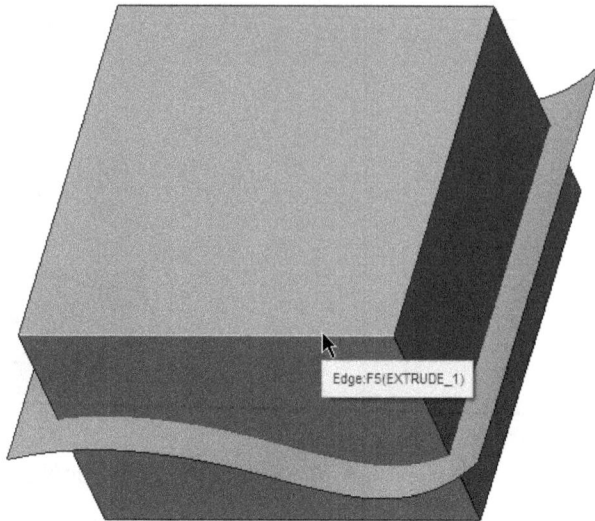

Edge:F5(EXTRUDE_1)

Figure 10–71

5. If required, click in the *Loop Reference* collector and select the top surface of the model, so the chain shown in Figure 10–72 highlights.

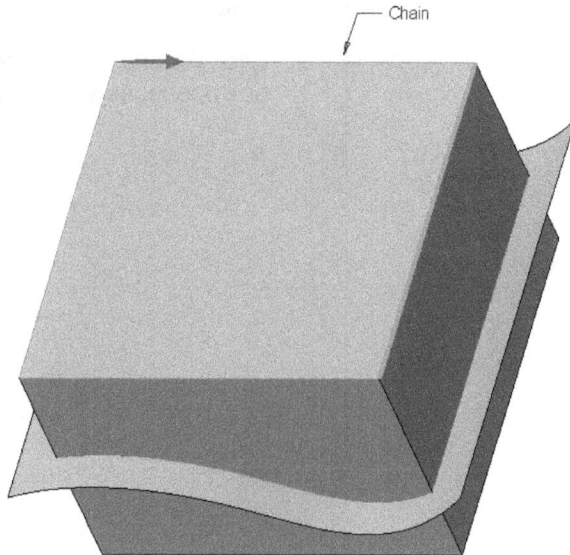

Chain

Figure 10–72

6. Click **Add** in the Chain dialog box.

7. Select the bottom edge shown in Figure 10–73.

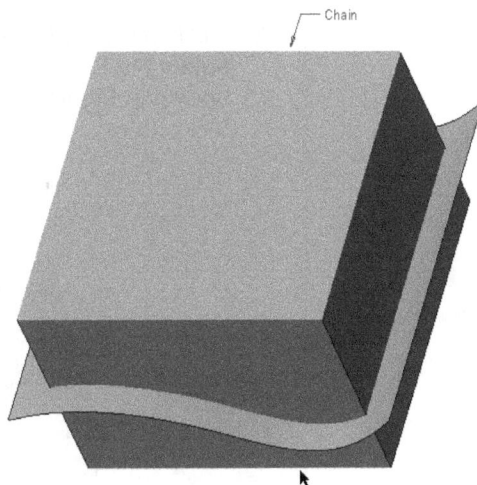

Figure 10–73

8. If required, select in the *Loop Reference* collector and select the bottom planar surface to create the second loop shown in Figure 10–74.

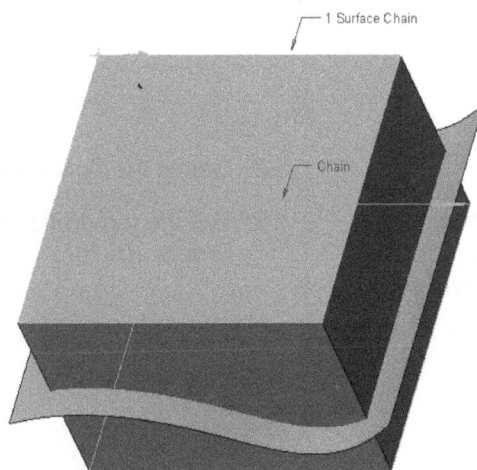

Figure 10–74

9. Click **OK** in the Chain dialog box.

Task 4 - Define the pull direction and draft angles.

1. Click in the Pull direction collector in the dashboard, and select the top planar surface of the model, so it displays as shown in Figure 10–75.

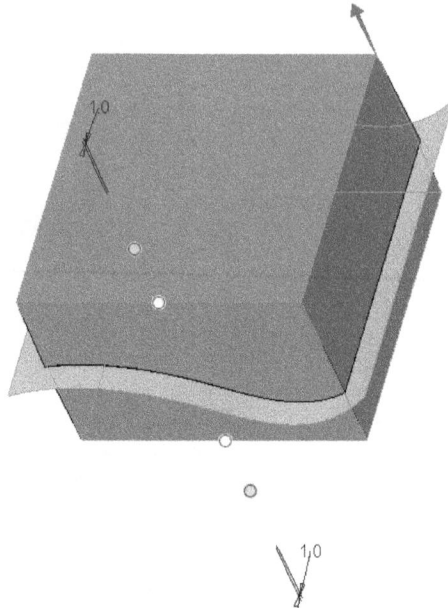

Figure 10–75

2. Select the Split panel.

*Note the default Side options setting of **Draft sides independently**.*

3. Set the top draft to **10** and the bottom to **20**, as shown in Figure 10–76.

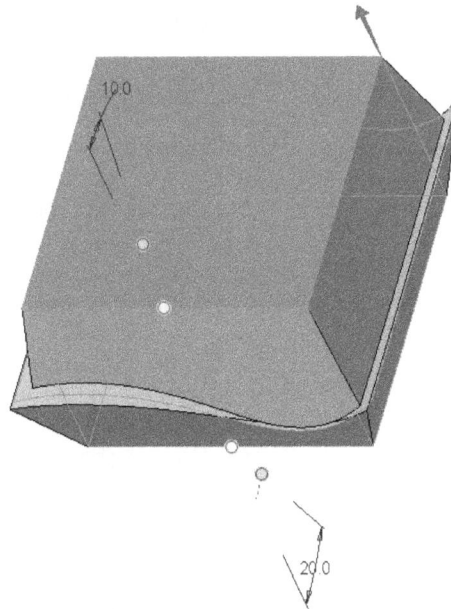

Figure 10–76

4. In the Split panel, select **Draft sides dependently** from the Side options drop-down list.

5. Click ✔ (OK).

6. In the Model Tree, click **Extrude 2** and select ✎ (Hide) in the mini toolbar.

7. The model displays as shown in Figure 10–77.

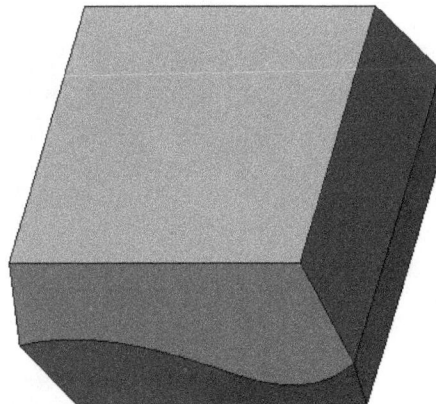

Figure 10–77

8. Save the part and erase it from memory.

Practice 10d | Link

Practice Objective

- Create various draft and round features to create the final geometry.

A good design practice is to leave the creation of most draft and rounds as late as possible in model creation. This enables you to ensure that these features interact with all of the other geometry in the intended way.

In this practice, you are provided with a part in which all of the features except drafts and rounds have been defined. You will add these features to the part so that the resulting geometry displays as shown in Figure 10–78.

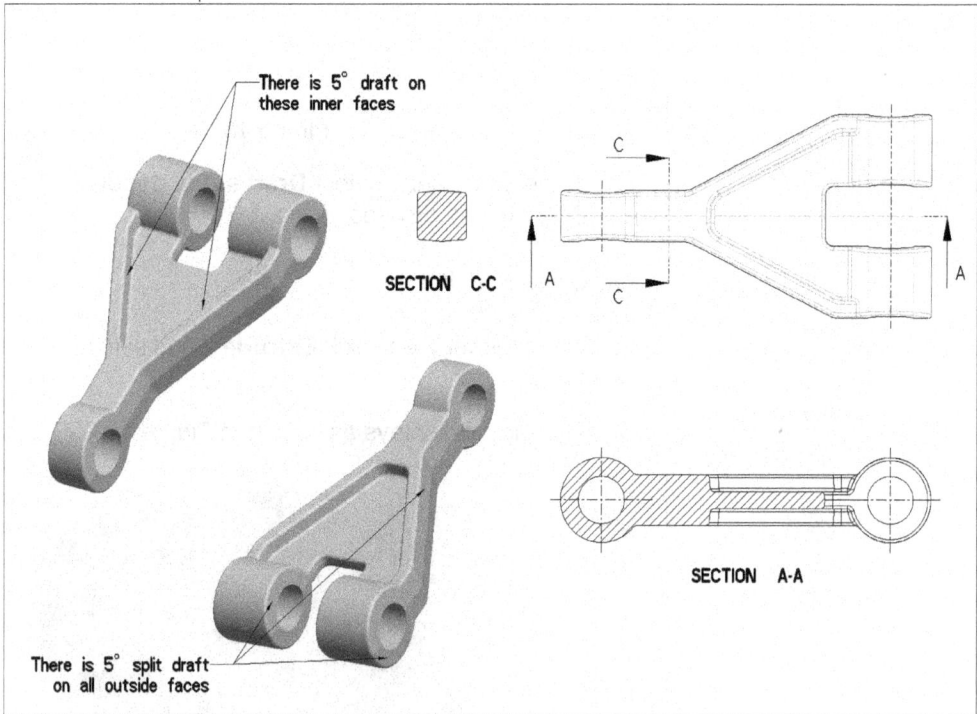

There is 5° draft on these inner faces

SECTION C-C

There is 5° split draft on all outside faces

SECTION A-A

Figure 10–78

Consider the order of the draft and round creation and how they will interact and affect the overall geometry of the part.

1. Set the working directory to the *Draft_Link* folder.

2. Open **link.prt**.

3. Add draft and round features to complete the support part. Use dimension values such as 10, 2, and 5 for the radii and 5° for all of the draft angles.

4. Save the part and erase it from memory.
   - **Hint:** Add the rounds after the draft.
   - **Hint:** Use datum RIGHT as the Draft Hinge and split reference.

Practice 10e | Exclude Areas

Practice Objectives

- Create a draft feature on a set of surfaces.
- Remove surfaces that already meet the draft requirement.

In this practice, you will use **Exclude areas with draft** to remove a set of surfaces that already meet the required draft.

Task 1 - Open the draft.prt model.

1. Set the Working Directory to the *Exclude_Areas* folder.

2. Open **draft.prt**.

3. Set the model display as follows:

   - ⁑ *(Datum Display Filters)*: All Off

   - ⁓ *(Spin Center)*: Off

   - ▢ *(Display Style)*: ▢ (Shading With Edges)

Task 2 - Measure the angle between the angled surface and the top of the model.

1. In the ribbon, select the *Analysis* tab.

2. Expand 📏 (Measure) and select ⟁ (Angle).

3. Select the surface shown in Figure 10–79.

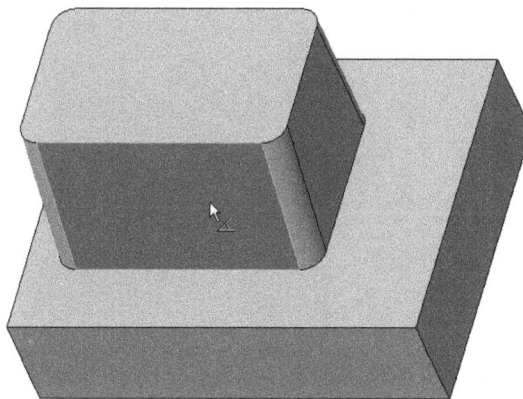

Figure 10–79

4. Press and hold <Ctrl> and select the surface shown in Figure 10–80.

Note the angle of approximately 78°.

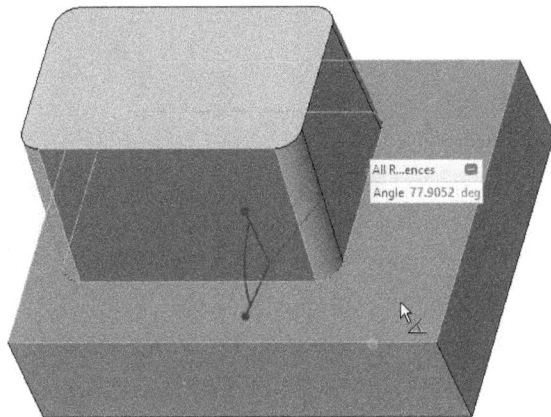

Figure 10–80

5. Click **Close**.

Task 3 - Draft the surfaces surrounding the boss at the top of the model.

---

1. Select the surface shown in Figure 10–81.

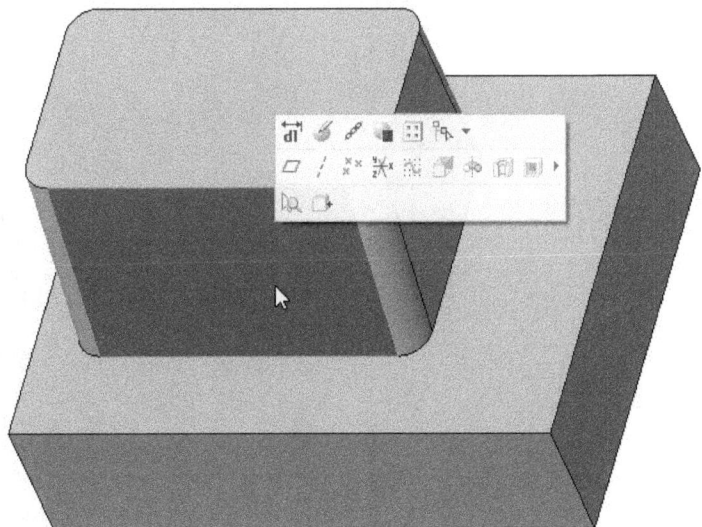

Figure 10–81

2. In the *Model* tab, in the Shapes group, click (Draft).

---

3. Select the surface shown in Figure 10–82 as the draft hinge.

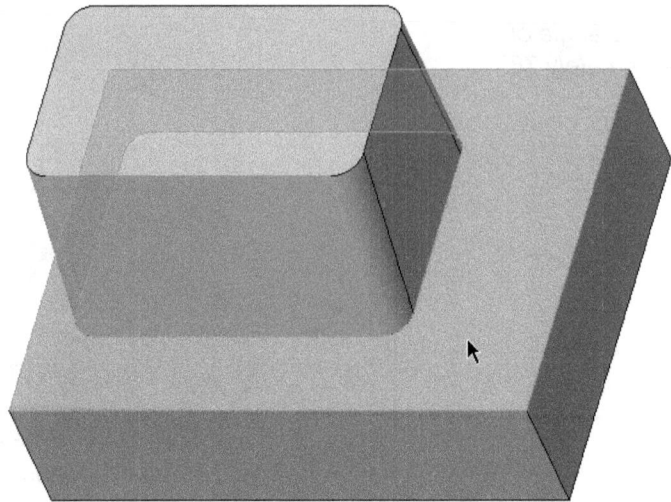

Figure 10–82

4. In the *Draft* dashboard, edit the Draft Angle to **2**.

5. Click ✎ (Reverse Angle) so the draft displays as shown in Figure 10–83.

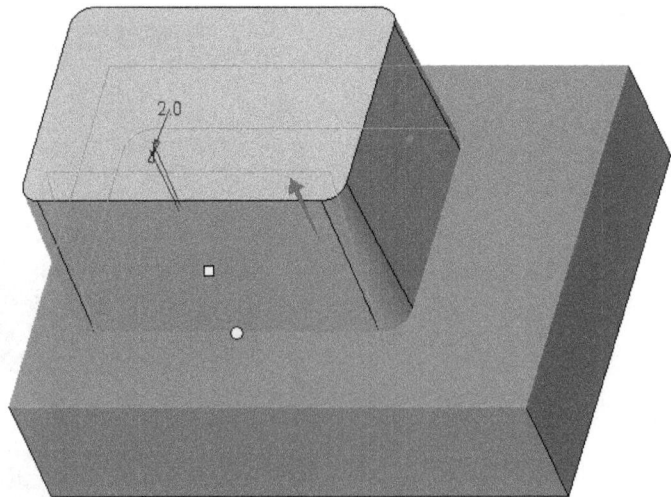

2,0

Figure 10–83

6. Click ✔ (OK).

7. Measure the angle between the drafted surface and the top of the base, as you did in Task 1. The angle should be 88° as shown in Figure 10–84.

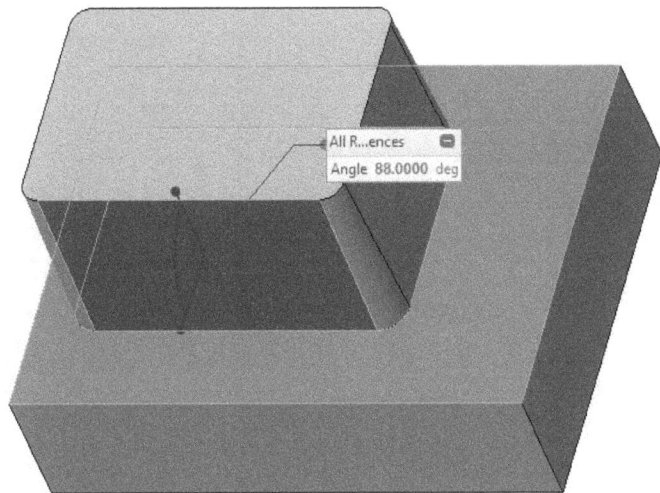

All R...ences
Angle 88.0000 deg

Figure 10–84

Task 4 - Remove the surface from the set of drafted surfaces.

Design Considerations

For functional purposes, you require the originally defined angle. Since this angle is greater than the defined draft angle, you can remove the surface from the set of drafted surfaces.

1. In the Model Tree, select the **Draft 1** feature.

2. In the mini toolbar, click 🖌 (Edit Definition).

3. Expand the Options panel, and select **Exclude areas with draft**.

4. The surface and adjacent tangent surfaces are removed from the set as shown in Figure 10–85.

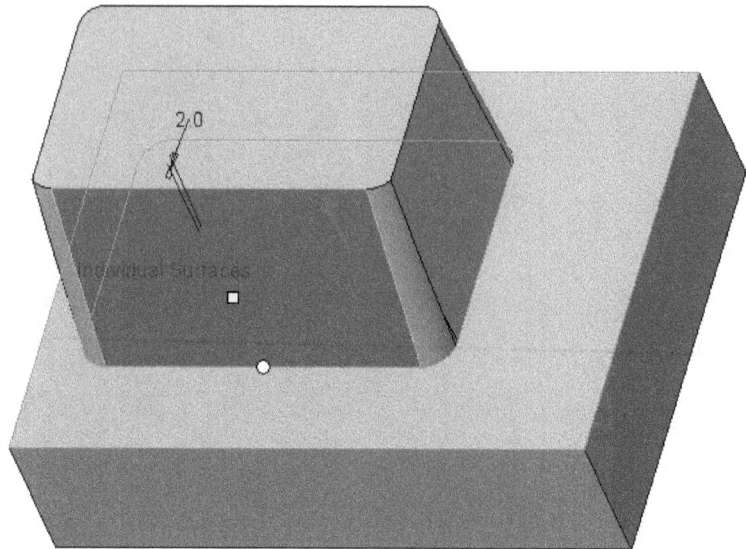

Figure 10–85

5. In the dashboard, click ✔ (OK).

6. Measure the angle between the angled surface and the top of the base, as you did in Task 1. The angle should be approximately 78° as shown in Figure 10–86.

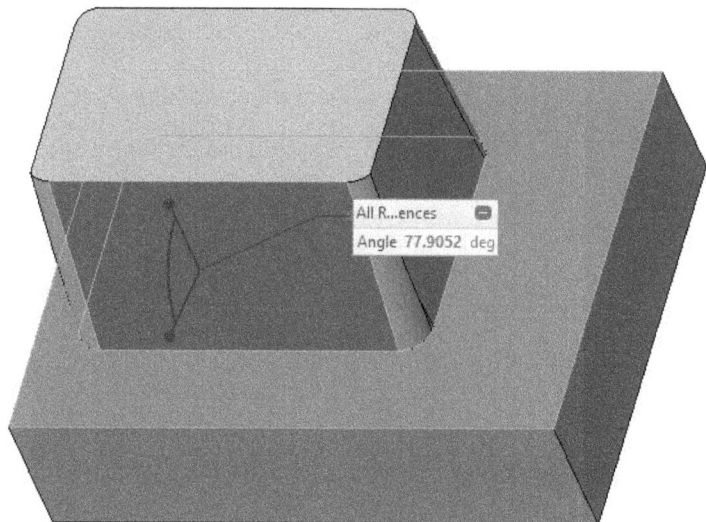

Figure 10–86

7. Note that the system has created a small surface in order to generate the required geometry, as shown in Figure 10–87.

Always verify the resulting geometry when using this option to ensure that it is acceptable.

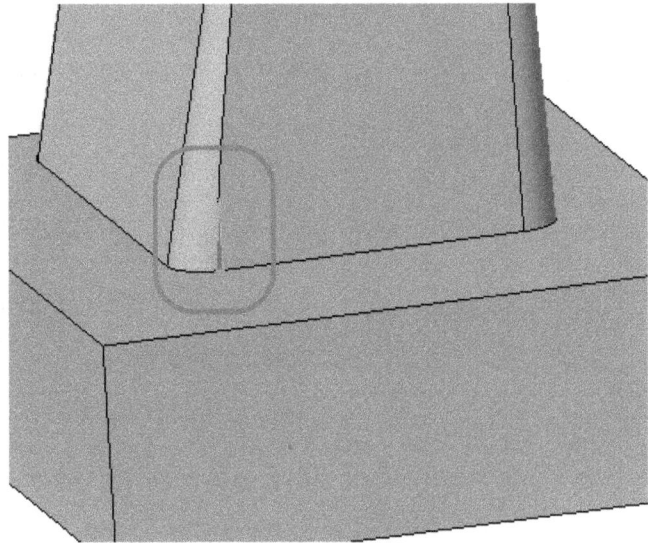

Figure 10–87

8. Close the file and erase it from memory.

Practice 10f | Handling Rounds in Draft

Practice Objective

- Create draft on surfaces that have adjacent rounds.

In this practice, you will review how Creo Parametric handles draft features on surfaces with adjacent rounds.

Task 1 - Open the baseplate.prt model.

1. Set the Working Directory to *Rounds_In_Draft*, if required.

2. Open **draft2.prt**.

3. Set the model display as follows:

   - *(Datum Display Filters)*: All Off
   - *(Spin Center)*: Off
   - *(Display Style)*: (Shading With Edges)

   The model displays as shown in Figure 10–88.

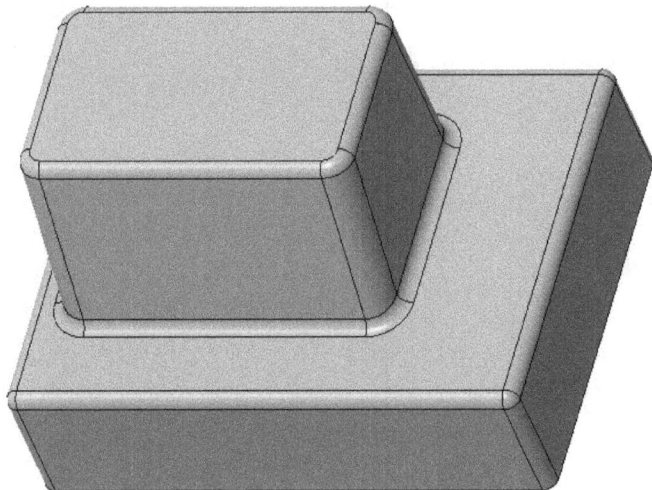

Figure 10–88

Task 2 - Create a draft on the boss.

1. Select the surface shown in Figure 10–89.

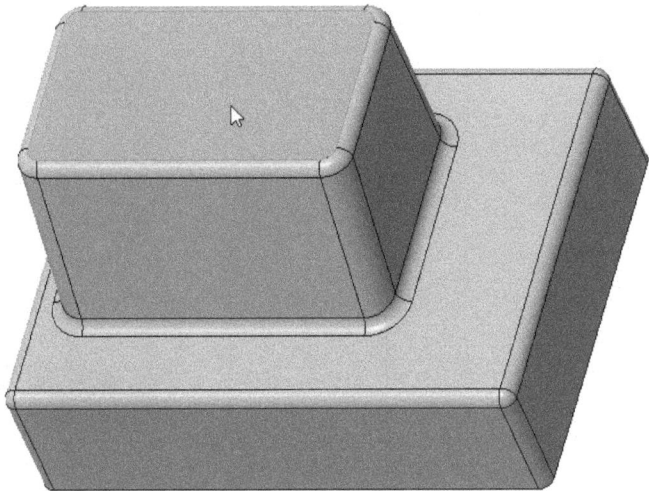

Figure 10–89

2. Press and hold <Shift> and select the surface shown in Figure 10–90.

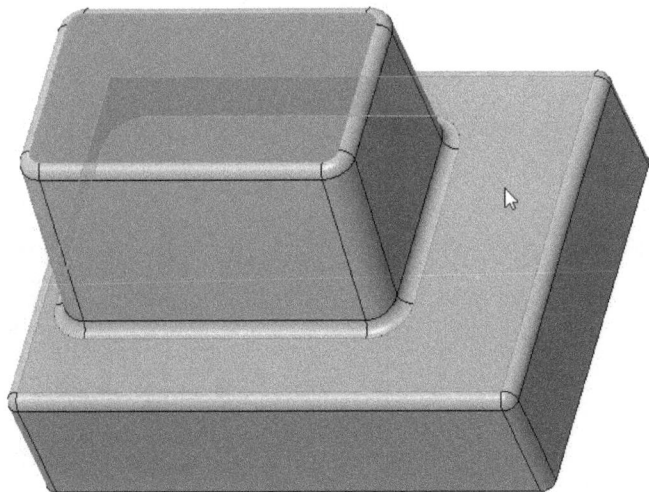

Figure 10–90

3. Release <Shift>, press and hold <Ctrl>, and select the top surface to remove it from the surface set.

4. In the *Model* tab, in the Engineering group, click ⬛ (Draft).

---

5. Select the top surface of the boss as the draft hinge. The draft previews as shown in Figure 10–91.

Note that the rounds highlight in a different color than the rest of the geometry.

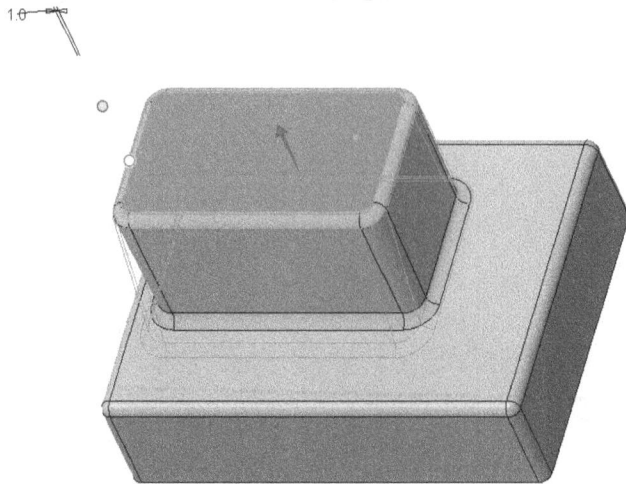

Figure 10–91

6. In the dashboard, edit the draft angle to **10** as shown in Figure 10–92.

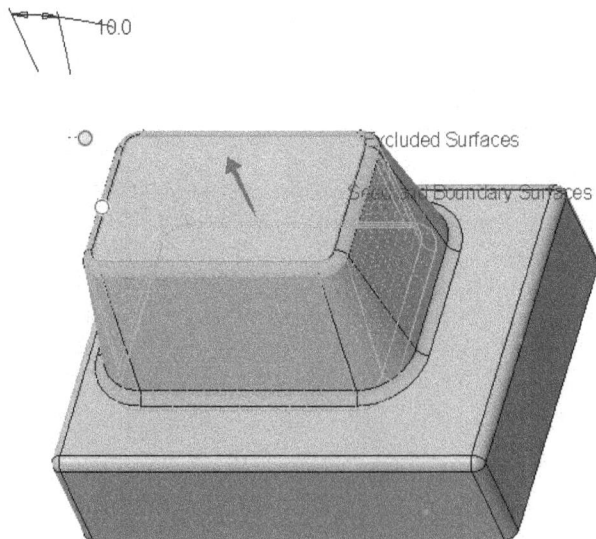

Figure 10–92

7. Drag the draft angle handle and note that the rounds move along with the drafted surface.

8. Edit the draft angle to **5** and click ✔ (OK).

Task 3 - Create another draft feature and investigate additional round handling capabilities.

1. Select the bottom surface of the model.

2. Hold <Shift> and select the surface shown in Figure 10–93.

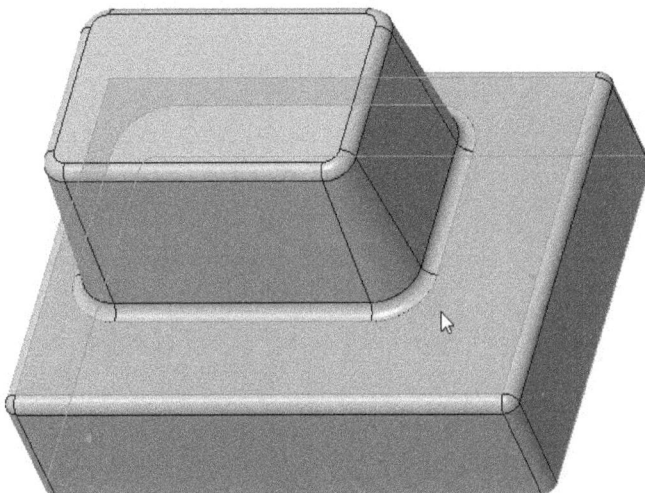

Figure 10–93

3. Note that the bottom surface is still included in the selection set. Hold <Ctrl> and select the surface to remove it, as shown in Figure 10–94.

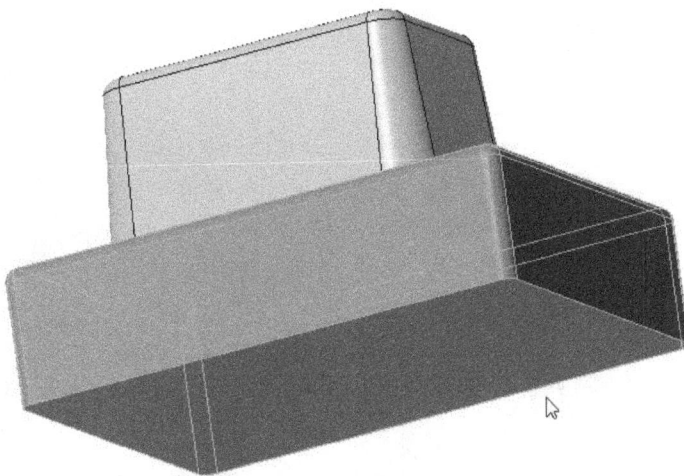

Figure 10–94

4. In the *Model* tab, in the Engineering group, click ⟋ (Draft).

5. Select the surface shown in Figure 10–95 as the draft hinge.

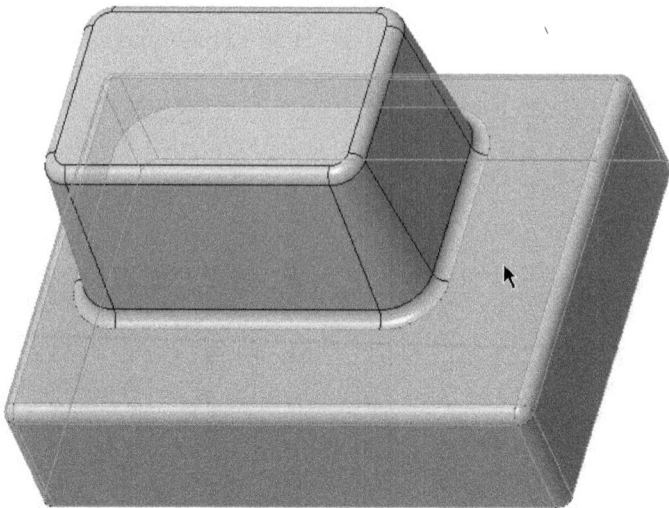

Figure 10–95

6. Edit the draft angle to **10** and flip the draft direction if required, so the model displays as shown in Figure 10–96.

The rounds that were included in the set of surfaces are also drafted, resulting in a varying radius.

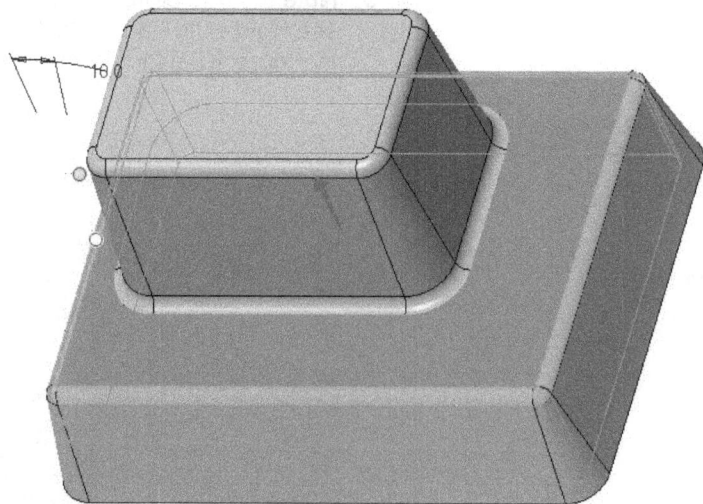

Figure 10–96

7. In the dashboard, remove the vertical rounds from the round set by clicking 🔧 (Exclude Inlying Rounds). The result displays as shown in Figure 10–97.

Note that in this case, the rounds maintain a constant radius.

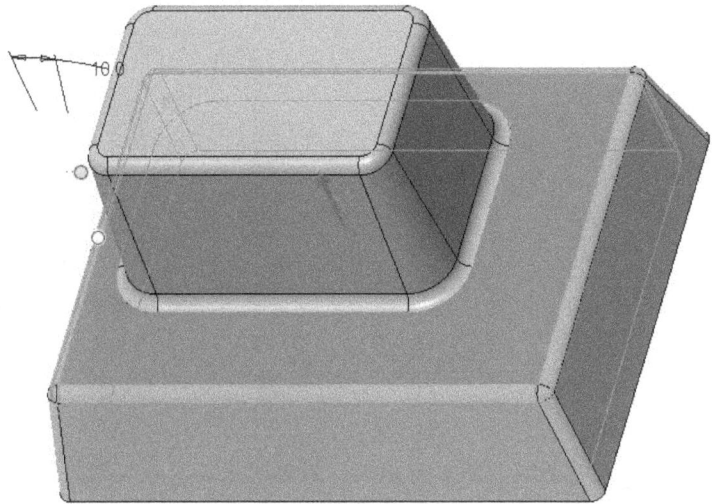

Figure 10–97

8. In the Options panel, disable the **Create round/chamfer geometry** option to remove the rounds completely, as shown in Figure 10–98.

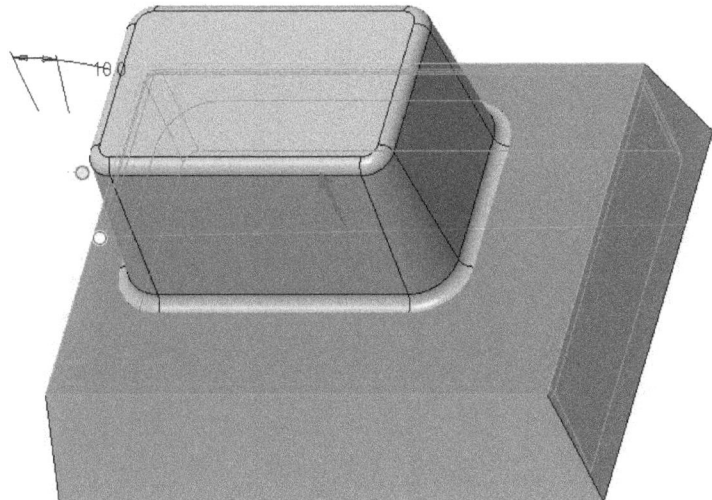

Figure 10–98

9. Enable the **Create round/chamfer geometry** option.

10. Click ✓ (OK). The completed model displays as shown in Figure 10–99.

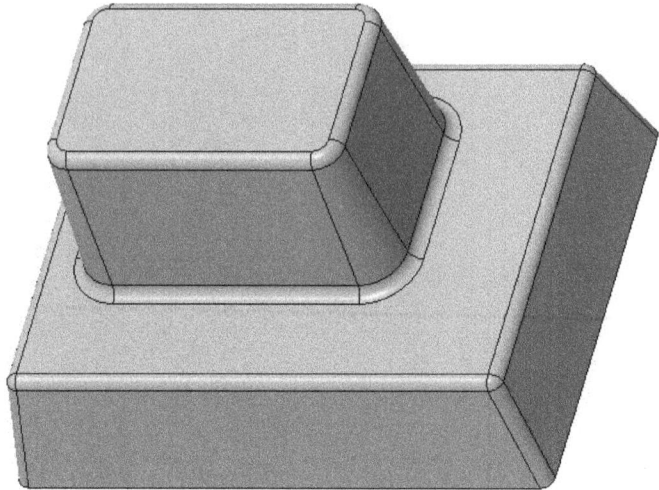

Figure 10–99

11. Close the model and erase it from memory.

Chapter Review Questions

1. Which of the following statements is true regarding creating a draft feature?

    a. Multiple surfaces can be selected for drafting by holding <Ctrl> as you are selecting the surfaces.

    b. Multiple surfaces can be selected as references when defining the draft hinge by holding <Ctrl> as you are selecting the surfaces.

    c. To define the draft hinge reference, you can only select an existing edge on the model.

    d. The pull direction reference must be a reference independent of the draft hinge reference.

2. What is the maximum angle range for a Variable Pull Direction Draft?

    a. -29.9° and +29.9°

    b. -59.9° and +59.9°

    c. -89.9° and +89.9°

    d. -179.9° and +179.9°

3. A Draft feature can be added to a surface adjacent to a round.

    a. True

    b. False

4. Which command enables you to specify multiple draft sets?

    a. ⬚ (Draft)

    b. ⬚ (Variable Pull Direction Draft)

5. A draft can be split so that the surface can have different angles on each side of the split reference. Which entities can be selected to split a draft? (Select all that apply.)

    a. Draft hinge

    b. Along a line.

    c. Along a curve.

    d. At a point.

6. What is the line or curve about which the drafted surfaces are pivoted is called?

   a. Draft hinge

   b. Pull direction

   c. Split draft

   d. Transition

7. What is the direction that is used to measure the draft angle called?

   a. Draft hinge

   b. Pull direction

   c. Split draft

   d. Transition

Answers: 1a, 2c, 3a, 4b, 5abc, 6a, 7b

Basic Surface Design

Creo Parametric enables you to create solid features from surfaces. Using this functionality, you can combine complex surface definitions to create solid features that would otherwise be difficult to create using standard construction methods.

Learning Objectives in This Chapter

- Understand how the surface modeling tools in the Creo Parametric 6.0 software can be used to create complex shapes that cannot be created using the basic solid modeling tools.
- Create simple surfaces using the **Surface** command in the Extrude, Revolve, Sweep, and Blend dashboards, so that the features are created as surfaces instead of solids.
- Create a fill surface by referencing a 2D closed sketch profile.
- Create a surface offset from an existing solid or nonsolid surface by a specified distance.
- Copy an existing solid or nonsolid surface to create a nonsolid surface.
- Create a surface that is defined by a series of planar and non-planar curves or edges to create a 3D surface.
- Combine individual surface features into one quilted surface that can be used as a single surface for modeling.
- Remove material from the model by referencing a datum curve, a datum plane, or a surface.
- Create solid geometry from a surface using the **Thicken** command.

11.1 Introduction to Surfaces

As with datum planes, surface features are non-solid and have zero thickness. However, surfaces do not have to be planar and can be selected anywhere, not just on the edges.

The term *quilt* is often used to describe surface features and can refer to a single surface feature or a group of merged (combined) surface features. Surfaces features can be used to do the following:

- Create surface models that can be converted to solid models.

- Create a *skin* over an imported wireframe model.

- Create complex solid cuts and protrusions.

- Define complex projected and formed curves.

Figure 11–1 is created using surfaces, these surfaces could then be used to create a solid.

Figure 11–1

Surface Display

When the non-solid surface displays in **Shaded** or **Shaded with Edges**, the geometry displays in violet blue. When displayed in **Wireframe**, **Hidden Line**, or **No-hidden Line**, the external edges (one-sided edges) display in yellow (quilt color), while the internal edges (two sided edges) display in magenta (manufacturing volume color). Since surfaces are non-solid geometry, you can add them individually to a part- or assembly-level layer and remove them from display by hiding the layer.

When you shade the model, surface features are shaded by default. The shading is controlled by the **shade_surface_feat** config.pro option (the default value is **yes**). This option can be set to **no** to prevent surface features from being shaded.

To remove surfaces from display, you do not have to add them to a layer. Right-click on the surface in the Graphic window or in the Model Tree and select **Hide**. To display the surface again, right-click on it in the Model Tree and select **Unhide**.

Surface features can be created using many different options. Selecting the correct option depends on the required geometry and your design intent.

You can create surface features in the following ways:

- Sketch the feature.

- Copy another feature.

- Offset an existing surface.

- Use selected boundaries.

Once the geometry for the surface has been defined, the surface can be created and used to create other features.

11.2 Surface Creation

When you create a new surface feature, the available options are similar to those for a solid.

Extrude

To create an extruded surface feature, click ⬚ (Extrude) in the *Model* tab or mini toolbar. Once the dashboard activates, ensure that ⬚ (Surface) is clicked to create a surface instead of a solid, as shown in the *Extrude* dashboard in Figure 11–2.

This icon is used to create surface features

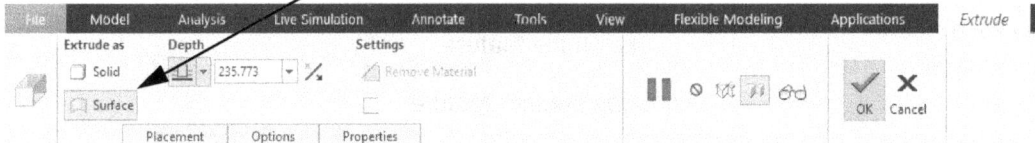

Figure 11–2

You can create extruded features as a closed or open volume. Figure 11–3 shows two extruded surface features. The feature on the left shows a closed volume and the feature on the right shows an open volume.

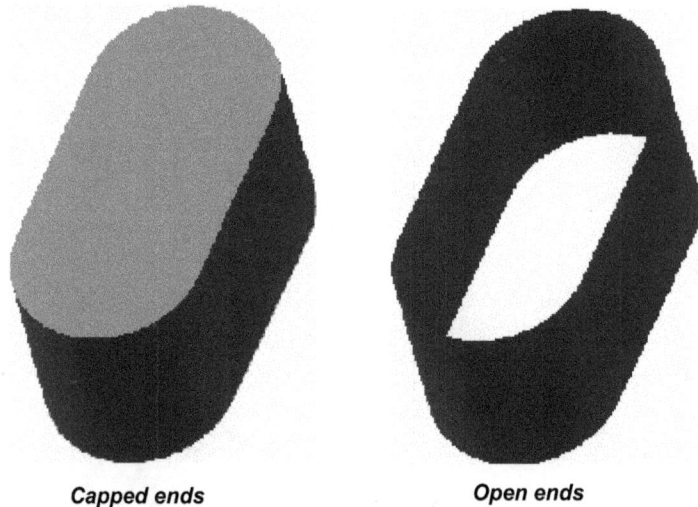

Capped ends   *Open ends*

Figure 11–3

To create a closed volume, click **Options** to open the Options panel and select the **Capped Ends** option. Clear this option to create an open volume.

Revolve

To create a revolved surface feature, click ⚙ (Revolve) in the *Model* tab. Once the dashboard displays, ensure that

▢ (Surface) is clicked to create a surface instead of a solid. Figure 11–4 shows two revolved surface features. The feature on the left shows a closed volume and the feature on the right shows an open volume.

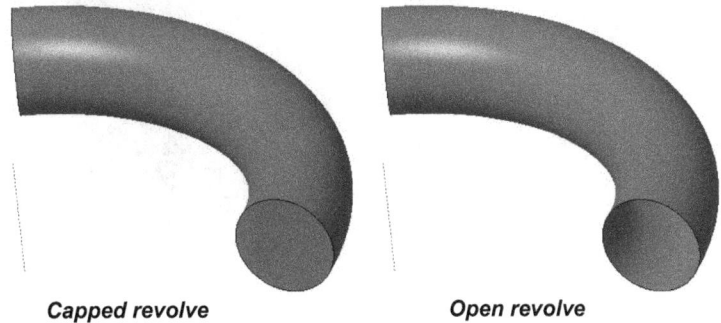

Capped revolve   *Open revolve*

Figure 11–4

Sweep

To create a swept surface feature, click ⬡ (Sweep) in the *Model* tab. Figure 11–5 shows two swept surface features. The feature on the top shows a closed volume and the bottom shows an open volume.

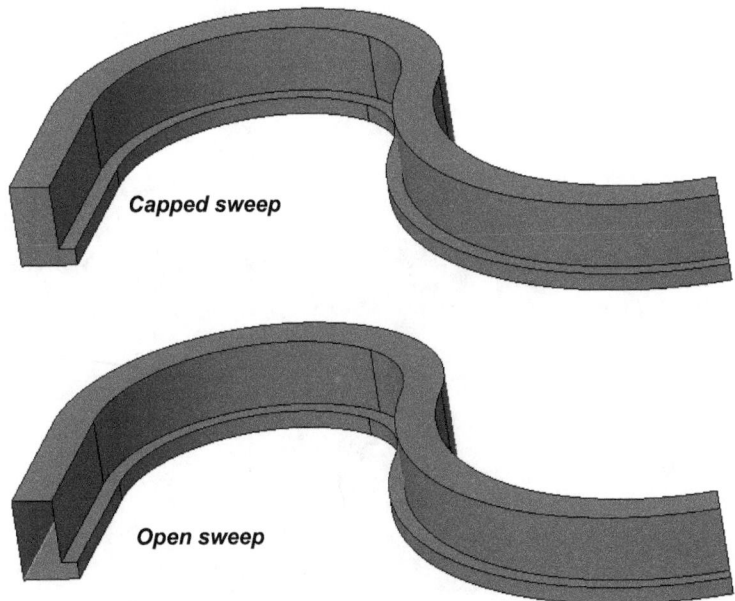

Capped sweep

Open sweep

Figure 11–5

Blend

To create blended surface features, select **Shapes>Blend** in the *Model* tab. Figure 11–6 shows two blended surface features. The feature on the left shows a closed volume and the feature on the right shows an open volume.

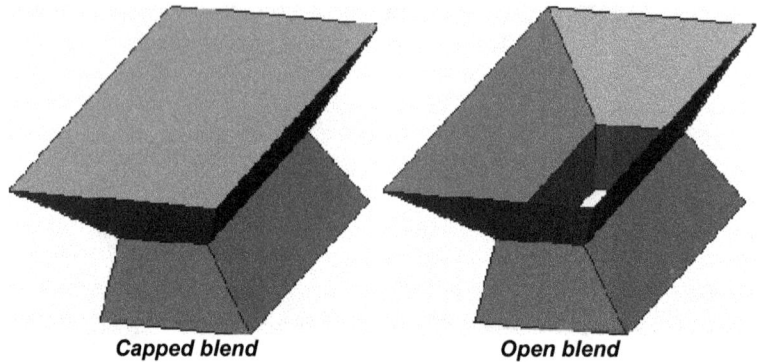

Capped blend   *Open blend*

Figure 11–6

Fill

To create a filled surface feature, click ☐ (Fill) in the *Model* tab. This option creates a planar surface using boundaries. To create the surface, you can either select an existing 2D sketch to define its boundaries or sketch the boundaries in the feature. To access Sketcher, right-click on the sketch and select **Define Internal Sketch**. A 2D sketch and the resulting flat surface are shown in Figure 11–7.

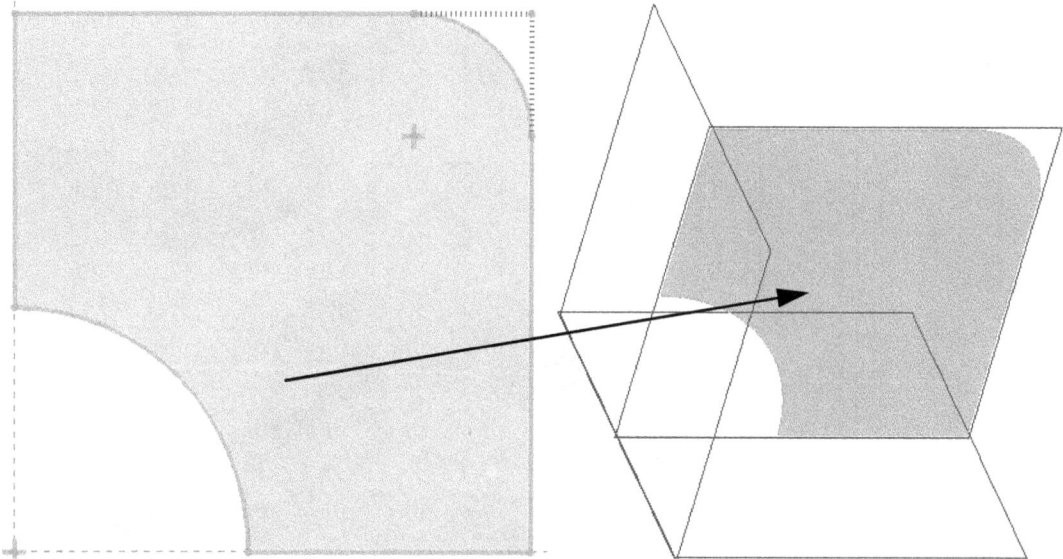

Figure 11–7

Offset

This option creates a quilt by offsetting it from another quilt or solid surface by a specified distance and in the normal direction. To create an offset surface feature, select the surface to offset and click ⬚ (Offset) in the *Model* tab. If the surface is not preselected, the **Offset** option is not available. The surface selected as the reference for an offset surface and the resulting geometry is shown in Figure 11–8.

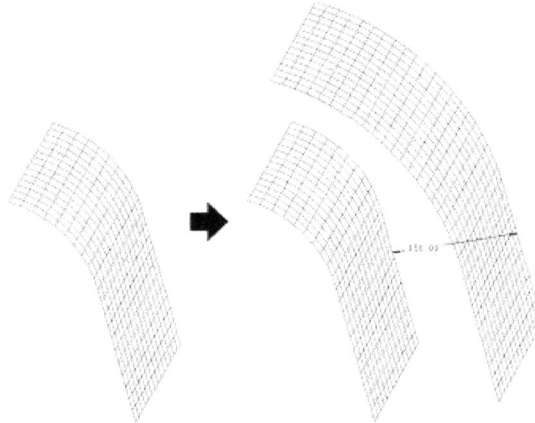

Figure 11–8

Copy

The **Copy** option enables you to copy solid surface(s) and quilts. This option creates a quilt that is a copy of an existing quilt, solid surface, or curve. The new quilt is created on top of the referenced surfaces. To copy a surface, select it and click ⬚ (Copy) and ⬚ (Paste). In Figure 11–9, a solid surface on the part is selected to create a copied surface feature. This new surface feature can be used in conjunction with other features to create additional geometry, as shown on the right.

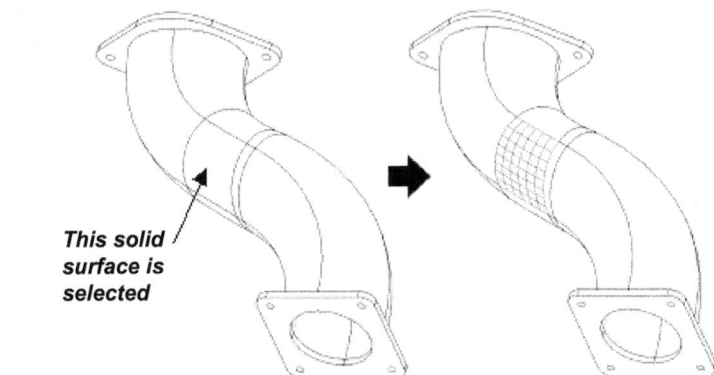

This solid surface is selected

Figure 11–9

Boundary Blend

To create a boundary blend surface feature, click ⌨ (Boundary Blend) in the *Model* tab. This option creates a surface between selected boundaries. The boundaries can be curves, edges, points, and vertices. The five datum curves shown in Figure 11–10 are used as boundaries to define the resulting surface.

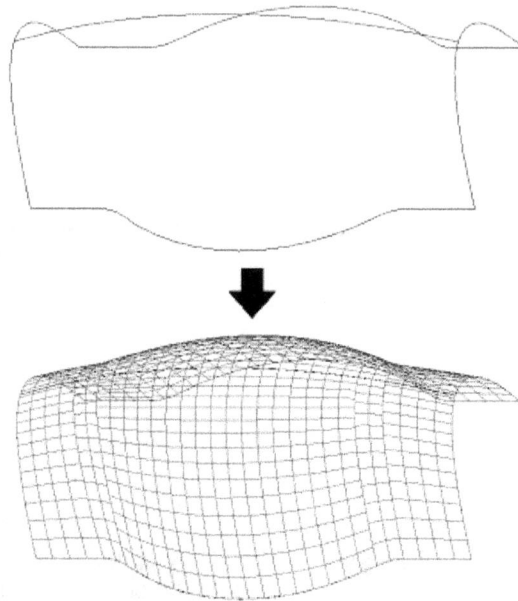

Figure 11–10

11.3 Merging Surface Features

Two adjacent or intersecting surface quilts can be merged to create a single quilt. The resulting surface merge feature consumes the original surfaces. If the surface merge is deleted, the original surfaces are restored.

How To: Merge Surface Features

1. To start the creation of the merge feature, select two or more quilts and click ⬠ (Merge) in the *Model* tab. The dashboard displays as shown in Figure 11–11.

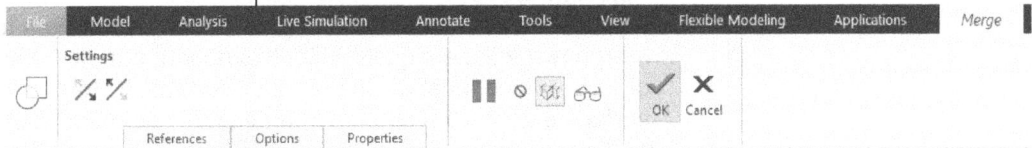

Figure 11–11

Consider the part shown in Figure 11–12.

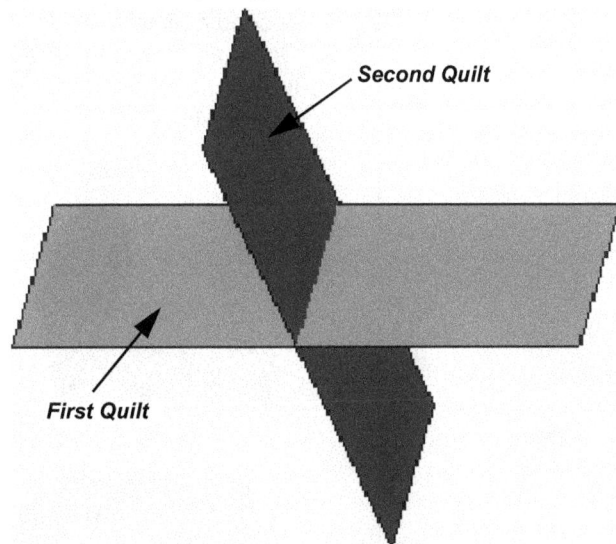

Figure 11–12

2. Define the merge feature using the Options panel and the dashboard icons as shown in Figure 11–13.

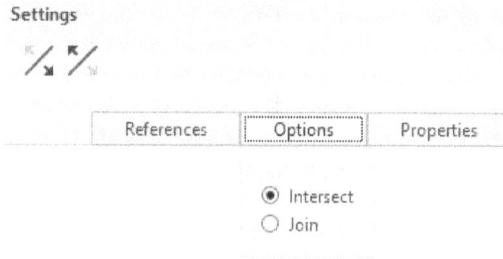

Settings

References   Options   Properties

⦿ Intersect
◯ Join

Figure 11–13

3. Select **Intersect** to merge two quilts that intersect. This option keeps portions of the original quilts. Select **Join** to merge two adjacent quilts. With this option, one of the edges of one surface must lie on the other surface. If the second surface extends beyond the intersection, you must select a portion to keep.

4. Use (Flip First Side) to change the side of the first quilt to keep and (Flip Second Side) to change the side of the second quilt to keep.

5. Once the merge feature has been defined, complete the feature. The four possible merge results are shown in Figure 11–14.

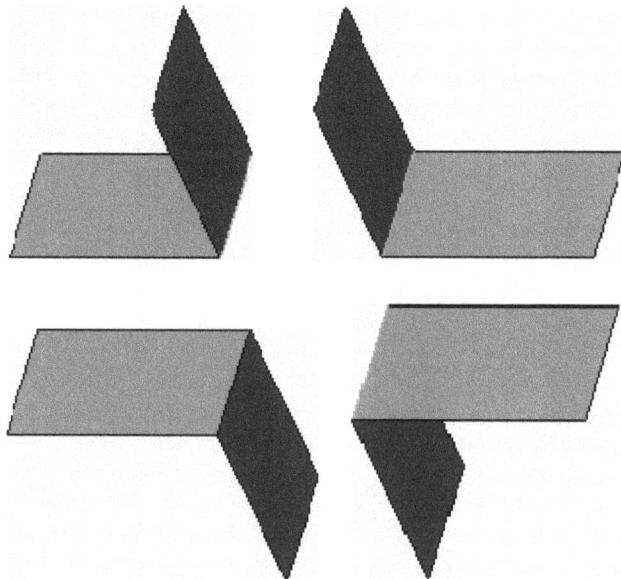

Figure 11–14

11.4 Trimming Surface Features

Portions of a surface can be removed using a selected datum curve or datum plane as a reference. This option is useful for achieving an irregular shape.

How To: Trim Surface Features

1. To access the **Trim** option, select the item to trim and click
   (Trim) in the *Model* tab. The *Trim* dashboard displays as shown in Figure 11–15.

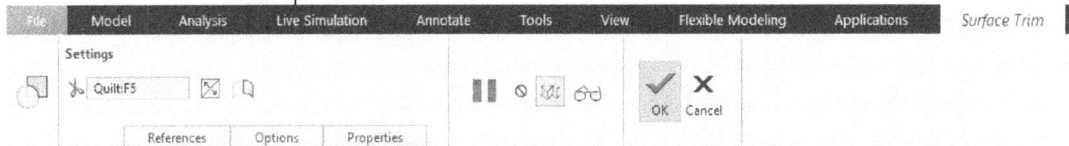

Figure 11–15

2. Select the trimming object in the Model Tree or on the model. Use (Flip Trimmed Surface) to select the surface side to keep.
3. Once the trimming references have been defined, complete the feature. A surface feature trimmed to a datum curve is shown in Figure 11–16.

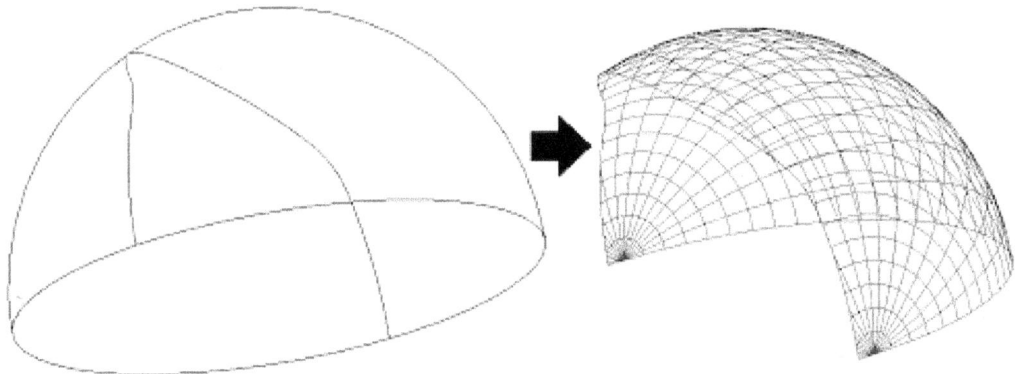

Figure 11–16

A surface that is trimmed to a datum plane is shown in Figure 11–17.

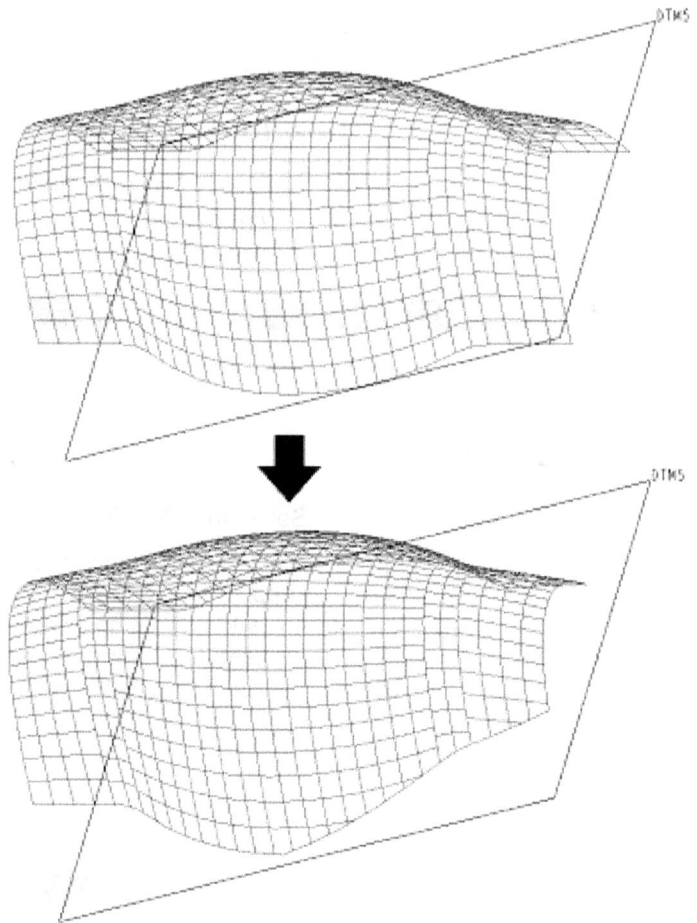

Figure 11–17

11.5 Remove Feature

The Remove feature enables you to remove a selected surface from a solid or surface quilt. Once removed, the geometry re-intersects the adjacent surfaces to recreate the geometry. In the example shown in Figure 11–18. The Remove feature was used to modify the geometry.

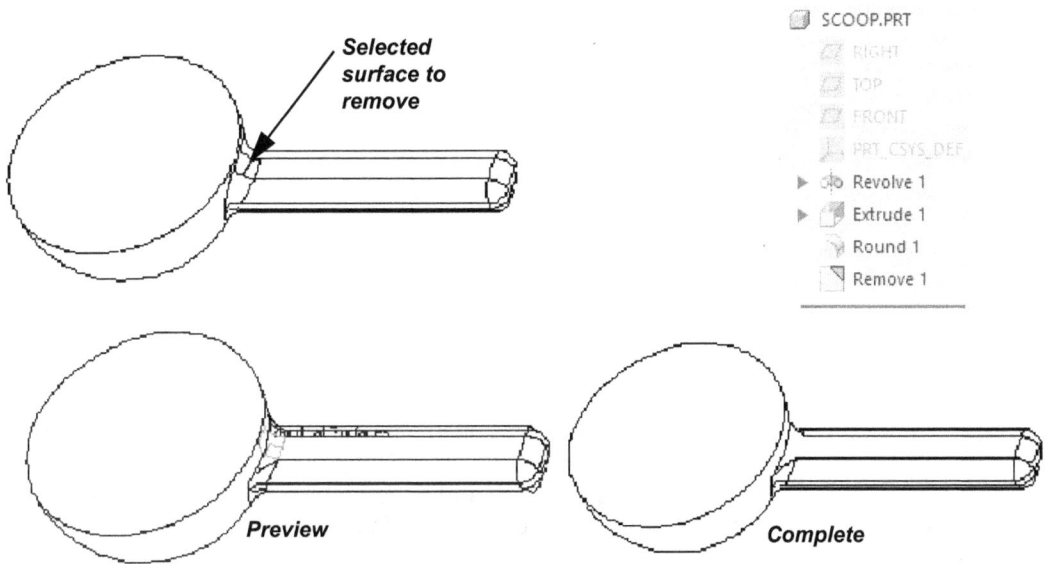

Figure 11–18

How To: Remove Surface Features

1. Select the item to remove and select **Editing>Remove**. The *Remove Surface* dashboard displays as shown in Figure 11–19.

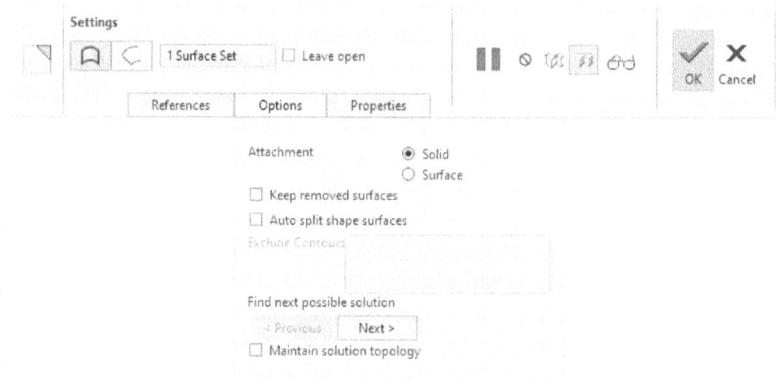

Figure 11–19

2. Specify additional options in the Options panel. The Remove feature can result in either a solid or a surface. You can also click **Next** to display additional solutions.
3. Once surfaces and options have been defined, complete the feature. A removed surface is shown in Figure 11–20.

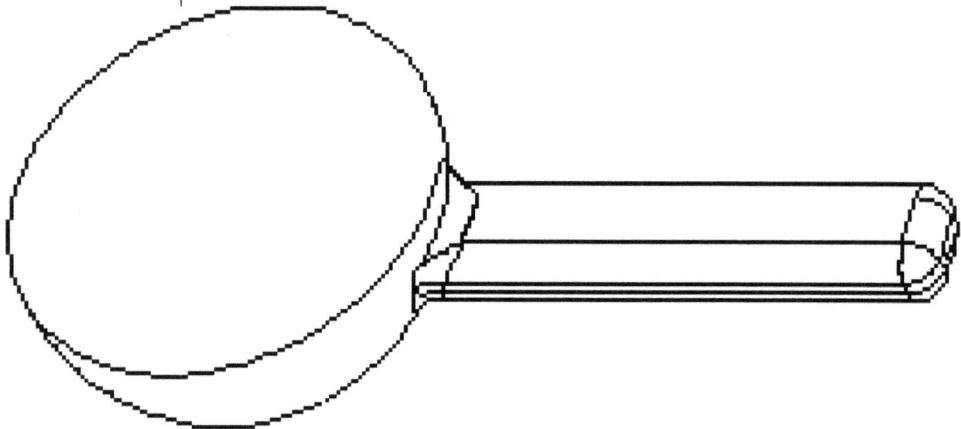

Figure 11–20

11.6 Thicken

The **Thicken** option enables you to create a thin feature. It thickens a selected section by a specified thickness and uses this volume for adding or removing material. To create a thicken feature, select the surface that is to be thickened and click

⬜ (Thicken). The *Thicken* dashboard activates as shown in Figure 11–21.

Select this icon to remove material

Select this icon to add material

Reference quilt

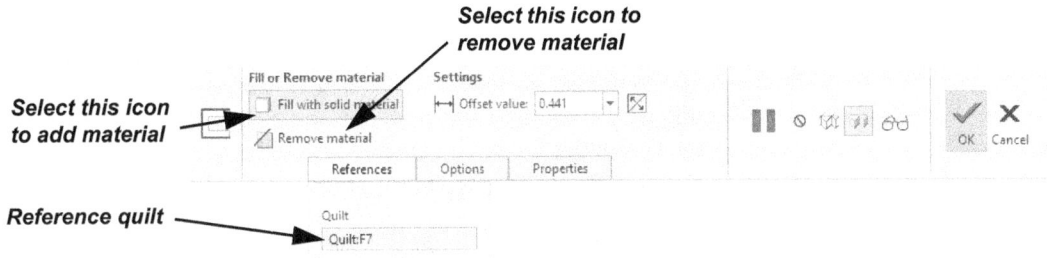

Figure 11–21

The protrusion shown on the right in Figure 11–22 is created using the **Thicken** option. In this situation you could have created this as one feature using a thin protrusion, but when extruding complex shapes that cannot be easily sketched, this is a valuable tool.

Surface quilt

Solid created using Thicken option

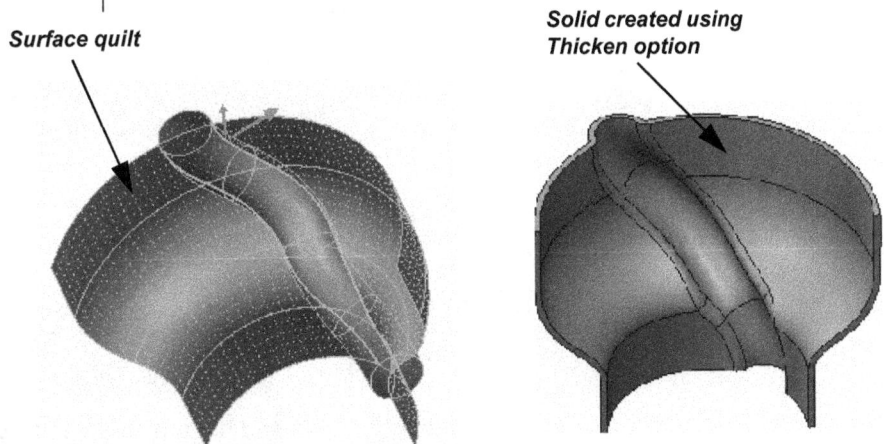

Figure 11–22

Practice 11a | Thicken Quilt

Practice Objectives

- Create a non-solid surface using the Revolve and Sweep commands and a projected datum curve as the trajectory.
- Combine individual surface features into one quilted surface that can be used as a single surface to thicken.
- Create solid geometry from the merged surfaces using the Thicken command.

In this practice, you will create a part using surfaces and then create a solid from the surfaces. To create the geometry, you will begin by creating a revolved surface as the base feature. You will then create a projected curve that will be used as the trajectory for a swept surface feature. Once the sweep has been created, you will merge the revolve and the sweep and then add rounds. To complete the part, you will thicken the final surface geometry to create the final solid, as shown in Figure 11–23.

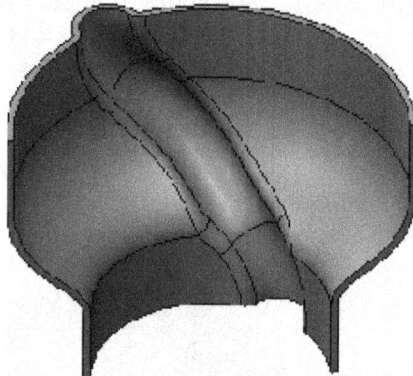

Figure 11–23

Task 1 - Create a new part.

1. Set the working directory to the *Thicken_Quilt* folder.

2. Create a new part and set the *Name* to **housing**.

3. Set the model display as follows:

   - ⁺⁄⊹ *(Datum Display Filters)*: All Off
   - ⋟ *(Spin Center)*: Off
   - ◻ *(Display Style)*: ⬚ (Shading With Edges)

Task 2 - Create a revolved surface.

1. In the Model Tree, select datum plane **FRONT** as the sketching plane and click ⟲ (Revolve) in the mini toolbar.

2. Sketch the section shown in Figure 11–24. The section consists of one vertical centerline, two vertical lines, and a three-point spline sketched between them. Make the spline tangent to the lines at its two end points.

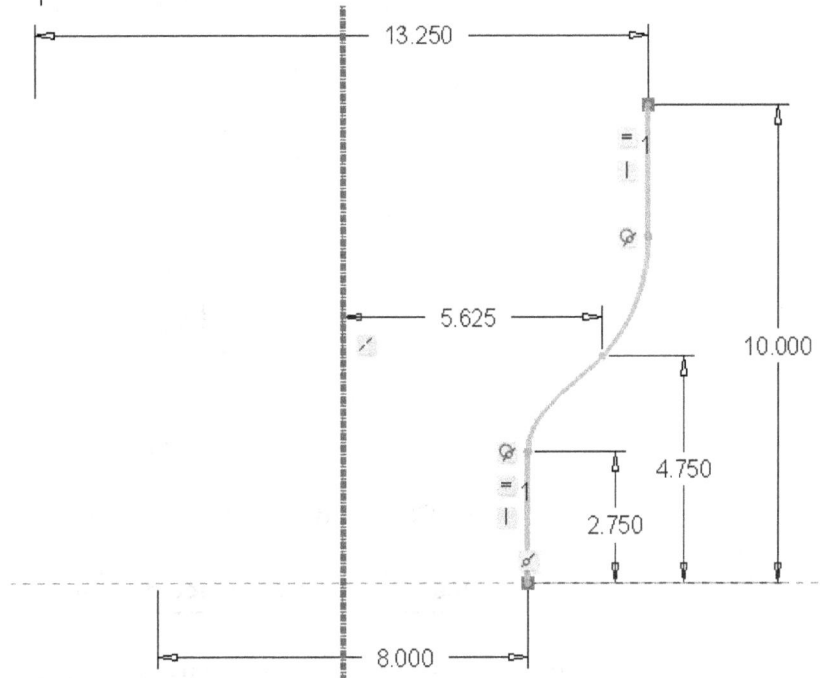

Figure 11–24

3. Complete the sketch.

4. Click **OK** in the Solid Surface Switch Option dialog box. as shown in Figure 11–25.

Since you have an open section with no solid geometry, the system must create a surface feature and it is simply informing you of that.

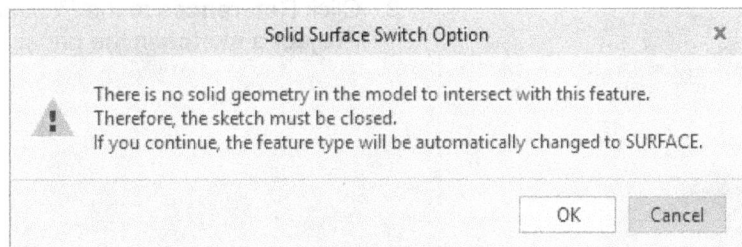

Figure 11–25

5. Modify the *Angle* to **180** and use ⚘ (Change Angle Direction) in the *Revolve* dashboard so that the default view of the model displays as shown in Figure 11–26.

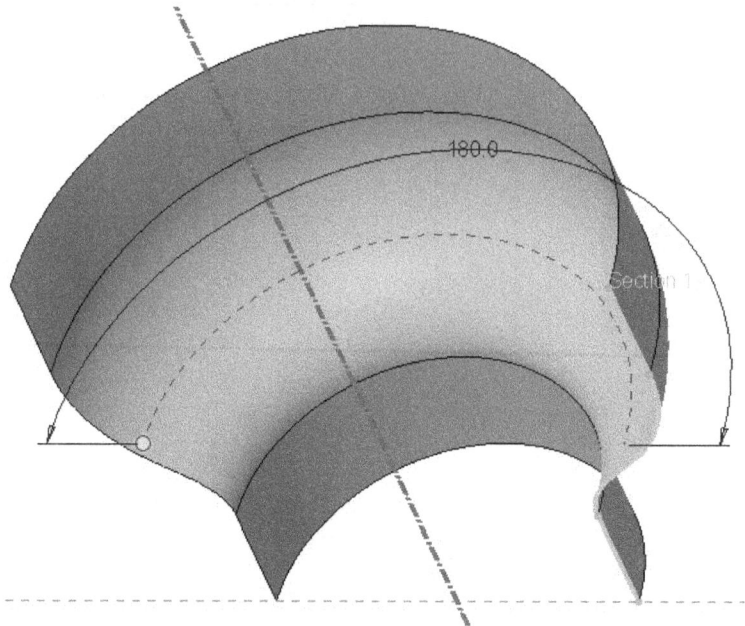

Figure 11–26

6. Click ✔ (OK) to complete the feature.

Task 3 - Create a projected datum curve.

Design Considerations

The swept geometry requires a trajectory to follow the surface of the revolve. Because this surface is not planar, you must project the curve onto the surface. Once this curve has been created, it can be used as the trajectory to create a swept surface.

1. Click ⌇ (Project) in the Editing group of the *Model* tab.

2. Click **References** in the *Projected Curve* dashboard. Select **Project a sketch** in the panel as shown in Figure 11–27.

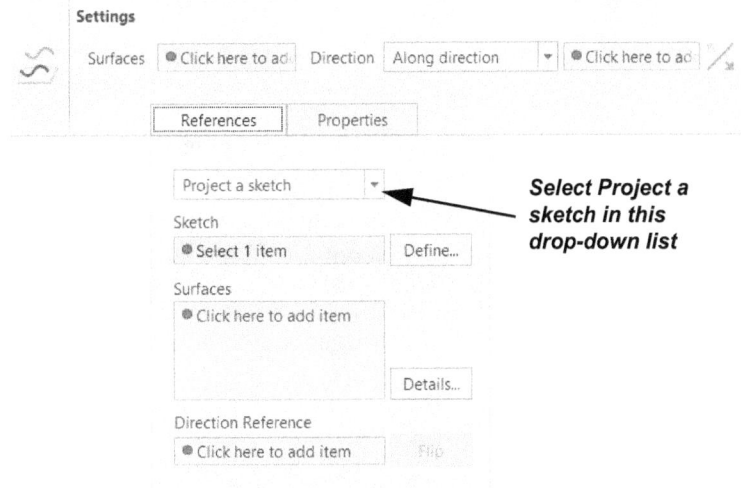

Figure 11–27

*You can also click **Define** in the References panel.*

3. Right-click and select **Define Internal Sketch**.

4. Select datum plane **FRONT** as the sketching plane and accept the viewing direction and default orientation references.

5. Click **Sketch** to sketch the section.

You can click ∿ and hold <Alt> to pick the references.

6. Sketch the three-point spline as shown in Figure 11–28. Add angular dimensions to the end points to make them perpendicular to the edges of the surface.

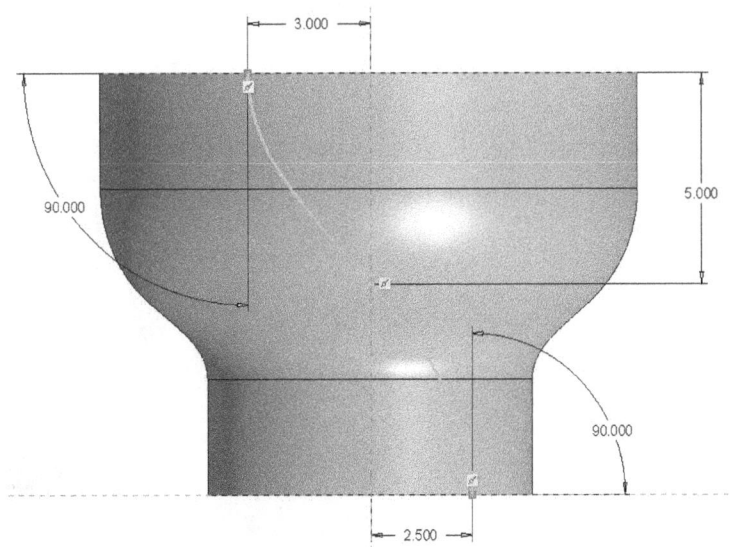

Figure 11–28

7. Complete the sketch.

8. Use <Ctrl> to select all three sections of the surface onto which to project the sketched curve.

9. Ensure that the *Direction* in the dashboard is set to **Along direction**.

10. Right-click and select **Select Direction reference**. Select datum plane **FRONT** as the direction reference.

If you expand the References panel, the *Projected Curve* dashboard should display as shown in Figure 11–29.

Figure 11–29

11. Click ✔ (OK) to complete the feature. The completed curve displays as shown in Figure 11–30.

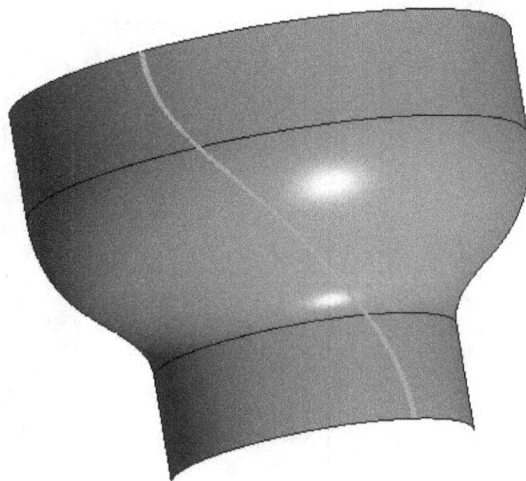

Figure 11–30

Task 4 - Create a swept surface.

Design Considerations

In this task, you will create a swept surface using the projected curve as the trajectory.

1. Click ✎ (Sweep) in the *Model* tab and click ⌒ (Surface).

2. Select the projected curve you just created. The part displays as shown in Figure 11–31.

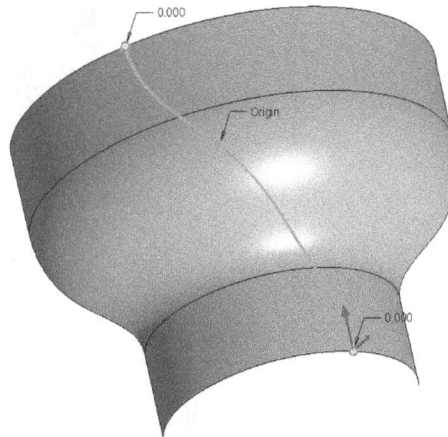

Figure 11–31

3. Click ✎ (Create or Edit Section) in the *Sweep* dashboard.

4. Sketch a circular cross-section with a *Diameter* of **2.00**, as shown in Figure 11–32.

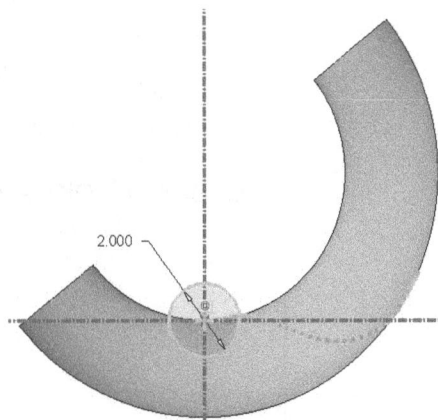

Figure 11–32

Your model might be oriented differently depending on how the start point was oriented.

5. Complete the sketch and the feature.

6. Press <Ctrl>+<D> to change to the default orientation. The model displays as shown in Figure 11–33.

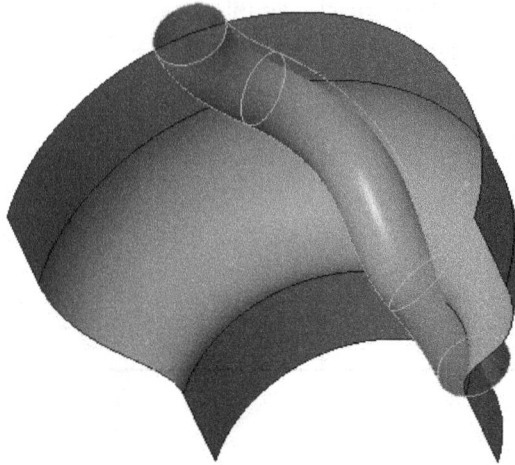

Figure 11–33

Task 5 - Merge the two surfaces.

Design Considerations

Now that the two surface features have been created, you will manipulate them to obtain the required surface geometry. Once you have this created, you will be able to create the solid geometry.

1. Select the revolved surface and the swept surface.

2. Click ⏛ (Merge) in the mini toolbar to merge the two surfaces.

3. Click ⟋ (Flip Second Side) to define the appropriate side of the quilt to keep.

4. Click ✔ (OK), and the model displays as shown in Figure 11–34.

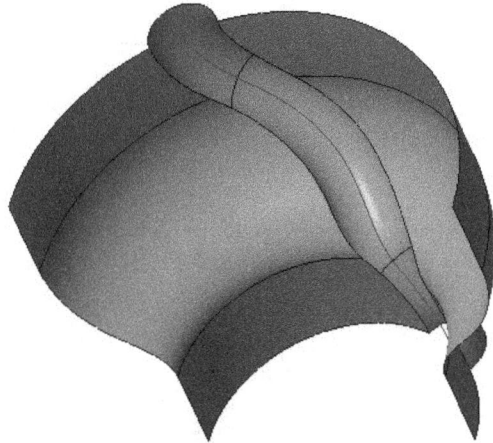

Figure 11–34

5. Hide the **03__PRT_ALL_CURVES** default layer since the projected datum curve is no longer required.

Task 6 - Create rounds at the intersection of the two surfaces.

---

1. Create a round with a *Radius* of **0.5** on the two edges shown in Figure 11–35.

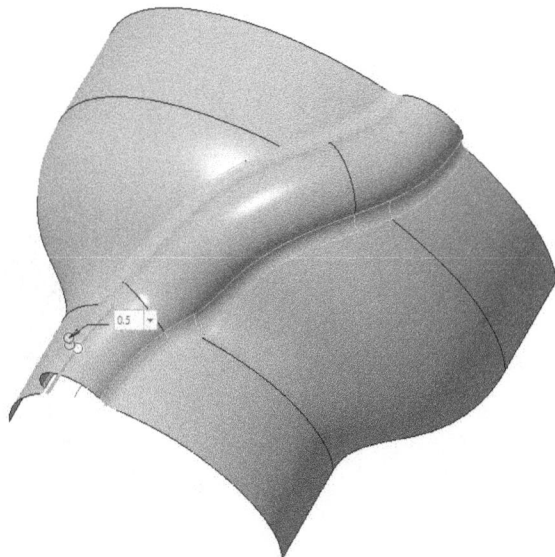

Figure 11–35

Task 7 - Create solid geometry.

Design Considerations

Now that all of the surface geometry has been created, you can use the **Thicken** operation to create the solid geometry. Once completed, review the model and note how, by adding the round before thickening, the round is on the inside and outside of the model. If the round was added after thickening, you would have to select four edges to round.

1. Select the merged surface.

2. Click ☐ (Thicken) in the *Model* tab.

3. Add the material to the outside of the quilt and set the *Thickness* to **0.25**, as shown in Figure 11–36.

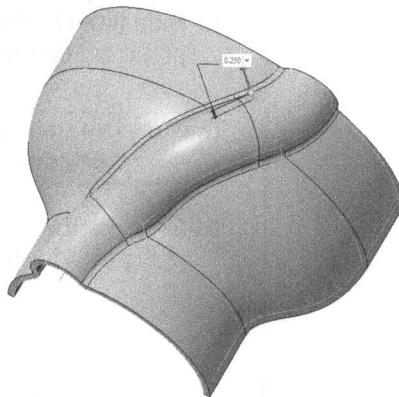

Figure 11–36

- The completed part displays as shown in Figure 11–37.

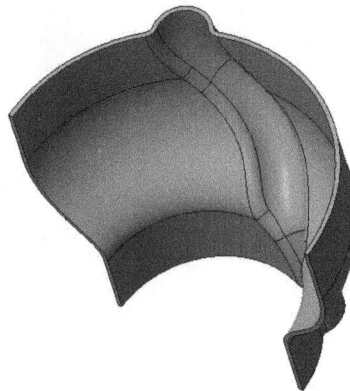

Figure 11–37

4. Save the part and erase it from memory.

Practice 11b | Surface Rounds

Practice Objectives

- Create a round and use the Options panel to create the round as a surface.
- Extend and trim the surface round to achieve the required surface.
- Use solidify to patch the round surface geometry to the solid geometry.

In this practice, you will work on a model that requires a surface to create the round correctly.

Task 1 - Open a part file.

1. Set the working directory to the *Surface_Rounds* folder.

2. Open **spacer_block.prt**.

3. Set the model display as follows:

   - ⅍ *(Datum Display Filters)*: All Off

   - ⅀ *(Spin Center)*: Off

   - ▢ *(Display Style)*: ▢ (Shading With Edges)

Task 2 - Create an edge round.

1. Create a round with a *Radius* of **0.5** on the edge shown in Figure 11–38.

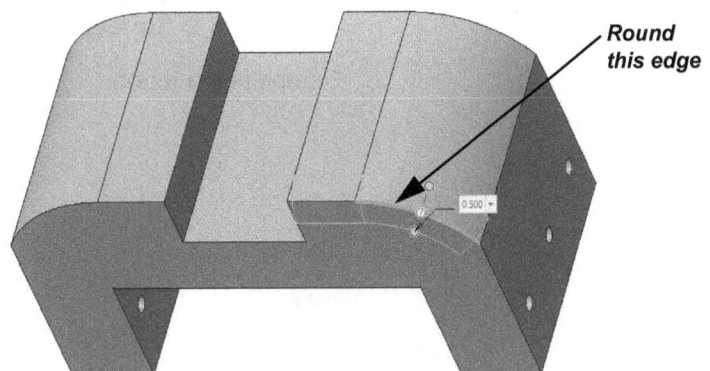

Round this edge

Figure 11–38

2. Enable ◉◉ (Verify Mode) in the *Round* dashboard to preview the round.

3. Select the **Note** option for Item 1 and Item 2 in the Troubleshooter dialog box. The part displays as shown in Figure 11–39.

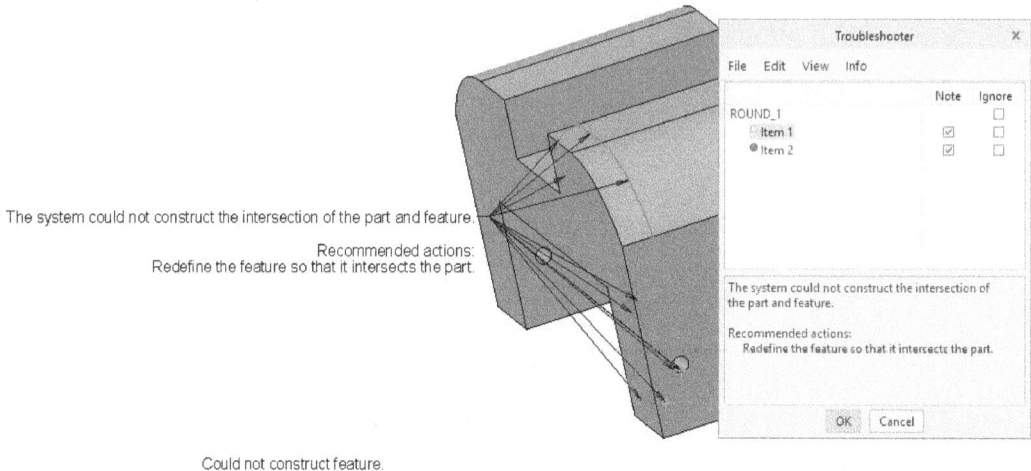

The system could not construct the intersection of the part and feature.

Recommended actions:
Redefine the feature so that it intersects the part.

Could not construct feature.

Figure 11–39

Design Considerations

This round failed because as the rolling ball attempted to follow the contour created by the convex surface of the part, the round geometry never reached the outside of the part and therefore it could not be created. This prevents the system from being able to attach the round to the part as a solid. You need to complete this round using surfacing techniques.

4. Click ▶ (Resume) to resume feature creation.

5. Open the Options panel in the *Round* dashboard and change *Attachment* to **Surface**.

6. Complete the round.

7. Set the display to ⬚ (No Hidden). The surface geometry representing the round displays inside the solid geometry, as shown in Figure 11–40.

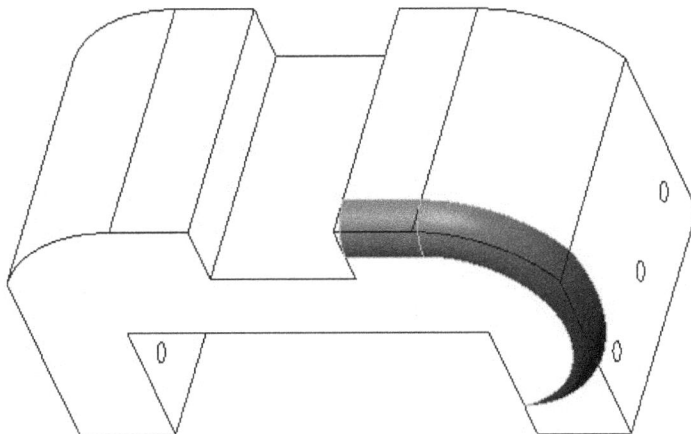

Figure 11–40

Task 3 - Create datum planes that can be used to trim the surface.

1. Create a datum plane **Through** the edge and **Tangent** to the surface shown in Figure 11–41.

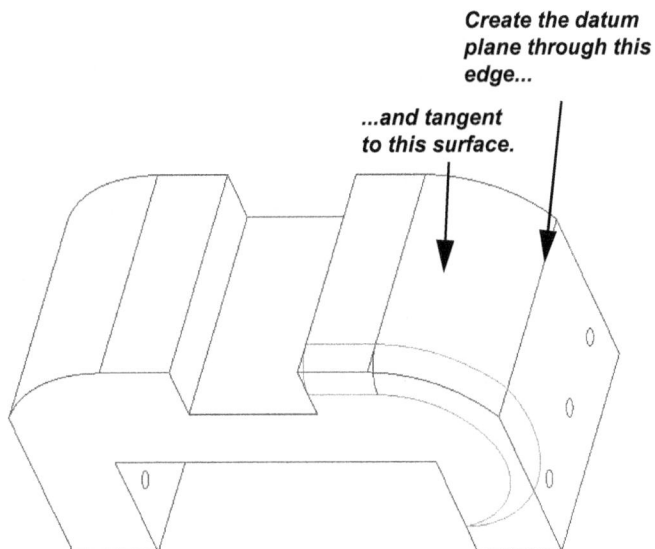

Create the datum plane through this edge...

...and tangent to this surface.

Figure 11–41

2. Create a second datum plane **Through** the edge and **Normal** to the datum plane that you just created, as shown in Figure 11–42.

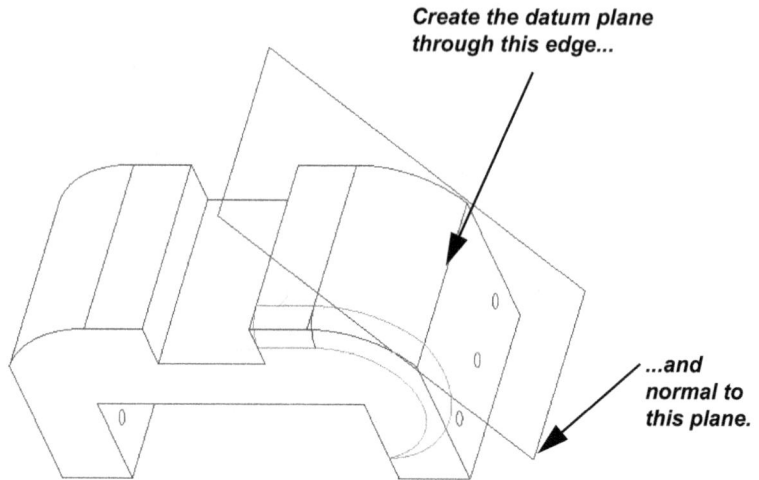

Create the datum plane through this edge...

...and normal to this plane.

Figure 11–42

The completed datum planes display as shown in Figure 11–43.

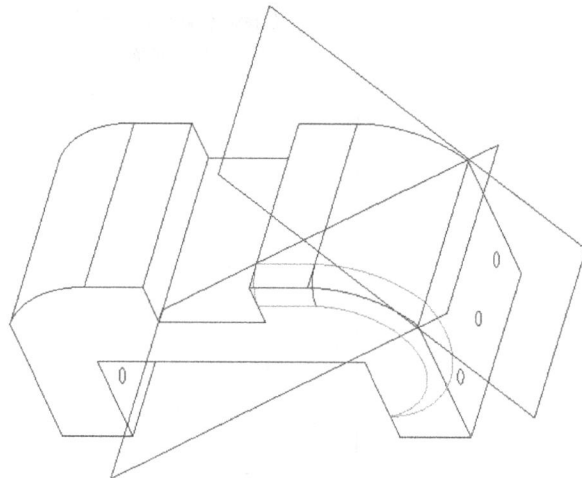

Figure 11–43

Task 4 - Trim a surface feature.

1. Set the selection filter to **Quilt** and select the surface round.

2. Click ⬛ (Trim) in the *Model* tab and select **DTM2** from the Model Tree. Select the arrow head, if required, to point toward the side to keep, as shown in Figure 11–44.

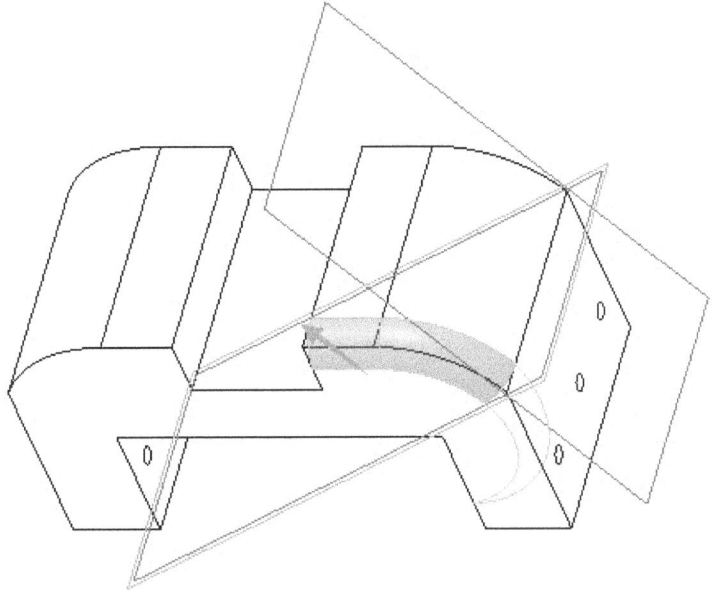

Figure 11–44

3. Complete the trim and hide the datum planes. The trimmed surface displays as shown in Figure 11–45.

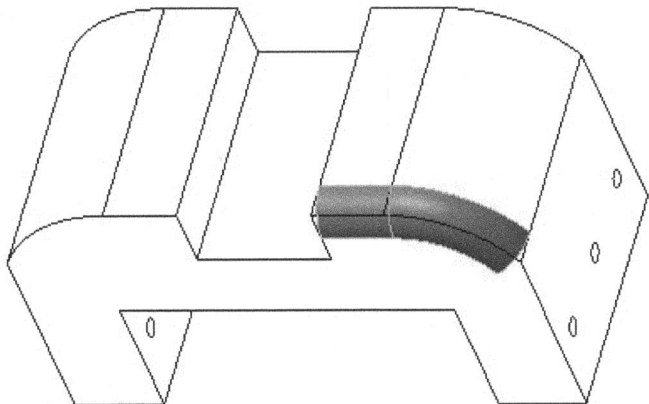

Figure 11–45

Task 5 - Extend the surface round so that it passes beyond the right side of the part.

1. Change the selection filter to **Geometry** and select the edge of the surface, as shown in Figure 11–46.

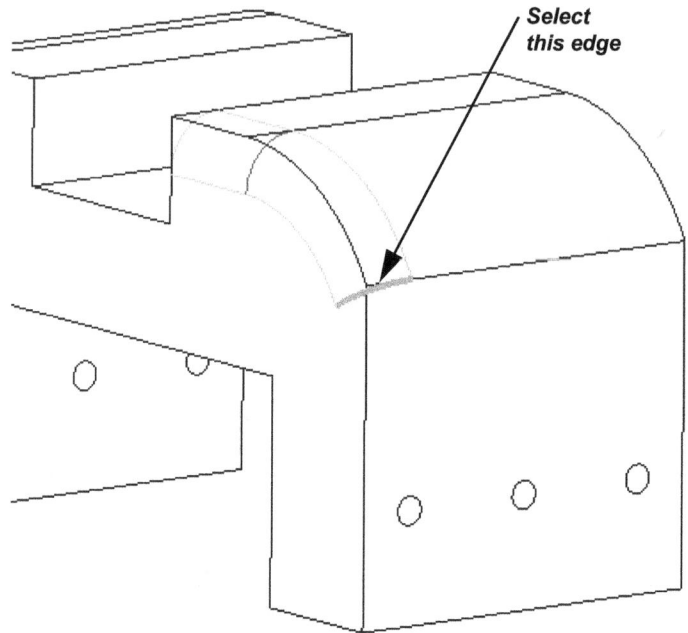

Select this edge

Figure 11–46

2. Click ⊡ (Extend) in the *Model* tab.

3. Open the Options panel, expand the Method drop-down list, and select **Tangent** as shown in Figure 11–47.

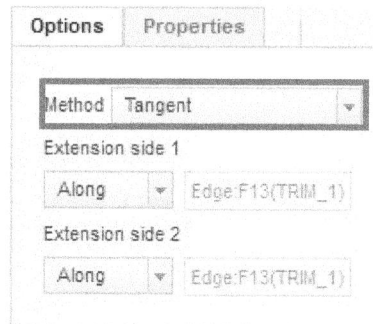

Figure 11–47

4. Set the extension *Distance* to **1.00**, as shown in Figure 11–48 and complete the feature.

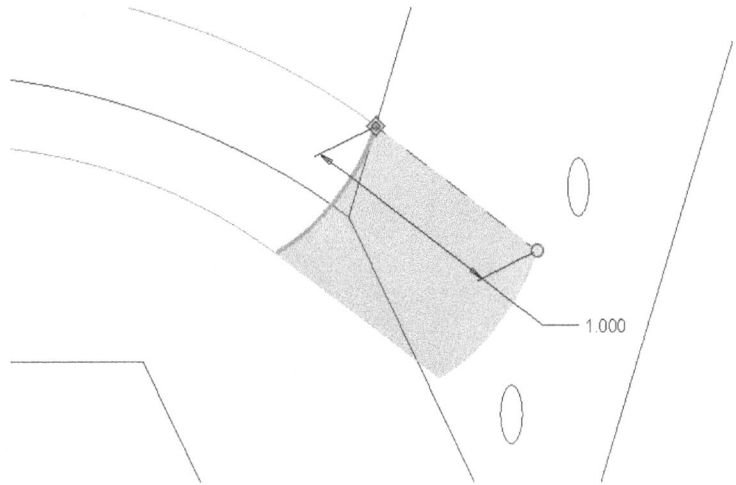

— 1.000

Figure 11–48

Design Considerations

The **Tangent** option was used for the **Extend** operation so that the extension would remain tangent to the existing surface round, as shown in Figure 11–49.

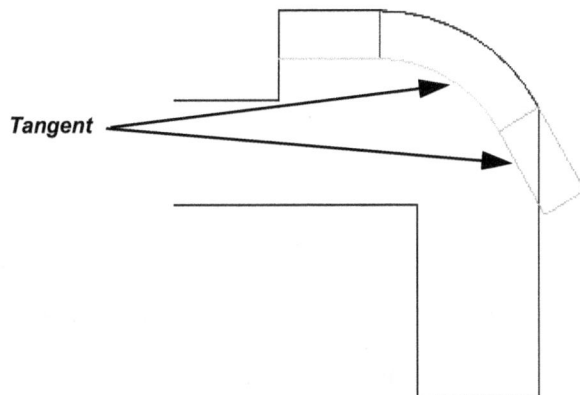

Tangent

Figure 11–49

Task 6 - Trim the extended surface.

1. Create a datum plane through the surface, as shown in Figure 11–50.

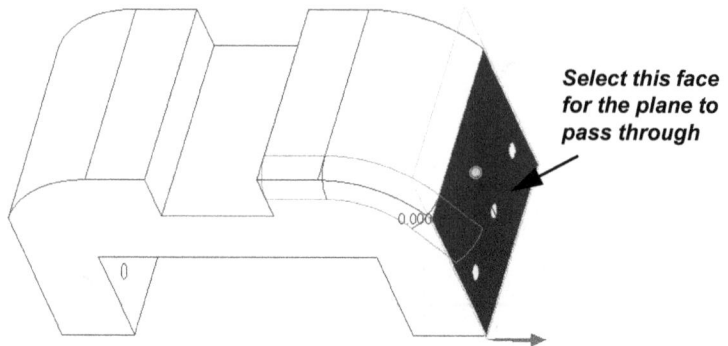

Select this face for the plane to pass through

Figure 11–50

2. Ensure that the selection filter is set to **Quilts** and select the surface round.

3. Trim the surface round with the datum plane that you just created, as shown in Figure 11–51.

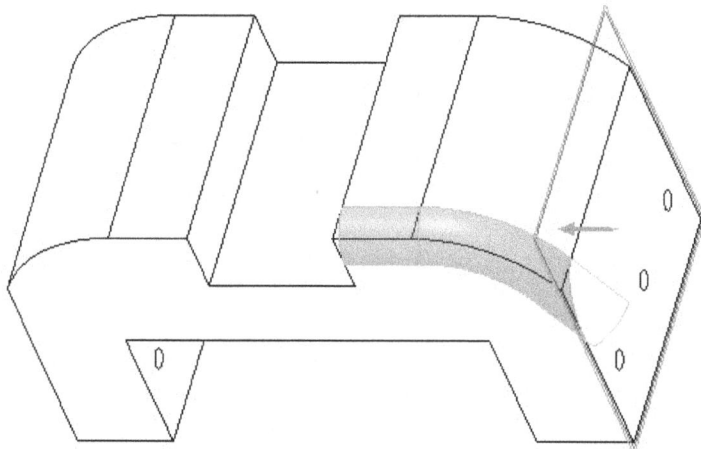

Figure 11–51

4. Hide datum plane **DTM3**. The part displays as shown in Figure 11–52.

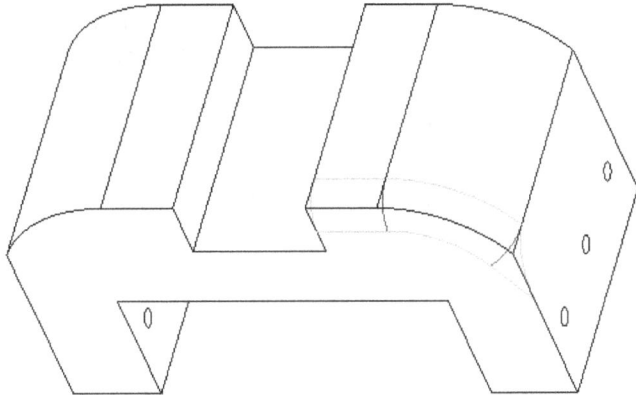

Figure 11–52

Task 7 - Perform a Solidify operation to complete the round geometry.

1. Select the surface round.

2. Click ☐ (Solidify) in the *Model* tab.

3. Click ✔ (OK) to complete the operation.

4. Set the display to ☐ (Shading With Edges), and the completed part displays as shown in Figure 11–53.

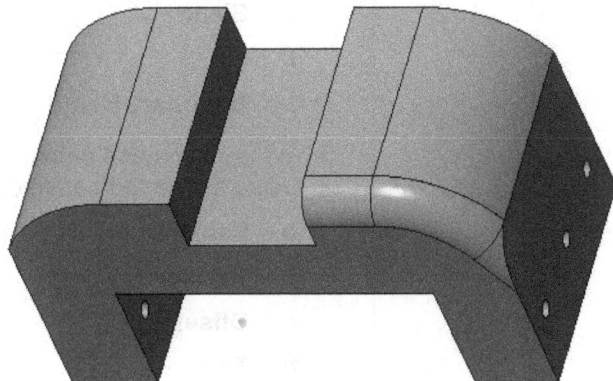

Figure 11–53

5. Hide the surface quilt.

6. Save the part and erase it from memory.

Chapter Review Questions

1. Which of the following options are examples of what surfaces can be used for? (Select all that apply.)

   a. Creation of complex geometry.

   b. Creation of datum features.

   c. Creation of shell features.

   d. Creation of drafts.

2. Surface geometry has a very slight thickness value.

   a. True

   b. False

3. Does the profile of an extruded surface need to be closed or can it be open?

   a. Open only

   b. Closed only

   c. Either Open or Closed

4. Which option can you use to create a surface from a closed 2D sketch? (Select all that apply.)

   a. **Extrude**

   b. **Revolve**

   c. **Sweep**

   d. **Blend**

   e. **Fill**

   f. **Boundary Blend**

5. Which command permits portions of a surface to be removed using a selected datum curve or datum plane as a reference?

   a. **Remove**

   b. **Thicken**

   c. **Offset**

   d. **Trim**

6. Which option can you use to combine two or more surfaces?

   a. **Solidify**

   b. **Merge**

   c. **Offset**

   d. **Boundary Blend**

7. Which command adds or removes material by a specified thickness, using a selected non-solid surface?

   a. **Offset**

   b. **Extend**

   c. **Thicken**

   d. **Trim**

8. Which option creates a surface between selected boundaries? The boundaries can be curves, edges, points, and vertices.

   a. **Offset**

   b. **Extend**

   c. **Boundary Blend**

   d. **Fill**

User-Defined Features

A user-defined feature is commonly referred to as a UDF. This duplication technique helps to reduce the time spent on duplicating a collection of features or components that are used repeatedly in the same or different models. This functionality results in time being saved and thus increasing efficiency for designers.

Learning Objectives in This Chapter

- Learn the creation process and elements for a user-defined feature.
- Learn to quickly duplicate features in the same or different models using the user-defined feature.
- Compare and use one of the duplication techniques to create geometry that best follows the design intent of the model.

12.1 Creating User-Defined Features

A user-defined feature (UDF) is a group of one or more features or components that are created for duplication purposes. For example, the features of the boss shown in Figure 12–1 are selected to create a user-defined feature.

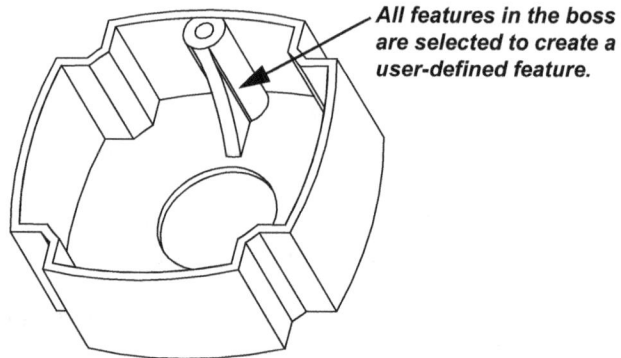

All features in the boss are selected to create a user-defined feature.

Figure 12–1

General Steps

Use the following general steps to create a UDF:

1. Start the creation of a UDF.
2. Define the type of UDF.
3. Select the features to include in the UDF.
4. Define the placement information of the UDF.
5. Define the optional elements, if required.
6. Complete the UDF.
7. Create a UDF library, if required.

Step 1 - Start the creation of a UDF.

You can also press <Enter> to accept a UDF name.

To start the creation of a UDF, select the *Tools* tab, click (UDF Library) and select **Create** in the **UDF** menu. Enter a descriptive name for the UDF and press <Enter> to accept the name.

Step 2 - Define the type of UDF.

The **UDF OPTIONS** menu displays after you finish entering a name for the UDF. Select **Stand Alone** or **Subordinate** to define the type of UDF. Click **Done** to continue.

A Stand Alone UDF copies all of the information from the original model and stores it in the UDF. If this option is selected, click **Yes** or **No** in the Confirmation window to specify whether to create a reference model. A reference model is a copy (**udf_name_gp.prt**) of the original that displays the required references as you are prompted for selection on a new model. For a Stand Alone UDF, a reference model is not required, but it can be helpful in placing the UDF.

A Subordinate UDF obtains values directly from the original model. To place a Subordinate UDF, ensure that the original model used to create the UDF file is easily identified in a search path or working directory. Subordinate UDFs automatically generate a reference model.

The UDF dialog box opens as shown in Figure 12–2.

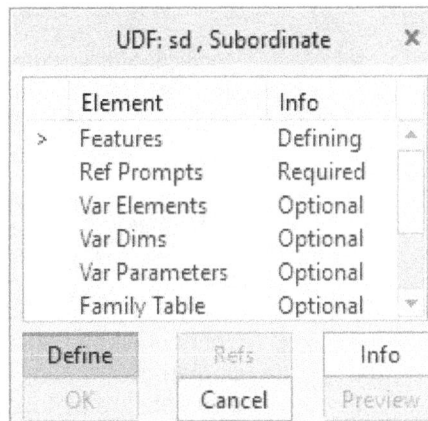

	Element	Info
>	Features	Defining
	Ref Prompts	Required
	Var Elements	Optional
	Var Dims	Optional
	Var Parameters	Optional
	Family Table	Optional

UDF: sd , Subordinate

Define | Refs | Info
OK | Cancel | Preview

Figure 12–2

Step 3 - Select the features to include in the UDF.

Use <Ctrl> to select multiple features.

Once you have defined the type of UDF, you are prompted to select the feature(s) you want to include in the UDF. They can be selected directly on the model or in the Model Tree. Once selected, select **Done** in the **SELECT FEAT** menu and **Done/Return** in the **UDF FEATS** menu.

When creating the features to be used in a UDF, care should be taken to minimize the number of references used. If multiple features can all use the same parent references, creation and placement of the UDF is simplified dramatically.

Step 4 - Define the placement information of the UDF.

Assign descriptive prompts for external references so that the intent of the reference can be easily identified.

Enter a name for each of the external references required to place the UDF. In some cases, the reference might be used by more than one feature in the UDF. Select **Single** if only one prompt is required for all references or **Multiple** if multiple prompts are required.

Once all of the prompts have been entered, select **Next** in the **MOD PRMPT** menu to scroll through and verify all of the prompts. Use the **SET PROMPT** menu to make changes and select **Done/Return** when complete.

Step 5 - Define the optional elements, if required.

Optional elements can be used to further define the UDF. Double-click on any element in the dialog box to define it. These elements are as follows.

Element	Description
Var Elements	Specifies any feature element in the UDF as variable, such as the depth of a cut. When the UDF is placed, the cut can be specified as **Thru All** in one situation and **Blind** in another.
Var Dims	Specifies dimensions of any feature in the UDF as variable. When placing the UDF, the prompts for the dimension values display in the message window.

Dim Values	Modifies the values of invariable dimensions on the UDF. This option is only available for standalone UDFs.
Var Parameters	Specifies parameters in the UDF as variable. When placing the UDF, the prompts for the dimension values display in the message window.
Family Table	Creates a family table that is stored with the UDF. When placing the UDF, the **INSTANCES** menu displays and an instance must be selected before placement.
Units	Sets the UDF's length units. This option is only available for standalone UDFs.
Pro/Program	Creates a program in the UDF that is copied to the program of the part during placement. The program is executed after the UDF has been placed. This option is only available with subordinate UDFs.
Ext Symbols	Defines relations involving symbols (dimensions and parameters) to be variable in the UDF. For example, a dimension has a relation d2=width, where width is a parameter. The **width** parameter can be added to the UDF and the relation can be maintained.

Step 6 - Complete the UDF.

Click **OK** in the UDF dialog box to complete the creation of the UDF. The UDF is stored independent of the source file using the name format, **udf_name.gph**. The UDF file stores the selected features, their dimensions, any relations that might exist between the selected features, and a list of references for placing the UDF.

The following restrictions apply to UDFs:

- Only parameters used in relations are copied with the UDF to the target part. This is accomplished using the variable element **Ext Symbols**.

- A UDF created in Part mode can be used in Assembly mode provided it does not contain features that are not permitted as assembly features. Features that are acceptable in Assembly mode are: **Hole**, **Cut**, and **Pipe**.

- User-defined transitions on advanced rounds included in a UDF are removed. The transition must be redefined in the new feature.

Step 7 - Create a UDF library, if required.

The same feature can be used in multiple parts. You can make features easier to find by creating a UDF library. A UDF library centrally locates all of the UDFs so that users can access a database of previously-created features.

*To rename a UDF, select **Tools>UDF Library>Dbms> Rename** and enter a new name for the file. To copy a UDF, select **Tools>UDF Library> Dbms>Save As** and copy the UDF with a new filename.*

By default, the UDF is saved to the current working directory. To save a UDF to the library directory, select **Dbms** in the **UDF** menu. The **DBMS** menu displays, enabling you to use the standard database management options for saving the UDF.

Creo Parametric has a configuration file option called **pro_group_dir** that can be set in the config.pro to specify a UDF library directory. All **udf_name.gph** and **udf_name_gp.prt** files can be manually moved into this directory. When placing a UDF, Creo Parametric accesses the specified **pro_group_dir** to locate the required UDF.

12.2 Placing User-Defined Features

A UDF can be placed in the same part in which it was created or it can be placed in any other part. A UDF reduces the time spent on duplicating a collection of features or components that are used repeatedly in the same or different models, as shown in Figure 12–3.

When placing a UDF, you have the option of varying dimension values in the new instance.

A user-defined feature is duplicated in the same model

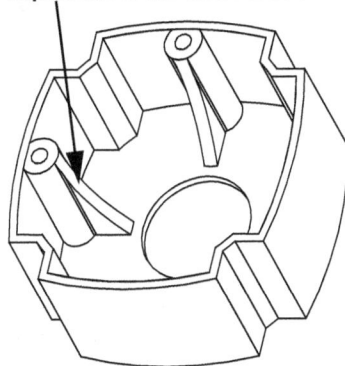

A user-defined feature is duplicated in a different model

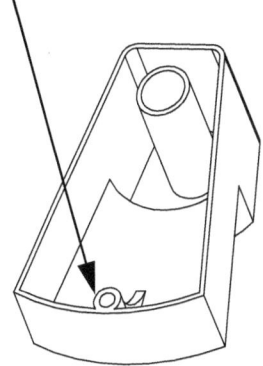

Figure 12–3

General Steps

Use the following general steps to place a UDF:

1. Start the placement of the UDF.
2. Set the UDF placement options.
3. Edit the definition of variable elements, if required.
4. Complete the placement of the UDF.
5. Manipulate the UDF.

Step 1 - Start the placement of the UDF.

Features that are added or removed from a UDF cannot be updated. You must replace the UDF.

To start placing the UDF, select the *Model* tab and click
(User-Defined Feature). Enter or select the name of the UDF in the Open dialog box.

Step 2 - Set the UDF placement options.

Once you have specified the UDF that you want to place, the Insert User-Defined Feature dialog box opens as shown in Figure 12–4 and the options are as follows.

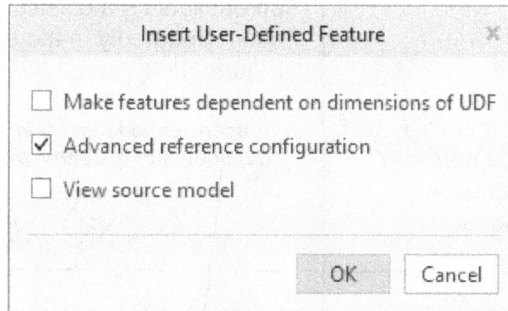

Insert User-Defined Feature ✕

☐ Make features dependent on dimensions of UDF
☑ Advanced reference configuration
☐ View source model

OK   Cancel

Figure 12–4

Option	Description
Make features dependent on dimensions of UDF	Sets dependency between UDF and its placed copy. When selected, the placed copy of UDF follows dimensional changes made in the original UDF. By default, this option is cleared and an independent copy of the UDF is placed.
Advanced reference configuration	When selected, the User Defined Features Placement dialog box opens when placing the UDF. Select the features to include in the UDF. When this option is cleared, the Edit Definition environment displays for features missing references.
View source model	Enables you to retrieve and display the UDF reference model in a separate window. Retrieving the reference model helps you to identify the original placement references as you place the UDF.

Click **OK** once the Insert User-Defined Feature dialog box has been configured correctly.

When the **Advanced reference configuration** option is selected in the Insert User-Defined Feature dialog box, the User Defined Feature Placement dialog box opens when placing the UDF, as shown in Figure 12–5.

If you clear the **Advanced reference configuration** option, the User Defined Feature Placement dialog box does not open. Instead, Creo Parametric invokes the edit definition environment for every feature with missing references.

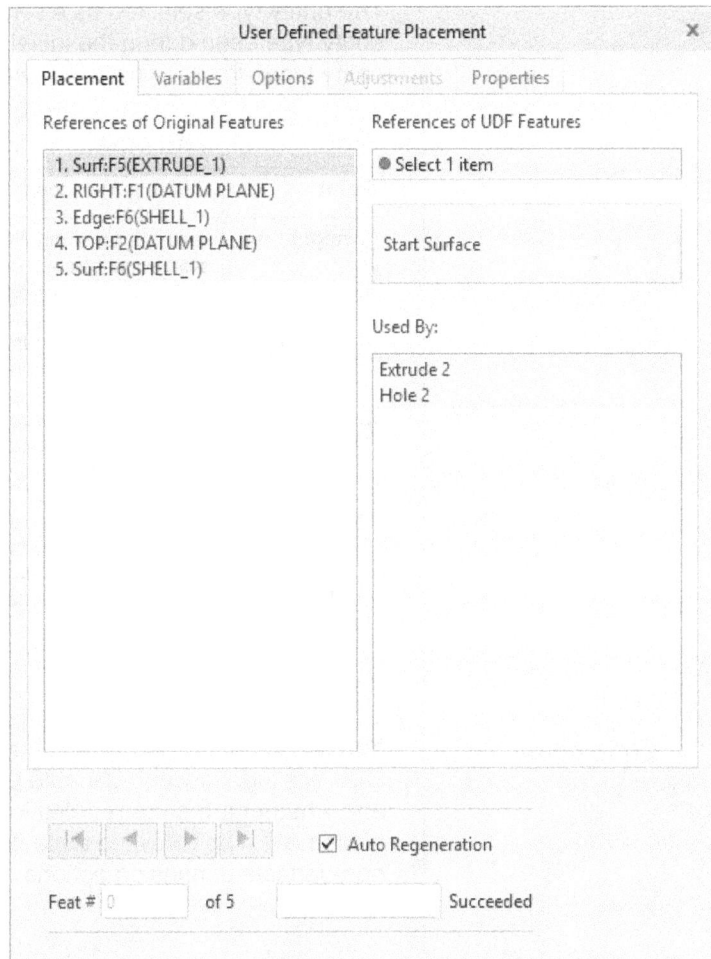

Figure 12–5

Placement Tab

The *Placement* tab (shown in Figure 12–5, above) enables you to review the original references used to place the features that form the UDF and to select the appropriate references in the current model. Once an item is selected in the dialog box, the reference is highlighted on the model.

The entity type selected as a reference must be similar to the entity type used during the initial creation of the feature. The entity types for each category are described as follows:

Option	Description
Point	Datum points, coordinate systems, and vertices.
Straight Line	Datum axis, straight datum curves or segments, straight solid edge, straight surface edge (one- and two-sided), and straight imported 2D entities.
Curve Line	Nonlinear datum curves and segments, nonlinear solid edges, nonlinear surface edges one- and two-sided), and imported nonlinear entities.
Planar	Datum planes, flat quilt surfaces, flat surface features, and flat solid surfaces.
Nonplanar	Nonplanar surface features, nonplanar quilt surfaces, and nonplanar solid surfaces.
On-Surface Coordinate System	On-Surface Coordinate System.

Options Tab

You can use the *Options* tab shown in Figure 12–6 to specify the UDF scaling, how non-variable UDF dimensions are dealt with, and whether a feature redefinition is possible after UDF placement. The following table describes options for scaling and non-variable dimension options.

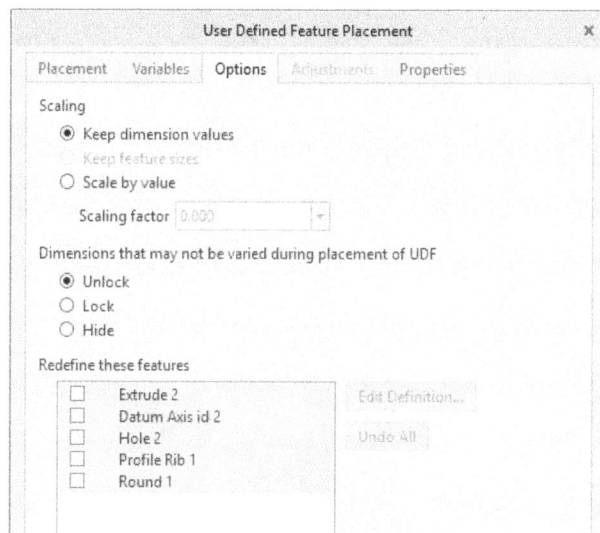

Figure 12–6

Option	Description
Scaling Options	
Keep dimension values	Maintains dimensional values regardless of differences in units between UDF and target model.
Keep feature size	Maintains size of original UDF by rescaling all dimensional values. Option is only available when UDF and target model have different units.
Scale by value	Enables you to enter a scale value for all dimensions. Option disregards any varying units in UDF and target model.
Non-variable dimension options	
Unlock	**Displays invariable dimensions so that values can be modified. Option is only available if UDF was created as independent.**
Lock	**Displays invariable dimensions so that values are read-only and cannot be modified.**
Hide	**Prevents display of invariable dimensions.**

Variables Tab

The *Variables* tab shown in Figure 12–7 displays when dimensions have been specified as variable during UDF creation. It enables you to modify dimensional values according to your needs. If no dimensions were specified as variable, this tab is not available.

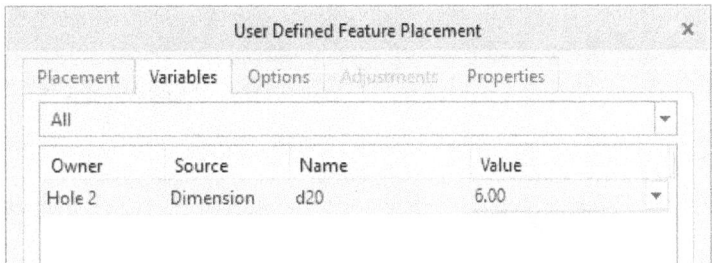

Figure 12–7

Once all of the UDF options have been defined, click ✔ (OK).

Step 3 - Edit the definition of variable elements, if required.

If **Var Elements** were specified when the UDF was created, Creo Parametric invokes the Edit Definition environment for the variable feature. Redefine the elements as required and complete the feature. This functionality is only available for an independent copy of a UDF.

Step 4 - Complete the placement of the UDF.

To complete the UDF placement, select **Done** in the **GRP PLACE** menu. If a program was created with the UDF, the **GET INPUT** menu displays to run the program.

The models shown in Figure 12–8 display newly placed UDFs in both the same and a different model.

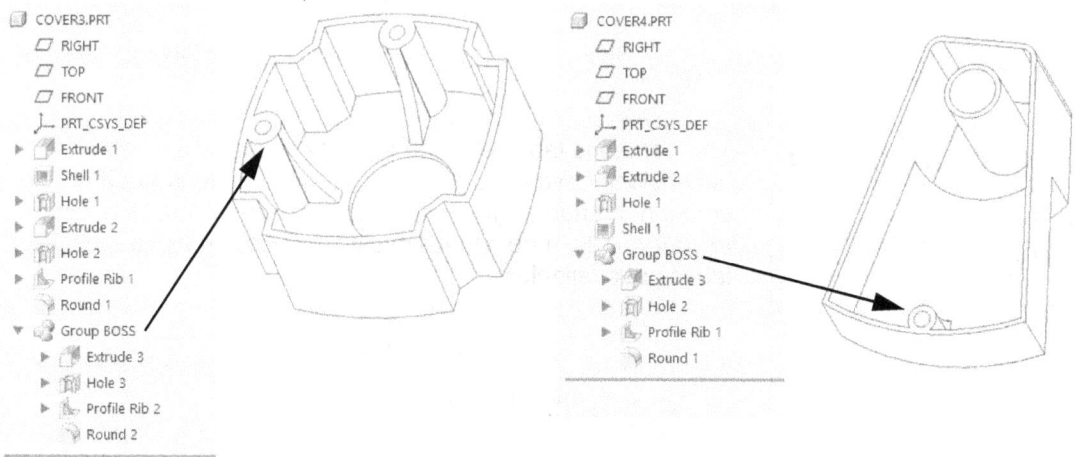

Figure 12–8

Step 5 - Manipulate the UDF.

Once the UDF has been placed, several options are available to manipulate it. You can replace the UDF group with another, make a dependent UDF independent, or update a dependent UDF.

Replace UDF

The **Replace** option replaces an existing UDF group with another. It can only be used if the replacing UDF group has the same number of references, lists them in the same order, and the references are the same type (e.g., surface, edge, or axis).

To replace a UDF, select the UDF group in the Model Tree, right-click and select **Replace**. The Replace Group dialog box opens as shown in Figure 12–9.

Figure 12–9

- **Manually retrieve UDF:** Enables you to open the replacing UDF from the disk.

- **Family Table:** Enables you to select an instance from a family table.

Make Dependent UDF Group Independent

You can convert a dependent UDF group to independent using the **Disassociate** option. To disassociate a UDF group, select it in the Model Tree, right-click and select **Disassociate**. Careful consideration should be given when using this option as there is no confirmation of this action and you cannot undo it.

12.3 Comparing Duplication Techniques

By selecting a method that best suits your design needs, you can design more efficiently. A comparison of the six duplication methods is as follows.

	Number of features to be copies	Number of instances	Copy to same or new part
Pattern	One	Multiple	Same
Copy/Paste	Multiple (single recommended)	One	Same or New
Copy/Paste Special (includes Move)	Multiple	One	Same or New
Mirror	Multiple	One	Same
Local Groups	Multiple (consecutive features)	Multiple (using patterning)	Same
UDF	Multiple	One copy	New (libraries of parts)

Practice 12a | Create User-Defined Features

Practice Objectives

- Create a stand-alone user-defined feature and specify the command prompts to locate the features.
- Place a independent user-defined feature on a different model by selecting new references.
- Ungroup the resulting user-defined features and change the dimension of the rib.

You have learned to copy features in an existing model as well as to different models. This process is time-consuming if you are copying the same feature multiple times in multiple models. In this practice, you will create the UDF from one model and then place the UDF in a second model to more efficiently copy features. The model shown at the top of Figure 12–10 will be the model that is used to create the UDF. The model shown at the bottom will be used to place the UDF.

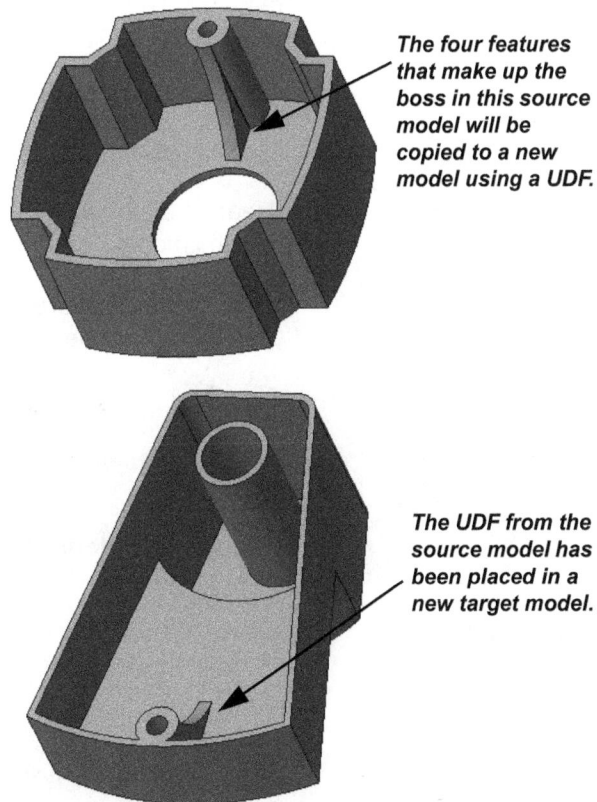

The four features that make up the boss in this source model will be copied to a new model using a UDF.

The UDF from the source model has been placed in a new target model.

Figure 12–10

Task 1 - Open a part file.

1. Set the working directory to the *Create_UDF* folder.

2. Open **cover3.prt**.

3. Set the model display as follows:

   - ⬩ ⚎ *(Datum Display Filters)*: All Off

   - ⬩ ⚘ *(Spin Center)*: Off

   - ⬩ ◻ *(Display Style)*: ◻ (Shading With Edges)

Task 2 - Create the UDF.

Design Considerations

In this task, you will create a UDF of the four features that make up the boss. Consider the following design requirements:

- The features (extrude, hole, rib, and round) must always remain independent from the features in the source part.

- The features (extrude, hole, rib, and round) must always remain independent from the features in the UDF.

- The diameter of the hole might vary depending on the part.

- Create the UDF with a reference model so that it gets stored with the model. This is recommended in case other designers need to use the UDF. Consequently, they can fully understand the references that are required if the assigned prompts are not descriptive enough.

1. Select the *Tools* tab and click ⚙ (UDF Library).

2. Select **Create** in the **UDF** menu and set the UDF *Name* to **boss**.

3. Select **Stand Alone>Done** in the **UDF OPTIONS** menu.

You can also press <Enter> to accept the reference part creation.

4. The message window prompts *Do you want to include a reference part?* Click **Yes** to create a reference part to help you select references during placement. The UDF dialog box opens.

5. Press and hold <Ctrl> and select **Extrude 2**, **Hole 2**, **Profile Rib 1**, and **Round 1**. You can select these features directly in the model or in the Model Tree.

In some cases, the references are used multiple times. In these cases, you can specify one or more reference prompts to correctly identify the reference.

6. Select **Done>Done/Return** in the **UDF FEATS** menu.

7. The next step is to enter reference prompts to identify the references for placing the UDF. Read the message window for the required reference that corresponds to the highlighted reference on the model.

8. Select **Single>Done/Return** to ensure that you are only prompted for one prompt for the current highlighted surface. Then, do the following:

   • When prompted to *Enter prompt for the surface in reference color:*, enter **Start Surface**.

   • Select **Single>Done/Return.** When prompted to *Enter prompt for the surface in reference color:*, enter **Horizontal Ref**.

   • When prompted to *Enter prompt for the surface in reference color:*, enter **Side Wall**.

   • When prompted to *Enter prompt for the surface in reference color:*, enter **Orientation Ref**.

   • When prompted to *Enter prompt for the surface in reference color:*, enter **Depth Ref**.

9. The **MOD PRMPT** menu displays. It enables you to review all of the reference prompts that were specified. If required, you can select **Enter Prompt** to enter a new prompt for any of the references.

10. Select **Next** to toggle through all of the references. Select **Done/Return** when you are satisfied with the prompts.

11. The message window now prompts you that all of the elements have been defined. The UDF has been created, but to meet the design requirement that the hole diameter must vary, select the optional element **Var Dims** and click **Define**.

12. All of the dimensions that are required to create the features display. Select the dimension for the diameter of the hole (this value is currently 6). Select **Done/Return** in the **VAR DIMS** menu.

13. Select **Done/Return** and enter **Diameter of Hole** as the prompt for the dimension value. This prompt is used when the UDF is placed in any model that requires an entry to set the variable dimension for the hole.

14. Click **OK>Done/Return** to complete the definition of the UDF.

15. Save the part and erase it from memory.

Task 3 - Place the UDF.

Design Considerations

In this task, you will place the UDF that you created in the previous task. Instead of placing the UDF in the same model, you will open a new model to place it. The UDF will be placed as independent to ensure that any changes made to the UDF will not affect the newly placed instance. To ensure that all of the dimensions are visible, select the **Unlock** option for the dimension display.

1. Open **cover4.prt**. The part displays as shown in Figure 12–11.

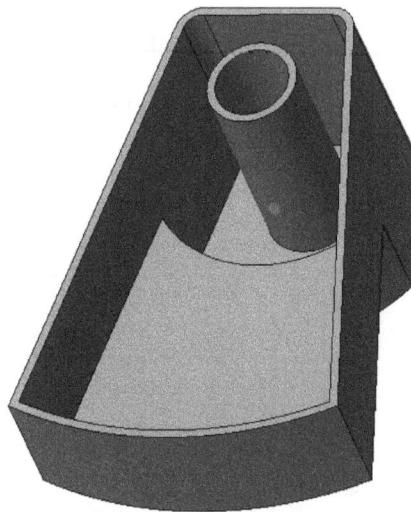

Figure 12–11

2. Click ⬚ (User-Defined Feature) in the *Model* tab.

3. A listing of all of the UDFs displays in the Open dialog box. Double-click on **boss.gph** in the list.

4. The Insert User-Defined Feature dialog box opens. Select the options as shown in Figure 12–12 to create an independent UDF copy. This ensures that if any changes are made to the UDF, they are not reflected in the **cover4** part.

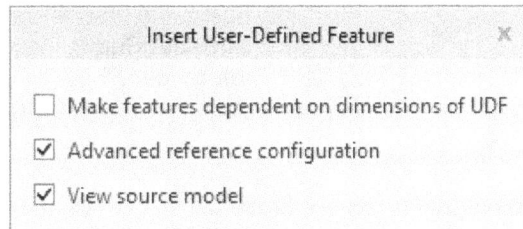

Figure 12–12

5. Click **OK**. The User Defined Feature Placement dialog box opens, as shown in Figure 12–13. The Creo Parametric window containing the reference part **boss_gp.prt** is also displayed. All of the references required to place the UDF are listed in the *References of Original Features* area.

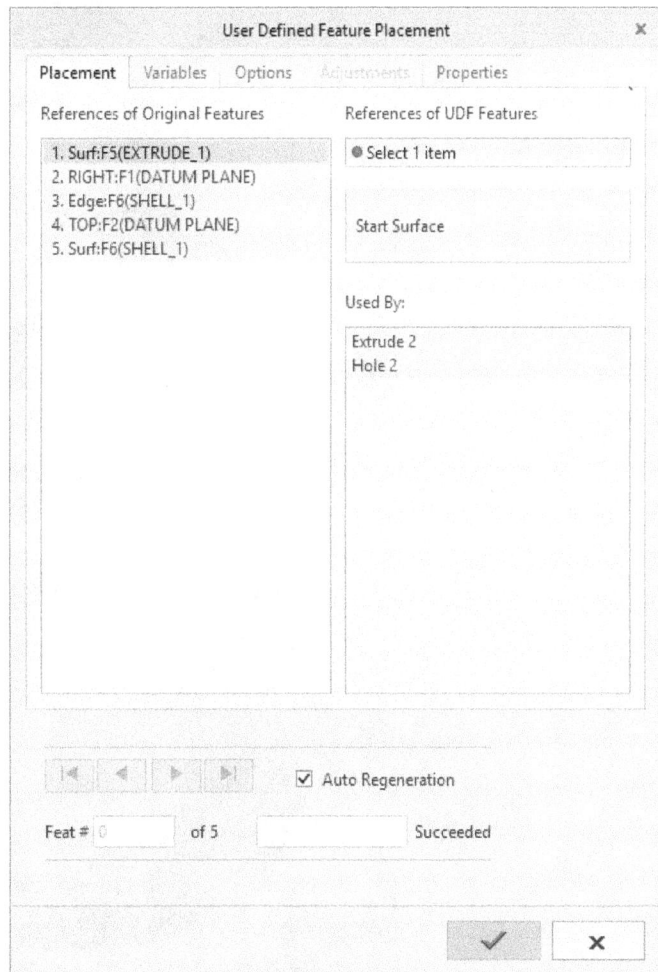

Figure 12–13

6. Select the first reference **(Surf:F5(EXTRUDE_1)) - Start Surface**. Select the surface shown in Figure 12–14 as the reference.

Figure 12–14

7. Select the second reference **(RIGHT:F1(DATUM PLANE)) - Horizontal Ref**. Select datum plane **RIGHT** as the reference.

8. Select the third reference **(Edge:F6(SHELL_1)) - Side Wall**. Select the edge shown in Figure 12–15 as the reference.

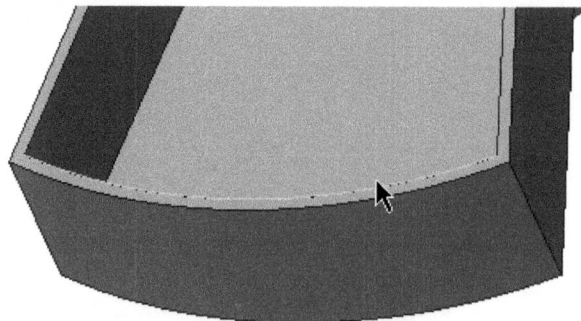

Figure 12–15

9. Select the fourth reference **(TOP:F2(DATUM PLANE)) - Orientation Ref**. Select datum plane **TOP** as the reference.

10. Select the fifth reference **(Surf:F6(SHELL_1)) - Depth Ref**. Select the surface shown in Figure 12–16 as the reference.

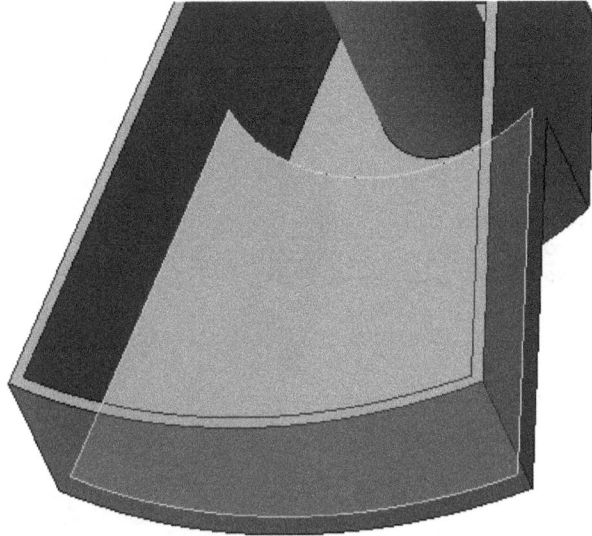

Figure 12–16

11. Select the *Options* tab. Select the **Scale by value** option and set the *Scaling factor* value to **2**.

12. Leave the **Unlock** option enabled for invariable dimensions.

13. Select the *Variables* tab. Set the hole *Diameter* to **16**.

14. Select the *Adjustments* tab.

15. Select the **Orientation Items**, and select **Section Orientation: PROFILE_RIB_1**. Click **Flip** so that the arrow points in the correct direction to add material, as shown in Figure 12–17.

Material added
to wrong side of
rib, so will fail.

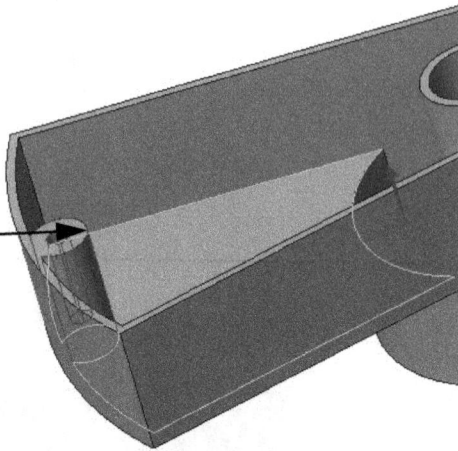

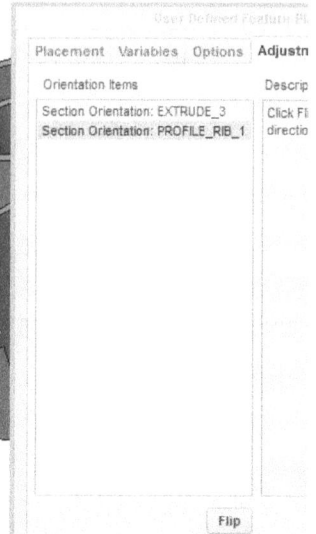

Flip the
direction and
the rib is
created.

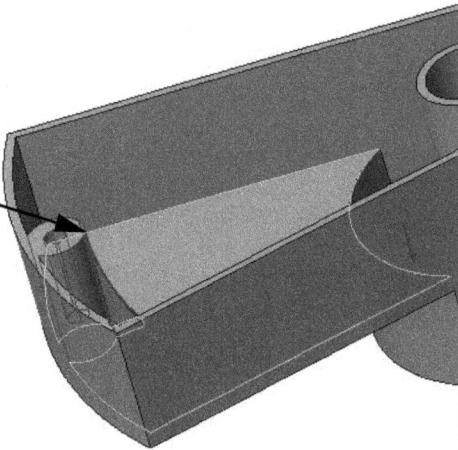

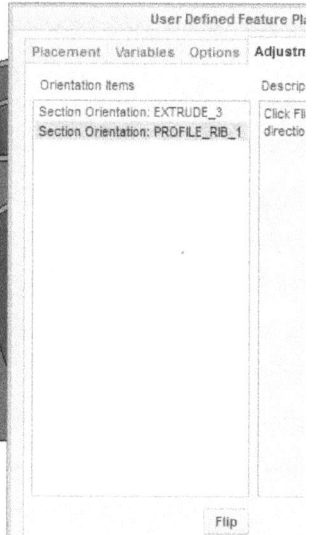

Figure 12–17

16. Click ✔ (OK) to finish placing the UDF. The UDF is placed as a group and all of the group functionality can be used on this group. The part displays as shown in Figure 12–18.

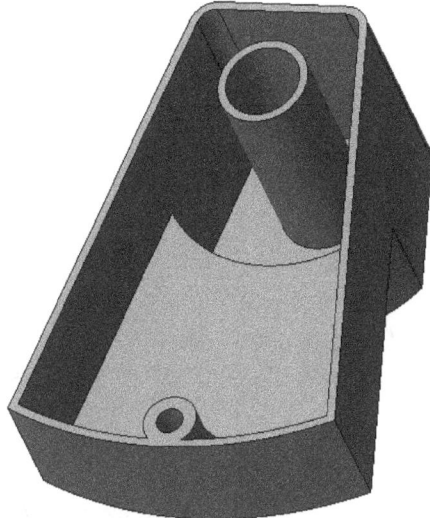

Figure 12–18

Task 4 - Modify the features created by a UDF.

1. Click on the **Group BOSS UDF** and select ✎ (Ungroup) in the mini toolbar.

2. Select the **Profile Rib** feature in the Model Tree and select ⊢d1⊣ (Edit Dimensions) in the mini toolbar.

3. Modify the *150* radius dimension to **70**, and then regenerate. The model displays as shown in Figure 12–19.

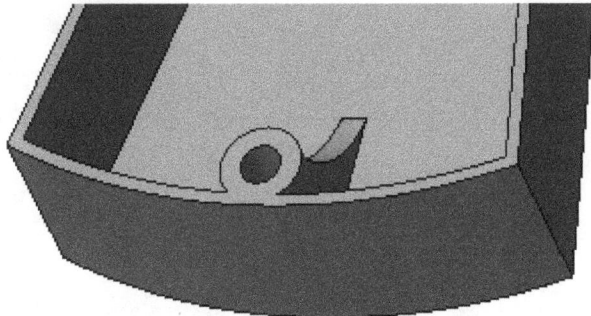

Figure 12–19

4. Save the part and erase it from memory.

Practice 12b | Manifold

Practice Objectives

- Create a user-defined feature and specify the command prompts to locate the features.
- Place the user-defined feature by selecting new references.

In this practice, you will create and place a UDF with limited instruction.

Task 1 - Open a part file.

Design Considerations

In this task, you will investigate the source part (the one you use to create the UDF) and the target part (the one into which you place the UDF).

1. Set the working directory to the *Manifold_UDF* folder.

2. Open **cartridge_valve_bore.prt**.

3. Set the model display as follows:

   - *(Datum Display Filters)*: (Axis Display) only

   - *(Spin Center)*: Off

   - *(Display Style)*: (Hidden Line)

4. The **VALVE_BORE** hole feature is a sketched coaxial hole. Edit the definition of the **VALVE_BORE** hole feature to display its references, as shown in Figure 12–20.

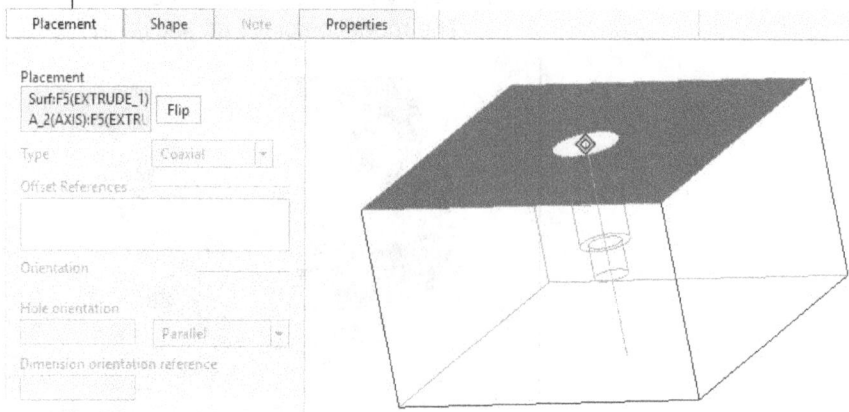

Figure 12–20

5. Exit the *Hole* tab without making any changes.

6. Open **manifold.prt**. The part displays as shown in Figure 12–21.

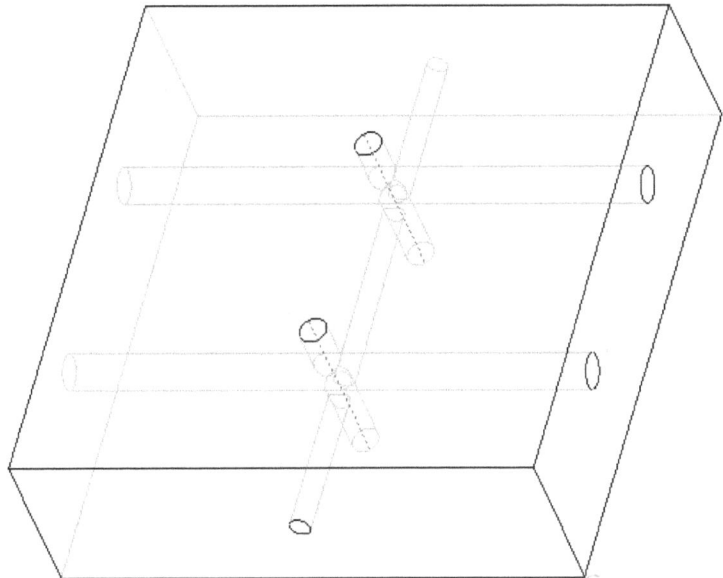

Figure 12–21

Design Considerations

Your design intent is to create a UDF of the **VALVE_BORE** hole and the chamfer that references it, and then place two instances of it referencing the two axes.

Task 2 - Create and place a UDF.

1. Return to the CARTRIDGE_VALVE_BORE.PRT window.

2. Create a UDF of the **VALVE_BORE** hole and include Chamfer 1.

3. Set the UDF *Name* to **C1_Valve**.

4. Place two instances of the UDF in the manifold part, as shown in Figure 12–22.

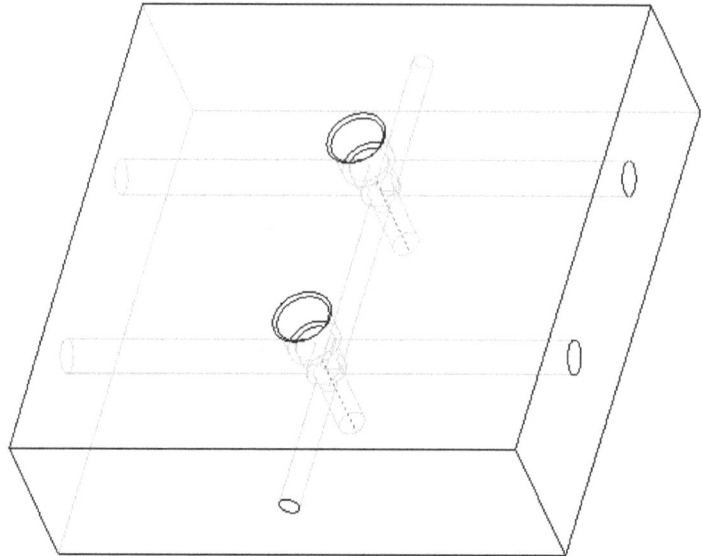

Figure 12–22

Design Considerations

A cross-section of the completed manifold part is shown in Figure 12–23. When cartridge valves are inserted into the bores created by the **C1_Valve** UDF, the valves control fluid flow through the internal passages of the manifold.

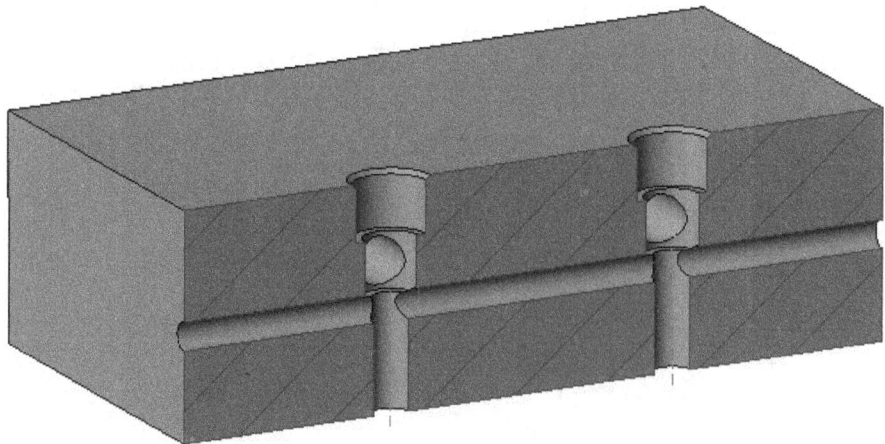

Figure 12–23

5. Save both parts and erase them from memory.

Chapter Review Questions

1. Only one feature can be selected to create a UDF.

    a. True

    b. False

2. Subordinate UDFs automatically generate a reference model.

    a. True

    b. False

3. The number of references used to create a feature that will be used to create a UDF does not matter.

    a. True

    b. False

4. Which of the following is not an optional element in the UDF dialog box?

    a. Var Dims

    b. Ref Prompts

    c. Units

    d. Var Elements

5. User-defined transitions on advanced rounds included in a UDF are removed.

    a. True

    b. False

6. The entity type selected as a reference must be similar to the entity type used during the initial creation of the feature.

    a. True

    b. False

7. Once the UDF has been placed, which option(s) are available to manipulate it? (Select all that apply.)

    a. Replace the UDF group with another.

    b. Make a dependent UDF independent.

    c. Update a Dependent UDF.

    d. Remove one of the grouped features from the UDF.

Answers: 1b, 2a, 3b, 4c, 5a, 6a, 7abcd

Part Family Tables

A part family table is a design tool that enables you to quickly and easily create variations in a design. Family tables can be used to create similar models instead of recreating the same model each time.

Learning Objectives in This Chapter

- Create a family table by adding columns and instances to vary in the table.
- Learn to patternize an existing instance to create additional instances with varying values for selected columns.
- Verify existing instances in a pattern table to ensure that the instance can be created.
- Learn to retrieve an existing instance in a pattern table.
- Note the different results when a dimension is modified, features are added, or features are removed between the generic part and an instance part.

13.1 Creating Part Family Tables

Family tables are created and stored in a model. A family table can be as simple as a variation in the features in the model or can be used to identify the steps in a manufacturing process. A family table can be created for any model by adding items, such as dimensions, parameters, or features. Once the items have been added, variations of the model can be created. These variations are known as instances. An example of a part family table is shown in Figure 13–1.

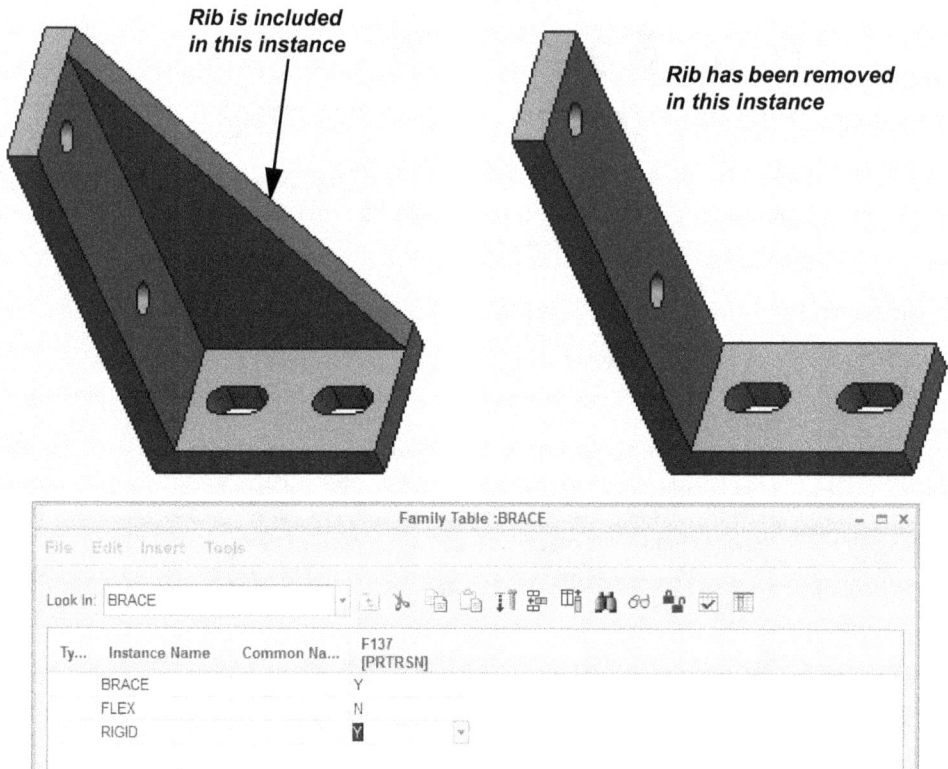

Figure 13–1

General Steps

Use the following general steps to create a part family table:

1. Open the family table editor.
2. Add items to the family table.
3. Add instances to the family table.
4. Manipulate the family table instances.
5. Create a multi-level family table, if required.
6. Verify the family table.
7. Retrieve an instance.

Step 1 - Open the family table editor.

A family table is created in the original (generic) model. To open the Family Table editor, select the *Tools* tab and click ▦ (Family Table). You can also select **Model Intent>Family Table** in the *Model* tab. The Family Table dialog box opens as shown in Figure 13–2.

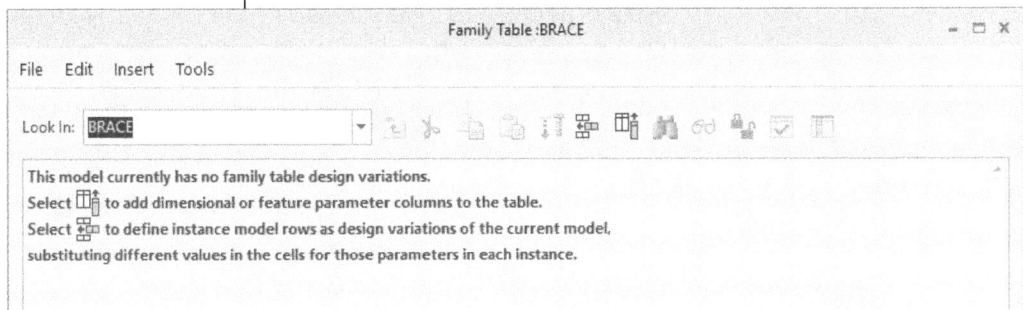

Figure 13–2

Step 2 - Add items to the family table.

Begin creating the family table by adding any items that are going to be varied in the instances. Remember the design intent of the model when selecting items to add to a family table. Consider which design variations are required and can be created.

*When you select the **Parameters** option, the Parameter dialog box opens. Parameters can be selected in the dialog box.*

To start adding items to the family table, click ▥ (Add Column). The Family Items dialog box opens. Items, such as dimensions, features, parameters, groups and pattern tables, can be added to the table. Select the type of item that you want to add in the *Add Item* area in the dialog box and select the item on the screen or Model Tree. Items are added as columns in the family table. The order in which the items are selected is the order in which they display in the family table.

For example, the brace shown in Figure 13–3 must be available in several versions. Depending on where the brace is used, it might need a different height. If the height of the brace increases, additional holes must be added to the side of the brace. Additionally, the rib along the back of the brace is not always required. Therefore, some instances must be created with the rib suppressed. The dimensions and features that affect the different variations of the brace all need to be added to the family table so they can be manipulated. Figure 13–3 also displays all of the required items listed in the Family Items dialog box.

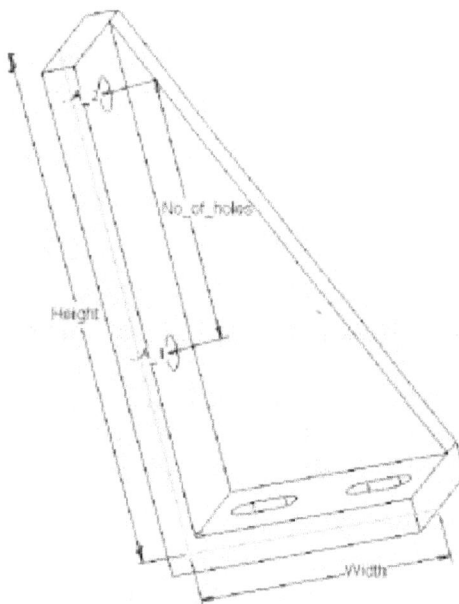

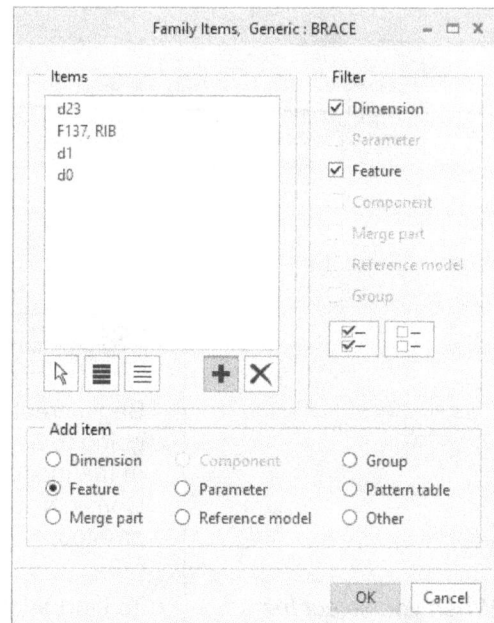

Figure 13–3

Once you finish adding the items to include in the family table, click **OK** to return to the Family Table dialog box.

Step 3 - Add instances to the family table.

The rows of the table represent the unique instances of the generic part. Instances can be added by editing the family table or patterning an existing instance. To add instances, click

(Add Instance) in the Family Table dialog box. Each row added represents one instance. Figure 13–4 shows three instances added to the family table.

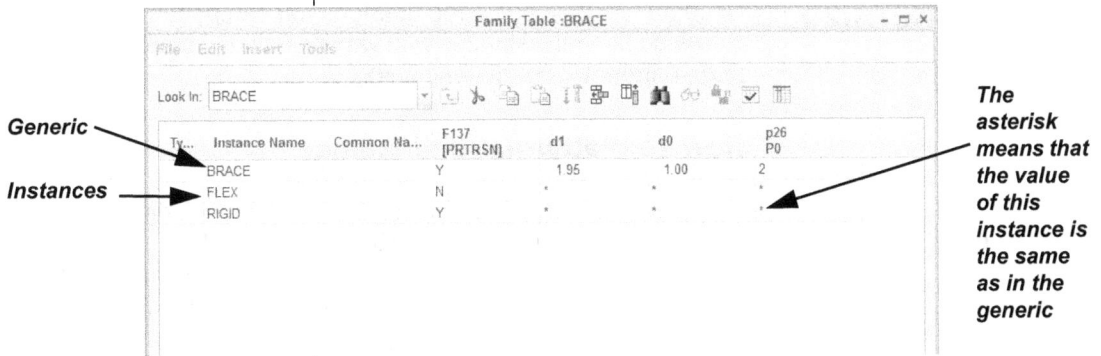

Generic

Instances

The asterisk means that the value of this instance is the same as in the generic

Figure 13–4

Step 4 - Manipulate the family table instances.

Once the columns and rows have been added to the table, you can change the values for each item to suit the requirements for a specific instance.

Feature Manipulation

A feature that is added to a family table can be suppressed in the instances. Suppress a feature in an instance by entering **N** in the appropriate cell. For example, in the instances **1456** and **1536** the rib feature is suppressed, as shown in Figure 13–5.

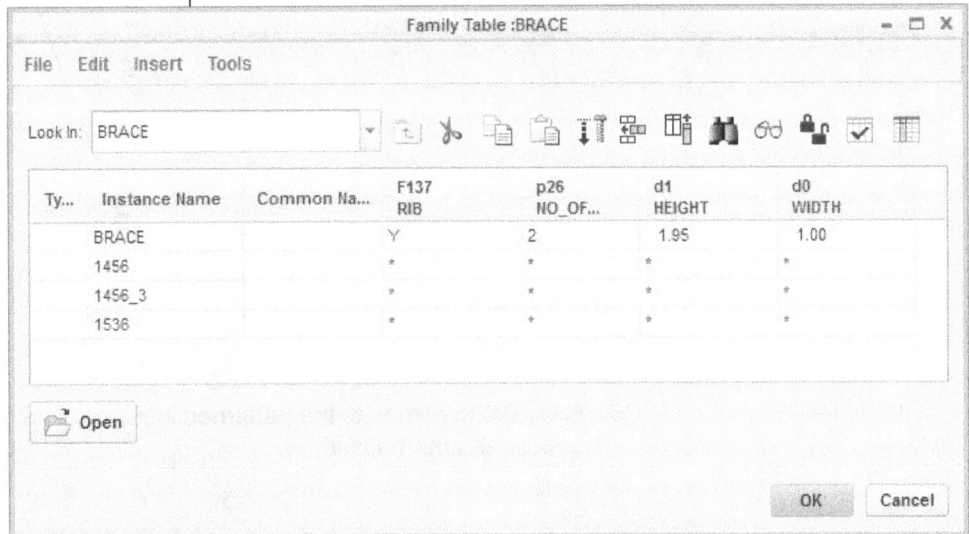

Figure 13–5

Patternize

Once an instance has been created, you can patternize it to create additional instances with varying values for selected items (e.g., parameters or dimensions).

How To: Patternize an Instance

1. Click ↓Ⅱ (Patternize). The Patternize Instance dialog box opens as shown in Figure 13–6.
2. Enter the number of instances required in the *Quantity* field.
3. In the *Items* area at the bottom of the dialog box, use

    ≫ (Add Item) to move the items that you want to vary from the left side to the right side.
4. Enter an incremental value in the *Increment* field for each varying item. A positive value indicates an increasing increment and a negative value indicates a decreasing increment.

    The dialog box shown in Figure 13–7 is set to create three instances, with the *Height* increasing by 1.5 and the *No_of_holes* increasing by 1.0.

Figure 13–6

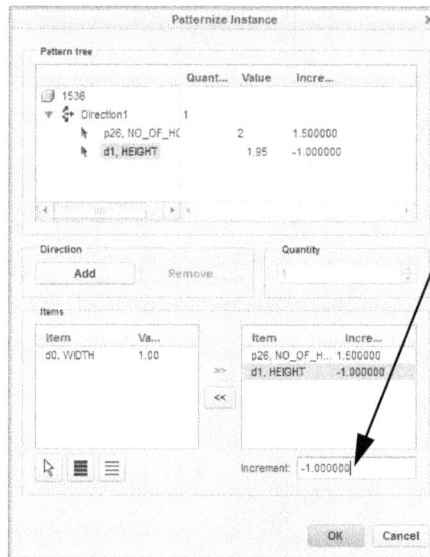

Enter negative values for the increment if you want the increment to decrease

Figure 13–7

5. Click **OK** to complete the patterned instance. The family table populates automatically.

Step 5 - Create a multi-level family table, if required.

Every instance can be used as the generic for its own family table. This results in multi-level family tables or nested family tables. Multi-level family tables enable you to effectively manage large amounts of data.

For example, the brace family table shown in Figure 13–8 currently has three instances. If each instance has six different brace widths, the table would require eighteen rows of data. Creating a separate family table for each instance makes the data easier to manage.

The part family table in Figure 13–8 shows an instance with its own family table. ▢ in the *Type* column of instance **1456** indicates that it has its own family table.

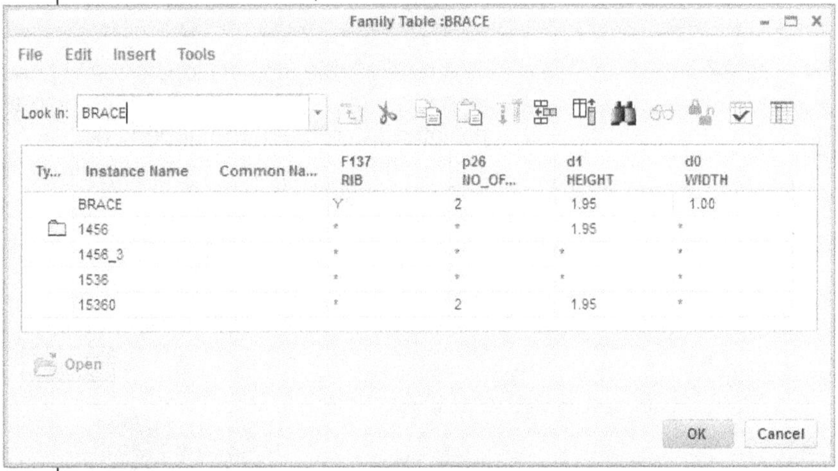

Figure 13–8

Step 6 - Verify the family table.

*To display all of the items that belong to the family table in the Family Tree dialog box, right-click on any instance or the generic name and select **Show Table**.*

The model must successfully regenerate to open an instance. To verify that instances are valid, click ☑ (Verify) in the Family Table dialog box. The Family Tree dialog box opens, enabling you to select individual instances or regenerate all of the instances in the family table. The regeneration status of each instance displays in the *Verify status* column in the dialog box. The regeneration status is also written to a file called **<model_name>.tst**.

shows the Family Tree dialog box after the instances have been verified. Note that instance **CONFIG3** has failed regeneration. The instance values must be adjusted so that the model can regenerate and the instance can be opened.

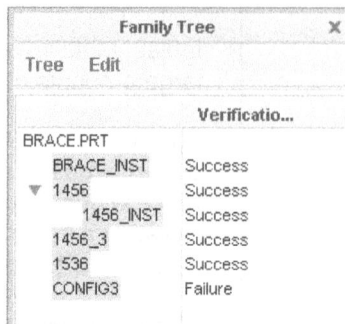

Figure 13–9

Step 7 - Retrieve an instance.

The family table information, including each instance, is stored with the generic part file. When opening the part, you are prompted to retrieve the generic or one of the instances, as shown in Figure 13–10. The *By Column* tab can be used to select by parameter.

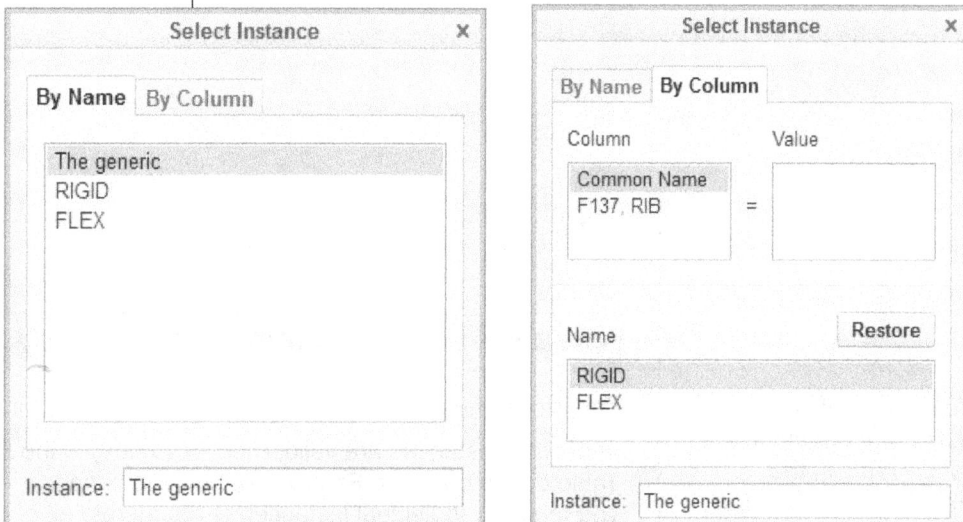

Figure 13–10

An instance can also be opened directly from the generic by selecting **Model Intent>Family Table**. Select the instance in the Family Table dialog box and click **Open**.

The generic model can also be opened from an instance model. To open a generic model or any other instance from an instance model, right-click on the model name in the Model Tree and select **Open Generic**. In the Select Instance dialog box, select the *By Name tab*. Select a generic model or instance name from the list, as shown on the left in Figure 13–11. Click **Open** to open the selected generic or instance. Alternatively, you can select the *By Column* tab to select the model by its column value in the family table, as shown on the right.

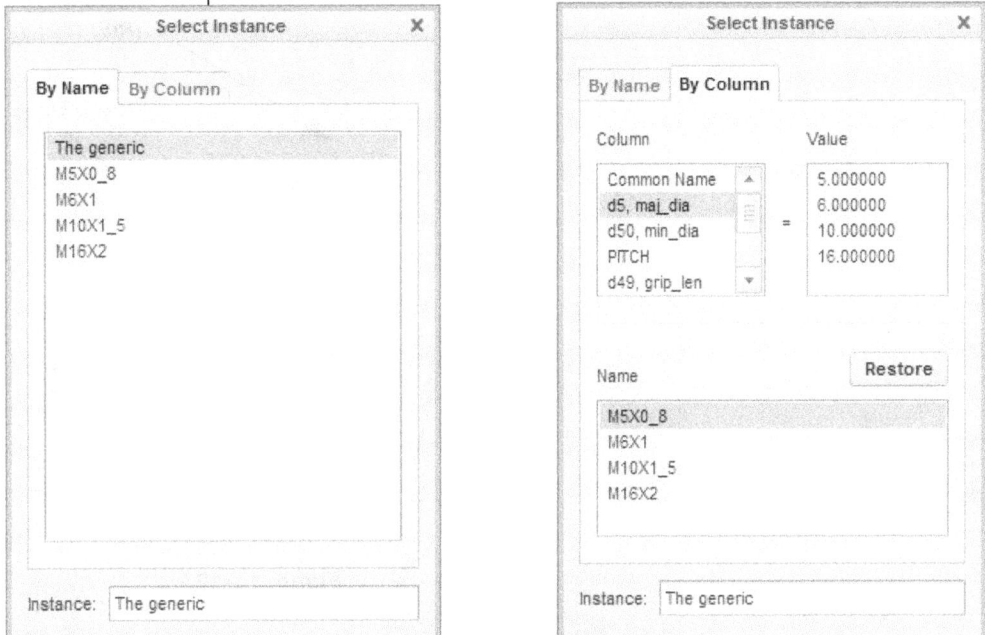

Figure 13–11

Instance Index

The instance index file (stored in the current working directory as **<current_directory_name>.idx**) enables you to open instances by name. The instance index file contains cross-references for all of the Creo Parametric files with family tables in that directory. Once you have verified the instances and saved the generic model file, an instance index file is automatically created or updated to include the newly saved generic part and its instances. You can also manually create or update the instance index file by selecting **File>Manage Session>Update Index**.

To remove the instances from display when opening the file, set the **config.pro** option **menu_show_instances** to **No**.

13.2 Modifying Family Tables

Models are constantly modified to reach the final design. The following examples describe how to manage changes to a generic model that contains family table instances. The features and dimensions shown in Figure 13–12 are used as family table items.

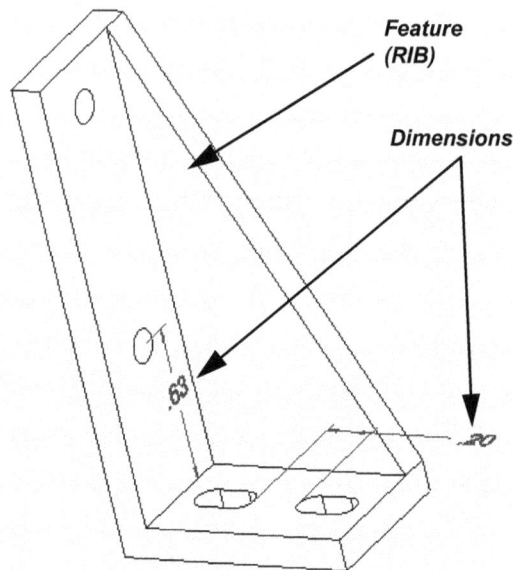

Figure 13–12

Modify Family Table Dimensions

To modify a dimension in an instance, open the instance and change the value using the standard modification techniques or use the Family Table editor by selecting the cell and entering a new value. An example is shown in Figure 13–13. Any modifications made to an instance also update in the Family Table editor.

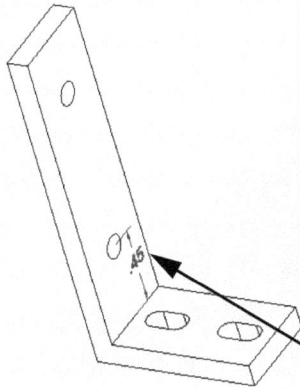

Dimension to be modified in the FLEX instance

Figure 13–13

Modify Non-family Table Dimensions

Any modifications to items that do not belong to the family table can be modified in the generic or in an instance, as shown in Figure 13–14. These changes are reflected in the generic and all instances.

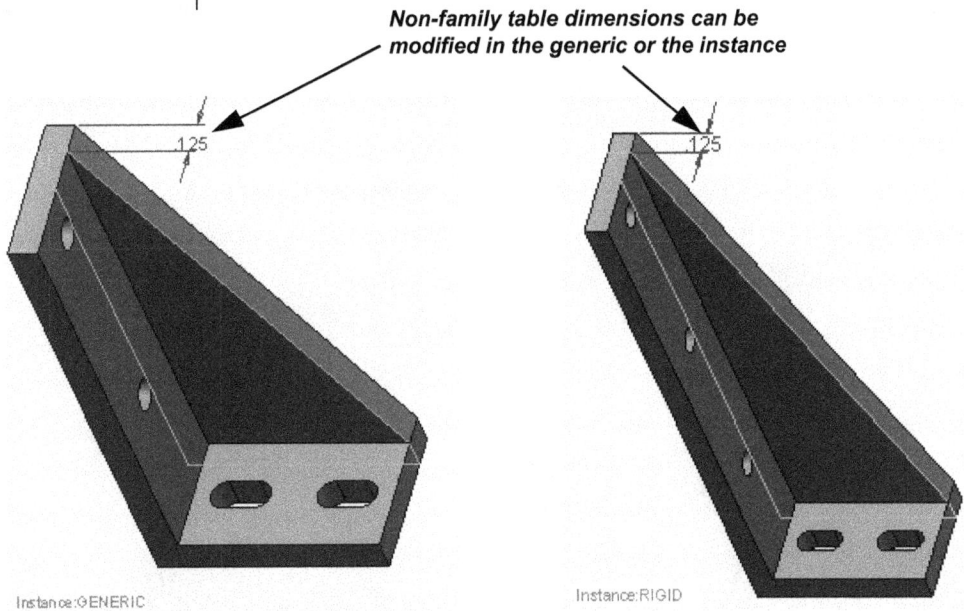

Non-family table dimensions can be modified in the generic or the instance

Instance:GENERIC

Instance:RIGID

Figure 13–14

Add Features to the Generic Model

Adding a feature to the generic is reflected in the generic and in all instances, as shown in Figure 13–15. The feature is not added to the family table, unless you explicitly add it.

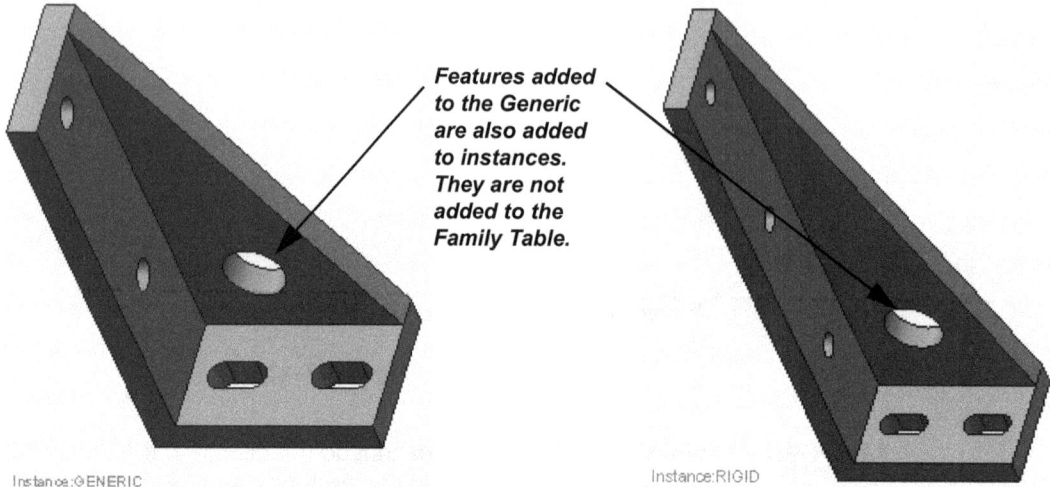

Features added to the Generic are also added to instances. They are not added to the Family Table.

Instance:GENERIC

Instance:RIGID

Figure 13–15

Add Features to an Instance

Adding a feature to an instance creates an additional column in the family table. The generic is permanently marked as **N** to prevent the feature from displaying in the generic model. By default, all of the other instances are assigned with an asterisk (*) to maintain the same status as the generic, but this can be modified in the Family Table editor. Features added to an instance are not added to the generic, as shown in Figure 13–16. To resume features added to the instance in generic model, select **Operations>Resume>Resume**.

Features added to an instance are not added to the generic. The feature's presence in other instances depends on the value in the Family Table.

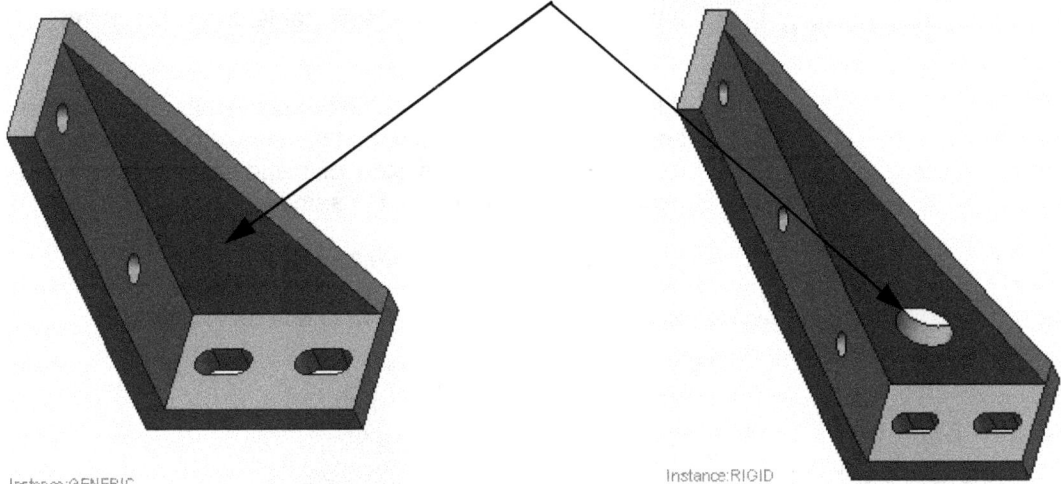

Instance:GENERIC

Instance:RIGID

Type	Instance Name	Com...	F137 RIB	p26 NO_OF...	d1 HEIGHT	d0 WIDTH	F302 [HOLE_1]
	BRACE		Y	2	1.95	1.00	N
	FLEX		N	3	2.95	0.45	*
	RIGID		Y	3	2.95	0.55	Y

Figure 13–16

Delete Features From an Instance

If a feature is deleted from an instance, the following scenarios might occur:

- If the feature exists in the family table, the value of the instance is changed to **N**.

- If the feature does not exist in the family table, the item is added to the family table and the value is changed to **N**. The generic is assigned the value of **Y** and all other instances are assigned as * to maintain the same status as the generic.

An example is shown in Figure 13–17.

Features deleted in an instance are marked as N in the Family Table

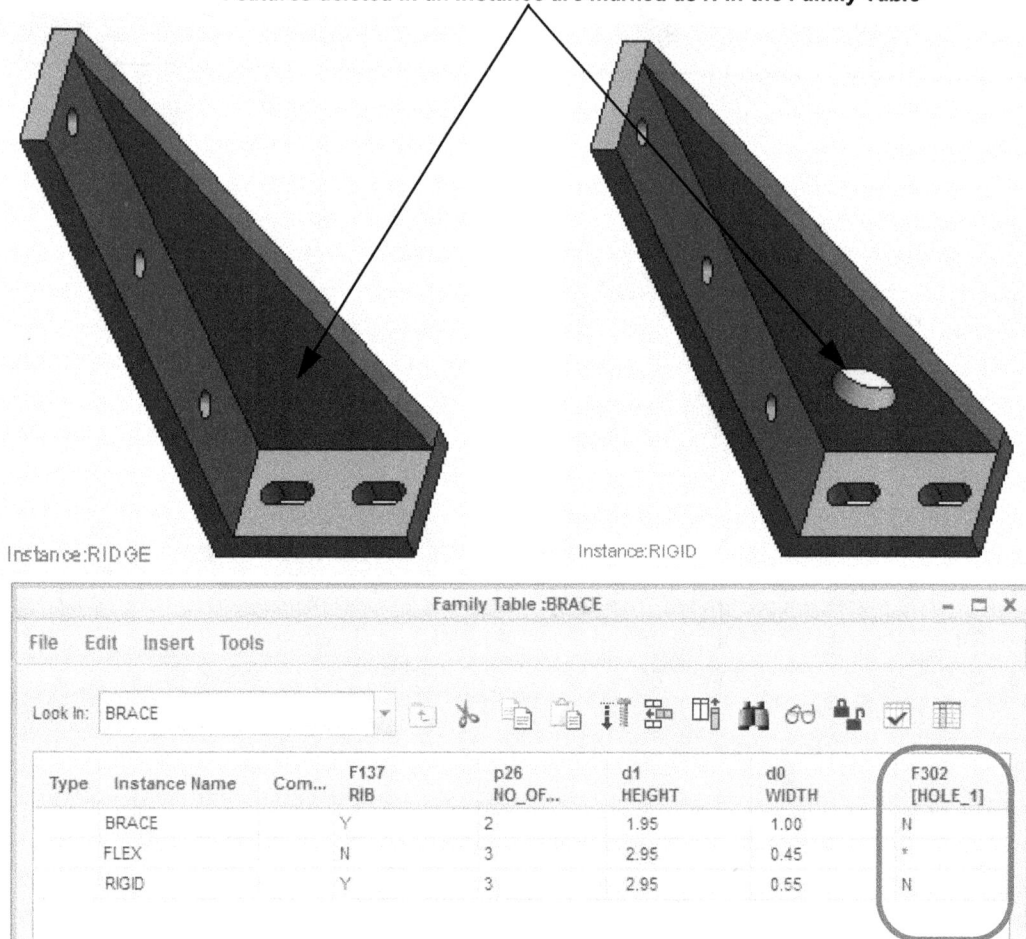

Instance:RIDGE

Instance:RIGID

Type	Instance Name	Com...	F137 RIB	p26 NO_OF...	d1 HEIGHT	d0 WIDTH	F302 [HOLE_1]
	BRACE		Y	2	1.95	1.00	N
	FLEX		N	3	2.95	0.45	*
	RIGID		Y	3	2.95	0.55	N

Family Table :BRACE

File   Edit   Insert   Tools

Look In: BRACE

Figure 13–17

Delete Features From the Generic

If a feature is deleted from the generic it is also deleted from all of the instances. If the item is a family table item, the column is removed from the table, as shown in Figure 13–18.

Features deleted from the generic are also deleted from all instances

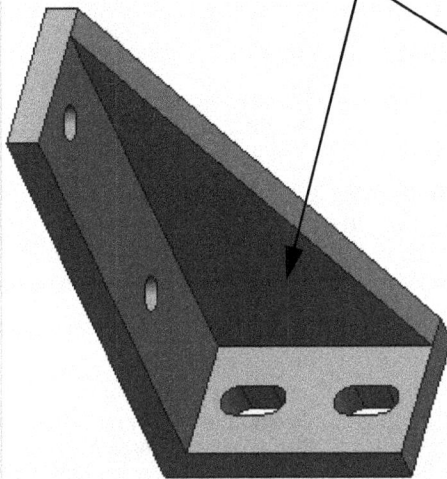

Instance:GENERIC

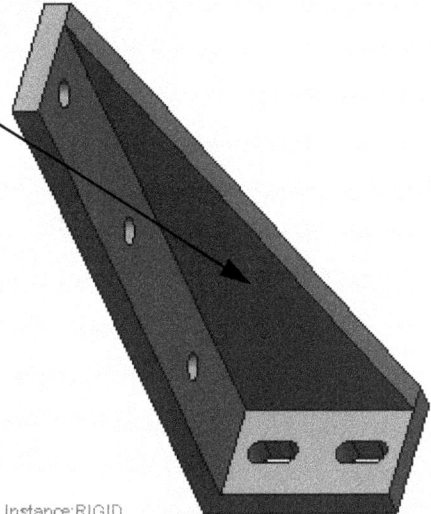

Instance:RIGID

Family Table :BRACE   – ☐ ✕

File   Edit   Insert   Tools

Look In: BRACE

Type	Instance Name	Com...	F137 RIB	p26 NO_OF...	d1 HEIGHT	d0 WIDTH	F302 [HOLE_1]
	BRACE		Y	2	1.95	1.00	N
	FLEX		N	3	2.95	0.45	*
	RIGID		Y	3	2.95	0.55	N

Figure 13–18

Practice 13a | Family Tables I

Practice Objectives

- Create a family table by adding columns and instances to vary in the table.
- Open the instances in the family table to create a multi-level family table.
- Verify existing instances in a family table to ensure that the instance can be created.

In this practice, you will open an existing model and create two family table instances in it. The family table instances will be created so that they either include or do not include the RIB support feature shown in Figure 13–19. Once the instances have been created in the generic you will open each instance and create instances within them to control the support holes along the side of the model.

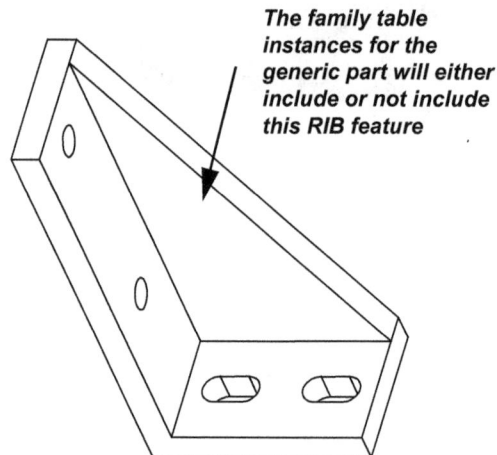

The family table instances for the generic part will either include or not include this RIB feature

Figure 13–19

Task 1 - Open a part file.

1. Set the working directory to the *Family_Tables_I* folder.

2. Open **brace.prt**.

3. Set the model display as follows:

- ✗⁄᷿ *(Datum Display Filters)*: All Off

- ⟑ *(Spin Center)*: Off

- ⬛ *(Display Style)*: ⬜ (Shading With Edges)

4. Select the *Tools* tab and click ⬛ (Model Player). Step through the creation of the part to see how it was built.

*You can also check for relations in the Model tab by selecting **Model Intent>Relations and Parameters** or **Model Intent>Relations**.*

5. Check for relations by clicking ᵈ= (Relations) in the *Tools* tab. What is this relation used for?

6. Review the model and the Model Tree, as shown in Figure 13–20.

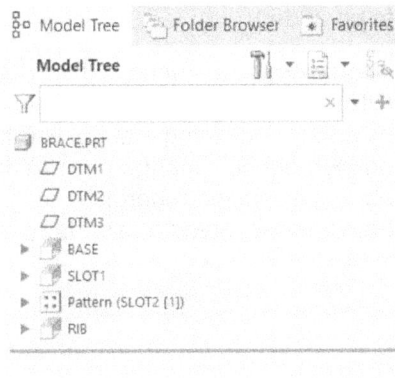

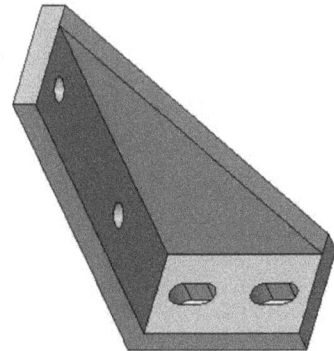

Figure 13–20

Task 2 - Define a family table.

Design Considerations

In this task the solid feature, RIB, will be added to the family table that will enable you to either include or not include it in the model. This RIB is included in some situations where the brace is required to be rigid and it is removed if the brace is required to be flexible. Both scenarios can reside in the same model using a family table.

When you close the Family Tree dialog box, it can hide behind the main Graphics window. To return it, minimize and maximize the application.

Do not press <Enter>. Doing so creates another instance.

1. In the *Model* tab, select **Model Intent>Family Table**.

2. Click ⬚ (Add Column) to add an item to the family table. The Family Item dialog box opens.

3. Select **Feature** in the *Add Item* area in the dialog box.

4. Select **RIB** in the Model Tree. This feature will be the only item in the table. Click **OK** in the Family Items dialog box.

5. Click ⬚ (Add Instance) in the Family Table dialog box to add an instance to the table.

6. Select the cell containing the name **BRACE_INST** and set the *Name* of this instance to **FLEX**.

7. Select the cell containing the asterisk (*) symbol and select **N** in the drop-down list. This indicates that the RIB feature is not to be added.

8. Add a second instance called **RIGID**. This instance has the RIB feature added. The * symbol displays in the *RIB* column by default indicating that the RIB feature's existence is based on the generic. Change this to **Y** to ensure that the RIB is always displayed regardless of its status in the generic. The Family Table dialog box updates as shown in Figure 13–21.

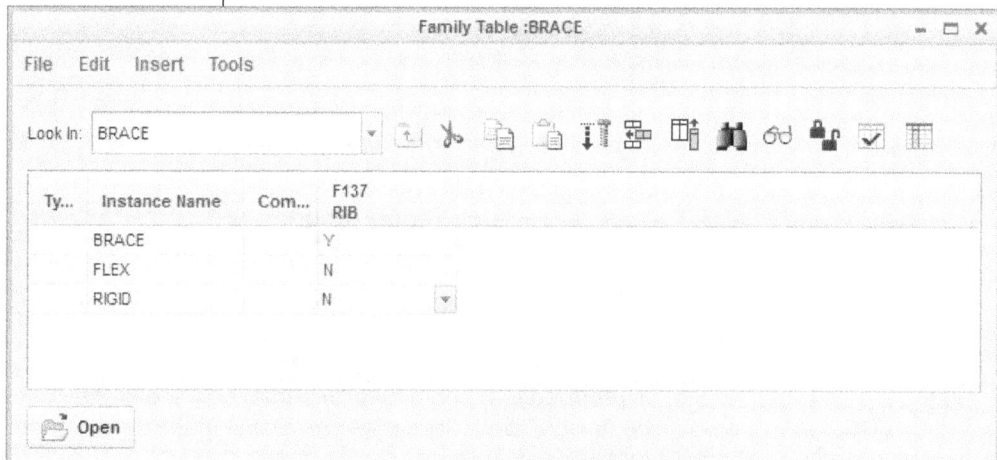

Figure 13–21

9. Confirm that the instances can be regenerated by clicking ☑ (Verify). The Family Tree dialog box opens with all of the instances selected.

10. Click **VERIFY**. The *Verify Status* column displays **Success** for each instance.

11. Read the message window. The system creates a text file called **brace.tst** in your current working directory that lists all of the instances and their regeneration status of **success** or **failure**.

Task 3 - Create a family table in each instance.

Design Considerations

Similar to creating instances in the generic model, each family table instance can also have instances of its own. In this task, you will add instances to both the **RIGID** and **FLEX** models that vary the number of support holes along the side of the model. This is required because depending on the design intent, the brace might need to be secured in multiple locations. These instances will be driven using the dimension that drives the number of holes in the support hole pattern. Because of the relation that had been added previously, the height of the model is dependent on the number of holes and updates automatically.

1. In the Family Table dialog box, select the row containing the **FLEX** instance and click **Open** to open it. The instance opens in a new Creo Parametric window.

2. Select **Model Intent>Family Table**.

3. Click ⬚ (Add Column) to add an item to the family table. The Family Items dialog box opens.

4. Leave **Dimension** selected in the *Add Item* area of the dialog box. Select the pattern in the Model Tree. The dimensions for the pattern display on the model. The pattern duplicates two cuts in the model as indicated by the **2 Cuts** parameter on the model. Select the number **2** to add the number of pattern instances (cuts) to the family table.

5. Click **OK**. A column has been added for **p0**, the parameter controlling the number of pattern instances.

6. Create instances with the following information:

Instance Name	Value for p0
279207-1-A	1
279207-2-A	2
279207-3-A	3

7. Verify the instances by clicking ✔ (Verify) and clicking **VERIFY**.

8. Close the Family Tree dialog box.

9. Select **279207-1-A** in the *Instance Name* column and click ᠔ (Preview) to display the instance.

10. Close the Preview window.

11. Click **OK** to close the Family Table dialog box.

12. Close the window containing the **FLEX** instance.

13. Select in the window containing the generic part.

14. Create a similar family table for the **RIGID** instance of the bracket. Use the following information:

Instance Name	Value for p0
279207-2-B	2
279207-3-B	3
279207-4-B	4

15. Verify the instances.

16. Examine the instances to confirm that the relations that control the height of the brace are working correctly.

17. Close the window containing the **RIGID** instance.

18. Save the part and erase it from memory.

Practice 13b	# (Optional) Family Tables II

Practice Objectives

- Create a family table by adding columns and instances to vary in the table.
- Learn to patternize an existing instance to create additional instances with varying values for selected columns.
- Retrieve an existing instance in a pattern table by name or by a value.

In this practice, you will create family table instances in a bolt part. Instances will be created in the generic model and in the generic's instances to form a multi-level family table. This is done so that all of the combinations of the bolt can be located in one model instead of having multiple models with similar dimension values. Using this approach can help reduce the number of models that exist in your company database. The model that will be used is shown in Figure 13–22.

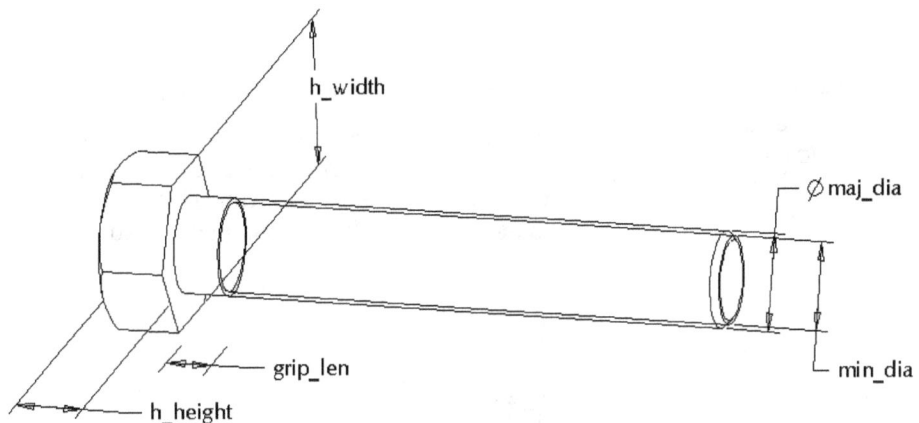

Figure 13–22

Task 1 - Open a part file.

1. Set the working directory to the *Family_Tables_II* folder.

2. Open **hex_bolt.prt**.

3. Set the model display as follows:

- ^{×⁄} *(Datum Display Filters)*: All Off

- ✶ *(Spin Center)*: Off

- ▱ *(Display Style)*: ▱ (No Hidden)

4. Select the *Tools* tab and click 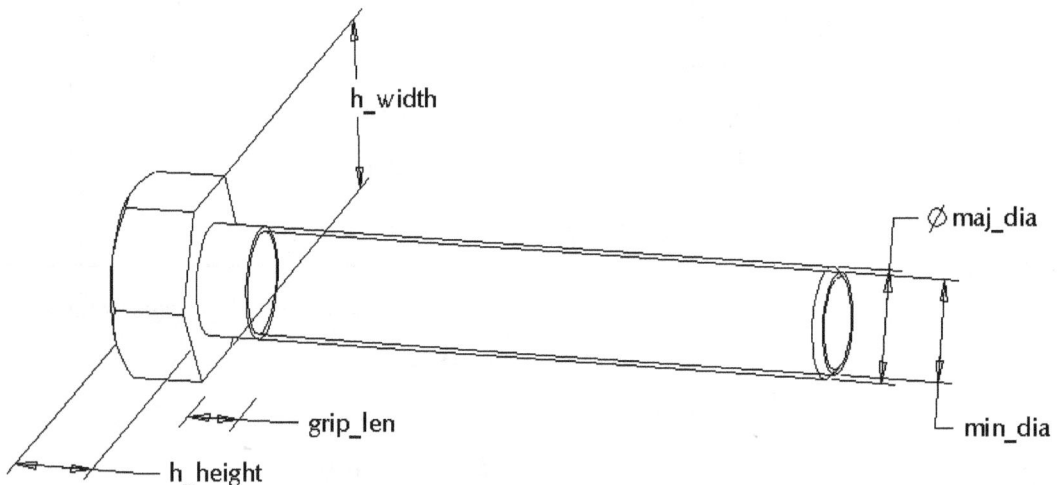 (Model Player) and step through the creation of the part to see how it was built.

Task 2 - Create a family table.

Design Considerations

In this task, you will create a family table that contains a combination of dimensions and parameters. All of the values for these items will be varied to obtain all of the required instances in the generic bolt model. The dimensions that are selected have previously assigned user-defined names to help you easily identify them and their intent in the model creation. To rename dimensions in this way, right-click on the dimension and select **Properties**, select the *Dimension Text* tab, and enter a name for the dimension. By default the dimension value is always visible, but if you switch to the dimension symbol (select the *Tools* tab and click (Switch Dimensions)), the new descriptive name replaces the d# format.

1. Create a family table by clicking (Family Table) in the *Tools* tab.

Remember that columns are arranged according to the order in which you add items to the family table.

2. Add the dimensions shown in Figure 13–23 to the family table. Click (Switch Dimensions) in the *Tools* tab to toggle between dimension values and names. The grip_len dimension is associated with **DTM4**. The **min_dia** dimension is associated with the cosmetic thread.

Figure 13–23

3. Add another column to the family table for the part parameter called **PITCH**. In the Family Items dialog box, select **Parameter**.

4. Select **PITCH** in the Select Parameter dialog box and click **Insert Selected**. Close the Select Parameter dialog box.

5. Click **OK** in the Family Item dialog box.

6. In the Family Table dialog box, select a cell in the *PITCH* column. Press and hold <Ctrl>. Select a cell in *H_HEIGHT* column. Select **Edit>Swap Two Columns**. The location of the two columns is reversed. Continue to swap columns to obtain the order shown in the following table.

7. Click ▦ (Add Instance) to create the following instances:

Name	maj_dia	min_dia	PITCH	grip_len	h_width	h_height
M5x0_8	5.0	4.567	0.80	2.4	8.0	3.875
M6x1	6.0	5.459	1.00	3.0	10.0	4.375
M10x1_5	10.0	9.188	1.50	4.5	16.0	6.850
M16x2	16.0	14.917	2.00	6.0	24.0	10.750

8. Click ☑ (Verify) to confirm that the instances can all be regenerated successfully.

Task 3 - Pattern instances to create second level family tables.

Design Considerations

In this task, you will create a second level of family tables in the generic's instances. To create all of the previous instances you entered all of the instance names and values manually. In this task, you will use additional family table functionality that enables you to pattern the first instance to create all of the subsequent instances. Using this technique will save you considerable time in creating instances in a model.

1. In the Family Table dialog box, select the row containing the **M5X0_8** instance and click **Open** to open it. The instance opens in a new Creo Parametric window.

2. Click **Model Intent>** ▦ (Family Table) in the *Model* tab. Add a column for the dimension named **fas_len** as shown in Figure 13–24.

You can also select
Model Intent>Family Table *in the Model tab.*

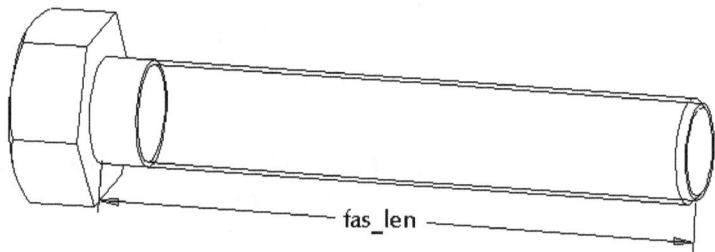

Figure 13–24

3. Create an instance called **m5x0_8_0** with a value of **20.0** for the **fas_len** dimension.

4. Select the cell containing the **m5x0_8_0** instance name and click ↓↑ (Patternize) to patternize the instance.

5. In the Patternize Instance dialog box, enter **7** in the *Quantity* field and press <Enter>.

6. In the *Items* area in the dialog box, select the **d1,FAS_LEN** entry in the left column and click ⟫ (Add Item) to move it to the right column.

7. Set the *Increment* field to **5.0** and press <Enter>. The dialog box updates as shown in Figure 13–25.

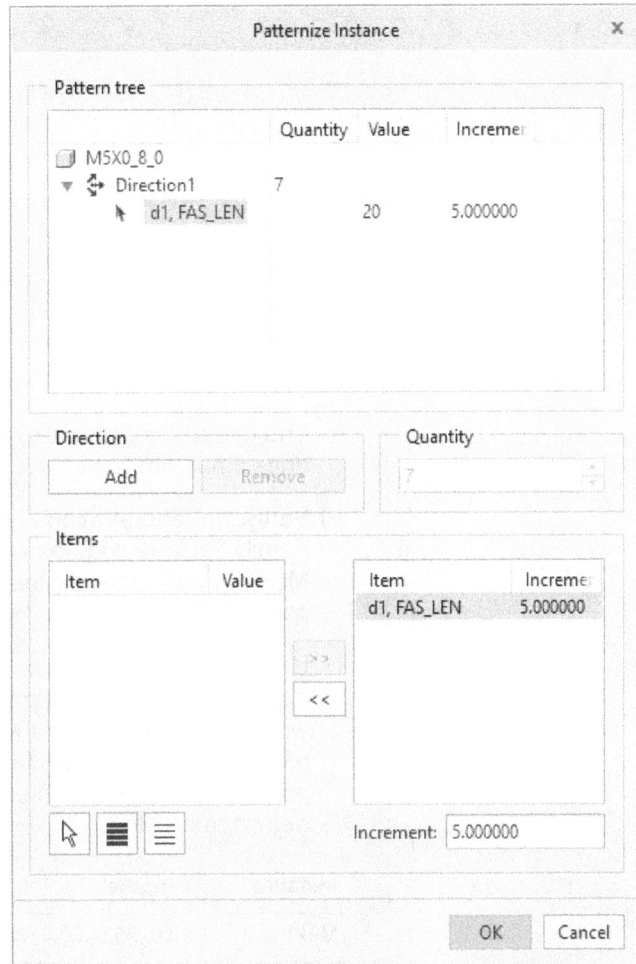

Figure 13–25

8. Click **OK** to close the Patternize Instance dialog box. The Family Table dialog box updates as shown in Figure 13–26.

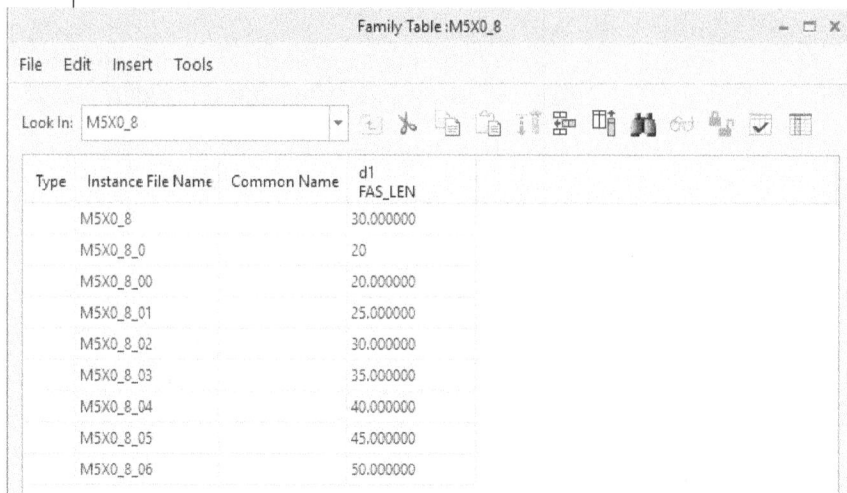

Type	Instance File Name	Common Name	d1 FAS_LEN
	M5X0_8		30.000000
	M5X0_8_0		20
	M5X0_8_00		20.000000
	M5X0_8_01		25.000000
	M5X0_8_02		30.000000
	M5X0_8_03		35.000000
	M5X0_8_04		40.000000
	M5X0_8_05		45.000000
	M5X0_8_06		50.000000

Figure 13–26

9. The patternize action recreates the first instance. Delete it once it has been created.

10. Verify the regeneration of each of the instances. Close the Family Table dialog box and the window containing the **M5X0_8** part. Activate the window containing the generic part.

11. Use the **Patternize** option to create family tables for the other **hex_bolt** instances, using the following values. Close the window and activate the window containing the generic part after each second-level family table has been created. The patternize action recreates the first instance. Delete it once it has been created.

Instance	Lengths
M6x1	20.0, 25.0, 30.0, 35.0, 40.0, 45.0, 50.0, 55.0, 60.0
M10x1_5	20.0, 25.0, 30.0, 35.0, 40.0, 45.0, 50.0, 55.0, 60.0, 65.0, 70.0
M16x2	30.0, 35.0, 40.0, 45.0, 50.0, 55.0, 60.0, 65.0, 70.0

12. When the second-level family tables are complete, 36 unique models are created. Activate the window containing the generic part and save the file.

13. Save the generic part, close the window, and erase all files not displayed.

Task 4 - Open instances.

Design Considerations

Once models have been created with family tables instances, it can be difficult to locate these instances when it is time to use them in assemblies. In this task, you will learn how to find and open instances by name or parameter value.

1. Open **hex_bolt.prt**.

2. The Select Instance dialog box opens. The generic model and the first-level family table instances are listed in the dialog box. The *By Name* and *By Column* tabs display in the dialog box. The *By Name* tab is the default. Double-click on M6X1 in the list. The second-level family table instances for M6x1 display in the dialog box. Select any instance name and click **Open**.

3. Close the window and open **hex_bolt** again.

4. The *By Column* tab enables you to open an instance based on the value of one or more items in the family table. Select the *By Column* tab. Select **PITCH** in the **Column** menu. The *Value* area displays all of the values for the **PITCH** parameter as listed in the family table. Selecting one of these values selects the corresponding instance. Select **2.000000**.

5. Double-click on the name of the instance that displays in the *Name* area to open it. It is possible for more than one instance to have the same value for a parameter.

6. The second level family table instances display in the *Name* area in the Select Instance dialog box. The dimension **d1**, (named **fas_len**) is the only one listed in the *Column* area. Select **50.000000** in the *Value* area. Open the instance.

7. Close the window and erase it from memory.

8. Open a **hex_bolt** instance with a grip length of **6.0** and an overall length of **65.0**. What is the name of this instance?

9. Save the part and erase it from memory.

Chapter Review Questions

1. A family table can be created for any model by adding which type of item? (Select all that apply.)

   a. Dimensions

   b. Group

   c. Parameters

   d. Features

2. Which icon is used to patternize and create additional instances with varying values for selected items?

   a.

   b.

   c.

   d.

3. Which symbol or icon indicates multi-level family tables or nested family tables?

   a. Y

   b. There is no icon or symbol.

   c. *

   d.

4. Any modifications to items that do not belong to the family table cannot be modified in an instance.

   a. True

   b. False

5. Adding a new feature to the generic results in which of the following scenarios?

   a. Creates an additional column in the family table.

   b. Adds the new feature to only the generic.

   c. Adds the new feature to the generic and is reflected in all of the instances.

   d. Cannot add a new feature to the generic.

6. Adding a new feature to an instance results in which of the following scenarios?

    a. Creates an additional column in the family table.

    b. Adds the new feature to only the generic and that instance.

    c. Adds the new feature to the generic and is reflected in all of the instances.

    d. Cannot add a new feature to an instance.

7. If a feature is deleted from an instance, which of the following scenarios might occur? (Select all that apply.)

    a. If the feature exists in the family table, the value of the instance is changed to **N**.

    b. If the feature does not exist in the family table, the item is added to the family table and the value is changed to **N**. The generic is assigned the value of **Y** and all of the other instances are assigned as * to maintain the same status as the generic.

    c. Cannot delete a feature from an instance.

    d. The feature is removed from the family table.

8. If a feature is deleted from the generic, which of the following scenarios might occur?

    a. If the item is a family table item, the value of the generic is changed to **N**.

    b. Cannot delete a feature from the generic.

    c. The feature is removed from the generic.

    d. If the item is a family table item, the column is removed from the table.

Answers: 1abcd, 2c, 3d, 4b, 5c, 6a, 7ab, 8d

Sharing Data

Creo Parametric provides several methods for distributing the geometry of one model into another one. These methods are known as data sharing. Two data sharing methods (Inheritance and Merge/Cut Out), enable you to add or remove material from the current model. Both can copy the geometry as dependent or independent. The inheritance method provides you with access to individual features, which form the copied geometry, and enables you to work with them independently on the original model. The Merge/Cut Out method copies the geometry as a single item.

Learning Objectives in This Chapter

- Create an external Merge feature that contains associate model geometry without a common assembly.
- Create an external inheritance feature that copies all of the geometry and feature data from a source model into a target model.

14.1 Merge Feature

An external merge feature is similar to a merge feature in Assembly mode. However, an external merge feature can be created without creating a common assembly. By using the external merge feature, you can add an associative feature that contains all of the geometry from the source model.

The external merge feature adds material to existing model geometry, as shown in Figure 14–1. The external cut out feature removes material, as shown in Figure 14–2.

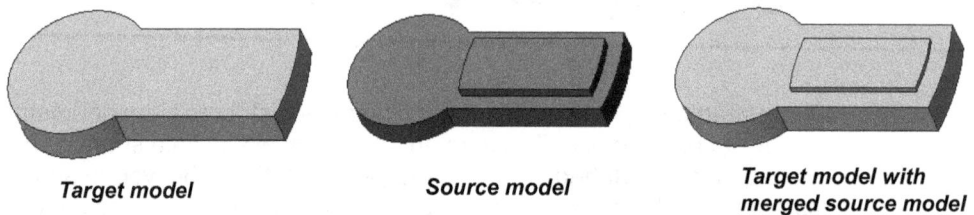

Target model   *Source model*   *Target model with merged source model*

Figure 14–1

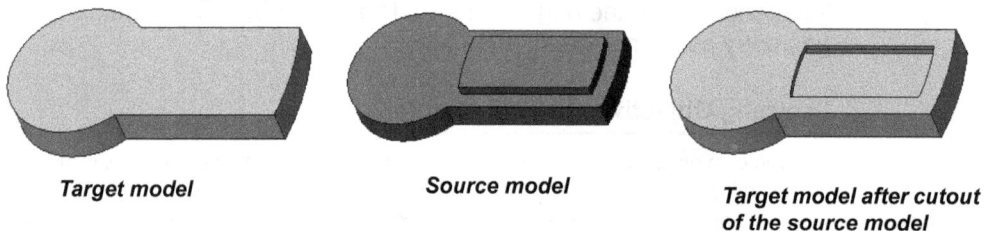

Target model   *Source model*   *Target model after cutout of the source model*

Figure 14–2

General Steps

Use the following general steps to create a merge/cut out feature:

1. Start the creation of the merge/cut out feature.
2. Open the reference model and assemble it.
3. Constrain the reference model.
4. Set the feature options.
5. Specify the material removal, if required.
6. Complete the feature.

Step 1 - Start the creation of the merge/cut out feature.

To create a merge/cut out feature, select **Get Data>Merge/ Inheritance** in the *Model* tab while working on the part.

The *Merge/Inheritance* tab displays as shown in Figure 14–3 and the system prompts you to open a reference model.

Figure 14–3

Step 2 - Open the reference model and assemble it.

Specify the reference model to open by clicking 🗁 (Open File) in the *Merge/Inheritance* dashboard, and selecting the reference model. The reference model displays in a small separate window. The Component Placement dialog box also opens to enable the reference model to be constrained. The Model Tree for the feature also displays below the current Model Tree.

Step 3 - Constrain the reference model.

Constrain the reference model in the current model using the Component Placement dialog box, as shown in Figure 14–4.

(Specify Placement) in the tab enables you to redefine the assembly constraints.

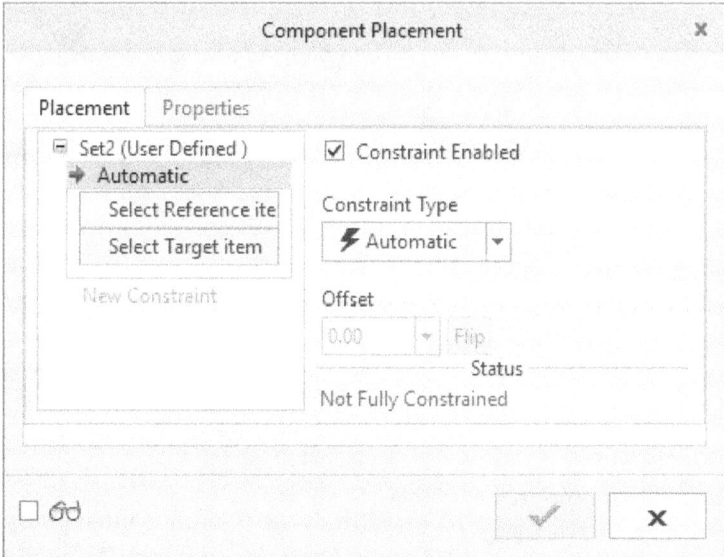

Figure 14–4

Step 4 - Set the feature options.

The Options panel shown in Figure 14–5 enables you to specify a dependency of the external merge feature on the original reference model by selecting the **Automatic Update** (default) or **Manual Update** option.

*You can also right-click and select **Automatic Update** (default) or **Manual Update**.*

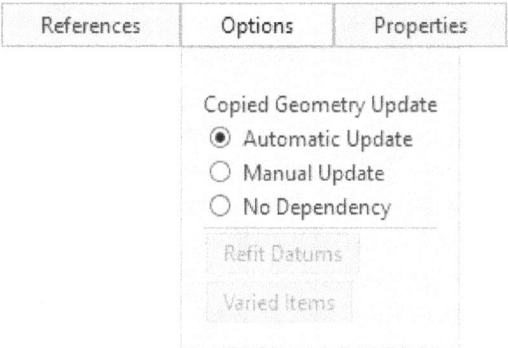

Figure 14–5

Step 5 - Specify the material removal, if required.

Click ⬚ (Remove Material) in the *Merge/Inheritance* dashboard to create a cutout feature. Click ⬚ (Add Material) to return to the external merge feature.

Step 6 - Complete the feature.

To complete the feature, click ✔ (OK) in the dashboard.

The external merge feature displays in the Model Tree as a single item, as shown in Figure 14–6. The external merge feature cannot be modified in the target part.

- When the geometry is merged, the Model Tree of the target part lists a single external merge feature for the copied geometry. The copied geometry cannot be modified in the target part.

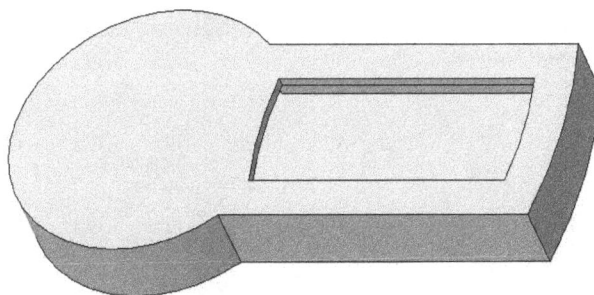

Figure 14–6

14.2 Inheritance Feature

An inheritance feature enables you to associatively copy all of the geometry and feature data of one part (the source model) into another part (the target model). The inheritance feature is similar to the **Merge** operation, but provides greater control of the geometry in the target model. The geometry of the source model can be added or removed from the target model.

When the geometry is copied using an inheritance feature, the Model Tree of the target part lists the inheritance feature and can be expanded to display the list of copied features. An example of the creation of the inheritance feature is shown in Figure 14–7.

The linkage shown is copied into the **LINK_MACHINED.PRT** using an inheritance feature. Features that form the external inheritance feature can be modified in the target part.

When the geometry is copied using an inheritance feature, the Model Tree of the target part lists the inheritance feature and can be expanded to display the list of copied features.

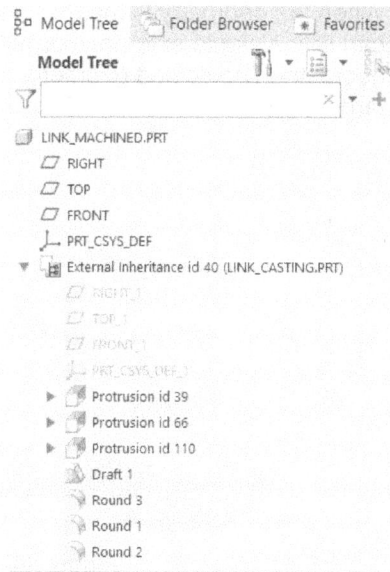

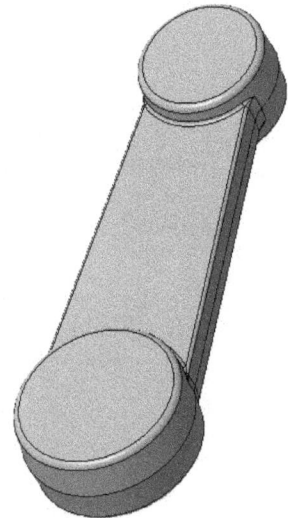

Figure 14–7

Inheritance features can only be created in a model that has the same units as the source model.

When creating an inheritance feature, you can specify dimensions that can be varied from within the target model. You can also specify features where the status (i.e., suppressed or regenerated) can be selected. Changes made to the inherited geometry in the target part do not affect the geometry of the base part. Conversely, changes made to the geometry of the base model are updated in the inherited geometry of the target model.

An inheritance feature displays in the Model Tree and can be expanded to display its included features.

Inheritance features are beneficial in analysis and manufacturing applications. Because you can control and modify features in the inherited model without affecting the source model, you can avoid having to create a family table and saving your model as a new version. For example, an NC model can be created and all of the rounds can be removed in the inherited model. This one-way associativity prevents any changes from being made to the design model.

General Steps

Use the following general steps to create an inheritance feature:

1. Start the creation of the inheritance feature.
2. Open the reference model.
3. Constrain the reference model.
4. Select an inheritance icon.
5. Set the feature options.
6. Specify the material removal, if required.
7. Complete the feature.

Step 1 - Start the creation of the inheritance feature.

To create an inheritance feature, select **Get Data>Merge/Inheritance**. The *Merge/Inheritance* dashboard displays as shown in Figure 14–8 and the system prompts you to open a reference model.

Figure 14–8

Step 2 - Open the reference model.

Specify the reference model to open by clicking 📂 (Open File) in the *Merge/Inheritance* dashboard, and selecting the reference model. The reference model displays in a separate window. The Component Placement dialog box also opens to enable the reference model to be constrained.

Step 3 - Constrain the reference model.

(Specify Placement) in the tab enables you to redefine assembly constraints.

Constrain the reference model in the current model using the Component Placement dialog box, as shown in Figure 14–9.

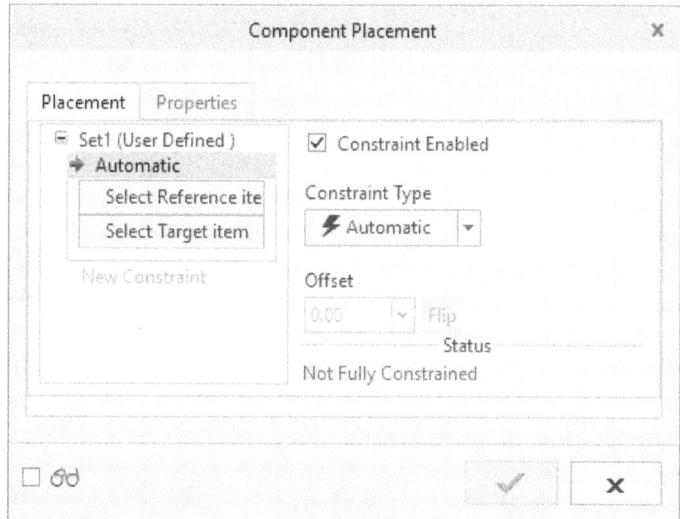

Figure 14–9

Step 4 - Select an inheritance icon.

By default, an external merge feature is created. Click (Toggle Inheritance) in the dashboard to specify that you want to create the inheritance feature. Click (Toggle Inheritance) again to return to the external merge feature.

Step 5 - Set the feature options.

*You can also right-click and select **Dependent**.*

The Options panel shown in Figure 14–10, enables you to specify a dependency of the external merge/cut out feature in the original reference model by selecting the **Dependent** option.

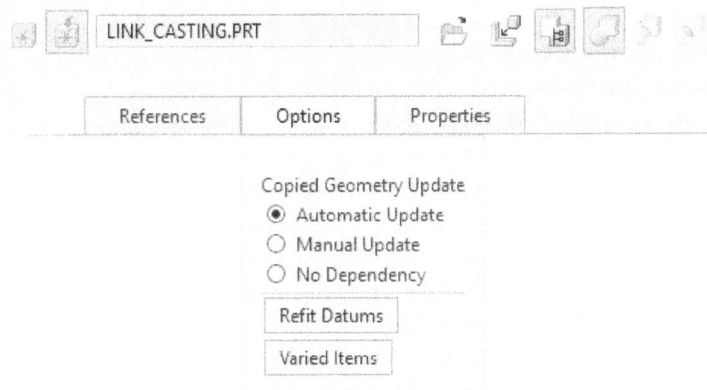

Figure 14–10

Varied Items

Click **Varied Items** in the Options panel to specify any varied items. You can also right-click and select **Varied Items**. A window containing the reference model and the Varied Items dialog box opens.

For example, to specify varied dimensions, select the *Dimensions* tab and select dimensions in the separate model window. The selected dimensions are listed in the *Dimensions* tab, as shown in Figure 14–11. Use the *New Value* column to enter the new dimension values.

You can only select a varied item in the separate window if

✚ *(Add) is depressed. To remove a varied item from the list, select it*

and click ▬ *(Remove).*

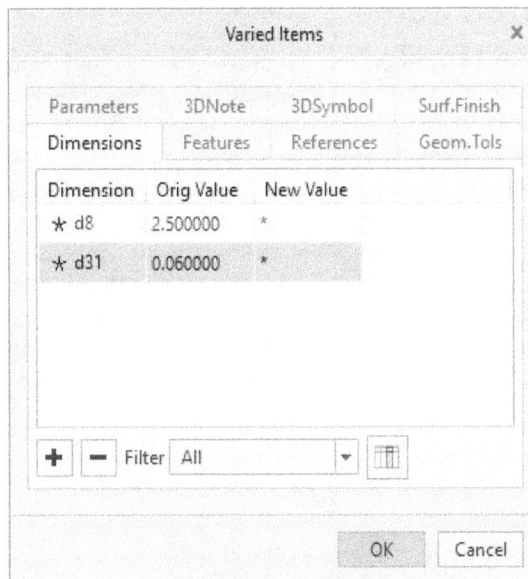

Figure 14–11

You can only select a varied item in the separate window, if ✚ is depressed. To remove a varied item from the list, select it and click ▬.

To specify varied features, activate the *Features* tab and select the features to vary in the separate model window. The selected features are listed in the *Features* tab, as shown in Figure 14–12. Use the *New Status* column to select one of the predefined values: **Resumed**, **Suppressed**, or **Erased**.

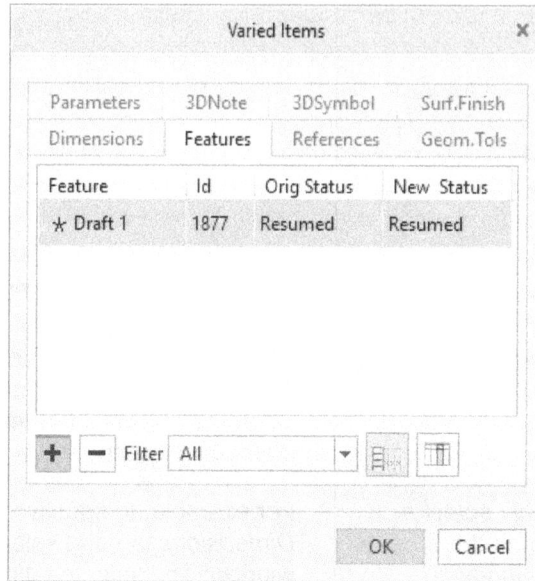

Figure 14–12

Varied Items Outside the Tab

Items can also be varied once the **Inheritance** feature has been placed. For example, to specify a varied dimension, select the feature in the Model Tree, right-click and select **Edit**. Select the dimension in the Graphics window, right-click and select **Value**. Select **Yes** at the *Please confirm adding this dimension to the Inherited Vardim table* prompt and enter the new dimension value. The dimension is added to the *Dimension* tab in the Varied Items dialog box.

To specify a varied feature, select the feature in the Model Tree, right-click and select **Suppress**, and confirm the suppress action. The feature is added into *Features* tab in the Varied Items dialog box in the *Suppressed* status.

Step 6 - Specify the material removal, if required.

To create an external inheritance cut feature click ◿ (Remove Material) in the *Merge/Inheritance* dashboard. Click ◿ (Remove Material) again to return to the external inheritance feature.

Step 7 - Complete the feature.

Click ✓ (OK) in the dashboard to complete the feature.

Practice 14a | Inheritance Features

Practice Objectives

- Create an inheritance feature and note that the individual features are located in the Model Tree.
- Modify the new features in the new part and note that the changes did not affect the source model.
- Note that the associativity is one-way, by modifying the source model and noting the new part changes.

In this practice, you will create a new part that represents a cast part post-machining. You will use the inheritance feature to capture this design intent.

Task 1 - Open a part file.

1. Set the working directory to the *Inheritance_Features* folder

2. Open **link_casting.prt**.

3. Set the model display as follows:

- ⅍ *(Datum Display Filters)*: All Off

- ⌖ *(Spin Center)*: Off

- ▢ *(Display Style)*: ▢ (Shading With Edges)

Design Considerations

The **link_casting** part is a cast part and is represented in its cast state. Display the features in the Model Tree and note that the part has draft and rounds.

Task 2 - Create a new part file and insert an inheritance feature.

1. Create a new part named **link_machined**.

2. Select **Get Data>Merge/Inheritance** to create an inheritance feature.

3. Click 📂 (Open File) in the *Merge/Inheritance* dashboard, and sele⟨
   link_casting.prt as the model from which to inherit the geometry.
   Click **Open**.

4. In the Component Placement dialog box, select **Default** in the
   Constraint Type drop-down list and click ✔ (OK).

5. Click 📇 (Toggle Inheritance) in the dashboard to specify that you
   want to create an inheritance feature.

6. Click ✔ (OK) in the *Merge/Inheritance* dashboard.

7. Expand the inheritance feature in the Model Tree to display the
   individual features from the source model, as shown in
   Figure 14–13.

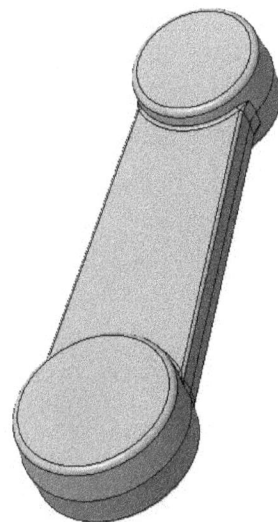

Figure 14–13

Task 3 - Create machined features.

**Design
Considerations**

In this task, you will create two holes that represent the part in a
post-machined state.

1. Enable the display of datum axes.

2. Create a **1.25** diameter through all coaxial hole, as shown in Figure 14–14.

3. Create a **1.75** diameter through all coaxial hole, as shown in Figure 14–15.

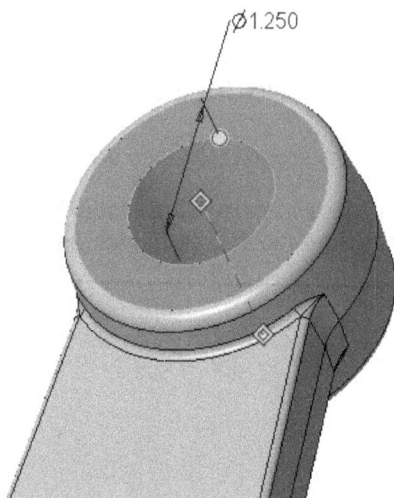

Figure 14–14

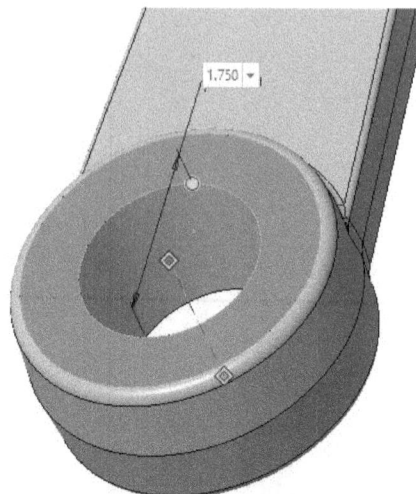

Figure 14–15

The machined part displays as shown in Figure 14–16.

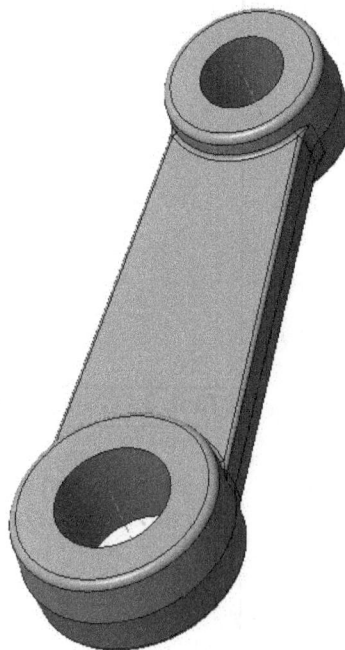

Figure 14–16

4. Switch to the **link_casting.prt** window. The casting part remains unchanged.

5. Edit the base feature (**Protrusion id 39**) and change the *Length* value of *10* to **12**, as shown in Figure 14–17.

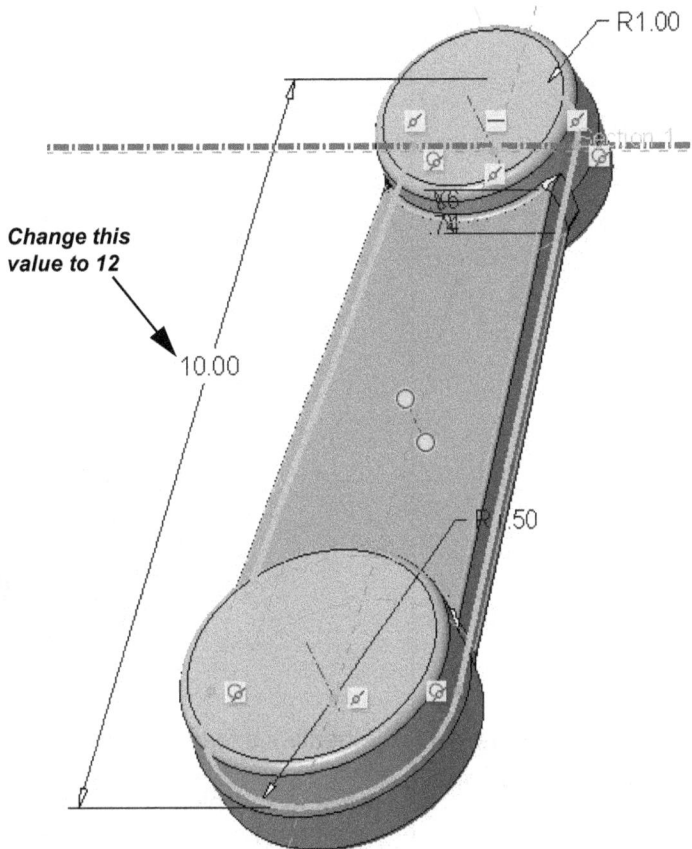

Change this value to 12

R1.00

10.00

R1.50

Figure 14–17

6. Regenerate the part.

7. Switch to the **link_machined.prt** window and regenerate. The part displays as shown in Figure 14–18.

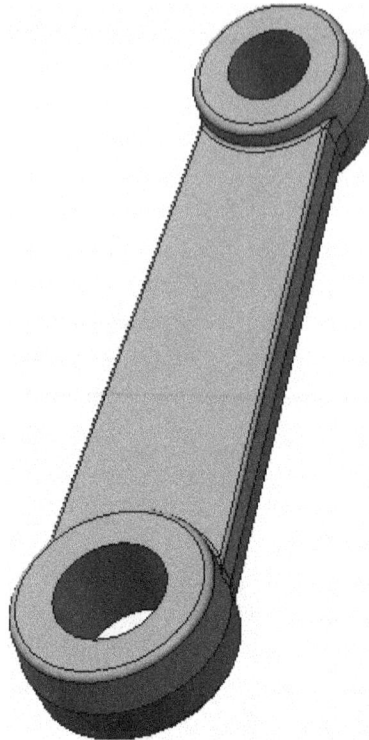

Figure 14–18

Design Considerations

Inheritance features provide one-way associativity. They offer functionality that enables features to be created in the target part while maintaining the original geometry in the source part. Additionally, changes made to the source part are reflected in the target part.

8. Save both parts and erase them from memory.

Practice 14b | Merge to Remove Material

Practice Objectives

- Merge independent geometry into the target model using constraints.
- Modify the source file to ensure that the changes are not reflected in the merged geometry of the target model.
- Change the merged geometry to Dependent and ensure that the geometry changes are reflected in the target model.
- Merge dependent geometry into the target model to remove material.

In this practice you will create a merge feature to cut out material from a security key-fob, as shown in Figure 14–19.

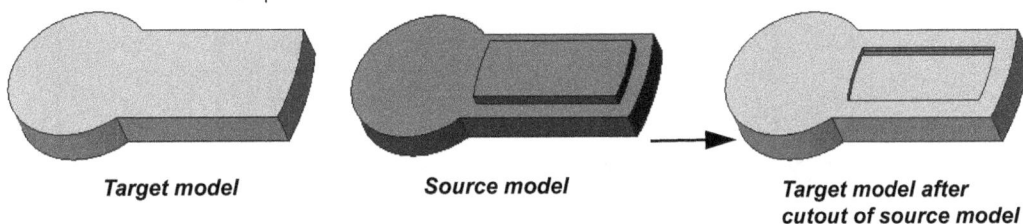

Target model   *Source model*   *Target model after cutout of source model*

Figure 14–19

Task 1 - Open a part file.

1. Set the working directory to the *Merge_Remove* folder.

2. Open **window.prt**.

3. Set the model display as follows:
    - ⚹ *(Datum Display Filters)*: ↳ (Csys Display) only
    - ⤙ *(Spin Center)*: Off
    - ◻ *(Display Style)*: ▱ (Shading With Edges)

4. Review the model which displays as shown in Figure 14–20.

This will be used to hollow out and create a window in the main part.

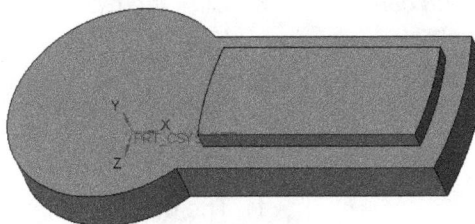

Figure 14–20

5. Close the part.

Task 2 - Create an independent external merge feature.

1. Open **cover.prt**.

2. Select **Get Data>Merge/Inheritance**.

3. Click 📂 (Open File) in the *Merge/Inheritance* tab and select **window.prt** as the model you want to merge into **cover.prt**.

4. Click **Open**.

5. Change the constraint type to **Coincident** in the Component Placement dialog box

6. Select the coordinate system **PRT_CSYS_DEF** in the cover and window parts, as shown in Figure 14–21.

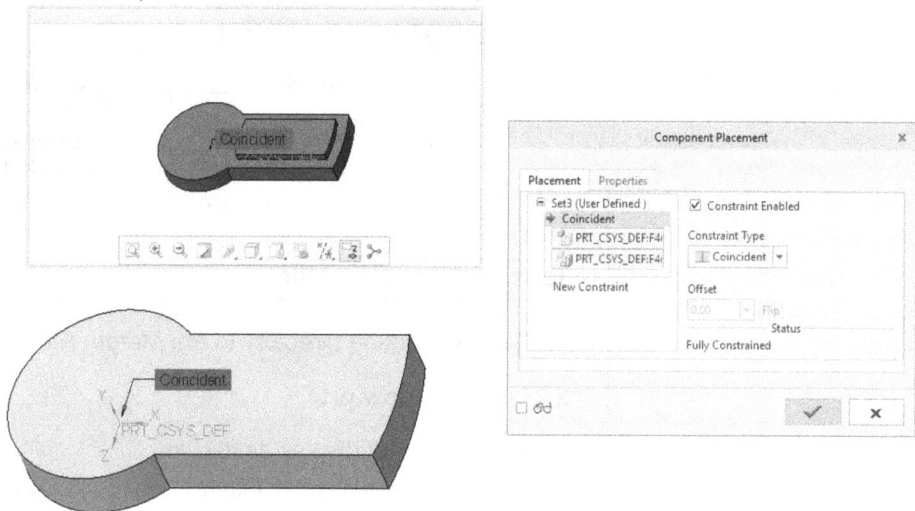

Figure 14–21

7. Once you have defined the assembly constraint, click ✓ (OK) to close the Component Placement dialog box.

*Alternatively, you can clear the **Dependent** option in the Options panel.*

8. Click the Options panel, and note that the dependency is set to Automatic Updates.

9. Click 🗗 (Remove Material) in the dashboard.

10. Click ✓ (OK).

11. The model displays as shown in Figure 14–22.

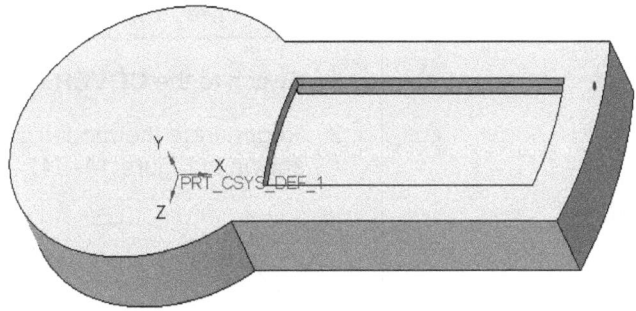

Figure 14–22

Task 3 - Modify window.prt.

1. Open **window.prt**.

2. Select the **Extrude 2** feature in the Model Tree and select
   $\overset{\longleftrightarrow}{d1}$ (Edit Dimensions) in the mini toolbar.

3. Edit the *3.00* dimension to **5.00** as shown in Figure 14–23.

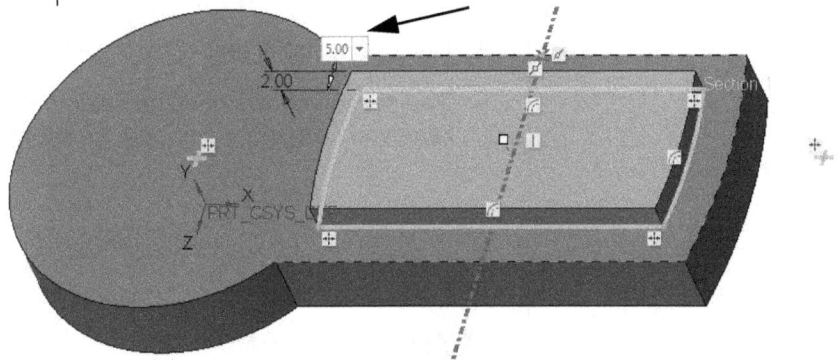

Figure 14–23

4. Regenerate the model.

Task 4 - Verify the dependence of the window in the cover.

1. Switch to the **COVER.PRT** window.

2. Regenerate the model. The model geometry updates as shown in Figure 14–24.

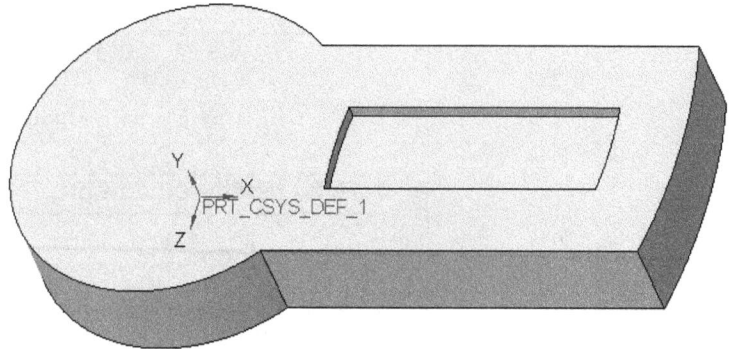

Figure 14–24

3. In the Model Tree, expand Sections.

4. Select Section **A** and click ◆ (Activate) in the mini toolbar.

5. The section shows how the volume of the window part was removed from the cover part, as shown in Figure 14–25.

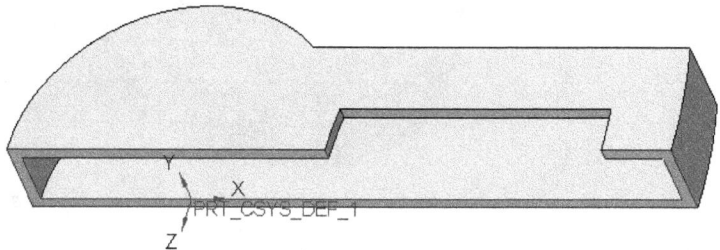

Figure 14–25

6. Save both parts and erase them from memory.

Chapter Review Questions

1. Which of the following advantages are true for an external merge feature? (Select all that apply.)

   a. External merge features can be created without an assembly.

   b. You can add associative features that contain all of the geometry of the source model.

   c. External merge features can add or remove material to the existing model geometry.

   d. External merge features can be converted to surface geometry.

2. Which icon enables you to redefine the assembly constraints used for Merge Features?

   a.

   b.

   c.

   d.

3. The external merge feature displays in the Model Tree as a single item and cannot be modified in the target part.

   a. True

   b. False

4. Which of the following is a true statement about the external inheritance feature? (Select all that apply.)

   a. You can specify dimensions that can be varied from within the target model.

   b. Changes made to the inherited geometry in the target part do not affect the geometry of the base part.

   c. Changes made to the inherited geometry in the target part do affect the geometry of the base part.

   d. Changes made to the geometry of the base model are updated in the inherited geometry of the target model.

5. Which icon enables you to create an inheritance feature?

   a.

   b.

   c.

   d.

Chapter

15

Part View Manager

The View Manager enables you to create various display states of a part, all in the same part file. Simplified representations can be used to simplify the part and reduce retrieval time as well as create a state representative of a stage in the design process. Combination states can be created with a combination of a cross-section, simplified representation, and/or orientation. These states are saved with the part file and can be used for drawing view creation.

Learning Objectives in This Chapter

- Learn the two types of cross-sections that can be created in a part, assembly, and drawing.
- Learn how to create a 3D cross-section in the drawing by creating a Zone in the part or assembly.
- Learn the system-defined simplified representations that are created automatically and can be used to simplify large assemblies.
- Learn to create a user-defined simplified representation to simplify the display and add the representation to the drawing.
- Define different appearance states for your model using the *Appearance* tab in the View Manager dialog box.
- Create a combination state using the View Manager dialog box to define an orientation, simplified representation, and cross-section.

15.1 3D Cross-sections

A cross-section defines a slice through a model as shown in Figure 15–1. Cross-sections can be created in both parts and assemblies using the View Manager dialog box. Two types of cross-sections that can be created and used in a drawing are as follows.

Option	Description
Planar	A planar cross-section is created using a datum plane in the location of the required slice, as shown on the left in Figure 15–1.
Offset	An offset cross-section is created by sketching a cut line to define the required cross-section, as shown on the right in Figure 15–1.

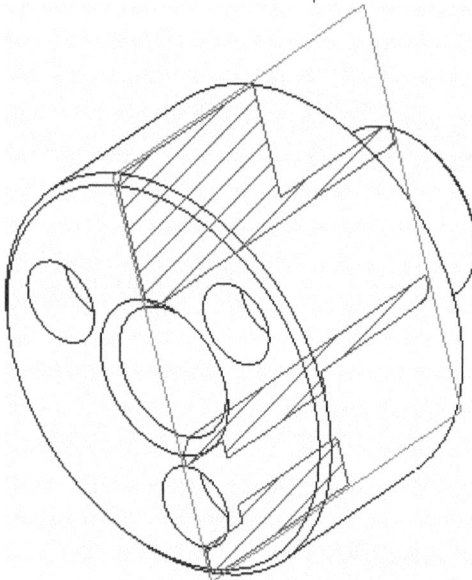

Planar cross-section

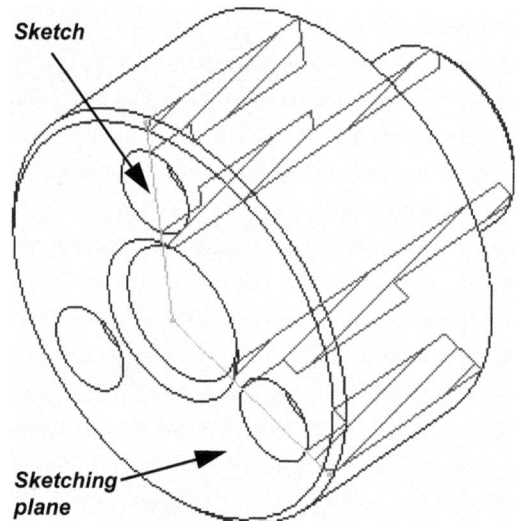

Sketch

Sketching plane

Offset cross-section

Figure 15–1

3D Cross-sections

To create a 3D Cross-section in a view you have to create a zone in the 3D object. The differences between using 3D or 2D cross-sections are as follows:

- In the 2D cross-section you cannot switch off hatching and the projection and auxiliary views are not included in the section.

- By default, in the 3D cross-section, hatching is switched off (optional) and the projection and auxiliary views are also included. Dependent views reference the scale and orientation and the 3D cross-section of the parent view.

- In the 3D cross-section you cannot display the section's arrows.

Creating a Zone

Zones are typically used in Simplified Representations. However, you can also use them as 3D cross-sections in a drawing. You can create zones similar to cross-sections in parts/assemblies.

How To: Create a Zone

1. Select the *View* tab. Expand (Section) and select **Zone**.
2. Zones can be defined based on planar surfaces, closed surfaces, within a specified distance from an entity, and offset from a coordinate system. These options are selected in the drop-down list at the bottom of the dialog box. Zones used to define 3D cross-sections are typically defined by auxiliary planes or opened quilt surfaces, as shown in Figure 15–2.

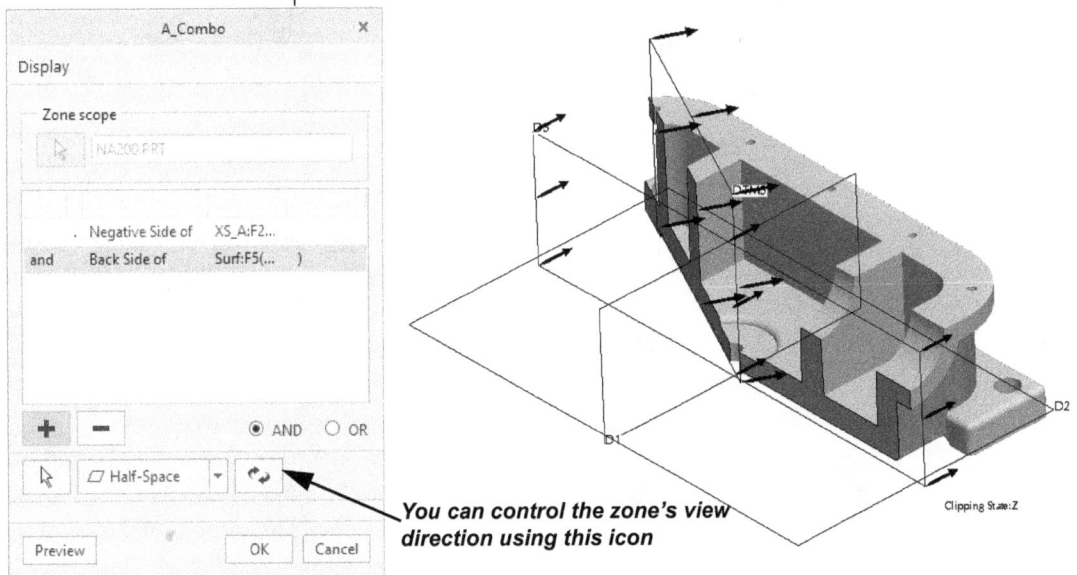

You can control the zone's view direction using this icon

Figure 15–2

3. Click ✚ (Add Reference) to continue adding references to define the zone. You can combine multiple conditions with different reference types to complete the zone. To remove a zone condition click ━ (Remove Reference).
4. Once the zone has been defined, click **OK** to close the dialog box.

How To: Place a Zone in a Drawing

1. To create a view with a 3D cross-section in the drawing you must first place a General view.
2. Right-click on the general view and select **Properties**. In the Drawing View dialog box, select the **Sections** category.
3. Select the **3D Cross-section** option, and select the previously created zone in the drop-down list, as shown in Figure 15–3.

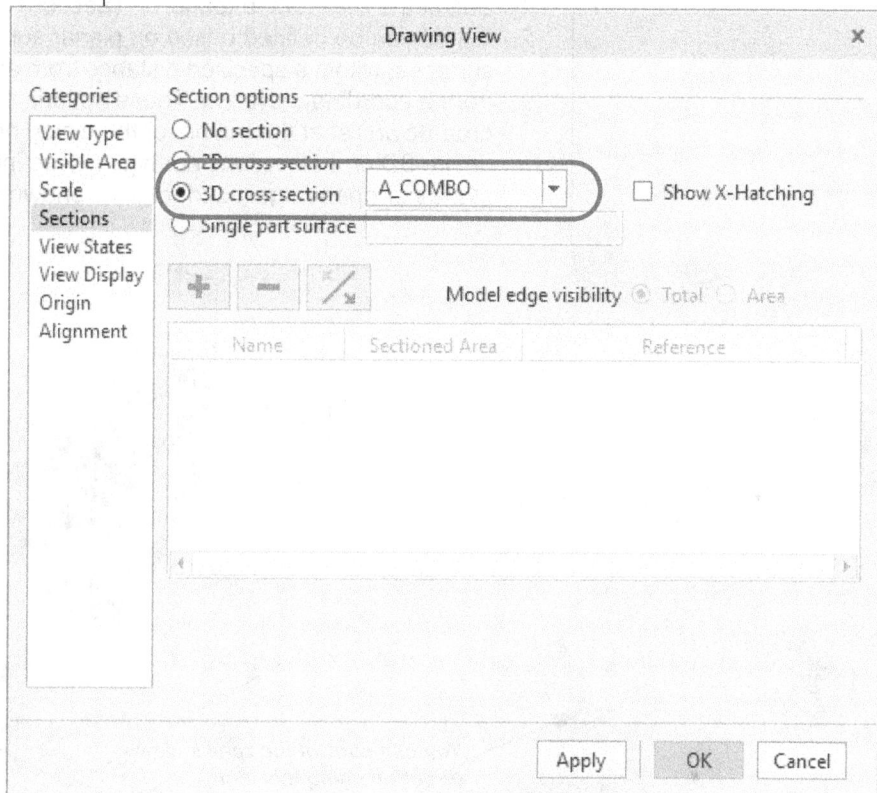

Figure 15–3

4. Select the **Show X-Hatching** option to display cross-hatching on the drawing view, as shown in Figure 15–4.

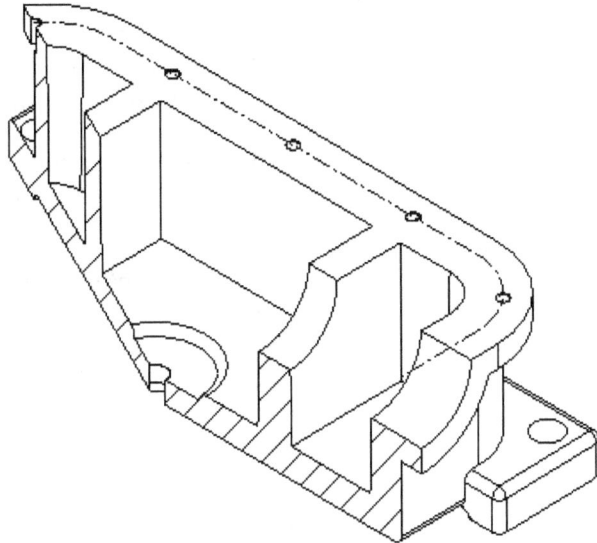

1:2

Figure 15–4

Orientation of such a view and creation of its projection views follows the same rules as standard views. The only difference is that these projection/auxiliary views also reference the 3D cross-section of the parent view.

15.2 System-Defined Simplified Representations

Parts have two system-defined Simplified Representation states:

- The Master representation (**Master Rep**) is the default representation of the model, and contains all part geometry.

- The Automatic representation (**Automatic Rep**) retrieves the minimum required data into session and is used to retrieve your part as fast as possible.

Note that only features included in the representation are retrieved in an Automatic representation, and all other features remain excluded. If you have worked with Simplified Representations in Creo Parametric 3.0 or earlier, you should be aware that the representation types such as Symbolic, Graphic, Geometry and so on are now obsolete.

You can control the handling of simplified representations from previous releases using the configuration option *hide_pre_creo4_reps*:

- **yes:** Hides all simplified representations created in Creo Parametric 3.0 and earlier, except for **Exclude** simplified representations. By default, when opening a part, it opens as an Automatic representation.

- **no:** Maintains all simplified representations for Creo 3.0 and earlier.

- **maintain_master:** (Default) Hides all simplified representations for Creo 3.0 and earlier, except for **Master** and **Exclude** simplified representations.

15.3 User-Defined Simplified Representations

You can create user-defined simplified representations in an assembly to simplify the display and help ease the regeneration times of working with large assemblies.

General Steps

Use the following general steps to create and display a user-defined simplified representation:

1. Open the View Manager.
2. Create a new simplified representation.
3. Define the representation settings.
4. Save the simplified representation.
5. Redefine the simplified representation, as required.

Step 1 - Open the View Manager.

User-defined simplified representations are created in View Manager. To open View Manager, click ▣ (View Manager) in the In-graphics toolbar, or select the *Tools* tab, click ▣ (Manage Views), and select the *Simp Rep* tab.

Step 2 - Create a new simplified representation.

To delete a simplified representation, select Edit>Remove or right-click and select Remove.

Click **New** in the *Simp Rep* area in View Manager. Enter a name for the simplified rep and press <Enter>. The new representation is now active, as indicated by the adjacent green arrow.

Step 3 - Define the representation settings.

You can select an edit method for a simplified representation manually using the Model Tree, selecting directly on the model.

The **EDIT METHOD** menu displays as shown in Figure 15–5.

Figure 15–5

Attributes

The **Attributes** option enables you to create an accelerated simplified representation. This permits a saved file to be retrieved more quickly because you retrieve an accelerated version of the file.

Using the **Whole Model** option, the representation uses the entire model and is fully modifiable and associative. An accelerator file is created with an *.XRP extension. Additionally, there can only be one accelerator file per part. Accelerator files are not versioned.

Using the **GeomSnpshot** option shown in Figure 15–6, you cannot make any modifications to features.

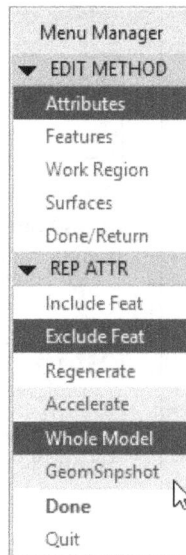

Figure 15–6

Features

The **Features** option shown in Figure 15–7 enables you to exclude features from the part. Unlike suppressing features, excluded features are not affected by parent/child relationships.

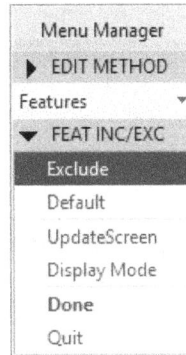

Figure 15–7

Work Regions

A simplified representation that is created using a work region (shown in Figure 15–8) removes a portion of the model from the display. A work region behaves like a cut feature

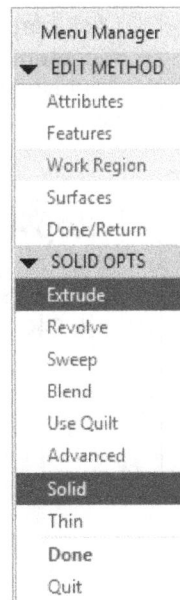

Figure 15–8

Surfaces

The **Surfaces** option enables you to create a simplified representation by copying solid surfaces from the part. When this representation is active (shown in Figure 15–9), only the selected surfaces are visible.

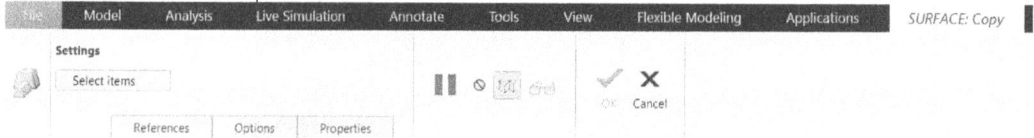

Figure 15–9

To display the Simp Rep settings in the Model Tree, click Options in the Listings page of the View Manager and select Add Column.

The features in the model can be set to one of two settings, accessed by clicking **Properties** in the View Manager. The settings and their icons are described as follows:

Option	Icon	Description
Exclude		Selected features of the master representation are excluded as members of the simplified representation.
Include		Selected features of the master representation are included as members of the simplified representation.

Click **List** to return to the listing of simplified reps. The current representation is temporarily modified with the new settings and displayed with a plus (+) symbol appended to the end of its name.

Step 4 - Save the simplified representation.

To save the changes to the simplified rep, click **Edit>Save** and click **OK**.

Step 5 - Redefine the simplified representation, as required.

You might need to make changes to the simplified representation once it has been created. Click **Edit>Redefine**. The **EDIT METHOD** menu opens, as shown in Figure 15–10.

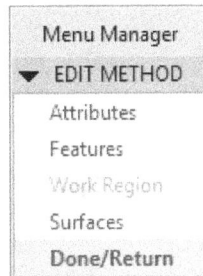

Menu Manager

▼ EDIT METHOD

Attributes

Features

Work Region

Surfaces

Done/Return

Figure 15–10

Drawing Models

To use a part simplified representation in a drawing, select the *Layout* tab and click ✎ (Drawing Models). Select **Set/Add Rep** in the **DWG MODELS** menu, as shown in Figure 15–11. This Simplified Representation is used for all new views until a different representation is selected.

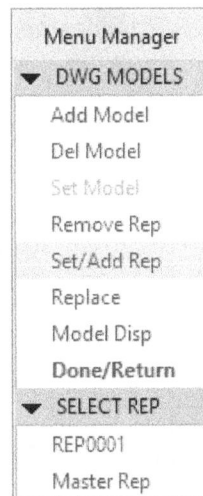

Menu Manager

▼ DWG MODELS

Add Model

Del Model

Set Model

Remove Rep

Set/Add Rep

Replace

Model Disp

Done/Return

▼ SELECT REP

REP0001

Master Rep

Figure 15–11

To remove a Simplified Representation from the drawing, you must first delete all of the views in which it is included and then select the *Layout* tab, click ✎ (Drawing Models), and select **Remove Rep**.

15.4 Appearance States

You can define different appearance states for your model using the *Appearance* tab in the View Manager dialog box. You can define and switch between different color combinations for your designs.

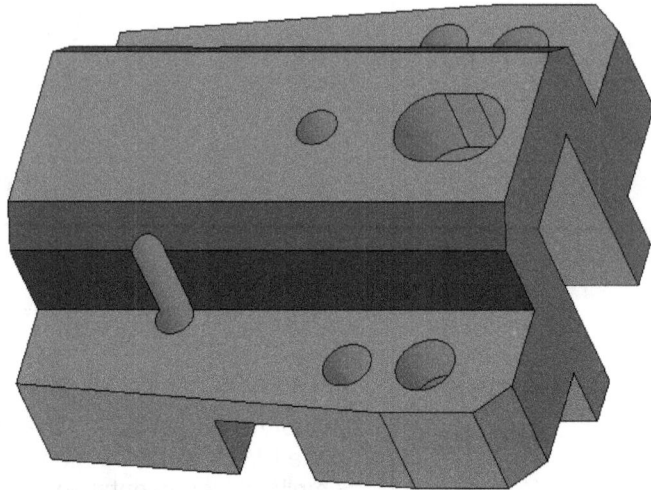

Figure 15–12

Apply appearances to surface or features in your model. In the *Appearance* tab of the View Manager, click **New** and enter a name. You can repeat this for as many different combinations of colors, textures, etc. that you require. This enables you to quickly change the appearance for various use cases.

15.5 View Manager States

Combination states can be created in the *All* tab in the View Manager in a model (part or assembly), and can be used during the placement of a view in a drawing. Combination states enable you to quickly define many properties, such as orientation and simplified representation, in the 3D model and reuse this information when creating 2D views.

The Reference Originals references the original display states (orientation, Simplified Rep, or Cross Sections) or you can select **Create Copies** to create copies of the originals as shown in Figure 15–13.

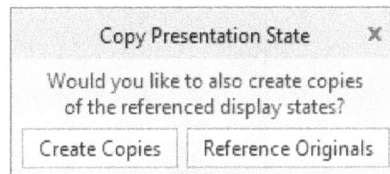

Figure 15–13

Define the required combination of display states as shown in Figure 15–14.

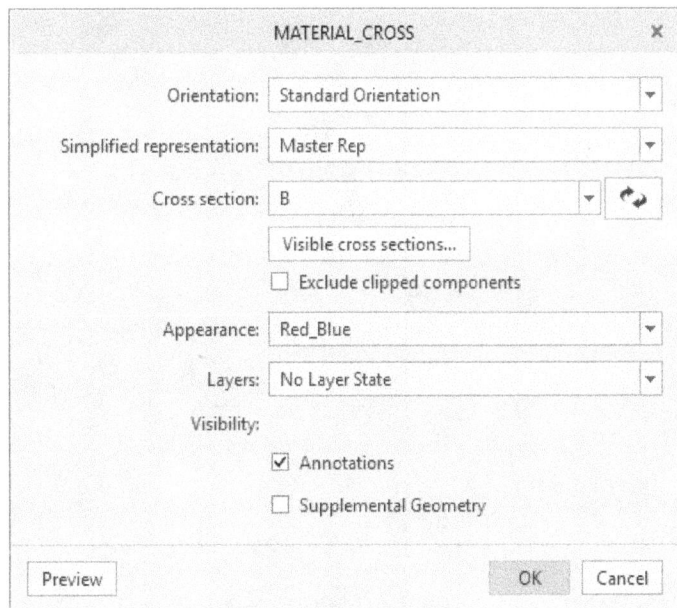

Figure 15–14

During the placement of the General View in the drawing the system prompts you to select one of the named combinations to be used for the view, as shown in Figure 15–15.

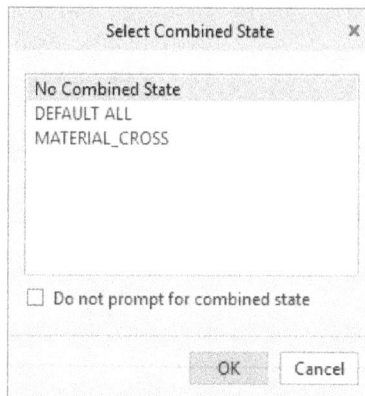

Figure 15–15

Practice 15a	# Part Display States

Practice Objectives

- Create a zone to use in a simplified representation to simplify the model.
- Create a 2D planar section in the part and use it to create a combination state.

In this practice, you will create a 3D cross-section, 2D cross-section, simplified rep, and combination view state.

Task 1 - Open a part file.

1. Set the working directory to the *Part_Display_States* folder.

2. Open **na200.prt**.

3. Set the model display as follows:

    - *(Datum Display Filters)*: All Off

    - *(Spin Center)*: Off

    - *(Display Style)*: (Shading With Edges)

Task 2 - Create a 3D cross-section.

You can also click in the Tools tab.

1. In the In-graphics toolbar, click (View Manager) to open the View Manager.

2. Select the *Sections* tab, expand **New** and select **Zone**.

3. Edit the name to **A_COMBO** and press <Enter>.

4. Select datum plane **XS_A**.

5. Add another plane by clicking ✚ (Add Reference) and select the planar surface shown in Figure 15–16. Click ↻ (Change Orientation) to change the direction of the arrows to point to the part.

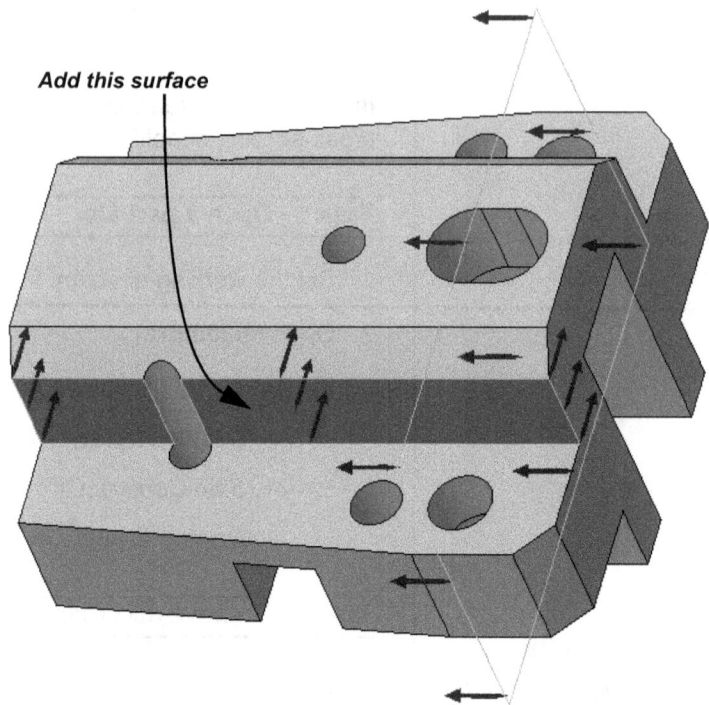

Arrows in all of the Zone references used for the 3D cross-section have to be oriented in the same direction.

Add this surface

Figure 15–16

6. Click **OK**.

7. Expand the **Footer** in the Model Tree to display the zone **A_COMBO**, as shown Figure 15–17.

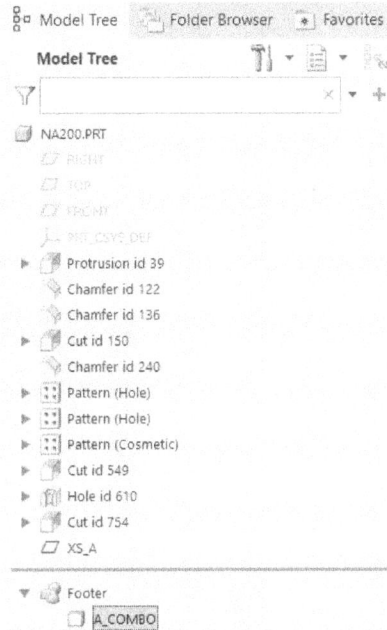

Figure 15–17

8. In the View Manager, double-click on **No Cross Section** to remove the section from display.

Task 3 - Create a simplified representation.

In this task, you will create a simplified rep of the **na200** part. The simplified rep will exclude all of the features except for the base feature. This represents the part in its raw material state, before any machining operations.

1. Select the *Simp Rep* tab.

2. Click **New** to create a new *Simp Rep*. Set the *Name* to **Before_Machining** and press <Enter>.

3. Select **Features** in the **EDIT METHOD** menu. **Exclude** is the default option.

4. Select **Chamfer id 122**, hold <Shift>, and select the datum plane **XS_A** as shown in Figure 15–18.

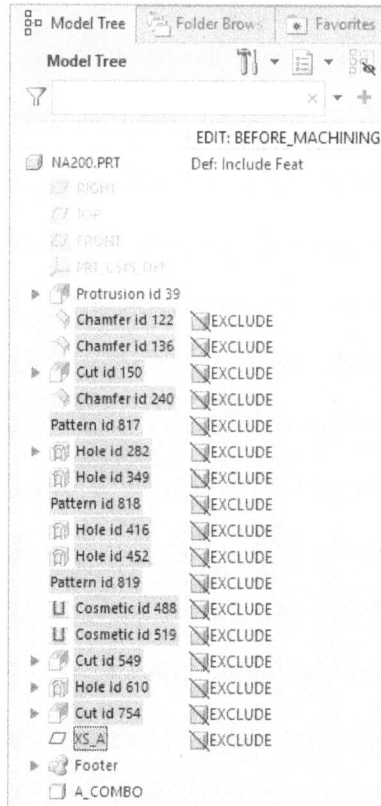

Figure 15–18

5. Select **Done>Done Return**. The part displays as shown in Figure 15–19.

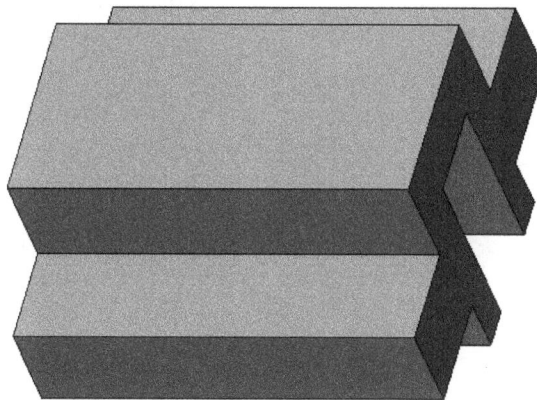

Figure 15–19

Task 4 - Create a 2D cross-section.

1. Double-click on **Master Rep**.

2. Close the View Manager.

3. Create a datum plane **Through** the **HOLE** and **Offset** from **XS_A**, as shown in Figure 15–20. Set the *Offset* value to **315**.

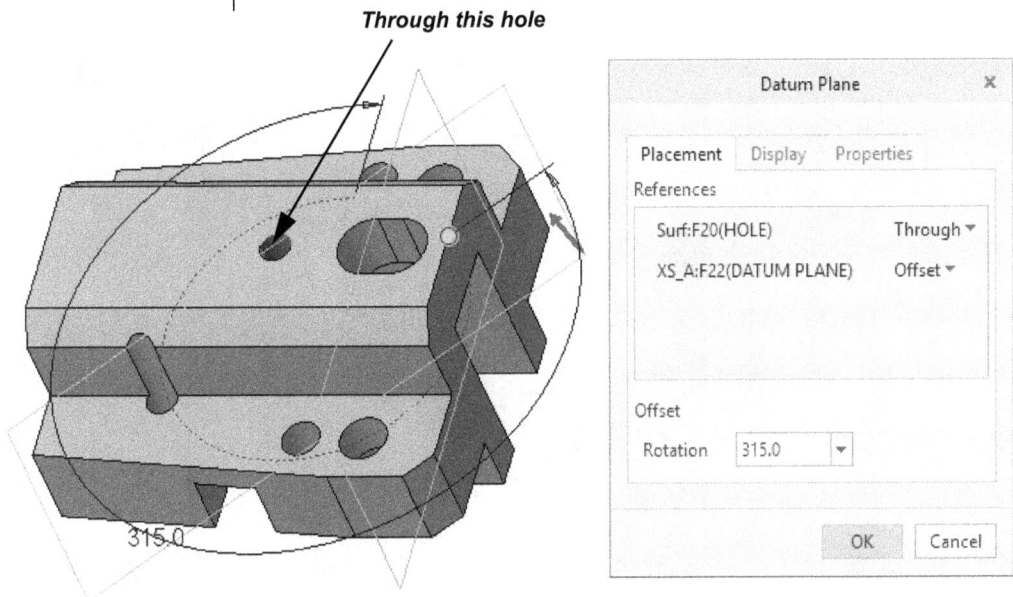

Through this hole

Figure 15–20

4. In the *Properties* tab, set the datum plane *Name* to **XS_B**, as shown in Figure 15–21.

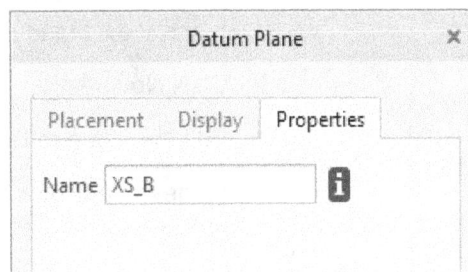

Figure 15–21

5. Click **OK** in the Datum Plane dialog box.

6. In the In-graphics toolbar, click ▦ (View Manager) to open the View Manager.

7. Select the *Sections* tab, expand **New** and **Planar**.

8. Edit the name to **B** and press <Enter>.

9. Complete the section. The part displays as shown in Figure 15–22.

Figure 15–22

10. Select cross-section B in the Model Tree and select ⊗ (Deactivate) in the mini toolbar to remove the section from the display.

Task 5 - Create an Appearance State.

---

1. In the View Manager, select the *Appearance* tab.

2. Click **New**.

3. Edit the name to **Blue_Red** and press <Enter>.

4. In the ribbon, click the *View* tab (leave the View Manager open).

5. Expand ◯ (Appearances) and select ● (ptc-painted-red).

If the indicated colors are not in your color palette, use another color of your choice.

6. Hold control, and select the two surfaces shown in Figure 15–23.

Select these two surfaces

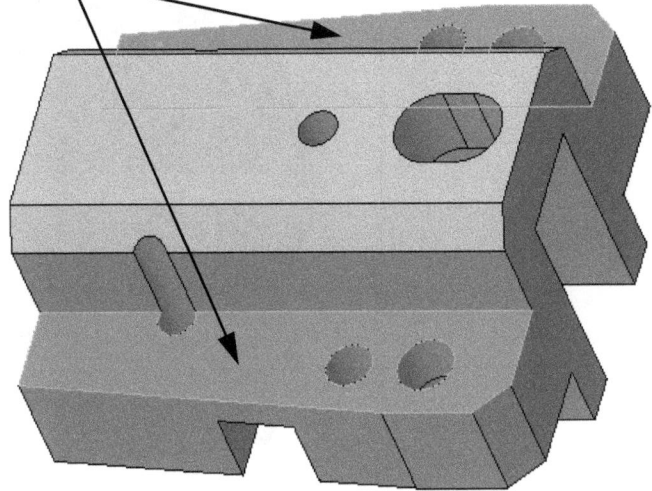

Figure 15–23

7. Press the middle mouse button.

8. Expand ⬤ (Appearances) and select ⬤ (ptc-metallic-blue).

9. Select the surface shown in Figure 15–24.

Select this surface

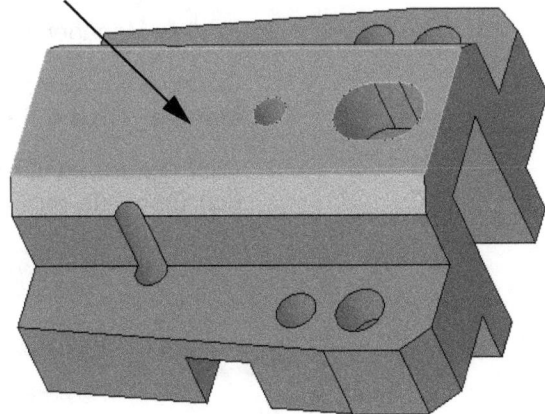

Figure 15–24

10. Press the middle mouse button. The model updates as shown in Figure 15–25.

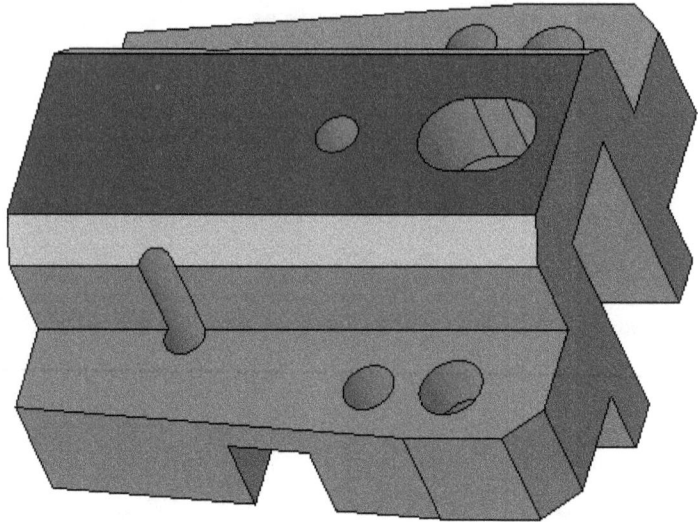

Figure 15–25

Task 6 - Create a combination view state.

In this task, you will create a view state that is a combination of a selected orientation, simplified rep, and cross-section.

1. Open View Manager if it has been closed.

2. In View Manager, select the *ALL* tab.

3. Create a combination state and set the *Name* to **Material_Cross**. Press <Enter>.

4. Click **Reference Originals** in the New Presentation State dialog box, as shown in Figure 15–26.

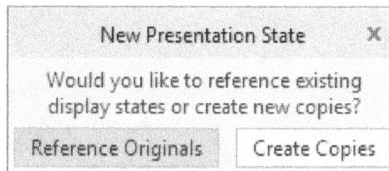

Figure 15–26

5. Select **Edit>Redefine** and enter the parameters shown in Figure 15–27.

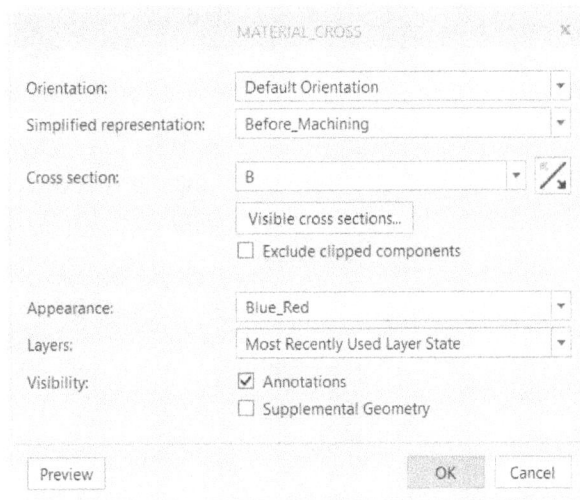

MATERIAL_CROSS		✕
Orientation:	Default Orientation	▼
Simplified representation:	Before_Machining	▼
Cross section:	B	▼
	Visible cross sections...	
	☐ Exclude clipped components	
Appearance:	Blue_Red	▼
Layers:	Most Recently Used Layer State	▼
Visibility:	☑ Annotations	
	☐ Supplemental Geometry	
Preview	OK	Cancel

Figure 15–27

6. Click **OK**. The part in its combination state displays as shown in Figure 15–28.

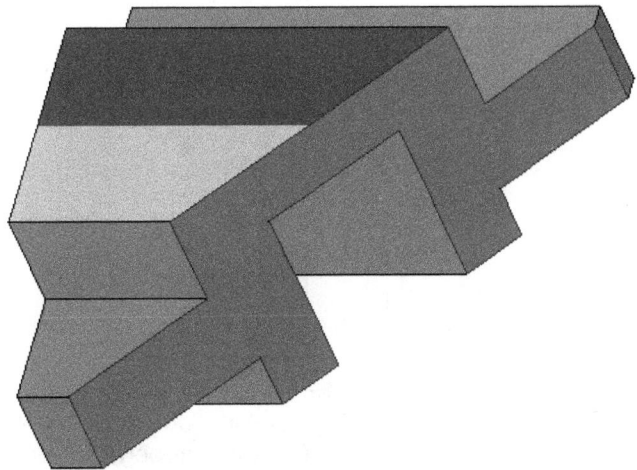

Figure 15–28

7. Save the part and erase it from memory.

Chapter Review Questions

1. Which of the following actions can be initiated in the Model Tree of a part? (Select all that apply.)

   a. Activate a cross-section.

   b. Edit Hatching

   c. Convert a Planar section to an Offset section

   d. Rename a section

2. Which of the following icons enables you to create a zone? (Select all that apply.)

   a.

   b.

   c.

   d.

3. You cannot display a cross-section's arrows on the 3D model.

   a. True

   b. False

4. The Master Rep is the default representation for the part, and it contains all geometry by default.

   a. True

   b. False

5. The Automatic representation retrieves the minimum required data into session, and is used to retrieve your part as fast as possible.

   a. True

   b. False

6. Combination states enable you to quickly define which of the following properties? (Select all that apply.)

   a. Orientation

   b. Simplified Representation

   c. Layers

   d. Cross-section

Answers: 1abd, 2ab, 3a, 4a, 5a, 6abcd

Pro/PROGRAM

Creo Parametric enables you to automate the control of the design intent in a model using relations. Pro/PROGRAM is a tool that is valuable for automating various configurations of similar features. It is also valuable for designers wanting to automate various configurations of part and assembly designs.

Learning Objectives in This Appendix

- Learn to create a part program to automate the design process.
- Learn the different sections of the program and how to make changes to the program.

A.1 Part Pro/PROGRAM

Pro/PROGRAM is a module of Creo Parametric used to automate the design and redesign process of similar models. It enables you to quickly and easily output parametric parts, assemblies, and drawings.

A part created in Creo Parametric automatically generates a program. This default program is a list of steps indicating how the part was created. It consists of features, elements, dimension values, and references arranged in the order in which the model features were created. The program includes subsections where user-defined specifics can be added.

A Creo Parametric part program consists of the following sections:

- Version, revnum, and model name

- Input variables

- Relations

- Features

- Mass properties

These sections are manipulated to automate the design of the model. The generic model must contain all of the features required to create the required design variations.

Figure A–1 shows an example of a default program. Note the sub-sections.

Features are removed from this listing for readability.

```
                              VERSION 3.0
                              REVNUM 702
                              LISTING FOR PART BRACKET
```

Input Section ──────▶
```
                              INPUT
                              END INPUT
```

Relations ──────▶
Section
```
                              RELATIONS
                              END RELATIONS
```

Add Feature ──────▶
Section
```
                              ADD FEATURE (initial number 1)
                              INTERNAL FEATURE ID  1
```

```
                              DATUM PLANE

                                NO.     ELEMENT NAME     INFO
                                ---     ------------     ------------
                                1       Feature Name     Defined
                                2       Constraints      Defined
                                2.1     Constraint #1    Defined
                                2.1.1   Constr Type      X Axis
                                3       Flip Datum Dir   Defined
                                4       Fit              Defined
                                4.1     Fit Type         Default

                              NAME = RIGHT

                                  FEATURE IS IN LAYER(S) :
                                    01___PRT_ALL_DTM_PLN - OPERATION = SHOWN
                                    01___PRT_DEF_DTM_PLN - OPERATION = HIDDEN

                              END ADD

                                . . .
```

Add Another ──────▶
Feature
```
                              ADD FEATURE (initial number 5)
                              INTERNAL FEATURE ID  40
                              PARENTS = 1(#1) 5(#3) 3(#2)
```

```
                              PROTRUSION: Extrude

                                NO.     ELEMENT NAME      INFO
                                ---     ------------      ------------
                                1       Feature Name      Defined
                                2       Extrude Feat type Solid
                                3       Material          Add
                                4       Section           Defined
                                4.1     Setup Plane       Defined
                                4.1.1   Sketching Plane   TOP:F2(DATUM PLANE)
                                4.1.2   View Direction    Side 1
                                4.1.3   Orientation       Right
                                4.1.4   Reference         RIGHT:F1(DATUM PLANE)
                                4.2     Sketch            Defined
                                5       Feature Form      Solid
                                6       Direction         Side 2
                                7       Depth             Defined
                                7.1     Side One          Defined
                                7.1.1   Side One Depth    None
                                7.2     Side Two          Defined
                                7.2.1   Side Two Depth    Variable
                                7.2.2   Value             2.00

                              SECTION NAME = Section 1


                              FEATURE'S DIMENSIONS:
                              d0 = (Displayed:) 2.00
                                   (  Stored:) 2.0 ( 0.01, -0.01 )
                              d2 = (Displayed:) 9.00
                                   (  Stored:) 9.0 ( 0.01, -0.01 )
                              d1 = (Displayed:) 5.50
                                   (  Stored:) 5.5 ( 0.01, -0.01 )
                              END ADD


                              ADD FEATURE (initial number 6)
                              INTERNAL FEATURE ID  67
                              PARENTS = 40(#5)


                              ROUND: General

                                NO.     ELEMENT NAME      INFO
                                ---     ------------      ------------
                                1       Feature Name      Defined
```

Figure A–1

General Steps

Use the following general steps to create a part program:

1. Start the creation of the program.
2. Add input statements.
3. Add relations.
4. Edit the body of the program, as required.
5. Fix errors, as required.
6. Incorporate the changes.
7. Run the program.

Step 1 - Start the creation of the program.

To start the creation of a program, select the *Tools* tab>**Model Intent>Program** to open the **PROGRAM** menu, as shown in Figure A–2.

Figure A–2

Select **Edit Design** in the **PROGRAM** menu to start editing the program. A system editor opens displaying the default program. When editing the design for the first time, the program design is accessed in the model. This is because an edited program file does not exist. Relations that have been added to the model are also displayed in the program.

Step 2 - Add input statements.

When the system editor opens, you can add input statements to the program to prompt the user for information.

The *Input* area at the beginning of the program is denoted by the lines INPUT / END INPUT. It contains input variables that are used to apply parameters in the program. These parameters can be used to drive the design of the part. The input variables that are added must be included within the INPUT / END INPUT lines and must contain the correct syntax. Input statements can contain the following:

- Parameter name

- Parameter type

- Prompt

Input variables must always begin with a parameter name or dimension symbol and can be any one of the three input types as follows.

Input Type	Description
Number	Input contains numeric value.
String	Input contains string of alphanumeric characters. Enables input of parameters or model names, but not user attributes.
Yes_No	Input contains **Yes** or **No** value.

Descriptive prompts can be designed for user inputs. When adding prompts to the program, always do the following:

- Enclose the prompt in quotes.

- Add the prompt immediately after the input variable.

Examples of input statements are shown in Figure A–3.

The current value is always displayed when you are prompted for the new value.

Figure A–3

Step 3 - Add relations.

When you finish adding input statements to the program, you must add relations to relate parameters and dimensions in the model.

The *Relation* area is below the *Input* area in the program, and is denoted by the lines RELATIONS / END RELATIONS. It enables you to create relations between the parameters and dimensions in the program. It contains model relations that were created using the options in the Relation dialog box as well as relations entered when you edited the program.

Relation statements follow input statements, as shown in Figure A–4.

Relations in Pro/PROGRAM can be commented as part and feature relations are commented. Use the /* syntax before the comment.

```
INPUT
diameter number
"Enter the diameter of the counterbore hole."
length number
"Enter the length of the cylinder."
d2 number
"Enter the depth of the counterbore hole."
material string
"Enter the material type."
round yes_no
"Add the round? (yes or no)"
END INPUT

RELATIONS
/* Relations govern the parameter values for the specified dim
outside_dia = d0
thickness = d5
inside_dia = outside_dia – thickness
d6 = length
END RELATIONS
```

Figure A–4

Step 4 - Edit the body of the program, as required.

You can use the program once input statements and relations have been added. However, you might want to edit the body of the program to further build intelligence into the model. You can capture the logic for the required design variations using the following statements:

Conditional Statements

A conditional statement can be included in the input, relation, or main body of the program. You can use IF-ENDIF and IF-ELSE-ENDIF conditional statements in Pro/PROGRAM.

The example shown in Figure A–5 uses conditional statements in the input, relations, and main body of the program.

The user entry in this specific program is denoted with a bullet and all information from the default program displays in bold.

Any features used in a program must be added to the original model. Conditional statements are then used to control the features / components.

*Relations that equate a parameter to a model dimension (e.g., d4 =depth) can be eliminated by renaming the dimension symbol to the parameter name. Select the feature dimension (dimension turns green), right-click and select **Value**, then type in the parameter name. You are prompted to confirm the creation of the relation.*

```
VERSION
REVNUM 1198
LISTING FOR GENERIC PART BRACKET

INPUT
• HOLE YES_NO
• "DO YOU WANT TO ADD THE HOLE?"
• DEPTH NUMBER
• "WHAT IS THE DEPTH OF THE BRACKET?"
END INPUT

RELATIONS
• D15=DEPTH
END RELATIONS
```

> Note: The addition of some features has been removed for readability.

```
• IF DEPTH > 5
ADD FEATURE (initial number 5)
INTERNAL FEATURE ID  709
PARENTS = 45(#4)

ROUND: General
```

NO.	ELEMENT NAME	INFO	STATUS
1	Round Type	Simple	Defined
2	Attributes	Constant, Edge Chain	Defined
3	References		Defined
4	Radius	Value = 0.4000	Defined
5	Round Extent		Optional
6	Attach Type	Make Solid - Feature has solid geometry	Defined

```
FEATURE'S DIMENSIONS:
d51 = .40R
END ADD
• ENDIF
```

> Note: The addition of some features has been removed for readability.

```
• IF HOLE == YES
ADD FEATURE (initial number 11)
INTERNAL FEATURE ID  225
PARENTS = 45(#4)

HOLE
```

NO.	ELEMENT NAME	INFO
1	Hole	Defined
1.1	Hole Type	Defined
1.2	Diameter	Defined
1.3	Depth	Defined
1.3.1	Side One	Defined
1.3.1.1	Side One Depth	Thru Next
1.3.2	Side Two	Defined
1.3.2.1	Side Two Depth	None
1.4	Flip	Defined
2	Placement	Defined
2.1	Primary Reference	Surf:F4(PROTRUSION)
2.2	Placement Type	Coaxial
2.3	CoAxial Reference	A_1(AXIS):F4(PROTRUSION)
3	Feature Name	Defined

```
PLACEMENT = COAXIAL

FEATURE'S DIMENSIONS:
d28 = 4.50 Dia
END ADD
• ENDIF
```

> Note: The addition of some features has been removed for readability.

Figure A–5

Interact Statements

Interact statements can also be used to add components to an assembly. Note that use of the Interact function displays feature creation menus that pre-date Wildfire and Creo Parametric.

Interact statements are similar to the Insert Mode functionality. They can be used to create features in a part. New features can be inserted anywhere between features (i.e., after END ADD and before ADD FEATURE) using an interact statement.

When the program encounters an interact statement, it interrupts the program and regeneration stops. It freezes the model at the time of the interact statement until all of the new features have been added. Once a new feature has been created, Creo Parametric prompts you whether any other features are to be added (*Do you want to insert more features?*). Program execution continues if you select **No**, while **Yes** enables you to continue adding features. When the part finishes regenerating, the feature(s) that have been created replace the interact statement.

In the following example, an interact statement is used so that a new feature can be added. The interact statement can be built into a conditional statement or can be stand-alone. What does the program in Figure A–6 have to look like to incorporate the following conditions?

- HOLE = YES

- DEPTH = 2

- If the DEPTH is less than 5, a Chamfer feature can be added to replace rounded edges that have not been regenerated in the model.

After program execution, the INTERACT statement is removed and replaced with a chamfer feature.

```
VERSION
REVNUM 1198
LISTING FOR GENERIC PART BRACKET

INPUT
HOLE YES_NO
"DO YOU WANT TO ADD THE HOLE?"
DEPTH NUMBER
"WHAT IS THE DEPTH OF THE BRACKET?"
END INPUT

RELATIONS
D15=DEPTH
END RELATIONS
```

... | *Note: The addition of some features has been removed for readability.*

```
IF DEPTH > 5
ADD FEATURE (initial number 5)
INTERNAL FEATURE ID   709
PARENTS = 45(#4)

ROUND: General
```

NO.	ELEMENT NAME	INFO	STATUS
1	Round Type	Simple	Defined
2	Attributes	Constant, Edge Chain	Defined
3	References		Defined
4	Radius	Value = 0.4000	Defined
5	Round Extent		Optional
6	Attach Type	Make Solid - Feature has solid geometry	Defined

```
FEATURE'S DIMENSIONS:
d51 = .40R
END ADD
• ELSE
•  INTERACT
ENDIF
```

... | *Note: The addition of some features has been removed for readability.*

```
IF HOLE == YES
ADD FEATURE (initial number 11)
INTERNAL FEATURE ID   225
PARENTS = 45(#4)

HOLE
```

NO.	ELEMENT NAME	INFO
1	Hole	Defined
1.1	Hole Type	Defined
1.2	Diameter	Defined
1.3	Depth	Defined
1.3.1	Side One	Defined
1.3.1.1	Side One Depth	Thru Next
1.3.2	Side Two	Defined
1.3.2.1	Side Two Depth	None
1.4	Flip	Defined
2	Placement	Defined
2.1	Primary Reference	Surf:F4(PROTRUSION)
2.2	Placement Type	Coaxial
2.3	CoAxial Reference	A_1(AXIS):F4(PROTRUSION)
3	Feature Name	Defined

```
PLACEMENT = COAXIAL

FEATURE'S DIMENSIONS:
d28 = 4.50 Dia
END ADD
ENDIF
```

... | *Note: The addition of some features has been removed for readability.*

Figure A–6

Suppressing Features

Suppressing features in Creo Parametric removes the feature from the display and the regeneration sequence. Features can be suppressed from the program using one of the following methods:

- Use parameters to suppress the feature as shown in Figure A–7.

```
INPUT
HOLE YES_NO
"Do you want to add the hole?"
END INPUT
RELATIONS
END RELATIONS
    .
    .
    .
If HOLE == YES
   ADD FEATURE (initial number 5)
   INTERNAL FEATURE ID  28
   PARENTS = 7(#4)
   HOLE: Straight
   NO. ELEMENT NAME     INFO                    STATUS
   --- ------------ -----------                 ------
    1  Placmnt Type Linear                      Defined
    2  Placmnt Refs                             Defined
    3  Side         One Side                    Defined
    4  Depth        Through All                 Defined
    5  Diameter     D = 2                       Defined
    6  Direction                                Defined
   PLACEMENT = LINEAR
   FEATURE'S DIMENSIONS:
   d5 = 5.00
   d6 = 5.00
   d7 = 2.00 Dia
   END ADD
ENDIF
```

Figure A–7

- Add a **Suppressed** command to the body of the program. as shown in Figure A–8.

*Using the **Suppressed** command is equivalent to selecting features and clicking (Suppress) in the mini toolbar.*

```
INPUT
END INPUT
RELATIONS
END RELATIONS
    .
    .
    .
ADD SUPPRESSED FEATURE (initial number 5)
INTERNAL FEATURE ID  28
PARENTS = 7(#4)
HOLE: Straight
NO. ELEMENT NAME     INFO                    STATUS
--- ------------ -----------                 ------
 1  Placmnt Type Linear                      Defined
 2  Placmnt Refs                             Defined
 3  Side         One Side                    Defined
 4  Depth        Through All                 Defined
 5  Diameter     D = 2                       Defined
 6  Direction                                Defined
PLACEMENT = LINEAR
FEATURE'S DIMENSIONS:
d5 = 5.00
d6 = 5.00
d7 = 2.00 Dia
END ADD
```

Figure A–8

The Model Tree is a good reference for determining which features are suppressed in a model. Figure A–9 shows the Model Tree in the various situations that are encountered when using the **Suppressed** command in a program.

To display suppressed features and their status, you need to modify the Model Tree display, using

$\boxed{\parallel}$ *▾>Tree Columns*

and $\boxed{\parallel}$ *▾>Tree Filters in the Model Tree menu.*

Original Part

Hole 2 suppressed using a parameter and conditional command

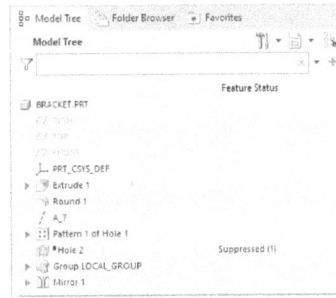

Hole suppressed using Suppressed command

Figure A–9

Reorder and Deletion

The program design is invalid if a member of a pattern is deleted.

Features can be reordered and deleted from the program. To accomplish this, edit the program and delete or rearrange the program as required. Note that feature reordering and deletion can cause the following failures in parent/child relationships:

- Deleting parents causes failures in child features during regeneration.

- Reordering children before parents causes failures during regeneration.

Remember that the order in which features are listed in the program defines the order in which they are regenerated.

Editing Dimensions

Dimensions can be edited directly inside a program using one of the following methods:

- Replace the dimension statement with **MODIFY d# = <value>** as shown in Figure A–10.

```
If HOLE == YES
  ADD FEATURE (initial number 5)
  /* Hole is required if the mass of the model is > 5lbs.
  INTERNAL FEATURE ID  28
  PARENTS = 7(#4)
  HOLE: Straight
   NO. ELEMENT NAME     INFO                                   STATUS
   --- ------------ ----------                                 ------
    1  Placmnt Type Linear                                     Defined
    2  Placmnt Refs                                            Defined
    3  Side         One Side                                   Defined
    4  Depth        Through All                                Defined
    5  Diameter     D = 2                                      Defined
    6  Direction                                               Defined
  PLACEMENT = LINEAR
  FEATURE'S DIMENSIONS:
  Modify d5 = 5.00
  d6 = 5.00
  d7 = 2.00 Dia
  END ADD
ENDIF
```

Figure A–10

- Specify a new value via relations **d# = <value>** as shown in Figure A–11.

```
RELATIONS
/* This equation equates the depth.
D4 = (D2+D4)/2
D4 = DEPTH
"What is the depth of the block?"
D8 = 9
END RELATIONS
```

Figure A–11

Step 5 - Fix errors, as required.

Program files are temporary files saved as <part_name>.pls or <asm_name>.als.

When changes are made to the program and those changes are saved, a program file is generated that contains the latest design specifications. If the program finds an error, you must fix the error before continuing.

Step 6 - Incorporate the changes.

Once any errors have been corrected, two designs exist. One *from model* and one *from file*. You must decide whether to incorporate the new changes (*from file*) into the model (*from model*). The scenarios are as follows.

Option	Description
Incorporate Changes	If changes are incorporated into the design from the file into the model, the file is deleted and only the design program exists.
Do Not Incorporate Changes	If changes are not incorporated into the design, two options become available in the **WHICH DESIGN** menu the next time the design is edited.
From Model	Opens the program design that was last incorporated into the model.
From File	Opens the program design from the file.

Step 7 - Run the program.

Once a program has been added to a model, you can run it by regenerating the model or editing the program and incorporating the changes. While the program is running, values can be entered using any of the following:

- Entering new values at the message window prompt.

- Maintaining the current values.

- Reading values from a text file.

Creating Instances

The **Instantiate** option in the **PROGRAM** menu enables you to quickly create family table instances of the model. This option is available after you execute a program design by regenerating the model or editing the program. When you enter a name for each instance, the family table is created automatically and consists of all of the input parameters. Each instance is added by giving the value for their respective parameters.

Process Flowchart

A part that uses Pro/PROGRAM has a logical sequence. The flowchart in Figure A–12 outlines this sequence with the various possibilities that can be encountered.

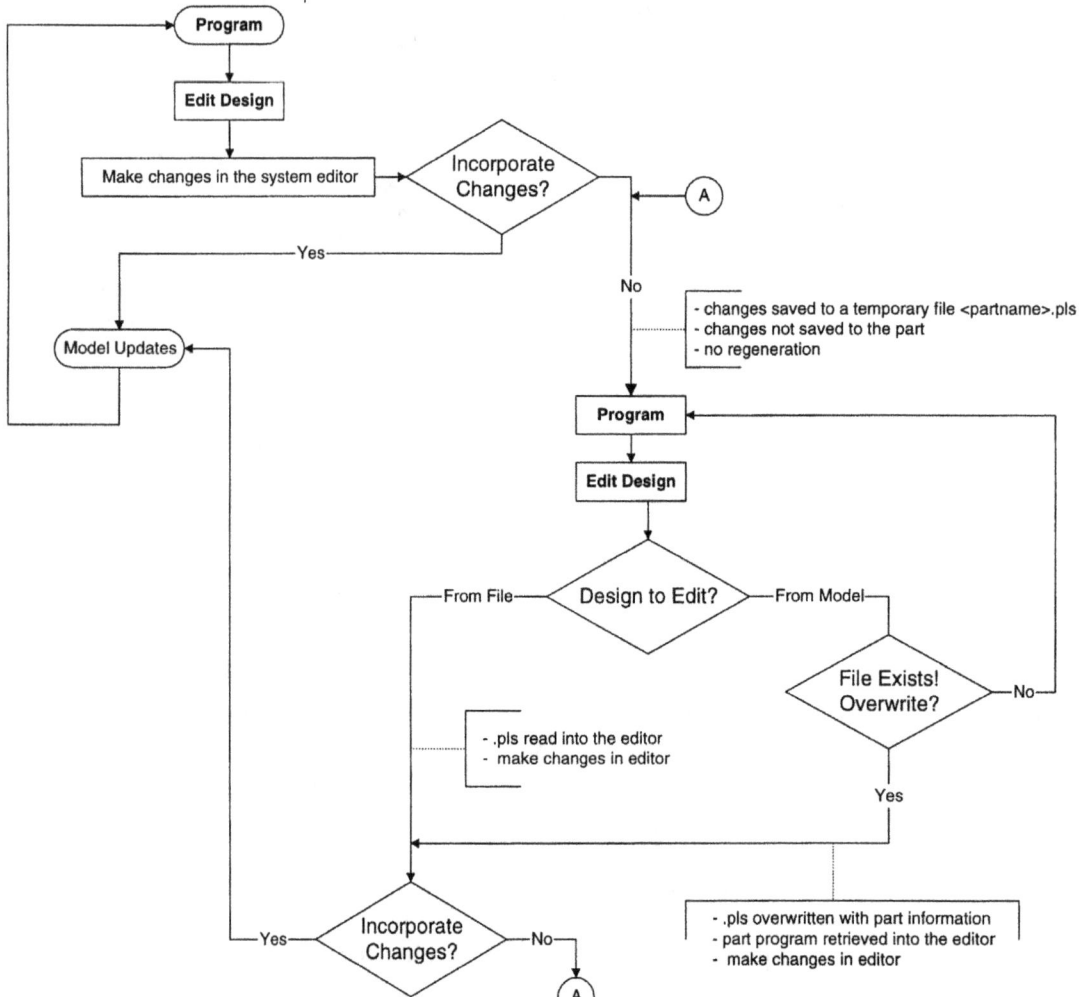

Figure A–12

Practice A1

Part PROGRAM

Practice Objectives

- Add input statements to the program that enable you to enter a value for the width and depth of the part.
- Enter information to drive the program.
- Edit the program and enter a relation that establishes a relationship with the width dimension of the model.
- Edit the program so that it prompts the user to include or exclude the round on the model.
- Edit the program so that it prompts the user to enter the number of holes to add to the model.

In this practice, you will create and run a part program. The relations and input statements will be used to control the round and hole features on the part.

Task 1 - Open a part file.

1. Set the working directory to the *Appendix A* folder.

2. Open **bracket.prt**.

3. Set the model display as follows:

   - ⅍ *(Datum Display Filters)*: All Off
   - ⅀ *(Spin Center)*: Off
   - ⬚ *(Display Style)*: ⬚ (Shading With Edges)

4. Use the Model Player to become familiar with the creation sequence of the model. Becoming familiar with the feature sequence helps when it comes to reading and understanding the information in the program.

Design Considerations

The design intent of a model can be easily captured in a part program. Consider the following design criteria:

- Variable number of holes, equally spaced around the center hole

- Variable width

- Variable length

- Include round, yes or no

Task 2 - Create a relation.

1. Create a relation that spaces the patterned holes equally around the center hole. Consider the design intent and that the number of holes is variable.

2. Modify the number of holes to **6** and regenerate the model. The part displays as shown in Figure A–13.

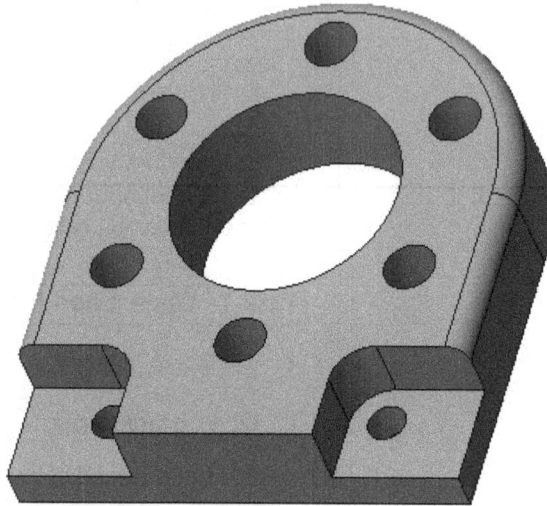

Figure A–13

Task 3 - Add input statements to the program.

Design Considerations

In this task, you will add input statements to the program that will enable you to prompt for a value for the width and depth of the part. To do this you will add information in the *Input* area.

1. Select the *Tools* tab and select **Model Intent>Program**.

2. Select **Edit Design** in the **PROGRAM** menu. The system editor opens and the default program displays. Scroll through the program. Note the *Input*, *Relations*, and *Feature* areas. Why is there a relation in the *Relations* area?

The highlight denotes user entry.

3. Edit the *Input* area to contain the information highlighted in Figure A–14.

```
INPUT
width number
"Enter the width of the part"
d1 number
"Enter the depth of the part"
END INPUT

RELATIONS
d11=360/p12
END RELATIONS
```

Figure A–14

4. Close the editor window. Confirm that you want to save the program.

5. In the confirmation dialog box, you are prompted: *Do you want to incorporate your changes into the model?*. Click **No**.

6. Select **Edit Design** in the **PROGRAM** menu. Because you did not incorporate changes to the program you are prompted for which program to edit. The From File program contains all of the information that you entered in the input statement.

7. To retain all of the input statement information, select **From File**. Otherwise, all of the information that was just entered and not incorporated will be lost.

8. Close the editor window.

9. At the message prompt to incorporate the changes, click **Yes**.

Task 4 - Enter information to drive the program.

1. The **GET INPUT** menu displays. It is used to enter information to drive the part program. The options are as follows:

Option	Description
Current Vals	Retains the current values for the input variables.
Enter	Enables you to enter your own input variables.
Read File	Reads data for the input variables from a file.

2. Select **Enter** in the **GET INPUT** menu. The **INPUT SEL** menu displays, listing all of the input variables that were entered in the input statement.

3. Select **WIDTH** and **D1**. Select **Done Sel**.

4. The message window now prompts for the user entry. The prompts display as written in the input statement and include the current value in brackets. Enter **10** at the *Enter the width of the part* prompt.

5. Accept the default value for the depth of the part by pressing <Enter>. The message area at the bottom of the screen displays *Part 'BRACKET' not changed since last regen*. Why? The value for the width is a new value and causes a regeneration of the model. A relation is missing that tells Creo Parametric how to equate the parameter width.

Task 5 - Add a relation.

Design Considerations

In a previous task you added input statements to prompt for width and depth values. Simply assigning an input statement and parameter does not affect the model geometry. To update the geometry, a relationship must be established to define how the parameter is related to the model. In this task you will create a relation that equates the width with a dimension on the model. In the case of the depth, a parameter was not used in the input statement. A dimension value was used and a relation is not required.

1. Edit the program by selecting **Edit Design** in the **PROGRAM** menu.

2. Add the relation shown in Figure A–15 to equate the width with dimension **d2**.

The highlight denotes user entry.

```
INPUT
 WIDTH NUMBER
  "Enter the width of the part"
 D1 NUMBER
  "Enter the depth of the part"
END INPUT

RELATIONS
D11=360/P12
d2=width
END RELATIONS
```

Figure A–15

3. Exit the editor, saving all of the changes.

4. Incorporate the changes that were just made to the program.

5. Enter new values for both width and **d1**. Set the *Width* to **10** and the *Depth* to **12**. The model regenerates as shown in Figure A–16.

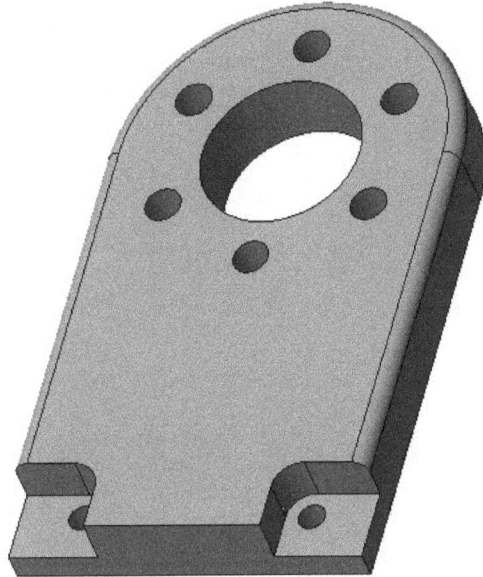

Figure A–16

Design Considerations

What is the difference between the two methods used to drive a dimension with a program?

Situation 1: Width

The parameter width was set up to drive the width of the part. In this case, a second step was required. You had to write an equation that equated the width to **d2**.

Situation 2: d15

The dimension **d1** was used in the input statement and the program knew that the user entry would govern the value.

Both methods work in the same way. Situation 1 offers a solution that involves more input but enables you to use the **width** parameter in other sections of the program.

Task 6 - Generate a user entry that prompts you to select whether to include the round or not.

Design Considerations

In some situations, the round on the top edge shown in Figure A–17 is required to help reduce the weight of the model. In this task you will edit the program so that it prompts the user include the round on the top edge of the model or not. The input statement alone does not affect the inclusion of the round. A conditional statement needs to be added that surrounds the feature in the program.

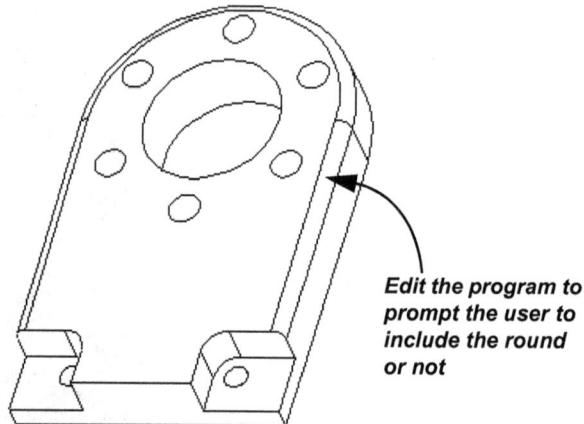

Edit the program to prompt the user to include the round or not

Figure A–17

The highlight denotes user entry.

1. Edit the program and add the input statement shown in Figure A–18.

```
INPUT
  WIDTH NUMBER
  "Enter the width of the part"
  D1 NUMBER
  "Enter the depth of the part"
  round yes_no
  "Should the round be added to the part?"
END INPUT

RELATIONS
D11=360/P12
D2=WIDTH
END RELATIONS
```

Figure A–18

The highlight denotes user entry.

2. Scroll down to where the features have been added. Find the round and add the statements shown in Figure A–19 (hint: feature 6).

```
IF ROUND==YES
ADD FEATURE (initial number 6)
INTERNAL FEATURE ID   67
PARENTS = 40(#5)


ROUND: General

NO.              ELEMENT NAME        INFO
---              ------------        ------------
1                Feature Name        Defined
2                Sets                1 Set
2.1              Set 0               Defined
2.1.1            Shape options       Constant
2.1.2            Conic               Defined
2.1.2.1          Conic Type          Plain
2.1.3            References                            Defined
2.1.3.1          Reference type      Edge Chain
2.1.3.2          Curve Collection    3 Selections
2.1.4            Spine               Defined
2.1.4.1          Ball/Spine          Rolling Ball
2.1.5            Extend Surfaces     Disable
2.1.6            Radii                                1 Points
2.1.6.1          Rad 0                                Defined
2.1.6.1.1        D1                  Defined
2.1.6.1.1.1      Distance type       Enter Value
2.1.6.1.1.2      Distance value      0.40
2.1.7            Pieces              1 of 1 Included, 0 Trimmed, 0 Extended
3                Attach type         Make Solid
4                Transitions         Defined


FEATURE'S DIMENSIONS:
d4 = (Displayed:) .40R
     (    Stored:) 0.4 ( 0.01, -0.01 )
END ADD
ENDIF
```

Figure A–19

3. Incorporate the changes in the model.

4. Select **Enter** and select the round.

5. Click **No** when prompted whether the round should be added to the part. The model regenerates as shown in Figure A–20.

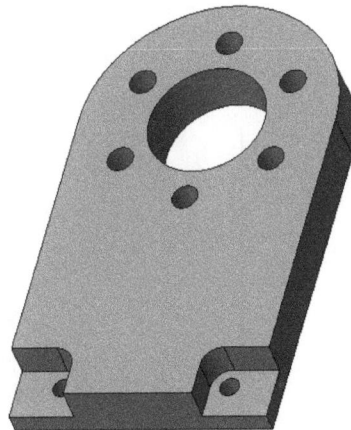

Figure A–20

Task 7 - Add an input statement for the number of holes.

Design Considerations

In the second task you created a relation that equally spaced the pattern of holes. In this task you will further your work with the hole pattern to create a user entry for the number of holes that are required in the model. By doing so in the program, you do not have to manually edit the dimension value on the model, you can enter the value when the program is run.

The highlight denotes user entry.

1. Edit the program and add the input statement and relation shown in Figure A–21.

```
INPUT
 WIDTH NUMBER
 "Enter the width of the part"
 D1 NUMBER
 "Enter the depth of the part"
 ROUND YES_NO
 "Should the round be added to the part?"
 holes number
 "Enter the number of holes"
END INPUT

RELATIONS
p12=holes
D11=360/P12
D2=WIDTH
END RELATIONS
```

Figure A–21

2. Exit the program. Save and incorporate the changes into the model.

3. Set the hole values to **4**. The part regenerates as shown in Figure A–22.

Figure A–22

4. Regenerate the model. The **GET INPUT** menu displays and recognizes that a program is driving the part.

5. Enter values to vary the parameters.

6. Save the part and erase it from memory.

Additional Practices

This appendix contains additional exercises that enable you to practice some of the tasks covered in this guide.

Practice B1

Advanced Variable Section Sweep

Practice Objective

- Create a Sweep with a variable section, using only a drawing for instructions.

The drawing in Figure B–1 shows a channel with an elliptical cross-section.

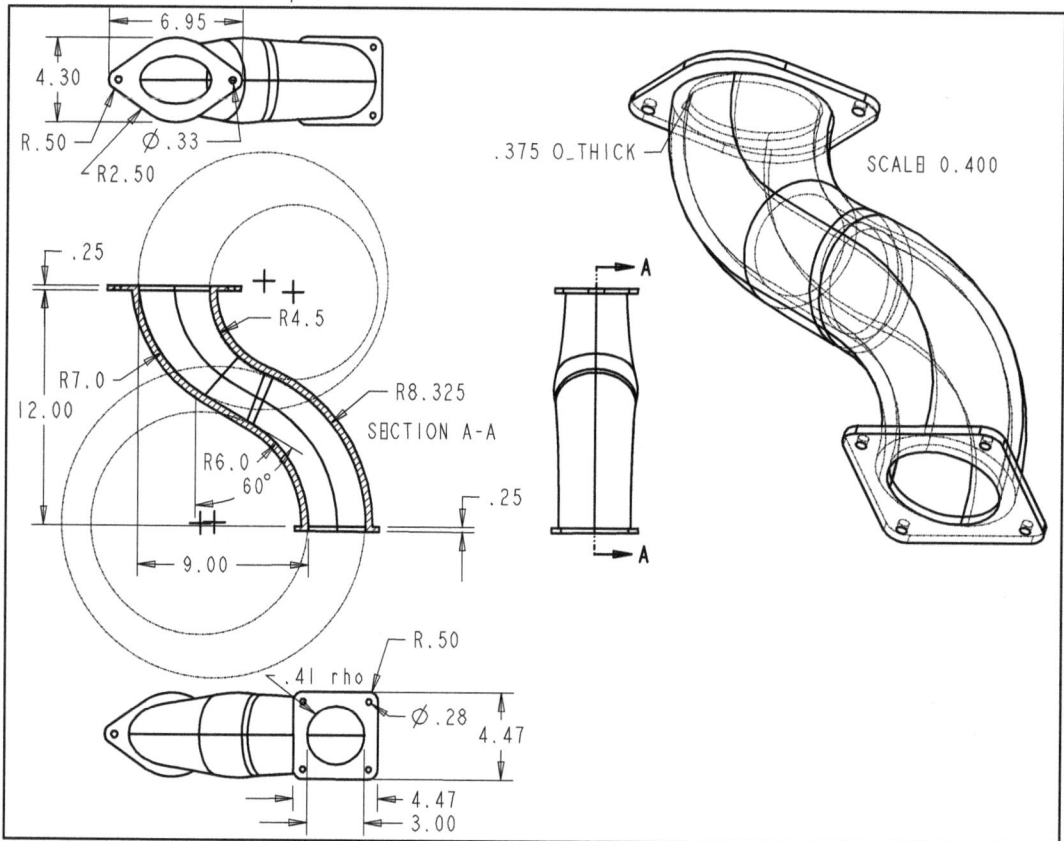

6.95
4.30
R.50
Ø.33
R2.50
.25
R4.5
R7.0
12.00
R8.325
SECTION A-A
R6.0
60°
.25
9.00
.375 O_THICK
SCALE 0.400
A
A
R.50
.41 rho
Ø.28
4.47
4.47
3.00

Figure B–1

Task 1 - Create a new part.

1. Set the working directory to the *Appendix B* folder

2. Create a new part called **adv_vss.prt**.

Use the following guidelines when creating the part:

- The channel has an elliptical cross-section with varying major and minor axes.

- The major axis of the ellipse is controlled by two datum curves. The dimensions for the sketched datum curves are shown in Section A-A of the drawing. Use the datum curve on the right side as the Origin trajectory and the datum curve on the left side as the X-vector trajectory (as shown in Figure B–1).

- A Sketcher relation using known dimensions that sets the cross-sectional area of the ellipse equal to 7 controls the minor axis of the ellipse. The area of an ellipse is shown in Figure B–2.

$$AREA = \pi ab$$

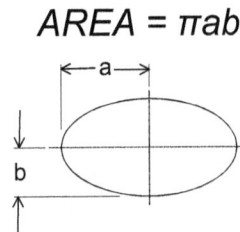

Figure B–2

Consider the most appropriate feature sequence before beginning the model.

Practice B2 | Pro/PROGRAM

Practice Objective

- Create a program that controls the part to incorporate the design intent.

Task 1 - Create a part that uses a program to incorporate design intent.

1. Set the working directory to the *Appendix B* folder

2. Create the part shown in Figure B–3. Consider the following design criteria.

    - User entry should control the number of holes.
    - User entry should control whether the holes are included or not.
    - The flange thickness can vary.

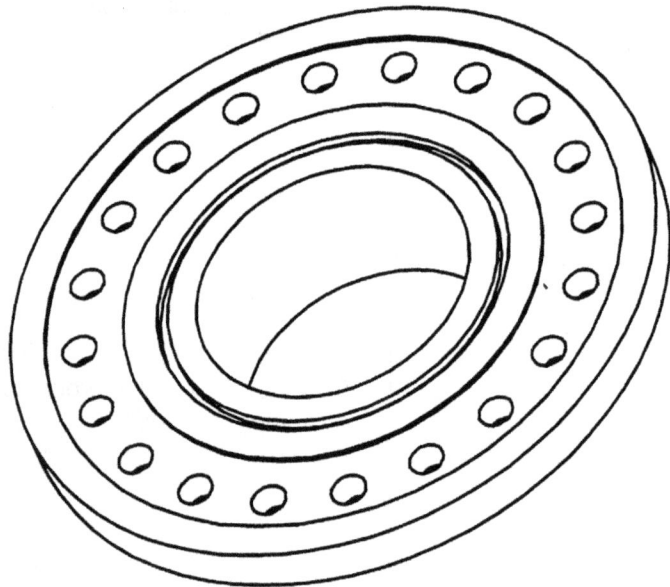

Figure B–3

3. Write a program that controls the specifications listed in Step 1. Include a conditional statement that only prompts you for the diameter of the holes if the holes are included in the part.

Practice B3

Remove Surface

Practice Objective

- Use the **Remove** command to remove an unwanted surface from an imported IGES part.

In this practice you will remove a surface, to modify the model shown in Figure B–4.

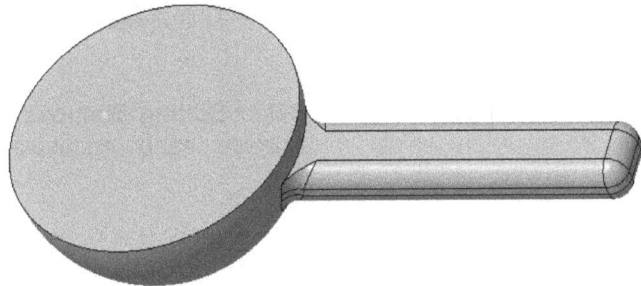

Figure B–4

When you open an .IGS file, making changes is difficult. The **Remove** tool enables you to remove unwanted surfaces from a model. It can be used on solid and non-solid surfaces.

1. Set the working directory to the *Appendix B* folder.

2. In the *Home* tab, click 🗁 (Open).

3. In the Open dialog box, select **IGES (.igs, .iges)** from the Type drop-down list.

4. Double-click on **scoop.igs**.

5. In the Import New Model dialog box, select **Use templates** and click **OK**.

6. Turn off the display of datum entities.

7. Set the display to 🗇 (Shading With Edges).

8. Select the surface shown in Figure B–5.

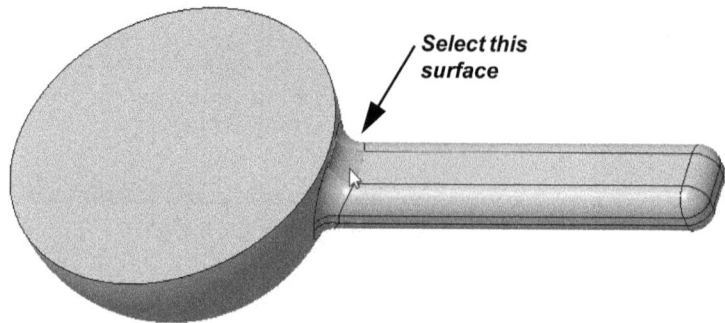

Figure B–5

9. Select **Editing>Remove** in the *Model* tab. The *Remove Surface* dashboard displays as shown in Figure B–6.

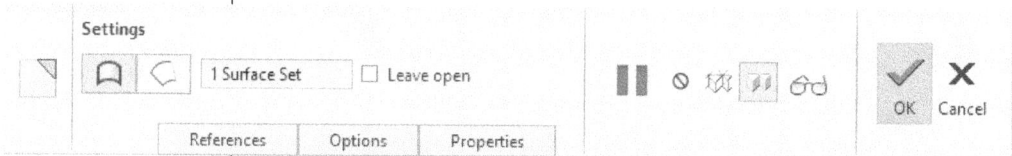

Figure B–6

10. Click the Options panel.

11. Click next until the preview displays as shown in Figure B–7.

*Multiple solutions exist, so clicking **Next** enables you to step through them.*

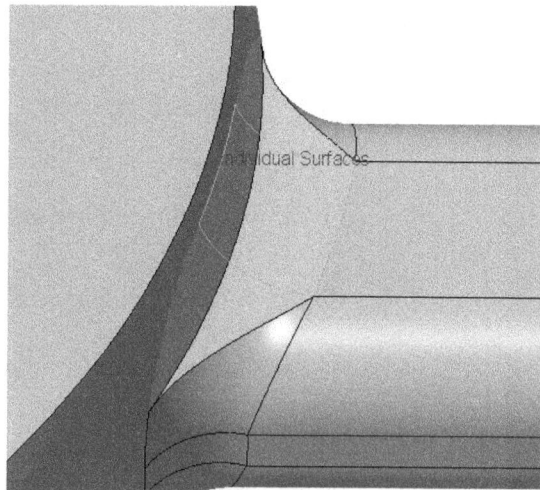

Figure B–7

12. Complete the feature. The model displays as shown in Figure B–8.

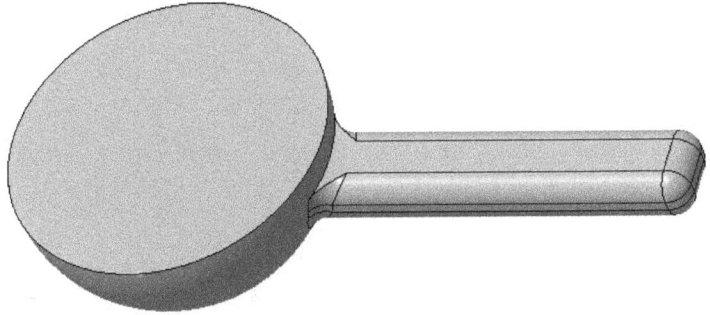

Figure B–8

www.ingramcontent.com/pod-product-compliance
Lightning Source LLC
Chambersburg PA
CBHW060937210326
41598CB00031B/4657